CW00621234

Paper 2.5

FINANCIAL REPORTING

International Stream

For exams in December 2006 and June 2007

Study Text

ACC

In this June 2006 new edition

- A **user-friendly format** for easy navigation

- **Exam-centred topic coverage**, directly linked to ACCA's syllabus and study guide

- **Exam focus points** showing you what the examiner will want you to do

- Regular **fast forward** summaries emphasising key points

- **Questions** and **quick quizzes** to test your understanding

- **Exam question bank** containing exam standard questions with answers

- A full index

BPP's **i-Learn** and **i-Pass** products also support this paper.

FOR EXAMS IN DECEMBER 2006 AND JUNE 2007

First edition 2001
Sixth edition June 2006

ISBN 0 7517 2678 8 (Previous edition 0 7517 2329 0)

British Library Cataloguing-in-Publication Data
A catalogue record for this book
is available from the British Library

Published by

BPP Professional Education
Aldine House, Aldine Place
London W12 8AW

www.bpp.com

Printed in Great Britain by W M Print
Frederick Street
Walsall
West Midlands
WS2 9NE

We are grateful to the Association of Chartered
Certified Accountants for permission to reproduce past
examination questions. The suggested solutions in the
exam answer bank have been prepared by BPP
Professional Education.

Contents

Introduction

The introduction pages contain lots of valuable advice and information. They include tips on studying for and passing the exam, also the content of the syllabus and what has been examined.

The BPP Effective Study Package – How the BPP Study Text can help you pass – Help yourself study for your ACCA exams – Syllabus and Study Guide – The exam paper – Oxford Brookes BSc (Hons) in Applied Accounting –ACCA professional development requirements – Syllabus mindmap

Computer-based learning products from BPP

If you want to reinforce your studies by **interactive** learning, try BPP's **i-Learn** product, covering major syllabus areas in an interactive format. For **self-testing**, try **i-Pass,** which offers a large number of **objective test questions**, particularly useful where objective test questions form part of the exam.

Learn Online

Learn Online uses BPP's wealth of teaching experience to produce a fully **interactive** e-learning resource **delivered via the Internet**. The site offers comprehensive **tutor support** and features areas such as **study, practice**, **email service**, **revision** and **useful resources**.

Visit our website www.bpp.com/acca/learnonline to sample aspects of Learn Online free of charge.

Learning to Learn Accountancy

BPP's ground-breaking **Learning to Learn Accountancy** book is designed to be used both at the outset of your ACCA studies and throughout the process of learning accountancy. It challenges you to consider how you study and gives you helpful hints about how to approach the various types of paper which you will encounter. It can help you **focus your studies on the subject and exam**, enabling you to **acquire knowledge, practise and revise efficiently and effectively**.

The BPP Effective Study Package

Recommended period of use	The BPP Effective Study Package
From the outset and throughout	**Learning to Learn Accountancy** Read this invaluable book as you begin your studies and refer to it throughout your studies.
Three to twelve months before the exam	**Study Text and i-Learn** Use the Study Text to acquire knowledge, understanding, skills and the ability to apply techniques. Use BPP's **i-Learn** product to reinforce your learning.
Throughout	**Learn Online** Study, practise, revise and use other helpful resources with BPP's fully interactive e-learning site, including full tutor support.
Throughout	**i-Pass** **i-Pass**, our computer-based testing package, provides objective test questions in a variety of formats and is ideal for self-assessment.
One to six months before the exam	**Practice & Revision Kit** Try the numerous examination-format questions in our Kit and compare your answers with the suggested solutions. Examiners emphasise that tackling exam-standard questions is essential preparation for your exams. Then attempt the two mock exams.
From three months before the exam until the last minute	**Passcards** Work through these short, memorable notes which are focused on the topics most likely to come up in your exam and which you can take anywhere.
One to six months before the exam	**Success CDs** The CDs cover the vital elements of your syllabus in less than 90 minutes per subject. They also contain exam hints to help you fine tune your strategy.

You can purchase these products by visiting www.bpp.com/mybpp

How the BPP Study Text can help you pass

> It provides you with the knowledge and understanding, skills and application techniques that you need to be successful in your exams

This Study Text has been targeted at the **Financial Reporting** syllabus.

- It is **comprehensive**. It covers the syllabus content. No more, no less.

- It is written at the **right level**. Each chapter is written with ACCA's syllabus and study guide in mind.

- It is aimed at the **exam**. We have taken account of recent exams, guidance the examiner has given and the assessment methodology.

> It allows you to study in the way that best suits your learning style and the time you have available, by following your personal Study Plan (see page (viii))

You may be studying at home on your own or you may be attending a full-time course. You may like to read every word, or you may prefer to skim-read and practise questions the rest of the time. However you study, you will find the BPP Study Text meets your needs in designing and following your personal Study Plan.

> It ties in with the other components of the BPP Effective Study Package to ensure you have the best possible chance of passing the exam (see page (v))

BPP
PROFESSIONAL EDUCATION

Help yourself study for your ACCA exams

Exams for professional bodies such as ACCA are very different from those you have taken at college or university. You will be under **greater time pressure before** the exam — as you may be combining your study with work. Here are some hints and tips.

The right approach

1 **Develop the right attitude**

Believe in yourself	Yes, there is a lot to learn. But thousands have succeeded before and you can too.
Remember why you're doing it	You are studying for a good reason: to advance your career.

2 **Focus on the exam**

Read through the Syllabus and Study Guide	These tell you what you are expected to know and are supplemented by **Exam focus points** in the text.
Study the Exam paper section	Past papers are likely to be good guides to what you should expect in the exam.

3 **The right method**

See the whole picture	Keeping in mind how all the detail you need to know fits into the whole picture will help you understand it better. <ul><li>The **Introduction** of each chapter puts the material in context.</li><li>The **Syllabus content, Study guide** and **Exam focus points** show you what you need to **grasp**.</li></ul>
Use your own words	To absorb the information (and to practise your written communication skills), you need to **put it into your own words**. <ul><li>**Take notes.**</li><li>Answer the **questions** in each chapter.</li><li>Draw **mindmaps**. We have an example for the whole syllabus.</li><li>Try **'teaching' a subject** to a colleague or friend.</li></ul>
Give yourself cues to jog your memory	The BPP Study Text uses **bold** to **highlight key points**. <ul><li>Try **colour coding** with a highlighter pen.</li><li>Write **key points** on cards.</li></ul>

4 **The right recap**

Review, review, review	Regularly reviewing a topic in summary form can **fix it in your memory**. The BPP Study Text helps you review in many ways. <ul><li>**Chapter roundups** summarise the 'Fast forward' key points in each chapter. Use them to recap each study session.</li><li>The **Quick quiz** actively tests your grasp of the essentials.</li><li>Go through the **Examples** in each chapter a second or third time.</li></ul>

Developing your personal Study Plan

BPP's **Learning to Learn Accountancy** book emphasises the need to use a study plan. Planning and sticking to the plan are key elements of learning successfully.
There are five steps you should work through.

Step 1   **How do you learn?**

First you need to be aware of your style of learning. BPP's **Learning to Learn Accountancy** book commits a chapter to this **self-discovery**. What types of intelligence do you display when learning? You might be advised to brush up on certain study skills before launching into this Study Text.

BPP's **Learning to Learn Accountancy** book helps you to identify what intelligences you show more strongly and then details how you can tailor your study process to your preferences. It also includes handy hints on how to develop intelligences you exhibit less strongly, but which might be needed as you study accountancy.

Step 2   **What do you prefer to do first?**

If you prefer to get to grips with a theory before seeing how it is applied, we suggest you concentrate first on the explanations we give in each chapter before looking at the examples and case studies. If you prefer to see first how things work in practice, skim through the detail in each chapter, and concentrate on the examples and case studies, before supplementing your understanding by reading the detail.

Step 3   **How much time do you have?**

Work out the time you have available per week, given the following.

- The standard you have set yourself
- The time you need to set aside later for work on the Practice & Revision Kit and Passcards
- The other exam(s) you are sitting
- Practical matters such as work, travel, exercise, sleep and social life

Hours

Note your time available in box A.   A [   ]

Step 4   **Allocate your time**

- Take the time you have available per week for this Study Text shown in box A, multiply it by the number of weeks available and insert the result in box B.   B [   ]

- Divide the figure in box B by the number of chapters in this text and insert the result in box C.   C [   ]

Remember that this is only a rough guide. Some of the chapters in this book are longer and more complicated than others, and you will find some subjects easier to understand than others.

Step 5   Implement

Set about studying each chapter in the time shown in box C, following the key study steps in the order suggested by your particular learning style.

This is your personal **Study Plan**. You should try to combine it with the study sequence outlined below. You may want to modify the sequence to adapt it to your **personal style**.

> BPP's **Learning to Learn Accountancy** gives further guidance on developing a study plan, and deciding where and when to study.

Tackling your studies

The best way to approach this Study Text is to tackle the chapters in order. Taking into account your individual learning style, you could follow this sequence for each chapter.

Key study steps	Activity
Step 1 **Topic list**	This topic list helps you navigate each chapter; each numbered topic is a numbered section in the chapter.
Step 2 **Introduction**	This sets your objectives for study by giving you the big picture in terms of the context of the chapter. The content is referenced to the Study Guide, and Exam guidance shows how the topic is likely to be examined. The Introduction tells you **why** the topics covered in the chapter need to be studied.
Step 3 **Knowledge brought forward boxes**	These highlight information and techniques that it is assumed you have 'brought forward' with you from your earlier studies. Remember that you may be tested on these areas in the exam. If you are unsure of these areas, you should consider revising your more detailed study material from earlier papers.
Step 4 **Fast forward**	Fast forward boxes give you a quick summary of the content of each of the main chapter sections. They are listed together in the roundup at the end of each chapter to help you review each chapter quickly.
Step 5 **Explanations**	Proceed methodically through each chapter, particularly focussing on areas highlighted as significant in the chapter introduction, or areas that are frequently examined.
Step 6 **Key terms and Exam focus points**	• Key terms can often earn you **easy marks** if you state them clearly and correctly in an exam answer. They are highlighted in the index at the back of this text. • Exam focus points state how the topic has been or may be examined, difficulties that can occur in questions about the topic, and examiner feedback on common weaknesses in answers.
Step 7 **Note taking**	Take brief notes, if you wish. Don't copy out too much. Remember that being able to record something yourself is a sign of being able to understand it. Your notes can be in whatever format you find most helpful; lists, diagrams, mindmaps.
Step 8 **Examples**	Work through the examples very carefully as they illustrate key knowledge and techniques.
Step 9 **Case studies**	Study each one, and try to add flesh to them from your own experience. They are designed to show how the topics you are studying come alive in the real world.
Step 10 **Questions**	Attempt each one, as they will illustrate how well you've understood what you've read.

Key study steps	Activity
Step 11 **Answers**	Check yours against ours, and make sure you understand any discrepancies.
Step 12 **Chapter roundup**	Review it carefully, to make sure you have grasped the significance of all the important points in the chapter.
Step 13 **Quick quiz**	Use the Quick quiz to check how much you have remembered of the topics covered and to practise questions in a variety of formats.
Step 14 **Question practice**	Attempt the Question(s) suggested at the very end of the chapter. You can find these in the Exam Question Bank at the end of the Study Text, along with the answers so you can see how you did. If you have bought i-Pass, use this too.

Short of time: Skim study technique?

You may find you simply do not have the time available to follow all the key study steps for each chapter, however you adapt them for your particular learning style. If this is the case, follow the **skim study** technique below.

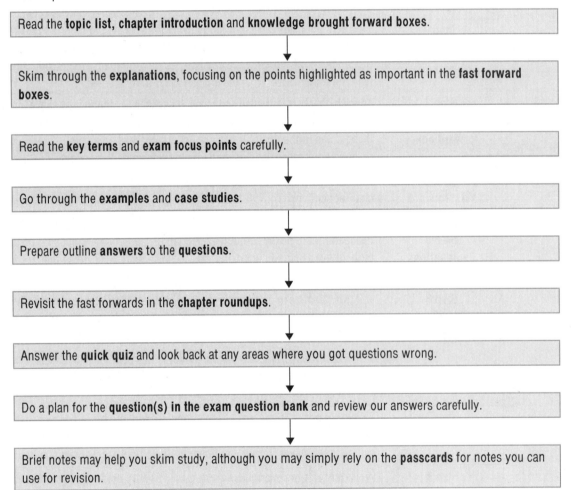

Read the **topic list, chapter introduction** and **knowledge brought forward boxes**.

Skim through the **explanations**, focusing on the points highlighted as important in the **fast forward boxes**.

Read the **key terms** and **exam focus points** carefully.

Go through the **examples** and **case studies**.

Prepare outline **answers** to the **questions**.

Revisit the fast forwards in the **chapter roundups**.

Answer the **quick quiz** and look back at any areas where you got questions wrong.

Do a plan for the **question(s) in the exam question bank** and review our answers carefully.

Brief notes may help you skim study, although you may simply rely on the **passcards** for notes you can use for revision.

Moving on...

When you are ready to start revising, you should still refer back to this Study Text.

- As a source of **reference** (you should find the index particularly helpful for this)

- As a way to **review** (the Fast forwards, Exam focus points, Chapter roundups and Quick quizzes help you here)

Remember to keep careful hold of this Study Text – you will find it invaluable in your work.

More advice on Study Skills can be found in BPP's **Learning to Learn Accountancy** book.

Syllabus

Aim

To build on the basic techniques in Paper 1.1 *Preparing Financial Statements* and to develop knowledge and understanding of more advanced financial accounting concepts and principles. Candidates will be required to apply this understanding by preparing and interpreting financial reports in a practical context.

Objectives

On completion of this paper candidates should be able to:

- Appraise and apply specified accounting concepts and theories to practical workplace situations

- Appraise and apply the international regulatory framework of financial reporting

- Prepare financial statements for different entities to comply with specified International Accounting Standards, International Financial Reporting Standards and other related pronouncements

- Prepare group financial statements (excluding group cash flow statements) to include a single subsidiary. An associate or joint venture may also be included.

- Analyse, interpret and report on financial statements (including cash flow statements) and related information to a variety of user groups

- Discuss and apply the requirements of other specified International Accounting Standards/ International Financial Reporting Standards.

- Demonstrate the skills expected in Part 2

Position of the paper in the overall syllabus

Paper 2.5 builds on the techniques developed at Paper 1.1 *Preparing Financial Statements* and tests the conceptual and technical financial accounting knowledge that candidates will require in order to progress to the higher level analytical, judgmental and communication skills of Paper 3.6 *Advanced Corporate Reporting*.

Paper 2.5 also provides essential financial accounting knowledge and principles that need to be fully understood by auditors, thus it forms some of the prerequisite knowledge of Paper 2.6 *Audit and Internal Review*, and the option Paper 3.1 *Audit and Assurance Services*.

Prerequisite knowledge of Paper 2.5 is largely the basic knowledge and skills demonstrated at Paper 1.1, but many recent accounting standards require the use of discounting techniques which candidates will have acquired at Paper 2.4 *Financial Management and Control*.

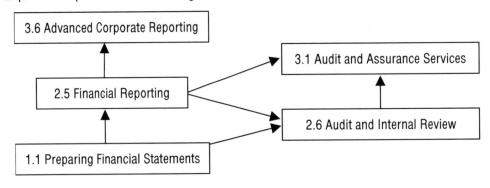

1   **Accounting principles, concepts and theory**

(a)   The IASB's Framework for the Preparation and Presentation of Financial Statements
(b)   Agency theory
(c)   Price level changes, capital maintenance

2   **Regulatory framework**

(a)   The structure of the International Accounting Standards Board (IASB)
(b)   The standard setting process
(c)   The role of the International Financial Reporting Interpretations Committee (IFRIC)
(d)   The IASB's relationship with the International Organisation of Securities Commissions (IOSCO)

3   **Preparation and presentation of financial statements for companies limited by liability and other entities**

(a)   Accounting for share capital and reserves

(i)   Issue and redemption of shares
(ii)   The principle of maintenance of capital
(iii)   The principle of distributable profits

(b)   Tangible and intangible non-current assets

(c)   Net current assets

(d)   Earnings per share

(e)   Tax in company accounts including:

(i)   Current tax
(ii)   Deferred tax

(f)   IASs, IFRSs and SIC/IFRIC pronouncements as specified in the examinable documents

4   **Preparation of consolidated financial statements**

(a)   Definition of subsidiary companies

(b)   Exclusions from consolidations

(c)   Preparation of consolidated income statements and balance sheets including:

(i)   Elimination of intra-group transactions
(ii)   Fair value adjustments

(d)   Associates and joint ventures

5   **Analysis and interpretation of financial statements and related information**

(a)   Analysis of corporate information
(b)   Preparation of reports on financial performance for various user groups
(c)   Preparation and analysis of cash flow statements of a single company
(d)   Related party transactions
(e)   Segmental information

Excluded topics

The following topics are specifically excluded from the syllabus.

- Partnership and branch financial statements
- Preparing group financial statements involving more than one subsidiary
- Piecemeal acquisitions, disposal of subsidiaries and group reconstructions

- Foreign currency translation/consolidations, hedging, hyperinflationary economies
- Financial statements of banks and similar financial institutions
- Group cash flows
- Schemes of reorganisation/reconstruction
- Company/share valuation
- Derivative financial instruments
- Accounting for retirement benefit costs/plans
- International Exposure Drafts and Discussion Drafts/Papers

Key areas of the syllabus

The key topic areas are as follows.

Accounting principles and concepts, accounting theory

- Framework for the Preparation and Presentation of Financial Statements
- Revenue recognition
- Substance over form

Preparation of financial statements of companies limited by liability

- Presentation of financial statements
- Accounting and disclosure requirements of the International Accounting Standards/International Financial Reporting Standards

Preparation of consolidated financial statements

- Definitions of subsidiaries: exclusions from consolidation
- Simple groups

Analysis and interpretation of financial statements

- Preparation of reports for various user groups
- Preparation and analysis of cash flow statements

Other topic areas

Note that these may be examined as part of a question within the above key areas or as a substantial part of a separate optional question.

- Accounting for leases
- Construction contracts
- Earnings per share
- Impairment of assets, provisions
- Non-current assets held for sale and discontinued operations
- Goodwill and other intangible assets

Paper 2.5

Financial Reporting
(International)

Study Guide

1 REVIEW OF BASIC CONCEPTS, FRAMEWORK FOR THE PREPARATION AND PRESENTATION OF FINANCIAL STATEMENTS

- Discuss what is meant by a conceptual framework and GAAP

- Describe the objectives of financial statements and the qualitative characteristics of financial information

- Define the elements of financial statements

- Apply the above definitions to practical situations

- Revision of Paper 1.1 – prepare the final accounts of a company from a trial balance.

2 ACCOUNTING CONCEPTS, ACCOUNTING THEORY

- Outline the concept of 'comprehensive income'.

- Explain the principle of fair value

- Discuss and apply accounting policies

- Describe the deficiencies of historic cost accounts (HCA) during periods of rising prices and explain principal alternatives to HCA.

3 REVENUE RECOGNITION

- Outline the principles of the timing of revenue recognition

- Explain the concept of substance over form in relation to recognising sales revenue

- Explain the principle of realised profits

- Discuss the various points in the production and sales cycle where it may, depending on circumstances, be appropriate to recognise gains and losses – give examples of this

- Describe the IASC's 'balance sheet approach' to revenue recognition within its Framework and compare this to the requirements of relevant accounting standards.

4 THE STRUCTURE OF THE IASB'S REGULATORY FRAMEWORK

- Describe the constitution of the IASB and its objectives

- Describe the influence of national standard setters and the International Organisation of Securities Commissions (IOSCO) on IASs and IFRSs

- Outline the International Accounting Standard Setting process and the role of the International Financial Reporting Interpretations Committee (IFRIC).

5 Preparation of financial statements for companies

- State the objectives of accounting standards on Presentation of Financial Statements

- Describe the structure and content of financial statements

- Discuss 'fair presentation' and the accounting concepts/principles in relevant accounting standards

- Prepare the financial statements of companies in accordance with International Accounting Standards/International Financial Reporting Standards

- Describe the main issues involved when a company adopts International Financial Reporting Standards (IFRSs) for the first time

- Apply the requirements of the IASB to the preparation of financial statements for a first time adopter of International Financial Reporting Standards

6&7 ACCOUNTING POLICIES, CHANGES IN ACCOUNTING ESTIMATES AND ERRORS; NON-CURRENT ASSETS HELD FOR SALE AND DISCONTINUED OPERATIONS

- Explain the needs for accounting standards in the above areas
- Discuss the importance of identifying and reporting the results of a discontinued operation
- Define discontinued operations
- Describe the circumstances where assets meet the criteria of 'held for sale'
- Discuss the accounting treatment of non-current assets held for sale
- Prepare financial statements in accordance with requirements of the relevant accounting standards in the above areas
- Describe the circumstances where a change in accounting policy is permitted
- Define and account for errors, changes in accounting estimates and changes in accounting policies
- Explain and illustrate the contents and purpose of the statement of changes in equity

8 SHARE CAPITAL AND RESERVES

- Explain the need for an accounting standard on financial instruments
- Distinguish between debt and equity capital
- Apply the requirements of relevant accounting standards to the issuing and finance costs of:
  - (i) equity and preference shares
  - (ii) debt instruments with no conversion rights, and
  - (iii) convertible debt (compound financial instruments)
- Explain and apply general principles relating to the purchase or redemption of shares
- Discuss the advantages of companies being able to redeem/purchase their own shares
- Discuss the principles relating to profits available for distribution

9 NON-CURRENT ASSETS - TANGIBLE

- Define the initial cost of a non-current asset (including a self-constructed asset) and apply this to various examples of expenditure distinguishing between capital and revenue items
- Describe and be able to identify, subsequent expenditure that may be capitalised
- State and appraise the effects of accounting standards of the revaluation of property, plant and equipment
- Account for gains and losses on the disposal of revalued assets
- Calculate depreciation on:
  - (i) revalued assets, and
  - (ii) assets that have two or more major components
- Apply the provisions of accounting standards on Accounting for Government Grants and Disclosure of Government Assistance
- Discuss the way in which the treatment of investment properties differs from other properties
- Apply the requirements of accounting standards on investment properties

10 LEASES

- Define the essential characteristics of a lease
- Describe and apply the method of determining a lease type (ie an operating or finance lease)
- Explain the effect on the financial statements of a finance lease being incorrectly treated as an operating lease
- Account for operating leases in financial statements
- Account for finance leases in the financial statements of lessors and lessees
- Outline the principles of accounting standard on leasing and its main disclosure requirements. Note: the net cash investment method will not be examined.

11 INTANGIBLE ASSETS

- Discuss the nature and possible accounting treatments of both internally generated and purchased goodwill

- Distinguish between goodwill and other intangible assets

- Describe the criteria for the initial recognition and measurement of intangible assets

- Describe the subsequent accounting treatment, including the principle of impairment tests in relation to purchased goodwill

- Describe the circumstances in which the goodwill calculation results in a negative amount and its subsequent accounting treatment.

- Describe and apply the requirements of accounting standards on internally generated assets other than goodwill (eg research and development)

12 IMPAIRMENT OF ASSETS

- Define the recoverable amount of an asset; define impairment losses

- Give examples of, and be able to identify, circumstances that may indicate that an impairment of an asset has occurred

- Describe what is meant by a cash-generating unit

- State the basis on which impairment losses should be allocated, and allocate a given impairment loss to the assets of a cash-generating unit

13 LIABILITIES – PROVISIONS, CONTINGENT LIABILITIES

AND CONTINGENT ASSETS

- Explain why an accounting standard on provisions is necessary – give examples of previous abuses in this area

- Define provisions, legal and constructive obligations, past events and the transfer of economic benefits

- State when provisions may and may not be made, and how they should be accounted for

- Explain how provisions should be measured

- Define contingent assets and liabilities – give examples and describe their accounting treatment

- Be able to identify and account for:

    (i)   warranties/guarantees

    (ii) onerous contracts

    (iii) environmental and similar provisions

- Discuss the validity of making provisions for future repairs or refurbishments

14 INVENTORY AND CONSTRUCTION CONTRACTS

- Review the principles of inventory valuation covered in paper 1.1.

- Define a construction contract and describe why recognising profit before completion is generally considered to be desirable and the circumstances where it may not be; discuss if this may be profit smoothing

- Describe the ways in which contract cost may

be recognised

- Calculate and disclose the amounts to be shown in the financial statements for construction contracts

15 EARNINGS PER SHARE

- Explain the importance of comparability in relation to the calculation of earnings per share (eps) and its importance as a stock market indicator

- Explain why the trend of eps may be a more accurate indicator of performance than a company's profit trend

- Define earnings and the basic number of shares

- Calculate the eps in accordance with relevant accounting standards in the following circumstances

    (i)   basic eps

    (ii) where there has been a bonus issue of shares/stock split during the year, and

    (iii) where there has been a rights issue of shares during the year

- Explain the relevance to existing shareholders of the diluted eps, and describe the circumstances that will give rise to a future dilution of the eps

- Calculate the diluted eps in the following circumstances;

    (i)   where convertible debt or preference shares are in issue; and

    (ii) where share options and warrants exist

16 TAXATION IN FINANCIAL STATEMENTS

- Account for current tax liabilities and assets in accordance with relevant accounting standards

- Describe the general principles of government sales taxes (eg VAT or GST)

- Explain the effect of taxable temporary differences on accounting and taxable profits

- Outline the principles of accounting for deferred tax

- Outline the requirements of relevant accounting standards relating to deferred tax assets and liabilities

- Calculate and record deferred tax amounts in the financial statements

17 ACCOUNTING FOR THE SUBSTANCE OF TRANSACTIONS

- Explain the importance of recording the substance rather than the legal form of transactions – give examples of previous abuses in this area

- Describe the features which may indicate that the substance of transactions may differ from their legal form

- Explain and apply the principles of recognition and derecognition of assets and liabilities

- Be able to recognise the substance of transactions in general, and specifically account for the following types of transaction:

(i) goods sold on sale or return/consignment goods

(ii) sale and repurchase/ leaseback agreement

(iii) factoring of accounts receivable

18 & 19

BUSINESS COMBINATIONS - INTRODUCTION

- Describe the concept of a group and the objective and usefulness of consolidated financial statements

- Explain the different methods which could be used to prepare consolidated financial statements

- Explain and apply the definition of subsidiary companies

- Describe the circumstances and reasoning for subsidiaries to be excluded from consolidated financial statements in accordance with relevant accounting standards

- Prepare a consolidated balance sheet for a simple group dealing with pre and post acquisition profits minority interest and consolidated goodwill

- Explain the need for using coterminous year ends and uniform accounting policies when preparing consolidated financial statements

- Describe how the above is achieved in practice

- Prepare a consolidated income statement for a simple group, including an example where an acquisition occurs during the year and there is a minority interest

20 BUSINESS COMBINATIONS – INTRA-GROUP ADJUSTMENTS

- Explain why intra-group transactions should be eliminated on consolidation

- Explain the nature of a dividend paid out of pre-acquisition profits

- Account for the effects (in the income statement and balance sheet) of intra-group trading and other transactions including:

(i) unrealised profits in inventory and non-current assets

(ii) intra-group loans and interest and other intra-group charges, and

(iii) intra-group dividends including those paid out of pre-acquisition profits

21 BUSINESS COMBINATIONS – FAIR VALUE ADJUSTMENTS

- Explain why it is necessary for both the consideration paid for a subsidiary and the subsidiary's identifiable assets and liabilities to be accounted for at their fair values when preparing consolidated financial statements

- Prepare consolidated financial statements dealing with fair value adjustments (including their effect on consolidated goodwill) in in respect of:

(i) depreciating and non-depreciating non-current assets

(ii) inventory

(iii) monetary liabilities (basic discounting techniques may be required)

(iv) assets and liabilities (including contingencies), not included in the subsidiary's own balance sheet

22 & 23

BUSINESS COMBINATIONS – ASSOCIATES AND JOINT VENTURES

- Define associates and joint ventures (ie jointly controlled operations, assets and entities)

- Distinguish between equity accounting and proportional consolidation

- Describe the two formats of proportional consolidation

- Prepare consolidated financial statements to include a single subsidiary and an associated company or a joint venture

24 ANALYSIS AND INTERPRETATION OF FINANCIAL STATEMENTS

- Calculate useful financial ratios for a single company or for group financial statements

- Analyse and interpret ratios to give an assessment of a company's performance in comparison with:

(i) a company's previous period's financial statements

(ii) another similar company for the same period

(iii) industry average ratios

- Discuss the effect that changes in accounting policies or the use of different accounting policies between companies can have on the ability to interpret performance

- Discuss how the interpretation of current cost accounts or general (current) purchasing power accounts would differ from that of historic cost accounts

- Discuss the limitations in the use of ratio analysis for assessing corporate performance, outlining other information that may be of relevance

Note: the content of reports should draw upon knowledge acquired in other sessions

These sessions concentrate on the preparation of reports and report writing skills

25 & 26

CASH FLOW STATEMENTS

- Prepare a cash flow statement, including relevant notes, for an individual company in accordance with relevant accounting standards. Note: questions may specify the use of the direct or indirect method

- Appraise the usefulness of, and interpret the information in, a cash flow statement

27 RELATED PARTY DISCLOSURES

- Define and apply the definition of related parties in accordance with relevant accounting standards

- Describe the potential to mislead users when related party transactions are included in a company's financial statements

- Adjust financial statements (for comparative purposes) for the effects of non-commercial related party transactions

- Describe the disclosure requirements of related party transactions

28 SEGMENT REPORTING

- Discuss the usefulness and problems associated with the provision of segment information

- Define a reportable segment and the information that is to be reported (primary and secondary formats)

- Prepare segment reports in accordance with relevant accounting standards

- Assess the performance of a company based on the information contained in its segment report

The exam paper

Approach to examining the syllabus

The examination is a three hour paper in two sections. It will contain both computational and discursive elements. Some questions will adopt a scenario/case study approach.

The Section A compulsory question will be the preparation of group financial statements and/or extracts thereof, may include a small related discussion element. Computations will be designed to test an understanding of principles. At least one of the optional questions in Section B will be a conceptual/discursive question that may include illustrative numerical calculations.

An individual question may often involve elements that relate to different areas of the syllabus. For example, a question on the preparation of financial statements for public issue could include elements relating to several accounting standards. In scenario questions candidates may be expected to comment on management's chosen accounting treatment and determine a more appropriate one, based on circumstances described in the question.

Questions on topic areas that are also included in Paper 1.1 will be examined at an appropriately greater depth in Paper 2.5. Some International Accounting Standards are very detailed and complex. At Paper 2.5 candidates need to be aware of the principles and key elements of these standards. Candidates will also be expected to have an appreciation of the need for accounting standards and why they have been introduced.

Number of marks

Section A: One compulsory question	25
Section B: Choice of 3 from 4 questions (25 marks each)	75
	100

Additional information

Candidates need to be aware that questions involving knowledge of new examinable regulations will not be set until at least six months after the last day of the month in which the regulation was issued.

The Study Guide provides more detailed guidance on the syllabus. Examinable documents are listed in the 'Exam Notes' section of the *Student Accountant*.

Analysis of past papers

The analysis below shows the topics which have been examined in all sittings of the current syllabus so far and in the Pilot Paper.

December 2005

Section A

1   Consolidated balance sheet

Section B

2   Income statements; balance sheet; basic and diluted eps
3   Impairment
4   Cash flow statements
5   Non-current assets; related parties

June 2005

Section A

1   Consolidated balance sheet

Section B

2   Restatement of income statement and balance sheet; statement of changes in equity
3   IFRS 1
4   Cash flow statement
5   Decontamination costs; events after balance sheet date; contingencies; substance of transactions

December 2004

Section A

1   Calculation of goodwill on acquisition; prepare consolidated income statement; show movement on consolidated retained profits

Section B

2   Preparation of company income statement and balance sheet
3   Function of the business within IASCF; standard setting process; global accounting standards discussion
4   Cash flow statement by indirect method; report analysing the financial performance
5   Share capital, reserves and dividends; advantages of companies being able to purchase and then cancel their own shares.

June 2004

Section A

1   Consolidated balance sheet with associate

Section B

2   Adjustments and redrafting of balance sheet
3   Intangibles: discussion and application
4   Cash flow statements
5   Construction contracts: discussion and application

December 2003

Section A

1   Consolidated balance sheet; discussion of negative goodwill

Section B

2   Preparation of income statement; substance over form
3   IAS 37: discussion and examples
4   Problems of ratio analysis; ratio analysis report
5   Deferred tax; events after balance sheet date; construction contracts

June 2003

Section A

1   Consolidated financial statements; discussion of unrealised profit

Section B

2   Preparation of financial statements; sale and repurchase
3   Revenue recognition; government grant and the IASB Framework
4   Cash flow statement with ratio analysis
5   Defects of historical cost; CPP, CCA; EPS; dividend cover

December 2002

Section A

1   Consolidated income statement and balance sheet; discussion of uniting of interest method

Section B

2   Preparation of financial statements
3   Creative accounting, substance over form and off balance sheet finance
4   Preparation of cash flow statement; commentary
5   Discontinuing operations; earnings per share

June 2002

Section A

1   Consolidated balance sheet for subsidiary and associate

Section B

2   Redraft balance sheet to allow for additional items of information
3   Impairment losses: discussion and numerical example
4   Report on financial performance of subsidiary
5   Construction contracts; revaluation

December 2001

Section A

1   Consolidated balance sheet; non-consolidation of subsidiaries

Section B

2   Preparation of financial statements; earnings per share
3   IAS 16: cost; revaluation
4   Preparation of cash flow statement
5   Change of accounting policy; investment properties; after the balance sheet date events

Pilot paper

Section A

1   Consolidated financial statements; status of investment

Section B

2   Preparation of financial statements including adjustments relating to non-current assets
3   Revenue recognition
4   Re-stating financial statements and re-calculating profits
5   Financial instruments; impairment; discontinuing operations

Oxford Brookes BSc (Hons) in Applied Accounting

The standard required of candidates completing Part 2 is that required in the final year of a UK degree. Students completing Parts 1 and 2 will have satisfied the examination requirement for an honours degree in Applied Accounting, awarded by Oxford Brookes University.

To achieve the degree, you must also submit two pieces of work based on a **Research and Analysis Project.**

- A 5,000 word **Report** on your chosen topic, which demonstrates that you have acquired the necessary research, analytical and IT skills.

- A 1,500 word **Key Skills Statement**, indicating how you have developed your interpersonal and communication skills.

BPP was selected by the ACCA and Oxford Brookes University to produce the official text *Success in your Research and Analysis Project* to support students in this task. The book pays particular attention to key skills not covered in the professional examinations.

BPP also offers courses and mentoring services.

For further information, please see BPP's website: www.bpp.com/bsc

ACCA professional development requirements

Soon, you will possess a professional qualification. You know its value by the effort you have put in. To uphold the prestige of the qualification, ACCA, with the other professional bodies that form the International Federation of Accountants (IFAC), requires its members to undertake continuous professional development (CPD). This requirement applies to all members, not just those with a practising certificate. Happily, BPP Professional Education is here to support you in your professional development with materials, courses and qualifications.

> For further information, please see ACCA's website: www.accaglobal.com

Professional development with BPP

You do not have to do exams for professional development (PD) – but you need relevant technical updating and you may also benefit from other work-related training. BPP can provide you with both. Visit our professional development website, www.bpp.com/pd for details of our PD courses in accounting, law, general business skills and other important areas. Offering defined hours of structured CPD, and delivered by top professionals throughout the year and in many locations, our courses are designed to fit around your busy work schedule. Our unique PD passport will give you access to these PD services at an attractive discount.

> For further information, please see BPP's website: www.bpp.com/pd

Master of Business Administration (MBA)

ACCA and Oxford Brookes University, a leading UK university, have worked together on an MBA programme. The MBA, accredited by AMBA (the Association of MBAs), lasts 21 months for ACCA members, and is taught by distance learning with online seminars delivered to a global student base over the Internet. BPP provides the user-friendly materials. As an ACCA member, you will receive credits towards this MBA and you can begin your studies when you have completed your ACCA professional exams. Flexibility, global reach and value for money underpin a high quality learning experience.

The qualification features an introductory module (*Foundations of Management*). Other modules include *Global Business Strategy, Managing Self Development*, and *Organisational Change and Transformation*.

Research Methods are also taught, as they underpin the **research dissertation**.

> For further information, please visit: www.accaglobal.com, www. brookes.ac.uk or www.bpp.com/mba

Diploma in International Financial Reporting

The ACCA's Diploma in International Financial Reporting is designed for those whose country-specific accounting knowledge needs to be supplemented by knowledge of international accounting standards. BPP offers books and courses in this useful qualification – it also earns you valuable CPD points.

For further information, please see ACCA's website: www.accaglobal.com and BPP's website: www.bpp.com/dipifr

Tax and financial services

If you are interested in tax, BPP offers courses for the ATT (tax technician) and CTA (Chartered Tax Adviser, formerly ATII) qualifications. You can also buy our user-friendly CTA texts to keep up-to-date with tax practice.

For further information, please see BPP's website: www.bpp.com/att and www.bpp.com/cta

If your role involves selling financial services products, such as pensions, or offering investment advice, BPP provides learning materials and training for relevant qualifications. BPP also offers training for specialist financial markets qualifications (eg CFA®) and insolvency.

For further information, please see BPP's website: www.bpp.com/financialadvisers

Other business qualifications

BPP supports many business disciplines, such as market research, marketing, human resources management and law. We are the official provider of distance learning programmes for the Market Research Society. We train for the Chartered Institute of Personnel and Development qualification, with a number of other supporting qualifications in training and personnel management. BPP's law school is an industry leader.

Visit www.bpp.com for further details of all that we can offer you. BPP's personalised online information service, My BPP, will help you keep track of the details you submit to BPP.

Syllabus mindmap

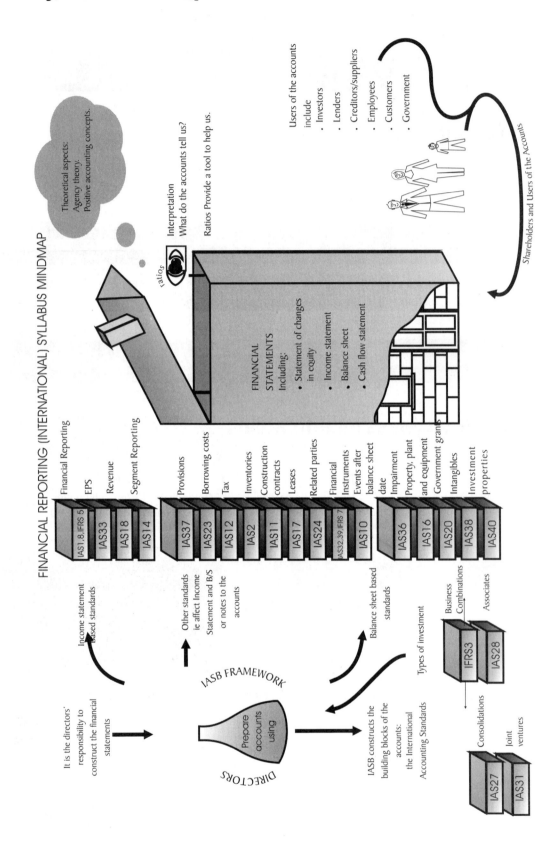

FINANCIAL REPORTING (INTERNATIONAL) SYLLABUS MINDMAP

Theoretical aspects:
Agency theory.
Positive accounting concepts.

Interpretation
What do the accounts tell us?
Ratios Provide a tool to help us.

Users of the accounts
include
. Investors
. Lenders
. Creditors/suppliers
. Employees
. Customers
. Government

Shareholders and Users of the Accounts

FINANCIAL
STATEMENTS
Including:
• Statement of changes
  in equity
• Income statement
• Balance sheet
• Cash flow statement

Financial Reporting — IAS1,8,IFRS 5
EPS — IAS33
Revenue — IAS18
Segment Reporting — IAS14

Provisions — IAS37
Borrowing costs — IAS23
Tax — IAS12
Inventories — IAS2
Construction contracts — IAS11
Leases — IAS17
Related parties — IAS24
Financial Instruments — IAS32,39,IFRS 7
Events after balance sheet date — IAS10

Impairment — IAS36
Property, plant and equipment — IAS16
Government grants — IAS20
Intangibles — IAS38
Investment properties — IAS40

Income statement based standards

Other standards ie affect Income Statement and B/S or notes to the accounts

Balance sheet based standards

It is the directors' responsibility to construct the financial statements

IASB FRAMEWORK

DIRECTORS

Prepare accounts using

IASB constructs the building blocks of the accounts: the International Accounting Standards

Types of investment

Business Combinations — IFRS3
Associates — IAS28

Consolidations
Joint ventures — IAS27, IAS31

Part A
The Regulatory Framework

Revision of basic accounts and concepts

Introduction

Paper 2.5 *Financial Reporting* has a demanding syllabus to cover, but don't let this put you off. As long as you give yourself plenty of time to work through the whole syllabus, you should not find any of the subject areas too complicated.

This chapter acts mainly as revision, so that you are sure of the skills and knowledge you have brought from your earlier studies. If you have any doubts, go back to your earlier study material and revise those aspects which seem unclear.

IAS 1 *Presentation of financial statements* has been revised recently following the issue of IFRS 5. Only that part of IAS 1 which deals with accounting policies is covered here. The remainder of IAS 1 will be dealth with in Chapter 3.

Study guide

Section 1 – Review of basic concepts and the Framework for the preparation and presentation of financial statements

- Revision of Paper 1.1 – prepare the final accounts of a company from a trial balance.

1 Introduction to paper 2.5

FAST FORWARD

Paper 2.5 covers a demanding syllabus, but if your approach is methodical, and you leave yourself enough time, you will succeed.

1.1 Fundamentals

Paper 2.5 is obviously a harder paper than Paper 1.1. Most of that difficulty stems from the **breadth of the syllabus,** which covers the bulk of financial accounting topics. You will find, however, that you are only expected to understand the simpler aspects of complicated areas, such as in group accounts.

Exam focus point

> Your aim should be to set aside enough time to work through the whole of the BPP Study Text for Paper 2.5 well before the exam.
>
> Go to the introductory pages of this text. Make sure you read the following.
>
> - Syllabus
> - Study Guide
> - Further guidance from the ACCA
> - Format of the examination paper

In particular, look at the **key areas of the syllabus** highlighted by the examiner. By the end of your studies for Paper 2.5, you should be happy with your skills and knowledge in all these areas.

1.2 International accounting standards (IASs and IFRSs)

Which IASs and IFRSs are examinable under Paper 2.5? You studied only a limited number for Paper 1.1, but in Paper 2.5 the bulk of IASs and IFRSs are examinable. There are still some exclusions, however, and these will not be covered until you tackle Paper 3.6 *Advanced Corporate Reporting.*

A list of current IASs and IFRSs (as at June 2006) is given below. Only those examinable by the ACCA are included. Those you have studied for Paper 1.1 are noted, as are those which are not examinable until you reach Paper 3.6.

IAS		Examinable in Paper		
No	**Title**	**1.1**	**2.5**	**3.6**
1	Presentation of financial statements	✓	✓	✓
2	Inventories	✓	✓	✓
7	Cash flow statements	✓	✓	✓
8	Accounting policies, changes in accounting estimates and errors	✓	✓	✓
10	Events after the balance sheet date	✓	✓	✓
11	Construction contracts		✓	✓
12	Income taxes		✓	✓

BPP
PROFESSIONAL EDUCATION

IAS		Examinable in Paper		
No	**Title**	**1.1**	**2.5**	**3.6**
14	Segment reporting		✓	✓
16	Property, plant and equipment	✓	✓	✓
17	Leases		✓	✓
18	Revenue	✓	✓	✓
19	Employee benefits			✓
20	Accounting for government grants and disclosure of government assistance		✓	✓
21	The effects of changes in foreign exchange rates			✓
23	Borrowing costs		✓	✓
24	Related party disclosures		✓	✓
27	Consolidated and separate financial statements		✓	✓
28	Investments in associates		✓	✓
29	Financial reporting in hyperinflationary economies			✓
31	Interests in joint ventures		✓	✓
32	Financial instruments: disclosure and presentation		✓	✓
33	Earnings per share		✓	✓
34	Interim financial reporting			✓
36	Impairment of assets		✓	✓
37	Provisions, contingent liabilities and contingent assets	✓	✓	✓
38	Intangible assets	✓	✓	✓
39	Financial instruments: recognition and measurement		✓	✓
40	Investment property		✓	✓
41	Agriculture			✓
IFRS		**Examinable in Paper**		
No	**Title**	**1.1**	**2.5**	**3.6**
1	First time adoption of International Financial Reporting Standards		✓	✓
2	Share-based payment			✓
3	Business combinations	✓	✓	✓
4	Insurance contracts			✓
5	Non-current assets held for sale and discontinued operations	✓	✓	✓
6	Exploration for and evaluation of mineral resources			✓
7	Financial instruments: disclosures		✓	

Exposure drafts and discussion drafts are not examinable at Paper 2.5.

1.3 Keeping up to date

In the case of subjects such as financial accounting and auditing you must keep up to date. In particular, you should read the *Student Accountant* every month. As well as all relevant articles, you must check the

'**Exam Notes**' **section** before your exam. This lists all the relevant examinable documents for each sitting. You should make sure that you have covered all the documents listed for your sitting of this paper.

Working through **articles** relevant to Paper 2.5 is an excellent way of checking that you understand a subject.

Set aside one or two nights a month to read through *Student Accountant.*

1.4 Be professional!

Before we go on to some revision topics, which should get you back into the swing of financial accounting, here is an important reminder.

Paper 2.5 is a Professional level exam.

You must demonstrate a professional approach in the exam. This does not only apply to **what you write,** but **how you write it.** Start cultivating the right approach now!

1.5 Section summary

Your overall approach to Paper 2.5 should be:

- Spend plenty of time on this paper: it is a big leap from your earlier studies
- Read Student Accountant every month
- Read the introductory pages of this Study Text, particularly the further guidance from the examiner
- Be professional!

2 The regulatory system of accounting

FAST FORWARD   This is just an outline, you will deal with the regulatory system in more detail in Chapter 2.

2.1 Introduction

The purpose of this section is to give a general picture of some of the **factors which have shaped financial accounting**. We will concern ourselves with the accounts of limited liability companies because the limited liability company is the type of organisation whose accounts are most closely regulated by statute or otherwise.

The following **factors** can be identified.

- National/local legislation
- Accounting concepts and individual judgement
- Accounting standards
- Other international influences
- Generally accepted accounting principles (GAAP)
- True and fair view (or presented fairly)

2.2 National/local legislation

Limited liability companies may be **required by law** to prepare and publish accounts annually. The form and content of the accounts may be regulated primarily by national legislation, but must also comply with International Financial Reporting Standards (IFRS).

2.3 Accounting concepts and individual judgement

Financial statements are prepared on the basis of a number of **fundamental accounting assumptions and conventions** as we will see below. Many figures in financial statements are derived from the application of judgement in putting these assumptions into practice.

It is clear that different people exercising their judgement on the same facts can arrive at very **different conclusions**. Suppose, for example, that an accountancy training firm has an excellent reputation amongst students and employers. How would you value this? The firm may have relatively little in the form of assets which you can touch, perhaps a building, desks and chairs. If you simply drew up a balance sheet showing the cost of the assets owned, then the business would not seem to be worth much, yet its income earning potential might be high. This is true of many service organisations where the people are among the most valuable assets.

Other examples of areas where the judgement of different people may differ are as follows.

- **Valuation of buildings** in times of rising property prices.

- **Research and development**: is it right to treat this only as an expense? In a sense it is an investment to generate future revenue.

- Accounting for **inflation**.

- **Brands** such as 'Mars Bar' or 'Walkman'. Are they assets in the same way that a fork lift truck is an asset?

Working from the same data, different groups of people would produce very different financial statements. If the exercise of judgement is completely unfettered, any **comparability** between the accounts of different organisations will disappear. This will be all the more significant in cases where deliberate manipulation occurs in order to present accounts in the most favourable light.

2.4 Accounting standards

In an attempt to deal with some of the subjectivity, and to achieve comparability between different organisations, accounting standards have been developed. These are developed at both a **national level** (in most countries) and an **international level**. In this text we are concerned with International Accounting Standards (IASs) and a brief summary of the current regime for producing IASs is given here. We go into much more depth in Chapter 2.

2.4.1 International Accounting Standards

International Accounting Standards (IASs) are produced by the **International Accounting Standards Board (IASB)**. The IASB was set up in 1973 (as the International Accounting Standards Committee) to work for the improvement and harmonisation of financial reporting. The IASB develops IASs through an international process that involves the world-wide accountancy profession, the preparers and users of financial statements, and national standard setting bodies. New Standards are now called *International Financial Reporting Standards* (IFRS). **Throughout this text, any reference to IFRSs includes both IASs and IFRSs.**

2.4.2 Objectives of the IASB

Here is a reminder of the formal objectives of the IASB.

(a) To **develop**, in the public interest, a single set of high quality, understandable and enforceable **global accounting standards** that require high quality, transparent and comparable information in general purpose financial statements.

(b) To promote the use and **rigorous application** of those standards

(c)   To work actively with national standard setters to bring about **convergence of national accounting standards and IFRS** to high quality solutions

The IASB is discussed in detail in Chapter 2.

2.5 Other international influences

There are a few **other international bodies** worth mentioning. You are not required to follow their workings in detail, but knowledge of them will aid your studies and should help your general reading around the subject area.

2.5.1 IASB and the EC/intergovernmental bodies

The European Commission has acknowledged the role of the IASB in harmonising world-wide accounting rules and EC representatives attend IASB Board meetings and have joined Steering Committees involved in setting IFRSs. This should bring to an end the idea of a separate layer of European reporting rules.

The EC has also set up a committee to investigate where there are conflicts between EU norms and international standards so that compatibility can be achieved. In turn, the IASB has used EC directives in its work.

All listed entities in member states must use IFRSs in their consolidated financial statements from 2005.

The IASB also works closely with the United Nations Working Groups of Experts on International Standards of Accounting and Reporting (UN IASR group), and with the Working Group in Accounting Standards of the Organisation for Economic Co-operation and Development (OECD Working group). These bodies support harmonisation and improvement of financial reporting, but they are not standard-setting bodies and much of their output draws on the work of the IASB (eg using the IASB's *Framework* document).

2.5.2 United Nations (UN)

The UN has a Commission and Centre on Transnational Reporting Corporations through which it gathers information concerning the activities and reporting of multinational companies. The UN processes are highly **political** and probably reflect the attitudes of the governments of developing countries to multinationals. For example, there is an inter-governmental working group of 'experts' on international standards of accounting and reporting which is dominated by the non-developed countries.

2.5.3 International Federation of Accountants (IFAC)

The IFAC is a private sector body established in 1977 and which now consists of over 100 professional accounting bodies from around 80 different countries. The IFAC's main objective is to co-ordinate the accounting profession on a global scale by issuing and establishing international standards on auditing, management accounting, ethics, education and training. You are already familiar with the **International Standards on Auditing** produced by the IAASB, an IFAC body. The IFAC has separate committees working on these topics and also organises the World Congress of Accountants, which is held every five years. The IASB is affiliated with IFAC.

2.5.4 Organisation for Economic Co-operation and Development (OECD)

The OECD was established in 1960 by the governments of 21 countries to 'achieve the highest sustainable economic growth and employment and a rising standard of living in member countries while maintaining financial stability and, thus, to contribute to the world economy'. The OECD supports the work of the IASB but also undertakes its **own research** into accounting standards via *ad hoc* working groups. For example, in 1976 the OECD issued guidelines for multinational companies on financial reporting and non-financial disclosures. The OECD appears to work on behalf of developed countries to protect them from the extreme proposals of the UN.

2.6 Generally Accepted Accounting Practice (GAAP)

We also need to consider some important terms which you will meet in your financial accounting studies. GAAP, as a term, has sprung up in recent years and signifies **all the rules, from whatever source, which govern accounting**. The rules may derive from:

(a)   Local (national) company legislation
(b)   National and international accounting standards
(c)   Statutory requirements in other countries (particularly the US)
(d)   Stock exchange requirements

GAAP will be considered in more detail in Chapter 2.

2.7 True and fair view (or presented fairly)

It is a requirement of national legislation (in some countries) that the financial statements should give a true and fair view of (or 'present fairly, in all material respects') the financial position of the entity as at the end of the financial year.

The terms 'true and fair view' and 'present fairly, in all material respects' are not defined in accounting or auditing standards. Despite this, a company's managers may depart from any of the provisions of accounting standards if these are inconsistent with the requirement to give a true and fair view. This is commonly referred to as the 'true and fair override'. It has been treated as an important **loophole** in the law in different countries and has been the cause of much argument and dissatisfaction within the accounting profession.

3 IAS 1 Presentation of financial statements

FAST FORWARD

IAS 1 has been revised recently.

Here we will look at the general requirements of IAS 1 and what it says about **accounting policies**. The rest of the standard, on the format and content of financial statements, current assets and liabilities and so on, will be covered in Chapter 3.

3.1 Objectives and scope

The main objective of IAS 1 is:

'to prescribe the basis for presentation of general purpose financial statements, in order to ensure comparability both with the entity's own financial statements of previous periods and with the financial statements of other entities.'

IAS 1 applies to all **general purpose financial statements** prepared in accordance with IFRSs, ie those intended to meet the needs of users who are not in a position to demand reports tailored to their specific needs.

3.2 Purpose of financial statements

The **objective of financial statements** is to provide information about the financial position, performance and cash flows of an entity that is useful to a wide range of users in making economic decisions. They also show the result of **management stewardship** of the resources of the entity.

In order to fulfil this objective, financial statements must provide information about the following aspects of an entity's results.

- Assets
- Liabilities
- Equity
- Income and expenses (including gains and losses)
- Cash flows

Along with other information in the notes and related documents, this information will assist users in predicting the entity's **future cash flows**.

3.3 Responsibility for financial statements

Responsibility for the preparation and presentation of an entity's financial statements rests with the **board of directors** (or equivalent).

3.4 Components of financial statements

As you will already know, a complete set of financial statements includes the following components.

- Balance sheet

- Income statement

- Statement showing *either*:

  - All changes in equity, *or*

  - Changes in equity other than those arising from capital transactions with and/or distributions to owners

- Cash flow statement

- Accounting policies and explanatory notes

In addition, IAS 1 recognises that many entities wish to present, outside the financial statements, a **financial review** by management (which is *not* part of the financial statements), explaining the main features of the entity's performance and position, and the principal uncertainties it faces. The report may include a review of the following.

(a) **Factors/influences determining performance**: changes in the environment in which the entity operates, the entity's response to those changes and their effect, and the entity's policy for investment to maintain and enhance performance, including its dividend policy

(b) Entity's **sources of funding**, the policy on **gearing** and its **risk management policies**

(c) **Strengths and resources** of the entity whose value is not reflected in the balance sheet under IFRSs

IFRSs are only concerned with the financial statements, so IAS 1 has no mandatory rules concerning such a review.

3.5 Fair presentation and compliance with IFRS

Most importantly, financial statements should **present fairly** the financial position, financial performance and cash flows of an entity. **Compliance with IFRS** is presumed to result in financial statements that achieve a fair presentation.

The following points made by IAS 1 expand on this principle.

(a) **Compliance with IFRS** should be disclosed

(b) **All relevant IFRS** must be followed if compliance with IFRS is disclosed

(c) Use of an **inappropriate accounting treatment** cannot be rectified either by disclosure of accounting policies or notes/explanatory material

There may be (very rare) circumstances when management decides that compliance with a requirement of an IFRS would be misleading. **Departure from the IFRS** is therefore required to achieve a fair presentation. The following should be disclosed in such an event.

(a) Management confirmation that the financial statements fairly present the entity's financial position, performance and cash flows

(b) Statement that all IFRS have been complied with *except* departure from one IFRS to achieve a fair presentation

(c) Details of the nature of the departure, why the IFRS treatment would be misleading, and the treatment adopted

(d) Financial impact of the departure

3.5.1 Extreme case disclosures

In very rare circumstances, management may conclude that compliance with a requirement in a Standard or interpretation may be so **misleading** that it would **conflict with the objective** of Financial Statements set out in the *Framework*, but the relevant regulatory framework prohibits departure from the requirements. In such cases the entity needs to reduce the perceived misleading aspects of compliance by **disclosing**:

(a) The title of the Standard, the nature of the requirement and the reason why management has reached its conclusion.

(b) For each period, the adjustment to each item in the Financial Statements that would be necessary to achieve fair presentation.

IAS 1 states what is required for a fair presentation.

(a) Selection and application of **accounting policies**

(b) **Presentation of information** in a manner which provides relevant, reliable, comparable and understandable information

(c) **Additional disclosures** where required

The IAS then goes on to consider certain important assumptions which underpin the preparation and presentation of financial statements, which we might call **fundamental assumptions.**

3.6 Going concern

Key term

> The entity is normally viewed as a **going concern**, that is, as continuing in operation for the foreseeable future. Financial statements are prepared on a going concern basis unless management intends to liquidate the entity or to cease trading.

This assumption is based on the notion that, when preparing a normal set of accounts, it is always expected that the business will **continue to operate** in approximately the same manner for the foreseeable future (at least the next 12 months should be considered). In particular, the entity will not go into liquidation or scale down its operations in a material way.

The main significance of the going concern assumption is that the assets of the business **should not be valued at their 'break-up' value**, which is the amount that they would sell for if they were sold off piecemeal and the business were thus broken up.

If the going concern assumption is not followed, that fact must be disclosed, together with:

- The **basis** on which the financial statements have been prepared
- The **reasons** why the entity is not considered to be a going concern

3.7 Accrual basis of accounting

> **Accrual basis of accounting.** Items are recognised as assets liabilities, equity, income and expenses when they satisfy the definition and recognition criteria for those elements in the *Framework*.   *(IAS 1)*

Entities should prepare their financial statements on the basis that transactions are recorded in them, not as the cash is paid or received, but as the revenues or expenses are **earned or incurred** in the accounting period to which they relate.

According to the accrual assumption, then, in computing profit revenue earned must be **matched against** the expenditure incurred in earning it.

3.8 Consistency of presentation

To maintain consistency, the presentation and classification of items in the financial statements should **stay the same from one period to the next**. **There are two exceptions.**

(a)   There is a significant change in the **nature of the operations** or a review of the financial statements presentation indicates a **more appropriate presentation**.

(b)   A change in presentation is **required by an IFRS**.

3.9 Materiality and aggregation

All material items should be presented separately in the financial statements.

Amounts which are **immaterial** can be aggregated with amounts of a similar nature or function and need not be presented separately.

> **Materiality.** Omissions or misstatement of items are material if they could, individually or collectively, influence the economic decisions of users taken on the basis of the financial statements. Materiality depends on the size and nature of the omission or misstatement judged in the surrounding circumstances. The size or nature of the item, or a combination of both, could be the determining factor.   *(IAS 1)*

An error which is too trivial to affect anyone's understanding of the accounts is referred to as **immaterial**. In preparing accounts it is important to assess what is material and what is not, so that time and money are not wasted in the pursuit of excessive detail.

Determining whether or not an item is material is a very **subjective exercise**. There is no absolute measure of materiality. It is common to apply a convenient rule of thumb (for example to define material items as those with a value greater than 5% of the net profit disclosed by the accounts). But some items disclosed in accounts are regarded as particularly sensitive and even a very small misstatement of such an item would be regarded as a material error. An example in the accounts of a limited liability company might be the amount of remuneration paid to directors of the company.

The assessment of an item as material or immaterial may **affect its treatment in the accounts**. For example, the income statement of a business will show the expenses incurred by the business grouped under suitable captions (heating and lighting expenses, rent and property taxes etc); but in the case of very small expenses it may be appropriate to lump them together under a caption such as 'sundry expenses', because a more detailed breakdown would be inappropriate for such immaterial amounts.

In assessing whether or not an item is material, it is not only the amount of the item which needs to be considered. The **context** is also important.

(a) If a balance sheet shows non-current assets of $2 million and inventories of $30,000 an error of $20,000 in the depreciation calculations might not be regarded as material, whereas an error of $20,000 in the inventory valuation probably would be. In other words, the total of which the erroneous item forms part must be considered.

(b) If a business has a bank loan of $50,000 and a $55,000 balance on bank deposit account, it might well be regarded as a material misstatement if these two amounts were displayed on the balance sheet as 'cash at bank $5,000'. In other words, incorrect presentation may amount to material misstatement even if there is no monetary error.

Users are assumed to have a personal knowledge of business and economic activities and accounting and a willingness to study the information with reasonable diligence.

3.10 Offsetting

IAS 1 does not allow **assets and liabilities to be offset** against each other unless such a treatment is required or permitted by another IFRS.

Income and expenses can be offset only when:

(a) an IAS requires/permits it; *or*

(b) gains, losses and related expenses arising from the same/similar transactions are not material (aggregate).

3.11 Comparative information

IAS 1 requires comparative information to be disclosed for the previous period for all **numerical information**, unless another IAS permits/requires otherwise. Comparatives should also be given in narrative information where helpful.

Comparatives should be **reclassified** when the presentation or classification of items in the financial statements is amended (see IAS 8: Chapter 12).

3.12 Disclosure of accounting policies

There should be a specific section for accounting policies in the notes to the financial statements and the following should be disclosed there.

(a) **Measurement bases** used in preparing the financial statements

(b) Each **specific accounting policy** necessary for a proper understanding of the financial statements

To be clear and understandable it is essential that financial statements should disclose the accounting policies used in their preparation. This is because **policies may vary**, not only from entity to entity, but also from country to country. As an aid to users, all the major accounting policies used should be disclosed in the same place.

There is a wide range of policies available in many accounting areas. Examples where such differing policies exist are as follows, although the list is not exhaustive and it contains some items which you will only meet later on in this text.

- **General**

  - Consolidation policy

  - Conversion/translation of foreign currencies, including the treatment of exchange gains/losses

  - Overall valuation policy (eg historical cost, general purchasing power, replacement value)

  - Events subsequent to the balance sheet date

  - Leases, hire purchase or instalment transactions and related interest

  - Taxes

  - Construction contracts

  - Franchises

- **Assets**

  - Receivables
  - Inventories and related cost of goods sold
  - Depreciable assets and depreciation
  - Growing crops
  - Land held for development and related development costs
  - Investments: subsidiary and associate companies and other investments
  - Research and development
  - Patents and trademarks
  - Goodwill

- **Liabilities and provisions**

  - Warranties
  - Commitments and contingencies
  - Pension costs and retirement plans
  - Severance and redundancy payments

- **Profits and losses**

  - Methods of revenue recognition

  - Maintenance, repairs and improvements

  - Gains and losses on disposals of property

  - Reserve accounting, statutory or otherwise, including direct charges and credits to surplus accounts

Try the following questions as revision of IAS 1.

| Question | Quality |

Compare the following two income statements prepared for a sole trader who wishes to show them to the bank manager to justify continuation of an overdraft facility.

YEAR ENDED 31 DECEMBER 20X7

	$	$
Sales revenue		25,150
Less: production costs	10,000	
selling and administration	7,000	
		17,000
Gross profit		8,150
Less interest charges		1,000
Profit after interest		7,150

YEAR ENDED 31 DECEMBER 20X8

	$
Sales revenue less selling costs	22,165
Less production costs	10,990
Gross profit	11,175
Less administration and interest	3,175
Net profit	8,000

Which accounting concept is being ignored here? Justify your choice.

How do you think the changes in the format of these financial statements affect the quality of the accounting information presented?

Answer

The accounting assumption breached here is that of **consistency**. This concept holds that accounting information should be presented in a way that facilitates comparisons from period to period.

In the income statement for 20X7 sales revenue is shown separately from selling costs. Also interest and administration charges are treated separately.

The new format is poor in itself, as we cannot know whether any future change in 'sales revenue less selling costs' is due to an increase in sales revenue or a decline in selling costs. A similar criticism can be levelled at the lumping together of administration costs and interest charges. It is impossible to divide the two.

It is not possible to 'rewrite' 20X7's accounts in terms of 20X8, because we do not know the breakdown in 20X7 between selling and administration costs.

The business's bank manager will not, therefore, be able to assess the business's performance, and might wonder if the sole trader has 'something to hide'. Thus the value of this accounting information is severely affected.

Question

Valuation

You are in business in a small town, whose main source of economic prosperity is the tourist trade. On 25 March 20X8 the town celebrated the 1,000th anniversary of its existence. The town held a number of festivals to mark this occasion and to bring in more tourists.

Your business has had the good fortune to be involved in the event. You have made 1,000 commemorative mugs. These were all made by 31 December 20X7 to be ready at the beginning of the year. They cost 40 cents each to make and during the anniversary year they were for sale at 75 cents each. At the end of the anniversary year, there are 200 still unsold. You estimate that you are unlikely to sell any more at 75 cents, but you might be able to sell them at 30 cents each.

Required

Which fundamental accounting assumptions and other matters will you consider when assessing a value for the mugs in your balance sheets:

(a) At the end of 20X7?

(b) At the end of 20X8?

On the basis of your considerations, note down the value of the mugs you would include in the balance sheet at 31 December 20X7 and 31 December 20X8.

Answer

The accounting assumption mainly involved is **accruals**. **Prudence** is also important when determining the accounting policy.

The accruals assumption states that income and expenditure should be matched in the same period if reasonably possible, whereas prudence dictates that revenue should not be anticipated. However, you are reasonably certain of selling the mugs, so you would value them in the balance sheet at the beginning of the year at *cost*, as an *asset* (rather than treating them as an expense in the income statement for that earlier year).

At 31 December 20X8 you have 200 spare, whose selling price is less than the cost of making them. Prudence dictates therefore that they are valued in the balance sheet at the lower of these two amounts (ie sales value if it is lower than cost).

You could argue that valuing them at a lower amount means a conflict with the accruals assumption, because the loss is accounted for before the sale. This is true. Normally, when accruals and prudence conflict, prudence should prevail.

As a consequence, at 31 December 20X7, the mugs would be valued at 40 cents each. At 31 December 20X8, the remaining mugs would be valued at 30 cents each.

Question

Materiality

You work for a multinational company and you are preparing two accounting documents.

(a) A statement for a customer, listing invoices and receipts, and detailing the amounts owed

(b) A report sent to the senior management of a division, who want a brief comparative summary of how well the firm is doing in Thailand and in Malaysia

How would considerations of **materiality** influence your preparation of each document?

Answer

Materiality as a 'fundamental concept' does have strict limitations. It refers primarily to financial *reporting*, but has no bearing at all on detailed procedural matters such as bank reconciliations or statements of account sent to customers.

Consequently, the statement sent to the customer, described in option (a), must be accurate to the last cent, however large it is. After all, if you receive a bill from a company for $147.50, you do not 'round it up' to $150 when you pay. Nor will the company billing you be prepared to 'round it down' to $145. A customer pays an agreed price for an agreed product or service. Paying more is effectively giving money away, and if you are going to do that, there might be worthier beneficiaries of your generosity. Paying less exposes your creditor to an unfair loss.

On the other hand, if you are preparing a performance report comparing how well the company is doing in Thailand and Malaysia, entirely different considerations apply.

There is little point in being accurate to the last cent (and inconsistencies might occur from the choice of currency rate used). This is because senior management are interested in the broad picture, and they are looking to identify comparisons between the overall performance of each division.

Assume that Thailand profits were $1,233,750.57 and profits in Malaysia were $1,373,370.75.

Malaysia	Thailand
$	$
1,373,370.75	1,233,750.57
or	or
$'000	$'000
1,373	1,234

The rounded figures are much easier to understand, and so the relative performance is easier to compare. Considerations of materiality would allow you to ignore the rounding differences, because they are so small and the information is used for comparative purposes only.

3.13 Section summary

Accounting policies are extremely important.

- Accounting policies must be **appropriate** and **applied consistently**

- Financial statements complying with IASs will normally **present fairly** the results of the entity

- Important **concepts** are: going concern, accruals, consistency, materiality, prudence and substance over form

- All accounting policies should be **fully disclosed**

4 Revision of basic accounts

FAST FORWARD

> The Study Guide requires you to be able to prepare a basic set of company accounts from a trial balance.

In the next part of this text we move on to the mechanics of preparing financial statements. It would be useful at this point to refresh your memory of the basic accounting you have already studied and these questions will help you. Make sure that you understand everything before you go on.

Question   **Basics**

A friend has bought some shares in a company quoted on a local stock exchange and has received the latest accounts. There is one page he is having difficulty in understanding.

Briefly, but clearly, answer his questions.

(a) What is a balance sheet?
(b) What is an asset?
(c) What is a liability?
(d) What is share capital?
(e) What are reserves?
(f) Why does the balance sheet balance?
(g) To what extent does the balance sheet value my investment?

Answer

(a)   A **balance sheet** is a statement of the assets, liabilities and capital of a business as at a stated date. It is laid out to show either total assets as equivalent to total liabilities and capital or net assets as equivalent to capital. Other formats are also possible but the top half (or left hand) total will always equal the bottom half (or right hand) total. Some balance sheets are laid out vertically and others horizontally.

(b)   An **asset** is a resource controlled by a business and is expected to be of some future benefit. Its value is determined as the historical cost of producing or obtaining it (unless an attempt is being made to reflect rising prices in the accounts, in which case a replacement cost might be used). Examples of assets are:

(i)   Plant, machinery, land and other **non-current assets**

(ii)   **Current** assets such as inventories, cash and debts owed to the business with reasonable assurance of recovery: these are assets which are not intended to be held on a continuing basis in the business

(c)   A **liability** is an amount owed by a business, other than the amount owed to its proprietors (capital). Examples of liabilities are:

(i)   Amounts owed to the government (sales or other taxes)
(ii)   Amounts owed to suppliers
(iii)   Bank overdraft
(iv)   Long-term loans from banks or investors

It is usual to differentiate between 'current' and 'long-term' liabilities. The former fall due within a year of the balance sheet date.

(d)   **Share capital** is the permanent investment in a business by its owners. In the case of a limited company, this takes the form of *shares* for which investors subscribe on formation of the company. Each share has a **nominal** or **par** (ie face) **value** (say $1). In the balance sheet, total issued share capital is shown at its par value.

(e)   If a company issues shares for more than their par value (at a **premium**) then (usually) by law this premium must be recorded separately from the par value in a 'share premium account'. This is an example of a reserve. It belongs to the shareholders but cannot be distributed to them, because it is a **capital reserve**. Other capital reserves include the revaluation reserve, which shows the surpluses arising on revaluation of assets which are still owned by the company.

Share capital and capital reserves are not distributable except on the winding up of the company, as a guarantee to the company's creditors that the company has enough assets to meet its debts. This is necessary because shareholders in limited liability companies have 'limited liability'; once they have paid the company for their shares they have no further liability to it if it becomes insolvent. The proprietors of other businesses are, by contrast, personally liable for business debts.

Revenue reserves constitute accumulated profits (less losses) made by the company and can be distributed to shareholders as **dividends**. They too belong to the shareholders, and so are a claim on the resources of the company.

(f)   Balance sheets do not always balance on the first attempt, as all accountants know! However, once errors are corrected, all balance sheets balance. This is because in **double entry bookkeeping** every transaction recorded has a dual effect. Assets are always equal to liabilities plus capital and so capital is always equal to assets less liabilities. This makes sense as the owners of the business are entitled to the net assets of the business as representing their capital plus accumulated surpluses (or less accumulated deficit).

(g) The balance sheet is not intended as a statement of a business's worth at a given point in time. This is because, except where some attempt is made to adjust for the effects of rising prices, assets and liabilities are recorded at **historical cost** and on a prudent basis. For example, if there is any doubt about the recoverability of a debt, then the value in the accounts must be reduced to the likely recoverable amount. In addition, where non-current assets have a finite useful life, their cost is gradually written off to reflect the use being made of them.

Sometimes non-current assets are **revalued** to their market value but this revaluation then goes out of date as few assets are revalued every year.

The balance sheet figure for capital and reserves therefore bears **no relationship** to the market value of shares. Market values are the product of a large number of factors, including general economic conditions, alternative investment returns (eg interest rates), likely future profits and dividends and, not least, market sentiment.

Question

Company financial statements

The accountant of Fiddles Co, a limited liability company, has begun preparing final accounts but the work is not yet complete. At this stage the items included in the list of account balances are as follows.

	$'000
Land	100
Buildings	120
Plant and machinery	170
Depreciation provision	120
Ordinary shares of $1	100
Reserve balance brought forward	200
Trade accounts receivable	200
Trade accounts payable	110
Inventory	190
Operating profit	80
Loan stock (16%)	180
Allowance for receivables	3
Bank balance (asset)	12
Suspense	1

Notes (i) to (vii) below are to be taken into account.

(i) The accounts receivable control account figure, which is used in the list of account balances, does not agree with the total of the sales ledger. A contra of $5,000 has been entered correctly in the individual ledger accounts but has been entered on the wrong side of both control accounts.

A batch total of sales of $12,345 had been entered in the double entry system as $13,345, although the individual ledger accounts entries for these sales were correct. The balance of $4,000 on the sales returns account has inadvertently been omitted from the trial balance though correctly entered in the ledger records.

(ii) A standing order of receipt from a regular customer for $2,000, and bank charges of $1,000, have been completely omitted from the records.

(iii) A receivable for $1,000 is to be written off. The allowance for receivables balance is to be adjusted to 1% of receivables.

(iv) The opening inventory figure had been overstated by $1,000 and the closing inventory figure had been understated by $2,000.

(v)   Any remaining balance on the suspense account should be treated as purchases if a debit balance and as sales if a credit balance.

(vi)   The loan stock was issued three months before the year end. No entries have been made as regards interest.

Required

(a)   Prepare journal entries to cover items in notes (i) to (v) above. You are not to open any new accounts and may use only those accounts included in the list of account balances as given.

(b)   Prepare final accounts for internal use within the limits of the available information. For presentation purposes all the items arising from notes (i) to (vii) above should be regarded as material.

Answer

(a)   JOURNAL ENTRIES FOR ADJUSTMENTS

		Debit $	Credit $
(i)	Trade accounts payable	10,000	
	Trade accounts receivable		10,000
	Operating profit	1,000	
	Trade accounts receivable		1,000
	Operating profit	4,000	
	Suspense		4,000
(ii)	Bank	2,000	
	Trade accounts receivable		2,000
	Operating profit	1,000	
	Bank		1,000
(iii)	Operating profit	1,000	
	Trade accounts receivable		1,000
	Allowance for receivables (W1)	1,140	
	Operating profit		1,140
(iv)	Inventories	2,000	
	Operating profit		2,000
	Reserves brought forward	1,000	
	Operating profit		1,000
(v)	Suspense	3,000	
	Operating profit		3,000

(b) FIDDLES CO
     BALANCE SHEET

	$	$	$
Assets			
Non-current assets			
Land and buildings		220,000	
Plant and machinery		170,000	
Depreciation		(120,000)	
			270,000
Current assets			
Inventories (190 + 2)		192,000	
Accounts receivable (W1)	186,000		
Less allowance	(1,860)		
		184,140	
Bank (12 + 2 – 1)		13,000	
			389,140
Total assets			659,140
Equity and liabilities			
Equity			
Share capital		100,000	
Revenue reserves		271,940	
			371,940
Non-current liabilities			
Loan stock			180,000
Current liabilities			
Accounts payable (110 – 10)		100,000	
Loan stock interest payable		7,200	
			107,200
Total equity and liabilities			659,140

FIDDLES CO
INCOME STATEMENT

	$
Operating profit (W2)	80,140
Debenture interest ($180,000 × 16% × 3/12)	(7,200)
	72,940
Revenue reserves brought forward ($200,000 – 1,000)	199,000
Revenue reserves carried forward	271,940

Workings

1 *Accounts receivable*

	$
Per opening trial balance	200,000
Contra	(10,000)
Miscasting	(1,000)
Standing order	(2,000)
Written off	(1,000)
	186,000
Allowance b/f	3,000
Allowance required	1,860
Journal	1,140

2   *Operating profit*

		$
Per question		80,000
Wrong batch total		(1,000)
Returns		(4,000)
Bank charges		(1,000)
Irrecoverable debt		(1,000)
Allowance for receivables		1,140
Inventory (2,000 + 1,000)		3,000
Suspense (sales)		3,000
		80,140

Chapter roundup

- Paper 2.5 covers a **demanding syllabus**, but if your approach is methodical and you leave yourself enough time you will succeed.

- You will cover the **bulk of IASs** in Paper 2.5, but the more complex will be left until you reach Paper 3.6. Those standards covered in Paper 1.1 are also of less importance in Paper 2.5.

- You must stay **up to date** by reading the *Students' Newsletter*. You will find articles relevant to Paper 2.5 extremely helpful and they may even give pointers about the exam!

- The regulatory system of accounting exists on both the national and international level. You should be aware of the regulatory system in your own country, but for this paper your main concern is the **International Accounting Standards Board** and its workings. More detail will be given in Chapter 2.

- **IAS 1** has recently been revised.

- **Accounting policies** are extremely important. You should be able to define all the key terms highlighted in this chapter: going concern, accruals accounting, consistency and materiality.

- At this stage in your studies, you should be confident in your knowledge of:

  - **Double entry bookkeeping**
  - **Basic accounting definitions**
  - **Simple balance sheet**
  - **Simple income statement**

- If you still feel a little rusty, go back to your old study material (which you should still have!) and practise a few questions.

Quick quiz

1   Where can you find guidance from the examiner on Paper 2.5?

2   Which IFRSs are examinable under Paper 2.5?

3   What are the objectives of the IASB?

Answers to quick quiz

1   Syllabus
    Study Guide
    Further guidance from the ACCA/*Student Accountant*/ACCA website

2   Look back to Section 1.2

3   See paragraph 2.4.2

Now try the questions below from the Exam Question Bank

Number	Level	Marks	Time
Q1	Introductory	n/a	n/a
Q2	Introductory	n/a	n/a

The regulatory framework

2

Topic list	Syllabus reference
1 The International Accounting Standards Board (IASB)	2(a)-(d)
2 Setting of International Financial Reporting Standards	2(b)
3 Criticisms of the IASB	2(a)-(d)
4 Conceptual framework and GAAP	1(a), 2(a)-(d)

Introduction

We have already discussed the IASB and IFRSs to some extent. Here we are concerned with the IASB's relationship with other bodies, and with the way the IASB operates and how IFRSs are produced.

Later in this text we look at some of the theory behind what appears in the accounts. The most important document in this area is the IASB's *Framework for the preparation and presentation of financial statements*. Since it was published, all IFRSs have been based on the principles it contains. We will look at it in detail in Chapter 19, but it is introduced here.

Study guide

Section 4 – The structure of the IASB's regulatory framework

- Describe the constitution of the IASB and its objectives

- Describe the influence of national standard setters and the International Organisation of Securities Commissions (IOSCO) on IASs and IFRSs

- Outline the international accounting standard setting process and the role of the International Financial Reporting Interpretations Committee (IFRIC)

Exam guide

You may be asked about these topics as part of a longer question.

1 The International Accounting Standards Board (IASB)

FAST FORWARD   You should be able to describe the organisation of the IASB.

1.1 Introduction

The International Accounting Standards Board is an independent, privately-funded accounting standard setter based in London.

In March 2001 the IASC Foundation was formed as a not-for-profit corporation incorporated in the USA. The IASC Foundation is the parent entity of the IASB.

From April 2001 the IASB assumed accounting standard setting responsibilities from its predecessor body, the International Accounting Standards Committee (IASC). This restructuring was based upon the recommendations made in the *Recommendations on Shaping IASC for the Future.*

1.2 How the IASB is made up

The 14 members of the IASB come from nine countries and have a variety of backgrounds with a mix of auditors, preparers of financial statements, users of financial statements and an academic. The Board consists of 12 full-time members and two part-time members.

1.3 Objectives of the IASB

The formal objectives of the IASB, formulated in its mission statement are:

(a)   To develop, in the public interest, a single set of high quality, understandable and enforceable global accounting standards that require high quality, transparent and comparable information in general purpose financial statements

(b)   To provide the use and vigorous application of those standards

(c)   To work actively with national accounting standard setters to bring about convergence of national accounting standards and IFRS to high quality solutions.

1.4 Structure of the IASB

The structure of the IASB has the following main features.

(a) The IASC Foundation is an independent corporation having two main bodies – the Trustees and the IASB.

(b) The IASC Foundation trustees appoint the IASB members, exercise oversight and raise the funds needed.

(c) The IASB has sole responsibility for setting accounting standards.

(d) There are also two further bodies, the Standards Advisory Council and the International Financial Reporting Interpretations Committee (see below).

The structure can be illustrated as follows.

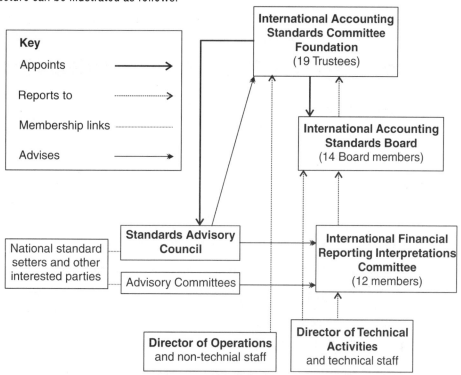

Trustees. The Trustees comprise a group of nineteen individuals, with diverse geographic and functional backgrounds. The Trustees appoint the Members of the Board, the International Financial Reporting Interpretations Committee and the Standards Advisory Council. In addition to monitoring IASC's effectiveness and raising its funds, the Trustees will approve IASC's budget and have responsibility for constitutional changes. Trustees were appointed so that initially there were six from North America, six from Europe, four from Asia Pacific, and three others from any area, as long as geographic balance is maintained.

(a) The International Federation of Accountants (IFAC) suggested candidates to fill five of the nineteen Trustee seats and international organisations of preparers, users and academics each suggested one candidate.

(b) The remaining eleven Trustees are 'at-large' in that they were not selected through the constituency nomination process.

Standards Advisory Council. The Standards Advisory Council provides a formal vehicle for further groups and individuals with diverse geographic and functional backgrounds to give advice to the Board and, at times, to advise the Trustees.

International Financial Reporting Interpretations Committee. The IFRIC provides timely guidance on the application and interpretation of International Financial Reporting Standards.

Question

In accounting terms what do you think are:

(a) The advantages to international harmonisation?

(b) The barriers to international harmonisation?

Answer

(a) Advantages of global harmonisation

The advantages of harmonisation will be based on the benefits to users and preparers of accounts, as follows.

     (i) Investors, both individual and corporate, would like to be able to compare the financial results of different companies internationally as well as nationally in making investment decisions.

     (ii) Multinational companies would benefit from harmonisation for many reasons including the following.

         (1) Better access would be gained to foreign investor funds.

         (2) Management control would be improved, because harmonisation would aid internal communication of financial information.

         (3) Appraisal of foreign entities for take-overs and mergers would be more straightforward.

         (4) It would be easier to comply with the reporting requirements of overseas stock exchanges.

         (5) Preparation of group accounts would be easier.

         (6) A reduction in audit costs might be achieved.

         (7) Transfer of accounting staff across national borders would be easier.

     (iii) Governments of developing countries would save time and money if they could adopt international standards and, if these were used internally, governments of developing countries could attempt to control the activities of foreign multinational companies in their own country. These companies could not 'hide' behind foreign accounting practices which are difficult to understand.

     (iv) Tax authorities. It will be easier to calculate the tax liability of investors, including multinationals who receive income from overseas sources.

     (v) Regional economic groups usually promote trade within a specific geographical region. This would be aided by common accounting practices within the region.

     (vi) Large international accounting firms would benefit as accounting and auditing would be much easier if similar accounting practices existed throughout the world.

(b) Barriers to harmonisation

     (i) Different purposes of financial reporting. In some countries the purpose is solely for tax assessment, while in others it is for investor decision-making.

     (ii) Different legal systems. These prevent the development of certain accounting practices and restrict the options available.

     (iii) Different user groups. Countries have different ideas about who the relevant user groups are and their respective importance. In the USA investor and creditor groups are given prominence, while in Europe employees enjoy a higher profile.

(iv)   Needs of developing countries. Developing countries are obviously behind in the standard setting process and they need to develop the basic standards and principles already in place in most developed countries.

(v)   Nationalism is demonstrated in an unwillingness to accept another country's standard.

(vi)   Cultural differences result in objectives for accounting systems differing from country to country.

(vii)   Unique circumstances. Some countries may be experiencing unusual circumstances which affect all aspects of everyday life and impinge on the ability of companies to produce proper reports, for example hyperinflation, civil war, currency restriction and so on.

(viii)   The lack of strong accountancy bodies. Many countries do not have strong independent accountancy or business bodies which would press for better standards and greater harmonisation.

1.5 The IASB and current accounting standards

The IASB's predecessor body, the IASC, had issued 41 International Accounting Standards (IASs) and on 1 April 2001 the IASB adopted all of these standards and now issues its own International Financial Reporting Standards (IFRSs). So far seven new IFRS have been issued.

1.6 The IASB and IOSCO

The International Organisation of Securities Commissions (IOSCO) is the representative of the world's securities markets regulators. High quality information is vital for the operation of an efficient capital market, and differences in the quality of the accounting policies and their enforcement between countries leads to inefficiencies between markets. IOSCO has been active in encouraging and promoting the improvement and quality of IFRSs over the last ten years. Most recently, this commitment was evidenced by the agreement between IASC and IOSCO to work on a programme of 'core standards' which could be used by publicly listed entities when offering securities in foreign jurisdictions.

The 'core standards' project resulted in fifteen new or revised IFRSs and was completed in 1999 with the issue of IAS 39 *Financial instruments: recognition and measurement.* IOSCO spent a year reviewing the results of the project and released a report in May 2000 which recommended to all its members that they allow multinational issuers to use IASs, as supplemented by reconciliation, disclosure and interpretation where necessary to address outstanding substantive issues at a national or regional level.

IASB staff and IOSCO continue to work together to resolve outstanding issues and to identify areas where new IASB standards are needed.

1.7 European Commission and IFRSs

All listed entities in member states must use IFRSs in their consolidated financial statements from 2005.

To this end the IASB has undertaken an **improvements project**, dealing with **revisions to IFRS**, for example in the area of materiality, presentation, leases, related parties and earnings per share. This has been matched in, for example, the UK, by a **convergence project**, bringing UK GAAP into line with IFRSs where these are better.

2 Setting of International Financial Reporting Standards

You must understand the due process involved in producing IFRSs.

International Financial Reporting Standards (IFRSs) are set in a similar manner to the setting of the previous IASs in accordance with the IASB's due process.

2.1 Due process

The overall agenda of the IASB will initially be set by discussion with the Standards Advisory Council. The process for developing an individual standard would involve the following steps.

Step 1 During the early stages of a project, IASB may establish an **Advisory Committee** to give advice on issues arising in the project. Consultation with the Advisory Committee and the Standards Advisory Council occurs throughout the project.

Step 2 IASB may develop and publish **Discussion Documents** for public comment.

Step 3 Following the receipt and review of comments, IASB would develop and publish an **Exposure Draft** for public comment.

Step 4 Following the receipt and review of comments, the IASB would issue a final **International Financial Reporting Standard**.

The period of exposure for public comment is normally 90 days. However, in exceptional circumstances, proposals may be issued with a comment period of 60 days. Draft IFRIC Interpretations are exposed for a 60 day comment period.

2.2 Co-ordination with national standard setters

Close co-ordination between IASB due process and due process of national standard setters is important to the success of the IASB's mandate.

The IASB is exploring ways in which to integrate its due process more closely with national due process. Such integration may grow as the relationship between IASB and national standard setters evolves. In particular, the IASB is exploring the following procedure for projects that have international implications.

(a) IASB and national standard setters would co-ordinate their work plans so that when the IASB starts a project, national standard setters would also add it to their own work plans so that they can play a full part in developing international consensus. Similarly, where national standard setters start projects, the IASB would consider whether it needs to develop a new Standard or review its existing Standards. Over a reasonable period, the IASB and national standard setters should aim to review all standards where significant differences currently exist, giving priority to the areas where the differences are greatest.

(b) National standards setters would not be required to vote for IASB's preferred solution in their national standards, since each country remains free to adopt IASB standards with amendments or to adopt other standards. However, the existence of an international consensus is clearly one factor that members of national standard setters would consider when they decide how to vote on national standards.

(c) The IASB would continue to publish its own Exposure Drafts and other documents for public comment.

(d) National standard setters would publish their own exposure document at approximately the same time as IASB Exposure Drafts and would seek specific comments on any significant divergences between the two exposure documents. In some instances, national standard setters may include in their exposure documents specific comments on issues of particular relevance to their country or include more detailed guidance than is included in the corresponding IASB document.

(e) National standard setters would follow their own full due process, which they would ideally choose to integrate with the IASB's due process. This integration would avoid unnecessary delays in completing standards and would also minimise the likelihood of unnecessary differences between the standards that result.

2.3 IASB liaison members

Seven of the full-time members of the IASB have formal liaison responsibilities with national standard setters in order to promote the convergence of national accounting standards and International Accounting Standards. The IASB envisages a partnership between the IASB and these national standard setters as they work together to achieve convergence of accounting standards world-wide.

The countries with these liaison members are Australia and New Zealand, Canada, France, Germany, Japan, UK and USA.

In addition all IASB members have contact responsibility with national standards setters not having liaison members and many countries are also represented on the Standards Advisory Council.

2.4 Current IASs

The current list is as follows. Compare it with the list in Chapter 1 to see which are examinable by ACCA.

International Accounting Standards		Date of issue
IAS 1 (revised)	Presentation of financial statements	Dec 2003
IAS 2 (revised)	Inventories	Dec 2003
IAS 7 (revised)	Cash flow statements	Dec 1992
IAS 8 (revised)	Accounting policies, changes in accounting estimates and errors	Dec 2003
IAS 10 (revised)	Events after the balance sheet date	Dec 2003
IAS 11 (revised)	Construction contracts	Dec 1993
IAS 12 (revised)	Income taxes	Nov 2000
IAS 14 (revised)	Segment reporting	Aug 1997
IAS 16 (revised)	Property, plant and equipment	Dec 2003
IAS 17 (revised)	Leases	Dec 2003
IAS 18 (revised)	Revenue	Dec 1993
IAS 19 (revised)	Employee benefits	Dec 2004
IAS 20	Accounting for government grants and disclosure of government assistance	Jan 1995
IAS 21 (revised)	The effects of changes in foreign exchange rates	Dec 2003
IAS 23 (revised)	Borrowing costs	Dec 1993
IAS 24 (revised)	Related party disclosures	Dec 2003
IAS 26	Accounting and reporting by retirement benefit plans	Jan 1995
IAS 27 (revised)	Consolidated and separate financial statements	Dec 2003
IAS 28 (revised)	Investments in associates	Dec 2003
IAS 29	Financial reporting in hyperinflationary economies	Jan 1995

International Accounting Standards		Date of issue
IAS 30	Disclosure in the financial statements of banks and similar financial institutions (not examinable)	Jan 1995
IAS 31 (revised)	Interests in joint ventures	Dec 2003
IAS 32 (revised)	Financial instruments: disclosure and presentation	Dec 2003
IAS 33 (revised)	Earnings per share	Dec 2003
IAS 34	Interim financial reporting	Feb 1998
IAS 36 (revised)	Impairment of assets	Mar 2004
IAS 37	Provisions, contingent liabilities and contingent assets	Sept 1998
IAS 38 (revised)	Intangible assets	Mar 2004
IAS 39 (revised)	Financial instruments: recognition and measurement	Dec 2004
IAS 40	Investment property	Dec 2003
IAS 41	Agriculture	Feb 2001
IFRS 1	First time adoption of International Financial Reporting Standards	June 2003
IFRS 2	Share-based payment	Feb 2004
IFRS 3	Business combinations	Mar 2004
IFRS 4	Insurance contracts	Mar 2004
IFRS 5	Non-current assets held for sale and discontinued operations	Mar 2004
IFRS 6	Exploration for and evaluation of mineral resources	Dec 2004
IFRS 7	Financial instruments: disclosures	Aug 2005

Various exposure drafts and discussion papers are currently at different stages within the IFRS process, but these are not of concern to you at this stage. By the end of your financial accounting studies, however, you will know *all* the standards, exposure drafts and discussion papers!

2.5 Benchmark and allowed alternative treatment

Many of the old IASs permitted two accounting treatments for like transactions or events. One treatment is designated as the **benchmark treatment** (effectively the **preferred treatment**) and the other is known as the **alternative treatment**. However, as the standards are revised, many alternatives are being eliminated.

2.6 Interpretation of IFRSs

The IASB has developed a procedure for issuing interpretations of its standards. In September 1996, the IASC Board approved the formation of a **Standing Interpretations Committee (SIC)** for this task. This has been renamed under the IASB as the **International Financial Reporting Interpretations Committee** (IFRIC).

The duties of the IFRIC are:

(a) To interpret the application of International Financial Reporting Standards and provide timely guidance on financial reporting issues not specifically addressed in IFRSs or IASs in the context of the IASB's Framework, and undertake other tasks at the request of the Board.

(b) To have regard to the Board's objective of working actively with national standard setters to bring about convergence of national accounting standards and IFRSs to high quality solutions.

BPP
PROFESSIONAL EDUCATION

(c)   To publish, after clearance by the Board, Draft Interpretations for public comment and consider comments made within a reasonable period before finalising an Interpretation.

(d)   To report to the Board and obtain Board approval for final Interpretations.

In developing interpretations, the 12-person IFRIC will work closely with **similar national committees**. If no more than three of its members vote against an interpretation, the SIC will ask the Board to approve the interpretation for issue; as is the case for IFRSs, three-quarters of the Board must vote in favour of an interpretation. Interpretations will be formally published after approval by the Board.

Exam focus point

> For Paper 2.5 the only examinable SIC is SIC-10. IFRIC 4 is also examinable.

2.7 Scope and application of IFRSs

2.7.1 Scope

Any limitation of the applicability of a specific IFRS is made clear within that standard. IFRSs are **not intended to be applied to immaterial items, nor are they retrospective**. Each individual IFRS lays out its scope at the beginning of the standard.

2.7.2 Application

Within each individual country **local regulations** govern, to a greater or lesser degree, the issue of financial statements. These local regulations include accounting standards issued by the national regulatory bodies and/or professional accountancy bodies in the country concerned.

The IASC **concentrated on essentials** when producing IFRSs. This means that the IASC tried not to make IFRSs too complex, because otherwise they would be impossible to apply on a worldwide basis.

2.8 World-wide effect of IFRSs and the IASB

The IASB, and before it the IASC, has now been in existence for around 25 years, and it is worth looking at the effect it has had in that time.

As far as **Europe** is concerned, the consolidated financial statements of many of Europe's top multinationals are now prepared in conformity with national requirements, EC directives and IFRSs. Furthermore, IFRSs are having a growing influence on national accounting requirements and practices. Many of these developments have been given added impetus by the internationalisation of capital markets.

In **Japan**, the influence of the IASC had, until recently, been negligible. This was mainly because of links in Japan between tax rules and financial reporting. The Japanese Ministry of Finance set up a working committee to consider whether to bring national requirements into line with IFRSs. The Tokyo Stock Exchange has announced that it will accept financial statements from foreign issuers that conform with home country standards.

This was widely seen as an attempt to attract foreign issuers, in particular companies from Hong Kong and Singapore. As these countries base their accounting on international standards, this action is therefore implicit acknowledgement by the Japanese Ministry of Finance of IFRS requirements.

America and Japan have been two of the developed countries which have been most reluctant to accept accounts prepared under IFRSs, but recent developments suggest that such financial statements may soon be acceptable on these important stock exchanges.

In **America**, the Securities and Exchange Commission (SEC) agreed in 1993 to allow foreign issuers (of shares, etc) to follow IFRS treatments on certain issues, including cash flow statements under IAS 7. The overall effect is that, where an IFRS treatment differs from US GAAP, these treatments will now be acceptable. The SEC is now supporting the IASB because it wants to attract foreign listings.

Exam focus point

While it will be more important to keep up to date with current developments for Paper 3.6, you will impress the Paper 2.5 examiner if you show familiarity with some of the above topics.

3 Criticisms of the IASB

FAST FORWARD

You need to be able to understand the problems that can arise.

We will begin by looking at some of the general problems created by **accounting standards**.

3.1 Accounting standards and choice

It is sometimes argued that companies should be given a choice in matters of financial reporting on the grounds that accounting standards are detrimental to the quality of such reporting. There are arguments on both sides.

In favour of accounting standards (both national and international), the following points can be made.

- They **reduce or eliminate confusing variations** in the methods used to prepare accounts.
- They provide a **focal point for debate** and discussions about accounting practice.
- They oblige companies to **disclose the accounting policies** used in the preparation of accounts.
- They are a less rigid alternative to enforcing conformity by means of **legislation**.
- They have obliged companies to **disclose more accounting information** than they would otherwise have done if accounting standards did not exist, for example IAS 33 *Earnings per share*.

Many companies are reluctant to disclose information which is not required by national legislation. However, the following arguments may be put forward **against standardisation** and **in favour of choice**.

- A set of rules which give backing to one method of preparing accounts might be **inappropriate in some circumstances**. For example, IAS 16 on depreciation is inappropriate for investment properties (properties not occupied by the entity but held solely for investment), which are covered by IAS 40 on investment property.
- Standards may be subject to **lobbying or government pressure** (in the case of national standards). For example, in the USA, the accounting standard FAS 19 on the accounts of oil and gas companies led to a powerful lobby of oil companies, which persuaded the SEC (Securities and Exchange Commission) to step in. FAS 19 was then suspended.
- Many national standards are not based on a **conceptual framework of accounting**, although IFRSs are (see Chapter 19).
- There may be a **trend towards rigidity**, and away from flexibility in applying the rules.

3.2 Political problems

Any international body, whatever its purpose or activity, faces enormous political difficulties in attempting to gain **international consensus** and the IASB is no exception to this. How can the IASB reconcile the financial reporting situation between economies as diverse as third-world developing countries and sophisticated first-world industrial powers?

Developing countries are suspicious of the IASB, believing it to be dominated by the **USA.** This arises because acceptance by the USA listing authority, the Securities and Exchange Commission (SEC), of IASs is seen as a major hurdle to be overcome. For all practical purposes it is the American market which must be persuaded to accept IFRSs.

Developing countries are being catered for to some extent by the issue of a standard on **agriculture**, which is generally of much more relevance to such countries.

There are also tensions between the **UK/US model** of financial reporting and the **European model**. The UK/US model is based around investor reporting, whereas the European model is mainly concerned with tax rules, so shareholder reporting has a much lower priority.

The break-up of the former USSR and the move in many **Eastern European countries** to free-market economies has also created difficulties. It is likely that these countries will have to 'catch up' to international standards as their economies stabilise.

You must keep up to date with the IASB's progress and the problems it encounters in the financial press. You should also be able to discuss:

- **Due process** of the IASB
- **Use and application** of IFRSs
- **Future work** of the IASB
- **Criticisms** of the IASB

4 Conceptual framework and GAAP

FAST FORWARD

> The IASB's *Framework* provides the backbone of the IASB's conceptual framework.

4.1 The search for a conceptual framework

Key term

> A **conceptual framework**, in the field we are concerned with, is a statement of generally accepted theoretical principles which form the frame of reference for financial reporting.

These theoretical principles provide the basis for the development of new accounting standards and the evaluation of those already in existence. The financial reporting process is concerned with providing information that is useful in the business and economic decision-making process. Therefore a conceptual framework will form the **theoretical basis** for determining which events should be accounted for, how they should be measured and how they should be communicated to the user. Although it is theoretical in nature, a conceptual framework for financial reporting has highly practical final aims.

The **danger of not having a conceptual framework** is demonstrated in the way some countries' standards have developed over recent years; standards tend to be produced in a haphazard and fire-fighting approach. Where an agreed framework exists, the standard-setting body act as an architect or designer, rather than a fire-fighter, building accounting rules on the foundation of sound, agreed basic principles.

The lack of a conceptual framework also means that fundamental principles are tackled more than once in different standards, thereby producing **contradictions and inconsistencies** in basic concepts, such as those of prudence and matching. This leads to ambiguity and it affects the true and fair concept of financial reporting.

Another problem with the lack of a conceptual framework has become apparent in the USA. The large number of **highly detailed standards** produced by the Financial Accounting Standards Board (FASB) has created a financial reporting environment governed by specific rules rather than general principles. This would be avoided if a cohesive set of principles were in place.

A conceptual framework can also bolster standard setters **against political pressure** from various 'lobby groups' and interested parties. Such pressure would only prevail if it was acceptable under the conceptual framework.

4.2 Advantages and disadvantages of a conceptual framework

Advantages

(a) The situation is avoided whereby standards are developed on a patchwork basis, where a particular accounting problem is recognised as having emerged, and resources were then channelled into **standardising accounting practice** in that area, without regard to whether that particular issue was necessarily the most important issue remaining at that time without standardisation.

(b) As stated above, the development of certain standards (particularly national standards) have been subject to considerable **political interference** from interested parties. Where there is a conflict of interest between user groups on which policies to choose, policies deriving from a conceptual framework will be **less open to criticism** that the standard-setter buckled to external pressure.

(c) Some standards may concentrate on the **income statement** whereas some may concentrate on the **valuation of net assets** (balance sheet).

Disadvantages

(a) Financial statements are intended for a **variety of users**, and it is not certain that a single conceptual framework can be devised which will suit all users.

(b) Given the diversity of user requirements, there may be a need for a variety of accounting standards, each produced for a **different purpose** (and with different concepts as a basis).

(c) It is not clear that a conceptual framework makes the task of **preparing and then implementing** standards any easier than without a framework.

Before we look at the IASB's attempt to produce a conceptual framework, we need to consider another term of importance to this debate: generally accepted accounting principles (or practice); or GAAP.

4.3 Generally Accepted Accounting Practice (GAAP)

Key term

> **GAAP** signifies all the rules, from whatever source, which govern accounting.

In individual countries this is seen primarily as a **combination** of:

- National company law
- National accounting standards
- Local stock exchange requirements

Although those sources are the basis for the GAAP of individual countries, the concept also includes the effects of **non-mandatory sources** such as:

- International accounting standards
- Statutory requirements in other countries

In many countries, like the UK, GAAP does not have any statutory or regulatory authority or definition, unlike other countries, such as the USA. The term is mentioned rarely in legislation, and only then in fairly limited terms.

There are different views of GAAP in different countries. The UK position can be explained in the following extracts from *UK GAAP* (Davies, Paterson & Wilson, Ernst & Young, 5th edition).

> 'Our view is that GAAP is a dynamic concept which requires constant review, adaptation and reaction to changing circumstances. We believe that use of the term "principle" gives GAAP an unjustified and inappropriate degree of permanence. GAAP changes in response to changing

business and economic needs and developments. As circumstances alter, accounting practices are modified or developed accordingly..... We believe that GAAP goes far beyond mere rules and principles, and encompasses contemporary permissible accounting **practice**.

It is often argued that the term "generally accepted" implies that there must exist a high degree of practical application of a particular accounting practice. However, this interpretation raises certain practical difficulties. For example, what about new areas of accounting which have not, as yet, been generally applied? What about different accounting treatments for similar items - are they all generally accepted?

'It is our view that "generally accepted" does **not** mean "generally adopted or used". We believe that, in the UK context, GAAP refers to accounting practices which are regarded as permissible by the accounting profession. The extent to which a particular practice has been adopted is, in our opinion, not the overriding consideration. Any accounting practice which is legitimate in the circumstances under which it has been applied should be regarded as GAAP. The decision as to whether or not a particular practice is permissible or legitimate would depend on one or more of the following factors:

- Is the practice addressed either in the accounting standards, statute or other official pronouncements?

- If the practice is not addressed in UK accounting standards, is it dealt with in International Accounting Standards, or the standards of other countries such as the US?

- Is the practice consistent with the needs of users and the objectives of financial reporting?

- Does the practice have authoritative support in the accounting literature?

- Is the practice being applied by other companies in similar situations?

- Is the practice consistent with the fundamental concept of "true and fair"?'

This view is not held in all countries, however. In the USA particularly, the equivalent of a 'true and fair view' is 'fair presentation in accordance with GAAP'. Generally accepted accounting principles are defined as those principles which have 'substantial authoritative support'. Therefore accounts prepared in accordance with accounting principles for which there is not substantial authoritative support are presumed to be misleading or inaccurate.

The effect here is that 'new' or 'different' accounting principles are not acceptable unless they have been adopted by the mainstream accounting profession, usually the standard-setting bodies and/or professional accountancy bodies. This is much more rigid than the UK view expressed above.

A **conceptual framework** for financial reporting can be defined as an attempt to codify existing GAAP in order to reappraise current accounting standards and to produce new standards.

4.4 The IASB's framework

In July 1989 the old IASC produced a document, *Framework for the preparation and presentation of financial statements* (*'Framework'*). The *Framework* is, in effect, the **conceptual framework** upon which all IASs are based and hence which determines how financial statements are prepared and the information they contain.

The *Framework* consists of several sections or chapters, following on after a preface and introduction. These **chapters** are as follows.

- The objective of financial statements
- Underlying assumptions
- Qualitative characteristics of financial statements
- The elements of financial statements

- Recognition of the elements of financial statements
- Measurement of the elements of financial statements
- Concepts of capital and capital maintenance

In your Paper 1.1 studies, you looked at the preface and introduction to the *Framework* and the first three chapters. In Chapter 19 we will go over these again and then look at the remaining chapters, as a detailed knowledge of the whole document is required for Paper 2.5.

Chapter roundup

- You should be able to describe the **organisation of the IASB** and its relationships with intergovernmental bodies, professional accountancy bodies, national standard setting bodies and IOSCO.

- You must understand the **due process** involved in producing international standards, their scope and application and moves by the IASB to interpret them. You should keep an eye on the work of the IASB in the accountancy press, so you are completely up to date.

- The IASB has been **criticised** because of dominance by the USA.

- The IASB's *Framework* provides the backbone of the IASB's **conceptual framework**. IASs are based on this **Framework**.

Quick quiz

1   What recent decisions will have a beneficial effect on global harmonisation of accounting?

2   One objective of the IASB is to promote the preparation of financial statements using the euro.

    True   ☐

    False   ☐

3   How many IASs and IFRSs have been published?

4   A conceptual framework is:

    A   A theoretical expression of accounting standards
    B   A list of key terms used by the IASB
    C   A statement of theoretical principles which form the frame of reference for financial reporting
    D   The proforma financial statements

5   Which of the following are chapters in the IASB *Framework?*

    A   Subsidiaries, associates and joint ventures
    B   Profit measurement in financial statements
    C   The objective of financial statements
    D   Accounting for interests in other entities
    E   Recognition of the elements of financial statements
    F   Presentation of financial information
    G   Substance of transactions in financial statements
    H   Qualitative characteristics of financial statements
    I   Quantitative characteristics of financial statements
    J   Measurement of the elements of financial statements
    K   Concepts of capital and capital maintenance
    L   The elements of financial statements.

6   What development at the IASB will aid users' interpretation of IFRSs?

7   Which of the following arguments is not in favour of accounting standards, but is in favour of accounting choice?

     A   They reduce variations in methods used to produce accounts
     B   They oblige companies to disclose their accounting policies
     C   They are a less rigid alternative to legislation
     D   They may tend towards rigidity in applying the rules

Answers to quick quiz

1   The IOSCO endorsement, and the EC requirement that listed companies should use IFRS from 2005.

2   False

3   41 IAS and 7 IFRSs

4   C

5   C, E, H, J, K and L.

6   The formation of the International Financial Reporting Interpretations Committee (IFRIC).

7   D   The other arguments are all in favour of accounting standards.

Now try the question below from the Exam Question Bank

Number	Level	Marks	Time
Q3	Introductory	n/a	n/a

Part B

Preparing the financial statements of companies limited by liability

Presentation of published financial statements

Topic list	Syllabus reference
1 Limited liability	3(a)-(f)
2 IAS 1 Presentation of financial statements	3(a)-(f)
3 Balance sheet	3(a)-(f)
4 The current/non-current distinction	3(a)-(f)
5 Income statement	3(a)-(f)
6 Changes in equity	3(a)-(f)
7 Notes to the financial statements	3(a)-(f)

Introduction

The bulk of this Study Text looks at the accounts of limited liability companies, either single companies (Part B of the text) or groups of companies (Part D).

We begin in this chapter by looking at the overall **content and format** of company financial statements. These are governed by IAS 1 (revised) *Presentation of financial statements*.

We looked at what IAS 1 says about **accounting concepts and policies** in Chapter 1. The rest of the standard is considered here.

Study guide

Section 5 – Presentation of financial statements for companies

- State the objectives of accounting standards on presentation of financial statements
- Describe the structure and content of financial statements
- Discuss 'fair presentation' and the accounting concepts/principles in relevant accounting standards
- Prepare the financial statements of companies in accordance with International Accounting Standards/International Financial Reporting Standards

Exam guide

Knowledge of IAS 1 will be assumed to be 'second nature' at this level.

1 Limited liability

FAST FORWARD Limited liability offers various advantages to companies, although there are disadvantages as well.

1.1 Fundamental differences

There are some fundamental differences in the accounts of limited liability companies **compared to sole traders or partnerships**, of which the following are perhaps the most significant.

(a) The **national legislation** governing the activities of limited liability companies tends to be very extensive. Amongst other things such legislation may define certain minimum accounting records which must be maintained by companies; they may specify that the annual accounts of a company must be filed with a government bureau and so available for public inspection; and they often contain detailed requirements on the minimum information which must be disclosed in a company's accounts. Businesses which are not limited liability companies (non-incorporated businesses) often enjoy comparative freedom from statutory regulation.

(b) The **owners of a company** (its members or shareholders) may be very numerous. Their capital is shown differently from that of a sole trader; and similarly the 'appropriation account' of a company is different.

1.2 Limited liability

You may be able to recognise the relative **advantages and disadvantages** of limited liability. Sole traders and partnerships are, with some significant exceptions, generally fairly small concerns. The amount of capital involved may be modest, and the proprietors of the business usually participate in managing it. Their liability for the debts of the business is unlimited, which means that if the business runs up debts that it is unable to pay, the proprietors will become personally liable for the unpaid debts, and would be required, if necessary, to sell their private possessions in order to repay them. For example, if a sole trader has some capital in his business, but the business now owes $40,000 which it cannot repay, the trader might have to sell his house to raise the money to pay off his business debts.

Limited liability companies offer **limited liability to their owners**. This means that the maximum amount that an owner stands to lose in the event that the company becomes insolvent and cannot pay off its debts, is his share of the capital in the business. Thus limited liability is a major advantage of turning a business into a limited liability company. However, in practice banks or other lenders will normally seek personal guarantees from shareholders before making loans or granting an overdraft facility and so the advantage of limited liability is lost to a small owner managed business.

There are also disadvantages to limited liability.

(a)   Compliance with national legislation
(b)   Compliance with national accounting standards and/or IASs/IFRSs
(c)   Any formation and annual registration costs

As a business grows, it needs **more capital** to finance its operations, and significantly more than the people currently managing the business can provide themselves. One way of obtaining more capital is to invite investors from outside the business to invest in the ownership or equity of the business. These new co-owners would not usually be expected to help with managing the business. To such investors, limited liability is very attractive.

Investments are always risky undertakings, but with limited liability the investor knows the maximum amount that he stands to lose when he puts some capital into a company.

1.3 The accounting records of limited liability companies

There is almost always a **national legal requirement** for companies to keep accounting records which are sufficient to show and explain the company's transactions. The records will probably:

(a)   Disclose the company's current financial position at any time

(b)   Contain:

   (i)   Day-to-day entries of money received and spent
   (ii)   A record of the company's assets and liabilities
   (iii) Where the company deals in goods

        (1)   A statement of inventories held at the year end, and supporting inventory count records

        (2)   With the exception of retail sales, statements of goods bought and sold which identify the sellers and buyers of those goods

(c)   Enable the managers of the company to ensure that the **final accounts** of the company give a true and fair view of the company's profit or loss and balance sheet position.

The detailed requirements of accounting records which must be maintained will vary from country to country.

Question   Regulation

How are limited liability companies regulated in your country?

2 IAS 1 Presentation of financial statements

IAS 1 covers the form and content of financial statements.

As well as covering accounting policies and other general considerations governing financial statements, IAS 1 *Presentation of financial statements* give substantial guidance on the form and content of published financial statements. The standard looks at the balance sheet and income statement (the cash flow statement is covered by IAS 7). First of all, some general points are made about financial statements.

2.1 Profit or loss for the period

The income statement is the most significant indicator of a company's financial performance. So it is important to ensure that it is not misleading.

The income statement will be misleading if costs incurred in the current year are deducted not from the current year profits but from the balance of accumulated profits brought forward. This presents the current year's results more favourably.

IAS 1 stipulates that all items of income and expense recognised in a period shall be included in profit or loss unless a **Standard** or an **Interpretation** requires otherwise.

Circumstances where items may be excluded from profit or loss for the current year include the correction of errors and the effect of changes in accounting policies. These are covered in IAS 8.

2.2 How items are disclosed

IAS 1 specifies disclosures of certain items in certain ways.

- Some items must appear on the **face of the balance sheet or income statement**
- Other items can appear in a **note to the financial statements** instead
- **Recommended formats** are given which enterprises may or may not follow, depending on their circumstances

Obviously, disclosures specified by **other standards** must also be made, and we will mention the necessary disclosures when we cover each statement in turn. Disclosures in both IAS 1 and other standards must be made either on the face of the statement or in the notes unless otherwise stated, ie disclosures cannot be made in an accompanying commentary or report.

2.3 Identification of financial statements

As a result of the above point, it is most important that enterprises **distinguish the financial statements** very clearly from any other information published with them. This is because all IASs apply *only* to the financial statements (ie the main statements and related notes), so readers of the annual report must be able to differentiate between the parts of the report which are prepared under IASs, and other parts which are not.

The enterprise should **identify each component** of the financial statements very clearly. IAS 1 also requires disclosure of the following information in a prominent position. If necessary it should be repeated wherever it is felt to be of use to the reader in his understanding of the information presented.

- **Name** of the reporting enterprise (or other means of identification)
- Whether the accounts cover the **single enterprise** only or a group of enterprises
- The **balance sheet date** or the period covered by the financial statements (as appropriate)
- The **reporting currency**
- The **level of precision** used in presenting the figures in the financial statements

Judgement must be used to determine the best method of presenting this information. In particular, the standard suggests that the approach to this will be very different when the financial statements are communicated electronically.

The **level of precision** is important, as presenting figures in thousands or millions of units makes the figures more understandable. The level of precision must be disclosed, however, and it should not obscure necessary details or make the information less relevant.

2.4 Reporting period

It is normal for enterprises to present financial statements **annually** and IAS 1 states that they should be prepared at least as often as this. If (unusually) an enterprise's balance sheet date is changed, for whatever reason, the period for which the statements are presented will be less or more than one year. In such cases the enterprise should also disclose:

(a) the **reason(s) why** a period other than one year is used; and

(b) the fact that the comparative figures given **are not in fact comparable** (in particular for the income statement, changes in equity, cash flows and related notes).

For practical purposes, some enterprises prefer to use a period which **approximates to a year**, eg 52 weeks, and the IAS allows this approach as it will produce statements not materially different from those produced on an annual basis.

2.5 Timeliness

If the publication of financial statements is delayed too long after the balance sheet date, their usefulness will be severely diminished. The standard states that enterprises should be able to produce their financial statements **within six months of the balance sheet date.** An enterprise with consistently complex operations cannot use this as a reason for its failure to report on a timely basis. Local legislation and market regulation imposes specific deadlines on certain enterprises.

IAS 1 looks at the balance sheet and the income statement. We will not give all the detailed disclosures as some are outside the scope of your syllabus. Instead we will look at a **'proforma' set of accounts** based on the Standard.

3 Balance sheet

FAST FORWARD   IAS 1 suggests a format for the balance sheet.

IAS 1 discusses the distinction between current and non-current items in some detail, as we shall see in the next section. First of all we can look at the **suggested format** of the balance sheet (given in an appendix to the standard) and then look at further disclosures required.

3.1 Balance sheet example

The example given by the standard is as follows.

XYZ GROUP
BALANCE SHEET AS AT 31 DECEMBER 20X8

	20X8 $'000	20X8 $'000	20X7 $'000	20X7 $'000
Assets				
Non-current assets				
Property, plant and equipment	X		X	
Goodwill	X		X	
Other intangible assets	X		X	
Investments in associates	X		X	
Available-for-sale investments	X̲		X̲	
		X		X
Current assets				
Inventories	X		X	
Trade receivables	X		X	
Other current assets	X		X	
Cash and cash equivalents	X̲		X̲	
		X̲		X̲
Total assets		X̲		X̲
Equity and liabilities				
Equity attributable to equity holders of the parent				
Share capital	X		X	
Other reserves	X		X	
Retained earnings	X̲		X̲	
		X		X
Minority interest		X̲		X̲
Total equity		X̲		X̲
Non-current liabilities				
Long-term borrowings	X		X	
Deferred tax	X		X	
Long-term provisions	X̲		X̲	
Total non-current liabilities		X		X
Current liabilities				
Trade and other payables	X		X	
Short-term borrowings	X		X	
Current portion of long-term borrowings	X		X	
Current tax payable	X		X	
Short-term provisions	X̲		X̲	
Total current liabilities		X̲		X̲
Total liabilities		X̲		X̲
Total equity and liabilities		X̲		X̲

IAS 1 specifies various items which must appear on the **face of the balance sheet** as a minimum disclosure.

(a)   Property, plant and equipment (Chapter 5)
(b)   Investment property (Chapter 5)
(c)   Intangible assets (Chapter 6)
(d)   Financial assets (excluding amounts shown under (e), (h) and (i)) (Chapter 8)
(e)   Investments accounted for using the equity method (Chapter 17)
(f)   Biological assets (outside the scope of the 2.5 syllabus)
(g)   Inventories (Chapter 7)
(h)   Trade and other receivables

(i)   Cash and cash equivalents (Chapter 22)
(j)   Trade and other payables
(k)   Provisions (Chapter 11)
(l)   Financial liabilities (other than (j) and (k))
(m)   Current tax liabilities as in IAS 12 (Chapter 10)
(n)   Minority interests (Chapter 15)
(o)   Issued capital and reserves

We will look at these items in the chapters marked.

Any **other line items**, headings or sub-totals should be shown on the face of the balance sheet when it is necessary for an understanding of the entity's financial position.

The example shown above is for illustration only (although we will follow the format in this Study Text). The IAS, however, does not prescribe the order or format in which the items listed should be presented. It simply states that they **must be presented separately** because they are so different in nature or function from each other.

Whether additional items are presented separately depends on judgements based on the assessment of the following factors.

(a)   **Nature and liquidity of assets and their materiality**. Thus goodwill and assets arising from development expenditure will be presented separately, as will monetary/non-monetary assets and current/non-current assets.

(b)   **Function within the entity.** Operating and financial assets, inventories, receivables and cash and cash equivalents are therefore shown separately.

(c)   **Amounts, nature and timing of liabilities**. Interest-bearing and non-interest-bearing liabilities and provisions will be shown separately, classified as current or non-current as appropriate.

The standard also requires separate presentation where **different measurement bases** are used for assets and liabilities which differ in nature or function. According to IAS 16, for example, it is permitted to carry certain items of property, plant and equipment at cost or at a revalued amount.

3.2 Information presented either on the face of the balance sheet or by note

Further **sub-classification** of the line items listed above should be disclosed either on the face of the balance sheet or in notes to the balance sheet. The classification will depend upon the nature of the entity's operations. As well as each item being sub-classified by its nature, any amounts payable to or receivable from any **group company or other related party** should also be disclosed separately.

The sub-classification details will in part depend on the requirements of IASs. The size, nature and function of the amounts involved will also be important and the factors listed above should be considered. **Disclosures** will vary from item to item and IAS 1 gives the following examples.

(a)   **Tangible assets** are classified by class as described in IAS 16, *Property, plant and equipment*

(b)   **Receivables** are analysed between amounts receivable from trade customers, other members of the group, receivables from related parties, prepayments and other amounts

(c)   **Inventories** are sub-classified, in accordance with IAS 2 *Inventories,* into classifications such as merchandise, production supplies, materials, work in progress and finished goods

(d)   **Provisions** are analysed showing separately provisions for employee benefit costs and any other items classified in a manner appropriate to the entity's operations

(e)   **Equity capital and reserves** are analysed showing separately the various classes of paid in capital, share premium and reserves

The standard then lists some **specific disclosures** which must be made, either on the face of the balance sheet or the related notes.

(a)   **Share capital disclosures** (for each class of share capital)

    (i)   Number of shares authorised

    (ii)   Number of shares issued and fully paid, and issued but not fully paid

    (iii)   Par value per share, or that the shares have no par value

    (iv)   Reconciliation of the number of shares outstanding at the beginning and at the end of the year

    (v)   Rights, preferences and restrictions attaching to that class including restrictions on the distribution of dividends and the repayment of capital

    (vi)   Shares in the entity held by the entity itself or by related group companies

    (vii)   Shares reserved for issuance under options and sales contracts, including the terms and amounts

(b)   Description of the nature and purpose of **each reserve** within owners' equity

Some types of entity have no share capital, eg partnerships. Such entities should disclose information which is **equivalent** to that listed above. This means disclosing the movement during the period in each category of equity interest and any rights, preferences or restrictions attached to each category of equity interest.

4 The current/non-current distinction

FAST FORWARD

You should appreciate the distinction between current and non-current assets and liabilities and their different treatments.

4.1 The current/non-current distinction

An entity must present **current** and **non-current** assets as separate classifications on the face of the balance sheet. A presentation based on liquidity should only be used where it provides more relevant and reliable information, in which case all assets and liabilities must be presented broadly **in order of liquidity**.

In either case, the entity should disclose any portion of an asset or liability which is expected to be recovered or settled **after more than twelve months**. For example, for an amount receivable which is due in instalments over 18 months, the portion due after more than twelve months must be disclosed.

The IAS emphasises how helpful information on the **operating cycle** is to users of financial statements. Where there is a clearly defined operating cycle within which the entity supplies goods or services, then information disclosing those net assets that are continuously circulating as **working capital** is useful.

This distinguishes them from those net assets used in the long-term operations of the entity. Assets that are expected to be realised and liabilities that are due for settlement within the operating cycle are therefore highlighted.

The liquidity and solvency of an entity is also indicated by information about the **maturity dates** of assets and liabilities. As we will see later, IAS 32 *Financial instruments: disclosure and presentation* requires disclosure of maturity dates of both financial assets and financial liabilities. (Financial assets include trade and other receivables; financial liabilities include trade and other payables.) In the case of non-monetary assets, eg inventories, such information is also useful.

4.2 Current assets

Key term

> An asset should be classified as a **current asset** when it:
>
> - is expected to be realised in, or is held for sale or consumption in, the normal course of the entity's operating cycle; or
> - is held primarily for trading purposes or for the short-term and expected to be realised within twelve months of the balance sheet date; or
> - is cash or a cash equivalent asset which is not restricted in its use.
>
> All other assets should be classified as non-current assets. *(IAS 1)*

Non-current assets includes tangible, intangible, operating and financial assets of a long-term nature. Other terms with the same meaning can be used (eg 'fixed', 'long-term').

The term 'operating cycle' has been used several times above and the standard defines it as follows.

Key term

> The **operating cycle** of an entity is the time between the acquisition of materials entering into a process and its realisation in cash or an instrument that is readily convertible into cash. *(IAS 1)*

Current assets therefore include inventories and trade receivables that are sold, consumed and realised as part of the normal operating cycle. **This is the case even where they are not expected to be realised within twelve months**.

Current assets will also include **marketable securities** if they are expected to be realised within twelve months of the balance sheet date. If expected to be realised later, they should be included in non-current assets.

4.3 Current liabilities

Key term

> A liability should be classified as a **current liability** when it:
>
> - is expected to be settled in the normal course of the entity's operating cycle; or
> - is due to be settled within twelve months of the balance sheet date; or
> - the entity does not have an unconditional right to defer settlement of the liability for at least twelve months after the balance sheet date.
>
> All other liabilities should be classified as non-current liabilities. *(IAS 1)*

The categorisation of current liabilities is very similar to that of current assets. Thus, some current liabilities are part of the **working capital** used in the normal operating cycle of the business (ie trade payables and accruals for employee and other operating costs). Such items will be classed as current liabilities **even where they are due to be settled more than twelve months after the balance sheet date.**

There are also current liabilities which are not settled as part of the normal operating cycle, but which are due to be settled within twelve months of the balance sheet date. These include bank overdrafts, income taxes, other non-trade payables and the current portion of interest-bearing liabilities. Any interest-bearing liabilities that are used to finance working capital on a long-term basis, and that are not due for settlement within twelve months, should be classed as **non-current liabilities**.

A **long-term financial liability** due to be **settled within twelve months** of the balance sheet date should be classified as a **current liability**, even if an agreement to refinance, or to reschedule payments, on a long-term basis is completed after the balance sheet date and before the financial statements are authorised for issue.

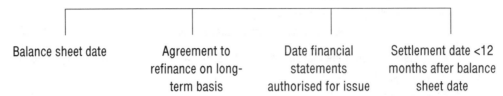

A **long-term financial liability** that is payable on **demand** because the entity **breached** a **condition** of its loan agreement should be classified as **current** at the balance sheet date even if the **lender** has agreed **after the balance sheet date**, and **before** the financial statements are **authorised for issue**, **not** to **demand payment** as a consequence of the breach.

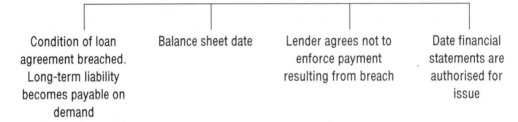

However, if the **lender** has **agreed** by the **balance sheet date** to provide a **period of grace** ending **at least twelve months after the balance sheet date** within which the entity can rectify the breach and during that time the lender cannot demand immediate repayment, the liability is classified as **non-current**.

5 Income statement

Once again, IAS 1 suggests a format for the income statement.

IAS 1 offers **two possible formats** for the income statement, the difference between the two being the classification of expenses: by function or by nature.

5.1 Examples of income statements

XYZ GROUP
INCOME STATEMENT FOR THE YEAR ENDED 31 DECEMBER 20X8

Illustrating the classification of expenses by function

	20X8 $'000	20X7 $'000
Revenue	X	X
Cost of sales	(X)	(X)
Gross profit	X	X
Other income	X	X
Distribution costs	(X)	(X)
Administrative expenses	(X)	(X)
Other expenses	(X)	(X)
Finance costs	(X)	(X)
Share of profit of associates	X	X
Profit before tax	X	X
Income tax expense	(X)	(X)
Profit for the period	X	X
Attributable to:		
Equity holders of the parent	X	X
Minority interest	X	X
	X	X

Illustrating the classification of expenses by nature

	20X8 $'000	20X7 $'000
Revenue	X	X
Other operating income	X	X
Changes in inventories of finished goods and work in progress	(X)	X
Work performed by the enterprise and capitalised	X	X
Raw material and consumables used	(X)	(X)
Employee benefits expense	(X)	(X)
Depreciation and amortisation expense	(X)	(X)
Impairment of property, plant and equipment	(X)	(X)
Other expenses	(X)	(X)
Finance costs	(X)	(X)
Share of profit of associates	X	X
Profit before tax	X	X
Income tax expense	(X)	(X)
Profit for the period	X	X
Attributable to:		
Equity holders of the parent	X	X
Minority interest	X	X
	X	X

5.2 Information presented on the face of the income statement

The standard lists the following as the **minimum** to be disclosed on the face of the income statement.

(a)   Revenue

(b)   Finance costs

(c)   Share of profits and losses of associates and joint ventures accounted for using the equity method

(d)   Pre-tax gain or loss recognised on the disposal of assets or settlement of liabilities attributable to discontinued operations

(e)   Tax expense

(f)   Profit or loss

The following items must be disclosed on the face of the income statement as allocations of profit or loss for the period.

(a)   Profit or loss **attributable to minority interest**

(b)   Profit or loss **attributable to equity holders of the parent**

The allocated amounts must not be presented as items of income or expense. There is a similar requirement for the statement of changes in equity or statement of recognised income and expense. (These relate to group accounts, covered later in this text.)

Income and expense items can only be **offset** when, and only when:

(a)   It is permitted or required by an IFRS, or

(b)   Gains, losses and related expenses arising from the same or similar transactions and events are immaterial, in which case they can be aggregated.

5.3 Information presented either on the face of the income statement or in the notes

An analysis of expenses must be shown either on the face of the income statement (as above, which is encouraged by the standard) or by note, using a classification based on *either* the nature of the expenses or their function. This **sub-classification of expenses** indicates a range of components of financial performance; these may differ in terms of stability, potential for gain or loss and predictability.

5.3.1 Nature of expense method

Expenses are not reallocated amongst various functions within the entity, but are aggregated in the income statement **according to their nature** (eg purchase of materials, depreciation, wages and salaries, transport costs). This is by far the easiest method, especially for smaller entities.

5.3.2 Function of expense/cost of sales method

You are likely to be more familiar with this method. Expenses are classified according to their function as part of cost of sales, distribution or administrative activities. This method often gives **more relevant information** for users, but the allocation of expenses by function requires the use of judgement and can be arbitrary. Consequently, perhaps, when this method is used, entities should disclose **additional information** on the nature of expenses, including staff costs, and depreciation and amortisation expense.

Which of the above methods is chosen by an entity will depend on **historical and industry factors**, and also the **nature of the organisation**. Under each method, there should be given an indication of costs which are likely to vary (directly or indirectly) with the level of sales or production. The choice of method should fairly reflect the main elements of the entity's performance.

5.4 Dividends

IAS 1 also requires disclosure of the amount of **dividends per share** (declared or proposed) for the period covered by the financial statements. This may be shown either on the face of the income statement or in the statement of changes in equity.

Further points

(a) All requirements previously set out in other Standards for the presentation of particular line items on the face of the balance sheet and income statement are now dealt with in IAS 1. These line items are: biological assets; liabilities and assets for current tax and deferred tax; and pre-tax gain or loss recognised on the disposal of assets or settlement of liabilities attributable to discontinued operations.

(b) The section that set out the **presentation requirements** for the **net profit or loss** for the period in **IAS 8** has now been **transferred** to **IAS 1** instead.

(c) The following **disclosures** are **no longer required:**

(i) The results of operating activities, as a line item on the face of the income statement. **'Operating activities'** are **not defined in IAS 1**

(ii) **Extraordinary items**, as a line item on the face of the income statement (note that the disclosure of 'extraordinary items' is now **prohibited**)

(iii) The **number** of an **entity's employees**

(d) An entity must disclose, in the summary of significant accounting policies and/or other notes, the **judgements** made by management in **applying** the **accounting policies** that have the **most significant effect** on the amounts of items recognised in the financial statements.

(e) An entity must disclose in the notes information regarding **key assumptions** about the **future**, and other sources of **measurement uncertainty**, that have a significant **risk of** causing a **material adjustment** to the carrying amounts of assets and liabilities within the **next financial year**.

6 Changes in equity

FAST FORWARD

The revised IAS 1 requires a statement of changes in equity.

6.1 Format

The statement can be in the format illustrated below (showing all changes in equity) or in the form of a statement of recognised income and expense.

XYZ GROUP
STATEMENT OF CHANGES IN EQUITY FOR THE YEAR ENDED 31 DECEMBER 20X8

	Attributable to equity holders of the parent						
	Share capital $'000	Other reserves $'000	Translation reserve $'000	Retained earnings $'000	Total $'000	Minority interest $'000	Total equity $'000
Balance at 31 December 20X7 brought forward	X	X	(X)	X	X	X	X
Changes in equity for 20X8							
Loss on property revaluation		(X)			(X)	(X)	(X)
Available-for-sale investments:							
Valuation gains/losses) taken to equity		(X)			(X)		(X)
Transferred to profit or loss on Sale		X			X		X
Cash flow hedges:							
Gains/(losses) taken to equity		X			X	X	X
Transferred to profit or loss for the period		(X)			(X)	(X)	(X)
Transferred to initial carrying Amount of hedged items		(X)			(X)		(X)
Exchange differences on translating foreign operations			(X)		(X)	(X)	(X)
Tax on items taken directly to or transferred from equity		X	X		X	X	X
Net income recognised directly in equity		(X)	(X)		(X)	(X)	(X)
Profit for the period		–	–	X	X	X	X
Total recognised income and expense for the period		(X)	(X)	X	X	X	X
Dividends				(X)	(X)	(X)	(X)
Issue of share capital	X				X		X
Balance at 31 December 20X8	X	X	(X)	X	X	X	X

6.2 Statement of recognised income and expense

This is an alternative method of presenting changes in equity. If this method is used, the notes to the financial statements must include a reconciliation of opening and closing balances of share capital, reserves and accumulated profit, as illustrated in the statement of changes in equity. (The previous version of IAS 1 referred to the statement of recognised gains and losses.)

XYZ GROUP
STATEMENT OF RECOGNISED INCOME AND EXPENSE
FOR THE YEAR ENDED 31 DECEMBER 20X8

	20X8 $'000	20X7 $'000
Gain/(loss) on revaluation of properties	(X)	X
Available-for-sale investments:		
Valuation gains/(losses) taken to equity	(X)	(X)
Transferred to profit or loss on sale	X	(X)
Cash flow hedges:		
Gains/(losses) taken to equity	X	X
Transferred to profit or loss for the period	(X)	X
Transferred to the initial carrying amount of hedged items	(X)	(X)
Exchange differences on translation of foreign operations	(X)	(X)
Tax on items taken directly to or transferred from equity	X	(X)
Net income recognised directly in equity	X	X
Net profit for the period	X	X
Total recognised income and expense for the period	X	X
Attributable to:		
Equity holders of the parent	X	X
Minority interest	X	X
	X	X
Effect of changes in accounting policy:		
Equity holders of the parent		(X)
Minority interest		(X)
		(X)

7 Notes to the financial statements

Some items need to be disclosed by way of note.

7.1 Contents of notes

The notes to the financial statements will **amplify** the information given in the balance sheet, income statement and statement of changes in equity. We have already noted above the information which the IAS allows to be shown by note rather than on the face of the statements. To some extent, then, the contents of the notes will be determined by the level of detail shown on the **face of the statements**.

7.2 Structure

The notes to the financial statements should perform the following functions.

(a) Provide information about the **basis on which the financial statements were prepared** and which **specific accounting policies** were chosen and applied to significant transactions/events

(b) Disclose any information, not shown elsewhere in the financial statements, which is **required by IFRSs**

(c) Show any additional information that is necessary for a **fair presentation** which is not shown on the face of the financial statements

The way the notes are presented is important. They should be given in a **systematic manner** and **cross referenced** back to the related figure(s) in the balance sheet, income statement or cash flow statement.

Notes to the financial statements will amplify the information shown therein by giving the following.

    (a)   More **detailed analysis** or breakdowns of figures in the statements

    (b)   **Narrative information** explaining figures in the statements

    (c)   **Additional information**, eg contingent liabilities and commitments

IAS 1 suggests a **certain order** for notes to the financial statements. This will assist users when comparing the statements of different entities.

    (a)   Statement of **compliance** with IFRSs

    (b)   Statement of the **measurement basis** (bases) and accounting policies applied

    (c)   **Supporting information** for items presented on the face of each financial statement in the same order as each line item and each financial statement is presented

    (d)   **Other disclosures**, eg:

        (i)   Contingent liabilities, commitments and other financial disclosures

        (ii)   Non-financial disclosures

The order of specific items may have to be varied occasionally, but a systematic structure is still required.

7.3 Presentation of accounting policies

The accounting policies section should describe the following.

    (a)   The **measurement basis** (or bases) used in preparing the financial statements

    (b)   The **other accounting policies** used, as required for a proper understanding of the financial statements

This information may be shown in the notes or sometimes as a **separate component** of the financial statements.

The information on measurement bases used is obviously fundamental to an understanding of the financial statements. Where **more than one basis is used**, it should be stated to which assets or liabilities each basis has been applied.

7.4 Other disclosures

An entity must disclose in the notes:

    (a)   The amount of dividends proposed or declared before the financial statements were authorised for issue but not recognised as a distribution to equity holders during the period, and the amount per share

    (b)   The amount of any cumulative preference dividends not recognised

IAS 1 ends by listing some **specific disclosures** which will always be required if they are not shown elsewhere in the financial statements.

    (a)   The **domicile and legal form** of the entity, its **country of incorporation** and the **address of the registered office** (or, if different, principal place of business)

    (b)   A description of the **nature of the entity's operations** and its **principal activities**

    (c)   The name of the **parent entity** and the **ultimate parent entity** of the group

The accountant of Wislon Co has prepared the following list of account balances as at 31 December 20X7.

	$'000
50c ordinary shares (fully paid)	350
7% $1 preferred shares (fully paid)	100
10% debentures (secured)	200
Accumulated profits 1.1.X7	242
General reserve 1.1.X7	171
Land and buildings 1.1.X7 (cost)	430
Plant and machinery 1.1.X7 (cost)	830
Aggregate depreciation	
Buildings 1.1.X7	20
Plant and machinery 1.1.X7	222
Inventory 1.1.X7	190
Sales	2,695
Purchases	2,152
Preferred dividend	7
Ordinary dividend	8
Debenture interest	10
Wages and salaries	254
Light and heat	31
Sundry expenses	113
Suspense account	135
Trade accounts receivable	179
Trade accounts payable	195
Cash	126

Notes

(a) Sundry expenses include $9,000 paid in respect of insurance for the year ending 1 September 20X8. Light and heat does not include an invoice of $3,000 for electricity for the three months ending 2 January 20X8, which was paid in February 20X8. Light and heat also includes $20,000 relating to salesmen's commission.

(b) The suspense account is in respect of the following items.

	$'000
Proceeds from the issue of 100,000 ordinary shares	120
Proceeds from the sale of plant	300
	420
Less consideration for the acquisition of Mary & Co	285
	135

(c) The net assets of Mary & Co were purchased on 3 March 20X7. Assets were valued as follows

	$'000
Investments	231
Inventory	34
	265

All the inventory acquired was sold during 20X7. The investments were still held by Wislon at 31.12.X7. Goodwill has not been impaired in value.

(d) The property was acquired some years ago. The buildings element of the cost was estimated at $100,000 and the estimated useful life of the assets was fifty years at the time of purchase. As at 31 December 20X7 the property is to be revalued at $800,000.

(e)   The plant which was sold had cost $350,000 and had a net book value of $274,000 as on 1.1.X7. $36,000 depreciation is to be charged on plant and machinery for 20X7.

(f)   The debentures have been in issue for some years. The 50c ordinary shares all rank for dividends at the end of the year.

(g)   The management wish to provide for:

    (i)   Debenture interest due
    (ii)   A transfer to general reserve of $16,000
    (iii) Audit fees of $4,000

(h)   Inventory as at 31 December 20X7 was valued at $220,000 (cost).

(i)   Taxation is to be ignored.

Required

Prepare the financial statements of Wislon Co as at 31 December 20X7. You do not need to produce notes to the statements.

Answer

(a)   Normal adjustments are needed for accruals and prepayments (insurance, light and heat, debenture interest and audit fees). The debenture interest accrued is calculated as follows.

	$'000
Charge needed in income statement (10% × $200,000)	20
Amount paid so far, as shown in list of account balances	10
Accrual: presumably six months' interest now payable	10

The accrued expenses shown in the balance sheet comprise:

	$'000
Debenture interest	10
Light and heat	3
Audit fee	4
	17

(b)   The misposting of $20,000 to light and heat is also adjusted, by reducing the light and heat expense, but charging $20,000 to salesmen's commission.

(c)   Depreciation on the building is calculated as $\dfrac{\$100,000}{50} = \$2,000$.

The NBV of the property is then $430,000 – $20,000 – $2,000 = $408,000 at the end of the year. When the property is revalued a reserve of $800,000 – $408,000 = $392,000 is then created.

(d)   The profit on disposal of plant is calculated as proceeds $300,000 (per suspense account) less NBV $274,000, ie $26,000. The cost of the remaining plant is calculated at $830,000 – $350,000 = $480,000. The depreciation provision at the year end is:

	$'000
Balance 1.1.X7	222
Charge for 20X7	36
Less depreciation on disposals (350 – 274)	(76)
Accumulated depreciate	182

(e)   Goodwill arising on the purchase of Mary & Co is:

	$'000
Consideration (per suspense account)	285
Assets at valuation	265
Goodwill	20

This is shown as an asset on the balance sheet. The investments, being owned by Wislon at the year end, are also shown on the balance sheet, whereas Mary's inventory, acquired and then sold, is added to the purchases figure for the year.

(f) The other item in the suspense account is dealt with as follows.

	$'000
Proceeds of issue of 100,000 ordinary shares	120
Less nominal value 100,000 × 50c	50
Excess of consideration over par value (= share premium)	70

(g) The transfer to general reserve increases it to $171,000 + $16,000 = $187,000.

We can now prepare the financial statements.

WISLON CO
INCOME STATEMENT
FOR THE YEAR ENDED 31 DECEMBER 20X7

	$'000	$'000	$'000
Revenue			2,695
Less cost of sales			
Opening inventory		190	
Purchases (2,152 + 34)		2,186	
		2,376	
Less closing inventory		220	
			2,156
Gross profit			539
Profit on disposal of plant			26
			565
Expenses			
Wages, salaries and commission (254 + 20)		274	
Sundry expenses (113 – 6)		107	
Light and heat (31 – 20 + 3)		14	
Depreciation: buildings		2	
plant		36	
Audit fees		4	
Debenture interest		20	
			457
Net profit			108

WISLON CO
BALANCE SHEET AS AT 31 DECEMBER 20X7

	$'000	$'000
Assets		
Non-current assets		
Property, plant and equipment		
Property at valuation		800
Plant: cost	480	
aggregate depreciation	182	
		298
Goodwill		20
Investments		231
Current assets		
Inventory	220	
Trade accounts receivable	179	
Prepayments	6	
Cash	126	
		531
Total assets		1,880
Equity and liabilities		
Equity		
50c ordinary shares	400	
7% $1 preferred shares	100	
	500	
Share premium	70	
Revaluation surplus	392	
General reserve	187	
Accumulated profits	319	
		1,468
Non-current liabilities		
10% debentures (secured)		200
Current liabilities		
Trade accounts payable	195	
Accrued expenses	17	
		212
Total equity and liabilities		1,880

WISLON CO
STATEMENT OF CHANGES IN EQUITY
FOR THE YEAR ENDED 31 DECEMBER 20X7

	Share capital $'000	Share premium $'000	Revaluation reserve $'000	General reserve $'000	Accumulated profits $'000	Total $'000
At 1.1.X7	450	–	–	171	242	863
Surplus on revaluation of properties			392			392
Net gains not recognised in the income statement	–	–	392	–	–	392
Net profit for the period					108	108
Dividends					(15)	(15)
Transfer to reserve				16	(16)	–
Issue of share capital	50	70				120
Balance at 31.12.X7	500	70	392	187	319	1,468

Chapter roundup

- **Limited liability** offers various advantages to companies, although there are disadvantages.

- IAS 1 *Presentation of financial statements* covers **accounting concepts** as described in Chapter 1.

- IAS 1 also covers the **form and content of** financial statements. The main components are:

    - Balance sheet
    - Income statement
    - Statement of recognised income and expenses (changes in equity)
    - Cash flow statement (see Chapter 14)
    - Notes to the financial statements

- Each component must be **identified clearly**.

- IAS 1 suggests **formats** for the balance sheet and income statement, but these are not rigid. Certain items are specified, however, for **disclosure on the face of the financial statements.**

- You should appreciate the distinction between **current and non-current** assets and liabilities and the difference in treatment for operating cycle items and other non-operating items which are due after twelve months.

- The revised IAS 1 requires a statement of changes in equity.

Quick quiz

1   Limited liability means that the shareholders of a company are not legally accountable.

   True   ☐

   False   ☐

2   IAS 1 states that entities should produce their financial statements within .... months of the balance sheet date.

3   Which of the following are examples of current assets?

   (a)   Property, plant and equipment
   (b)   Prepayments
   (c)   Cash equivalents
   (d)   Manufacturing licences
   (e)   Accumulated profits

4   Provisions must be disclosed on the face of the balance sheet.

   True   ☐

   False   ☐

5   Which of the following must be disclosed on the face of the income statement?

   (a)   Tax expense
   (b)   Analysis of expenses
   (c)   Net profit or loss for the period.

6   What is the alternative to the statement of changes in equity?

7   Fill in the blanks.

The accounting policies section of the notes describes:

The .... used in preparing the financial statements and...................................... required for a proper understanding of the financial statements.

Answers to quick quiz

1   False. It means that if the company becomes insolvent, the maximum that an owner stands to lose is his share capital in the business.

2   Six

3   (b) and (c) only

4   True

5   (a) and (c) only. (b) may be shown in the notes.

6   The statement of recognised income and expense.

7   Measurement basis (or bases)
     Specific accounting policies

Now try the question below from the Exam Question Bank

Number	Level	Marks	Time
Q4	Introductory	n/a	n/a

Distributable profits and capital transactions

Topic list	Syllabus reference
1 Revenue recognition	1(a), 3(a)
2 Distributable profits	3(a)
3 Redemption of shares	3(a)

Introduction

The topics in this chapter are relevant to all types of accounting transactions, providing a theoretical framework for the topics already covered and for accounting in general.

A great deal of national legislation governing distributions and capital transactions is concerned with protection of creditors; the aim is to prevent companies favouring shareholders over creditors.

Study guide

Section 3 – Revenue recognition

- Outline the principles of the timing of revenue recognition

- Explain the concept of substance over form in relation to recognising sales revenue

- Explain the principle of realised profits

- Discuss the various points in the production and sales cycle where it may, depending on circumstances be appropriate to recognise gains and losses – give examples of this

- Describe the IASB's 'balance sheet approach' to revenue recognition within its *Framework* and compare this to the requirements of relevant accounting standards

Section 8 – Share capital and reserves

- Explain and apply general principles relating to the purchase or redemption of shares
- Discuss the advantages of companies being able to redeem/purchase their own shares
- Discuss the principles relating to profits available for distribution

1 Revenue recognition

FAST FORWARD

> Revenue recognition is straightforward in most business transactions, but some situations are more complicated.

1.1 Introduction

Accruals accounting is based on the **matching of costs with the revenue they generate**. It is crucially important under this convention that we can establish the point at which revenue may be recognised so that the correct treatment can be applied to the related costs. For example, the costs of producing an item of finished goods should be carried as an asset in the balance sheet until such time as it is sold; they should then be written off as a charge to the trading account. Which of these two treatments should be applied cannot be decided until it is clear at what moment the sale of the item takes place.

The decision has a **direct impact on profit** since under the prudence concept it would be unacceptable to recognise the profit on sale until a sale had taken place in accordance with the criteria of revenue recognition.

Revenue is generally recognised as **earned at the point of sale**, because at that point four criteria will generally have been met.

- The product or service has been **provided to the buyer**.

- The buyer has **recognised his liability** to pay for the goods or services provided. The converse of this is that the seller has recognised that ownership of goods has passed from himself to the buyer.

- The buyer has indicated his **willingness to hand over cash** or other assets in settlement of his liability.

- The **monetary value** of the goods or services has been established.

At earlier points in the business cycle there will not in general be **firm evidence** that the above criteria will be met. Until work on a product is complete, there is a risk that some flaw in the manufacturing process will necessitate its writing off; even when the product is complete there is no guarantee that it will find a buyer.

At later points in the business cycle, for example when cash is received for the sale, the recognition of revenue may occur in a period later than that in which the related costs were charged. Revenue recognition would then depend on fortuitous circumstances, such as the cash flow of a company's customers, and might fluctuate misleadingly from one period to another.

However, there are times when revenue is **recognised at other times than at the completion of a sale**. For example, in the recognition of profit on long-term construction contracts. Under IAS 11 *Construction contracts* (see Chapter 7) contract revenue and contract costs associated with the construction contract should be recognised as revenue and expenses respectively by reference to the stage of completion of the contract activity at the balance sheet date.

(a)   Owing to the length of time taken to complete such contracts, to defer taking profit into account until completion may result in the income statement reflecting, not so much a fair view of the activity of the company during the year, but rather the results relating to contracts which have been completed by the year end.

(b)   Revenue in this case is recognised when production on, say, a section of the total contract is complete, even though no sale can be made until the whole is complete.

1.2 IAS 18 *Revenue*

IAS 18 governs the recognition of revenue in specific (common) types of transaction. Generally, recognition should be when it is probable that **future economic benefits** will flow to the enterprise and when these benefits can be **measured reliably**.

Income, as defined by the IASB's *Framework* document (see Chapter 20), includes both revenues and gains. Revenue is income arising in the ordinary course of an enterprise's activities and it may be called different names, such as sales, fees, interest, dividends or royalties.

1.3 Scope

IAS 18 covers the revenue from specific types of transaction or events.

- **Sale of goods** (manufactured products and items purchased for resale)
- **Rendering of services**
- Use by others of enterprise assets yielding **interest, royalties and dividends**

Interest, royalties and dividends are included as income because they arise from the use of an enterprise's assets by other parties.

Key terms

> **Interest** is the charge for the use of cash or cash equivalents or amounts due to the enterprise.
>
> **Royalties** are charges for the use of non-current assets of the enterprise, eg patents, computer software and trademarks.
>
> **Dividends** are distributions of profit to holders of equity investments, in proportion with their holdings, of each relevant class of capital.

The standard specifically **excludes** various types of revenue arising from leases, insurance contracts, changes in value of financial instruments or other current assets, natural increases in agricultural assets and mineral ore extraction.

1.4 Definitions

The following definitions are given in the standard.

Key terms

> **Revenue** is the gross inflow of economic benefits during the period arising in the course of the ordinary activities of an enterprise when those inflows result in increases in equity, other than increases relating to contributions from equity participants.
>
> **Fair value** is the amount for which an asset could be exchanged, or a liability settled, between knowledgeable, willing parties in an arm's length transaction.   *(IAS 18)*

Revenue **does not include** sales taxes, value added taxes or goods and service taxes which are only collected for third parties, because these do not represent an economic benefit flowing to the entity. The same is true for revenues collected by an agent on behalf of a principal. Revenue for the agent is only the commission received for acting as agent.

1.5 Measurement of revenue

When a transaction takes place, the amount of revenue is usually decided by the **agreement of the buyer and seller**. The revenue is actually measured, however, as the **fair value of the consideration received**, which will take account of any trade discounts and volume rebates.

1.6 Identification of the transaction

Normally, each transaction can be looked at **as a whole**. Sometimes, however, transactions are more complicated, and it is necessary to break a transaction down into its **component parts**. For example, a sale may include the transfer of goods and the provision of future servicing, the revenue for which should be deferred over the period the service is performed.

At the other end of the scale, **seemingly separate transactions must be considered together** if apart they lose their commercial meaning. An example would be to sell an asset with an agreement to buy it back at a later date. The second transaction cancels the first and so both must be considered together.

1.7 Sale of goods

Revenue from the sale of goods should only be recognised when *all* these conditions are satisfied.

    (a)   The enterprise has transferred the **significant risks and rewards** of ownership of the goods to the buyer

    (b)   The enterprise has **no continuing managerial involvement** to the degree usually associated with ownership, and no longer has effective control over the goods sold

    (c)   The amount of revenue can be **measured reliably**

    (d)   It is probable that the **economic benefits** associated with the transaction will flow to the enterprise

    (e)   The **costs incurred** in respect of the transaction can be measured reliably

The transfer of risks and rewards can only be decided by examining each transaction. Mainly, the transfer occurs at the same time as either the **transfer of legal title**, or the **passing of possession** to the buyer - this is what happens when you buy something in a shop.

If **significant risks and rewards remain with the seller**, then the transaction is *not* a sale and revenue cannot be recognised, for example if the receipt of the revenue from a particular sale depends on the buyer receiving revenue from his own sale of the goods.

It is possible for the seller to retain only an **'insignificant' risk of ownership** and for the sale and revenue to be recognised. The main example here is where the seller retains title only to ensure collection of what is owed on the goods. This is a common commercial situation, and when it arises the revenue should be recognised on the date of sale.

The probability of the enterprise receiving the revenue arising from a transaction must be assessed. It may only become probable that the economic benefits will be received when an uncertainty is removed, for example government permission for funds to be received from another country. Only when the uncertainty is removed should the revenue be recognised. This is in contrast with the situation where revenue has already been recognised but where the **collectability of the cash** is brought into doubt. Where recovery has ceased to be probable, the amount should be recognised as an expense, *not* an adjustment of the revenue previously recognised. These points also refer to services and interest, royalties and dividends below.

Matching should take place, ie the revenue and expenses relating to the same transaction should be recognised at the same time. It is usually easy to estimate expenses at the date of sale (eg warranty costs, shipment costs, etc). Where they cannot be estimated reliably, then revenue cannot be recognised; any consideration which has already been received is treated as a liability.

1.8 Rendering of services

When the outcome of a transaction involving the rendering of services can be estimated reliably, the associated revenue should be recognised by reference to the **stage of completion of the transaction** at the balance sheet date. The outcome of a transaction can be estimated reliably when *all* these conditions are satisfied.

(a) The amount of revenue can be **measured reliably**

(b) It is probable that the **economic benefits** associated with the transaction will flow to the enterprise

(c) The **stage of completion** of the transaction at the balance sheet date can be measured reliably

(d) The **costs incurred** for the transaction and the costs to complete the transaction can be measured reliably

The parties to the transaction will normally have to agree the following before an enterprise can make reliable estimates.

(a) Each party's **enforceable rights** regarding the service to be provided and received by the parties

(b) The **consideration** to be exchanged

(c) The **manner and terms of settlement**

There are various methods of determining the stage of completion of a transaction, but for practical purposes, when services are performed by an indeterminate number of acts over a period of time, revenue should be recognised on a **straight line basis** over the period, unless there is evidence for the use of a more appropriate method. If one act is of more significance than the others, then the significant act should be carried out *before* revenue is recognised.

In uncertain situations, when the outcome of the transaction involving the rendering of services cannot be estimated reliably, the standard recommends a **no loss/no gain approach**. Revenue is recognised only to the extent of the expenses recognised that are recoverable.

This is particularly likely during the **early stages of a transaction**, but it is still probable that the enterprise will recover the costs incurred. So the revenue recognised in such a period will be equal to the expenses incurred, with no profit.

Obviously, if the costs are not likely to be reimbursed, then they must be recognised as an expense immediately. **When the uncertainties cease to exist**, revenue should be recognised as laid out in the first paragraph of this section.

1.9 Interest, royalties and dividends

When others use the enterprise's assets yielding interest, royalties and dividends, the revenue should be recognised on the bases set out below when:

(a)   it is probable that the **economic benefits** associated with the transaction will flow to the enterprise; and

(b)   the amount of the revenue can be **measured reliably**.

The revenue is recognised on the following bases.

(a)   **Interest** is recognised on a time proportion basis that takes into account the effective yield on the asset

(b)   **Royalties** are recognised on an accruals basis in accordance with the substance of the relevant agreement

(c)   **Dividends** are recognised when the shareholder's right to receive payment is established

It is unlikely that you would be asked about anything as complex as this in the exam, but you should be aware of the basic requirements of the standard. The **effective yield** on an asset mentioned above is the rate of interest required to discount the stream of future cash receipts expected over the life of the asset to equate to the initial carrying amount of the asset.

Royalties are usually recognised on the same basis that they accrue **under the relevant agreement**. Sometimes the true substance of the agreement may require some other systematic and rational method of recognition.

Once again, the points made above about **probability and collectability** on sale of goods also apply here.

1.10 Disclosure

The following items should be disclosed.

(a)   The **accounting policies** adopted for the recognition of revenue, including the methods used to determine the stage of completion of transactions involving the rendering of services

(b)   The amount of each **significant category of revenue** recognised during the period including revenue arising from:

(i)   The sale of goods
(ii)   The rendering of services
(iii)   Interest
(iv)   Royalties
(v)   Dividends

(c)   The amount of revenue arising from **exchanges of goods or services** included in each significant category of revenue

Any **contingent gains or losses**, such as those relating to warranty costs, claims or penalties should be treated according to IAS 37 *Provisions, contingent liabilities and contingent assets* (covered in your earlier studies).

Question
Recognition

Given that prudence is the main consideration, discuss under what circumstances, if any, revenue might be recognised at the following stages of a sale.

(a)   Goods are acquired by the business which it confidently expects to resell very quickly.
(b)   A customer places a firm order for goods.
(c)   Goods are delivered to the customer.
(d)   The customer is invoiced for goods.
(e)   The customer pays for the goods.
(f)   The customer's cheque in payment for the goods has been cleared by the bank.

Answer

(a)   A sale must never be recognised before the goods have even been ordered by a customer. There is no certainty about the value of the sale, nor when it will take place, even if it is virtually certain that goods will be sold.

(b)   A sale must never be recognised when the customer places an order. Even though the order will be for a specific quantity of goods at a specific price, it is not yet certain that the sale transaction will go through. The customer may cancel the order, the supplier might be unable to deliver the goods as ordered or it may be decided that the customer is not a good credit risk.

(c)   A sale will be recognised when delivery of the goods is made only when:

(i)   the sale is for cash, and so the cash is received at the same time; or
(ii)   the sale is on credit and the customer accepts delivery (eg by signing a delivery note).

(d)   The critical event for a credit sale is usually the despatch of an invoice to the customer. There is then a legally enforceable debt, payable on specified terms, for a completed sale transaction.

(e)   The critical event for a cash sale is when delivery takes place and when cash is received; both take place at the same time.

It would be too cautious or 'prudent' to await cash payment for a credit sale transaction before recognising the sale, unless the customer is a high credit risk and there is a serious doubt about his ability or intention to pay.

(f)   It would again be over-cautious to wait for clearance of the customer's cheques before recognising sales revenue. Such a precaution would only be justified in cases where there is a very high risk of the bank refusing to honour the cheque.

2 Distributable profits

FAST FORWARD You need to be able to discuss the meaning of distributable and realisable profits.

Exam focus point

This is an important section, which you **must** look at.

2.1 Introduction

A **distribution** may be defined by national legislation, but we can state here that it is generally every description of distribution of a company's assets to members (shareholders) of the company, whether in cash or otherwise, with the **exception** of the following.

    (a)   An issue of **bonus shares**

    (b)   The **redemption or purchase of the company's own shares** out of capital (including the proceeds of a new issue) or out of unrealised profits

    (c)   The **reduction of share capital** by:

        (i)   reducing the liability on shares in respect of share capital not fully paid up, or
        (ii)   paying off paid-up share capital

    (d)   A distribution of assets to shareholders in a **winding up** of the company

In general, in most circumstances, **companies must not make a distribution except out of profits available for the purpose.** These available profits are:

    (a)   Its **accumulated realised profits**, insofar as these have not already been used for an earlier distribution or for 'capitalisation'

    (b)   **Minus its accumulated realised losses**, insofar as these have not already been written off in a reduction or reconstruction scheme

Capital profits and revenue profits (if realised) are taken together and capital losses and revenue losses (if realised) are similarly grouped together. **Unrealised profits** cannot be distributed (for example profit on the revaluation of non-current assets); nor must a company apply unrealised profits to pay up debentures or any unpaid amounts on issued shares.

Capitalisation of realised profits is the use of profits for one of two purposes.

    (a)   To issue bonus shares
    (b)   As a transfer to any reserve for the redemption of capital (a **capital redemption reserve**)

Some countries may impose **further restrictions on the distributions of all companies**, or perhaps listed companies or other public interest companies.

For example, such a company may not be able to make a distribution if at the time either of these apply.

    (a)   The amount of its net assets is less than the combined total of its called-up share capital plus its undistributable reserves.

    (b)   The distribution will reduce the amount of its net assets to below the combined total of its called-up share capital plus its undistributable reserves.

'Undistributable reserves' are likely to include the following, although national legislation may dictate otherwise.

    (a)   The **share premium account** (capital paid in excess of par)

    (b)   Any reserve for the **redemption of capital**

(c)   Any **accumulated surplus** of unrealised profits over unrealised losses

(d)   Any **other reserve** which cannot be distributed, whether by statute, or the company's memorandum or articles of association (ie constitution)

Where such a restriction applies, all **accumulated distributable profits, both realised and unrealised, must exceed the accumulated realised and unrealised losses of the company** before any distribution can be made. The difference between the profits and losses is the maximum possible distribution.

In contrast with the basic definition of distributable profits, this restriction includes consideration of **unrealised** profits and losses, so that if unrealised losses exceed unrealised profits, the amount of distributions which can be made will be reduced by the amount of the 'deficit'.

2.2 Example: basic distributable profits vs special restrictions

Huddle Co is a private company and Publimco is a listed company. Both companies have a financial year ending on 31 December. On 31 December 20X5, the balance sheets of the companies, by a remarkable coincidence, were identical, as follows.

	Huddle Co		Publimco	
	$'000	$'000	$'000	$'000
Net assets		365		365
Share capital		300		300
Share premium account		60		60
Unrealised losses on asset revaluations		(25)		(25)
Realised profits	50		50	
Realised losses	(20)		(20)	
		30		30
		365		365

What is the maximum distribution that each company can make, if Huddle Co's distributable profits follow the basic definition, but Publimco has special restrictions over its distributable profits as noted above?

Solution

(a)   The distributable profits of Huddle Co are $30,000.

(b)   The distributable profits of Publimco are further restricted to $30,000 – $25,000 = $5,000 (or alternatively, $365,000 – $300,000 – $60,000 = $5,000. This is the surplus of net assets over share capital plus undistributable reserves, which in this example are represented by the share premium account).

2.3 Realised and distributable profits

National legislation may define **realised profits** but in other countries the definition may not be clear. As a general 'rule of thumb' we can state that profits in the **income statement** are realised, while **unrealised profits** are **credited directly to reserves**.

IAS 1 *Presentation of financial statements* provides a framework for recognising realised profits. If IAS 1, particularly the **prudence concept** is followed, income statement profits will be realisable.

2.3.1 Exceptions

In the case of **sale of revalued non-current assets**, the **unrealised profit on revaluation** previously credited to the revaluation reserve may not pass through the income statement. It may nevertheless be regarded as **distributable**, unless local legislation states otherwise.

Where an asset has been revalued, the **increase in depreciation charge** can be treated as a realised profit.

Development expenditure is a realised loss in the year in which it is incurred, except when the costs are capitalised within IAS 38 guidelines, in which case the costs are amortised as realised losses over a number of years.

Provisions are generally treated as realised losses.

2.4 The relevant accounts

Which accounts should be used to determine the distributable profits? These are the **most recent audited annual accounts** of the company, prepared in compliance with national standards and legislation, or IFRSs. If the accounts are qualified by the auditors, the auditors must state in their report whether they consider that the proposed distribution would contravene any relevant legislation.

Companies may also be permitted to base a distribution on **interim accounts**, which need not be audited. However, in general, such interim accounts must be properly prepared and comply with IFRSs and show a true and fair view.

Question	Implications

Explain the implications of the following items to profits available for distribution in a company, based on the provisions of relevant IFRSs.

(a)   Research and development activities

(b)   Net deficit on a revaluation reserve arising from an overall deficit on the revaluation of non-current assets

(c)   Excess depreciation

(d)   Goodwill arising on consolidation

Answer

(a)   For the purposes of calculating realised profits, development expenditure carried forward in the balance sheet should be treated as a realised loss. This means that development expenditure may not be regarded as part of net assets.

   If, however, there are special circumstances which, in the opinion of the directors, justify the treatment of development expenditure as an asset and not as a loss, then this requirement need not apply. It is generally considered that, if the development expenditure qualifies for treatment as an asset under the provisions of IAS 38, then it may be treated as an asset and not a loss for the purposes of calculating distributable profits.

(b)   A revaluation reserve is a non-distributable reserve because it reflects unrealised profits and losses. An impairment in value causing an overall deficit on the revaluation reserve should be taken to the income statement, ie it is a realised loss and therefore reduces distributable profits.

(c)   Excess depreciation is the depreciation on revalued assets in excess of cost. Since excess depreciation is regarded as the realisation (through use) of part of the corresponding revaluation reserve, it is added back to profits available for distribution.

(d)   The normal treatment of such goodwill is to capitalise it but not amortise it. Instead an annual impairment review has to be carried out and any impairment charged to the income statement.

   Where this treatment is adopted, any amount written off for impairment is considered a realised loss and reduces distributable profits.

3 Redemption of shares

FAST FORWARD You must be able to carry out simple calculations on this topic.

3.1 Introduction

Limited liability companies may be permitted to cancel unissued shares and in that way reduce their **authorised** share capital. That change does not alter the financial position of any company.

If a limited liability company wishes to **reduce its issued share capital** (and incidentally its authorised capital of which the issued capital is part) it may do so provided that certain conditions are met (set by national legislation). For example:

(a)   It must have the power to do so in its **articles** of association
(b)   It must pass a **special resolution**
(c)   It must obtain **confirmation** of the reduction **from the court**

Requirement (a) is usually a matter of procedure. Articles usually contain the necessary power. If not, the company in general meeting would first pass a special resolution to alter the articles appropriately and then proceed to pass a special resolution to reduce the capital.

There are various basic methods of reducing share capital, and three of the most common are discussed here.

(a)   **Extinguish or reduce liability on partly paid shares**. A company may have issued $1 (par) shares 75c paid up. The outstanding liability of 25c per share may be eliminated altogether by reducing each share to 75c (par) fully paid or some intermediate figure, eg 80c (par) 75c paid. Nothing is returned to the shareholders but the company gives up a claim against them for money which it could call up whenever needed.

(b)   **Cancel paid up share capital which has been lost or which is no longer represented by available assets.** Suppose that the issued shares are $1 (par) fully paid but the net assets now represent a value of only 50c per share. The difference is probably matched by a debit balance on the retained reserves. The company could reduce the par value of its $1 shares to 50c (or some intermediate figure) and apply the amount to write off the debit balance wholly or in part. It would then be able to resume payment of dividends out of future profits without being obliged to make good past losses. The resources of the company are not reduced by this procedure of part cancellation of nominal value of shares but it avoids having to rebuild lost capital by retaining profits.

(c)   **Pay off part of the paid up share capital out of surplus assets.** The company might repay to shareholders, say, 30c in cash per $1 share by reducing the par value of the share to 70c. This reduces the assets of the company by 30c per share.

3.2 Role of court in reduction of capital

In many countries the sanction of the court (or equivalent) may be required for a redemption of shares or reduction in capital. The purpose here is **creditor protection**. The reduction in capital must not put at risk a company's ability to pay its debts. If it did so, then shareholders would be favoured over creditors for distributions from the company. Creditors may be allowed to petition the court against the proposed transaction, but the company may be able to override this by paying off its creditors. The details will vary from country to country.

3.3 Share premium account

Whenever a company obtains for its shares a consideration in excess of their par value, it must usually transfer the excess to a share premium account (capital in excess of par account). The general rule is that the **share premium account is subject to the same restrictions as share capital**. However, it may be possible to make a bonus issue using the share premium account (reducing share premium in order to increase issued share capital).

Examples of the **other likely permitted uses of share premium** are to pay:

(a) Capital expenses such as preliminary expenses of forming the company
(b) A discount on the issue of shares or debentures
(c) A premium (if any) paid on redemption of debentures

Some companies may also be able to use a share premium account in purchasing or redeeming their own shares out of capital. It must be emphasised that these rules will vary from country to country according to national legislation.

3.4 Redemption or purchase by a company of its own shares

In some countries, there is a **general prohibition** against any voluntary acquisition by a company of its own shares. In other countries, it is possible for a company to voluntarily acquire and keep its own shares, although there may be a limit on the time for which they can be held. For the rest of the chapter, however, we will assume that any of its own shares purchased by a company cannot be held and must be **cancelled immediately**.

Even where purchase of own shares is prohibited, there may be **exceptions**. For example, a company may:

(a) Purchase its own shares in compliance with an **order of the court**
(b) Issue **redeemable shares** and then redeem them
(c) Purchase its own shares under certain **specified procedures**
(d) **Forfeit** or accept the surrender of its shares
(e) Accept shares as a **gift**

There may be **conditions** for the issue and redemption of redeemable shares. Again these will vary from country to country, but these are good examples of the likely rules.

(a) The **articles** must give authority for the issue of redeemable shares. Articles do usually provide for it, but if they do not, the articles must be altered before the shares are issued.

(b) **Redeemable shares** may only be issued if at the time of issue the company also has issued shares which are not redeemable: a company's capital may not consist entirely of redeemable shares.

(c) Redeemable shares may only be redeemed if they are **fully paid**.

(d) The terms of redemption must **provide for payment on redemption**.

(e) The shares may be redeemed out of **distributable profits**, or the proceeds of a new issue of shares, or capital (this may be restricted for some special companies) in accordance with the relevant rules.

(f) Any **premium payable** on redemption must be provided out of distributable profits (subject to any exceptions).

One way to preserve reserves for creditor protection is to prevent companies from redeeming shares except by transferring a sum equal to the par value of shares redeemed from distributable profit reserves to a non-distributable reserve, which here we will call the '**capital redemption reserve**'. This reduction in distributable reserves is an example of the **capitalisation of profits**, where previously distributable profits become undistributable.

Such regulations prevent companies from reducing their share capital investment so as to put creditors of the company at risk.

3.5 Example: capitalisation of profits

Suppose, for example, that Muffin Co had $100,000 of preferred shares, redeemable in the very near future at par. A balance sheet of the company is currently as follows.

Assets	$	$
Cash		100,000
Other assets		300,000
		400,000
Equity and liabilities		
Equity		
Ordinary shares	30,000	
Retained earnings	150,000	
		180,000
Liabilities		
Redeemable preferred shares	100,000	
Trade accounts payable	120,000	
		220,000
		400,000

Now if Muffin were able to redeem the preferred shares without making any transfer from the retained earnings to a capital redemption reserve, the effect of the share redemption on the balance sheet would be as follows.

Assets	$
Non-cash assets	300,000
Equity and liabilities	
Equity	
Ordinary shares	30,000
Retained earnings	150,000
	180,000
Trade accounts payable	120,000
	300,000

In this example, the company would still be able to pay dividends out of profits of up to $150,000. If it did, the creditors of the company would be highly vulnerable, financing $120,000 out of a total of $150,000 assets of the company.

Regulations suggested above will prevent such extreme situations arising. On redemption of the preferred shares, Muffin would have been required to transfer $100,000 from its retained earnings to a non-distributable reserve, called here a capital redemption reserve. The effect of the redemption of shares on the balance sheet would have been:

Assets	$	$
Non-cash assets		300,000
Equity and liabilities		
Equity		
Ordinary shares	30,000	
Reserves		
Distributable (retained earnings)	50,000	
Non-distributable (capital redemption reserve)	100,000	
		180,000
Trade accounts payable		120,000
		300,000

The maximum distributable profits are now $50,000. If Muffin paid all these as a dividend, there would still be $250,000 of assets left in the company, just over half of which would be financed by non-distributable equity capital.

3.6 Further possible rules

When a company redeems some shares, or purchases some of its own shares, they should normally be redeemed:

(a) **Out of distributable profits,** OR

(b) **Out of the proceeds** of a new issue of shares.

In addition, if there is any premium on redemption, it may be the rule that **the premium must be paid out of distributable profits**, except that if the shares were issued at a premium, then any premium payable on their redemption may be paid out of the proceeds of a new share issue made for the purpose, up to an amount equal to the lesser of:

(a) the aggregate premiums received on issue of the redeemable shares; and

(b) the balance on the share premium account (including premium on issue of the new shares).

This may seem complicated, but it makes logical sense. A numerical example might help.

3.7 Example: redemption of shares

Suppose that Jingle Co intends to redeem 10,000 shares of $1 each at a premium of 5 cents per share. The redemption must be financed in one of the following ways.

(a) Out of distributable profits (10,000 × $1.05 = $10,500).

(b) Out of the proceeds of a new share issue (say, by issuing 10,000 new $1 shares at par). The premium of $500 must be paid out of distributable profits.

(c) Out of a combination of a new share issue and distributable profits.

(d) Out of the proceeds of a new share issue where the redeemable shares were issued at a premium. For example, if the redeemable shares had been issued at a premium of 3c per share, then (assuming that the balance on the share premium account after the new share issue was at least $300) $300 of the premium on redemption could be debited to the share premium account and only $200 need be debited to distributable profits.

The following rules may also assist.

(a) Where a company redeems shares or purchases its own shares wholly out of distributable profits, it must transfer to the capital redemption reserve an amount equal to the par value of the shares redeemed.

In example (a) above the accounting entries would be:

		$	$
DEBIT	Share capital account	10,000	
	Retained earnings (premium on redemption)	500	
CREDIT	Cash		10,500
DEBIT	Retained earnings	10,000	
CREDIT	Capital redemption reserve		10,000

(b) Where a company redeems shares or purchases its shares wholly or partly out of the proceeds of a new share issue, it must transfer to the capital redemption reserve an amount by which the par value of the shares redeemed exceeds the *aggregate* proceeds from the new issue (ie par value of new shares issued plus share premium).

In example (b) the accounting entries would be:

		$	$
DEBIT	Share capital account (redeemed shares)	10,000	
	Retained earnings (premium)	500	
CREDIT	Cash (redemption of shares)		10,500
DEBIT	Cash (from new issue)	10,000	
CREDIT	Share capital account		10,000

No credit to the capital redemption reserve is necessary because there is no decrease in the creditors' buffer.

(c) If the redemption in the same example as in (b) were made by issuing 5,000 new $1 shares at par, and paying $5,500 out of distributable profits:

		$	$
DEBIT	Share capital account (redeemed shares)	10,000	
	Retained earnings (premium)	500	
CREDIT	Cash (redemption of shares)		10,500
DEBIT	Cash (from new issue)	5,000	
CREDIT	Share capital account		5,000
DEBIT	Retained earnings	5,000	
CREDIT	Capital redemption reserve		5,000

(d) In the example (d) above (assuming a new issue of 10,000 $1 shares at a premium of 8c per share) the accounting entries would be:

		$	$
DEBIT	Cash (from new issue)	10,800	
CREDIT	Share capital account		10,000
	Share premium account		800
DEBIT	Share capital account (redeemed shares)	10,000	
	Share premium account	300	
	Retained earnings	200	
CREDIT	Cash (redemption of shares)		10,500

No capital redemption reserve is required, as in (b) above. The redemption is financed entirely by a new issue of shares.

Exam focus point

The examiner has indicated that he will not examine small company redemption of shares out of capital.

3.8 Commercial reasons for altering capital structure

These include the following.

- Greater **security of finance**
- Better **image** for third parties
- A **'neater' balance sheet**
- **Borrowing repaid** sooner
- **Cost of borrowing** reduced

Set out below are the summarised balance sheets of A Co and B Co at 30 June 20X5.

	A $'000	B $'000
Net assets	520	380
Capital and reserves		
Called up share capital $1 ordinary shares	300	300
Share premium account	60	60
Retained earnings	160	20
	520	380

On 1 July 20X5 A Co and B Co each purchased 50,000 of their own ordinary shares as follows.

A Co purchased its own shares at 150c each. The shares were originally issued at a premium of 20c. The redemption was partly financed by the issue at par of 5,000 10% redeemable preferred shares of $1 each.

B Co purchased its own shares out of capital at a price of 80c each.

A Co can only purchase its own shares using distributable profits.

B Co can purchase its own shares out of capital. All shares must be cancelled on purchase.

Required

Prepare the summarised balance sheets of A Co and B Co at 1 July 20X5 immediately after the above transactions have been effected.

Answer

Workings for A Co

	$	$
Cost of redemption (50,000 × $1.50)		75,000
Premium on redemption (50,000 × 50c)		25,000
No premium arises on the new issue.		
Distributable profits		
Retained earnings before redemption		160,000
Premium on redemption (must come out of distributable profits, no premium on new issue)		(25,000)
		135,000
Remainder of redemption costs	50,000	
Proceeds of new issue 5,000 × $1	(5,000)	
Remainder out of distributable profits		(45,000)
Balance on retained earnings		90,000
Transfer to capital redemption reserve		
Par value of shares redeemed		50,000
Proceeds of new issue		(5,000)
Balance on CRR		45,000

BALANCE SHEET OF A CO AS AT 1 JULY 20X5

	$'000
Net assets	450
Equity	
Ordinary shares	250
Share premium	60
Capital redemption reserve	45
	355
Retained earnings	90
	445
Liability: preferred shares	5
	450

Workings for B Co

	$
Cost of redemption (50,000 × 80c)	40,000
Discount on redemption (50,000 × 20c)	10,000
Cost of redemption	40,000
Distributable profits	(20,000)
Permissible capital payment (PCP)	20,000
Transfer to capital redemption reserve	
Par value of shares redeemed	50,000
PCP	20,000
Balance on capital redemption reserve	30,000

BALANCE SHEET OF B CO AS AT 1 JULY 20X5

	$'000
Net assets	340
Equity	
Ordinary shares	250
Share premium	60
Capital redemption reserve	30
	340

Chapter roundup

- **Revenue recognition** is straightforward in most business transactions, but some situations are more complicated. It is necessary to determine the **substance of each transaction, rather than the legal form**.

- IAS 18 *Revenue* is concerned with the **recognition of revenues** arising from fairly common transactions.

  - The sale of goods
  - The rendering of services
  - The use by others of enterprise assets yielding interest, royalties and dividends

- Generally revenue is recognised when the enterprise has transferred to the buyer the **significant risks and rewards of ownership** and when the revenue can be **measured reliably**.

- You should be able to calculate **maximum distributions available to companies** and to discuss the meaning of distributable and realised profits.

- You must be able to carry out **simple calculations** showing the amounts to be transferred to the **capital redemption reserve** on purchase or redemption of own shares, how the amount of any **premium** on redemption would be treated, and how much the **permissible capital payment** would be for a company.

Quick quiz

1   To which purposes can a share premium account normally be applied?

(i)   Writing off share/debenture issue expenses
(ii)   Paying a premium on redemption
(iii)   Issuing fully paid bonus shares to members

Which is correct?

A   (i) and (ii)
B   (i) and (iii)
C   (ii) and (iii)
D   All the above

2   Revenue recognition is governed by IAS ....

3   What are the profits generally available for distribution?

4   A company cannot make a distribution if this will reduce its net assets to below the value of its called up share capital plus undistributable reserves.

True   ☐

False   ☐

5   If a company has not got the power to reduce its issued share capital, per the articles of association, then it can never do so.

True   ☐

False   ☐

6   A company can redeem shares out of which sources of funds?

(i)   Distributable profits
(ii)   Proceeds of new shares
(iii)   The share premium account

A   All three
B   (i) and (ii)
C   (ii) and (iii)
D   (i) and (iii)

Answers to quick quiz

1   D (see Section 3.3)

2   18

3   See Section 2.1

4   True

5   False, it can pass a special resolution to change the articles.

6   B   Only if specifically permitted by local statute can a company redeem shares out of capital (share premium account).

Now try the question below from the Exam Question Bank

Number	Level	Marks	Time
Q5	Examination	25	45 mins

Accounting for tangible non-current assets

Topic list	Syllabus reference
1 Depreciation accounting	3(b)
2 IAS 16 *Property, plant and equipment*	3(b)
3 IAS 20 *Government grants*	3(b)
4 IAS 40 *Investment property*	3(b)
5 IAS 36 *Impairment of assets*	3(b)

Introduction

IAS 16 should be familiar to you from your earlier studies, as should the mechanics of accounting for depreciation, revaluations of long-term (non-current) assets and disposals of non-current assets. Some questions are given here for revision purposes.

IAS 20 on government grants is a straightforward standard and you should have few problems with it.

IAS 40 deals with investment properties, which can be treated differently from other property under IAS 16.

IAS 36 on impairment is a topical standard.

IAS 16, 36 and **40** have recently been revised.

Study guide

Section 9 – Non-current assets – tangible

- Define the initial cost of a non-current asset (including a self-constructed asset) and apply this to various examples of expenditures distinguishing between capital and revenue items

- Describe, and be able to identify, subsequent expenditure that may be capitalised

- State and appraise the effects of accounting standards on the revaluation of property, plant and equipment

- Account for gains and losses on the disposal of revalued assets

- Calculate depreciation on:

    - revalued assets, and
    - assets that have two or more major components

- Apply the provisions of accounting standards on accounting for government grants and disclosure of government assistance

- Discuss the way in which the treatment of investment properties differs from other properties

- Apply the requirements of accounting standards on investment properties

Section 12 – Impairment of assets

- Define the recoverable amount of an asset; define impairment losses

- Give examples of, and be able to identify, circumstances that may indicate that an impairment of an asset has occurred

- Describe what is meant by a cash-generating unit

- State the basis on which impairment losses should be allocated, and allocate a given impairment loss to the assets of a cash-generating unit

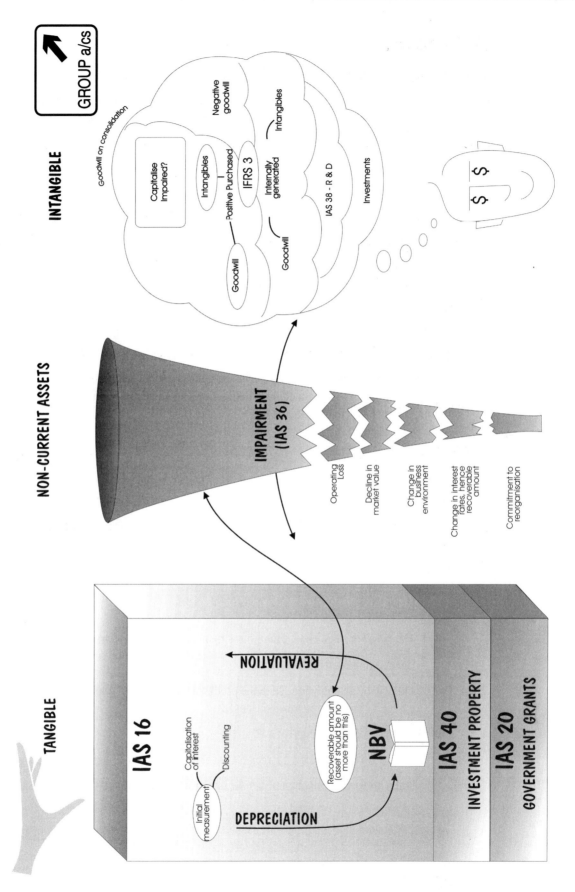

1 Depreciation accounting

Where assets held by an entity have a **limited useful life** to that entity it is necessary to apportion the value of an asset used in a period against the revenue it has helped to create.

1.1 Non-current assets

If an asset's life extends over more than one accounting period, it earns profits over more than one period. It is a **non-current asset**.

With the exception of land held on freehold or very long leasehold, **every non-current asset eventually wears out over time**. Machines, cars and other vehicles, fixtures and fittings, and even buildings do not last for ever. When a business acquires a non-current asset, it will have some idea about how long its useful life will be, and it might decide what to do with it.

(a)   Keep on using the non-current asset until it becomes **completely worn out**, useless, and worthless.

(b)   **Sell off** the non-current asset at the end of its useful life, either by selling it as a second-hand item or as scrap.

Since a non-current asset has a cost, and a limited useful life, and its value eventually declines, it follows that a charge should be made in the income statement to reflect the use that is made of the asset by the business. This charge is called **depreciation**.

1.2 Scope

Depreciation accounting is governed by IAS 16 *Property, plant and equipment* which we will look at in Section 2 of this chapter. However, this section will deal with some of the IAS 16 definitions concerning depreciation.

Key terms

> - **Depreciation** is the result of systematic allocation of the depreciable amount of an asset over its estimated useful life. Depreciation for the accounting period is charged to net profit or loss for the period either directly or indirectly.
>
> - **Depreciable assets** are assets which:
>   - Are expected to be used during more than one accounting period
>   - Have a limited useful life
>   - Are held by an entity for use in the production or supply of goods and services, for rental to others, or for administrative purposes
>
> - **Useful life** is one of two things.
>   - The period over which a depreciable asset is expected to be used by the entity, or
>   - The number of production or similar units expected to be obtained from the asset by the entity.
>
> - **Depreciable amount** of a depreciable asset is the historical cost or other amount substituted for cost in the financial statements, less the estimated residual value.
>
> *(IAS 16)*

An 'amount substituted for cost' will normally be a **current market value** after a revaluation has taken place.

1.3 Depreciation

IAS 16 requires the depreciable amount of a depreciable asset to be allocated on a **systematic basis** to each accounting period during the useful life of the asset. **Every part of an item of property, plant and equipment with a cost that is significant in relation to the total cost of the item must be depreciated separately**.

One way of defining depreciation is to describe it as a means of **spreading the cost** of a non-current asset over its useful life, and so matching the cost against the full period during which it earns profits for the business. Depreciation charges are an example of the application of the accrual assumption to calculate profits.

There are situations where, over a period, an asset has **increased in value**, ie its current value is greater than the carrying value in the financial statements. You might think that in such situations it would not be necessary to depreciate the asset. The standard states, however, that this is irrelevant, and that depreciation should still be charged to each accounting period, based on the depreciable amount, irrespective of a rise in value.

An entity is required to begin depreciating an item of property, plant and equipment when it is available for use and to continue depreciating it until it is derecognised even if it is idle during the period.

1.4 Useful life

The following factors should be considered when **estimating the useful life** of a depreciable asset.

- Expected **physical wear and tear**
- **Obsolescence**
- Legal or other **limits** on the use of the assets

Once decided, the useful life should be **reviewed at least every financial year end** and depreciation rates adjusted for the current and future periods if expectations vary significantly from the original estimates. The effect of the change should be disclosed in the accounting period in which the change takes place.

The assessment of useful life requires **judgement** based on previous experience with similar assets or classes of asset. When a completely new type of asset is acquired (ie through technological advancement or through use in producing a brand new product or service) it is still necessary to estimate useful life, even though the exercise will be much more difficult.

The standard also points out that the physical life of the asset might be longer than its useful life to the entity in question. One of the main factors to be taken into consideration is the **physical wear and tear** the asset is likely to endure. This will depend on various circumstances, including the number of shifts for which the asset will be used, the entity's repair and maintenance programme and so on. Other factors to be considered include obsolescence (due to technological advances/improvements in production/reduction in demand for the product/service produced by the asset) and legal restrictions, eg length of a related lease.

1.5 Residual value

In most cases the residual value of an asset is **likely to be immaterial**. If it is likely to be of any significant value, that value must be estimated at the date of purchase or any subsequent revaluation. The amount of residual value should be estimated based on the current situation with other similar assets, used in the same way, which are now at the end of their useful lives. Any expected costs of disposal should be offset against the gross residual value.

1.6 Depreciation methods

Consistency is important. The depreciation method selected should be applied consistently from period to period unless altered circumstances justify a change. When the method *is* changed, the effect should be quantified and disclosed and the reason for the change should be stated.

Various methods of allocating depreciation to accounting periods are available, but whichever is chosen must be applied **consistently** (as required by IAS 1: see Chapter 1), to ensure comparability from period to period. Change of policy is not allowed simply because of the profitability situation of the entity.

You should be familiar with the various **accepted methods of allocating depreciation** and the relevant calculations and accounting treatments, which are revised in questions at the end of this section.

1.7 Disclosure

An accounting policy note should disclose the **valuation bases** used for determining the amounts at which depreciable assets are stated, along with the other accounting policies: see IAS 1.

IAS 16 also requires the following to be disclosed for each major class of depreciable asset.

- **Depreciation methods** used
- **Useful lives** or the depreciation rates used
- **Total depreciation** allocated for the period
- **Gross amount** of depreciable assets and the related accumulated depreciation

1.8 What is depreciation?

The need to depreciate non-current assets arises from the **accruals assumption**. If money is expended in purchasing an asset then the amount expended must at some time be charged against profits. If the asset is one which contributes to an entity's revenue over a number of accounting periods it would be inappropriate to charge any single period (eg the period in which the asset was acquired) with the whole of the expenditure. Instead, some method must be found of spreading the cost of the asset over its useful economic life.

This view of depreciation as a process of allocation of the cost of an asset over several accounting periods is the view adopted by IAS 16. It is worth mentioning here two **common misconceptions** about the purpose and effects of depreciation.

(a) It is sometimes thought that the net book value (NBV) of an asset is equal to its net realisable value and that the object of charging depreciation is to **reflect the fall in value of an asset over its life**. This misconception is the basis of a common, but incorrect, argument which says that freehold properties (say) need not be depreciated in times when property values are rising. It is true that historical cost balance sheets often give a misleading impression when a property's NBV is much below its market value, but in such a case it is open to a business to incorporate a revaluation into its books, or even to prepare its accounts based on current costs. This is a separate problem from that of allocating the property's cost over successive accounting periods.

(b) Another misconception is that depreciation is provided **so that an asset can be replaced at the end of its useful life**. This is not the case.

(i) If there is no intention of replacing the asset, it could then be argued that there is no need to provide for any depreciation at all.

(ii) If prices are rising, the replacement cost of the asset will exceed the amount of depreciation provided.

The following questions are for revision purposes only.

Question | Depreciation methods

A lorry bought for a business cost $17,000. It is expected to last for five years and then be sold for scrap for $2,000. Usage over the five years is expected to be:

Year 1	200 days
Year 2	100 days
Year 3	100 days
Year 4	150 days
Year 5	40 days

Required

Work out the depreciation to be charged each year under:

(a) The straight line method
(b) The reducing balance method (using a rate of 35%)
(c) The machine hour method

Answer

(a) Under the straight line method, depreciation for each of the five years is:

$$\text{Annual depreciation} = \frac{\$(17,000 - 2,000)}{5} = \$3,000$$

(b) Under the reducing balance method, depreciation for each of the five years is:

Year	Depreciation		
1	35% × $17,000	=	$5,950
2	35% × ($17,000 − $5,950) = 35% × $11,050	=	$3,868
3	35% × ($11,050 − $3,868) = 35% × $7,182	=	$2,514
4	35% × ($7,182 − $2,514) = 35% × $4,668	=	$1,634
5	Balance to bring book value down to $2,000 = $4,668 − $1,634 − $2,000	=	$1,034

(c) Under the machine hour method, depreciation for each of the five years is calculated as follows.

Total usage (days) = 200 + 100 + 100 + 150 + 40 = 590 days

$$\text{Depreciation per day} = \frac{\$(17,000 - 2,000)}{590} = \$25.42$$

Year	Usage (days)	Depreciation ($) (days × $25.42)
1	200	5,084.00
2	100	2,542.00
3	100	2,542.00
4	150	3,813.00
5	40	1,016.80
		14,997.80

Note. The answer does not come to exactly $15,000 because of the rounding carried out at the 'depreciation per day' stage of the calculation.

Question

(a)   What are the purposes of providing for depreciation?

(b)   In what circumstances is the reducing balance method more appropriate than the straight-line method? Give reasons for your answer.

Answer

(a)   The accounts of a business try to recognise that the cost of a non-current asset is gradually consumed as the asset wears out. This is done by gradually writing off the asset's cost in the income statement over several accounting periods. This process is known as depreciation, and is an example of the accruals assumption. IAS 16 *Property, plant and equipment* requires that depreciation should be allocated on a systematic basis to each accounting period during the useful life of the asset.

With regard to the accrual principle, it is fair that the profits should be reduced by the depreciation charge; this is not an arbitrary exercise. Depreciation is not, as is sometimes supposed, an attempt to set aside funds to purchase new non-current assets when required. Depreciation is not generally provided on freehold land because it does not 'wear out' (unless it is held for mining etc).

(b)   The reducing balance method of depreciation is used instead of the straight line method when it is considered fair to allocate a greater proportion of the total depreciable amount to the earlier years and a lower proportion to the later years on the assumption that the benefits obtained by the business from using the asset decline over time.

In favour of this method it may be argued that it links the depreciation charge to the costs of maintaining and running the asset. In the early years these costs are low and the depreciation charge is high, while in later years this is reversed.

Question

A business purchased two rivet-making machines on 1 January 20X5 at a cost of $15,000 each. Each had an estimated life of five years and a nil residual value. The straight line method of depreciation is used.

Owing to an unforeseen slump in market demand for rivets, the business decided to reduce its output of rivets, and switch to making other products instead. On 31 March 20X7, one rivet-making machine was sold (on credit) to a buyer for $8,000.

Later in the year, however, it was decided to abandon production of rivets altogether, and the second machine was sold on 1 December 20X7 for $2,500 cash.

Prepare the machinery account, provision for depreciation of machinery account and disposal of machinery account for the accounting year to 31 December 20X7.

Answer

MACHINERY ACCOUNT

		$			$
20X7			*20X7*		
1 Jan	Balance b/f	30,000	31 Mar	Disposal of machinery account	15,000
			1 Dec	Disposal of machinery account	15,000
		30,000			30,000

PROVISION FOR DEPRECIATION OF MACHINERY

20X7		$	20X7		$
31 Mar	Disposal of machinery account*	6,750	1 Jan	Balance b/f	12,000
1 Dec	Disposal of machinery account**	8,750	31 Dec	Income statement***	3,500
		15,500			15,500

*   Depreciation at date of disposal = $6,000 + $750
** Depreciation at date of disposal = $6,000 + $2,750
*** Depreciation charge for the year = $750 + $2,750

DISPOSAL OF MACHINERY

20X7		$	20X7		$
31 Mar	Machinery account	15,000	31 Mar	Account receivable (sale price)	8,000
			31 Mar	Provision for depreciation	6,750
1 Dec	Machinery	15,000	1 Dec	Cash (sale price)	2,500
			1 Dec	Provision for depreciation	8,750
			31 Dec	Income statement (loss on disposal)	4,000
		30,000			30,000

You should be able to calculate that there was a loss on the first disposal of $250, and on the second disposal of $3,750, giving a total loss of $4,000.

Workings

1   At 1 January 20X7, accumulated depreciation on the machines will be:

2 machines × 2 years × $\dfrac{\$15,000}{5}$ per machine pa = $12,000, or $6,000 per machine

2   Monthly depreciation is $\dfrac{\$3,000}{12}$ = $250 per machine per month

3   The machines are disposed of in 20X7.

(a)   On 31 March – after 3 months of the year. Depreciation for the year on the machine = 3 months × $250 = $750.

(b)   On 1 December – after 11 months of the year. Depreciation for the year on the machine = 11 months × $250 = $2,750.

2 IAS 16 Property, plant and equipment

This standard covers all aspects of accounting for property, plant and equipment. This represents the bulk of items which are **'tangible' non-current assets**. The standard was revised in December 2003.

2.1 Scope

IAS 16 should be followed when accounting for property, plant and equipment *unless* another international accounting standard requires a **different treatment**.

IAS 16 **does not apply** to the following.

(a) Biological assets related to agricultural activity

(b) Mineral rights and mineral reserves, such as oil, gas and other non-regenerative resources

However, the standard applies to property, plant and equipment used to develop these assets.

2.2 Definitions

The standard gives a large number of definitions.

Key terms

- **Property, plant and equipment** are tangible assets that:

  – are held for use in the production or supply of goods or services, for rental to others, or for administrative purposes; and

  – are expected to be used during more than one period.

- **Cost** is the amount of cash or cash equivalents paid or the fair value of the other consideration given to acquire an asset at the time of its acquisition or construction.

- **Residual value** is the net amount which the entity expects to obtain for an asset at the end of its useful life after deducting the expected costs of disposal.

- **Entity specific value** is the present value of the cash flows an entity expects to arise from the continuing use of an asset and from its disposal at the end of its useful life, or expects to incur when settling a liability.

- **Fair value** is the amount for which an asset could be exchanged between knowledgeable, willing parties in an arm's length transaction.

- **Carrying amount** is the amount at which an asset is recognised in the balance sheet after deducting any accumulated depreciation and accumulated impairment losses.

- An **impairment loss** is the amount by which the carrying amount of an asset exceeds its recoverable amount.

(IAS 16)

2.3 Recognition

In this context, recognition simply means incorporation of the item in the business's accounts, in this case as a non-current asset. The recognition of property, plant and equipment depends on two criteria.

(a) It is probable that **future economic benefits** associated with the asset will flow to the entity

(b) The cost of the asset to the entity can be **measured reliably**

These recognition criteria apply to **subsequent expenditure** as well as costs incurred initially. There are no longer any separate criteria for recognising subsequent expenditure.

Property, plant and equipment can amount to **substantial amounts** in financial statements, affecting the presentation of the company's financial position (in the balance sheet) and the profitability of the entity, through depreciation and also if an asset is wrongly classified as an expense and taken to the income statement.

2.3.1 First criterion: future economic benefits

The **degree of certainty** attached to the flow of future economic benefits must be assessed. This should be based on the evidence available at the date of initial recognition (usually the date of purchase). The entity should thus be assured that it will receive the rewards attached to the asset and it will incur the

BPP)))
PROFESSIONAL EDUCATION

associated risks, which will only generally be the case when the rewards and risks have actually passed to the entity. Until then, the asset should not be recognised.

2.3.2 Second criterion: cost measured reliably

It is generally easy to measure the cost of an asset as the **transfer amount on purchase**, ie what was paid for it. **Self-constructed assets** can also be measured easily by adding together the purchase price of all the constituent parts (labour, material etc) paid to external parties.

2.4 Separate items

Most of the time assets will be identified individually, but this will not be the case for **smaller items**, such as tools, dies and moulds, which are sometimes classified as inventory and written off as an expense.

Major components or spare parts, however, should be recognised as property, plant and equipment.

For very **large and specialised items**, an apparently single asset should be broken down into its composite parts. This occurs where the different parts have different useful lives and different depreciation rates are applied to each part, eg an aircraft, where the body and engines are separated as they have different useful lives.

2.5 Safety and environmental equipment

When such assets as these are acquired they will qualify for recognition where they enable the entity to **obtain future economic benefits** from related assets in excess of those it would obtain otherwise. The recognition will only be to the extent that the carrying amount of the asset and related assets does not exceed the total recoverable amount of these assets.

2.6 Initial measurement

Once an item of property, plant and equipment qualifies for recognition as an asset, it will initially be **measured at cost**.

2.6.1 Components of cost

The standard lists the components of the cost of an item of property, plant and equipment.

- **Purchase price**, less any trade discount or rebate

- **Import duties** and non-refundable purchase taxes

- **Directly attributable costs** of bringing the asset to working condition for its intended use, eg:
    - The cost of site preparation
    - Initial delivery and handling costs
    - Installation costs
    - Testing
    - Professional fees (architects, engineers)

- Initial estimate of the unavoidable cost of dismantling and removing the asset and restoring the site on which it is located

The revised IAS 16 provides **additional guidance on directly attributable** costs included in the cost of an item of property, plant and equipment.

(a)   These costs bring the asset to the location and working conditions necessary for it to be capable of operating in the manner intended by management, including those costs to test whether the asset is functioning properly.

(b)   They are determined after deducting the net proceeds from selling any items produced when bringing the asset to its location and condition.

The revised standard also states that income and related expenses of operations that are **incidental** to the construction or development of an item of property, plant and equipment should be **recognised** in the income statement.

The following costs **will not be part of the cost** of property, plant or equipment unless they can be attributed directly to the asset's acquisition, or bringing it into its working condition.

- Administration and other general overhead costs
- Start-up and similar pre-production costs
- Initial operating losses before the asset reaches planned performance

All of these will be recognised as an **expense** rather than an asset.

In the case of **self-constructed assets**, the same principles are applied as for acquired assets. If the entity makes similar assets during the normal course of business for sale externally, then the cost of the asset will be the cost of its production under IAS 2 *Inventories*. This also means that abnormal costs (wasted material, labour or other resources) are excluded from the cost of the asset. An example of a self-constructed asset is when a building company builds its own head office.

2.6.2 Exchanges of assets

The revised IAS 16 specifies that exchange of items of property, plant and equipment, regardless of whether the assets are similar, are measured at **fair value**, **unless the exchange transaction lacks commercial substance** or the fair value of neither of the assets exchanged can be **measured reliably**. If the acquired item is not measured at fair value, its cost is measured at the carrying amount of the asset given up.

Expenditure incurred in replacing or renewing a component of an item of property, plant and equipment must be **recognised in the carrying amount of the item**. The carrying amount of the replaced or renewed component must be derecognised. A similar approach is also applied when a separate component of an item of property, plant and equipment is identified in respect of a major inspection to enable the continued use of the item.

2.7 Measurement subsequent to initial recognition

The standard offers two possible treatments here, essentially a choice between keeping an asset recorded at **cost** or revaluing it to **fair value**.

(a)   **Cost model.** Carry the asset at its cost less depreciation and any accumulated impairment loss.

(b)   **Revaluation model.** Carry the asset at a revalued amount, being its fair value at the date of the revaluation less any subsequent accumulated depreciation and subsequent accumulated impairment losses. The revised IAS 16 makes clear that the **revaluation model is available only if the fair value of the item can be measured reliably**.

2.7.1 Revaluations

The **market value** of land and buildings usually represents fair value, assuming existing use and line of business. Such valuations are usually carried out by professionally qualified valuers.

In the case of **plant and equipment**, fair value can also be taken as **market value**. Where a market value is not available, however, depreciated replacement cost should be used. There may be no market value where types of plant and equipment are sold only rarely or because of their specialised nature (ie they would normally only be sold as part of an ongoing business).

The frequency of valuation depends on the **volatility of the fair values** of individual items of property, plant and equipment. The more volatile the fair value, the more frequently revaluations should be carried out. Where the current fair value is very different from the carrying value then a revaluation should be carried out.

Most importantly, when an item of property, plant and equipment is revalued, **the whole class of assets to which it belongs should be revalued.**

All the items within a class should be **revalued at the same time**, to prevent selective revaluation of certain assets and to avoid disclosing a mixture of costs and values from different dates in the financial statements. A rolling basis of revaluation is allowed if the revaluations are kept up to date and the revaluation of the whole class is completed in a short period of time.

How should any **increase in value** be treated when a revaluation takes place? The debit will be the increase in value in the balance sheet, but what about the credit? IAS 16 requires the increase to be credited to a **revaluation surplus** (ie part of owners' equity), *unless* the increase is reversing a previous decrease which was recognised as an expense. To the extent that this offset is made, the increase is recognised as income; any excess is then taken to the revaluation reserve.

2.8 Example: revaluation reserve

Binkie Co has an item of land carried in its books at $13,000. Two years ago a slump in land values led the company to reduce the carrying value from $15,000. This was taken as an expense in the income statement. There has been a surge in land prices in the current year, however, and the land is now worth $20,000.

Account for the revaluation in the current year.

Solution

The double entry is:

DEBIT	Asset value (balance sheet)	$7,000	
CREDIT	Income statement		$2,000
	Revaluation surplus		$5,000

The case is similar for a **decrease in value** on revaluation. Any decrease should be recognised as an expense, except where it offsets a previous increase taken as a revaluation surplus in owners' equity. Any decrease greater than the previous upwards increase in value must be taken as an expense in the income statement.

2.9 Example: revaluation decrease

Let us simply swap round the example given above. The original cost was $15,000, revalued upwards to $20,000 two years ago. The value has now fallen to $13,000.

Account for the decrease in value.

Solution

The double entry is:

DEBIT	Revaluation surplus	$5,000	
DEBIT	Income statement	$2,000	
CREDIT	Asset value (balance sheet)		$7,000

There is a further complication when a **revalued asset is being depreciated**. As we have seen, an upward revaluation means that the depreciation charge will increase. Normally, a revaluation surplus is only realised when the asset is sold, but when it is being depreciated, part of that surplus is being realised as the asset is used. The amount of the surplus realised is the difference between depreciation charged on the revalued amount and the (lower) depreciation which would have been charged on the asset's original cost. **This amount can be transferred to retained (ie realised) earnings but *not* through the income statement.**

2.10 Example: revaluation and depreciation

Crinckle Co bought an asset for $10,000 at the beginning of 20X6. It had a useful life of five years. On 1 January 20X8 the asset was revalued to $12,000. The expected useful life has remained unchanged (ie three years remain).

Account for the revaluation and state the treatment for depreciation from 20X8 onwards.

Solution

On 1 January 20X8 the carrying value of the asset is $10,000 − (2 × $10,000 ÷ 5) = $6,000. For the revaluation:

DEBIT	Asset value (balance sheet)	$6,000	
CREDIT	Revaluation surplus		$6,000

The depreciation for the next three years will be $12,000 ÷ 3 = $4,000, compared to depreciation on cost of $10,000 ÷ 5 = $2,000. So each year, the extra $2,000 can be treated as part of the surplus which has become realised:

DEBIT	Revaluation surplus	$2,000	
CREDIT	Retained earnings		$2,000

This is a movement on owners' equity only, not an item in the income statement.

2.11 Depreciation

The standard states:

- The **depreciable amount** of an item of property, plant and equipment should be allocated on a systematic basis over its useful life.

- The **depreciation method** used should reflect the pattern in which the asset's economic benefits are consumed by the entity.

- The **depreciation charge** for each period should be recognised as an expense unless it is included in the carrying amount of another asset.

Land and buildings are dealt with separately even when they are acquired together because land normally has an unlimited life and is therefore not depreciated. In contrast buildings do have a limited life and must be depreciated. Any increase in the value of land on which a building is standing will have no impact on the determination of the building's useful life.

Depreciation is usually treated as an **expense**, but not where it is absorbed by the entity in the process of producing other assets. For example, depreciation of plant and machinery can be incurred in the production of goods for sale (inventory items). In such circumstances, the depreciation is included in the cost of the new assets produced.

2.11.1 Review of useful life

A review of the **useful life** of property, plant and equipment should be carried out **at least at each financial year end** and the depreciation charge for the current and future periods should be adjusted if expectations have changed significantly from previous estimates. Changes are changes in accounting estimates and are accounted for prospectively as adjustments to future depreciation.

2.11.2 Review of depreciation method

The **depreciation method** should also be reviewed **at least at each financial year end** and, if there has been a significant change in the expected pattern of economic benefits from those assets, the method should be changed to suit this changed pattern. When such a change in depreciation method takes place the change should be accounted for as a **change in accounting estimate** and the depreciation charge for the current and future periods should be adjusted.

2.11.3 Impairment of asset values

An **impairment loss** should be treated in the same way as a **revaluation decrease** ie the decrease should be **recognised as an expense**. However, a revaluation decrease (or impairment loss) should be charged directly against any related revaluation surplus to the extent that the decrease does not exceed the amount held in the revaluation surplus in respect of that same asset.

A **reversal of an impairment** loss should be treated in the same way as a **revaluation increase**, ie a revaluation increase should be recognised as income to the extent that it reverses a revaluation decrease or an impairment loss of the same asset previously recognised as an expense.

2.12 Retirements and disposals

When an asset is permanently **withdrawn from use, or sold or scrapped**, and no future economic benefits are expected from its disposal, it should be withdrawn from the balance sheet.

Gains or losses are the difference between the estimated net disposal proceeds and the carrying amount of the asset. They should be recognised as income or expense in the income statement.

2.13 Derecognition

An entity is required to **derecognise the carrying amount** of an item of property, plant or equipment that it disposes of on the date the **criteria for the sale of goods** in IAS 18 *Revenue* would be met. This also applies to parts of an asset.

An entity cannot classify as revenue (ie in the top line of the income statement) a gain it realises on the disposal of an item of property, plant and equipment.

2.14 Disclosure

The standard has a long list of disclosure requirements, for each class of property, plant and equipment.

(a) **Measurement bases** for determining the gross carrying amount (if more than one, the gross carrying amount for that basis in each category)

(b) **Depreciation methods** used

 (c) **Useful lives** or depreciation rates used

 (d) **Gross carrying amount** and accumulated depreciation (aggregated with accumulated impairment losses) at the beginning and end of the period

 (e) **Reconciliation** of the carrying amount at the beginning and end of the period showing:

  (i) Additions

  (ii) Disposals

  (iii) Acquisitions through business combinations (see Chapter 15)

  (iv) Increases/decreases during the period from revaluations and from impairment losses

  (v) Impairment losses recognised in the income statement

  (vi) Impairment losses reversed in the income statement

  (vii) Depreciation

  (viii) Net exchange differences (from translation of statements of foreign entity)

  (ix) Any other movements.

The financial statements should also disclose the following.

 (a) Any recoverable amounts of property, plant and equipment

 (b) Existence and amounts of **restrictions on title**, and items pledged as security for liabilities

 (c) Accounting policy for **the estimated costs of restoring the site**

 (d) Amount of expenditures on account of **items in the course of construction**

 (e) Amount of commitments to **acquisitions**

Revalued assets require further disclosures.

 (a) Basis used to revalue the assets

 (b) Effective date of the revaluation

 (c) Whether an independent valuer was involved

 (d) Nature of any indices used to determine replacement cost

 (e) Carrying amount of each class of property, plant and equipment that would have been included in the financial statements had the assets been carried at cost less accumulated depreciation and accumulated impairment losses.

 (f) Revaluation surplus, indicating the movement for the period and any restrictions on the distribution of the balance to shareholders.

The standard also **encourages disclosure** of additional information, which the users of financial statements may find useful.

 (a) The carrying amount of temporarily idle property, plant and equipment

 (b) The gross carrying amount of any fully depreciated property, plant and equipment that is still in use

 (c) The carrying amount of property, plant and equipment retired from active use and held for disposal

 (d) The fair value of property, plant and equipment when this is materially different from the carrying amount

The following format (with notional figures) is commonly used to disclose non-current assets movements.

	Total $	Land and buildings $	Plant and equipment $
Cost or valuation			
At 1 January 20X4	50,000	40,000	10,000
Revaluation surplus	12,000	12,000	–
Additions in year	4,000	–	4,000
Disposals in year	(1,000)	–	(1,000)
At 31 December 20X4	65,000	52,000	13,000
Depreciation			
At 1 January 20X4	16,000	10,000	6,000
Charge for year	4,000	1,000	3,000
Eliminated on disposals	(500)	–	(500)
At 31 December 20X4	19,500	11,000	8,500
Net book value			
At 31 December 20X4	45,500	41,000	4,500
At 1 January 20X4	34,000	30,000	4,000

Question
Balance sheet items

(a) In a balance sheet prepared in accordance with IAS 16, what does the net book value (carrying value) represent?

(b) In a set of financial statements prepared in accordance with IAS 16, is it correct to say that the net book value (carrying value) figure in a balance sheet cannot be greater than the market (net realisable) value of the partially used asset as at the balance sheet date? Explain your reasons for your answer.

Answer

(a) In simple terms the net book value of an asset is the cost of an asset less the 'accumulated depreciation', that is all depreciation charged so far. It should be emphasised that the main purpose of charging depreciation is to ensure that profits are fairly reported. Thus depreciation is concerned with the income statement rather than the balance sheet. In consequence the net book value figure in the balance sheet can be quite arbitrary. In particular, it does not necessarily bear any relation to the market value of an asset and is of little use for planning and decision making.

An obvious example of the disparity between net book value and market value is found in the case of buildings, which may be worth more than ten times as much as their net book value.

(b) Net book value can in some circumstances be higher than market value (net realisable value). IAS 16 *Property, plant and equipment* states that the value of an asset cannot be greater than its 'recoverable amount'. However 'recoverable amount' as defined in IAS 16 is the amount recoverable from further use. This may be higher than the market value.

This makes sense if you think of a specialised machine which could not fetch much on the secondhand market but which will produce goods which can be sold at a profit for many years.

Exam focus point

Property and/or other non-current assets are likely to be tested as they have come up on a number of papers.

3 IAS 20 Government grants

It is common for entities to receive government grants for various purposes (grants may be called subsidies, premiums, etc). They may also receive other types of assistance which may be in many forms. The treatment of government grants is covered by IAS 20 *Accounting for government grants and disclosure of government assistance.*

3.1 Scope

IAS 20 does *not* cover the following situations.

- Accounting for government grants in financial statements reflecting the effects of **changing prices**

- Government assistance given in the form of **'tax breaks'**

- Government acting as **part-owner** of the entity

3.2 Definitions

These definitions are given by the standard.

Key terms

- **Government.** Government, government agencies and similar bodies whether local, national or international.

- **Government assistance.** Action by government designed to provide an economic benefit specific to an entity or range of entities qualifying under certain criteria.

- **Government grants.** Assistance by government in the form of transfers of resources to an entity in return for past or future compliance with certain conditions relating to the operating activities of the entity. They exclude those forms of government assistance which cannot reasonably have a value placed upon them and transactions with government which cannot be distinguished from the normal trading transactions of the entity.

- **Grants related to assets.** Government grants whose primary condition is that an entity qualifying for them should purchase, construct or otherwise acquire non-current assets. Subsidiary conditions may also be attached restricting the type or location of the assets or the periods during which they are to be acquired or held.

- **Grants related to income.** Government grants other than those related to assets.

- **Forgivable loans.** Loans which the lender undertakes to waive repayment of under certain prescribed conditions.

- **Fair value.** The amount for which an asset could be exchanged, or a liability settled, between knowledgeable, willing parties in an arm's length transaction.

You can see that there are many **different forms** of government assistance: both the type of assistance and the conditions attached to it will vary. Government assistance may have encouraged an entity to undertake something it otherwise would not have done.

How will the receipt of government assistance affect the financial statements?

(a)   An appropriate method must be found to account for any **resources transferred.**

(b)   The extent to which an entity has **benefited** from such assistance during the reporting period should be shown.

3.3 Government grants

An entity should not recognise government grants (including non-monetary grants at fair value) until it has **reasonable assurance** that:

- The entity will comply with any **conditions** attached to the grant
- The entity will **actually receive** the grant

Even if the grant has been received, this does not prove that the conditions attached to it have been or will be fulfilled.

It makes no difference in the treatment of the grant whether it is received in cash or given as a reduction in a liability to government, ie the **manner of receipt is irrelevant**.

Any related **contingency** should be recognised under IAS 37 *Provisions, contingent liabilities and contingent assets*, once the grant has been recognised.

In the case of a **forgivable loan** (as defined in key terms above) from government, it should be treated in the same way as a government grant when it is reasonably assured that the entity will meet the relevant terms for forgiveness.

3.3.1 Accounting treatment of government grants

There are two methods which could be used to account for government grants, and the arguments for each are given in IAS 20.

(a) **Capital approach**: credit the grant directly to shareholders' interests.
(b) **Income approach**: the grant is credited to the income statement over one or more periods.

Question   **Capital approach or income approach**

Can you think of the different arguments used in support of each method?

Answer

The standard gives the following arguments in support of each method.

Capital approach

(a) The grants are a **financing device**, so should go through the balance sheet. In the income statement they would simply offset the expenses which they are financing. No repayment is expected by the Government, so the grants should be credited directly to shareholders' interests.

(b) Grants are **not earned**, they are incentives without related costs, so it would be wrong to take them to the income statement.

Income approach

(a) The grants are **not received from shareholders** so should not be credited directly to shareholders' interests.

(b) Grants are **not given or received for nothing**. They are earned by compliance with conditions and by meeting obligations. There are therefore associated costs with which the grant can be matched in the income statement as these costs are being compensated by the grant.

(c) Grants are an extension of **fiscal policies** and so as income taxes and other taxes are charged against income, so grants should be credited to income.

IAS 20 requires grants to be recognised under the **income approach**, ie grants are recognised as income over the relevant periods to match them with related costs which they have been received to compensate. This should be done on a systematic basis. **Grants should not, therefore, be credited directly to shareholders' interests.**

It would be against the accruals assumption to credit grants to income on a receipts basis, so a **systematic basis of matching** must be used. A receipts basis would only be acceptable if no other basis was available.

It will usually be easy to identify the **costs related to a government grant**, and thereby the period(s) in which the grant should be recognised as income, ie when the costs are incurred. Where grants are received in relation to a depreciating asset, the grant will be recognised over the periods in which the asset is depreciated *and* in the same proportions.

Question	Recognition

Arturo Co receives a government grant representing 50% of the cost of a depreciating asset which costs $40,000. How will the grant be recognised if Arturo Co depreciates the asset:

(a)   over four years straight line; or

(b)   at 40% reducing balance?

The residual value is nil. The useful life is four years.

Answer

The grant should be recognised in the same proportion as the depreciation.

(a)   *Straight line*

		Depreciation $	Grant income $
Year	1	10,000	5,000
	2	10,000	5,000
	3	10,000	5,000
	4	10,000	5,000

(b)   *Reducing balance*

		Depreciation $	Grant income $
Year	1	16,000	8,000
	2	9,600	4,800
	3	5,760	2,880
	4 (remainder)	8,640	4,320

In the case of **grants for non-depreciable assets**, certain obligations may need to be fulfilled, in which case the grant should be recognised as income over the periods in which the cost of meeting the obligation is incurred. For example, if a piece of land is granted on condition that a building is erected on it, then the grant should be recognised as income over the building's life.

There may be a **series of conditions** attached to a grant, in the nature of a package of financial aid. An entity must take care to identify precisely those conditions which give rise to costs which in turn determine the periods over which the grant will be earned. When appropriate, the grant may be split and the parts allocated on different bases.

An entity may receive a grant as compensation for expenses or losses which it has **already incurred**. Alternatively, a grant may be given to an entity simply to provide immediate financial support where no future related costs are expected. In cases such as these, the grant received should be recognised as income of the period in which it becomes receivable.

3.3.2 Non-monetary government grants

A non-monetary asset may be transferred by government to an entity as a grant, for example a piece of land, or other resources. The **fair value** of such an asset is usually assessed and this is used to account for both the asset and the grant. Alternatively, both may be valued at a nominal amount.

3.3.3 Presentation of grants related to assets

There are two choices here for how government grants related to assets (including non-monetary grants at fair value) should be shown in the balance sheet.

(a) Set up the grant as **deferred income.**

(b) **Deduct the grant** in arriving at the **carrying amount** of the asset.

These are considered to be acceptable alternatives and we can look at an example showing both.

Example: accounting for grants related to assets

A company receives a 20% grant towards the cost of a new item of machinery, which cost $100,000. The machinery has an expected life of four years and a nil residual value. The expected profits of the company, before accounting for depreciation on the new machine or the grant, amount to $50,000 per annum in each year of the machinery's life.

Solution

The results of the company for the four years of the machine's life would be as follows.

(a) *Reducing the cost of the asset*

	Year 1 $	Year 2 $	Year 3 $	Year 4 $	Total $
Profits					
Profit before depreciation	50,000	50,000	50,000	50,000	200,000
Depreciation*	20,000	20,000	20,000	20,000	80,000
Profit	30,000	30,000	30,000	30,000	120,000

*The depreciation charge on a straight line basis, for each year, is ¼ of $(100,000 – 20,000) = $20,000.

Balance sheet at year end (extract)

	$	$	$	$
Non-current asset at cost	80,000	80,000	80,000	80,000
Depreciation	20,000	40,000	60,000	80,000
Net book value	60,000	40,000	20,000	–

(b) *Treating the grant as deferred income*

	Year 1 $	Year 2 $	Year 3 $	Year 4 $	Total $
Profits					
Profit before grant & dep'n	50,000	50,000	50,000	50,000	200,000
Depreciation	(25,000)	(25,000)	(25,000)	(25,000)	(100,000)
Grant	5,000	5,000	5,000	5,000	20,000
Profit	30,000	30,000	30,000	30,000	120,000

Balance sheet at year end (extract)

Non-current asset at cost	100,000	100,000	100,000	100,000
Depreciation	(25,000)	(50,000)	(75,000)	(100,000)
Net book value	75,000	50,000	25,000	–
Deferred income				
Government grant				
deferred income	15,000	10,000	5,000	–

Whichever of these methods is used, the **cash flows** in relation to the purchase of the asset and the receipt of the grant are often disclosed separately because of the significance of the movements in cash flow.

3.3.4 Presentation of grants related to income

These grants are a credit in the income statement, but there is a choice in the method of disclosure.

(a)   Present as a **separate credit** or under a general heading, eg 'other income'

(b)   **Deduct from the related expense**

Some would argue that offsetting income and expenses in the income statement is not good practice. Others would say that the expenses would not have been incurred had the grant not been available, so offsetting the two is acceptable. Although both methods are acceptable, disclosure of the grant may be necessary for a **proper understanding** of the financial statements, particularly the effect on any item of income or expense which is required to be separately disclosed.

3.3.5 Repayment of government grants

If a grant must be repaid it should be accounted for as a **revision of an accounting estimate** (see IAS 8).

(a)   **Repayment of a grant related to income:** apply first against any unamortised deferred income set up in respect of the grant; any excess should be recognised immediately as an expense.

(b)   **Repayment of a grant related to an asset**: increase the carrying amount of the asset or reduce the deferred income balance by the amount repayable. The cumulative additional depreciation that would have been recognised to date in the absence of the grant should be immediately recognised as an expense.

It is possible that the circumstances surrounding repayment may require a review of the **asset value** and an impairment of the new carrying amount of the asset.

3.4 Government assistance

Some forms of government assistance are excluded from the definition of government grants.

(a)   Some forms of government assistance **cannot reasonably have a value placed on them**, eg free technical or marketing advice, provision of guarantees.

(b)   There are transactions with government which **cannot be distinguished from the entity's normal trading transactions**, eg government procurement policy resulting in a portion of the entity's sales. Any segregation would be arbitrary.

Disclosure of such assistance may be necessary because of its significance; its nature, extent and duration should be disclosed. Loans at low or zero interest rates are a form of government assistance, but the imputation of interest does not fully quantify the benefit received.

3.5 Disclosure

Disclosure is required of the following.

- **Accounting policy** adopted, including method of presentation
- **Nature and extent** of government grants recognised and other forms of assistance received
- **Unfulfilled conditions and other contingencies** attached to recognised government assistance

3.6 SIC 10 *Government assistance – no specific relation to operating activities*

In some countries government assistance to entities may be aimed at encouragement or long-term support of business activities either in certain regions or industry sectors. Conditions to receive such assistance may not be specifically related to the operating activities of the entity. Examples of such assistance are transfers of resources by governments to entities which:

(a) Operate in a particular industry
(b) Continue operating in recently privatised industries
(c) Start or continue to run their business in underdeveloped areas

The issue is whether such government assistance is a 'government grant' within the scope of IAS 20 and, therefore, should be accounted for in accordance with this Standard.

Government assistance to entities meets the definition of government grants in IAS 20, even if there are no conditions specifically relating to the operating activities of the entity other than the requirement to operate in certain regions or industry sectors. Such grants should therefore not be credited directly to equity.

4 IAS 40 Investment property

FAST FORWARD

> An entity may own land or a building **as an investment** rather than for use in the business. It may therefore generate cash flows largely independently of other assets which the entity holds.

4.1 Definitions

Consider the following definitions.

Key terms

> **Investment property** is property (land or a building – or part of a building – or both) held (by the owner or by the lessee under a finance lease) to earn rentals or for capital appreciation or both, rather than for:
>
> (a) Use in the production or supply of goods or services or for administrative purposes, or
> (b) Sale in the ordinary course of business
>
> **Owner-occupied property** is property held by the owner (or by the lessee under a finance lease) for use in the production or supply of goods or services or for administrative purposes.
>
> **Fair value** is the amount for which an asset could be exchanged between knowledgeable, willing parties in an arm's length transaction.
>
> **Cost** is the amount of cash or cash equivalents paid or the fair value of other consideration given to acquire an asset at the time of its acquisition or construction.
>
> **Carrying amount** is the amount at which an asset is recognised in the balance sheet.

Key terms

> A property interest that is held by a lessee under an **operating lease** may be classified and accounted for as an **investment property**, if and only if the property would otherwise meet the definition of an investment property and the lessee uses the IAS 40 **fair value model**. This classification is available on a property-by-property basis.

Examples of investment property include:

(a)   **Land held for long-term capital appreciation** rather than for short-term sale in the ordinary course of business

(b)   A **building** owned by the reporting entity (or held by the entity under a finance lease) and **leased out under an operating lease**

Question   Investment

Rich Co owns a piece of land. The directors have not yet decided whether to build a factory on it for use in its business or to keep it and sell it when its value has risen.

Would this be classified as an investment property under IAS 40?

Answer

Yes. If an entity has not determined that it will use the land either as an owner-occupied property or for short-term sale in the ordinary course of business, the land is considered to be held for capital appreciation.

4.2 IAS 40

IAS 40 *Investment property* was published in March 2000 and has recently been revised. Its objective is to prescribe the accounting treatment for investment property and related disclosure requirements.

The standard includes investment property held under a finance lease or leased out under an operating lease. However, the current IAS 40 does not deal with matters covered in IAS 17 *Leases*.

You now know what **is** an investment property under IAS 40. Below are examples of items that are **not investment property.**

Type of non-investment property	Applicable IAS
Property intended for sale in the ordinary course of business	IAS 2 *Inventories*
Property being constructed or developed on behalf of third parties	IAS 11 *Construction contracts*
Owner-occupied property	IAS 16 *Property, plant and equipment*
Property being constructed or developed for future use as investment property	IAS 16 until construction or development is complete, then treat as investment property

4.3 Recognition

Investment property should be recognised as an asset when **two conditions** are met.

(a)   It is **probable** that the **future economic benefits** that are associated with the investment property will **flow to the entity**.

(b)   The **cost** of the investment property can be **measured reliably**.

4.4 Initial measurement

An investment property should be measured initially at its **cost,** including transaction costs.

A property interest held under a lease and classified as an investment property shall be accounted for **as if it were a finance lease**. The asset is recognised at the lower of the fair value of the property and the present value of the minimum lease payments. An equivalent amount is recognised as a liability.

4.5 Measurement subsequent to initial recognition

IAS 40 requires an entity to **choose between two models.**

*   **The fair value model**
*   **The cost model**

Whatever policy it chooses should be applied to **all of its investment property**.

Where an entity chooses to classify a property held under an **operating lease** as an investment property, there is **no choice**. The **fair value model must be used** for **all the entity's investment property**, regardless of whether it is owned or leased.

4.5.1 Fair value model

Key terms

(a)   After initial recognition, an entity that chooses the **fair value model** should measure all of its investment property at fair value, except in the extremely rare cases where this cannot be measured reliably. In such cases it should apply the IAS 16 cost model.

(b)   A gain or loss arising from a change in the fair value of an investment property should be recognised in net profit or loss for the period in which it arises.

(c)   The fair value of investment property should reflect market conditions at the balance sheet date.

This was the first time that the IASB has allowed a fair value model for non-financial assets. This is not the same as a revaluation, where increases in carrying amount above a cost-based measure are recognised as revaluation surplus. Under the fair-value model all changes in fair value are recognised in the income statement.

The standard elaborates on **issues relating to fair value.**

(a)   Fair value assumes that an arm's length transaction has taken place between '**knowledgeable, willing parties'**, ie both buyer and seller are reasonably informed about the nature and characteristics of the investment property.

(b)   A willing buyer is **motivated but not compelled** to buy. A willing seller is neither an over-eager nor a forced seller, nor one prepared to sell at any price or to hold out for a price not considered reasonable in the current market.

(c)   **Fair value is not the same as 'value in use'** as defined in IAS 36 *Impairment of assets*. Value in use reflects factors and knowledge specific to the entity, while fair value reflects factors and knowledge relevant to the market.

(d)   In determining fair value an entity **should not double count assets**. For example, elevators or air conditioning are often an integral part of a building and should be included in the investment property, rather than recognised separately.

(e)   In those rare cases where the **entity cannot determine the fair value of an investment property reliably**, the cost model in **IAS 16** must be applied until the investment property is disposed of. The **residual value must be assumed to be zero**.

4.5.2 Cost model

The cost model is the **cost model in IAS 16.** Investment property should be measured at **depreciated cost, less any accumulated impairment losses.** An entity that chooses the cost model should **disclose the fair value of its investment property.**

4.5.3 Changing models

Once the entity has chosen the fair value or cost model, it should apply it to all its investment property. It **should not change from one model to the other unless the change will result in a more appropriate presentation.** IAS 40 states that it is highly unlikely that a change from the fair value model to the cost model will result in a more appropriate presentation.

4.6 Transfers

Transfers to or from investment property should **only** be made **when there is a change in use**. For example, owner occupation commences so the investment property will be treated under IAS 16 as an owner-occupied property.

When there is a transfer from investment property carried at fair value to owner-occupied property or inventories, the property's cost for subsequent accounting under IAS 16 or IAS 2 should be its fair value at the date of change of use.

Conversely, an owner-occupied property may become an investment property and need to be carried at fair value. An entity should apply IAS 16 up to the date of change of use. It should treat any difference at that date between the carrying amount of the property under IAS 16 and its fair value as a revaluation under IAS 16.

4.7 Disposals

Derecognise (eliminate from the balance sheet) an investment property on disposal or when it is permanently withdrawn from use and no future economic benefits are expected from its disposal.

Any **gain or loss** on disposal is the difference between the net disposal proceeds and the carrying amount of the asset. It should generally be **recognised as income or expense in the income statement.**

Compensation from third parties for investment property that was impaired, lost or given up shall be recognised in profit or loss when the compensation becomes receivable.

4.8 Disclosure requirements

These relate to:

- Choice of fair value model or cost model
- Whether property interests held as operating leases are included in investment property
- Criteria for classification as investment property
- Assumptions in determining fair value
- Use of independent professional valuer (encouraged but not required)
- Rental income and expenses
- Any restrictions or obligations

4.8.1 Fair value model – additional disclosures

An entity that adopts this must also disclose a **reconciliation** of the carrying amount of the investment property at the beginning and end of the period.

4.8.2 Cost model – additional disclosures

These relate mainly to the depreciation method. In addition, an entity which adopts the cost model **must disclose the fair value** of the investment property.

4.9 Decision tree

The decision tree below summarises which IAS apply to various kinds of property.

Exam focus point

> Learn this decision tree – it will help you tackle most of the problems you are likely to meet in the exam!

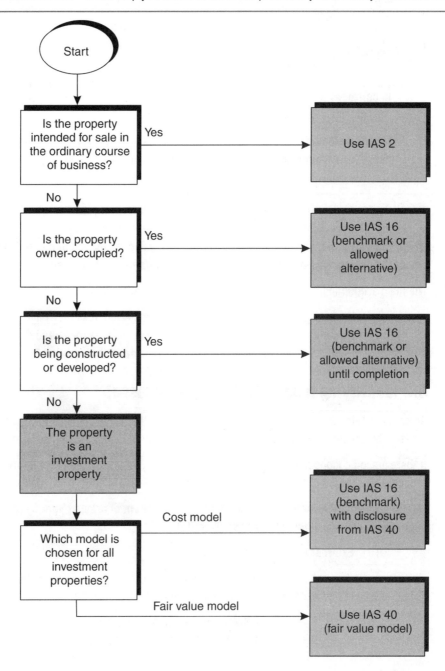

5 IAS 36 Impairment of assets

Impairment is determined by comparing the carrying amount of the asset with its recoverable value.

There is an established principle that assets should not be carried at above their recoverable amount. An entity should write down the carrying value of an asset to its recoverable amount if the carrying value of an asset is not recoverable in full. IAS 36 was published in June 1998 and has recently been revised. It puts in place a detailed methodology for carrying out impairment reviews and related accounting treatments and disclosures.

5.1 Scope

IAS 36 applies to all tangible, intangible and financial assets except inventories, assets arising from construction contracts, deferred tax assets, assets arising under IAS 19 *Employee benefits* and financial assets within the scope of IAS 32 *Financial instruments: disclosure and presentation*. This is because those IASs already have rules for recognising and measuring impairment. Note also that IAS 36 does not apply to non-current assets held for sale, which are dealt with under IFRS 5 *Non-current assets held for sale and discontinued operations*.

Key terms

> - **Impairment**: a fall in the value of an asset, so that its 'recoverable amount' is now less than its carrying value in the balance sheet.
>
> - **Carrying amount**: is the net value at which the asset is included in the balance sheet (ie after deducting accumulated depreciation and any impairment losses).
>
> *(IAS 36)*

The basic principle underlying IAS 36 is relatively straightforward. If an asset's value in the accounts is higher than its realistic value, measured as its 'recoverable amount', the asset is judged to have suffered an impairment loss. It should therefore be reduced in value, by the amount of the **impairment loss**. The amount of the impairment loss should be **written off against profit** immediately.

The main accounting issues to consider are therefore as follows.

(a)   How is it possible to **identify when** an impairment loss may have occurred?

(b)   How should the **recoverable amount** of the asset be measured?

(c)   How should an 'impairment loss' be **reported in the accounts**?

5.2 Identifying a potentially impaired asset

An entity should assess at each balance sheet date whether there are any indications of impairment to any assets. The concept of **materiality** applies, and only material impairment needs to be identified.

If there are indications of possible impairment, the entity is required to make a formal estimate of the **recoverable amount** of the assets concerned.

IAS 36 suggests how **indications of a possible impairment** of assets might be recognised. The suggestions are based largely on common sense.

(a)   **External sources of information**

(i)   A fall in the asset's market value that is more significant than would normally be expected from passage of time over normal use.

(ii)   A significant change in the technological, market, legal or economic environment of the business in which the assets are employed.

(iii)   An increase in market interest rates or market rates of return on investments likely to affect the discount rate used in calculating value in use.

(iv)   The carrying amount of the entity's net assets being more than its market capitalisation.

(b)   **Internal sources of information**: evidence of obsolescence or physical damage, adverse changes in the use to which the asset is put, or the asset's economic performance

Even if there are no indications of impairment, the following assets must **always** be tested for impairment annually.

(a)   An intangible asset with an **indefinite useful life**

(b)   **Goodwill** acquired in a business combination

5.3 Measuring the recoverable amount of the asset

What is an asset's recoverable amount?

Key term

> The **recoverable amount of an asset** should be measured as the *higher value* of:
>
> (a)   the asset's fair value less costs to sell; and
>
> (b)   its value in use.   *(IAS 36)*

An asset's fair value less costs to sell is the amount net of selling costs that could be obtained from the sale of the asset. Selling costs include sales transaction costs, such as legal expenses.

(a)   If there is **an active market** in the asset, the net selling price should be based on the **market value**, or on the price of recent transactions in similar assets.

(b)   If there is **no active market** in the assets it might be possible to **estimate** a net selling price using best estimates of what 'knowledgeable, willing parties' might pay in an arm's length transaction.

Net selling price **cannot** be reduced, however, by including within selling costs any **restructuring or reorganisation expenses**, or any costs that have already been recognised in the accounts as liabilities.

The concept of 'value in use' is very important.

Key term

> The **value in use** of an asset is measured as the present value of estimated future cash flows (inflows minus outflows) generated by the asset, including its estimated net disposal value (if any) at the end of its expected useful life.

The cash flows used in the calculation should be **pre-tax cash flows** and a **pre-tax discount rate** should be applied to calculate the present value.

The calculation of **value in use** must reflect the following.

(a)   An estimate of the **future cash flows** the entity expects to derive from the asset

(b)   Expectations about **possible variations** in the amount and timing of future cash flows

(c)   The **time value of money**

(d)   The price for bearing the **uncertainty** inherent in the asset, and

(e)   **Other factors** that would be reflected in pricing future cash flows from the asset

Calculating a value in use therefore calls for estimates of future cash flows, and the possibility exists that an entity might come up with **over-optimistic estimates** of cash flows. The IAS therefore states the following.

(a)   Cash flow projections should be based on **'reasonable and supportable'** assumptions.

(b)   Projections of cash flows, normally up to a maximum period of five years, should be based on the most **recent budgets or financial forecasts**.

(c)   Cash flow projections beyond this period should be obtained by extrapolating short-term projections, using either a **steady or declining growth rate** for each subsequent year (unless a rising growth rate can be justified). The long term growth rate applied should not exceed the average long term growth rate for the product, market, industry or country, unless a higher growth rate can be justified.

5.4 Composition of estimates of future cash flows

These should include the following.

(a)   Projections of **cash inflows** from **continuing use** of the asset

(b)   Projections of **cash outflows** necessarily incurred to **generate the cash inflows** from continuing use of the asset

(c)   **Net cash flows** received/paid on **disposal** of the asset at the end of its useful life

There is an underlying principle that future cash flows should be estimated for the asset in its current condition. Future cash flows relating to restructurings to which the entity is not yet committed, or to future costs to add to, replace part of, or service the asset are excluded.

Estimates of future cash flows should **exclude** the following.

(a)   Cash inflows/ outflows from financing activities
(b)   Income tax receipts/payments

The amount of net cash inflow/outflow on **disposal** of an asset should assume an arm's length transaction.

Foreign currency future cash flows should be forecast in the currency in which they will arise and will be discounted using a rate appropriate for that currency. The resulting figure should then be translated into the reporting currency at the spot rate at the balance sheet date.

The **discount rate** should be a current pre-tax rate (or rates) that reflects the current assessment of the time value of money and the risks specific to the asset. The discount rate should not include a risk weighting if the underlying cash flows have already been adjusted for risk.

5.5 Recognition and measurement of an impairment loss

The rule for assets at historical cost is:

Rule to learn

If the recoverable amount of an asset is lower than the carrying amount, the carrying amount should be reduced by the difference (ie the impairment loss) which should be charged as an expense in the income statement.

The rule for assets held at a revalued amount (such as property revalued under IAS 16) is:

Rule to learn

The impairment loss is to be treated as a revaluation decrease under the relevant IAS.

In practice this means:

- To the extent that there is a revaluation surplus held in respect of the asset, the impairment loss should be charged to revaluation surplus.

- Any excess should be charged to the income statement.

The IAS goes into quite a large amount of detail about the important concept of cash generating units. As a basic rule, the recoverable amount of an asset should be calculated for the **asset individually**. However, there will be occasions when it is not possible to estimate such a value for an individual asset, particularly in the calculation of value in use. This is because cash inflows and outflows cannot be attributed to the individual asset.

If it is not possible to calculate the recoverable amount for an individual asset, the recoverable amount of the asset's cash generating unit should be measured instead.

Key term

> **A cash generating unit** is the smallest identifiable group of assets for which independent cash flows can be identified and measured.

Question	Cash generating unit I

Can you think of some examples of how a cash generating unit would be identified?

Answer

Here are two possibilities.

(a) A mining company owns a private railway that it uses to transport output from one of its mines. The railway now has no market value other than as scrap, and it is impossible to identify any separate cash inflows with the use of the railway itself. Consequently, if the mining company suspects an impairment in the value of the railway, it should treat the mine as a whole as a cash generating unit, and measure the recoverable amount of the mine as a whole.

(b) A bus company has an arrangement with a town's authorities to run a bus service on four routes in the town. Separately identifiable assets are allocated to each of the bus routes, and cash inflows and outflows can be attributed to each individual route. Three routes are running at a profit and one is running at a loss. The bus company suspects that there is an impairment of assets on the loss-making route. However, the company will be unable to close the loss-making route, because it is under an obligation to operate all four routes, as part of its contract with the local authority. Consequently, the company should treat all four bus routes together as a cash generating unit, and calculate the recoverable amount for the unit as a whole.

Question	Cash generating unit II

Minimart belongs to a retail store chain Maximart. Minimart makes all its retail purchases through Maximart's purchasing centre. Pricing, marketing, advertising and human resources policies (except for hiring Minimart's cashiers and salesmen) are decided by Maximart. Maximart also owns 5 other stores in the same city as Minimart (although in different neighbourhoods) and 20 other stores in other cities. All stores are managed in the same way as Minimart. Minimart and 4 other stores were purchased 5 years ago and goodwill was recognised.

What is the cash-generating unit for Minimart?

Answer

In identifying Minimart's cash-generating unit, an entity considers whether, for example:

(a)   Internal management reporting is organised to measure performance on a store-by-store basis.

(b)   The business is run on a store-by-store profit basis or on a region/city basis.

All Maximart's stores are in different neighbourhoods and probably have different customer bases. So, although Minimart is managed at a corporate level, Minimart generates cash inflows that are largely independent from those of Maximart's other stores. Therefore, it is likely that Minimart is a cash-generating unit.

Question

Cash generating unit III

Mighty Mag Publishing Co owns 150 magazine titles of which 70 were purchased and 80 were self-created. The price paid for a purchased magazine title is recognised as an intangible asset. The costs of creating magazine titles and maintaining the existing titles are recognised as an expense when incurred. Cash inflows from direct sales and advertising are identifiable for each magazine title. Titles are managed by customer segments. The level of advertising income for a magazine title depends on the range of titles in the customer segment to which the magazine title relates. Management has a policy to abandon old titles before the end of their economic lives and replace them immediately with new titles for the same customer segment.

What is the cash-generating unit for an individual magazine title?

Answer

It is likely that the recoverable amount of an individual magazine title can be assessed. Even though the level of advertising income for a title is influenced, to a certain extent, by the other titles in the customer segment, cash inflows from direct sales and advertising are identifiable for each title. In addition, although titles are managed by customer segments, decisions to abandon titles are made on an individual title basis.

Therefore, it is likely that individual magazine titles generate cash inflows that are largely independent one from another and that each magazine title is a separate cash-generating unit.

If an active market exists for the output produced by the asset or a group of assets, this asset or group should be identified as a cash generating unit, even if some or all of the output is used internally.

Cash generating units should be identified consistently from period to period for the same type of asset unless a change is justified.

The group of net assets less liabilities that are considered for impairment should be the same as those considered in the calculation of the recoverable amount. (For the treatment of goodwill and corporate assets see below.)

5.6 Example: Recoverable amount and carrying amount

Fourways Co is made up of four cash generating units. All four units are being tested for impairment.

(a)   Property, plant and equipment and separate intangibles would be allocated to be cash generating units as far as possible.

(b)   Current assets such as inventories, receivables and prepayments would be allocated to the relevant cash generating units.

(c)   Liabilities (eg payables) would be deducted from the net assets of the relevant cash generating units.

(d)   The net figure for each cash generating unit resulting from this exercise would be compared to the relevant recoverable amount, computed on the same basis.

5.7 Goodwill and the impairment of assets

5.7.1 Allocating goodwill to cash-generating units

Goodwill acquired in a business combination does not generate cash flows independently of other assets. It must be **allocated** to each of the acquirer's **cash-generating units** (or groups of cash-generating units) that are expected to benefit from the synergies of the combination. Each unit to which the goodwill is so allocated should:

(a)   Represent the **lowest level** within the entity at which the goodwill is monitored for internal management purposes

(b)   Not be **larger than a reporting segment** determined in accordance with IAS 14 *Segment reporting*

It may be impractical to complete the allocation of goodwill before the first reporting date after a business combination, particularly if the acquirer is accounting for the combination for the first time using provisional values (see Chapter 6). The initial allocation of goodwill must be completed before the end of the first reporting period after the acquisition date.

5.7.2 Testing cash-generating units with goodwill for impairment

There are two situations to consider.

(a)   Where goodwill has been allocated to a cash-generating unit

(b)   Where it has not been possible to allocate goodwill to a specific cash-generating unit, but only to a group of units

A cash-generating unit to which goodwill has been allocated is tested for impairment annually. The **carrying amount** of the unit, including goodwill, is **compared with the recoverable amount**. If the carrying amount of the unit exceeds the recoverable amount, the entity must recognise an impairment loss.

Where goodwill relates to a cash-generating unit but has not been allocated to that unit, the unit is tested for impairment by **comparing its carrying amount** (excluding goodwill) **with its recoverable amount**. The entity must recognise an impairment loss if the carrying amount exceeds the recoverable amount.

The annual impairment test may be performed at any time during an accounting period, but must be performed at the **same time every year**.

5.8 Corporate assets

Corporate assets are group or divisional assets such as a head office building, computer equipment or a research centre. Essentially, corporate assets are assets that do not generate cash inflows independently from other assets, hence their carrying amount cannot be fully attributed to a cash-generating unit under review.

In testing a cash generating unit for impairment, an entity should identify all the corporate assets that relate to the cash-generating unit.

(a) If a portion of the carrying amount of a corporate asset **can be allocated** to the unit on a reasonable and consistent basis, the entity compares the carrying amount of the unit (including the portion of the asset) with its recoverable amount.

(b) If a portion of the carrying amount of a corporate asset **cannot be allocated** to the unit on a reasonable and consistent basis, the entity:

(i) Compares the carrying amount of the unit (excluding the asset) with its recoverable amount and recognises any impairment loss

(ii) Identifies the smallest group of cash-generating units that includes the cash-generating unit to which the asset belongs and to which a portion of the carrying amount of the asset can be allocated on a reasonable and consistent basis

(iii) Compares the carrying amount of that group of cash-generating units (including the portion of the asset allocated to the group of units) with the recoverable amount of the group of units and recognises any impairment loss

5.9 Accounting treatment of an impairment loss

If, and only if, the recoverable amount of an asset is less than its carrying amount in the balance sheet, an impairment loss has occurred. This loss should be **recognised immediately**.

(a) The asset's **carrying amount** should be reduced to its recoverable amount in the balance sheet.

(b) The **impairment loss** should be recognised immediately in the income statement (unless the asset has been revalued in which case the loss is treated as a revaluation decrease; see Paragraph 5.5).

After reducing an asset to its recoverable amount, the **depreciation charge** on the asset should then be based on its new carrying amount, its estimated residual value (if any) and its estimated remaining useful life.

An impairment loss should be recognised for a **cash generating unit** if (and only if) the recoverable amount for the cash generating unit is less than the carrying amount in the balance sheet for all the assets in the unit. When an impairment loss is recognised for a cash generating unit, the loss should be allocated between the assets in the unit in the following order.

(a) First, to any assets that are obviously damaged or destroyed
(b) Next, to the **goodwill** allocated to the cash generating unit
(c) Then to all other assets in the cash-generating unit, on a **pro rata basis**

In allocating an impairment loss, the carrying amount of an asset should not be reduced below the highest of:

(a) Its fair value less costs to sell
(b) Its value in use (if determinable)
(c) Zero

Any remaining amount of an impairment loss should be recognised as a liability if required by other IASs.

5.10 Example 1: impairment loss

A company that extracts natural gas and oil has a drilling platform in the Caspian Sea. It is required by legislation of the country concerned to remove and dismantle the platform at the end of its useful life. Accordingly, the company has included an amount in its accounts for removal and dismantling costs, and is depreciating this amount over the platform's expected life.

The company is carrying out an exercise to establish whether there has been an impairment of the platform.

(a)   Its carrying amount in the balance sheet is $3m.

(b)   The company has received an offer of $2.8m for the platform from another oil company. The bidder would take over the responsibility (and costs) for dismantling and removing the platform at the end of its life.

(c)   The present value of the estimated cash flows from the platform's continued use is $3.3m.

(d)   The carrying amount in the balance sheet for the provision for dismantling and removal is currently $0.6m.

What should be the value of the drilling platform in the balance sheet, and what, if anything, is the impairment loss?

Solution

Fair value less costs to sell	=	$2.8m
Value in use	=	PV of cash flows from use less the carrying amount of the provision/liability = $3.3m – $0.6m = $2.7m
Recoverable amount	=	Higher of these two amounts, ie $2.8m
Carrying value	=	$3m
Impairment loss	=	$0.2m

The carrying value should be reduced to $2.8m

5.11 Example 2: impairment loss

A company has acquired another business for $4.5m: tangible assets are valued at $4.0m and goodwill at $0.5m.

An asset with a carrying value of $1m is destroyed in a terrorist attack. The asset was not insured. The loss of the asset, without insurance, has prompted the company to assess whether there has been an impairment of assets in the acquired business and what the amount of any such loss is.

The recoverable amount of the business (a single cash generating unit) is measured as $3.1m.

Solution

There has been an impairment loss of $1.4m ($4.5m – $3.1m).

The impairment loss will be recognised in the income statement. The loss will be allocated between the assets in the cash generating unit as follows.

(a)   A loss of $1m can be attributed directly to the uninsured asset that has been destroyed.
(b)   The remaining loss of $0.4m should be allocated to goodwill.

The carrying value of the assets will now be $3m for tangible assets and $0.1m for goodwill.

5.12 Reversal of an impairment loss

The annual assessment to determine whether there may have been some impairment should be **applied to all assets**, including assets that have already been impaired in the past.

In some cases, the recoverable amount of an asset that has previously been impaired might turn out to be **higher** than the asset's current carrying value. In other words, there might have been a reversal of some of the previous impairment loss.

(a) The reversal of the impairment loss should be **recognised immediately** as income in the income statement.

(b) The carrying amount of the asset should be increased to its **new recoverable amount**.

Rule to learn

> An impairment loss recognised for an asset in prior years should be recovered if, and only if, there has been a change in the estimates used to determine the asset's recoverable amount since the last impairment loss was recognised.

The asset cannot be revalued to a carrying amount that is higher than its value would have been if the asset had not been impaired originally, ie its **depreciated carrying value** had the impairment not taken place. Depreciation of the asset should now be based on its new revalued amount, its estimated residual value (if any) and its estimated remaining useful life.

An exception to this rule is for **goodwill**. An impairment loss for goodwill should not be reversed in a subsequent period.

Question

Reversal of impairment loss

A cash generating unit comprising a factory, plant and equipment etc and associated purchased goodwill becomes impaired because the product it makes is overtaken by a technologically more advanced model produced by a competitor. The recoverable amount of the cash generating unit falls to $60m, resulting in an impairment loss of $80m, allocated as follows.

	Carrying amounts before impairment $m	Carrying amounts after impairment $m
Goodwill	40	
Patent (with no market value)	20	
Tangible non-current assets (market value $60m)	80	60
Total	140	60

After three years, the entity makes a technological breakthrough of its own, and the recoverable amount of the cash generating unit increases to $90m. The carrying amount of the tangible non-current assets had the impairment not occurred would have been $70m.

Required

Calculate the reversal of the impairment loss.

Answer

The reversal of the impairment loss is recognised to the extent that it increases the carrying amount of the tangible non-current assets to what it would have been had the impairment not taken place, ie a reversal of the impairment loss of $10m is recognised and the tangible non-current assets written back to $70m. Reversal of the impairment is not recognised in relation to the goodwill and patent because the effect of the external event that caused the original impairment has not reversed – the original product is still overtaken by a more advanced model.

5.13 Disclosure

IAS 36 calls for substantial disclosure about impairment of assets. The information to be disclosed includes the following.

(a) For each class of assets, the amount of **impairment losses recognised** and the amount of any **impairment losses recovered** (ie reversals of impairment losses)

(b) For each individual asset or cash generating unit that has suffered a **significant impairment loss**, details of the nature of the asset, the amount of the loss, the events that led to recognition of the loss, whether the recoverable amount is fair value less costs to sell or value in use, and if the recoverable amount is value in use, the basis on which this value was estimated (eg the discount rate applied)

5.13.1 Compensation for the impairment or loss of items

An entity may receive monetary or non-monetary compensation from third parties for the impairment or loss of items of property, plant and equipment. The compensation may be used to restore the asset. Examples include:

- Reimbursement by insurance companies after an impairment of items of plant and equipment
- Physical replacement of an impaired or lost asset

The accounting treatment is as follows.

(a) Impairments of items of property, plant and equipment should be recognised under IAS 36, disposals should be recognised under IAS 16.

(b) Monetary or non-monetary compensation from third parties for items of property etc that were impaired, lost or given up, should be included in the income statement.

(c) The cost of assets restored, purchased, constructed as a replacement or received as compensation should be determined and presented under IAS 16.

5.14 Section summary

The main aspects of IAS 36 to consider are:

- **Indications** of impairment of assets
- **Measuring recoverable amount**, as net selling price or value in use
- **Measuring value in use**
- **Cash generating units**
- **Accounting treatment** of an impairment loss, for individual assets and cash generating units
- **Reversal** of an impairment loss

Chapter roundup

- This has been a long chapter with a lot to take in, so do not be surprised if it has taken you longer than you expected to work through it. Now that you have finally reached the end, you should understand the following points.

- The **cost of a non-current asset**, less its estimated residual value, is allocated fairly between accounting periods by means of depreciation. The provision for depreciation is both:

    - Charged against profit
    - Deducted from the value of the non-current asset in the balance sheet

- IAS 16 *Property, plant and equipment* provides the basic rules on **depreciation**, including important definitions of depreciation, depreciable assets, useful life and depreciable amount, all of which you should learn. You should be familiar with methods of depreciation from your Paper 1.1 studies.

- When a non-current asset is **revalued**, depreciation is charged on the revalued amount.

- When a non-current asset is **sold**, there is likely to be a profit or loss on disposal. This is the difference between the net sale price of the asset and its net book value at the time of disposal.

- IAS 16 *Property, plant and equipment* covers the major categories of **tangible non-current assets**. As well as depreciation, it also looks at recognition criteria, components of cost, revaluations etc.

- **Government grants** are the most common type of assistance from government and you must learn how to account for them as laid out in **IAS 20**.

- You should understand the arguments supporting the **income approach and the capital approach** to the treatment of government grants.

- You should be able to show both methods of dealing with **grants related to assets**.

- IAS 40 *Investment property* defines investment property as property **held to earn rentals or for capital appreciation** or both, rather than for:

    - Use in production or supply of goods or services
    - Sale in the ordinary course of business

- Entities can choose between:

    - A **fair value model**, with changes in fair value being measured
    - A **cost model** – usual treatment under IAS 16

- **IAS 36** *Impairment of assets* covers a controversial topic and it affects goodwill as well as tangible non-current assets.

- Impairment is determined by comparing the carrying amount of the asset with its **recoverable amount**.

- The recoverable amount of an asset is the higher of the asset's **fair value less costs to sell** and **its value in use**.

- When it is not possible to calculate the recoverable amount of a single asset, then that of its **cash generating unit** should be measured instead.

Quick quiz

1   Define depreciation.

2   Which of the following elements can be included in the production cost of a non-current asset?

    (i)   Purchase price of raw materials
    (ii)   Architect's fees
    (iii)   Import duties
    (iv)   Installation costs

3   Market value can usually be taken as fair value.

    True   ☐

    False   ☐

4   Define impairment.

5   Investment properties must always be shown at fair value.

    True   ☐

    False   ☐

6   What is the correct treatment for property being constructed for future use as investment property?

Answers to quick quiz

1   See Para 1.2

2   All of them.

3   True

4   See Para 5.1

5   False. The cost model may be used, provided it is used consistently.

6   Use IAS 16 until construction is complete, then IAS 40.

Now try the question below from the Exam Question Bank			
Number	**Level**	**Marks**	**Time**
Q6	Examination	25	45 mins

Intangible non-current assets

Topic list	Syllabus reference
1 IAS 38 *Intangible assets*	3(b)
2 Goodwill (IFRS 3)	3(b)

Introduction

We begin our examination of intangible non-current assets with a discussion of a recently revised IAS on the subject (**IAS 38**).

Goodwill and its treatment is a controversial area, as is the accounting for items similar to goodwill, such as brands. Goodwill is very important in **group accounts** and we will look at it again in Part C.

Study guide

Section 11 – Intangible assets

- Discuss the nature and possible accounting treatments of both internally generated and purchased goodwill

- Distinguish between goodwill and other intangible assets

- Describe the criteria for the initial recognition and measurement of intangible assets

- Describe the subsequent accounting treatment, including the principle of impairment tests in relation to purchased goodwill

- Describe the circumstances in which negative goodwill arises, and its subsequent accounting treatment and disclosure

- Describe and apply the requirements of accounting standards on internally generated assets other than goodwill (eg research and development)

1 IAS 38 Intangible assets

FAST FORWARD

Intangible assets are defined by IAS 38 as non-monetary assets without physical substance.

IAS 38 *Intangible assets* was originally published in September 1998. It has recently been revised to reflect changes introduced by IFRS 3 *Business combinations*.

1.1 The objectives of the standard

(a) To establish the criteria for when an intangible asset may or should be **recognised**
(b) To specify how intangible assets should be **measured**
(c) To specify the **disclosure requirements** for intangible assets

1.2 Scope

IAS 38 applies to all intangible assets with certain **exceptions**: deferred tax assets (IAS 12), leases that fall within the scope of IAS 17, financial assets, insurance contracts, assets arising from employee benefits (IAS 19) non-current assets held for sale and mineral rights and exploration and extraction costs for minerals etc (although intangible assets used to develop or maintain these rights are covered by the standard). It does *not* apply to goodwill acquired in a business combination, which is dealt with under IFRS 3 *Business combinations*.

1.3 Definition of an intangible asset

The definition of an intangible asset is a key aspect of the standard, because the rules for deciding whether or not an intangible asset may be **recognised** in the accounts of an entity are based on the definition of what an intangible asset is.

Key term

> An **intangible asset** is an identifiable non-monetary asset without physical substance The asset must be:
>
> (a) controlled by the entity as a result of events in the past, and
> (b) something from which the entity expects future economic benefits to flow.

Examples of items that might be considered as intangible assets include computer software, patents, copyrights, motion picture films, customer lists, franchises and fishing rights. An item should not be recognised as an intangible asset, however, unless it **fully meets the definition** in the standard. The guidelines go into great detail on this matter.

1.4 Intangible asset: must be identifiable

An intangible asset must be identifiable in order to distinguish it from goodwill. With non-physical items, there may be a problem with **'identifiability'**.

(a) If an intangible asset is **acquired separately through purchase**, there may be a transfer of a legal right that would help to make an asset identifiable.

(b) An intangible asset may be identifiable if it is **separable**, ie if it could be rented or sold separately. However, 'separability' is not an essential feature of an intangible asset.

1.5 Intangible asset: control by the entity

Another element of the definition of an intangible asset is that it must be under the control of the entity as a result of a past event. The entity must therefore be able to enjoy the future economic benefits from the asset, and prevent the access of others to those benefits. A **legally enforceable right** is evidence of such control, but is not always a *necessary* condition.

(a) Control over **technical knowledge or know-how** only exists if it is protected by a **legal right**.

(b) The skill of employees, arising out of the benefits of **training costs**, are most unlikely to be recognisable as an intangible asset, because an entity does not control the future actions of its staff.

(c) Similarly, **market share and customer loyalty** cannot normally be intangible assets, since an entity cannot control the actions of its customers.

1.6 Intangible asset: expected future economic benefits

An item can only be recognised as an intangible asset if economic benefits are expected to flow in the future from ownership of the asset. Economic benefits may come from the **sale** of products or services, or from a **reduction in expenditures** (cost savings).

An intangible asset, when recognised initially, must be measured at **cost**. It should be recognised if, and only if **both** the following occur.

(a) It is probable that the **future economic benefits** that are attributable to the asset will **flow to the entity.**

(b) The **cost can be measured reliably**.

Management has to exercise its judgement in assessing the degree of certainty attached to the flow of economic benefits to the entity. External evidence is best.

(a) If an intangible asset is **acquired separately**, its cost can usually be measured reliably as its purchase price (including incidental costs of purchase such as legal fees, and any costs incurred in getting the asset ready for use).

(b) When an intangible asset is acquired as **part of a business combination** (ie an acquisition or takeover), the cost of the intangible asset is its fair value at the date of the acquisition.

IFRS 3 explains that the fair value of intangible assets acquired in business combinations can normally be measured with sufficient reliability to be **recognised separately** from goodwill.

Quoted market prices in an active market provide the most reliable estimate of the fair value of an intangible asset. If no active market exists for an intangible asset, its fair value is the amount that the entity would have paid for the asset, at the acquisition date, in an arm's length transaction between knowledgeable and willing parties, on the basis of the best information available. In determining this amount, an entity should consider the outcome of recent transactions for similar assets. There are techniques for estimating the fair values of unique intangible assets (such as brand names) and these may be used to measure an intangible asset acquired in a business combination.

In accordance with IAS 20, intangible assets acquired by way of government grant and the grant itself may be recorded initially either at cost (which may be zero) or fair value.

1.7 Exchanges of assets

If one intangible asset is exchanged for another, the cost of the intangible asset is measured at fair value unless:

(a)   The exchange transaction lacks commercial substance, or

(b)   The fair value of neither the asset received nor the asset given up can be measured reliably.

Otherwise, its cost is measured at the carrying amount of the asset given up.

1.8 Internally generated goodwill

Rule to Learn

Internally generated goodwill may **not** be recognised as an **asset**.

The standard deliberately precludes recognition of internally generated goodwill because it requires that, for initial recognition, the cost of the asset rather than its fair value should be capable of being measured reliably and that it should be identifiable and controlled. Thus you do not recognise an asset which is subjective and cannot be measured reliably.

1.9 Research and development costs

1.9.1 Research

Research activities by definition do not meet the criteria for recognition under IAS 38. This is because, at the research stage of a project, it cannot be certain that future economic benefits will probably flow to the entity from the project. There is too much uncertainty about the likely success or otherwise of the project. **Research costs should therefore be written off as an expense as they are incurred**.

Examples of research costs

(a)   Activities aimed at obtaining new knowledge

(b)   The search for, evaluation and final selection of, applications of research findings or other knowledge

(c)   The search for alternatives for materials, devices, products, processes, systems or services

(d)   The formulation, design evaluation and final selection of possible alternatives for new or improved materials, devices, products, systems or services

1.9.2 Development

Development costs **may qualify** for recognition as intangible assets provided that the following **strict criteria** can be demonstrated.

(a)   The technical feasibility of completing the intangible asset so that it will be available for use or sale.

(b)   Its intention to complete the intangible asset and use or sell it.

(c)   Its ability to use or sell the intangible asset.

(d)   How the intangible asset will generate probable future economic benefits. Among other things, the entity should demonstrate the existence of a market for the output of the intangible asset or the intangible asset itself or, if it is to be used internally, the usefulness of the intangible asset.

(e)   Its ability to measure the expenditure attributable to the intangible asset during its development reliably.

In contrast with research costs development costs are incurred at a later stage in a project, and the probability of success should be more apparent. Examples of development costs include the following.

(a)   The design, construction and testing of pre-production or pre-use prototypes and models

(b)   The design of tools, jigs, moulds and dies involving new technology

(c)   The design, construction and operation of a pilot plant that is not of a scale economically feasible for commercial production

(d)   The design, construction and testing of a chosen alternative for new or improved materials, devices, products, processes, systems or services

1.9.3 Other internally generated intangible assets

The standard **prohibits** the recognition of **internally generated brands, mastheads, publishing titles and customer lists** and similar items as intangible assets. These all fail to meet one or more (in some cases all) the definition and recognition criteria and in some cases are probably indistinguishable from internally generated goodwill.

1.9.4 Cost of an internally generated intangible asset

The costs allocated to an internally generated intangible asset should be only costs that can be **directly attributed** or allocated on a reasonable and consistent basis to creating, producing or preparing the asset for its intended use. The principles underlying the costs which may or may not be included are similar to those for other non-current assets and inventory.

The cost of an internally operated intangible asset is the sum of the **expenditure incurred from the date when** the intangible asset first **meets the recognition criteria**. If, as often happens, considerable costs have already been recognised as expenses before management could demonstrate that the criteria have been met, this earlier expenditure should not be retrospectively recognised at a later date as part of the cost of an intangible asset.

Question	Treatment

Doug Co is developing a new production process. During 20X3, expenditure incurred was $100,000, of which $90,000 was incurred before 1 December 20X3 and $10,000 between 1 December 20X3 and 31 December 20X3. Doug Co can demonstrate that, at 1 December 20X3, the production process met the criteria for recognition as an intangible asset. The recoverable amount of the know-how embodied in the process is estimated to be $50,000.

How should the expenditure be treated?

Answer

At the end of 20X3, the production process is recognised as an intangible asset at a cost of $10,000. This is the expenditure incurred since the date when the recognition criteria were met, that is 1 December 20X3. The $90,000 expenditure incurred before 1 December 20X3 is expensed, because the recognition criteria were not met. It will never form part of the cost of the production process recognised in the balance sheet.

1.10 Recognition of an expense

All expenditure related to an intangible which does not meet the criteria for recognition either as an identifiable intangible asset or as goodwill arising on an acquisition should be **expensed as incurred**. The IAS gives examples of such expenditure.

- Start up costs
- Training costs
- Advertising costs
- Business relocation costs

Prepaid costs for services, for example advertising or marketing costs for campaigns that have been prepared but not launched, can still be recognised as a **prepayment**.

1.11 Measurement of intangible assets subsequent to initial recognition

The standard allows two methods of valuation for intangible assets after they have been first recognised.

Applying the **cost model**, an intangible asset should be **carried at its cost**, less any accumulated amortisation and less any accumulated impairment losses.

The **revaluation model** allows an intangible asset to be carried at a revalued amount, which is its **fair value** at the date of revaluation, less any subsequent accumulated amortisation and any subsequent accumulated impairment losses.

(a) The fair value must be able to be measured reliably with reference to an **active market** in that type of asset.

(b) The **entire class** of intangible assets of that type must be revalued at the same time (to prevent selective revaluations).

(c) If an intangible asset in a class of revalued intangible assets cannot be revalued because there is **no active market** for this asset, the asset should be carried at its **cost less any accumulated amortisation and impairment losses**.

(d) Revaluations should be made with such **regularity** that the carrying amount does not differ from that which would be determined using fair value at the balance sheet date.

Point to note

This treatment is **not** available for the **initial recognition** of intangible assets. This is because the cost of the asset must be reliably measured.

The guidelines state that there **will not usually be an active market** in an intangible asset; therefore the revaluation model will usually not be available. For example, although copyrights, publishing rights and film rights can be sold, each has a unique sale value. In such cases, revaluation to fair value would be inappropriate. A fair value might be obtainable however for assets such as fishing rights or quotas or taxi cab licences.

Where an intangible asset is revalued upwards to a fair value, the amount of the revaluation should be credited directly to equity under the heading of a **revaluation surplus**.

However, if a revaluation surplus is a **reversal of a revaluation decrease** that was previously charged against income, the increase can be recognised as income.

Where the carrying amount of an intangible asset is revalued downwards, the amount of the **downward revaluation** should be charged as an expense against income, unless the asset has previously been revalued upwards. A revaluation decrease should be first charged against any previous revaluation surplus in respect of that asset.

Question	Downward revaluation

An intangible asset is measured by a company at fair value. The asset was revalued by $400 in 20X3, and there is a revaluation surplus of $400 in the balance sheet. At the end of 20X4, the asset is valued again, and a downward valuation of $500 is required.

Required

State the accounting treatment for the downward revaluation.

Answer

In this example, the downward valuation of $500 can first be set against the revaluation surplus of $400. The revaluation surplus will be reduced to 0 and a charge of $100 made as an expense in 20X4.

When the revaluation model is used, and an intangible asset is revalued upwards, the cumulative revaluation **surplus may be transferred to retained earnings** when the surplus is eventually realised. The surplus would be realised when the asset is disposed of. However, the surplus may also be realised over time as the **asset is used** by the entity. The amount of the surplus realised each year is the difference between the amortisation charge for the asset based on the revalued amount of the asset, and the amortisation that would be charged on the basis of the asset's historical cost. The realised surplus in such case should be transferred from revaluation surplus directly to retained earnings, and should not be taken through the income statement.

1.12 Useful life

An entity should **assess** the useful life of an intangible asset, which may be **finite or indefinite**. An intangible asset has an indefinite useful life when there is **no foreseeable limit** to the period over which the asset is expected to generate net cash inflows for the entity.

Many factors are considered in determining the useful life of an intangible asset, including: expected usage; typical product life cycles; technical, technological, commercial or other types of obsolescence; the stability of the industry; expected actions by competitors; the level of maintenance expenditure required; and legal or similar limits on the use of the asset, such as the expiry dates of related leases. Computer software and many other intangible assets normally have short lives because they are susceptible to technological obsolescence. However, uncertainty does not justify choosing a life that is unrealistically short.

The useful life of an intangible asset that arises from **contractual or other legal rights** should not exceed the period of the rights, but may be shorter depending on the period over which the entity expects to use the asset.

1.13 Amortisation period and amortisation method

An intangible asset with a finite useful life should be amortised over its **expected useful life**.

(a) Amortisation should start when the asset is **available for use**.

(b) Amortisation should cease at the earlier of the date that the asset is classified **as held for sale** in accordance with IFRS 5 *Non-current assets held for sale and discontinued operations* and the date that the asset is **derecognised**.

(c) The amortisation method used should reflect the **pattern in which the asset's future economic benefits are consumed**. If such a pattern cannot be predicted reliably, the straight-line method should be used.

(d) The amortisation charge for each period should normally be recognised **in profit or loss**.

The **residual value** of an intangible asset with a finite useful life is **assumed to be zero** unless a third party is committed to buying the intangible asset at the end of its useful life or unless there is an active market for that type of asset (so that its expected residual value can be measured) and it is probable that there will be a market for the asset at the end of its useful life.

The amortisation period and the amortisation method used for an intangible asset with a finite useful life should be **reviewed at each financial year-end**.

1.14 Intangible assets with indefinite useful lives

An intangible asset with an indefinite useful life **should not be amortised**. (IAS 36 requires that such an asset is tested for impairment at least annually.)

The useful life of an intangible asset that is not being amortised should be **reviewed each year** to determine whether it is still appropriate to assess its useful life as indefinite. Reassessing the useful life of an intangible asset as finite rather than indefinite is an indicator that the asset may be impaired and therefore it should be tested for impairment.

Question

Intangible asset

It may be difficult to establish the useful life of an intangible asset, and judgement will be needed. Consider how to determine the useful life of a *purchased* brand name.

Answer

Factors to consider would include the following.

(a) Legal protection of the brand name and the control of the entity over the (illegal) use by others of the brand name (ie control over pirating)

(b) Age of the brand name

(c) Status or position of the brand in its particular market

(d) Ability of the management of the entity to manage the brand name and to measure activities that support the brand name (eg advertising and PR activities)

(e) Stability and geographical spread of the market in which the branded products are sold

(f) Pattern of benefits that the brand name is expected to generate over time

(g) Intention of the entity to use and promote the brand name over time (as evidenced perhaps by a business plan in which there will be substantial expenditure to promote the brand name)

1.15 Disposals/retirements of intangible assets

An intangible asset should be eliminated from the balance sheet when it is disposed of or when there is no further expected economic benefit from its future use. On disposal the gain or loss arising from the **difference between the net disposal proceeds and the carrying amount** of the asset should be taken to the income statement as a gain or loss on disposal (ie treated as income or expense).

1.16 Disclosure requirements

The standard has fairly extensive disclosure requirements for intangible assets. The financial statements should disclose the **accounting policies** for intangible assets that have been adopted.

For **each class of intangible assets**, disclosure is required of the following.

- The **method of amortisation** used

- The **useful life** of the assets or the amortisation rate used

- The **gross carrying amount**, the **accumulated amortisation** and the **accumulated impairment losses** as at the beginning and the end of the period

- A **reconciliation of the carrying amount** as at the beginning and at the end of the period (additions, retirements/disposals, revaluations, impairment losses, impairment losses reversed, amortisation charge for the period, net exchange differences, other movements)

- The carrying amount of **internally-generated intangible assets**

The financial statements should also disclose the following.

- In the case of intangible assets that are assessed as having an indefinite useful life, the carrying amounts and the reasons supporting that assessment

- For intangible assets acquired by way of a **government grant** and initially recognised at fair value, the **fair value initially recognised**, the **carrying amount**, and whether they are carried under the **cost model** or the **revaluation model** for subsequent remeasurements

- The carrying amount, nature and remaining amortisation period of any intangible asset that is **material to the financial statements of the entity as a whole**

- The existence (if any) and amounts of intangible assets whose **title is restricted** and of intangible assets that have been **pledged as security** for liabilities

- The amount of any **commitments for the future acquisition of intangible assets**

Where intangible assets are accounted for at revalued amounts, disclosure is required of the following.

- The **effective date of the revaluation** (by class of intangible assets)

- The **carrying amount** of revalued intangible assets

- The carrying amount that would have been shown (by class of assets) **if the cost model had been used**, and the amount of amortisation that would have been charged

- The amount of any **revaluation surplus** on intangible assets, as at the beginning and end of the period, and movements in the surplus during the year (and any restrictions on the distribution of the balance to shareholders)

The financial statements should also disclose the amount of research and development expenditure that have been charged as expenses of the period.

1.17 Section summary

- An intangible asset should be recognised if, and only if, it is probable that future economic benefits will flow to the entity and the cost of the asset can be measured reliably.

- An asset is initially recognised at cost and subsequently carried either at cost or revalued amount.

- Costs that do not meet the recognition criteria should be expensed as incurred.

- An intangible asset with a finite useful life should be amortised over its useful life. An intangible asset with an indefinite useful life should not be amortised.

Question	R&D

As an aid to your revision, list the examples given in IAS 38 of activities that might be included in either research or development.

Answer

IAS 38 gives these examples.

Research

- Activities aimed at obtaining new knowledge
- The search for applications of research findings or other knowledge
- The search for product or process alternatives
- The formulation and design of possible new or improved product or process alternatives

Development

- The evaluation of product or process alternatives

- The design, construction and testing of pre-production prototypes and models

- The design of tools, jigs, moulds and dies involving new technology

- The design, construction and operation of a pilot plant that is not of a scale economically feasible for commercial production

2 Goodwill (IFRS 3)

FAST FORWARD ❯❯ Purchased goodwill arising on consolidation is retained in the balance sheet as an intangible asset under IFRS 3. It must then be reviewed annually for impairment.

2.1 What is goodwill?

Goodwill is **created by good relationships** between a business and its customers.

- (a) By building up a **reputation** (by word of mouth perhaps) for high quality products or high standards of service

- (b) By **responding promptly and helpfully** to queries and complaints from customers

- (c) Through the **personality of the staff** and their attitudes to customers

The value of goodwill to a business might be **extremely significant**. However, goodwill is not usually valued in the accounts of a business at all, and we should not normally expect to find an amount for goodwill in its balance sheet. For example, the welcoming smile of the bar staff may contribute more to a bar's profits than the fact that a new electronic cash register has recently been acquired. Even so, whereas the cash register will be recorded in the accounts as a non-current asset, the value of staff would be ignored for accounting purposes.

On reflection, we might agree with this omission of goodwill from the accounts of a business.

(a) The goodwill is **inherent** in the business but it has not been paid for, and it does not have an 'objective' value. We can guess at what such goodwill is worth, but such guesswork would be a matter of individual opinion, and not based on hard facts.

(b) Goodwill **changes** from day to day. One act of bad customer relations might damage goodwill and one act of good relations might improve it. Staff with a favourable personality might retire or leave to find another job, to be replaced by staff who need time to find their feet in the job, etc. Since goodwill is continually changing in value, it cannot realistically be recorded in the accounts of the business.

2.2 Purchased goodwill

There is one exception to the general rule that goodwill has no objective valuation. This is **when a business is sold**. People wishing to set up in business have a choice of how to do it – they can either buy their own long-term assets and inventory and set up their business from scratch, or they can buy up an existing business from a proprietor willing to sell it. When a buyer purchases an existing business, he will have to purchase not only its long-term assets and inventory (and perhaps take over its accounts payable and receivable too) but also the goodwill of the business.

Purchased goodwill is shown in the balance sheet because it has been paid for. It has no tangible substance, and so it is an **intangible non-current asset**.

2.3 How is the value of purchased goodwill decided?

When a business is sold, there is likely to be some purchased goodwill in the selling price. But **how is the amount of this purchased goodwill decided**?

This is not really a problem for accountants, who must simply record the goodwill in the accounts of the new business. The value of the goodwill is a **matter for the purchaser and seller to agree upon in fixing the purchase/sale price**. However, two methods of valuation are worth mentioning here.

(a) The seller and buyer agree on a price for the business **without specifically quantifying the goodwill**. The purchased goodwill will then be the difference between the price agreed and the value of the tangible net assets in the books of the new business.

(b) However, the calculation of goodwill often precedes the fixing of the purchase price and becomes a **central element of negotiation**. There are many ways of arriving at a value for goodwill and most of them are related to the profit record of the business in question.

No matter how goodwill is calculated within the total agreed purchase price, the goodwill shown by the purchaser in his accounts will be **the difference between the purchase consideration and his own valuation of the tangible net assets acquired**. If A values his tangible net assets at $40,000, goodwill is agreed at $21,000 and B agrees to pay $61,000 for the business but values the tangible net assets at only $38,000, then the goodwill in B's books will be $61,000 – $38,000 = $23,000.

2.4 IFRS 3 *Business combinations*

IFRS 3 covers the accounting treatment of goodwill acquired in a business combination.

It is possible to define goodwill in different ways. The IFRS 3 definition of goodwill is different from the more traditional definition (eg in the previous IAS 22) and emphasises benefits, rather than the method of calculation.

Key terms

> - **Goodwill**. Future economic benefits arising from assets that are not capable of being individually identified and separately recognised.   *(IFRS 3)*
>
> - **Goodwill**. Any excess of the cost of acquisition over the acquirer's interest in the fair value of the identifiable assets and liabilities acquired as at the date of the exchange transaction.   *(IAS 22)*

Goodwill acquired in a business combination is **recognised as an asset** and is initially measured at **cost**. Cost is the excess of the cost of the combination over the acquirer's interest in the net fair value of the acquiree's identifiable assets, liabilities and contingent liabilities.

After initial recognition goodwill acquired in a business combination is measured **at cost less any accumulated impairment losses**. It is **not amortised**. Instead it is tested for impairment at least annually, in accordance with IAS 36 *Impairment of assets*.

Negative goodwill arises when the acquirer's interest in the net fair value of the acquiree's identifiable assets, liabilities and contingent liabilities exceeds the cost of the business combination. IFRS 3 refers to negative goodwill as the 'excess of acquirer's interest in the net fair value of acquiree's identifiable assets, liabilities and contingent liabilities over cost'.

Negative goodwill can arise as the result of **errors** in measuring the fair value of either the cost of the combination or the acquiree's identifiable net assets. It can also arise as the result of a **bargain purchase**.

Where there is negative goodwill, an entity should first **reassess** the amounts at which it has measured both the cost of the combination and the acquiree's identifiable net assets. This exercise should identify any errors.

Any negative goodwill remaining should be **recognised immediately in profit or loss** (that is, in the income statement).

IFRS 3 requires extensive **disclosures**. These include a **reconciliation** of the carrying amount of goodwill at the beginning and end of the period, showing separately:

(a) The gross amount and accumulated impairment losses at the beginning of the period
(b) Additional goodwill recognised during the period
(c) Impairment losses recognised during the period
(d) Net exchange differences arising during the period, and
(e) The gross amount and accumulated impairment losses at the end of the period

Question   Characteristics of goodwill

What are the main characteristics of goodwill which distinguish it from other intangible non-current assets? To what extent do you consider that these characteristics should affect the accounting treatment of goodwill? State your reasons.

Answer

Goodwill may be distinguished from other intangible non-current assets by reference to the following characteristics.

(a) It is incapable of realisation separately from the business as a whole.

(b) Its value has no reliable or predictable relationship to any costs which may have been incurred.

(c)   Its value arises from various intangible factors such as skilled employees, effective advertising or a strategic location. These indirect factors cannot be valued.

(d)   The value of goodwill may fluctuate widely according to internal and external circumstances over relatively short periods of time.

(e)   The assessment of the value of goodwill is highly subjective.

It could be argued that, because goodwill is so different from other intangible non-current assets it does not make sense to account for it in the same way. Thus the capitalisation and amortisation treatment would not be acceptable. Furthermore, because goodwill is so difficult to value, any valuation may be misleading, and it is best eliminated from the balance sheet altogether. However, there are strong arguments for treating it like any other intangible non-current asset. This issue remains controversial.

Chapter roundup

- **Intangible assets** are defined by **IAS 38** as non-monetary assets without physical substance. They must be:

  -   **Identifiable**
  -   **Controlled** as a result of a past event
  -   Able to provide **future economic benefits**

- Intangible assets should initially be measured at cost, but subsequently they can be carried at **cost or at a revalued amount**.

- **Internally-generated goodwill** cannot be recognised as an asset but other internally-generated assets may be, eg R & D.

- **Impairment** rules follow **IAS 36**. There are substantial disclosure requirements.

- If a business has **goodwill**, it means that the value of the business as a going concern is greater than the value of its separate tangible assets. The valuation of goodwill is extremely subjective and fluctuates constantly. For this reason, non-purchased goodwill is **not** shown as an asset in the balance sheet.

- When someone **purchases a business** as a going concern the purchaser and vendor will fix an agreed price which includes an element in respect of goodwill. The way in which goodwill is then valued is not an accounting problem, but a matter of agreement between the two parties.

- **Purchased goodwill** arising on a business combination is then retained in the balance sheet as an intangible asset under the requirements of **IFRS 3**. It must be reviewed for impairment annually.

Quick quiz

1   Intangible assets can only be recognised in a company's accounts if:

- It is probable that .... will flow to the entity
- The cost can be ....

2   What are the criteria which must be met before development expenditure can be deferred?

3   Start up costs must be expensed.

True ☐

False ☐

4   Peggy buys Phil's business for $30,000. The business assets are a bar valued at $20,000, inventories at $3,000 and receivables of $3,000. How much is goodwill valued at?

5   What method of accounting for goodwill arising on consolidation is required by IFRS 3?

6   How should negative goodwill be accounted for under IFRS 3?

Answers to quick quiz

1   Future economic benefits. Measured reliably.

2   See Para 1.9.2

3   True

4   $30,000 – $20,000 – $3,000 – $3,000 = $4,000

5   Cost less impairment losses

6   Recognised in profit or loss immediately

Now try the question below from the Exam Question Bank

Number	Level	Marks	Time
Q7	Examination	25	45 mins

Inventories and construction contracts

Topic list	Syllabus reference
1 Inventories and short-term WIP (IAS 2)	3(f)
2 IAS 11 *Construction contracts*	3(f)

Introduction

You have encountered inventory and its valuation in your earlier studies. Inventory and short-term work-in-progress valuation has a direct impact on a company's gross profit and it is usually a material item in any company's accounts. This is therefore an important subject area. If you have any doubts about accounting for inventories and methods of inventory valuation you would be advised to go back to your earlier study material and revise this topic.

Section 1 of this chapter goes over some of this ground again, concentrating on the effect of IAS 2. Section 2 goes on to discuss a new area, construction contracts, which are effectively long-term work in progress. You should find this topic fairly logical as long as you work through the examples and question carefully.

Study guide

Section 14 – Inventories and construction contracts

- Review the principles of inventory valuation covered in Paper 1.1

- Define a construction contract and describe why recognising profit before completion is generally considered to be desirable and the circumstances where it may not be; discuss if this may be profit smoothing

- Describe the ways in which contract revenue and contract cost may be recognised

- Calculate and disclose the amounts to be shown in the financial statements for construction contracts

Exam guide

The **pilot paper** contained a question on construction contracts. They are a good test of double entry. The examiner is likely to test them regularly, if only because they do not feature at Paper 3.6.

1 Inventories and short-term WIP (IAS 2)

FAST FORWARD

> Most of this is revision. However you should be aware that the use of LIFO is prohibited under the revised IAS 2.

1.1 Introduction

In most businesses the value put on inventory is an important factor in the determination of profit. Inventory valuation is, however, a highly subjective exercise and consequently there is a wide variety of different methods used in practice.

1.2 IAS 2 (revised) Inventories

IAS 2 was revised in December 2003. It lays out the required accounting treatment for inventories (sometimes called stocks) under the historical cost system. The major area of contention is the cost **value of inventory** to be recorded. This is recognised as an asset of the entity until the related revenues are recognised (ie the item is sold) at which point the inventory is recognised as an expense (ie cost of sales). Part or all of the cost of inventories may also be expensed if a write-down to **net realisable value** is necessary. The revised IAS also provides guidance on the cost formulas that are used to assign costs to inventories.

In other words, the fundamental accounting assumption of **accruals** requires costs to be matched with associated revenues. In order to achieve this, costs incurred for goods which remain unsold at the year end must be carried forward in the balance sheet and matched against future revenues.

1.3 Scope

The following items are **excluded** from the scope of the standard.

- Work in progress under **construction contracts** (covered by IAS 11 *Construction contracts*, see Section 2)

- **Financial instruments** (ie shares, bonds)

- **Biological assets**

Certain inventories are exempt from the standard's **measurement rules**, ie those held by:

- Producers of **agricultural and forest products**
- **Commodity-broker traders**

1.4 Definitions

The standard gives the following important definitions.

Key terms

- **Inventories** are assets:
  - held for sale in the ordinary course of business;
  - in the process of production for such sale; or
  - in the form of materials or supplies to be consumed in the production process or in the rendering of services.
- **Net realisable value** is the estimated selling price in the ordinary course of business less the estimated costs of completion and the estimated costs necessary to make the sale.
- **Fair value** is the amount for which an asset could be exchanged or a liability settled between knowledgeable, willing parties in an arm's length transaction. (*IAS 2*)

Inventories can **include** any of the following.

- **Goods purchased and held for resale**, eg goods held for sale by a retailer, or land and buildings held for resale
- **Finished goods** produced
- **Work in progress** being produced
- Materials and supplies awaiting use in the production process (**raw materials**)

1.5 Measurement of inventories

The standard states that '**Inventories should be measured at the lower of cost and net realisable value**.'

Exam focus point

This is a very important rule and you will be expected to apply it in the exam.

1.6 Cost of inventories

The cost of inventories will consist of all costs of:

- **Purchase**
- **Costs of conversion**
- **Other costs** incurred in bringing the inventories to their **present location and condition**

1.6.1 Costs of purchase

The standard lists the following as comprising the costs of purchase of inventories:

- **Purchase price** *plus*
- **Import duties** and other taxes *plus*
- Transport, handling and any other cost **directly attributable** to the acquisition of finished goods, services and materials *less*
- **Trade discounts**, rebates and other similar amounts

1.6.2 Costs of conversion

Costs of conversion of inventories consist of two main parts.

(a) Costs **directly related** to the units of production, eg direct materials, direct labour

(b) Fixed and variable **production overheads** that are incurred in converting materials into finished goods, allocated on a systematic basis.

You may have come across the terms 'fixed production overheads' or 'variable production overheads' elsewhere in your studies. The standard defines them as follows.

Key terms

> • **Fixed production overheads** are those indirect costs of production that remain relatively constant regardless of the volume of production, eg the cost of factory management and administration.
>
> • **Variable production overheads** are those indirect costs of production that vary directly, or nearly directly, with the volume of production, eg indirect materials and labour.   *(IAS 2)*

The standard emphasises that fixed production overheads must be allocated to items of inventory on the basis of the **normal capacity of the production facilities**. This is an important point.

(a) **Normal capacity** is the expected achievable production based on the average over several periods/seasons, under normal circumstances.

(b) The above figure should take account of the capacity lost through **planned maintenance**.

(c) If it approximates to the normal level of activity then the **actual level of production** can be used.

(d) **Low production** or **idle plant** will *not* result in a higher fixed overhead allocation to each unit.

(e) **Unallocated overheads** must be recognised as an expense in the period in which they were incurred.

(f) When production is **abnormally high**, the fixed production overhead allocated to each unit will be reduced, so avoiding inventories being stated at more than cost.

(g) The allocation of variable production overheads to each unit is based on the **actual use** of production facilities.

1.6.3 Other costs

Any other costs should only be recognised if they are incurred in bringing the inventories to their **present location and condition**.

The standard lists types of cost which **would not be included** in cost of inventories. Instead, they should be recognised as an **expense** in the period they are incurred.

(a) **Abnormal amounts** of wasted materials, labour or other production costs

(b) **Storage costs** (except costs which are necessary in the production process before a further production stage)

(c) **Administrative overheads** not incurred to bring inventories to their present location and conditions

(d) **Selling costs**

1.6.4 Techniques for the measurement of cost

Two techniques are mentioned by the standard, both of which produce results which **approximate to cost**, and so both of which may be used for convenience.

(a) **Standard costs** are set up to take account of normal production values: amount of raw materials used, labour time etc. They are reviewed and revised on a regular basis.

(b) **Retail method**: this is often used in the retail industry where there is a large turnover of inventory items, which nevertheless have similar profit margins. The only practical method of inventory valuation may be to take the total selling price of inventories and deduct an overall average profit margin, thus reducing the value to an approximation of cost. The percentage will take account of reduced price lines. Sometimes different percentages are applied on a department basis.

1.7 Cost formulas

Cost of inventories should be assigned by **specific identification** of their individual costs for:

(a) Items that are **not ordinarily interchangeable**
(b) Goods or services produced and segregated for **specific projects**

Specific costs should be attributed to individual items of inventory when they are segregated for a specific project, but not where inventories consist of a large number of interchangeable (ie identical or very similar) items. In the latter case the rule is as specified below.

1.7.1 Interchangeable items

Rule to learn

The cost of inventories should be assigned by using the **first-in, first-out (FIFO)** or **weighted average** cost formulas. The LIFO formula (last in, first out) is **not permitted** by the revised IAS 2.

You should be familiar with these methods from your Paper 1.1 studies. Under the weighted average cost method, a recalculation can be made after each purchase, **or alternatively only at the period end**.

1.8 Net realisable value (NRV)

As a general rule assets should not be carried at amounts greater than those expected to be realised from their sale or use. In the case of inventories this amount could fall below cost when items are **damaged or become obsolete**, or where the **costs to completion have increased** in order to make the sale.

In fact we can identify the principal situations in which **NRV is likely to be less than cost**, ie where there has been:

(a) An **increase in costs** or a **fall in selling price**

(b) A **physical deterioration** in the condition of inventory

(c) **Obsolescence** of products

(d) A decision as part of the company's marketing strategy to manufacture and sell products at a **loss**

(e) **Errors in production or purchasing**

A write down of inventories would normally take place on an item by item basis, but similar or related items may be **grouped together**. This grouping together is acceptable for, say, items in the same product line, but it is not acceptable to write down inventories based on a whole classification (eg finished goods) or a whole business.

The assessment of NRV should take place **at the same time** as estimates are made of selling price, using the most reliable information available. Fluctuations of price or cost should be taken into account if they relate directly to **events after the balance sheet date,** which confirm conditions existing at the end of the period.

The reasons why inventory is held must also be taken into account. Some inventory, for example, may be held to satisfy a firm contract and its NRV will therefore be the **contract price**. Any additional inventory of the same type held at the period end will, in contrast, be assessed according to general sales prices when NRV is estimated.

Net realisable value must be reassessed at the end of each period and compared again with cost. If the NRV has risen for inventories held over the end of more than one period, then the previous write down must be **reversed** to the extent that the inventory is then valued at the lower of cost and the new NRV. This may be possible when selling prices have fallen in the past and then risen again.

On occasion a write down to NRV may be of such size, incidence or nature that it must be **disclosed separately**.

1.9 Recognition as an expense

The following treatment is required **when inventories are sold**.

(a) The **carrying amount** is recognised as an expense in the period in which the related revenue is recognised

(b) The amount of any **write-down of inventories** to NRV and all losses of inventories are recognised as an expense in the period the write-down or loss occurs

(c) The amount of any **reversal of any write-down of inventories**, arising from an increase in NRV, is recognised as a reduction in the amount of inventories recognised as an expense in the period in which the reversal occurs

1.10 Disclosure

The financial statements should disclose the following.

(a) **Accounting policies** adopted in measuring inventories, including the cost formula used

(b) **Total carrying amount of inventories** and the carrying amount in classifications appropriate to the entity

(c) **Carrying amount** of inventories carried at fair value less costs to sell

(d) The amount of inventories **recognised as an expense** in the period

(e) The amount of any **write-down** of inventories **recognised as an expense** in the period

(f) The amount of any **reversal of any write-down** that is recognised as a reduction in the amount of inventories recognised as an expense in the period

(g) **Circumstances or events** that led to the reversal of a write-down of inventories

(h) Carrying amount of inventories **pledged as security for liabilities**

This information is of great relevance to users of financial statements, particularly the change in assets from period to period. The standard lists common **classifications for inventories**.

- Merchandise
- Production supplies
- Materials

- Work in progress
- Finished goods

The financial statements must also disclose one of two things.

(a)   The **cost of inventories** recognised as an expense during the period, or

(b)   The **operating costs**, applicable to revenues, recognised as an expense during the period, classified by their nature

The choice reflects differences in **the way the income statement can be presented**.

Where the entity discloses the amount of **operating costs** applicable to the revenues of the period, classified by their nature, then the costs recognised as an expense will be disclosed for:

(a)   Raw materials and consumables
(b)   Labour costs
(c)   Other operating costs
(d)   The net change in inventories for the period

Question	Valuation

You are the accountant at Water Pumps Co, and you have been asked to calculate the valuation of the company's inventory at cost at its year end of 30 April 20X5.

Water Pumps manufactures a range of pumps. The pumps are assembled from components bought by Water Pumps (the company does not manufacture any parts).

The company does not use a standard costing system, and work in progress and finished goods are valued as follows.

(a)   Material costs are determined from the product specification, which lists the components required to make a pump.

(b)   The company produces a range of pumps. Employees record the hours spent on assembling each type of pump, this information is input into the payroll system which prints the total hours spent each week assembling each type of pump. All employees assembling pumps are paid at the same rate and there is no overtime.

(c)   Overheads are added to the inventory value in accordance with IAS 2 *Inventories.* The financial accounting records are used to determine the overhead cost, and this is applied as a percentage based on the direct labour cost.

For direct labour costs, you have agreed that the labour expended for a unit in work in progress is half that of a completed unit.

The draft accounts show the following materials and direct labour costs in inventory.

	Raw materials	Work in progress	Finished goods
Materials ($)	74,786	85,692	152,693
Direct labour ($)		13,072	46,584

The costs incurred in April, as recorded in the financial accounting records, were as follows.

	$
Direct labour	61,320
Selling costs	43,550
Depreciation and finance costs of production machines	4,490
Distribution costs	6,570
Factory manager's wage	2,560
Other production overheads	24,820

	$
Purchasing and accounting costs relating to production	5,450
Other accounting costs	7,130
Other administration overheads	24,770

For your calculations assume that all work in progress and finished goods were produced in April 20X5 and that the company was operating at a normal level of activity.

Required

Calculate the value of overheads which should be added to work in progress and finished goods in accordance with IAS 2 *Inventories*.

Note. You should include details and a description of your workings and all figures should be calculated to the nearest $.

Answer

Calculation of overheads for inventories

Production overheads are as follows.

	$
Depreciation/finance costs	4,490
Factory manager's wage	2,560
Other production overheads	24,820
Accounting/purchasing costs	5,450
	37,320

Direct labour = $61,320

$\therefore$ Production overhead rate = $\dfrac{37,320}{61,320}$ = 60.86%

Inventory valuation

	Raw materials $	WIP $	Finished goods $	Total $
Materials	74,786	85,692	152,693	313,171
Direct labour	-	13,072	46,584	59,656
Production overhead (at 60.86% of labour)	-	7,956	28,351	36,307
	74,786	106,720	227,628	409,134

1.11 Consistency - different cost formulas for inventories

IAS 2 allows two cost formulas (FIFO or weighted average cost) for inventories that are ordinarily interchangeable or are not produced and segregated for specific projects. The issue is whether an entity may use different cost formulas for different types of inventories.

IAS 2 provides that an entity should use **the same cost formula for all inventories having similar nature and use to the entity.** For inventories with different nature or use (for example, certain commodities used in one business segment and the same type of commodities used in another business segment), different cost formulas may be justified. A difference in geographical location of inventories (and in the respective tax rules), by itself, is not sufficient to justify the use of different cost formulas.

BPP
PROFESSIONAL EDUCATION

2 IAS 11 Construction contracts

At this stage of your studies, the most difficult part of IAS 11 is the mastering of the valuation and disclosure clauses.

2.1 Introduction

Imagine that you are the accountant at a construction company. Your company is building a large tower block that will house offices, under a contract with an investment company. It will take three years to build the block and over that time you will obviously have to pay for building materials, wages of workers on the building, architects' fees and so on. You will receive periodic payments from the investment company at various predetermined stages of the construction. How do you decide, in each of the three years, **what to include as income and expenditure** for the contract in the income statement?

This is the problem tackled by IAS 11 *Construction contracts*.

2.2 Example: construction contract

A numerical example might help to illustrate the problem. Suppose that a contract is started on 1 January 20X5, with an estimated completion date of 31 December 20X6. The final contract price is $1,500,000. In the first year, to 31 December 20X5:

(a) Costs incurred amounted to $600,000.

(b) Half the work on the contract was completed.

(c) Certificates of work completed have been issued, to the value of $750,000. (*Note*. It is usual, in a construction contract, for a qualified person such as an architect or engineer to inspect the work completed, and if it is satisfactory, to issue certificates. This will then be the notification to the customer that progress payments are now due to the contractor. Progress payments are commonly the amount of valuation on the work certificates issued, minus a precautionary retention of 10%).

(d) It is estimated with reasonable certainty that further costs to completion in 20X6 will be $600,000.

What is the contract profit in 20X5, and what entries would be made for the contract at 31 December 20X5 if:

(a) Profits are deferred until the completion of the contract?

(b) A proportion of the estimated revenue and profit is credited to the income statement in 20X5?

Solution

(a) If profits were deferred until the completion of the contract in 20X6, the revenue and profit recognised on the contract in 20X5 would be nil, and the value of work in progress on 31 December 20X5 would be $600,000. IAS 11 takes the view that this policy is unreasonable, because in 20X6, the total profit of $300,000 would be recorded. Since the contract revenues are earned throughout 20X5 and 20X6, a profit of nil in 20X5 and $300,000 in 20X6 would be contrary to the accruals concept of accounting.

(b) **It is fairer to recognise revenue and profit throughout the duration of the contract.**

As at 31 December 20X5 revenue of $750,000 should be matched with cost of sales of $600,000 in the income statement, leaving an attributable profit for 20X5 of $150,000.

The only balance sheet entry as at 31 December 20X5 is a receivable of $750,000 recognising that the company is owed this amount for work done to date. No balance remains for work in progress, the whole $600,000 having been recognised in cost of sales.

2.3 What is a construction contract?

A contract which needs IAS 11 treatment does not have to last for a period of more than one year. The main point is that the contract activity **starts in one financial period and ends in another**, thus creating the problem: to which of two or more periods should contract income and costs be allocated? In fact the definition given in the IAS of a construction contract is very straightforward.

> **Construction contract.** A contract specifically negotiated for the construction of an asset or a combination of assets that are closely interrelated or interdependent in terms of their design, technology and function or their ultimate purpose or use.   *(IAS 11)*

The standard differentiates between fixed price contracts and cost plus contracts.

> - **Fixed price contract.** A contract in which the contractor agrees to a fixed contract price, or a fixed rate per unit of output, which in some cases is subject to cost escalation clauses.
>
> - **Cost plus contract.** A construction contract in which the contractor is reimbursed for allowable or otherwise defined costs, plus a percentage of these costs or a fixed fee.

Construction contracts may involve the building of one asset, eg a bridge, or a series of interrelated assets eg an oil refinery. They may also include **rendering of services** (eg architects) or restoring or demolishing an asset.

2.4 Combining and segmenting construction contracts

The standard lays out the factors which determine whether the construction of a **series of assets** under one contract should be treated as several contracts.

- **Separate proposals** are submitted for each asset
- **Separate negotiations** are undertaken for each asset; the customer can accept/reject each individually
- **Identifiable costs and revenues** can be separated for each asset

There are also circumstances where a **group of contracts** should be treated as **one single construction contract**.

- The group of contracts are negotiated as a **single package**
- Contracts are **closely interrelated**, with an overall profit margin
- The contracts are performed **concurrently** or **in a single sequence**

2.5 Contract revenue

Contract revenue will be the **amount specified in the contract**, subject to variations in the contract work, incentive payments and claims *if* these will probably give rise to revenue and *if* they can be reliably measured. The result is that contract revenue is measured at the **fair value** of received or receivable revenue.

The standard elaborates on the types of uncertainty, which depend on the outcome of future events, that affect the **measurement of contract revenue**.

- An **agreed variation** (increase/decrease)
- **Cost escalation clauses** in a fixed price contract (increase)
- **Penalties** imposed due to delays by the contractor (decrease)
- **Number of units** varies in a contract for fixed prices per unit (increase/decrease)

In the case of any variation, claim or incentive payment, two factors should be assessed to determine whether contract revenue should be recognised.

- Whether it is **probable** that the customer will accept the variation/claim, or that the contract is sufficiently advanced that the performance criteria will be met

- Whether the amount of the revenue can be **measured reliably**

2.6 Contract costs

Contract costs consist of:

- Costs relating **directly** to the contract

- Costs attributable to general contract activity which can be **allocated** to the contract, such as insurance, cost of design and technical assistance not directly related to a specific contract and construction overheads

- Any other costs which can be **charged to the customer** under the contract, which may include general administration costs and development costs

Costs that **relate directly** to a specific contract include the following.

- **Site labour costs**, including site supervision
- Costs of **materials** used in construction
- **Depreciation** of plant and equipment used on the contract
- Costs of **moving** plant, equipment and materials to and from the contract site
- Costs of **hiring** plant and equipment
- Costs of **design and technical assistance** that are directly related to the contract
- Estimated costs of **rectification and guarantee work**, including expected warranty costs
- **Claims from third parties**

General contract activity costs should be **allocated systematically and rationally**, and all costs with similar characteristics should be treated **consistently**. The allocation should be based on the **normal level** of construction activity. Borrowing costs may be attributed in this way (see IAS 23: Chapter 10).

Some costs **cannot be attributed** to contract activity and so the following should be **excluded** from construction contract costs.

- **General administration costs** (unless reimbursement is specified in the contract)
- **Selling costs**
- **R&D** (unless reimbursement is specified in the contract)
- **Depreciation** of idle plant and equipment not used on any particular contract

2.7 Recognition of contract revenue and expenses

Revenue and costs associated with a contract should be recognised according to the stage of completion of the contract at the balance sheet date, but *only when* the **outcome of the activity can be estimated reliably**. If a loss is predicted on a contract, then it should be recognised immediately. This is often known as the **percentage of completion method**.

A reliable estimate of the outcome of a construction contract can only be made when **certain conditions** have been met, and these conditions will be different for fixed price and cost plus contracts.

- **Fixed price contracts**

  - Probable that economic benefits of the contract will flow to the entity

  - Total contract revenue can be reliably measured

  - Stage of completion at the period end and costs to complete the contract can be reliably measured

  - Costs attributable to the contract can be identified clearly and be reliably measured (actual costs can be compared to previous estimates)

- **Cost plus contracts**

  - Probable that economic benefits of the contract will flow to the entity

  - Costs attributable to the contract (whether or not reimbursable) can be identified clearly and be reliably measured

The **percentage of completion method** is an application of the accruals assumption. Contract revenue is matched to the contract costs incurred in reaching the stage of completion, so revenue, costs and profit are attributed to the proportion of work completed.

We can **summarise** the treatment as follows.

- Recognise **contract revenue** as revenue in the accounting periods in which the work is performed

- Recognise **contract costs** as an expense in the accounting period in which the work to which they relate is performed

- Any **expected excess** of total contract costs over total contract revenue should be recognised as an expense immediately

- Any costs incurred which relate to **future activity** should be recognised as an asset if it is probable that they will be recovered (often called contract work in progress, ie amounts due from the customer)

- Where amounts have been recognised as contract revenue, but their **collectability** from the customer becomes doubtful, such amounts should be recognised as an expense, not a deduction from revenue

2.8 When can reliable estimates be made?

IAS 11 only allows contract revenue and costs to be recognised when the outcome of the contract can be predicted, ie when it is probable that the economic benefits attached to the contract will flow to the entity. IAS 11 states that this can only be when a contract has been agreed which establishes the following.

- The **enforceable rights** of each party in respect of the asset to be constructed
- The **consideration** that is to be exchanged
- **Terms and manner of settlement**

In addition, the entity should have an **effective internal financial budgeting and reporting system**, in order to review and revise the estimates of contract revenue and costs as the contract progresses.

2.9 Determining the stage of completion

How should you decide on the stage of completion of any contract? The standard lists several methods.

- **Proportion of contract costs incurred** for work carried out to date
- **Surveys** of work carried out
- **Physical proportion** of the contract work completed

2.10 Example: stage of completion

Centrepoint Co have a fixed price contract to build a tower block. The initial amount of revenue agreed is $220m. At the beginning of the contract on 1 January 20X6 our initial estimate of the contract costs is $200m. At the end of 20X6 our estimate of the total costs has risen to $202m.

During 20X7 the customer agrees to a variation which increases expected revenue from the contract by $5m and causes additional costs of $3m. At the end of 20X7 there are materials stored on site for use during the following period which cost $2.5m.

We have decided to determine the stage of completion of the contract by calculating the proportion that contract costs incurred for work to date bear to the latest estimated total contract costs. The contract costs incurred at the end of each year were 20X6: $52.52m, 20X7: $154.2m (including materials in store), 20X8 $205m.

Required

Calculate the stage of completion for each year of the contract and show how revenues, costs and profits will be recognised in each year.

Solution

We can summarise the financial data for each year end during the construction period as follows.

	20X6 $'000	20X7 $'000	20X8 $'000
Initial amount of revenue agreed in the contract	220,000	220,000	220,000
Variation	-	5,000	5,000
Total contract revenue	220,000	225,000	225,000
Contract costs incurred to date	52,520	154,200	205,000
Contract costs to complete	149,480	50,800	-
Total estimated contract costs	202,000	205,000	205,000
Estimated profit	18,000	20,000	20,000
Stage of completion	26.0%	74.0%	100.0%

The stage of completion has been calculated using the formula:

$$\frac{\text{Contract costs incurred to date}}{\text{Total estimated contract costs}}$$

The stage of completion in 20X7 is calculated by deducting the $2.5m of materials held for the following period from the costs incurred up to that year end, ie $154.2m – $2.5m = $151.7m. $151.7m/$205m = 74%.

Revenue, expenses and profit will be recognised in the income statements as follows.

	To date $'000	Recognised in prior years $'000	Recognised in current year $'000
20X6 Revenue ($220m × 26%)	57,200		
Costs ($202m × 26%)	52,520		
	4,680		
20X7 Revenue ($225m × 74%)	166,500	57,200	109,300
Costs ($205m × 74%)	151,700	52,520	99,180
	14,800	4,680	10,120
20X8 Revenue ($225m × 100%)	225,000	166,500	58,500
Costs ($205m × 100%)	205,000	151,700	53,300
	20,000	14,800	5,200

You can see from the above example that, when the stage of completion is determined using the contract costs incurred to date, only contract costs reflecting the work to date should be included in costs incurred to date.

- Exclude costs relating to **future activity**, eg cost of materials delivered but not yet used
- Exclude payments made to subcontractors **in advance** of work performed

2.11 Outcome of the contract cannot be predicted reliably

When the contract's outcome cannot be predicted reliably the following treatment should be followed.

- Only recognise revenue to the extent of contract costs incurred which are expected to be **recoverable**
- Recognise contract costs as an **expense** in the period they are incurred

This **no profit/no loss approach** reflects the situation near the beginning of a contract, ie the outcome cannot be reliably estimated, but it is likely that costs will be recovered.

Contract costs which **cannot be recovered** should be recognised as an expense straight away. IAS 11 lists the following situations where this might occur.

- The contract is **not fully enforceable**, ie its validity is seriously questioned
- The completion of the contract is subject to the outcome of **pending litigation or legislation**
- The contract relates to properties which will probably be **expropriated or condemned**
- The customer is **unable to meet its obligations** under the contract
- The contractor **cannot complete** the contract or in any other way meet its obligations under the contract

Where these **uncertainties cease to exist,** contract revenue and costs should be recognised as normal, ie by reference to the stage of completion.

2.12 Recognition of expected losses

Any loss on a contract should be **recognised as soon as it is foreseen**. The loss will be the amount by which total expected contract revenue is exceeded by total expected contract costs. The loss amount is not affected by whether work has started on the contract, the stage of completion of the work or profits on other contracts (unless they are related contracts treated as a single contract).

2.13 Changes in estimates

The effect of any change in the estimate of contract revenue or costs or the outcome of a contract should be accounted for as a **change in accounting estimate** under IAS 8 *Accounting policies, changes in accounting estimates and errors.*

2.14 Example: changes in estimates

The example below shows the effect of a change in estimate of costs on the figures that appear in the income statement and balance sheet.

Battersby Co enters into a three-year contract.

Estimated revenue = $20,000
Estimated total cost = $16,000.

However, during Year 2, management revises its estimate of total costs incurred and thus the outcome of the contract. As a result, during Year 2, a loss is recognised on the contract for the year, even though the contract will still be profitable overall.

	Year 1	Year 2	Year 3
	$	$	$
Estimated revenue	20,000	20,000	20,000
Estimated total cost	16,000	18,000	18,000
Estimated total profit	4,000	2,000	2,000
Cost incurred to date	$8,000	$13,500	$18,000
Percentage of completion	50%	75%	100%
Recognised profit/(loss) for year	$2,000	($500)	$500
Cumulative recognised profit	$2,000	$1,500	$2,000

Progress billings of $8,000, $8,000 and $4,000 are made on the last day of each year and are received in the first month of the following year. The balance sheet asset at the end of each year is:

	Year 1	Year 2	Year 3
	$	$	$
Costs incurred	8,000	13,500	18,000
Recognised profits	2,000	2,000	2,500
(Recognised losses)	-	(500)	(500)
(Progress billings)	(8,000)	(16,000)	(20,000)
Amount recognised as an asset/(liability)	2,000	(1,000)	0

In addition, at each year end, the entity recognises a trade receivable for the amount outstanding at the end of the year of $8,000, $8,000 and $4,000.

2.15 Disclosures

The following should be disclosed under IAS 11

- Contract revenue recognised as **revenue in the period**
- **Methods used** to determine the **contract revenue**
- **Methods used** to determine **stage of completion** of contracts which are in progress

For **contracts in progress** at the balance sheet date, show the following.

- **Total costs incurred** and recognised profits (less recognised losses) to date
- **Advances** received
- **Retentions** (progress billings not paid until the satisfaction of certain conditions)

Amounts owed by customers and to sub-contractors for contract work must be **shown gross as an asset and a liability respectively**. These are determined by comparing the total costs incurred plus recognised profits to the sum of recognised losses and progress billings, as you will see in the question below.

Any **contingent gains or losses**, eg due to warranty costs, claims, penalties or possible losses, should be disclosed in accordance with IAS 37 *Provisions, contingent liabilities and contingent assets*.

2.16 Example: disclosure

Suppose that Tract Ore Co finishes its first year of operations in which all contract costs were paid in cash and all progress billings and advances were received in cash. For contracts W, X and Z only:

(a) contract costs include costs of materials purchased for use in the contract which have not been used at the period end; and

(b) customers have advanced sums to the contractor for work not yet performed.

The relevant figures for all contracts at the end of Tract Ore's first year of trading are as follows.

	V $m	W $m	X $m	Y $m	Z $m	Total $m
Contract revenue recognised	37.7	135.2	98.8	52.0	14.3	338.0
Contract expenses recognised	28.6	117.0	91.0	65.0	14.3	315.9
Expected losses recognised	-	-	-	10.4	7.8	18.2
Recognised profits less recognised losses	9.1	18.2	7.8	(23.4)	(7.8)	3.9
Contract costs incurred in the period	28.6	132.6	17.0	65.0	26.0	369.2
Contract expenses recognised	28.6	117.0	28.6	65.0	14.3	315.9
Contract expenses that relate to future activity recognised as an asset	-	15.6	26.0	-	11.7	53.3
Contract revenue	37.7	135.2	98.8	52.0	14.3	338.0
Progress billings	26.0	135.2	98.8	46.8	14.3	321.1
Unbilled contract revenue	11.7	-	-	5.2	-	16.9
Advances	-	20.8	5.2	-	6.5	32.5

Required

Show the figures that should be disclosed under IAS 11.

Solution

Following IAS 11, the required disclosures would be as follows.

	$m
Contract revenue recognised in the period	338.0
Contract costs incurred and recognised profits (less recognised losses) to date (W)	373.1
Advances received	32.5
Gross amount due from customers for contract work: asset (W)	57.2
Gross amount due to customers for contract work: liability (W)	(5.2)

Workings

These amounts are calculated as follows.

	V $m	W $m	X $m	Y $m	Z $m	Total $m
Contract costs incurred	28.6	132.6	117.0	65.0	26.0	369.2
Recognised profits less recognised losses	9.1	18.2	7.8	(23.4)	(7.8)	3.9
	37.7	150.8	124.8	41.6	18.2	373.1
Progress billings	26.0	135.2	98.8	46.8	14.3	321.1
Due from customers	11.7	15.6	26.0		3.9	57.2
Due to customers				(5.2)		(5.2)

2.17 Section summary

In valuing long-term contracts and the other disclosures required under IAS 11, an organised approach is essential. The following suggested method breaks the process down into five logical steps.

Step 1 **Compare the contract value** and the **total costs** expected to be incurred on the contract. If a loss is foreseen (that is, if the costs to date plus estimated costs to completion exceed the contract value) then it must be charged against profits. If a loss has already been charged in previous years, then only the difference between the loss as previously and currently estimated need be charged.

Step 2 Using the percentage completed to date (or other formula given in the question), calculate sales revenue **attributable** to the contract for the period (for example percentage complete × total contract value, less of course, revenue taken in previous periods).

Step 3 **Calculate the cost of sales** on the contract for the period.

	$
Total contract costs × percentage complete (or follow instructions in question)	X
Less any costs charged in previous periods	(X)
	X
Add foreseeable losses in full (not previously charged)	X
Cost of sales on contract for the period	X

Step 4 **Deduct the cost of sales** for the period as calculated above (including any foreseeable loss) from work in progress at cost up to the total balance on the account. If the cost of sales transfer exceeds this balance, then show the excess as a provision for liabilities and charges or as an accrual.

Step 5 **Calculate cumulative sales revenue** on the contract (the total sales revenue recorded in respect of the contract in the income statement of all accounting periods since the inception of the contract). Compare this with total progress payments to date.

    (a)   If sales revenue exceeds advances from customers, an amount recoverable on the contracts is established and separately disclosed within receivables.

    (b)   If advances from customers as an asset exceed cumulative sales revenue then the excess is disclosed within payables.

2.18 Summary of accounting treatment

The following summarises the accounting treatment for long-term contracts - **make sure that you understand it.**

2.18.1 Income statement

    (a)   **Revenue and costs**

        (i)   Sales revenue and associated costs should be recorded in the income statement as the contract activity progresses.

        (ii)   Include an appropriate proportion of total contract value as sales revenue in the income statement.

        (iii)   The costs incurred in reaching that stage of completion are matched with this sales revenue, resulting in the reporting of results which can be attributed to the proportion of work completed.

        (iv)   Sales revenue is the value of work carried out to date.

    (b)   **Profit recognised in the contract**

        (i)   It must reflect the proportion of work carried out.

        (ii)   It should take into account any known inequalities in profitability in the various stages of a contract.

2.18.2 Balance sheet

(a)   **Inventories**

	$
Costs to date	X
Less transfer to income statement	(X)
	X
Less foreseeable losses	(X)
	X
Less advances in excess of revenue	(X)
WIP	X

(b)   **Receivables**

	$
Cumulative revenue recognised	X
Less advances	(X)
Amount recoverable on contracts	X

(c)   **Payables**. Where progress billings exceed both cumulative turnover and net WIP the excess should be included in payables under 'payments on account'.

(d)   **Provisions**. To the extent foreseeable future losses exceed WIP, the losses should be provided.

Question	Balance sheet disclosure

The main business of Santolina Co is construction contracts. At the end of September 20X3 there are two uncompleted contracts on the books, details of which are as follows.

CONTRACT	A	B
Date commenced	1.9.X3	1.4.X1
Expected completed date	23.12.X3	23.12.X3
	$	$
Final contract price	70,000	290,000
Costs to 30.9.X3	21,000	210,450
Value of work certified to 30.9.X3	20,000	230,000
Progress billings to 30.9.X3	20,000	210,000
Cash received to 30.9.X3	18,000	194,000
Estimated costs to completion at 30.9.X3	41,000	20,600

Required

Prepare calculations showing the amounts to be included in the balance sheet at 30 September 20X3 in respect of the above contracts.

Answer

Contract A is a short-term contract and will be included in the balance sheet as work in progress at cost less amounts received and receivable $(21,000 – 20,000) ie $1,000.

Contract B is a long-term contract and will be included in the balance sheet at cost plus attributable profit less amounts received and receivable.

The estimated final profit is:

	$
Final contract price	290,000
Less: costs to date	(210,450)
estimated future costs	(20,600)
Estimated final profit	58,950

The attributable profit is found as follows.

$$\text{Estimated final profit} \quad \times \quad \frac{\text{Work certified}}{\text{Total contract price}}$$

$$\$58,950 \quad \times \quad \frac{230,000}{290,000}$$

Attributable profit = $46,753

Long-term contract work in progress

CONTRACT B

	$
Costs to date	210,450
Attributable profit	46,753
Anticipated loss	-
	257,203
Progress payments received and receivable	210,000
Long-term construction contract	47,203

Exam focus point

A question is more likely to be set on long-term construction contracts than on inventory or short term WIP, simply because inventory and short term WIP were covered in depth for Paper 1.1.

Question

IAS 11 calculations

Haggrun Co has two contracts in progress, the details of which are as follows.

	Happy (profitable)	Grumpy (loss-making)
	$'000	$'000
Total contract price	300	300
Costs incurred to date	90	150
Estimated costs to completion	135	225
Progress payments invoiced and received	116	116

Required

Show extracts from the income statement and the balance sheet for each contract, assuming they are both:

(a) 40% complete; and
(b) 36% complete.

Answer

Happy contract

(a) *40% complete*

	$'000
Income statement	
Sales revenue (40% × 300)	120
Cost of sales (40% × 225)	90
Gross profit	30
Balance sheet	
Receivables (120 – 116)	4
Construction contract in progress (90 – 90)	-

(b) *36% complete*

	$'000
Income statement	
Sales revenue (36% × 300)	108
Cost of sales (36% × 225)	81
Gross profit	27
Balance sheet	
Receivables (108 – 116 = –8)	-
Construction contract in progress (90 – 81) =	9
Payables	8

Grumpy contract

(a) *40% complete*

Working

	$'000	$'000
Total contract price		300
Less: costs to date	150	
estimated costs to completion	225	
		375
Foreseeable loss		(75)

	$'000
Income statement	
Sales revenue (40% × 300)	120
Cost of sales (40% × 375)	(150)
	(30)
Provision for future losses (bal fig)	(45)
Gross loss	(75)
Balance sheet	$'000
Receivables (120 – 116)	4
Construction contract in progress (150 – 150)	-
Provision for future losses	(45)

BPP
PROFESSIONAL EDUCATION

(b)   *36% complete*

	$'000
Income statement	
Sales revenue (36% × 300)	108
Cost of sales (36% × 375)	(135)
	(27)
Provision for future losses (balancing figure)	(48)
Gross loss	(75)
Balance sheet	
Provisions: provisions for future losses*	41
*Provision for future losses	48
Less construction contract in progress (150 – 135 – 8)	7
	41

Chapter roundup

- IAS 2 *Inventories* requires that the balance sheet should show **inventories** classified in a manner appropriate to the entity. Common **classifications** are:

  Merchandise
  Production supplies
  Materials
  Work in progress
  Finished goods

- The use of **LIFO** is **prohibited** under the revised IAS 2.

- Full details are required of inventory carried at **NRV** as well as the reversal of any previous write down.

- The rules for calculating accounting entries on **construction contracts** can be summarised as follows.

  – Sales revenue taken on construction contracts should be debited to receivables (and credited to the income statement).

  – The amount at which contract work in progress is stated in accounts should be cost, less cost of sales to date, including any foreseeable losses.

  – Progress billings received and receivable should first be credited to receivables and any excess to payables.

- At this stage of your studies the most difficult aspect of IAS 11 to be mastered is the **valuation and disclosure of construction contracts**.

- You must be able both to calculate all the balances to be included in accounts and to discuss the reasons for IAS 11's provisions, along with alternative possibilities.

Quick quiz

1   Net realisable value = Selling price **less** .... **less** ....

2   Which inventory costing method is allowed under IAS 2?

    (a)   FIFO

    (b)   LIFO

3   Any expected loss on a construction contract must be recognised, in full, in the year it was identified.

    True   ☐

    False   ☐

4   List the five steps to be taken when valuing construction contracts.

5   Which items in the income statement and balance sheet are potentially affected by construction contracts?

Answers to quick quiz

1   Net realisable value = selling price costs to completion **less** costs necessary to make the sale.

2   (a) FIFO. LIFO is not allowed.

3   True

4   See paragraph 2.17

5   Income statement: revenue and cost of sales.
      Balance sheet: inventories, receivables, payables and provisions

Now try the question below from the Exam Question Bank

Number	Level	Marks	Time
Q8	Introductory	n/a	n/a

BPP
PROFESSIONAL EDUCATION

Financial instruments and borrowing costs

Topic list	Syllabus reference
1 Financial instruments	3(a), (f)
2 Presentation of financial instruments	3(a), (f)
3 Disclosure of financial instruments	3(a), (f)
4 Recognition of financial instruments	3(a), (f)
5 Measurement of financial instruments	3(a), (f)
6 IAS 23 *Borrowing costs*	3(f)

Introduction

IAS 32 is about a very complex issue, but you will only be asked
straightforward questions about the basic issues in the Paper 2.5 exam.
Presentation and disclosure issues are important but the fundamental
questions of recognition and measurement of financial instruments are not
tackled until Paper 3.6, so you should skim read sections 4 and 5.

The issue of the **capitalisation of borrowing costs** is closely related to tangible
non-current assets and you should refer back to Chapter 5.

Study guide

Section 8 – Share capital and reserves

- Explain the need for an accounting standard on financial instruments
- Distinguish between debt and equity capital
- Apply the requirements of relevant accounting standards to the issuing and finance costs of:
  - equity and preference shares
  - debt instruments with no conversion rights
  - convertible debt (compound financial instruments)

Exam guide

Financial instruments are generally tested as part of a question rather than as a full question.

Exam focus point

> Although the very complexity of this topic makes it a highly likely subject for an exam question in Paper 3.6, there are limits as to how complicated and detailed a question the examiner can set at Paper 2.5 with any realistic expectation of students being able to answer it. You should therefore concentrate on the essential points. To date, financial instruments have mainly been examined within a larger scenario based question. However, a more detailed question with a main focus on this topic cannot be ruled out.

1 Financial instruments

FAST FORWARD

Financial instruments can be very complex, particularly derivative instruments.

1.1 Introduction

If you read the financial press you will probably be aware of **rapid international expansion** in the use of financial instruments. These vary from straightforward, traditional instruments, eg bonds, through to various forms of so-called 'derivative instruments'.

We can perhaps summarise the reasons why a project on accounting for financial instruments was considered necessary as follows.

- (a) The **significant growth of financial instruments** over recent years has outstripped the development of guidance for their accounting.

- (b) The topic is of **international concern**, other national standard-setters are involved as well as the IASB.

- (c) There have been recent **high-profile disasters** involving derivatives (eg Barings) which, while not caused by accounting failures, have raised questions about accounting and disclosure practices.

The old IASC dealt with financial instruments in two stages:

- (a) IAS 32 *Financial instruments: disclosure and presentation*, which deals with:

  - (i) The classification of financial instruments between liabilities and equity
  - (ii) Presentation of certain compound instruments
  - (iii) The disclosure of information about financial instruments

(b)   IAS 39 *Financial instruments: recognition and measurement*, which deals with:

(i)   Recognition and derecognition

(ii)   The measurement of financial instruments

(iii)   Hedge accounting

1.2 Definitions

The most important definitions are common to both standards.

Key terms

- **Financial instrument.** Any contract that gives rise to both a financial asset of one entity and a financial liability or equity instrument of another entity.

- **Financial asset.** Any asset that is:

(a)   cash

(b)   an equity instrument of another entity

(c)   a contractual right to receive cash or another financial asset from another entity; or to exchange financial instruments with another entity under conditions that are potentially favourable to the entity, or

(d)   a contract that will or may be settled in the entity's own equity instruments and is:

    (i)   a non-derivative for which the entity is or may be obliged to receive a variable number of the entity's own equity instruments; or

    (ii)   a derivative that will or may be settled other than by the exchange of a fixed amount of cash or another financial asset for a fixed number of the entity's own equity instruments.

- **Financial liability.** Any liability that is:

(a)   a contractual obligation:

    (i)   to deliver cash or another financial asset to another entity, or

    (ii)   to exchange financial instruments with another entity under conditions that are potentially unfavourable; or

(b)   a contract that will or may be settled in the entity's own equity instruments and is:

    (i)   a non-derivative for which the entity is or may be obliged to deliver a variable number of the entity's own equity instruments; or

    (ii)   a derivative that will or may be settled other than by the exchange of a fixed amount of cash or another financial asset for a fixed number of the entity's own equity instruments.

- **Equity instrument.** Any contract that evidences a residual interest in the assets of an entity after deducting all of its liabilities.

- **Fair value** is the amount for which an asset could be exchanged, or a liability settled, between knowledgeable, willing parties in an arm's length transaction.

- **Derivative.** A financial instrument or other contract with all three of the following characteristics:

(a)   its value changes in response to the change in a specified interest rate, financial instrument price, commodity price, foreign exchange rate, index of prices or rates, credit rating or credit index, or other variable (sometimes called the 'underlying');

Key terms

> (b)   it requires no initial net investment or an initial net investment that is smaller than would be required for other types of contracts that would be expected to have a similar response to changes in market factors; and
>
> (c)   it is settled at a future date.   *(IAS 32 and IAS 39)*

Exam focus point

> These definitions are very important – particularly the first three – so learn them.

We should clarify some points arising from these definitions. Firstly, one or two terms above should be themselves defined.

(a)   A '**contract**' need not be in writing, but it must comprise an agreement that has 'clear economic consequences' and which the parties to it cannot avoid, usually because the agreement is enforceable in law.

(b)   An '**entity**' here could be an individual, partnership, incorporated body or government agency.

The definitions of **financial assets** and **financial liabilities** may seem rather circular, referring as they do to the terms financial asset and financial instrument. The point is that there may be a chain of contractual rights and obligations, but it will lead ultimately to the receipt or payment of cash *or* the acquisition or issue of an equity instrument.

Examples of **financial assets** include:

(a)   Trade receivables
(b)   Options
(c)   Shares (when held as an investment)

Examples of **financial liabilities** include:

(a)   Trade payables
(b)   Debenture loans payable
(c)   Redeemable preference (non-equity) shares
(d)   Forward contracts standing at a loss

As we have already noted, financial instruments include both of the following.

(a)   **Primary instruments**: eg receivables, payables and equity securities

(b)   **Derivative instruments**: eg financial options, futures and forwards, interest rate swaps and currency swaps, **whether recognised or unrecognised**

IAS 32 makes it clear that the following items are *not* financial instruments.

(a)   **Physical assets**, eg inventories, property, plant and equipment, leased assets and **intangible assets** (patents, trademarks etc)

(b)   **Prepaid expenses**, deferred revenue and most warranty obligations

(c)   Liabilities or assets that are **not contractual** in nature

(d)   Contractual rights/obligations that **do not involve transfer of a financial asset**, eg commodity futures contracts

Definitions

Can you give the reasons why physical assets and prepaid expenses do not qualify as financial instruments?

Answer

Refer to the definitions of financial assets and liabilities given above.

(a) **Physical assets**: control of these creates an opportunity to generate an inflow of cash or other assets, but it does not give rise to a present right to receive cash or other financial assets.

(b) **Prepaid expenses, etc**: the future economic benefit is the receipt of goods/services rather than the right to receive cash or other financial assets.

Contingent rights and obligations meet the definition of financial assets and financial liabilities respectively, even though many do not qualify for recognition in financial statements. This is because the contractual rights or obligations exist because of a past transaction or event (eg assumption of a guarantee).

1.3 Derivatives

A **derivative** is a financial instrument that **derives** its value from the price or rate of an underlying item. Common **examples** of derivatives include the following:

(a) **Forward contracts**: agreements to buy or sell an asset at a fixed price at a fixed future date

(b) **Futures contracts**: similar to forward contracts except that contracts are standardised and traded on an exchange

(c) **Options**: rights (but not obligations) for the option holder to exercise at a pre-determined price; the option writer loses out if the option is exercised

(d) **Swaps**: agreements to swap one set of cash flows for another (normally interest rate or currency swaps)

The nature of derivatives often gives rise to **particular problems**. The **value** of a derivative (and the amount at which it is eventually settled) depends on **movements** in an underlying item (such as an exchange rate). This means that settlement of a derivative can lead to a very different result from the one originally envisaged. A company which has derivatives is exposed to **uncertainty and risk** (potential for gain or loss) and this can have a very material effect on its financial performance, financial position and cash flows.

Yet because a derivative contract normally has **little or no initial cost**, under traditional accounting it **may not be recognised** in the financial statements at all. Alternatively it may be recognised at an amount which bears no relation to its current value. This is clearly **misleading** and leaves users of the financial statements unaware of the **level of risk** that the company faces. IASs 32 and 39 were developed in order to correct this situation.

1.4 Section summary

- Two accounting standards are relevant:

    - **IAS 32**: *Financial instruments: Disclosure and presentation*
    - **IAS 39**: *Financial instruments: Recognition and measurement*

- The definitions of **financial asset, financial liability** and **equity instrument** are fundamental to IAS 32 and IAS 39.
- Financial instruments include:
  - **Primary** instruments
  - **Derivative** instruments

2 Presentation of financial instruments

The objective of IAS 32 is:

'to enhance financial statement users' understanding of the significance of on-balance-sheet and off-balance-sheet financial instruments to an entity's financial position, performance and cash flows.'

2.1 Scope

IAS 32 should be applied in the presentation and disclosure of **all types of financial instruments**, whether recognised or unrecognised.

Certain items are **excluded** for example subsidiaries, associates and joint ventures, pensions and insurance contracts.

2.2 Liabilities and equity

The main thrust of IAS 32 here is that financial instruments should be presented according to their **substance, not merely their legal form**. In particular, entities which issue financial instruments should classify them (or their component parts) as **either financial liabilities, or equity**.

The classification of a financial instrument as a liability or as equity depends on the following.

- The **substance of the contractual arrangement** on initial recognition
- The definitions of a **financial liability** and an **equity instrument**

How should a **financial liability be distinguished from an equity instrument**? The critical feature of a **liability** is an **obligation** to transfer economic benefit. Therefore a financial instrument is a financial liability if there is a **contractual obligation** on the issuer either to deliver cash or another financial asset to the holder or to exchange another financial instrument with the holder under potentially unfavourable conditions to the issuer.

The financial liability exists **regardless of the way in which the contractual obligation will be settled**. The issuer's ability to satisfy an obligation may be restricted, eg by lack of access to foreign currency, but this is irrelevant as it does not remove the issuer's obligation or the holder's right under the instrument.

Where the above critical feature is *not* met, then the financial instrument is an **equity instrument**. IAS 32 explains that although the holder of an equity instrument may be entitled to a *pro rata* share of any distributions out of equity, the issuer does *not* have a contractual obligation to make such a distribution.

Although substance and legal form are often **consistent with each other**, this is not always the case. In particular, a financial instrument may have the legal form of equity, but in substance it is in fact a liability. Other instruments may combine features of both equity instruments and financial liabilities.

For example, many entities issue **preferred shares** which must be **redeemed** by the issuer for a fixed (or determinable) amount at a fixed (or determinable) future date. Alternatively, the holder may have the right to require the issuer to redeem the shares at or after a certain date for a fixed amount. In such cases, the issuer has an **obligation**. Therefore the instrument is a **financial liability** and should be classified as such.

The classification of the financial instrument is made when it is **first recognised** and this classification will continue until the financial instrument is removed from the entity's balance sheet.

2.3 Compound financial instruments

Some financial instruments contain both a liability and an equity element. In such cases, IAS 32 requires the component parts of the instrument to be **classified separately**, according to the substance of the contractual arrangement and the definitions of a financial liability and an equity instrument.

One of the most common types of compound instrument is **convertible debt**. This creates a primary financial liability of the issuer and grants an option to the holder of the instrument to convert it into an equity instrument (usually ordinary shares) of the issuer. This is the economic equivalent of the issue of conventional debt plus a warrant to acquire shares in the future.

Although in theory there are several possible ways of calculating the split, IAS 32 requires the following method:

(a) Calculate the value for the liability component.

(b) Deduct this from the instrument as a whole to leave a residual value for the equity component.

The reasoning behind this approach is that an entity's equity is its residual interest in its assets amount after deducting all its liabilities.

The **sum of the carrying amounts** assigned to liability and equity will always be equal to the carrying amount that would be ascribed to the instrument **as a whole**.

2.4 Example: valuation of compound instruments

Rathbone Co issues 2,000 convertible bonds at the start of 20X2. The bonds have a three year term, and are issued at par with a face value of $1,000 per bond, giving total proceeds of $2,000,000. Interest is payable annually in arrears at a nominal annual interest rate of 6%. Each bond is convertible at any time up to maturity into 250 common shares.

When the bonds are issued, the prevailing market interest rate for similar debt without conversion options is 9%. At the issue date, the market price of one common share is $3. The dividends expected over the three year term of the bonds amount to 14c per share at the end of each year. The risk-free annual interest rate for a three year term is 5%.

Required

What is the value of the equity component in the bond?

Solution

The liability component is valued first, and the difference between the proceeds of the bond issue and the fair value of the liability is assigned to the equity component. The present value of the liability component is calculated using a discount rate of 9%, the market interest rate for similar bonds having no conversion rights, as shown.

	$
Present value of the principal: $2,000,000 payable at the end of three years	1,544,367

$$(\$2m \times \frac{1}{(1.09)^3})^*$$

Present value of the interest: $120,000 payable annually in arrears for three years	303,755

$$(\$120,000 \times \frac{1-(1.09)^{-3}}{0.09})^*$$

Total liability component	1,848,122
Equity component (balancing figure)	151,878
Proceeds of the bond issue	2,000,000

* These figures can be obtained from discount and annuity tables.

The split between the liability and equity components remains the same throughout the term of the instrument, even if there are changes in the **likelihood of the option being exercised.** This is because it is not always possible to predict how a holder will behave. The issuer continues to have an obligation to make future payments until conversion, maturity of the instrument or some other relevant transaction takes place.

2.5 Interest, dividends, losses and gains

As well as looking at balance sheet presentation, IAS 32 considers how financial instruments affect the income statement (and movements in equity). The treatment varies according to whether interest, dividends, losses or gains relate to a financial liability or an equity instrument.

(a)   Interest, dividends, losses and gains relating to a financial instrument (or component part) classified as a **financial liability** should be recognised as **income or expense** in profit or loss.

(b)   Distributions to holders of a financial instrument classified as an **equity instrument** should be **debited directly to equity** by the issuer.

(c)   **Transaction costs** of an equity transaction shall be accounted for as a **deduction from equity** (unless they are directly attributable to the acquisition of a business, in which case they are accounted for under IFRS 3).

You should look at the requirements of IAS 1 *Presentation of financial statements* for further details of disclosure, and IAS 12 *Income taxes* for disclosure of tax effects.

2.6 Section summary

- Issuers of financial instruments must classify them as **liabilities** or **equity**

- The **substance** of the financial instrument is more important than its **legal form**

- The **critical feature of a financial liability** is the contractual obligation to deliver cash or another financial asset

- **Compound instruments** are split into equity and liability parts and presented accordingly

- **Interest, dividends, losses and gains** are treated according to whether they relate to a financial liability or an equity instrument

3 Disclosure of financial instruments

> One of the main purposes of IAS 32 is to provide full and useful disclosures relating to financial instruments. IFRS 7 revises, enhances and replaces the disclosures in IAS 30 and 32.

As well as specific monetary disclosures, **narrative commentary** by issuers is encouraged by the Standard. This will enable users to understand management's attitude to risk, whatever the current transactions involving financial instruments are at the period end.

3.1 Different aspects of risk

In undertaking transactions in financial instruments, an entity may assume or transfer to another party one or more of **different types of financial risk** as defined below. The disclosures required by the standard show the extent to which an entity is exposed to these different types of risk, relating to both recognised and unrecognised financial instruments.

Key terms

- **Market risk**. There are three types of market risk: currency risk, interest rate risk and price risk.

    - **Currency risk** is the risk that the value of a financial instrument will fluctuate due to changes in foreign exchange rates.

    - **Interest rate risk** is the risk that the value of a financial instrument will fluctuate due to changes in market interest rates.

    - **Price risk** is the risk that the value of a financial instrument will fluctuate as a result of changes in market prices whether those changes are caused by factors specific to the individual instrument or its issuer or factors affecting all securities traded in the market.

    The term 'market risk' embodies not only the potential for loss but also the potential for gain.

- **Credit risk**. The risk that one party to a financial instrument will fail to discharge an obligation and cause the other party to incur a financial loss.

- **Liquidity risk** (or funding risk). The risk that an entity will encounter difficulty in raising funds to meet commitments associated with financial instruments. Liquidity risk may result from an inability to sell a financial asset quickly at close to its fair value.

- **Cash flow interest rate risk**. The risk that future cash flows of a financial instrument will fluctuate because of changes in market interest rates. In the case of a floating rate debt instrument, for example, such fluctuations result in a change in the effective interest rate of the financial instrument, usually without a corresponding change in its fair value.

(IAS 32)

The standard does not prescribe the **format or location** for disclosure of information. A combination of narrative descriptions and specific quantified data should be given, as appropriate.

The **level of detail** required is a matter of judgement. Where a large number of very similar financial instrument transactions are undertaken, these may be grouped together. Conversely, a single significant transaction may require full disclosure.

Classes of instruments will be grouped together by management in a manner appropriate to the information to be disclosed.

Information must be disclosed about the following.

    (a)   Risk management policies and hedging activities
    (b)   Terms, conditions and accounting policies
    (c)   Interest rate risk

(d)   Credit risk

(e)   Fair value

(f)   Material items of income, expense, gains and losses resulting from financial assets and liabilities.

Exam focus point

The examiner has indicated that he will not set questions about the **financial risks** of financial instruments.

4 Recognition of financial instruments

FAST FORWARD

IAS 39 *Financial instruments: Recognition and measurement* establishes principles for recognising and measuring financial assets and financial liabilities.

Exam focus point

IAS 39 is possibly the most controversial or least satisfactory, of the core standards which IOSCO endorsed in May 2000. The core standards approved included all the then current IASs, except IAS 15, IAS 26, IAS 30, IAS 40 and IAS 41.

4.1 Scope

IAS 39 applies to **all entities** and to **all types of financial instruments except** those specifically excluded, for example investments in subsidiaries, associates and joint ventures.

4.2 Initial recognition

A financial asset or financial liability should be recognised on the balance sheet when the reporting entity becomes a party to the contractual provisions of the instrument.

Point to note

An important consequence of this is that all derivatives should be recognised on the balance sheet.

Notice that this is **different** from the recognition criteria in the *Framework* and in most other standards. Items are normally recognised when there is a probable inflow or outflow of resources and the item has a cost or value that can be measured reliably.

4.3 Example: initial recognition

An entity has entered into two separate contracts:

(a)   a firm commitment (an order) to buy a specific quantity of iron

(b)   a forward contract to buy a specific quantity of iron at a specified price on a specified date.

Contract (a) is a **normal trading contract**. The entity does not recognise a liability for the iron until the goods have actually been delivered. (Note that this contract is not a financial instrument because it involves a physical asset, rather than a financial asset.)

Contract (b) is a **financial instrument**. Under IAS 39, the entity recognises a financial liability (an obligation to deliver cash) on the **commitment date**, rather than waiting for the closing date in which the exchange takes place.

Note that planned future transactions, no matter how likely, are not assets and liabilities of an entity – the entity has not yet become a party to the contract.

4.4 Derecognition

Derecognition is the removal of a previously recognised financial instrument from an entity's balance sheet.

An entity should derecognise a **financial asset** when:

    (a)   the **contractual rights** to the cash flows from the financial asset **expire**; or

    (b)   it **transfers substantially all the risks and rewards of ownership** of the financial asset to another party.

Question   Examples

Can you think of an example of a situation in which:

    (a)   an entity has transferred substantially all the risks and rewards of ownership?
    (b)   an entity has retained substantially all the risks and rewards of ownership?

Answer

IAS 39 includes the following examples.

    (a)   (i)   An unconditional sale of a financial asset

            (ii)   A sale of a financial asset together with an option to repurchase the financial asset at its fair value at the time of repurchase

    (b)   (i)   A sale and repurchase transaction where the repurchase price is a fixed price or the sale price plus a lender's return

            (ii)   A sale of a financial asset together with a total return swap that transfers the market risk exposure back to the entity

Exam focus point

> The principle here is that of **substance over form**.

An entity should derecognise a **financial liability** when it is **extinguished** – ie, when the obligation specified in the contract is discharged or cancelled or expires.

It is possible for only **part** of a financial asset or liability to be derecognised. This is allowed if the part comprises:

    (a)   only specifically identified cash flows; or
    (b)   only a fully proportionate (pro rata) share of the total cash flows.

For example, if an entity holds a bond it has the right to two separate sets of cash inflows: those relating to the principal and those relating to the interest. It could sell the right to receive the interest to another party while retaining the right to receive the principal.

On derecognition, the amount to be included in net profit or loss for the period is calculated as follows:

Formula to learn

	$	$
Carrying amount of asset/liability (or the portion of asset/liability) transferred		X
Less: Proceeds received/paid	X	
Any cumulative gain or loss reported in equity	X	
		(X)
Difference to net profit/loss		X

Where only part of a financial asset is derecognised, the carrying amount of the asset should be allocated between the part retained and the part transferred based on their relative fair values on the date of transfer. A gain or loss should be recognised based on the proceeds for the portion transferred.

4.5 Section summary

- All financial assets and liabilities should be recognised on the balance sheet, including derivatives.

- Financial assets should be derecognised when the rights to the cash flows from the asset expire or where substantially all the risks and rewards of ownership are transferred to another party.

- Financial liabilities should be derecognised when they are extinguished.

5 Measurement of financial instruments

FAST FORWARD

All financial assets should be initially measured at cost.

5.1 Initial measurement

Financial instruments are initially measured at the **fair value** of the consideration given or received (ie, **cost**) **plus** (in most cases) **transaction costs** that are **directly attributable** to the acquisition or issue of the financial instrument.

The **exception** to this rule is where a financial instrument is designated as **at fair value through profit or loss** (this term is explained below). In this case, **transaction costs** are **not** added to fair value at initial recognition.

The fair value of the consideration is normally the transaction price or market prices. If market prices are not reliable, the fair value may be **estimated** using a valuation technique (for example, by discounting cash flows).

5.2 Subsequent measurement

For the purposes of measuring a financial asset held subsequent to initial recognition, IAS 39 classifies financial assets into four categories defined here.

Key terms

A **financial asset or liability at fair value through profit or loss** meets either of the following conditions:

(a)   It is classified as held for trading. A financial instrument is classified as held for trading if it is:

   (i)   acquired or incurred principally for the purpose of selling or repurchasing it in the near term;

   (ii)   part of a portfolio of identified financial instruments that are managed together and for which there is evidence of a recent actual pattern of short-term profit-taking; or

(iii)   a derivative (unless it is a designated and effective hedging instrument).

(b)   Upon initial recognition it is designated by the entity as at fair value through profit or loss. Any financial instrument may be so designated when it is initially recognised except for investments in equity instruments that do not have a quoted market price in an active market and whose fair value cannot be reliably measured.

Held-to-maturity investments are non-derivative financial assets with fixed or determinable payments and fixed maturity that an entity has the positive intent and ability to hold to maturity other than:

(a)   those that the entity upon initial recognition designates as at fair value through profit or loss;

(b)   those that the entity designates as available for sale; and

(c)   those that meet the definition of loans and receivables.

Key terms

Loans and receivables are non-derivative financial assets with fixed or determinable payments that are not quoted in an active market, other than:

(a)   those that the entity intends to sell immediately or in the near term, which should be classified as held for trading and those that the entity upon initial recognition designates as at fair value through profit or loss;

(b)   those that the entity upon initial recognition designates as available-for-sale; or

(c)   those for which the holder may not recover substantially all of the initial investment, other than because of credit deterioration, which shall be classified as available for sale.

An interest acquired in a pool of assets that are not loans or receivables (for example, an interest in a mutual fund or a similar fund) is not a loan or a receivable.

Available-for-sale financial assets are those financial assets that are not:

(a)   loans and receivables originated by the entity,

(b)   held-to-maturity investments, or

(c)   financial assets at fair value through profit or loss.   *(IAS 39)*

After initial recognition, all financial assets should be **remeasured to fair value**, without any deduction for transaction costs that may be incurred on sale or other disposal, except for:

(a)   **Loans and receivables**

(b)   **Held to maturity investments**

(c)   Investments in **equity instruments** that do not have a quoted market price in an active market and whose **fair value cannot be reliably measured** and derivatives that are linked to and must be settled by delivery of such unquoted equity instruments

Loans and receivables and **held to maturity investments** should be measured at **amortised cost** using the **effective interest method**.

Key terms

Amortised cost of a financial asset or financial liability is the amount at which the financial asset or liability is measured at initial recognition minus principal repayments, plus or minus the cumulative amortisation of any difference between that initial amount and the maturity amount, and minus any write-down (directly or through the use of an allowance account) for impairment or uncollectability.

The **effective interest method** is a method of calculating the amortised cost of a financial instrument and of allocating the interest income or interest expense over the relevant period.

The **effective interest rate** is the rate that exactly discounts estimated future cash payments or receipts through the expected life of the financial instrument to the net carrying amount.   *(IAS 39)*

5.3 Example: amortised cost

On 1 January 20X1 Abacus Co purchases a debt instrument for its fair value of $1,000. The debt instrument is due to mature on 31 December 20X5. The instrument has a principal amount of $1,250 and the instrument carries fixed interest at 4.72% that is paid annually.

How should Abacus Co account for the debt instrument over its five year term?

Solution

Abacus Co will receive interest of $59 (1,250 × 4.72%) each year and $1,250 when the instrument matures.

Abacus must allocate the discount of $250 and the interest receivable over the five year term at a constant rate on the carrying amount of the debt. To do this, it must apply the effective interest rate of 10%.

The following table shows the allocation over the years:

Year	Amortised cost at beginning of year	Income statement: Interest income for year (@10%)	Interest received during year (cash inflow)	Amortised cost at end of year
	$	$	$	$
20X1	1,000	100	(59)	1,041
20X2	1,041	104	(59)	1,086
20X3	1,086	109	(59)	1,136
20X4	1,136	113	(59)	1,190
20X5	1,190	119	(1,250+59)	-

Each year the carrying amount of the financial asset is increased by the interest income for the year and reduced by the interest actually received during the year.

Investments whose **fair value cannot be reliably measured** should be measured at **cost**.

5.4 Classification

There is a certain amount of flexibility in that **any** financial instrument can be designated as at fair value through profit or loss. However, this is a **once and for all choice** and has to be made on initial recognition. Once a financial instrument has been classified in this way it **cannot be reclassified**, even if it would otherwise be possible to measure it at cost or amortised cost.

In contrast, it is quite difficult for an entity **not** to remeasure financial instruments to fair value.

Exam focus point

> Notice that derivatives **must** be remeasured to fair value. This is because it would be misleading to measure them at cost.

For a financial instrument to be held to maturity it must meet several extremely narrow criteria. The entity must have a **positive intent** and a **demonstrated ability** to hold the investment to maturity. These conditions are not met if:

(a)   The entity intends to hold the financial asset for an undefined period

(b)   The entity stands ready to sell the financial asset in response to changes in interest rates or risks, liquidity needs and similar factors (unless these situations could not possibly have been reasonably anticipated)

(c)   The issuer has the right to settle the financial asset at an amount significantly below its amortised cost (because this right will almost certainly be exercised)

(d)   It does not have the financial resources available to continue to finance the investment until maturity

(e)   It is subject to an existing legal or other constraint that could frustrate its intention to hold the financial asset to maturity

In addition, an **equity** instrument is **unlikely** to meet the criteria for classification as held to maturity.

There is a **penalty** for selling or reclassifying a 'held-to-maturity' investment other than in certain very tightly defined circumstances. If this has occurred during the **current** financial year or during the **two preceding** financial years **no** financial asset can be classified as held-to-maturity.

If an entity can no longer hold an investment to maturity, it is no longer appropriate to use amortised cost and the asset must be re-measured to fair value. **All** remaining held-to-maturity investments must also be re-measured to fair value and classified as available-for-sale (see above).

5.5 Subsequent measurement of financial liabilities

After initial recognition, all financial liabilities should be measured at **amortised cost**, with the exception of financial liabilities at fair value through profit or loss (including most derivatives). These should be measured at **fair value**, but where the fair value **is not capable of reliable measurement**, they should be measured at **cost**.

Question   Bond

Galaxy Co issues a bond for $503,778 on 1 January 20X2. No interest is payable on the bond, but it will be held to maturity and redeemed on 31 December 20X4 for $600,000. The bond has **not** been designated as at fair value through profit or loss.

Required

Calculate the charge to the income statement of Galaxy Co for the year ended 31 December 20X2 and the balance outstanding at 31 December 20X2.

Answer

The bond is a 'deep discount' bond and is a financial liability of Galaxy Co. It is measured at amortised cost. Although there is no interest as such, the difference between the initial cost of the bond and the price at which it will be redeemed is a finance cost. This must be allocated over the term of the bond at a constant rate on the carrying amount.

To calculate amortised cost we need to calculate the effective interest rate of the bond:

$\dfrac{600,000}{503,778}$ = 1.191 over three years. $\sqrt[3]{1.191}$ = 1.06 per annum.

Therefore the interest rate is 6%.

The charge to the income statement is $30,226 (503,778 × 6%)

The balance outstanding at 31 December 20X2 is $534,004 (503,778 + 30,226)

5.6 Gains and losses

Instruments at **fair value through profit or loss**: gains and losses are recognised **in profit or loss** (ie, in the income statement).

Available for sale financial assets: gains and losses are recognised **directly in equity** through the statement of changes in equity. When the asset is derecognised the cumulative gain or loss previously recognised in equity should be recognised in profit and loss.

Financial instruments carried at **amortised cost**: gains and losses are recognised **in profit and loss** as a result of the amortisation process and when the asset is derecognised.

Financial assets and financial liabilities that are **hedged items**: special rules apply (but this is outside the scope of the 2.5 syllabus).

5.7 Impairment and uncollectability of financial assets

At each balance sheet date, an entity should assess whether there is any objective evidence that a financial asset or group of assets is impaired.

Where there is objective evidence of impairment, the entity should **determine the amount** of any impairment loss.

5.7.1 Financial assets carried at amortised cost

The impairment loss is the **difference** between the asset's **carrying amount** and its **recoverable amount**. The asset's recoverable amount is the present value of estimated future cash flows, discounted at the financial instrument's **original** effective interest rate.

The amount of the loss should be **recognised in profit or loss.**

If the impairment loss decreases at a later date (and the decrease relates to an event occurring **after** the impairment was recognised) the reversal is recognised in profit or loss. The carrying amount of the asset must not exceed the original amortised cost.

5.7.2 Financial assets carried at cost

Unquoted equity instruments are carried at cost if their fair value cannot be reliably measured. The impairment loss is the difference between the asset's **carrying amount** and the **present value of estimated future cash flows**, discounted at the current market rate of return for a similar financial instrument. Such impairment losses cannot be reversed.

5.7.3 Available for sale financial assets

Available for sale financial assets are carried at fair value and gains and losses are recognised directly in equity. Any impairment loss on an available for sale financial asset should be **removed from equity** and **recognised in net profit or loss for the period** even though the financial asset has not been derecognised.

The impairment loss is the difference between its **acquisition cost** (net of any principal repayment and amortisation) and **current fair value** (for equity instruments) or recoverable amount (for debt instruments), less any impairment loss on that asset previously recognised in profit or loss.

Impairment losses relating to equity instruments cannot be reversed. Impairment losses relating to debt instruments may be reversed if, in a later period, the fair value of the instrument increases and the increase can be objectively related to an event occurring after the loss was recognised.

5.8 Section summary

- On initial recognition, financial instruments are measured at **cost**.
- Subsequent measurement depends on how a financial asset is **classified**.

- Financial assets at **fair value through profit or loss** are measured at **fair value**; gains and losses are recognised in **profit or loss**.

- **Available for sale** assets are measured at **fair value**; gains and losses are taken to **equity**.

- **Loans and receivables** and **held to maturity** investments are measured at **amortised cost**; gains and losses are recognised in **profit or loss**.

- Financial **liabilities** are normally measured at **amortised cost**, unless they have been classified as at fair value through profit or loss.

6 IAS 23 *Borrowing costs*

FAST FORWARD

This standard looks at the treatment of borrowing costs, particularly where the related borrowings are applied to the construction of certain assets. These are what are usually called 'self-constructed assets', where an enterprise builds its own inventory or non-current assets over a substantial period of time.

6.1 Definitions

Only two definitions are given by the standard.

Key terms

> **Borrowing costs**. Interest and other costs incurred by an enterprise in connection with the borrowing of funds.
>
> **Qualifying asset**. An asset that necessarily takes a substantial period of time to get ready for its intended use or sale. *(IAS 23)*

The standard lists what may be **included in borrowing costs**.

- Interest on bank overdrafts and short-term and long-term borrowings
- Amortisation of discounts or premiums relating to borrowings
- Amortisation of ancillary costs incurred in connection with the arrangement of borrowings
- Finance charges in respect of finance leases recognised in accordance with IAS 17
- Exchange differences arising from foreign currency borrowings to the extent that they are regarded as an adjustment to interest costs

The standard also gives examples of qualifying assets.

- Inventories that require a substantial period of time to bring them to a saleable condition
- Manufacturing plants
- Power generation facilities
- Investment properties

Inventories produced in bulk over short periods and on a regular basis are **not qualifying assets**, nor are assets ready for sale or their intended use when purchased.

6.2 Benchmark treatment

The benchmark treatment for borrowing costs is the most straightforward and prudent. They should be **recognised as an expense** in the period in which they were incurred, regardless of how the borrowings were applied. The accounting policy adopted for borrowing costs should be disclosed.

6.3 Allowed alternative treatment: capitalisation

Under the alternative treatment, certain borrowing costs may be **capitalised**. Any other borrowing costs remaining must still be recognised as an expense as under the benchmark treatment.

Only borrowing costs that are **directly attributable** to the acquisition, construction or production of a qualifying asset can be capitalised as part of the cost of that asset. The standard lays out the criteria for determining which borrowing costs are eligible for capitalisation.

6.3.1 Borrowing costs eligible for capitalisation

Those borrowing costs directly attributable to the acquisition, construction or production of a qualifying asset must be identified. These are the borrowing costs that **would have been avoided** had the expenditure on the qualifying asset not been made. This is obviously straightforward where funds have been borrowed for the financing of one particular asset.

Difficulties arise, however, where the enterprise uses a **range of debt instruments** to finance a wide range of assets, so that there is no direct relationship between particular borrowings and a specific asset. For example, all borrowings may be made centrally and then lent to different parts of the group or enterprise. Judgement is therefore required, particularly where further complications can arise (eg foreign currency loans).

Once the relevant borrowings are identified, which relate to a specific asset, then the **amount of borrowing costs available for capitalisation** will be the actual borrowing costs incurred on those borrowings during the period, *less* any investment income on the temporary investment of those borrowings. It would not be unusual for some or all of the funds to be invested before they are actually used on the qualifying asset.

Question	Capitalisation

On 1 January 20X6 Stremans Co borrowed $1.5m to finance the production of two assets, both of which were expected to take a year to build. Production started during 20X6. The loan facility was drawn down on 1 January 20X6, and was utilised as follows, with the remaining funds invested temporarily.

	Asset A	Asset B
	$'000	$'000
1 January 20X6	250	500
1 July 20X6	250	500

The loan rate was 9% and Stremans Co can invest surplus funds at 7%.

Required

Ignoring compound interest, calculate the borrowing costs which may be capitalised for each of the assets and consequently the cost of each asset as at 31 December 20X6.

Answer

		Asset A $	Asset B $
Borrowing costs			
To 30 June 20X6	$250,000/$500,000 × 9% × 6/12	11,250	22,500
To 31 December 20X6	$500,000/$1,000,000 × 9% × 6/12	22,500	45,000
		33,750	67,500
Less investment income			
To 30 June 20X6	$250,000/$500,000 × 7% × 6/12	(8,750)	(17,500)
		25,000	50,000
		$	$
Cost of assets			
Expenditure incurred		500,000	1,000,000
Borrowing costs		25,000	50,000
		525,000	1,050,000

In a situation where **borrowings are obtained generally**, but are applied in part to obtaining a qualifying asset, then the amount of borrowing costs eligible for capitalisation is found by applying the 'capitalisation rate' to the expenditure on the asset.

The **capitalisation rate** is the weighted average of the borrowing costs applicable to the enterprise's borrowings that are outstanding during the period, *excluding* borrowings made specifically to obtain a qualifying asset. However, there is a cap on the amount of borrowing costs calculated in this way: it must not exceed actual borrowing costs incurred.

Sometimes one overall weighted average can be calculated for a group or enterprise, but in some situations it may be more appropriate to use a weighted average for borrowing costs for **individual parts of the group or enterprise**.

Question   Construction

Acruni Co had the following loans in place at the beginning and end of 20X6.

	1 January 20X6 $m	31 December 20X6 $m
10% Bank loan repayable 20X8	120	120
9.5% Bank loan repayable 20X9	80	80
8.9% debenture repayable 20X7	-	150

The 8.9% debenture was issued to fund the construction of a qualifying asset (a piece of mining equipment), construction of which began on 1 July 20X6.

On 1 January 20X6, Acruni Co began construction of a qualifying asset, a piece of machinery for a hydro-electric plant, using existing borrowings. Expenditure drawn down for the construction was: $£30m on 1 January 20X6, $20m on 1 October 20X6.

Required

Calculate the borrowing costs that can be capitalised for the hydro-electric plant machine.

Answer

Capitalisation rate = weighted average rate

$$= (10\% \times \frac{120}{120+80}) + (9.5\% \times \frac{80}{120+80}) = 9.8\%$$

Borrowing costs $= (\$30m \times 9.8\%) + (\$20m \times 9.8\% \times 3/12)$

$= \$3.43m$

6.3.2 Carrying amount exceeds recoverable amount

A situation may arise whereby the carrying amount (or expected ultimate cost) of the qualifying asset exceeds its recoverable amount or net realisable value. In these cases, the carrying amount must be **written down or written off**, as required by other IASs. In certain circumstances (again as allowed by other IASs), these amounts may be written back in future periods.

6.3.3 Commencement of capitalisation

Three events or transactions must be taking place for capitalisation of borrowing costs to be started.

(a) Expenditure on the asset is being incurred
(b) Borrowing costs are being incurred
(c) Activities are in progress that are necessary to prepare the asset for its intended use or sale

Expenditure must result in the payment of cash, transfer of other assets or assumption of interest-bearing liabilities. **Deductions from expenditure** will be made for any progress payments or grants received in connection with the asset. IAS 23 allows the **average carrying amount** of the asset during a period (including borrowing costs previously capitalised) to be used as a reasonable approximation of the expenditure to which the capitalisation rate is applied in the period. Presumably more exact calculations can be used.

Activities necessary to prepare the asset for its intended sale or use extend further than physical construction work. They encompass technical and administrative work prior to construction, eg obtaining permits. They do *not* include holding an asset when no production or development that changes the asset's condition is taking place, eg where land is held without any associated development activity.

6.3.4 Suspension of capitalisation

If active development is **interrupted for any extended periods**, capitalisation of borrowing costs should be suspended for those periods.

Suspension of capitalisation of borrowing costs is not necessary for **temporary delays** or for periods when substantial technical or administrative work is taking place.

6.3.5 Cessation of capitalisation

Once substantially all the activities necessary to prepare the qualifying asset for its intended use or sale are complete, then capitalisation of borrowing costs should cease. This will normally be when **physical construction of the asset is completed**, although minor modifications may still be outstanding.

The asset may be completed in **parts or stages**, where each part can be used while construction is still taking place on the other parts. Capitalisation of borrowing costs should cease for each part as it is completed. The example given by the standard is a business park consisting of several buildings.

6.3.6 Disclosure

The following should be disclosed in the financial statements in relation to borrowing costs.

(a) **Accounting policy** adopted

(b) Amount of borrowing costs **capitalised during the period**

(c) **Capitalisation rate** used to determine the amount of borrowing costs eligible for capitalisation

6.4 Consistency - capitalisation of borrowing costs

IAS 23 allows a choice.

(a) Recognise all borrowing costs as an expense in the period in which they are incurred (benchmark treatment).

(b) Capitalise borrowing costs that are directly attributable to the acquisition, construction or production of qualifying assets as part of the cost of that asset (allowed alternative treatment). The issue is whether an enterprise that has chosen a policy of capitalising borrowing costs should apply this policy to all qualifying assets or whether an enterprise may choose to capitalise borrowing costs for certain qualifying assets and not for others.

Where an enterprise adopts the allowed alternative treatment, that treatment should be applied consistently to all borrowing costs that are directly attributable to the acquisition, construction or production of all qualifying assets of the enterprise. If all the conditions laid down in IAS 23 are met, an enterprise should continue to capitalise such borrowing costs even if the carrying amount of the asset exceeds its recoverable amount. However, IAS 23 explains that the carrying amount of the asset should be written down to recognise impairment losses in such cases.

6.5 Section summary

- There are two treatments allowed for borrowing costs.

  - **Benchmark treatment**: write off in the period incurred
  - **Allowed alternative**: capitalise those costs directly attributable to qualifying assets

- You may be asked to discuss the pros and cons of the capitalisation of borrowing costs.

For capitalisation

- Borrowing costs are part of the **total cost** of bringing an asset into use.

- Capitalisation gives greater **comparability** between companies: a purchase price includes interest incurred by the seller, so a construction cost should also include interest.

Against capitalisation

- Finance costs are **not the most direct of costs** and may relate to the business as a whole.

- There will still be a lack of comparability due to **different financing policies**: businesses with loan financing will have higher values for assets than equity-backed businesses.

Chapter roundup

- Financial instruments can be very complex, particularly **derivative instruments**, although **primary instruments** are more straightforward.

- The important definitions to learn are:

  - **Financial asset**
  - **Financial liability**
  - **Equity instrument**

- Financial instruments must be classified as **liabilities** or **equity** according to their **substance**.

- The critical feature of a financial liability is the **contractual obligation to deliver cash** or another financial asset.

- **Compound instruments** are split into **equity** and **liability** components and presented in the balance sheet accordingly

- **IAS 39** *Financial instruments: recognition and measurement* is a recent and most controversial standard.

- The IAS states that **all financial assets and liabilities** should be **recognised on the balance sheet, including derivatives**.

- **Financial assets** should **initially** be measured at **cost = the fair value** of the consideration paid.

- Subsequently they should be **re-measured to fair value** except for

  (a) Loans and receivables not held for trading
  (b) Other **held-to-maturity investments**
  (c) Investments in **equity instruments** whose value **cannot be reliably measured**

- **IAS 23** *Borrowing costs* is also about financing, specially how borrowing costs associated with the construction of certain assets are dealt with.

- IAS 23 offers two treatments for borrowing costs.

  - **Benchmark**: write off in period incurred (prudence)
  - **Alternative**: capitalise (accrual)

Quick quiz

1   Which issues are dealt with by IAS 32?

2   Define the following.

(a)   Financial asset
(b)   Financial liability
(c)   Equity instrument

3   What is the critical feature used to identify a financial liability?

4   How should compound instruments be classified by the issuer?

5   When should a financial asset be de-recognised?

6   How are financial instruments initially measured?

7   After initial recognition, all financial liabilities should be measured at amortised cost. True or false?

Answers to quick quiz

1   Classification between liabilities and equity; presentation; disclosure

2   See Key Terms, paragraph 1.2

3   The contractual obligation to deliver cash or another financial asset to the holder

4   By calculating the present value of the liability component and then deducting this from the instrument as a whole to leave a residual value for the equity component.

5   Financial assets should be derecognised when the rights to the cash flows from the asset expire or where substantially all the risks and rewards of ownership are transferred to another party.

6   At cost

7   False. See paragraph 5.5

Now try the question below from the Exam Question Bank

Number	Level	Marks	Time
Q9	Introductory	n/a	n/a

Accounting for leases

9

Topic list	Syllabus reference
1 Types of lease	3(f)
2 Lessees	3(f)
3 Lessors	3(f)

Introduction

Leasing transactions are extremely common so this is an important practical subject. **Lease accounting is regulated by IAS 17**, which was introduced because of abuses in the use of lease accounting by companies.

These companies effectively 'owned' an asset and 'owed' a debt for its purchase, but showed neither the asset nor the liability on the balance sheet because they were not required to do so. This is called **'off balance sheet finance'**, a term which you will meet again later in this Text.

IAS 17 was revised in December 2003.

Study guide

Section 10 – Leases

- Define the essential characteristics of a lease
- Describe and apply the method of determining a lease type (ie an operating or finance lease)
- Explain the effect on the financial statements of a finance lease being incorrectly treated as an operating lease
- Account for operating leases in financial statements
- Account for finance leases in the financial statements of lessor and lessees
- Outline the principles of the accounting standard on leasing and its main disclosure requirements

Note. The net cash investment method will not be examined

Exam guide

At Paper 2.5 you are likely to be asked about the detailed accounting treatment. At Paper 3.6, you will be asked for critical comment and discussion. Issues of substance over form come up here, a 'Key area' for this exam.

1 Types of lease

> **FAST FORWARD**
>
> A finance lease is a means of acquiring the long-term use of an asset whereas an operating lease is a short-term rental agreement. However substance over form is essential.

1.1 What is a lease?

Where goods are acquired other than on immediate cash terms, arrangements have to be made in respect of the future payments on those goods. In the simplest case of **credit sales**, the purchaser is allowed a period of time (say one month) to settle the outstanding amount and the normal accounting procedure in respect of receivables/payables will be adopted. However, in recent years there has been considerable growth in leasing agreements (some types of lease are called **hire purchase agreements** in some countries).

IAS 17 *Leases* standardises the accounting treatment and disclosure of assets held under lease.

In a leasing transaction there is a **contract** between the lessor and the lessee for the hire of an asset. The lessor retains legal ownership but conveys to the lessee the right to use the asset for an agreed period of time in return for specified rentals. IAS 17 defines a lease and recognises two types.

Key terms

> - **Lease.** An agreement whereby the lessor conveys to the lessee in return for rent the right to use an asset for an agreed period of time.
> - **Finance lease.** A lease that transfers substantially all the risks and rewards incident to ownership of an asset. Title may or may not eventually be transferred.
> - **Operating lease.** A lease other than a finance lease.   *(IAS 17)*

A **finance lease** may be a **hire purchase agreement**. (The difference is that under a hire purchase agreement the customer eventually, after paying an agreed number of instalments, becomes entitled to exercise an option to purchase the asset. Under other leasing agreements, ownership remains forever with the lessor.)

In this chapter the **user** of an asset will often be referred to simply as the **lessee**, and the **supplier** as the **lessor**. You should bear in mind that identical requirements apply in the case of hirers and vendors respectively under hire purchase agreements.

To expand on the definition above, a finance lease should be presumed if at the inception of a lease the **present value of the minimum lease payments** is approximately equal to the **fair value of the leased asset**.

The present value should be calculated by using the **interest rate implicit in the lease**.

Key terms

> • **Minimum lease payments.** The payments over the lease term that the lessee is or can be required to make, excluding contingent rent, costs for services and taxes to be paid by and be reimbursed to the lessor, together with:
>
> (a) For a lessee, any amounts guaranteed by the lessee or by a party related to the lessee
>
> (b) For a lessor, any residual value guaranteed to the lessor by one of the following.
>
> > (i) The lessee
> > (ii) A party related to the lessee
> > (iii) An independent third party financially capable of meeting this guarantee
>
> However, if the lessee has the option to purchase the asset at a price which is expected to be sufficiently lower than fair value at the date the option becomes exercisable for it to be reasonably certain, at the inception of the lease, that the option will be exercised, the minimum lease payments comprise the minimum payments payable over the lease term to the expected date of exercise of this purchase option and the payment required to exercise it.
>
> • **Interest rate implicit in the lease.**
>
> The discount rate that, at the inception of the lease, causes the aggregate present value of
>
> (a) the minimum lease payments, and
> (b) the unguaranteed residual value
>
> to be equal to the sum of
>
> (a) the fair value of the leased asset, and
> (b) any initial direct costs.
>
> • **Initial direct costs** are **incremental costs** that are directly attributable to **negotiating** and **arranging** a lease, except for such costs incurred by manufacturer or dealer lessors. Examples of initial direct costs include amounts such as **commissions, legal fees** and relevant internal costs.
>
> • **Lease term.** The non-cancellable period for which the lessee has contracted to lease the asset together with any further terms for which the lessee has the option to continue to lease the asset, with or without further payment, when at the inception of the lease it is reasonably certain that the lessee will exercise the option.
>
> • A **non-cancellable lease** is a lease that is cancellable only in one of the following situations.
>
> (a) Upon the occurrence of some remote contingency
>
> (b) With the permission of the lessor
>
> (c) If the lessee enters into a new lease for the same or an equivalent asset with the same lessor
>
> (d) Upon payment by the lessee of an additional amount such that, at inception, continuation of the lease is reasonably certain

Key terms

- The **inception of the lease** is the earlier of the date of the lease agreement and the date of commitment by the parties to the principal provisions of the lease. As at this date:

  (a)   a lease is classified as either an operating lease or a finance lease; and

  (b)   in the case of a finance lease, the amounts to be recognised at the start of lease term are determined.

- **Economic life** is either:

  (a)   the period over which an asset is expected to be economically usable by one or more users, or

  (b)   the number of production or similar units expected to be obtained from the asset by one or more users.

- **Useful life** is the estimated remaining period, from the beginning of the lease term, without limitation by the lease term, over which the economic benefits embodied in the asset are expected to be consumed by the entity.

- **Guaranteed residual value** is:

  (a)   for a lessee, that part of the residual value which is guaranteed by the lessee or by a party related to the lessee (the amount of the guarantee being the maximum amount that could, in any event, become payable).

  (b)   for a lessor, that part of the residual value which is guaranteed by the lessee or by a third party unrelated to the lessor who is financially capable of discharging the obligations under the guarantee.

- **Unguaranteed residual value** is that portion of the residual value of the leased asset, the realisation of which by the lessor is not assured or is guaranteed solely by a party related to the lessor.

- **Gross investment in the lease** is the aggregate of:

  (a)   the minimum lease payments receivable by the lessor under a finance lease, and
  (b)   any unguaranteed residual value accruing to the lessor.

- **Net investment in the lease** is the gross investment in the lease discounted at the interest rate implicit in the lease.

- **Unearned finance income** is the difference between:

  (a)   the gross investment in the lease, and
  (b)   the net investment in the lease.

- The **lessee's incremental borrowing rate of interest** is the rate of interest the lessee would have to pay on a similar lease or, if that is not determinable, the rate that, at the inception of the lease, the lessee would incur to borrow over a similar term, and with a similar security, the funds necessary to purchase the asset.

- **Contingent rent** is that portion of the lease payments that is not fixed in amount but is based on a factor other than just the passage of time (eg percentage of sales, amount of usage, price indices, market rates of interest).

  (IAS 17)

There are further definitions in IAS 17, but (fortunately!) these go beyond the scope of your syllabus.

1.2 Accounting for leases: lessees and lessors

Operating leases do not really pose an accounting problem. The lessee pays amounts periodically to the lessor and these are **charged to the income statement**. The lessor treats the leased asset as a non-current asset and depreciates it in the normal way. Rentals received from the lessee are credited to the income statement in the lessor's books.

For assets held under **finance leases** (including hire purchase) this accounting treatment would not disclose the reality of the situation. If a **lessor** leases out an asset on a finance lease, the asset will probably never be seen on his premises or used in his business again. It would be inappropriate for a lessor to record such an asset as a non-current asset. In reality, what he owns is a **stream of cash flows receivable** from the lessee. **The asset is an amount receivable rather than a non-current asset.**

Similarly, a **lessee** may use a finance lease to fund the 'acquisition' of a major asset which he will then use in his business perhaps for many years. **The substance of the transaction is that he has acquired a non-current asset**, and this is reflected in the accounting treatment prescribed by IAS 17, even though in law the lessee may never become the owner of the asset.

Exam focus point

Questions on leasing could involve a discussion of the reasons for the different accounting treatments of operating and finance leases, from the perspectives of both the lessor and the lessee. Practical questions could involve preparation of the relevant ledger accounts and/or extracts from the financial statements.

The following summary diagram should help you when deciding whether a lease is an operating lease or a finance lease.

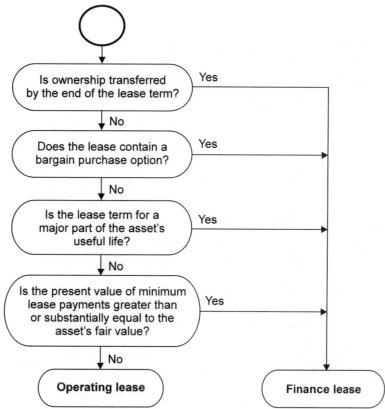

The revised IAS 17 states that when classifying a lease of **land and buildings** the **land** element is normally classified as an **operating lease unless title passes to the lessee** at the end of the contract.

2 Lessees

You must learn the disclosure requirements for both lessors and lessees.

2.1 Accounting treatment

IAS 17 requires that, when an asset changes hands under a **finance lease, lessor and lessee should account for the transaction as though it were a credit sale.** In the lessee's books therefore:

DEBIT   Asset account
CREDIT   Lessor (liability) account

The amount to be recorded in this way is the **lower of** the **fair value** and the **present value** of the **minimum lease payments**.

IAS 17 states that it is not appropriate to show liabilities for leased assets as deductions from the leased assets. A distinction should be made between **current and non-current** lease liabilities, if the entity makes this distinction for other liabilities.

The asset should be **depreciated** (on the bases set out in IASs 16 and 38) over the shorter of:

- The lease term
- The asset's useful life

If there is reasonable certainty of eventual ownership of the asset, then it should be depreciated over its useful life.

2.2 Apportionment of rental payments

When the lessee makes a rental payment it will comprise two elements.

(a)   An **interest charge** on the finance provided by the lessor. This proportion of each payment is interest payable and interest receivable in the income statements of the lessee and lessor respectively.

(b)   A repayment of part of the **capital cost** of the asset. In the lessee's books this proportion of each rental payment must be debited to the lessor's account to reduce the outstanding liability. In the lessor's books, it must be credited to the lessee's account to reduce the amount owing (the debit of course is to cash).

The accounting problem is to decide what proportion of each instalment paid by the lessee represents interest, and what proportion represents a repayment of the capital advanced by the lessor. There are two apportionment methods you may encounter:

- The **actuarial method**
- The **sum-of-the-digits method**

Exam focus point

An examination question would always make it clear which method should be used. In theory, the aim is that the income statement finance charge should reduce over the lease term in line with the outstanding liability. The examiners will not examine the **sum-of-the-digits method.**

The **actuarial method** is the best and most scientific method. It derives from the common-sense assumption that the interest charged by a lessor company will equal the rate of return desired by the company, multiplied by the amount of capital it has invested.

(a)   At the beginning of the lease the capital invested is equal to the fair value of the asset (less any initial deposit paid by the lessee).

(b)   This amount reduces as each instalment is paid. It follows that the interest accruing is greatest in the early part of the lease term, and gradually reduces as capital is repaid. In this section, we will look at a simple example of the actuarial method.

The **sum-of-the-digits** method approximates to the actuarial method, splitting the total interest (without reference to a rate of interest) in such a way that the greater proportion falls in the earlier years.

2.3 Example: apportionment methods

On 1 January 20X0 Bacchus Co, wine merchants, buys a small bottling and labelling machine from Silenus Co under a finance lease. The cash price of the machine was $7,710 while the amount to be paid was $10,000. The agreement required the immediate payment of a $2,000 deposit with the balance being settled in four equal annual instalments commencing on 31 December 20X0. The charge of $2,290 represents interest of 15% per annum, calculated on the remaining balance of the liability during each accounting period. Depreciation on the plant is to be provided for at the rate of 20% per annum on a straight line basis assuming a residual value of nil.

You are required to show the breakdown of each instalment between interest and capital.

Solution

In this example, enough detail is given to use any of the apportionment methods. In an examination question, you would normally be directed to use one method specifically.

Actuarial method

Interest is calculated as 15% of the outstanding *capital* balance at the beginning of each year. The outstanding capital balance reduces each year by the capital element comprised in each instalment. The outstanding capital balance at 1 January 20X0 is $5,710 ($7,710 fair value less $2,000 deposit).

	Total $	Capital $	Interest $
Capital balance at 1 Jan 20X0		5,710	
1st instalment			
(interest = $5,710 × 15%)	2,000	1,144	856
Capital balance at 1 Jan 20X1		4,566	
2nd instalment			
(interest = $4,566 × 15%)	2,000	1,315	685
Capital balance at 1 Jan 20X2		3,251	
3rd instalment			
(interest = $3,251 × 15%)	2,000	1,512	488
Capital balance at 1 Jan 20X3		1,739	
4th instalment			
(interest = $1,739 × 15%)	2,000	1,739	261
	8,000		2,290
Capital balance at 1 Jan 20X4		–	

2.4 Disclosure requirements for lessees

IAS 17 (revised) requires the following disclosures by lessees in respect of finance leases:

- The **net carrying amount** at the balance sheet date for each class of asset

- A **reconciliation** between the total of minimum lease payments at the balance sheet date, and their present value. In addition, an entity should disclose the total of minimum lease payments at the balance sheet date, and their present value, for each of the following periods:

- Not later than one year
- Later than one year and not later than five years
- Later than five years

- **Contingent rents** recognised in income for the period

- Total of **future minimum sublease payments** expected to be received under non-cancellable subleases at the balance sheet date

- A **general description** of the lessee's significant leasing arrangements including, but not limited to, the following:

  - The basis on which contingent rent payments are determined

  - The existence and terms of renewal or purchase options and escalation clauses

  - Restrictions imposed by lease arrangements, such as those concerning dividends, additional debt, and further leasing

IAS 17 encourages (but does not require) further disclosures, as appropriate.

2.5 Example: lessee disclosures

These disclosure requirements will be illustrated for Bacchus Co (above example). We will assume that Bacchus Co makes up its accounts to 31 December and uses the actuarial method to apportion finance charges.

Solution

The company's accounts for the first year of the lease, the year ended 31 December 20X0, would include the information given below.

BALANCE SHEET AS AT 31 DECEMBER 20X0 (EXTRACTS)

	$	$
Non-current assets		
Assets held under finance leases		
Plant and machinery at cost	7,710	
Less accumulated depreciation (20% × $7,710)	1,542	
		6,168
Current liabilities		
Obligations under finance leases		1,315
Non-current liabilities		
Obligations under finance leases		
$(1,512 + 1,739)		3,251

(Notice that only the outstanding **capital** element is disclosed under liabilities, ie the total of the minimum lease payments with future finance charges separately deducted.)

INCOME STATEMENT
FOR THE YEAR ENDED 31 DECEMBER 20X0 (EXTRACT)

	$
Interest payable and similar charges	
Interest on finance leases	856

For **operating leases** the disclosures are as follows.

(a) The total of future minimum lease payments under non-cancellable operating leases for each of the following periods:

(i) Not later than one year
(ii) Later than one year and not later than five years
(iii) Later than five years

(b) The total of future minimum sublease payments expected to be received under non-cancellable subleases at the balance sheet date

(c) Lease and sublease payments recognised in income for the period, with separate amounts for minimum lease payments, contingent rents, and sublease payments

(d) A general description of the lessee's significant leasing arrangements including, but not limited to, the following

  (i) The basis on which contingent rent payments are determined

  (ii) The existence and terms of renewal or purchase options and escalation clauses

  (iii) Restrictions imposed by lease arrangements, such as those concerning dividends, additional debt, and further leasing

The following diagram gives a useful summary of the **accounting treatment for a finance lease by a lessee.**

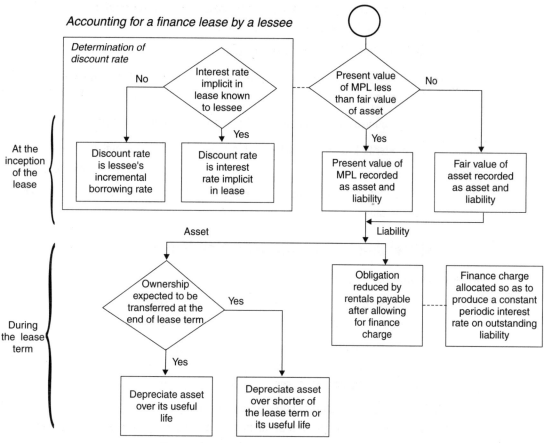

Accounting for a finance lease by a lessee

MPL = Minimum lease payments

3 Lessors

You must learn the disclosure requirements for lessors as well as lessees.

3.1 Accounting treatment: finance leases

In principle, accounting for a **finance lease** by a **lessor** is a **mirror image of the entries for the lessee.** The asset is recorded in the lessor's books as a receivable, *not* as a non-current asset, as follows.

DEBIT   Lessee (receivable) account
CREDIT   Non-current assets

The **income derived** from the lease is spread over accounting periods so as to give a constant periodic rate of return for the lessor. The complex methods of achieving this are beyond the scope of your syllabus, but they are based on the lessor's net investment in respect of the finance lease. You will look at these complex methods later in your studies.

3.2 Accounting treatment: operating leases

An **asset** held for use in operating leases by a lessor should be recorded as a non-current asset and depreciated over its useful life. The basis for depreciation should be consistent with the lessor's policy on similar non-lease assets and follow the guidance in IAS 16.

Income from an operating lease, excluding charges for services such as insurance and maintenance, should be recognised on **a straight-line basis** over the period of the lease, even if the receipts are not on such a basis, unless another systematic and rational basis is more representative of the time pattern in which the benefit from the leased asset is receivable.

Indirect costs should be treated in one of two ways

(a) **Deferred** and allocated to income over the lease term in proportion to the recognition of rent income

(b) Recognised as an **expense** in the income statement of the period they are incurred.

Lessors should refer to IAS 36 on **impairment** in order to determine whether a leased asset has become impaired.

A lessor who is a **manufacturer or dealer** should not recognise any selling profit on entering into an operating lease because it is not the equivalent of a sale.

3.3 Lessors' disclosures for operating leases

The following should be disclosed.

- For each class of asset, the **gross carrying amount**, the accumulated depreciation and accumulated impairment losses at the balance sheet date:

    - Depreciation recognised in income for the period
    - Impairment losses recognised in income for the period
    - Impairment losses reversed in income for the period

- The **future minimum lease payments** under non-cancellable operating leases in the aggregate and for each of the following periods:

    - Not later than one year
    - Later than one year and not later than five years
    - Later than five years

- Total **contingent rents** recognised in income

- A **general description** of the lessor's significant leasing arrangements

The accounts of Silenus Co for the year ended 31 December 20X0 would show the information given below.

BALANCE SHEET AS AT 31 DECEMBER 20X0 (EXTRACTS)

	$
Current assets	
Receivables	
Net investment in finance leases (note)	4,566

NOTES TO THE BALANCE SHEET

Net investment in finance leases	$
Falling due within one year	1,315
Falling due after more than one year	3,251
	4,566

3.4 Sale and leaseback transactions

Under this type of transaction, the holder of an asset **sells it** to another party and then immediately **leases it back again**. The sale price and the rental agreed are dependent upon each other, negotiated as a package. The treatment depends on the type of lease which results.

For **finance leases**, any apparent profit on sale should not be recognised as income, but should be deferred and amortised over the lease term. The transaction is effectively the raising of finance secured on an asset that continues to be held and is not disposed of.

For **operating leases**, any profit on sale is recognised immediately if the transaction was carried out at **fair value** (ie this is a normal sale). For transactions which are not at fair value, the following rules apply.

- **Sale price is below fair value**: recognise profit/loss immediately *unless* the loss is compensated by rentals below market value, in which case defer and amortise the loss in proportion to the rental payments over the period the asset is used.

- **Sale price is above fair value**: defer and amortise the excess above fair value over the period the asset is used.

- **Fair value is less than carrying amount**: the loss (fair value less carrying amount) should be recognised immediately.

Question

Lessor

Leisure Services Co are electrical wholesalers. On 2 May 20X3, they purchased on credit from TV Suppliers Co ten television sets for a total of $1,600. They offered these for sale for cash at $240 each or under a finance lease for a cash deposit of $40 and eight quarterly instalments of $30 each, the first instalment being payable after three months (at the end of which ownership would transfer to the buyer). In the week ended 16 May 20X3 they sold two sets for cash and four under leases for which the cash deposits were paid at the time of sale.

On 1 December 20X3 Leisure Services Co installed one of their sets permanently on their own premises in a closed circuit television installation to detect theft.

You are required to prepare the necessary accounts (except cash and TV Suppliers Co) with dates and narrations in the ledger of Leisure Services Co to record the above transactions, balance them and prepare an income statement up to 31 December 20X3.

Note. The amount of finance interest earned in the period, calculated on the sum of the digits method, can be included in the income statement after sales.

Answer

	$
Price structure	
Cost	160
Gross profit	80
Cash selling price	240
Lease interest	40
Lease selling price $(40 + (8 \times 30))$	280

With eight instalments, the sum of the digits is:

$$1 + 2 + \ldots + 7 + 8 = 36 \text{ or } \frac{8 \times 9}{2} = 36$$

Interest on the first instalment	$= 8/36 \times \$40 = \$9$
Interest on the second instalment	$= 7/36 \times \$40 = \$8$
Capital element in first instalment	$= \$(30 - 9) = \$21$
Capital element in second instalment	$= \$(30 - 8) = \$22$

Ledger accounts

NON-CURRENT ASSETS

20X3		$			
1 Dec	Purchases: closed circuit TV	160			

LEASE RECEIVABLES

20X3		$	20X3		$
16 May	Sales (4 × $240)	960	16 May	Bank: deposits	160
			16 Aug	Bank: 1st instalment (4 × $21)	84
			16 Nov	Bank: 2nd instalment (4 × $22)	88
			31 Dec	Balance c/f	628
		960			960

SALES

20X3		$	20X3		$
31 Dec	Trading account	1,440	16 May	Lease receivables	960
				Cash (2 × $240)	480
		1,440			1,440

PURCHASES

20X3		$	20X3		$
2 May	Creditors	1,600	1 Dec	Non-current assets	160
			31 Dec	Trading account	1,440
		1,600			1,600

LEASE INTEREST RECEIVABLE

20X3		$	20X3		$
31 Dec	Trading account	68	16 Aug	Bank: 1st instalment (4 × $9)	36
			16 Nov	Bank: 2nd instalment (4 × $9)	32
		68			68

INCOME STATEMENT TO 31 DECEMBER 20X3

	$	$
Sales		1,440
Lease interest receivable		68
		1,508
Purchases	1,440	
Less closing inventory (3 × $160)	480	
Cost of sales		960
Gross profit		548

Chapter roundup

- Under **finance leases**:

  - Assets acquired should be capitalised
  - Interest element of instalments should be charged against profit.

- **Operating leases** are **rental agreements** and all instalments are charged against profit.

- You must learn (through repeated practice) how to apply the actuarial and sum-of-the-digits methods of **interest allocation**.

- You must also learn the **disclosure requirements of IAS 17** (revised) for both lessors and lessees.

Quick quiz

1   (a)   ....leases transfer substantially all the risks and rewards of ownership.

    (b)   ....leases are usually short-term rental agreements with the lessor being responsible for the repairs and maintenance of the asset.

2   A business acquires an asset under a finance lease. What is the double entry?

3   What is the formula to calculate each period's interest using the sum of digits?

4   List the disclosures required under IAS 17 for lessees.

5   A lorry has an expected useful life of six years. It is acquired under a four year finance lease. Over which period should it be depreciated?

6   A company leases a photocopier under an operating lease which expires in June 20X2. Its office is leased under an operating lease due to expire in January 20X3. How should past and future operating leases be disclosed in its 31 December 20X1 accounts?

Answers to quick quiz

1   (a)   Finance leases
     (b)   Operating leases

2   DEBIT   Asset account
     CREDIT   Lessor account

3    $\dfrac{\text{Digit applicable to the instalment}}{\text{Sum of the digits}} \times$ Total finance charge

4   See Para 2.4.

5   The four year term, unless eventual ownership of the lorry is reasonably certain, in which case it should be depreciated over its useful life of six years.

6   The total operating lease rentals charged though the income statement should be disclosed. The payments committed to should be disclosed analysing them between those falling due in the next year and the second to fifth years.

Now try the question below from the Exam Question Bank

Number	Level	Marks	Time
Q10	Examination	25	45 mins

Accounting for taxation

10

Topic list	Syllabus reference
1 Sales tax	3(e)
2 Current tax	3(e)
3 Deferred tax	3(e)
4 Taxable in company accounts	3(e)
5 Presentation and disclosure of taxation	3(e)

Introduction

In almost all countries entities are taxed on the basis of their trading income. In some countries this may be called corporation or corporate tax, but we will follow the terminology of IAS 12 *Income taxes* and call it income tax.

In Section 1 we will look briefly at sales tax which should be revision from your earlier studies.

There are two aspects of income tax which must be accounted for: **current tax** and **deferred tax**. These will be discussed in Sections 2 and 3 respectively.

Note. Throughout this chapter we will assume a current corporate income tax rate of 30% and a current personal income tax rate of 20%, unless otherwise stated.

Study guide

Section 16 Taxation in financial statements

- Account for current tax liabilities and assets in accordance with relevant accounting standards

- Describe the general principles of government sales taxes (eg VAT or GST)

- Explain the effect of taxable temporary differences on accounting and taxable profits

- Outline the principle of accounting for deferred tax

- Outline the requirements of relevant accounting standards relating to deferred tax assets and liabilities

- Calculate and record deferred tax amounts in the financial statements

1 Sales tax

Sales tax is a tax on the supply of goods and services. Tax is collected at each transfer point in the chain from prime producer to final consumer. Eventually, the consumer bears the tax in full and any tax paid earlier in the chain can be recovered by the trader who paid it.

1.1 Example: Sales tax

A manufacturing company, Alyson Co, purchases raw materials at a cost of $1,000 plus sales tax at 17½%. From the raw materials Alyson Co makes finished products which it sells to a retail outlet, Barry Co, for $1,600 plus sales tax. Barry Co sells the products to customers at a total price of $2,000 plus VAT. How much sales tax is paid to the tax authorities at each stage in the chain?

Solution

	Value of goods sold $	Sales tax at 17½% $
Supplier of raw materials	1,000	175
Value added by Alyson Co	600	105
Sale to Barry Co	1,600	280
Value added by Barry Co	400	70
Sales to 'consumers'	2,000	350

1.2 How is sales tax collected?

Although it is the final consumer who eventually bears the full tax of $350, the sum is **collected and paid over to the tax authorities by the traders who make up the chain.** Each trader must assume that his customer is the final consumer and must collect and pay over sales tax at the appropriate rate on the full sales value of the goods sold. He is entitled to reclaim sales tax paid on his own purchases (inputs) and so makes a net payment to the tax authorities equal to the tax on value added by himself.

In the example above, the supplier of raw materials collects from Alyson Co sales tax of $175, all of which he pays over. When Alyson Co sells goods to Barry Co sales tax is charged at the rate of 17½% on $1,600 = $280. Only $105, however, is paid by Alyson Co because the company is entitled to deduct sales tax of $175 suffered on its own purchases. Similarly, Barry Co must charge its customers $350 in sales tax but need only pay over the net amount of $70 after deducting the $280 sales tax suffered on its purchase from Alyson Co.

1.3 Registered and non-registered persons

Traders whose sales (outputs) are below a certain minimum need not register for sales tax. Such traders neither charge sales tax on their outputs nor are entitled to reclaim sales tax on their inputs. They are in the same position as a final consumer.

All outputs of registered traders are either taxable or exempt. Traders carrying on exempt activities (such as banks) cannot charge sales tax on their outputs and consequently cannot reclaim sales tax paid on their inputs.

Taxable outputs are usually chargeable at one of **three rates**:

(a) **Zero rate (0%)**
(b) **Standard-rated (17½% in the UK)**
(c) **Lower standard-rated (5% on items like fuel in the UK)**

The tax authorities publish lists of supplies falling into each category. **Persons carrying on taxable activities** (even activities taxable at zero per cent) **are entitled to reclaim sales tax paid on their inputs.**

Some traders carry on a **mixture of taxable and exempt activities**. Such traders need to apportion the sales tax suffered on inputs and **can only reclaim the proportion relating to taxable outputs.**

1.4 Accounting for sales tax

As a general principle the treatment of sales tax in the accounts of a trader should reflect his role as a collector of the tax and **sales tax should not be included in income or in expenditure whether of a capital or of a revenue nature.**

1.4.1 Irrecoverable sales tax

Where the **trader bears the sales tax** himself, as in the following cases, this should be reflected in the accounts.

(a) **Persons not registered** for sales tax will suffer sales tax on inputs. This will effectively increase the cost of their consumable materials and their non-current assets and must be so reflected, ie shown **inclusive of sales tax.**

(b) **Registered persons** who also carry on **exempted** activities will have a residue of sales tax which falls directly on them. In this situation the costs to which this residue applies will be inflated by the **irrecoverable sales tax.**

(c) **Non-deductible inputs will be borne** by all traders (examples in the UK are tax on cars bought which are not for resale, entertaining expenses and provision of domestic accommodation for a company's directors).

Exam focus point

> Where sales tax is not recoverable it must be regarded as an inherent part of the cost of the items purchased and included in the I/S charge or balance sheet as appropriate.

1.5 Further points

Sales tax is charged on the price net of any discount and this general principle is carried to the extent that where a cash discount is offered, sales tax is charged on the net amount **even where the discount is not taken up.**

Most sales tax registered persons are obliged to record sales tax when a supply is received or made (effectively when a credit sales invoice is raised or a purchase invoice recorded). This has the effect that **the net sales tax liability has on occasion to be paid to the tax authorities before all output tax has**

been paid by customers. If a debt is subsequently written off, the sales tax element may not be recovered from the tax authorities for six months from the date of sale, even if the customer becomes insolvent.

Some small businesses can join the cash accounting scheme whereby sales tax is only paid to the tax authorities after it is received from customers. This delays recovery of input tax but improves cash flow overall, although it may involve extra record keeping. Irrecoverable debt relief is automatic under this scheme since if sales tax is not paid by the customer it is not due to the tax authorities.

Question	Sales tax

Sunglo Co is preparing accounts for the year ended 31 May 20X9. Included in its balance sheet as at 31 May 20X8 was a balance for sales tax recoverable of $15,000.

Its summary income statement for the year is as follows.

	$'000
Sales (all standard rated)	500
Purchases (all standard rated)	120
Gross profit	380
Expenses	(280)
Interest receivable	20
Profit before tax	120

	$'000
Note: expenses	
Wages and salaries	200
Entertainment expenditure	10
Other (all standard rated)	70
	280

Payments of $5,000, $15,000 and $20,000 have been made in the year and a repayment of $12,000 was received. What is the balance for sales tax in the balance sheet as at 31 May 20X9? Assume a 17.5% standard rate of sales tax.

Answer

SUNGLO CO: SALES TAX ACCOUNT

	$		$
Balance b/d	15,000	Sales ($500,000 × 17.5%)	87,500
Purchases ($120,000 × 17.5%)	21,000	Bank	12,000
Expenses ($70,000 × 17.5%)	12,250		
Bank	40,000		
Balance c/d	11,250		
	99,500		99,500

1.6 Disclosure requirements

The following accounting rules should be followed.

(a)   **Revenue** shown in the income statement should **exclude** sales tax on taxable outputs. If gross revenue must be shown then the sales tax in that figure must also be shown as a deduction in arriving at the revenue exclusive of sales tax.

(b)   **Irrecoverable sales tax** allocated to non-current assets and other items separately disclosed should be **included in their cost** where material and practical.

(c)   The **net amount due to (or from) the tax authorities** should be **included in the total for payables** (or receivables), and need not be separately disclosed.

2 Current tax

Current tax is the amount payable to the tax authorities in relation to the trading activities of the period.

2.1 Introduction

You may have assumed until now that accounting for income tax was a very simple matter for companies. You would calculate the amount of tax due to be paid on the company's taxable profits and (under the classical system) you would:

DEBIT   Tax charge (income statement)
CREDIT   Tax liability (balance sheet)

with this amount.

Indeed, this aspect of corporate taxation – **current tax** – *is* ordinarily straightforward. Complexities arise, however, when we consider the future tax consequences of what is going on in the accounts now. This is an aspect of tax called **deferred tax**, which we will look at in the next section.

2.2 IAS 12 *Income taxes*

IAS 12 covers both current and deferred tax. The parts relating to current tax are fairly brief, because this is the simple and uncontroversial area of tax.

2.3 Definitions

These are some of the definitions given in IAS 12. We will look at the rest later.

Key terms

> *   **Accounting profit**. Net profit or loss for a period before deducting tax expense.
>
> *   **Taxable profit (tax loss)**. The profit (loss) for a period, determined in accordance with the rules established by the taxation authorities, upon which income taxes are payable (recoverable).
>
> *   **Tax expense (tax income)**. The aggregate amount included in the determination of net profit or loss for the period in respect of current tax and deferred tax.
>
> *   **Current tax**. The amount of income taxes payable (recoverable) in respect of the taxable profit (tax loss) for a period.   *(IAS 12)*

Before we go any further, let us be clear about the difference between current and deferred tax.

(a)   **Current tax** is the amount *actually payable* to the tax authorities in relation to the trading activities of the entity during the period.

(b)   **Deferred tax** is an *accounting measure*, used to match the tax effects of transactions with their accounting impact and thereby produce less distorted results.

You should understand this a little better after working through Section 3.

2.4 Recognition of current tax liabilities and assets

IAS 12 requires any **unpaid tax** in respect of the current or prior periods to be recognised as a **liability**.

Conversely, any **excess tax** paid in respect of current or prior periods over what is due should be recognised as an asset.

Question	Current tax

In 20X8 Darton Co had taxable profits of $120,000. In the previous year (20X7) income tax on 20X7 profits had been estimated as $30,000.

Required

Calculate tax payable and the charge for 20X8 if the tax due on 20X7 profits was subsequently agreed with the tax authorities as:

(a) $35,000; or
(b) $25,000.

Any under or over payments are not settled until the following year's tax payment is due.

Answer

(a)

	$
Tax due on 20X8 profits ($120,000 × 30%)	36,000
Underpayment for 20X7	5,000
Tax charge and liability	41,000

(b)

	$
Tax due on 20X8 profits (as above)	36,000
Overpayment for 20X7	(5,000)
Tax charge and liability	31,000

Alternatively, the rebate due could be shown separately as income in the income statement and as an asset in the balance sheet. An offset approach like this is, however, most likely.

Taking this a stage further, IAS 12 also requires recognition as an asset of the benefit relating to any tax loss that can be **carried back** to recover current tax of a previous period. This is acceptable because it is probable that the benefit will flow to the entity *and* it can be reliably measured.

2.5 Example: tax losses carried back

In 20X7 Eramu Co paid $50,000 in tax on its profits. In 20X8 the company made tax losses of $24,000. The local tax authority rules allow losses to be carried back to offset against current tax of prior years.

Required

Show the tax charge and tax liability for 20X8.

Solution

Tax repayment due on tax losses = 30% × $24,000 = $7,200.

The double entry will be:

DEBIT   Tax receivable (balance sheet) $7,200
CREDIT   Tax repayment (income statement) $7,200

The tax receivable will be shown as an asset until the repayment is received from the tax authorities.

2.6 Measurement

Measurement of current tax liabilities (assets) for the current and prior periods is very simple. They are measured at the **amount expected to be paid to (recovered from) the tax authorities**. The tax rates (and tax laws) used should be those enacted (or substantively enacted) by the balance sheet date.

2.7 Recognition of current tax

Normally, current tax is recognised as income or expense and included in the net profit or loss for the period, except in two cases.

(a)   Tax arising from a **business combination** which is an acquisition is treated differently (see Part D of this text).

(b)   Tax arising from a transaction or event which is recognised **directly in equity** (in the same or a different period).

The rule in (b) is logical. If a transaction or event is charged or credited directly to equity, rather than to the income statement, then the related tax should be also. An example of such a situation is where, under IAS 8, an adjustment is made to the **opening balance of retained earnings** due to either a change in accounting policy that is applied retrospectively, or to the correction of a material prior period error.

2.8 Presentation

In the balance sheet, **tax assets and liabilities** should be shown separately from other assets and liabilities.

Current tax assets and liabilities can be **offset**, but this should happen only when certain conditions apply.

(a)   The entity has a **legally enforceable right** to set off the recognised amounts.

(b)   The entity intends to settle the amounts on a **net basis**, or to realise the asset and settle the liability at the same time.

The **tax expense (income)** related to the profit or loss from ordinary activities should be shown on the face of the income statement.

The **disclosure requirements** of IAS 12 are extensive and we will look at these later in the chapter.

3 Deferred tax

FAST FORWARD

> **IAS 12** requires full provision for **deferred** tax. It is unlikely that complicated numerical questions will be set in the exam so concentrate on **understanding** deferred tax.

Exam focus point

> This topic appears almost in every paper, so do work through the material thoroughly, learn and inwardly digest. The June 2004 paper included a deferred tax adjustment.

You may already be aware from your studies of taxation that accounting profits and taxable profits are not the same. There are several reasons for this but they may conveniently be considered under two headings.

(a)   **Permanent differences** arise because certain expenditure, such as entertainment of UK customers, is not allowed as a deduction for tax purposes although it is quite properly deducted in arriving at accounting profit. Similarly, certain income (such as UK dividend income) is not subject to tax, although it forms part of accounting profit.

(b)   **Timing differences** arise because certain items are included in the accounts of a period which is different from that in which they are dealt with for taxation purposes.

Deferred taxation is the tax attributable to timing differences.

> **Deferred tax.** Estimated future tax consequences of transactions and events recognised in the financial statements of the current and previous periods.

Deferred taxation is therefore a means of ironing out the tax inequalities arising from timing differences.

(a)   In years when **corporation tax is saved** by timing differences such as accelerated tax allowances, a charge for deferred taxation is made in the income statement and a provision set up in the balance sheet.

(b)   In years when **timing differences reverse**, because the depreciation charge exceeds the tax allowances available, a deferred tax credit is made in the income statement and the balance sheet provision is reduced.

You should be clear in your mind that the tax actually payable to the tax authorities is the **tax liability**. The credit balance on the deferred taxation account represents an estimate of tax saved because of timing differences but expected ultimately to become payable when those differences reverse.

The following are the main categories in which timing differences can occur.

(a)   **Accelerated tax allowances.** Tax deductions for the cost of a non-current asset are accelerated or decelerated, ie received before or after the cost of the non-current asset is recognised in the income statement.

(b)   **Pension liabilities** are accrued in the financial statements but are allowed for tax purposes only when paid or contributed at a later date (pensions are not in the paper 2.5 syllabus).

(c)   **Interest charges or development costs** are capitalised on the balance sheet but are treated as revenue expenditure and allowed as incurred for tax purposes.

(d)   **Intragroup profits in inventory**, unrealised at group level, are reversed on consolidation.

(e)   **Revaluations.** An asset is revalued in the financial statements but the revaluation gain becomes taxable only if and when the asset is sold.

(f)   **Unrelieved tax losses.** A tax loss is not relieved against past or present taxable profits but can be carried forward to reduce future taxable profits.

(g)   **Unremitted earnings of subsidiaries.** The unremitted earnings of subsidiary and associated undertakings and joint ventures are recognised in the group results but will be subject to further taxation only if and when remitted to the parent undertaking.

Deferred taxation is therefore an accounting convention which is introduced in order to apply the accruals concept to income reporting where timing differences occur. However, **deferred tax assets** are not included in accounts as a rule, because it would not be prudent, given that the recovery of the tax is uncertain.

3.1 Basis of provision

A comprehensive tax allocation system is one in which deferred taxation is computed for every instance of timing differences: **full provision**. The opposite extreme would be the **nil provision** approach ('**flow**

through method'), where only the tax payable in the period would be charged to that period. There is also a middle course called **partial provision** where the effect of timing differences is accepted for to the extent that it is probable that a liability or a asset well crystallise.

The **probability** that a liability or asset would crystallise was assessed by the directors on the basis of **reasonable assumptions**. They had to take into account all relevant information available up to the date on which they approved the financial statements, and also their intentions for the future. Ideally, financial projections of future plans had to be made for a number (undefined) of years ahead. The directors' judgement had to be exercised with prudence.

If a company predicted, for example, that capital expenditure would **continue at the same rate** for the foreseeable future, so that capital allowances and depreciation would remain at the same levels, then no originating or reversing differences of any significance to the continuing trend of the tax charge would arise and so no change to the provision for deferred tax needed to be made (unless there were other significant timing differences).

3.2 The three different methods compared

Under the **flow-through method**, the tax liability recognised is the expected legal tax liability for the period (ie no provision is made for deferred tax). The main **advantages** of the method are that it is straightforward to apply and the tax liability recognised is closer to many people's idea of a 'real' liability than that recognised under either full or partial provision.

The main **disadvantages** of flow-through are that it can lead to large fluctuations in the tax charge and that it does not allow tax relief for long-term liabilities to be recognised until those liabilities are settled. The method is not used internationally.

The **full provision method** has the **advantage** that it is consistent with general international practice. It also recognises that each timing difference at the balance sheet date has an effect on future tax payments. If a company claims an accelerated capital allowance on an item of plant, future tax assessments will be bigger than they would have been otherwise. Future transactions may well affect those assessments still further, but that is not relevant in assessing the position at the balance sheet date. The **disadvantage** of full provision is that, under certain types of tax system, it gives rise to large liabilities that may fall due only far in the future. The full provision method is the one prescribed by IAS 12.

The **partial provision method** addresses this disadvantage by providing for deferred tax only to the extent that it is expected to be paid in the foreseeable future. This has an obvious intuitive appeal, but its effect is that deferred tax recognised at the balance sheet date includes the tax effects of future transactions that have not been recognised in the financial statements, and which the reporting company has neither undertaken nor even committed to undertake at that date. It is difficult to reconcile this with the IASB's *Framework*, which defines assets and liabilities as arising from past events.

Exam focus point

> You need to understand the concept of deferred tax, it is unlikely that you will need to perform detailed calculations.

It is important that you understand the issues properly so consider the example below.

3.3 Example: The three methods compared

Suppose that Pamella Co begins trading on 1 January 20X7. In its first year it makes profits of $5m, the depreciation charge is $1m and the capital allowances on those assets is $1.5m. The rate of income tax is 33%.

Solution: Flow through method

The tax liability for the year is 33% $(5.0 + 1.0 – 1.5)m = $1.485m. The potential deferred tax liability of 33% × ($1.5m – $1m) is completely ignored and no judgement is required on the part of the preparer.

Solution: Full provision

The tax liability is $1.485m again, but the debit in the income statement is increased by the deferred tax liability of 33% × $0.5m = $165,000. The total charge to the income statement is therefore $1,650,000 which is an effective tax rate of 33% on accounting profits (ie 33% × $5.0m). Again, no judgement is involved in using this method.

Solution: Partial provision

Is a deferred tax provision necessary under partial provision? It is now necessary to look ahead at future capital expenditure plans. Will tax allowances exceed depreciation over the next few years? If *yes*, no provision for deferred tax is required. If *no*, then a reversal is expected, ie there is a year in which depreciation is greater than tax allowances. The deferred tax provision is made on the maximum reversal which will be created, and any not provided is disclosed by note.

If we assume that the review of expected future capital expenditure under the partial method required a deferred tax charge of $82,500 (33% × $250,000), we can then summarise the position.

3.4 Summary

The methods can be compared as follows.

Method	Provision	Disclosure
	$	$
Flow-through	–	–
Full provision	165,000	–
Partial provision	82,500	82,500

3.5 IAS 12 Income tax

IAS 12 requires entities to provide for tax timing differences on a **full, rather than partial provision basis.**

3.6 Objective

The objective of IAS 12 is to ensure that:

(a)   Future tax consequences of past transactions and events are recognised as liabilities or assets in the financial statements

(b)   The financial statements disclose any other special circumstances that may have an effect on future tax charges.

3.7 Scope

The IAS applies **to all financial statements that are intended to give a true and fair view** of a reporting entity's financial position and profit or loss (or income and expenditure) for a period. The IAS applies to taxes calculated on the basis of taxable profits, including withholding taxes paid on behalf of the reporting entity.

PROFESSIONAL EDUCATION

3.8 Recognition of deferred tax assets and liabilities

Remember!

> **Deferred tax** should be recognised in respect of **all timing differences that have originated but not reversed by the balance sheet date**.
>
> Deferred tax should **not be recognised on permanent differences.**

Question
Timing differences

Can you remember some examples of timing differences?

Answer

- Accelerated tax allowances
- Pension liabilities accrued but taxed when paid
- Interest charges and development costs capitalised but allowed for tax purposes when incurred
- Unrealised intra-group inventory profits reversed on consolidation
- Revaluation gains
- Tax losses
- Unremitted earnings of subsidiaries, associates and joint ventures recognised in group results.

Key term

> **Permanent differences.** Differences between an entity's taxable profits and its results as stated in the financial statements that arise because certain types of income and expenditure are non-taxable or disallowable, or because certain tax charges or allowances have no corresponding amount in the financial statements.

3.8.1 Allowances for non-current asset expenditure

Deferred tax **should be recognised** when the **allowances** for the cost of a non-current asset are **received before or after the cost of the non-current asset is recognised in the income statement.** However, if and when **all conditions** for retaining the allowances have been met, the **deferred tax should be reversed.**

If an asset is not being depreciated (and has not otherwise been written down to a carrying value less than cost), the timing difference is the amount of tax allowances received.

Most tax allowances are received on a **conditional basis**, ie they are repayable (for example, via a balancing charge) if the assets to which they relate are sold for more than their tax written-down value. However, some, such as industrial buildings allowances, are repayable only if the assets to which they relate are sold within a specified period. Once that period has expired, all conditions for retaining the allowance have been met. At that point, deferred tax that has been recognised (ie on the excess of the allowance over any depreciation) is reversed.

Question
Tax allowances

An industrial building qualifies for a tax allowance when purchased in 20X1. The building is still held by the company in 20Z6. What happens to the deferred tax?

Answer

All the conditions for retaining tax allowances have been met. This means that the timing differences have become permanent and the deferred tax recognised should be reversed. Before the 25 year period has passed, deferred tax should be provided on the difference between the amount of the industrial building allowance and any depreciation charged on the asset.

3.9 Measurement – discounting

IAS 12 states that deferred tax and liabilities **should not be discounted** because of the complexities and difficulties involved.

3.10 Section summary

- Deferred tax is tax relating to timing differences.
- Full provision must be made for tax timing differences.

Exam focus point

> Questions on deferred tax for Paper 2.5 should be fairly straightforward. It is likely to be tested as part of a larger question rather than a question in its own right.

4 Taxation in company accounts

FAST FORWARD

> The balance sheet liability for tax payable is the tax charge for the year. In the income statement the tax charge for the year is adjusted for transfers to or from deferred tax and for prior year under- or over-provisions.

We have now looked at the 'ingredients' of taxation in company accounts. There are two aspects to be learned:

(a) Taxation on profits in the income statement.
(b) Taxation payments due, shown as a liability in the balance sheet.

4.1 Taxation in the income statement

The tax on profit on ordinary activities is calculated by **aggregating**:

(a) **Income tax** on taxable profits
(b) **Transfers to or from deferred taxation**
(c) Any **under provision or overprovision** of income tax on profits of previous years

When corporation tax on profits is calculated for the income statement, **the calculation is only an estimate of what the company thinks its tax liability will be. In subsequent dealings with the tax authorities, a different corporation tax charge might eventually be agreed.**

The difference between the estimated tax on profits for one year and the actual tax charge finally agreed for the year is made as an adjustment to taxation on profits in the following year, **resulting in the disclosure of either an underprovision or an overprovision of tax.**

In the accounting year to 31 December 20X3, Neil Down Co made an operating profit before taxation of $110,000.

Income tax on the operating profit has been estimated as $45,000. In the previous year (20X2) income tax on 20X2 profits had been estimated as $38,000 but it was subsequently agreed at $40,500.

A transfer to the deferred taxation account of $16,000 will be made in 20X3.

Required

(a)   Calculate the tax on profits for 20X3 for disclosure in the accounts.
(b)   Calculate the amount of tax payable.

Answer

(a)

	$
Corporation tax on profits	45,000
Deferred taxation	16,000
Underprovision of tax in previous year $(40,500 – 38,000)$	2,500
Tax on profits for 20X3	63,500

(b)

	$
Tax payable on 20X3 profits	45,000

4.2 Taxation in the balance sheet

It should already be apparent from the previous examples that the corporation tax charge in the income statement will not be the same as corporation tax liabilities in the balance sheet.

In the balance sheet, there are several items which we might expect to find.

(a)   **Income tax may be payable** in respect of (say) interest payments paid in the last accounting return period of the year, or accrued.

(b)   If no tax is payable (or very little), then there might be an **income tax recoverable asset** disclosed in current assets (income tax is normally recovered by offset against the tax liability for the year).

(c)   There will usually be a **liability for tax**, possibly including the amounts due in respect of previous years but not yet paid.

(d)   We may also find a **liability on the deferred taxation account**. Deferred taxation is shown under 'provisions for liabilities and charges' in the balance sheet.

For the year ended 31 July 20X4 Norman Kronkest Co made taxable trading profits of $1,200,000 on which corporation tax is payable at 30%.

(a)   A transfer of $20,000 will be made to the deferred taxation account. The balance on this account was $100,000 before making any adjustments for items listed in this paragraph.

(b) The estimated tax on profits for the year ended 31 July 20X3 was $80,000, but tax has now been agreed at $84,000 and fully paid.

(c) Tax on profits for the year to 31 July 20X4 is payable on 1 May 20X5.

(d) In the year to 31 July 20X4 the company made a capital gain of $60,000 on the sale of some property. This gain is taxable at a rate of 30%.

Required

(a) Calculate the tax charge for the year to 31 July 20X4.

(b) Calculate the tax liabilities in the balance sheet of Norman Kronkest as at 31 July 20X4.

Answer

(a) *Tax charge for the year*

		$
(i)	Tax on trading profits (30% of $1,200,000)	360,000
	Tax on capital gain	18,000
	Deferred taxation	20,000
		398,000
	Underprovision of taxation in previous years $(84,000 – 80,000)	4,000
	Tax charge on ordinary activities	402,000
(ii)	*Note.* The income statement will show the following.	

	$
Operating profit (assumed here to be the same as taxable profits)	1,200,000
Profit from sale of asset (exceptional)	60,000
Profit on ordinary activities before taxation	1,260,000
Tax on profit on ordinary activities	402,000
Retained profits for the year	858,000

(b)

	$
Deferred taxation	
Balance brought forward	100,000
Transferred from income statement	20,000
Deferred taxation in the balance sheet	120,000

The tax liability is as follows.

	$
Payable on 1 May 20X5	
Tax on ordinary profits (30% of $1,200,000)	360,000
Tax on capital gain (30% of $60,000)	18,000
Due on 1 May 20X5	378,000

Summary

	$
Creditors liabilities	
Tax, payable on 1 May 20X5	378,000
Deferred taxation	120,000
	498,000

Note. It may be helpful to show the journal entries for these items.

		$	$
DEBIT	Tax charge (income statement)	402,000	
CREDIT	Tax payable		*382,000
	Deferred tax		20,000

* This account will show a debit balance of $4,000 until the underprovision is recorded, since payment has already been made: (360,000 + 18,000 + 4,000).

5 Presentation and disclosure of taxation

FAST FORWARD

IAS 12 contains rules for comprehensive presentation and disclosure of taxation items, which are summarised here.

5.1 Presentation of tax assets and liabilities

These should be **presented separately** from other assets and liabilities in the balance sheet. Deferred tax assets and liabilities should be distinguished from current tax assets and liabilities.

In addition, deferred tax assets/liabilities should *not* be classified as current assets/ liabilities, where an entity makes such a distinction.

There are only limited circumstances where **current tax** assets and liabilities may be **offset**. This should only occur if two things apply

(a)   The entity has a legally enforceable right to set off the recognised amounts.

(b)   The entity intends either to settle on a net basis, or to realise the asset and settle the liability simultaneously.

Similar criteria apply to the **offset of deferred tax assets and liabilities**.

5.2 Presentation of tax expense

The tax expense or income related to the profit or loss from ordinary activities should be presented on the **face of the income statement**.

5.3 Disclosure

As you would expect, the major components of tax expense or income should be disclosed separately. These will generally include the following.

- **Current tax expense** (income)

- Any adjustments recognised in the period for **current tax of prior periods** (ie for over/under statement in prior years)

- Amount of **deferred tax expense (income)** relating to the origination and reversal of **temporary differences**

- Amount of the benefit arising from a previously unrecognised tax loss, tax credit or temporary difference of a prior period that is used to **reduce current tax expense**

- Amount of the benefit from a previously unrecognised tax loss, tax credit or temporary difference of a prior period that is used to **reduce deferred tax expense**

- Deferred tax expense arising from the **write-down**, or reversal of a previous write-down, of a deferred tax asset

- Amount of tax expense (income) relating to those **changes in accounting policies** and **errors** which are included in the determination of net profit or loss for the period in accordance with IAS 8, because they cannot be accounted for retrospectively.

There are substantial additional disclosures required by the standard. All these items should be shown separately.

- Aggregate current and deferred tax relating to items that are charged or credited to **equity**

- An explanation of the relationship between **tax expense (income)** and **accounting profit** in either or both of the following forms

  - A numerical reconciliation between tax expense (income) and the product of accounting profit multiplied by the applicable tax rate(s), disclosing also the basis on which the applicable tax rate(s) is (are) computed, *or*

  - A numerical reconciliation between the average effective tax rate and the applicable tax rate, disclosing also the basis on which the applicable tax rate is computed

- An explanation of **changes in the applicable tax rate(s)** compared to the previous accounting period

- The amount (and expiry date, if any) of **deductible temporary differences**, unused tax losses, and unused tax credits for which no deferred tax is recognised in the balance sheet

- In respect of each type of **temporary difference**, and in respect of each type of **unused tax loss** and **unused tax credit**:

  - The amount of the deferred tax assets and liabilities recognised in the balance sheet for each period presented

  - The amount of the deferred tax income or expense recognised in the income statement, if this is not apparent from the changes in the amounts recognised in the balance sheet

- In respect of **discontinued operations**, the tax expense relating to

  - The gain or loss on discontinuance

  - The profit or loss from the ordinary activities of the discontinued operation for the period, together with the corresponding amounts for each prior period presented

In addition, an entity should disclose the amount of a deferred tax asset and the nature of the evidence supporting its recognition, when:

- The utilisation of the deferred tax asset is dependent on future taxable profits in excess of the profits arising from the reversal of existing taxable temporary differences, and

- The entity has suffered a loss in either the current or preceding period in the tax jurisdiction to which the deferred tax asset relates.

Chapter roundup

- There are two main systems under which companies can be taxed.

    - The **classical system**
    - The **imputation system**

- The classical system is much the **simpler**. A dividend is paid by Company A to Company B. No advanced tax is due on this dividend. No tax credit is imputed to Company B and no advanced tax is available to set off against the income tax liability.

- Taxation consists of **two components.**

    - Current tax
    - Deferred tax

- **Current tax** is the amount payable to the tax authorities in relation to the trading activities during the period. It is generally straightforward.

- **Deferred tax** is an accounting measure, used to match the tax effects of transactions with their accounting impact. It is quite complex.

- **Deferred tax assets and liabilities** arise from deductible and taxable temporary differences.

- **IAS 12** *Income taxes* covers both current and deferred tax. It has substantial presentation and disclosure requirements.

Quick quiz

1   What is the sales tax at $17\frac{1}{2}$% on sales of \$5,000, if 10% are zero-rated?

2   The tax expense related to the profit from ordinary activities should be shown on the face of the income statement.

    True   ☐

    False   ☐

3   Deferred tax liabilities are the amounts of income taxes payable in future periods in respect of
    ....

4   Give three examples of taxable temporary differences.

5   Which of the following methods of accounting for deferred tax is adopted by IAS 12?

    A   Flow-through method
    B   Differential method
    C   Full provision method
    D   Partial provision method

Answers to quick quiz

1     $787.50 [(90% × $5,000) × 17.5%]

2   True

3   Taxable temporary differences

4   Any three of:

- Interest revenue received in arrears
- Depreciation accelerated for tax purposes
- Development costs capitalised in the balance sheet
- Prepayments
- Sale of goods revenue recognised before the cash is received

5   C

Now try the question below from the Exam Question Bank

Number	Level	Marks	Time
Q11	Examination	25	45 mins

11

Events after the balance sheet date, provisions and contingencies

Topic list	Syllabus reference
1 Revision of IAS 10	3(f)
2 Provisions, contingent liabilities and contingent assets	3(f)

Introduction

You will have met these standards in your earlier studies. However, you may be asked in more detail about IAS 37 for Paper 2.5, given that the relevant Study Guide section is fairly detailed.

Study guide

Section 13 – Liabilities – provisions, contingent assets and liabilities

- Explain why an accounting standard on provisions is necessary – give examples of previous abuses in this area

- Define provisions, legal and constructive obligations, past events and the transfer of economic benefits

- State when provisions may and may not be made, and how they should be accounted for

- Explain how provisions should be measured

- Define contingent assets and liabilities – give examples and describe their accounting treatment

- Be able to identify and account for:
    - warranties/guarantees
    - onerous contracts
    - environmental and similar provisions

- Discuss the validity of making provisions for future repairs or refurbishments

1 Revision of IAS 10

FAST FORWARD
> IAS 10 should be familiar from your earlier studies, but it could still come up in part of a question.

You have already studied IAS 10 *Events after the balance sheet date* extensively.

Knowledge brought forward from earlier studies

IAS 10 Events after the balance sheet date

Definition

Events after the balance sheet date are those events, both favourable and unfavourable, that occur between the balance sheet date and the date on which the financial statements are authorised for issue. Two types of events can be identified:

- Those that provide further evidence of conditions that existed at the balance sheet date
- Those that are indicative of conditions that arose subsequent to the balance sheet date

Accounting treatment

- **Adjust** assets and liabilities where events after the B/S date provide further evidence of conditions existing at the B/S date.

- **Do not adjust**, but instead disclose, important events after the B/S date that do not affect the condition of assets/liabilities at the B/S date.

- **Equity dividends** for period declared after the B/S date but before the financial statements are approved should not be recognised as a liability but shown as a note in the financial statements.

Disclosure

- Nature of event
- Estimate of financial effect (or statement that estimate cannot be made)

2 Provisions, contingent liabilities and contingent assets

As we have seen with regard to post balance sheet events, financial statements must include **all the information necessary for an understanding of the company's financial position**. Provisions, contingent liabilities and contingent assets are 'uncertainties' that must be accounted for consistently if we are to achieve this understanding.

2.1 Objective

IAS 37 *Provisions, contingent liabilities and contingent assets* aims to ensure that appropriate **recognition criteria** and **measurement bases** are applied to provisions, contingent liabilities and contingent assets and that **sufficient information** is disclosed in the **notes** to the financial statements to enable users to understand their nature, timing and amount.

2.2 Provisions

You will be familiar with provisions for depreciation and doubtful debts from your earlier studies. The sorts of provisions addressed by IAS 37 are, however, rather different.

Before IAS 37, there was no accounting standard dealing with provisions. Companies wanting to show their results in the most favourable light used to make large 'one off' provisions in years where a high level of underlying profits was generated. These provisions, often known as 'big bath' provisions, were then available to shield expenditure in future years when perhaps the underlying profits were not as good.

In other words, provisions were used for profit smoothing. Profit smoothing is misleading.

Important

The key aim of IAS 37 is to ensure that **provisions are made only** where there are valid grounds for them.

IAS 37 views a provision as a liability.

Key terms

A **provision** is a **liability** of uncertain timing or amount.

A **liability** is an obligation of an entity to transfer economic benefits as a result of past transactions or events.
(IAS 37)

The IAS distinguishes provisions from other liabilities such as trade creditors and accruals. This is on the basis that for a provision there is **uncertainty** about the timing or amount of the future expenditure. Whilst uncertainty is clearly present in the case of certain accruals the uncertainty is generally much less than for provisions.

2.3 Recognition

IAS 37 states that a provision should be **recognised** as a liability in the financial statements when:

- An entity has a **present obligation** (legal or constructive) as a result of a past event
- It is probable that a **transfer of economic benefits** will be required to settle the obligation
- A **reliable estimate** can be made of the obligation

2.4 Meaning of obligation

It is fairly clear what a legal obligation is. However, you may not know what a **constructive obligation** is.

Key term

IAS 37 defines a **constructive obligation** as

'An obligation that derives from an entity's actions where:

- by an established pattern of past practice, published policies or a sufficiently specific current statement the entity has indicated to other parties that it will accept certain responsibilities; and

- as a result, the entity has created a valid expectation on the part of those other parties that it will discharge those responsibilities.'

Question

In which of the following circumstances might a provision be recognised?

(a) On 13 December 20X9 the board of an entity decided to close down a division. The accounting date of the company is 31 December. Before 31 December 20X9 the decision was not communicated to any of those affected and no other steps were taken to implement the decision.

(b) The board agreed a detailed closure plan on 20 December 20X9 and details were given to customers and employees.

(c) A company is obliged to incur clean up costs for environmental damage (that has already been caused).

(d) A company intends to carry out future expenditure to operate in a particular way in the future.

Answer

(a) No provision would be recognised as the decision has not been communicated.

(b) A provision would be made in the 20X9 financial statements.

(c) A provision for such costs is appropriate.

(d) No present obligation exists and under IAS 37 no provision would be appropriate. This is because the entity could avoid the future expenditure by its future actions, maybe by changing its method of operation.

2.4.1 Probable transfer of economic benefits

For the purpose of the IAS, a transfer of economic benefits is regarded as **'probable'** if the event is **more likely than not** to occur. This appears to indicate a probability of more than 50%. However, the standard makes it clear that where there is a number of similar obligations the probability should be based on considering the population as a whole, rather than one single item.

2.4.2 Example: transfer of economic benefits

If a company has entered into a warranty obligation then the probability of transfer of economic benefits may well be extremely small in respect of one specific item. However, when considering the population as a whole the probability of some transfer of economic benefits is quite likely to be much higher. If there is a **greater than 50% probability** of some transfer of economic benefits then a **provision** should be made for the **expected amount**.

2.4.3 Measurement of provisions

Important

> The amount recognised as a provision should be the best estimate of the expenditure required to settle the present obligation at the balance sheet date.

The estimates will be determined by the **judgement** of the entity's management supplemented by the experience of similar transactions.

Allowance is made for **uncertainty**. Where the provision being measured involves a large population of items, the obligation is estimated by weighting all possible outcomes by their associated probabilities, ie **expected value**.

Question   Warranty

Parker Co sells goods with a warranty under which customers are covered for the cost of repairs of any manufacturing defect that becomes apparent within the first six months of purchase. The company's past experience and future expectations indicate the following pattern of likely repairs.

% of goods sold	Defects	Cost of repairs if all items suffered from these defects $m
75	None	-
20	Minor	1.0
5	Major	4.0

What is the expected cost of repairs?

Answer

The cost is found using 'expected values' (75% × $nil) + (20% × $1.0m) + (5% × $4.0m) = $400,000.

Where the effect of the **time value of money** is material, the amount of a provision should be the **present value** of the expenditure required to settle the obligation. An appropriate **discount** rate should be used.

The discount rate should be a **pre-tax rate** that reflects current market assessments of the time value of money. **The discount rate(s) should not reflect risks for which future cash flow estimates have been adjusted.**

2.4.4 Future events

Future events which are reasonably expected to occur (eg new legislation, changes in technology) may affect the amount required to settle the entity's obligation and should be taken into account.

2.4.5 Expected disposal of assets

Gains from the expected disposal of assets should not be taken into account in measuring a provision.

2.4.6 Reimbursements

Some or all of the expenditure needed to settle a provision may be expected to be recovered from a third party. If so, the **reimbursement should be recognised only when it is virtually certain that reimbursement will be received if the entity settles the obligation.**

- The reimbursement should be treated as a separate asset, and the amount recognised should not be greater than the provision itself.

- The provision and the amount recognised for reimbursement may be netted off in the income statement.

2.4.7 Changes in provisions

Provisions should be renewed at each balance sheet date and adjusted to reflect the current best estimate. If it is no longer probable that a transfer of economic benefits will be required to settle the obligation, the provision should be reversed.

2.4.8 Use of provisions

A provision should be used only for expenditures for which the provision was originally recognised. Setting expenditures against a provision that was originally recognised for another purpose would conceal the impact of two different events.

2.4.9 Future operating losses

Provisions should not be recognised for future operating losses. They do not meet the definition of a liability and the general recognition criteria set out in the standard.

2.4.10 Onerous contracts

If an entity has a contract that is onerous, the present obligation under the contract **should be recognised and measured** as a provision. An example might be vacant leasehold property.

Key term

> An **onerous contract** is a contract entered into with another party under which the unavoidable costs of fulfilling the terms of the contract exceed any revenues expected to be received from the goods or services supplied or purchased directly or indirectly under the contract and where the entity would have to compensate the other party if it did not fulfil the terms of the contract.

2.5 Examples of possible provisions

It is easier to see what IAS 37 is driving at if you look at examples of those items which are possible provisions under this standard. Some of these we have already touched on.

(a) **Warranties**. These are argued to be genuine provisions as on past experience it is probable, ie more likely than not, that some claims will emerge. The provision must be estimated, however, on the basis of the class as a whole and not on individual claims. There is a clear legal obligation in this case.

(b) **Major repairs**. In the past it has been quite popular for companies to provide for expenditure on a major overhaul to be accrued gradually over the intervening years between overhauls. Under IAS 37 this is no longer possible as IAS 37 would argue that this is a mere intention to carry out repairs, not an obligation. The entity can always sell the asset in the meantime. The only solution is to treat major assets such as aircraft, ships, furnaces etc as a series of smaller assets where each part is depreciated over shorter lives. Thus any major overhaul may be argued to be replacement and therefore capital rather than revenue expenditure.

(c) **Self insurance**. A number of companies have created a provision for self insurance based on the expected cost of making good fire damage etc instead of paying premiums to an insurance company. Under IAS 37 this provision is no longer justifiable as the entity has no obligation until a fire or accident occurs. No obligation exists until that time.

(d) **Environmental contamination**. If the company has an environmental policy such that other parties would expect the company to clean up any contamination or if the company has broken current environmental legislation then a provision for environmental damage must be made.

(e) **Decommissioning or abandonment costs**. When an oil company initially purchases an oilfield it is put under a legal obligation to decommission the site at the end of its life. Prior to IAS 37 most oil companies set up the provision gradually over the life of the field so that no one year would be unduly burdened with the cost.

IAS 37, however, insists that a legal obligation exists on the initial expenditure on the field and therefore a liability exists immediately. This would appear to result in a large charge to profit and loss in the first year of operation of the field. However, the IAS takes the view that the cost of purchasing the field in the first place is not only the cost of the field itself but also the costs of putting it right again. Thus all the costs of abandonment may be capitalised.

(f) **Restructuring**. This is considered in detail below.

2.6 Provisions for restructuring

One of the main purposes of IAS 37 was to target abuses of provisions for restructuring. Accordingly, IAS 37 lays down **strict criteria** to determine when such a provision can be made.

Key term

> IAS 37 defines a **restructuring** as:
>
> A programme that is planned and is controlled by management and materially changes one of two things.
>
> - The scope of a business undertaken by an entity
> - The manner in which that business is conducted

The IAS gives the following **examples** of events that may fall under the definition of restructuring.

- The **sale or termination** of a line of business

- The **closure of business locations** in a country or region or the **relocation** of business activities from one country region to another

- **Changes in management structure**, for example, the elimination of a layer of management

- **Fundamental reorganisations** that have a material effect on the **nature and focus** of the entity's operations

The question is whether or not an entity has an obligation - legal or constructive - at the balance sheet date. For this to be the case:

- An entity must have a **detailed formal plan** for the restructuring

- It must have **raised a valid expectation** in those affected that it will carry out the restructuring by starting to implement that plan or announcing its main features to those affected by it

Important

> **A mere management decision is not normally sufficient**. Management decisions may sometimes trigger off recognition, but only if earlier events such as negotiations with employee representatives and other interested parties have been concluded subject only to management approval.

Where the restructuring involves the **sale of an operation** then IAS 37 states that no obligation arises until the entity has entered into a **binding sale agreement**. This is because until this has occurred the entity will be able to change its mind and withdraw from the sale even if its intentions have been announced publicly.

2.6.1 Costs to be included within a restructuring provision

The IAS states that a restructuring provision should include only the **direct expenditures** arising from the restructuring, which are those that are both:

- **Necessarily entailed** by the restructuring; and
- Not associated with the **ongoing activities** of the entity.

The following costs should specifically **not** be included within a restructuring provision.

- **Retraining** or relocating continuing staff
- **Marketing**
- **Investment in new systems** and distribution networks

2.7 Disclosure

Disclosures for provisions fall into two parts.

- Disclosure of details of the **change in carrying value** of a provision from the beginning to the end of the year

- Disclosure of the **background** to the making of the provision and the uncertainties affecting its outcome

2.8 Contingent liabilities

Now you understand provisions it will be easier to understand contingent assets and liabilities.

Key term

> IAS 37 defines a **contingent liability** as:
>
> - A possible obligation that arises from past events and whose existence will be confirmed only by the occurrence or non-occurrence of one or more uncertain future events not wholly within the entity's control; or
>
> - A present obligation that arises from past events but is not recognised because:
>
>   - It is not probable that a transfer of economic benefits will be required to settle the obligation; or
>
>   - The amount of the obligation cannot be measured with sufficient reliability.

As a rule of thumb, probable means more than 50% likely. **If an obligation is probable, it is not a contingent liability** - instead, a **provision is needed**.

2.8.1 Treatment of contingent liabilities

Contingent liabilities **should not be recognised in financial statements** but they **should be disclosed**. The required disclosures are:

- A brief description of the nature of the contingent liability
- An estimate of its financial effect
- An indication of the uncertainties that exist
- The possibility of any reimbursement

2.9 Contingent assets

Key term

IAS 37 defines a **contingent asset** as:

A possible asset that arises from past events and whose existence will be confirmed by the occurrence or non-occurrence of one or more uncertain future events not wholly within the entity's control.

A contingent asset must not be recognised. Only when the realisation of the related economic benefits is **virtually certain** should recognition take place. At that point, **the asset is no longer a contingent asset!**

2.10 Disclosure

2.10.1 Disclosure: contingent liabilities

A **brief description** must be provided of all material contingent liabilities unless they are likely to be remote. In addition, provide

- An estimate of their **financial effect**
- Details of **any uncertainties**
- The possibility of any reimbursement

2.10.2 Disclosure: contingent assets

Contingent assets must only be disclosed in the notes if they are **probable**. In that case a brief description of the contingent asset should be provided along with an estimate of its likely financial effect.

2.11 'Let out'

IAS 37 permits reporting entities to avoid disclosure requirements relating to provisions, contingent liabilities and contingent assets if they would be expected to **seriously prejudice** the position of the entity in dispute with other parties. However, this should only be employed in **extremely rare** cases. Details of the general nature of the provision/contingencies must still be provided, together with an explanation of why it has not been disclosed.

2.12 Flow chart

You must practise the questions below to get the hang of IAS 37. But first, study the flow chart, taken from IAS 37, which is a good summary of its requirements concerning provisions and contingent liabilities.

Exam focus point

If you learn this flow chart you should be able to deal with most questions you are likely to meet in an exam.

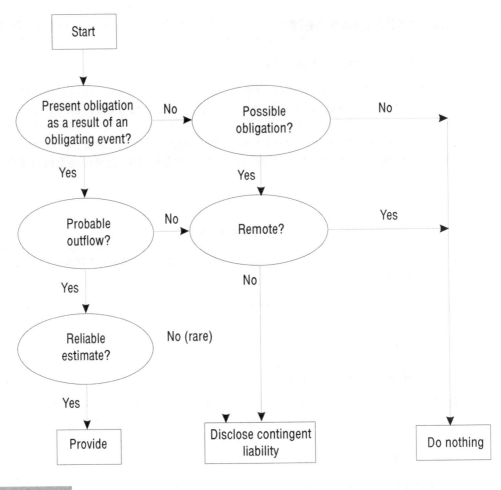

Question

During 20X0 Smack Co gives a guarantee of certain borrowings of Pony Co, whose financial condition at that time is sound. During 20X1, the financial condition of Pony Co deteriorates and at 30 June 20X1 Pony Co files for protection from its creditors.

What accounting treatment is required:

(a) At 31 December 20X0?
(b) At 31 December 20X1?

Answer

(a) *At 31 December 20X0*

There is a present obligation as a result of a past obligating event. The obligating event is the giving of the guarantee, which gives rise to a legal obligation. However, at 31 December 20X0 no transfer of economic benefits is probable in settlement of the obligation.

No provision is recognised. The guarantee is disclosed as a contingent liability unless the probability of any transfer is regarded as remote.

(b) *At 31 December 20X1*

As above, there is a present obligation as a result of a past obligating event, namely the giving of the guarantee.

At 31 December 20X1 it is probable that a transfer of economic benefits will be required to settle the obligation. A provision is therefore recognised for the best estimate of the obligation.

Question

Warren Co gives warranties at the time of sale to purchasers of its products. Under the terms of the warranty the manufacturer undertakes to make good, by repair or replacement, manufacturing defects that become apparent within a period of three years from the date of the sale. Should a provision be recognised?

Answer

Warren Co **cannot avoid** the cost of repairing or replacing all items of product that manifest manufacturing defects in respect of which warranties are given before the balance sheet date, and a provision for the cost of this should therefore be made.

Warren Co is obliged to repair or replace items that fail within the entire warranty period. Therefore, in respect of **this year's sales**, the obligation provided for at the balance sheet date should be the cost of making good items for which defects have been notified but not yet processed, **plus** an estimate of costs in respect of the other items sold for which there is sufficient evidence that manufacturing defects **will** manifest themselves during their remaining periods of warranty cover.

Question

After a wedding in 20X0 ten people died, possibly as a result of food poisoning from products sold by Callow Co. Legal proceedings are started seeking damages from Callow but it disputes liability. Up to the date of approval of the financial statements for the year to 31 December 20X0, Callow's lawyers advise that it is probable that it will not be found liable. However, when Callow prepares the financial statements for the year to 31 December 20X1 its lawyers advise that, owing to developments in the case, it is probable that it will be found liable.

What is the required accounting treatment:

(a)   At 31 December 20X0?
(b)   At 31 December 20X1?

Answer

(a)   *At 31 December 20X0*

On the basis of the evidence available when the financial statements were approved, there is no obligation as a result of past events. No provision is recognised. The matter is disclosed as a contingent liability unless the probability of any transfer is regarded as remote.

(b)   *At 31 December 20X1*

On the basis of the evidence available, there is a present obligation. A transfer of economic benefits in settlement is probable.

A provision is recognised for the best estimate of the amount needed to settle the present obligation.

2.13 Section summary

- The objective of IAS 37 is to ensure that appropriate recognition criteria and measurement bases are applied to provisions and contingencies and that sufficient information is disclosed.

- The IAS seeks to ensure that provisions are **only recognised** when a **measurable obligation** exists. It includes detailed rules that can be used to ascertain when an obligation exists and how to measure the obligation.

- The standard attempts to **eliminate** the **'profit smoothing'** which has gone on before it was issued.

Chapter roundup

- **IAS 10** should be familiar from your earlier studies, but it still could come up in part of a question.

- Under **IAS 37**, a **provision** should be recognised

  - When an entity has a **present obligation**, legal or constructive
  - It is probable that a **transfer of economic benefits** will be required to settle it
  - A **reliable estimate** can be made of its amount

- An entity **should not recognise a contingent asset or liability**, but they **should be disclosed**.

Quick quiz

1   Define events occurring after the balance sheet date.

2   A customer goes bankrupt after the balance sheet date and his debt must be written off.

Adjusting event   ☐

Non-adjusting event   ☐

3   Inventory is lost in a fire after the balance sheet date.

Adjusting event   ☐

Non-adjusting event   ☐

4   A provision is a .... of .... timing or amount.

5   A programme is undertaken by management which converts the previously wholly owned chain of restaurants they ran into franchises. Is this restructuring?

6   Define contingent asset and contingent liability.

Answers to quick quiz

1   Those events, unfavourable and favourable, which occur between the balance sheet date and the date on which the financial statements are authorised for issue.

2   Adjusting

3   Non-adjusting

4   Liability of uncertain timing or amount

5   Yes. The manner in which the business is conducted has changed

6   Refer to paragraphs 2.9 and 2.8 respectively

Now try the question below from the Exam Question Bank

Number	Level	Marks	Time
Q12	Examination	25	45 mins

Reporting financial performance

Topic list	Syllabus reference
1 IAS 8 *Accounting policies, changes in accounting estimates and errors*	3(f)
2 Accounting policies	3(f)
3 Changes in accounting policies	3(f)
4 Changes in accounting estimates	3(f)
5 Errors	3(f)
6 IFRS 5 *Non-current assets held for sale and discontinued operations*	3(f)
7 IFRS 1 *First-time adoption of International Financial Reporting Standards*	3(f)

Introduction

This long chapter is mainly concerned with the **income statement**. **IAS 8** deals with accounting policies. It also looks at certain circumstances and transactions which require different treatment to normal profit or loss items.

IFRS 5 on assets held for sale and discontinued operations is a recent and important standard.

IFRS 1 on first time adoption of IFRS is included for completeness, but in many ways is more relevant to the UK stream

Study guide

Section 5 – Preparation of financial statements for companies

- Describe the main issues involved when a company adopts International Financial Reporting Standards (IFRSs) for the first time
- Apply the requirements of the IASB to the preparation of financial statements for a first time adopter of International Financial Reporting Standards

Sections 6 and 7 – Accounting policies, changes in accounting estimates and errors; non-current assets held for sale and discontinued operations

- Explain the need for accounting standards in the above areas
- Discuss the importance of identifying and reporting the results of a discontinued operation; define discontinued operations
- Describe the circumstances where assets meet the criteria of 'held for sale'
- Discuss the accounting treatment of non-current assets held for sale
- Prepare financial statements in accordance with the requirements of relevant accounting standards in the above areas
- Describe the circumstances where a change in accounting policy is permitted
- Define and account for errors and changes in accounting estimates and changes in accounting policies
- Explain and illustrate the contents and purpose of the statement of changes in equity

1 IAS 8 *Accounting policies, changes in accounting estimates and errors*

FAST FORWARD

IAS 8 deals with the treatment of **changes in accounting estimates, changes in accounting policies and errors**, as defined below.

The standard was extensively revised in December 2003. The new title reflects the fact that the material on determining net profit or loss for the period has been transferred to IAS 1.

1.1 Definitions

The following definitions are given in the standard. Apart from the definition of accounting policies, most of the definitions are either new or heavily amended.

Key terms

- **Accounting policies** are the specific principles, bases, conventions, rules and practices adopted by an entity in preparing and presenting financial statements.

- A **change in accounting estimate** is an adjustment of the carrying amount of an asset or a liability or the amount of the periodic consumption of an asset, that results from the assessment of the present status of, and expected future benefits and obligations associated with, assets and liabilities. Changes in accounting estimates result from new information or new developments and, accordingly, are not corrections of errors.

- **Material**: as defined in IAS 1 (see Chapter 4)

- **Prior period errors** are omissions from, and misstatements in, the entity's financial statements for one or more prior periods arising from a failure to use, or misuse of, reliable information that:

    (a)   Was available when financial statements for those periods were authorised for issue, and

    (b)   Could reasonably be expected to have been obtained and taken into account in the preparation and presentation of those financial statements.

    Such errors include the effects of mathematical mistakes, mistakes in applying accounting policies, oversights or misinterpretations of facts, and fraud.

- **Retrospective application** is applying a new accounting policy to transactions, other events and conditions as if that policy had always been applied.

- **Retrospective restatement** is correcting the recognition, measurement and disclosure of amounts of elements of financial statements as if a prior period error had never occurred.

- **Prospective application** of a change in accounting policy and of recognising the effect of a change in an accounting estimate, respectively, are:

    (a)   Applying the new accounting policy to transactions, other events and conditions occurring after the date as at which the policy is changed; and

    (b)   Recognising the effect of the change in the accounting estimate in the current and future periods affected by the change.

- **Impracticable** Applying a requirement is impracticable when the entity cannot apply it after making every reasonable effort to do so. It is impracticable to apply a change in an accounting policy retrospectively or to make a retrospective restatement to correct an error if one of the following apply.

    (a)   The effects of the retrospective application or retrospective restatement are not determinable.

    (b)   The retrospective application or retrospective restatement requires assumptions about what management's intent would have been in that period.

    (c)   The retrospective application or retrospective restatement requires significant estimates of amounts and it is impossible to distinguish objectively information about those estimates that: provides evidence of circumstances that existed on the date(s) at which those amounts are to be recognised, measured or disclosed; and would have been available when the financial statements for that prior period were authorised for issue, from other information.

(IAS 8)

2 Accounting policies

FAST FORWARD

The material on the selection of appropriate accounting policies has been **transferred** into IAS 8 from IAS 1.

Accounting policies are determined by **applying the relevant IFRS or IFRIC** and considering any relevant Implementation Guidance issued by the IASB for that IFRS/IFRIC.

Where there is no applicable IFRS or IFRIC management should use its **judgement** in developing and applying an accounting policy that results in information that is **relevant** and **reliable**. Management should refer to:

    (a)   The requirements and guidance in IFRSs and IFRICs dealing with **similar** and **related** issues

(b)   The definitions, recognition criteria and measurement concepts for assets, liabilities and expenses in the *Framework*

Management may also consider the most recent pronouncements of **other standard setting bodies** that use a similar conceptual framework to develop standards, other accounting literature and accepted industry practices if these do not conflict with the sources above.

An entity must select and apply its accounting policies for a period **consistently** for similar transactions, other events and conditions, unless an IFRS or an IFRIC specifically requires or permits categorisation of items for which different policies may be appropriate. If an IFRS or an IFRIC requires or permits categorisation of items, an appropriate accounting policy must be selected and applied consistently to each category.

3 Changes in accounting policies

FAST FORWARD
You should be able to define and deal with changes in accounting policies.

3.1 Introduction

The same accounting policies are usually adopted from period to period, to allow users to analyse trends over time in profit, cash flows and financial position. **Changes in accounting policy will therefore be rare** and should be made only if required by one of three things.

(a)   By **statute**

(b)   By an **accounting standard setting body**

(c)   If the change will result in a **more appropriate presentation** of events or transactions in the financial statements of the entity

The standard highlights two types of event **which do not constitute changes in accounting policy**.

(a)   Adopting an accounting policy for a **new type of transaction** or event not dealt with previously by the entity.

(b)   Adopting a **new accounting policy** for a transaction or event which has not occurred in the past or which was not material.

In the case of tangible non-current assets, if a policy of revaluation is adopted for the first time then this is treated, not as a change of accounting policy under IAS 8, but as a revaluation under IAS 16 *Property, plant and equipment* (see Chapter 5). The following paragraphs do not therefore apply to a change in policy to adopt revaluations.

A change in accounting policy **must be applied retrospectively**. **Retrospective application** means that the new accounting policy is applied to transactions and events as if it had always been in use. In other words, at the earliest date such transactions or events occurred, the policy is applied from that date.

Prospective application is **no longer allowed** under the revised IAS 8 unless it is **impracticable** (see Key Terms) to determine the cumulative amount of charge.

3.2 Adoption of an IAS/IFRS

Where a new IAS or IFRS is adopted, IAS 8 requires any transitional provisions in the new IAS itself to be followed. If none are given in the IAS which is being adopted, then you should follow the general principles of IAS 8.

3.3 Other changes in accounting policy

IAS 8 requires **retrospective application**, *unless* it is **impracticable** to determine the cumulative amount of charge. Any resulting adjustment should be reported as an adjustment to the opening balance of retained earnings. Comparative information should be restated unless it is impracticable to do so.

This means that all comparative information must be restated **as if the new policy had always been in force**, with amounts relating to earlier periods reflected in an adjustment to opening reserves of the earliest period presented.

Prospective application is allowed only when it is impracticable to determine the cumulative effect of the change.

Certain **disclosures** are required when a change in accounting policy has a material effect on the current period or any prior period presented, or when it may have a material effect in subsequent periods.

  (a) Reasons for the change

  (b) Amount of the adjustment for the current period and for each period presented

  (c) Amount of the adjustment relating to periods prior to those included in the comparative information

  (d) The fact that comparative information has been restated or that it is impracticable to do so

An entity should also disclose information relevant to assessing the **impact of new IFRS** on the financial statements where these have **not yet come into force.**

Question	Change in accounting policy

Wick Co was established on 1 January 20X0. In the first three years' accounts development expenditure was carried forward as an asset in the balance sheet. During 20X3 the managers decided that for the current and future years, all development expenditure should be written off as it is incurred. This decision has not resulted from any change in the expected outcome of development projects on hand, but rather from a desire to favour the prudence concept. The following information is available.

(a) *Movements on the development account*

Year	*Development expenditure incurred and capitalised during year*	*Transfer from capitalised development expenditure account to income statement*
	$'000	$'000
20X0	525	-
20X1	780	215
20X2	995	360

(b) The 20X2 accounts showed the following.

	$'000
Retained earnings b/f	2,955
Retained earnings for the year	1,825
Retained earnings c/f	4,780

(c) The retained profit for 20X3 after charging the actual development expenditure for the year was $2,030,000.

Required

Show how the change in accounting policy should be reflected in the reserves in the company's 20X3 accounts in accordance with IAS 8.

Ignore taxation.

Answer

If the new accounting policy had been adopted since the company was incorporated, the additional income statement charges for development expenditure would have been:

	$'000
20X0	525
20X1 (780 – 215)	565
	1,090
20X2 (995 – 360)	635
	1,725

This means that the reserves brought forward at 1 January 20X3 would have been $1,725,000 less than the reported figure of $4,780,000; while the reserves brought forward at 1 January 20X2 would have been $1,090,000 less than the reported figure of $2,955,000.

The statement of reserves in Wick Co's 20X3 accounts should, therefore, appear as follows.

RETAINED EARNINGS

	20X3 $'000	Comparative (previous year) figures 20X2 $'000	
Retained earnings at the beginning of year			
Previously reported	4,780	2,955	
Retrospective change in accounting policy (note 1)	1,725	1,090	
Restated	3,055	1,865	
Retained earnings for the year	2,030	1,190	(note 2)
Retained earnings at the end of the year	5,085	3,055	

Notes

1   The accounts should include a note explaining the reasons for and consequences of the changes in accounting policy. (See above workings for 20X3 and 20X2.)

2   The retained profit shown for 20X2 is after charging the additional development expenditure of $635,000.

4 Changes in accounting estimates

FAST FORWARD

Once again, you need to be able to define and deal with changes in accounting estimates.

Estimates arise in relation to business activities because of the **uncertainties inherent within them**. Judgements are made based on the most up to date information and the use of such estimates is a necessary part of the preparation of financial statements. It does *not* undermine their reliability. Here are some examples of accounting estimates.

(a)   A necessary **bad debt provision**

(b)   **Useful lives** of depreciable assets

(c)   Provision for **obsolescence of inventory**

The rule here is that the **effect of a change in an accounting estimate** should be included in the determination of net profit or loss in one of:

(a)   The period of the change, if the change affects that period only

(b)   The period of the change *and* future periods, if the change affects both

Changes may occur in the circumstances which were in force at the time the estimate was calculated, or perhaps additional information or subsequent developments have come to light.

An example of a change in accounting estimate which affects only the **current period** is the bad debt estimate. However, a revision in the life over which an asset is depreciated would affect both the **current and future periods**, in the amount of the depreciation expense.

Reasonably enough, the effect of a change in an accounting estimate should be included in the **same income statement classification** as was used previously for the estimate. This rule helps to ensure **consistency** between the financial statements of different periods.

The **materiality** of the change is also relevant. The nature and amount of a change in an accounting estimate that has a material effect in the current period (or which is expected to have a material effect in subsequent periods) should be disclosed. If it is not possible to quantify the amount, this impracticability should be disclosed.

5 Errors

Here we deal with errors relating to a prior period.

5.1 Introduction

Errors discovered during a current period which **relate to a prior period** may arise through:

(a)   Mathematical mistakes

(b)   Mistakes in the application of accounting policies

(c)   Misinterpretation of facts

(d)   Oversights

(e)   Fraud

A more formal definition is given in the Key Terms in Paragraph 1.1.

Most of the time these errors can be **corrected through net profit or loss for the current period**. Where they are material prior period errors, however, this is not appropriate. The standard considers two possible treatments.

5.2 Accounting treatment

Prior period errors: correct retrospectively. There is no longer any allowed alternative treatment.

This involves:

(a)   Either restating the comparative amounts for the prior period(s) in which the error occurred,

(b)   Or, when the error occurred before the earliest prior period presented, restating the opening balances of assets, liabilities and equity for that period

so that the financial statements are presented **as if the error had never occurred**.

Only where it is **impracticable** to determine the cumulative effect of an error on prior periods can an entity correct an error **prospectively**.

Various **disclosures** are required.

(a) **Nature** of the prior period error

(b) For each prior period, to the extent practicable, the **amount** of the correction.

    (i) For each financial statement line item affected

    (ii) If IAS 33 applies, for basic and diluted earnings per share

(c) The amount of the correction at the **beginning of the earliest prior period** presented

(d) If **retrospective restatement is impracticable** for a particular prior period, the **circumstances** that led to the existence of that condition and a description of how and from when the error has been corrected. Subsequent periods need not repeat these disclosures

Question   Error

During 20X7 Global discovered that certain items had been included in inventory at 31 December 20X6, valued at $4.2m, which had in fact been sold before the year end. The following figures for 20X6 (as reported) and 20X7 (draft) are available.

	20X6	20X7 (draft)
	$'000	$'000
Sales	47,400	67,200
Cost of goods sold	(34,570)	(55,800)
Profit before taxation	12,830	11,400
Income taxes	(3,880)	(3,400)
Net profit	8,950	8,000

Reserves at 1 January 20X6 were $13m. The cost of goods sold for 20X7 includes the $4.2m error in opening inventory. The income tax rate was 30% for 20X6 and 20X7. No dividends have been declared or paid.

Required

Show the income statement for 20X7, with the 20X6 comparative, and retained earnings.

Answer

INCOME STATEMENT

	20X6	20X7
	$'000	$'000
Sales	47,400	67,200
Cost of goods sold (W1)	(38,770)	(51,600)
Profit before tax	8,630	15,600
Income tax (W2)	(2,620)	(4,660)
Net profit	6,010	10,940

RETAINED EARNINGS

	20X6	20X7
	$'000	$'000
Opening retained earnings		
As previously reported	13,000	21,950
Correction of prior period error (4,200 – 1,260)	–	(2,940)
As restated	13,000	19,010
Net profit for year	6,010	10,940
Closing retained earnings	19,010	29,950

Workings

1	Cost of goods sold	20X6	20X7
		$'000	$'000
	As stated in question	34,570	55,800
	Inventory adjustment	4,200	(4,200)
		38,770	51,600
2	Income tax	20X6	20X7
		$'000	$'000
	As stated in question	3,880	3,400
	Inventory adjustment (4,200 × 30%)	(1,260)	1,260
		2,620	4,660

6 IFRS 5 *Non-current Assets held for sale and Discontinued Operations*

FAST FORWARD

IFRS 5 requires assets 'held for sale' to be presented separately on the face of the balance sheet.

6.1 Background

IFRS 5 is the result of a short-term convergence project with the US Financial Accounting Standards Board (FASB). It replaces IAS 35 *Discontinuing operations*.

IFRS 5 requires assets and groups of assets that are 'held for sale' to be **presented separately** on the face of the balance sheet and the results of discontinued operations to be presented separately in the income statement. This is required so that users of financial statements will be better able to make **projections** about the financial position, profits and cash flows of the entity.

Key term

> **Disposal** group: a group of assets to be disposed of, by sale or otherwise, together as a group in a single transaction, and liabilities directly associated with those assets that will be transferred in the transaction. (In practice a disposal group could be a subsidiary, a cash-generating unit or a single operation within an entity.)   (*IFRS 5*)

IFRS 5 does not apply to certain assets covered by other accounting standards:

(a)   Deferred tax assets (IAS 12)

(b)   Assets arising from employee benefits (IAS 19)

(c)   Financial assets (IAS 39)

(d)   Investment properties accounted for in accordance with the fair value model (IAS 40)

(e)   Agricultural and biological assets that are measured at fair value less estimated point of sale costs (IAS 41)

(f)   Insurance contracts (IFRS 4)

6.2 Classification of assets held for sale

A non-current asset (or disposal group) should be classified as **held for sale** if its carrying amount will be recovered **principally through a sale transaction** rather than **through continuing use**. A number of detailed criteria must be met:

    (a)   The asset must be **available for immediate sale** in its present condition.

    (b)   Its sale must be **highly probable** (ie, significantly more likely than not).

For the sale to be highly probable, the following must apply.

    (a)   Management must be **committed** to a plan to sell the asset.

    (b)   There must be an active programme to **locate a buyer.**

    (c)   The asset must be marketed for sale at a **price that is reasonable** in relation to its current fair value.

    (d)   The sale should be expected to take place **within one year** from the date of classification.

    (e)   It is unlikely that significant changes to the plan will be made or that the plan will be withdrawn.

An asset (or disposal group) can still be classified as held for sale, even if the sale has not actually taken place within one year. However, the delay must have been **caused by events or circumstances beyond the entity's control** and there must be sufficient evidence that the entity is still committed to sell the asset or disposal group. Otherwise the entity must cease to classify the asset as held for sale.

If an entity acquires a disposal group (eg, a subsidiary) exclusively with a view to its subsequent disposal it can classify the asset as held for sale only if the sale is expected to take place within one year and it is highly probable that all the other criteria will be met within a short time (normally three months).

An asset that is to be **abandoned** should not be classified as held for sale. This is because its carrying amount will be recovered principally through continuing use. However, a disposal group to be abandoned may meet the definition of a discontinued operation and therefore separate disclosure may be required (see below).

Question

Held for sale

On 1 December 20X3, a company became committed to a plan to sell a manufacturing facility and has already found a potential buyer. The company does not intend to discontinue the operations currently carried out in the facility. At 31 December 20X3 there is a backlog of uncompleted customer orders. The company will not be able to transfer the facility to the buyer until after it ceases to operate the facility and has eliminated the backlog of uncompleted customer orders. This is not expected to occur until spring 20X4.

Required

Can the manufacturing facility be classified as 'held for sale' at 31 December 20X3?

Answer

The facility will not be transferred until the backlog of orders is completed; this demonstrates that the facility is not available for immediate sale in its present condition. The facility cannot be classified as 'held for sale' at 31 December 20X3. It must be treated in the same way as other items of property, plant and equipment: it should continue to be depreciated and should not be separately disclosed.

6.3 Measurement of assets held for sale

Key terms

> **Fair value:** the amount for which an asset could be exchanged, or a liability settled, between knowledgeable, willing parties in an arm's length transaction.
> **Costs to sell:** the incremental costs directly attributable to the disposal of an asset (or disposal group), excluding finance costs and income tax expense.
> **Recoverable amount:** the higher of an asset's fair value less costs to sell and its value in use.
> **Value in use:** the present value of estimated future cash flows expected to arise from the continuing use of an asset and from its disposal at the end of its useful life.

A non-current asset (or disposal group) that is held for sale should be measured at the **lower of** its **carrying amount** and **fair value less costs to sell**. Fair value less costs to sell is equivalent to net realisable value.

An impairment loss should be recognised where fair value less costs to sell is lower than carrying amount. Note that this is an exception to the normal rule. IAS 36 *Impairment of assets* requires an entity to recognise an impairment loss only where an asset's recoverable amount is lower than its carrying value. Recoverable amount is defined as the higher of net realisable value and value in use. IAS 36 does not apply to assets held for sale.

Non-current assets held for sale **should not be depreciated**, even if they are still being used by the entity.

A non-current asset (or disposal group) that is **no longer classified as held for sale** (for example, because the sale has not taken place within one year) is measured at the **lower of**:

(a) Its **carrying amount** before it was classified as held for sale, adjusted for any depreciation that would have been charged had the asset not been held for sale

(b) Its **recoverable amount** at the date of the decision not to sell

6.4 Presenting discontinued operations

Key terms

> Discontinued **operation:** a component of an entity that has either been disposed of, or is classified as held for sale, and:
> (a) Represents a separate major line of business or geographical area of operations
> (b) Is part of a single co-ordinated plan to dispose of a separate major line of business or geographical area of operations, or
> (c) Is a subsidiary acquired exclusively with a view to resale.
>
> **Component of an entity:** operations and cash flows that can be clearly distinguished, operationally and for financial reporting purposes, from the rest of the entity.

An entity should **present and disclose information** that enables users of the financial statements to evaluate the financial effects of **discontinued operations** and disposals of non-current assets or disposal groups.

An entity should disclose a **single amount** on the **face of the income statement** comprising the total of:

(a) The **post-tax profit or loss** of discontinued operations and

(b) The post-tax gain or loss recognised on the **measurement to fair value less costs to sell** or on the disposal of the assets or disposal group(s) constituting the discontinued operation.

An entity should also disclose an **analysis** of this single amount into:

(a)　The revenue, expenses and pre-tax profit or loss of discontinued operations

(b)　The related income tax expense

(c)　The gain or loss recognised on the measurement to fair value less costs to sell or on the disposal of the assets of the discontinued operation

(d)　The related income tax expense

This may be presented either on the face of the income statement or in the notes. If it is presented on the face of the income statement it should be presented in a section identified as relating to discontinued operations, ie separately from continuing operations. This analysis is not required where the discontinued operation is a newly acquired subsidiary that has been classified as held for sale.

An entity should disclose the **net cash flows** attributable to the operating, investing and financing activities of discontinued operations. These disclosures may be presented either on the face of the cash flow statement or in the notes.

Gains and losses on the remeasurement of a disposal group that is not a discontinued operation but is held for sale should be included in profit or loss from continuing operations.

6.5 Illustration

The following illustration is taken from the implementation guidance to IFRS 5. Profit for the period from discontinued operations would be analysed in the notes.

XYZ GROUP
INCOME STATEMENT
FOR THE YEAR ENDED 31 DECEMBER 20X2

	20X2 $'000	20X1 $'000
Continuing operations		
Revenue	X	X
Cost of sales	(X)	(X)
Gross profit	X	X
Other income	X	X
Distribution costs	(X)	(X)
Administrative expenses	(X)	(X)
Other expenses	(X)	(X)
Finance costs	(X)	(X)
Share of profit of associates	X	X
Profit before tax	X	X
Income tax expense	(X)	(X)
Profit for the period from continuing operations	X	X
Discontinued operations		
Profit for the period from discontinued operations	X	X
Profit for the period	X	X
Attributable to:		
Equity holders of the parent	X	X
Minority interest	X	X
	X	X

An alternative to this presentation would be to analyse the profit from discontinued operations in a separate column on the face of the income statement.

On 20 October 20X3 the directors of a parent company made a public announcement of plans to close a steel works. The closure means that the group will no longer carry out this type of operation, which until recently has represented about 10% of its total revenue. The works will be gradually shut down over a period of several months, with complete closure expected in July 20X4. At 31 December output had been significantly reduced and some redundancies had already taken place. The cash flows, revenues and expenses relating to the steel works can be clearly distinguished from those of the subsidiary's other operations.

Required

How should the closure be treated in the financial statements for the year ended 31 December 20X3?

Answer

Because the steel works is being closed, rather than sold, it cannot be classified as 'held for sale'. In addition, the steel works is not a discontinued operation. Although at 31 December 20X3 the group was firmly committed to the closure, this has not yet taken place and therefore the steel works must be included in continuing operations. Information about the planned closure could be disclosed in the notes to the financial statements.

6.6 Presentation of a non-current asset or disposal group classified as held for sale

Non-current assets and disposal groups classified as held for sale should be **presented separately** from other assets in the balance sheet. The liabilities of a disposal group should be presented separately from other liabilities in the balance sheet.

(a) Assets and liabilities held for sale **should not be offset**.

(b) The **major classes** of assets and liabilities held for sale should be **separately disclosed** either on the face of the balance sheet or in the notes.

6.7 Additional disclosures

In the period in which a non-current asset (or disposal group) has been either classified as held for sale or sold the following should be disclosed.

(a) A **description** of the non-current asset (or disposal group)

(b) A description of the **facts and circumstances** of the disposal

(c) Any **gain or loss** recognised when the item was classified as held for sale

(d) If applicable, the **segment** in which the non-current asset (or disposal group) is presented in accordance with IAS 14 *Segment reporting*

Where an asset previously classified as held for sale is **no longer held for sale**, the entity should disclose a description of the facts and circumstances leading to the decision and its effect on results.

7 IFRS 1 *First time adoption of International Financial Reporting Standards*

FAST FORWARD

IFRS 1 sets out the precise way in which companies should implement a **change from local accounting standards (their previous GAAP) to IASs and IFRSs.**

7.1 Background and definitions

One of the main reasons for issuing IFRS 1 is that listed companies in the EU are required to prepare their consolidated financial statements in accordance with IFRSs from 2005 onwards. Many companies in the EU (for example, in the UK) have made the transition to IFRS over the last few months.

The standard is intended to ensure that an entity's **first IFRS financial statements** contain **high quality information** that is transparent for users and comparable over all periods presented; provides a suitable starting point for accounting under IFRSs; and can be generated at a cost that does not exceed the benefits to users.

Key terms

- **Date of transition to IFRSs.** The beginning of the earliest period for which an entity presents full comparative information under IFRSs in its first IFRS financial statements.

- **Deemed cost** An amount used as a surrogate for cost or depreciated cost at a given date.

- **Fair value** The amount for which an asset could be exchanged, or a liability settled, between knowledgeable, willing parties in an arm's length transaction.

- **First IFRS financial statements** The first annual financial statements in which an entity adopts International Financial Reporting Standards (IFRSs), by an explicit and unreserved statement of compliance with IFRSs.

- **Opening IFRS balance sheet** An entity's balance sheet (published or unpublished) at the date of transition to IFRSs.

- **Previous GAAP** The basis of accounting that a first time adopter used immediately before adopting IFRSs.

- **Reporting date** The end of the latest period covered by financial statements or by an interim financial report.

(IFRS 1)

IFRS 1 **only applies** where an entity prepares IFRS financial statements **for the first time.** Changes in accounting policies made by an entity that already applies IFRSs should be dealt with by applying either IAS 8 or specific transitional requirements in other standards.

7.2 Making the transition to IFRS

An entity should:

(a) Select accounting policies that comply with IFRSs **at the reporting date** for the entity's first IFRS financial statements.

(b) Prepare an **opening IFRS balance sheet** at the **date of transition to IFRSs.** This is the starting point for subsequent accounting under IFRSs. The date of transition to IFRSs is the beginning of the earliest comparative period presented in an entity's first IFRS financial statements.

(c) **Disclose the effect** of the change in the financial statements.

7.3 Example: reporting date and opening IFRS balance sheet

An EU listed company has a 31 December year-end and is required to comply with IFRSs from 1 January 2005.

Required

What is the date of transition to IFRSs?

Solution

The company's first IFRS financial statements will be for the **year ended 31 December 2005**.

IFRS 1 requires that at least one year's comparative figures are presented in the first IFRS financial statements. The comparative figures will be for the year ended 31 December 2004.

Therefore the date of transition to IFRSs is **1 January 2004** and the company prepares an opening IFRS balance sheet at this date.

7.4 Preparing the opening IFRS balance sheet

IFRS 1 states that in its opening IFRS balance sheet an entity shall:

(a) **Recognise all assets and liabilities** whose recognition is required by IFRSs

(b) Not recognise items as assets or liabilities if IFRSs do not permit such recognition

(c) **Reclassify items** that it recognised under previous GAAP as one type of asset, liability or component of equity, but are a different type of asset, liability or component of equity under IFRSs

(d) **Apply IFRS in measuring** all recognised assets and liabilities

This involves restating the balance sheet prepared at the same date under the entity's previous GAAP so that it complies with IASs and IFRSs in force **at the first reporting date**. In our example above, the company prepares its opening IFRS balance sheet at **1 January 2004**, following accounting policies that comply with IFRSs in force at **31 December 2005**.

The accounting policies that an entity uses in its opening IFRS balance sheet may differ from those it used for the same date using its previous GAAP. The resulting adjustments are recognised directly **in retained earnings** (in equity) **at the date of transition**. (This is because the adjustments arise from events and transactions before the date of transition to IFRS.)

7.5 Exemptions from other IFRSs

A business may elect to use **any or all** of a range of exemptions. These enable an entity not to apply certain requirements of specific accounting standards retrospectively in drawing up its opening IFRS balance sheet. Their purpose is to ensure that the cost of producing IFRS financial statements does not exceed the benefits to users.

7.5.1 Business combinations

Exam focus point

You may want to come back to this paragraph after you have done Part D of this text on group accounts.

IFRS 3 need not be applied retrospectively to business combinations that occurred before the date of the opening IFRS balance sheet. This has the following consequences.

(a) Combinations keep the **same classification** (eg, acquisition, uniting of interests) as in the previous GAAP financial statements.

(b)   **All acquired assets and liabilities are recognised** other than:

- Some financial assets and financial liabilities derecognised under the previous GAAP (derivatives and special purpose entities must be recognised);

- Assets (including goodwill) and liabilities that were not recognised under previous GAAP and would not qualify for recognition under IFRSs.

Any resulting change is recognised by **adjusting retained earnings** (ie equity) unless the change results from the recognition of an intangible asset that was previously subsumed within goodwill.

(c)   **Items which do not qualify for recognition** as an asset or liability under IFRSs must be excluded from the opening IFRS balance sheet. For example, intangible assets that do not qualify for separate recognition under IAS 38 must be reclassified as part of goodwill.

(d)   The carrying amount of **goodwill** in the opening IFRS balance sheet is based on its carrying amount **under previous GAAP**. However, goodwill must be tested for impairment at the transition date.

7.5.2 Property, plant and equipment

An entity may measure an item of property, plant and equipment at its **fair value at the transition** date and then use the fair value as its **deemed** cost at that date.

An entity may use a **previous GAAP revaluation**, or a valuation for the purpose of a privatisation or initial public offering, as the deemed cost at the transition date, so long as the revaluation was **broadly comparable** to fair value or depreciated replacement cost at the date of the valuation.

These exemptions are also available for:

(a)   Investment properties measured under the cost model in IAS 40 *Investment property*

(b)   Intangible assets that meet the recognition criteria and the criteria for revaluation in IAS 38 *Intangible assets*

7.5.3 Compound financial instruments

IAS 32 requires compound financial instruments to be split at inception into separate liability and equity components. If the liability component is no longer outstanding at the date of the transition to IFRSs, the split is not required.

7.5.4 Designation of previously recognised financial instruments

When financial instruments are first recognised, they may be designated as financial assets or financial liabilities 'at fair value through profit or loss' or as 'available for sale' under IAS 39. An entity may make such a designation at the date of transition to IFRSs.

Question   **First time adopter**

Russell Co will adopt International Financial Reporting Standards (IFRSs) for the first time in its financial statements for the year ended 31 December 20X4.

In its previous financial statements for 31 December 20X2 and 20X3, which were prepared under local GAAP, the company made a number of routine accounting estimates, including accrued expenses. It also recognised a general provision for liabilities, calculated at a fixed percentage of its retained profits for the year. This is required under its local GAAP.

Subsequently, some of the accruals were found to be overestimates and some were found to be underestimates.

Required

Discuss how the matters above should be dealt with in the IFRS financial statements of Russell Co for the year ended 31 December 20X4.

Answer

Provided that the routine accounting estimates have been made in a manner consistent with IFRSs no adjustments are made in the first IFRS financial statements. The only exception to this is if the company has subsequently discovered that these estimates were in material error. Although there were some overestimates and some underestimates, this is probably not the case here.

The general provision is a different matter. This provision would definitely not have met the criteria for recognition under IAS 37 and therefore it will not be recognised in the opening IFRS balance sheet (1 January 20X3) or at subsequent year-ends.

7.6 Presentation and disclosure

An entity's first IFRS financial statements must include **at least one year of comparative information.**

Comparative information need not comply with IAS 32 and IAS 39; instead the entity may apply its previous GAAP and disclose this fact together with the nature of the main adjustments that would make the information comply with IAS 32 and IAS 39.

An entity must also **explain the effect** of the transition from previous GAAP to IFRSs on its financial position, financial performance and cash flows by providing **reconciliations**:

    (a)   Of **equity** reported under previous GAAP to equity under IFRSs at the **date of transition and at the balance sheet date**

    (b)   Of the **profit or loss** reported under previous GAAP to profit or loss reported under IFRSs for the period

The reconciliations must give sufficient detail to enable users to understand the material adjustments to the balance sheet and income statement.

If an entity presented a cash flow statement under its previous GAAP, it should also explain the material **adjustments to the cash flow statement**.

If an entity recognised or reversed any **impairment losses** for the first time in preparing its opening IFRS balance sheet, it must provide the disclosures that IAS 36 *Impairment of assets* would have required if the entity had recognised those impairment losses or reversals in the period beginning with the date of transition to IFRSs.

If an entity corrects **errors made under previous GAAP**, the reconciliations must distinguish the correction of errors from changes in accounting policies.

Where **fair value has been used as deemed cost** for a non-current asset in the opening IFRS balance sheet, the financial statements must disclose the aggregate of fair values and the aggregate adjustments to the carrying amounts reported under previous GAAP for each line in the opening IFRS balance sheet.

7.7 Managing the change to International Standards

The implementation of the above technical aspects is likely to entail careful management in most companies. Here are some of the **change management considerations** that should be addressed.

(a) **Accurate assessment of the task involved**. Underestimation or wishful thinking may hamper the effectiveness of the conversion and may ultimately prove inefficient.

(b) **Proper planning**. This should take place at the overall project level, but a **detailed** task **analysis** could be drawn up to **control work performed**.

(c) **Human resource management**. The project must be properly structured and staffed.

(d) **Training**. Where there are **skills gaps**, remedial training should be provided.

(e) **Monitoring and accountability**. A relaxed 'it will be alright on the night' attitude could spell danger. Implementation **progress** should be **monitored** and **regular meetings** set up so that participants can **personally account for what they are doing** as well as **flag up any problems** as early as possible. **Project drift should be avoided**.

(f) **Achieving milestones**. Successful completion of key steps and tasks should be appropriately acknowledged, ie what managers call 'celebrating success', so as to **sustain motivation and performance**.

(g) **Physical resourcing**. The need for IT **equipment** and **office space** should be properly assessed.

(h) **Process review**. Care should be taken not to perceive the change as a one-off quick fix. Any change in **future systems** and processes should be assessed and properly implemented.

(i) **Follow-up procedures**. As with general good management practice, the **follow up procedures** should be planned in to **make sure that the changes stick** and that any further changes are identified and addressed.

Chapter roundup

- **IAS 8** *Accounting policies, changes in accounting estimates and errors* is a very important standard with which you should be familiar from your Paper 1.1 studies. You should be able to define and deal with:

    - Selection of accounting policies
    - Changes in accounting policies
    - Changes in accounting estimates
    - Errors

- **IFRS 5** *Non-current assets held for sale and discontinued operations* requires assets 'held for sale' to be presented separately on the face of the balance sheet.

- The results of discontinued operations should be presented separately in the income statement.

- Another important aspect of reporting financial performance is **segment reporting**.

- **IAS 14** adopts a **management approach** to determining reporting segments.

- The most important **definitions** are of:

    - Business segments
    - Geographical segments

- These definitions include **factors** which are used to determine whether products/services are related or whether a geographical segment exists. You must **learn these** as the rest of the standard is based on them.

- Other definitions are also important. You should be particularly careful about what is **included in and excluded from**:

    - Segment revenue
    - Segment expense
    - Segment assets
    - Segment liabilities

- Do not worry too much about the detailed **disclosure requirements**. These are unlikely to be of great importance in the exam.

- **IFRS 1** sets out the precise way in which an entity should implement a change from old accounting standards to IAS and IFRS.

Quick quiz

1   How should a prior period error be corrected under IAS 8?

2   Give three circumstances when a change in accounting policy might be required.

3   When can a non-current asset be classified as held for sale?

4   How should an asset held for sale be measured?

5   How does IFRS 5 define a discontinued operation?

6   What approach should normally be taken when deciding whether business or geographical segments should be the primary reporting format?

7   What is the 'date of transition to IFRS' according to IFRS 1?

Answers to quick quiz

1   By adjusting the opening balance of retained earnings.

2   (a)   By statute
     (b)   By the IASB
     (c)   For a more appropriate presentation

3   See Para 6.2

4   See Para 6.3

5   See Para 6.4

6   See Para 8.1

7   The beginning of the earliest comparative period present in an entity's first IFRS financial statements.

Now try the question below from the Exam Question Bank

Number	Level	Marks	Time
Q13	Examination	25	45 mins

BPP
PROFESSIONAL EDUCATION

13

Earnings per share

Topic list	Syllabus reference
1 IAS 33 Earnings per share	3(d)(f)
2 Basic EPS	3(d)(f)
3 Effect on EPS of changes in capital structure	3(d)(f)
4 Diluted EPS	3(d)(f)
5 Presentation, disclosure and other matters	3(d)(f)

Introduction

Earnings per share (EPS) is widely used by investors as a measure of a company's performance and is of particular importance in:

(a) **Comparing the results** of a company over a **period of time**

(b) **Comparing the performance** of one company's equity against the performance of **another company's equity**, and also against the returns obtainable from loan stock and other forms of investment.

The purpose of any earnings yardstick is to achieve as far as possible clarity of meaning, comparability between one company and another, one year and another, and attributability of profits to the equity shares. IAS 33 *Earnings per share* goes some way to ensuring that all these aims are achieved.

Study guide

Section 15 – Earnings per share

- Explain the importance of comparability in relation to the calculation of earnings per share (EPS) and its importance as a stock market indicator

- Explain why the trend of EPS may be a more accurate indicator of performance than a company's profit trend

- Define earnings and the basic number of shares

- Calculate the EPS in accordance with relevant accounting standards in the following circumstances

  - basic EPS
  - where there has been a bonus issue of shares/stock split during the year
  - where there has been a rights issue of shares during the year

- Explain the relevance to existing shareholders of the diluted EPS, and describe the circumstances that will give rise to a future dilution of the EPS

- Calculate the diluted EPS where convertible debt or preference shares are in issue and where share options and warrants exist

1 IAS 33 *Earnings per share*

FAST FORWARD

IAS 33 is a fairly straightforward standard. Make sure you follow all the calculations through and you should then be able to tackle questions easily. IAS 33 was revised in December 2003, but the revisions are to areas not in your syllabus.

1.1 Objective

The objective of IAS 33 is to improve the **comparison** of the performance of different entities in the same period and of the same entity in different accounting periods by prescribing methods for determining the number of shares to be included in the calculation of earnings per share and other amounts per share and by specifying their presentation.

1.2 Definitions

The following definitions are given in IAS 33, some of which are given in other IASs.

Key terms

- **Ordinary shares**: an equity instrument that is subordinate to all other classes of equity instruments.

- **Potential ordinary share:** a financial instrument or other contract that may entitle its holder to ordinary shares.

- **Warrants or options**: financial instruments that give the holder the right to purchase ordinary shares.

- **Financial instrument**: any contract that gives rise to both a financial asset of one entity and a financial liability or equity instrument of another entity.

- **Equity instrument**: any contract that evidences a residual interest in the assets of an entity after deducting all of its liabilities.

                                                                                              (IAS 33)

1.2.1 Ordinary shares

There may be more than one class of ordinary shares, but ordinary shares of the same class will have the same rights to receive dividends. Ordinary shares participate in the net profit for the period **only after other types of shares**, eg preference shares.

1.2.2 Potential ordinary shares

IAS 33 identifies the following examples of financial instruments and other contracts generating potential ordinary shares.

(a) **Debt or equity instruments**, including preference shares, that are convertible into ordinary shares

(b) **Share warrants and options**

(c) **Employee plans** that allow employees to receive ordinary shares as part of their remuneration and other share purchase plans

(d) Shares that would be issued upon the satisfaction of **certain conditions** resulting from contractual arrangements, such as the purchase of a business or other assets

1.3 Scope

IAS 33 has the following scope restrictions.

(a) Only companies with (potential) ordinary shares which are **publicly traded** need to present EPS (including companies in the process of being listed).

(b) EPS need only be presented on the basis of **consolidated results** where the parent's results are shown as well.

(c) Where companies **choose** to present EPS, even when they have no (potential) ordinary shares which are traded, they must do so in accordance with IAS 33.

2 Basic EPS

FAST FORWARD

You should know how to calculate basic EPS.

2.1 Measurement

Basic EPS should be calculated by dividing the **net profit** or loss for the period attributable to ordinary shareholders by the **weighted average number of ordinary shares** outstanding during the period.

$$\text{Basic EPS} = \frac{\text{Net profit/(loss) attributable to ordinary shareholders}}{\text{Weighted average number of ordinary shares outstanding during the period}}$$

2.2 Earnings

Earnings includes **all items of income and expense** (including tax and minority interests) *less* net profit attributable to **preference shareholders**, including preference dividends.

Preference dividends deducted from net profit consist of:

(a) Preference dividends on non-cumulative preference shares declared in respect of the period

(b)   The full amount of the required preference dividends for cumulative preference shares for the period, *whether or not* they have been declared (*excluding* those paid/declared during the period in respect of previous periods)

2.3 Per share

The number of ordinary shares used should be the weighted average number of ordinary shares during the period. This figure (for all periods presented) should be **adjusted for events**, other than the conversion of potential ordinary shares, that have changed the number of shares outstanding without a corresponding change in resources.

The **time-weighting factor** is the number of days the shares were outstanding compared with the total number of days in the period; a reasonable approximation is usually adequate.

2.4 Example: weighted average number of shares

Justina Co, a listed company, has the following share transactions during 20X7.

Date	Details	Shares issued	Treasury shares*	Shares outstanding
1 January 20X7	Balance at beginning of year	200,000	30,000	170,000
31 May 20X7	Issue of new shares for cash	80,000	-	250,000
1 December 20X7	Purchase of treasury shares	-	25,000	225,000
31 December 20X7	Balance at year end	280,000	55,000	225,000

* Treasury shares are an entity's own shares acquired. In some countries own shares cannot be held, but must be cancelled on acquisition.

Required

Calculate the weighted average number of shares outstanding for 20X7.

Solution

The weighted average number of shares can be calculated in two ways.

(a) $(170,000 \times 5/12) + (250,000 \times 6/12) + (225,000 \times 1/12) = 214,583$ shares
(b) $(170,000 \times 12/12) + (80,000 \times 7/12) - (25,000 \times 1/12) = 214,583$ shares

2.5 Consideration

Shares are usually included in the weighted average number of shares from the **date consideration is receivable** which is usually the date of issue; in other cases consider the specific terms attached to their issue (consider the substance of any contract). The treatment for the issue of ordinary shares in different circumstances is as follows.

Consideration	Start date for inclusion
In exchange for cash	When cash is receivable
On the voluntary reinvestment of dividends on ordinary or preferred shares	The dividend payment date
As a result of the conversion of a debt instrument to ordinary shares	Date interest ceases accruing
In place of interest or principal on other financial instruments	Date interest ceases accruing
In exchange for the settlement of a liability of the entity	The settlement date

Consideration	Start date for inclusion
As consideration for the acquisition of an asset other than cash	The date on which the acquisition is recognised
For the rendering of services to the entity	As services are rendered

Ordinary shares issued as **purchase consideration** in an acquisition should be included as of the date of acquisition because the acquired entity's results will also be included from that date.

If ordinary shares are **partly paid**, they are treated as a fraction of an ordinary share to the extent they are entitled to dividends relative to fully paid ordinary shares.

Contingently issuable shares (including those subject to recall) are included in the computation when all necessary conditions for issue have been satisfied.

Question

Basic EPS

Flame Co is a company with a called up and paid up capital of 100,000 ordinary shares of $1 each and 20,000 10% preferred shares of $1 each. The company manufactures gas appliances. During its financial year to 31 December the company had to pay $50,000 compensation and costs arising from an uninsured claim for personal injuries suffered by a customer while on the company premises.

The gross profit was $200,000. Flame Co paid the required preferred share dividend and declared an ordinary dividend of 42c per share. Assuming an income tax rate of 30% on the given figures show the trading results and EPS of the company.

Answer

FLAME CO
TRADING RESULTS FOR YEAR TO 31 DECEMBER

	$	$
Gross profit		200,000
Expense		(50,000)
Profit before tax		150,000
Tax at 30%		(45,000)
Profit for the financial year		105,000
Less dividends		
Preferred *	2,000	
Ordinary	42,000	
		44,000
		61,000

EARNINGS PER SHARE

$$\frac{103,000 \, ^*}{100,000} = 103c$$

*($105,000 − $2,000 preferred div = $103,000)

3 Effect on EPS of changes in capital structure

You also need to know how to deal with EPS following changes in capital structure.

3.1 Introduction

We looked at the effect of issues of new shares or buy-backs of shares on basic EPS above. In these situations, the corresponding figures for EPS for the previous year will be comparable with the current year because, as the weighted average number of shares has risen or fallen, there has been a **corresponding increase or decrease in resources**. Money has been received when shares were issued, and money has been paid out to repurchase shares. It is assumed that the sales or purchases have been made at full market price.

3.2 Example: earnings per share with a new issue

On 30 September 20X2, Boffin Co made an issue at full market price of 1,000,000 ordinary shares. The company's accounting year runs from 1 January to 31 December. Relevant information for 20X1 and 20X2 is as follows.

	20X2	20X1
Shares in issue as at 31 December	9,000,000	8,000,000
Profits after tax and preferred dividend	$3,300,000	$3,280,000

Required

Calculate the EPS for 20X2 and the corresponding figure for 20X1.

Solution

	20X2	20X1
Weighted average number of shares		
9 months × 8 million	6,000,000	
3 months × 9 million	2,250,000	
	8,250,000	8,000,000
Earnings	$3,300,000	$3,280,000
EPS	40 cents	41 cents

In spite of the increase in total earnings by $20,000 in 20X2, the EPS is not as good as in 20X1, because there was extra capital employed for the final 3 months of 20X2.

There are other events, however, which change the number of shares outstanding, **without a corresponding change in resources**. In these circumstances it is necessary to make adjustments so that the current and prior period EPS figures are comparable.

Four such events are considered by IAS 33.

 (a) **Capitalisation or bonus issue** (sometimes called a stock dividend)
 (b) Bonus element in any other issue, eg a **rights issue** to existing shareholders
 (c) **Share split**
 (d) **Reverse share split** (consolidation of shares)

3.3 Capitalisation/bonus issue and share split/reverse share split

These two types of event can be considered together as they have a similar effect. In both cases, ordinary shares are issued to existing shareholders for **no additional consideration**. The number of ordinary shares has increased without an increase in resources.

This problem is solved by **adjusting the number of ordinary shares outstanding before the event** for the proportionate change in the number of shares outstanding as if the event had occurred at the beginning of the earliest period reported.

3.4 Example: earnings per share with a bonus issue

Greymatter Co had 400,000 shares in issue, until on 30 September 20X2 it made a bonus issue of 100,000 shares. Calculate the EPS for 20X2 and the corresponding figure for 20X1 if total earnings were $80,000 in 20X2 and $75,000 in 20X1. The company's accounting year runs from 1 January to 31 December.

Solution

	20X2	20X1
Earnings	$80,000	$75,000
Shares at 1 January	400,000	400,000
Bonus issue	100,000	100,000
	500,000 shares	500,000 shares
EPS	16c	15c

The number of shares for 20X1 must also be adjusted if the figures for EPS are to remain comparable.

3.5 Rights issue

A rights issue of shares is an issue of new shares to existing shareholders **at a price below the current market value**. The offer of new shares is made on the basis of x new shares for every y shares currently held; eg a 1 for 3 rights issue is an offer of 1 new share at the offer price for every 3 shares currently held. This means that there is a bonus element included.

To arrive at figures for EPS when a rights issue is made, we need to calculate first of all the **theoretical ex-rights price**. This is a weighted average value per share, and is perhaps explained most easily with a numerical example.

3.6 Example: theoretical ex-rights price

Suppose that Egghead Co has 10,000,000 shares in issue. It now proposes to make a 1 for 4 rights issue at a price of $3 per share. The market value of existing shares on the final day before the issue is made is $3.50 (this is the 'with rights' value). What is the theoretical ex-rights price per share?

Solution

	$
Before issue 4 shares, value $3.50 each	14.00
Rights issue 1 share, value $3	3.00
Theoretical value of 5 shares	17.00

Theoretical ex-rights price = $\dfrac{\$17.00}{5}$ = $3.40 per share

Note that this calculation can alternatively be performed using the total value and number of outstanding shares.

3.7 Procedures

The procedures for calculating the EPS for the current year and a corresponding figure for the previous year are now as follows.

(a) The **EPS for the corresponding previous period** should be multiplied by the following fraction. (*Note.* The market price on the last day of quotation is taken as the fair value immediately prior to exercise of the rights, as required by the standard.)

Formula to learn

$$\frac{\text{Theoretical ex - rights price}}{\text{Market price on last day of quotation (with rights)}}$$

(b)   To obtain the **EPS for the current year** you should:

(i)   Multiply the number of shares before the rights issue by the fraction of the year before the date of issue and by the following fraction

Formula to learn

$$\frac{\text{Market price on last day of quotation with rights}}{\text{Theoretical ex - rights price}}$$

(ii)   Multiply the number of shares after the rights issue by the fraction of the year after the date of issue and add to the figure arrived at in (i)

The total earnings should then be divided by the total number of shares so calculated.

3.8 Example: earnings per share with a rights issue

Brains Co had 100,000 shares in issue, but then makes a 1 for 5 rights issue on 1 October 20X2 at a price of $1. The market value on the last day of quotation with rights was $1.60.

Calculate the EPS for 20X2 and the corresponding figure for 20X1 given total earnings of $50,000 in 20X2 and $40,000 in 20X1.

Solution

Calculation of theoretical ex-rights price:

	$
Before issue 5 shares, value × $1.60	8.00
Rights issue 1 share, value × $1.00	1.00
Theoretical value of 6 shares	9.00

Theoretical ex-rights price = $\dfrac{\$9}{6}$ = $1.50

 EPS for 20X1

EPS as calculated before taking into account the rights issue = 40c ($40,000 divided by 100,000 shares).

$$\text{EPS} = \frac{1.50}{1.60} \times 40c = 37\tfrac{1}{2}c$$

(Remember: this is the corresponding value for 20X1 which will be shown in the financial statements for Brains Co at the end of 20X2.)

EPS for 20X2

Number of shares before the rights issue was 100,000. 20,000 shares were issued.

Stage 1:	$100,000 \times {}^{9}/_{12} \times \dfrac{1.60}{1.50}$ =	80,000
Stage 2:	$120,000 \times {}^{3}/_{12}$ =	30,000
		110,000

$$\text{EPS} = \frac{\$50,000}{110,000} = 45\tfrac{1}{2}c$$

The figure for total earnings is the actual earnings for the year.

Question | **Rights issue**

Marcoli Co has produced the following net profit figures for the years ending 31 December.

	$m
20X6	1.1
20X7	1.5
20X8	1.8

On 1 January 20X7 the number of shares outstanding was 500,000. During 20X7 the company announced a rights issue with the following details.

Rights: 1 new share for each 5 outstanding (100,000 new shares in total)
Exercise price: $5.00
Last date to exercise rights: 1 March 20X7

The market (fair) value of one share in Marcoli immediately prior to exercise on 1 March 20X7 = $11.00.

Required

Calculate the EPS for 20X6, 20X7 and 20X8.

Answer

Computation of theoretical ex-rights price

This computation uses the total fair value and number of shares.

$$\frac{\text{Fair value of all outstanding shares} + \text{total received from exercise of rights}}{\text{No shares outstanding prior to exercise} + \text{no shares issued in exercise}}$$

$$= \frac{(\$11.00 \times 500{,}000) + (\$5.00 \times 100{,}000)}{500{,}000 + 100{,}000} = \$10.00$$

Computation of EPS

		20X6 $	20X7 $	20X8 $
20X6	EPS as originally reported $\dfrac{\$1{,}100{,}000}{500{,}000}$	2.20		
20X6	EPS restated for rights issue = $\dfrac{\$1{,}100{,}000}{500{,}000} \times \dfrac{10}{11}$	2.00		
20X7	EPS including effects of rights issue $\dfrac{\$1{,}500{,}000}{(500{,}000 \times 2/12 \times 11/10) + (600{,}000 \times 10/12)}$		2.54	
20X8	EPS $= \dfrac{\$1{,}800{,}000}{600{,}000}$			3.00

4 Diluted EPS

Diluted EPS is complicated, but you should be able to deal with a fairly straightforward situation.

4.1 Introduction

At the end of an accounting period, a company may have in issue some **securities** which do not (at present) have any 'claim' to a share of equity earnings, but **may give rise to such a claim in the future**. These securities include:

(a) A **separate class of equity shares** which at present is not entitled to any dividend, but will be entitled after some future date

(b) **Convertible loan stock** or **convertible preferred shares** which give their holders the right at some future date to exchange their securities for ordinary shares of the company, at a pre-determined conversion rate

(c) **Options** or **warrants**

In such circumstances, the future number of ordinary shares in issue might increase, which in turn results in a fall in the EPS. In other words, a **future increase** in the **number of ordinary shares will cause a dilution or 'watering down' of equity**, and it is possible to calculate a **diluted earnings per share** (ie the EPS that would have been obtained during the financial period if the dilution had already taken place). This will indicate to investors the possible effects of a future dilution.

4.2 Earnings

The earnings calculated for basic EPS should be adjusted by the **post-tax** (including deferred tax) effect of:

(a) Any **dividends** on dilutive potential ordinary shares that were deducted to arrive at earnings for basic EPS

(b) **Interest recognised** in the period for the dilutive potential ordinary shares

(c) Any **other changes in income or expenses** (fees and discount, premium accounted for as yield adjustments) that would result from the conversion of the dilutive potential ordinary shares

The conversion of some potential ordinary shares may lead to changes in **other income or expenses**. For example, the reduction of interest expense related to potential ordinary shares and the resulting increase in net profit for the period may lead to an increase in the expense relating to a non-discretionary employee profit-sharing plan. When calculating diluted EPS, the net profit or loss for the period is adjusted for any such consequential changes in income or expense.

4.3 Per share

The number of ordinary shares is the weighted average number of ordinary shares calculated for basic EPS plus the weighted average number of ordinary shares that would be issued on the conversion of all the **dilutive potential ordinary shares** into ordinary shares.

It should be assumed that dilutive ordinary shares were converted into ordinary shares at the **beginning of the period** or, if later, at the actual date of issue. There are two other points.

(a) The computation assumes the most **advantageous conversion rate** or exercise rate from the standpoint of the holder of the potential ordinary shares.

(b) **Contingently issuable** (potential) ordinary shares are treated as for basic EPS; if the conditions have not been met, the number of contingently issuable shares included in the computation is based on the number of shares that would be issuable if the end of the reporting period was the end of the contingency period. Restatement is not allowed if the conditions are not met when the contingency period expires.

4.4 Example: diluted EPS

In 20X7 Farrah Co had a basic EPS of 105c based on earnings of $105,000 and 100,000 ordinary $1 shares. It also had in issue $40,000 15% Convertible Loan Stock which is convertible in two years' time at the rate of 4 ordinary shares for every $5 of stock. The rate of tax is 30%. In 20X7 gross profit of $200,000 and expenses of $50,000 were recorded, including interest payable of $6,000.

Required

Calculate the diluted EPS.

Solution

Diluted EPS is calculated as follows.

Step 1   **Number of shares**: the additional equity on conversion of the loan stock will be 40,000 × 4/5 = 32,000 shares

Step 2   **Earnings**: Farrah Co will save interest payments of $6,000 but this increase in profits will be taxed. Hence the earnings figure may be recalculated:

	$
Gross profit	200,000
Expenses (50,000 – 6,000)	(44,000)
Profit before tax	156,000
Tax expense (30%)	(46,800)
Earnings	109,200

Step 3   **Calculation**: Diluted EPS = $\dfrac{\$109{,}200}{132{,}000}$ = 82.7c

Step 4   **Dilution**: the dilution in earnings would be 105c – 82.7c = 22.3c per share.

Question   **Diluted EPS**

Ardent Co has 5,000,000 ordinary shares of 25 cents each in issue, and also had in issue in 20X4:

(a) $1,000,000 of 14% convertible loan stock, convertible in three years' time at the rate of 2 shares per $10 of stock;

(b) $2,000,000 of 10% convertible loan stock, convertible in one year's time at the rate of 3 shares per $5 of stock.

The total earnings in 20X4 were $1,750,000.

The rate of income tax is 35%.

Required

Calculate the basic EPS and diluted EPS.

Answer

(a)   Basic EPS = $\dfrac{\$1{,}750{,}000}{5 \text{ million}}$ = 35 cents

(b)   We must decide which of the potential ordinary shares (ie the loan stocks) are dilutive (ie would decrease the EPS if converted).

For the 14% loan stock, incremental EPS $= \dfrac{0.65 \times \$140,000}{200,000 \text{ shares}}$

$= 45.5c$

For the 10% loan stock, incremental EPS $= \dfrac{0.65 \times \$200,000}{1.2m \text{ shares}}$

$= 10.8c$

The effect of converting the 14% loan stock is therefore to **increase** the EPS figure, since the incremental EPS of 45.5c is greater than the basic EPS of 35c. The 14% loan stock is not dilutive and is therefore excluded from the diluted EPS calculation.

The 10% loan stock is dilutive.

Diluted EPS $= \dfrac{\$1.75m + \$0.13m}{5m + 1.2m} = 30.3c$

It should be assumed that options were exercised and that the assumed proceeds would have been received from the issue of shares at **fair value**. Fair value for this purpose is calculated on the basis of the average price of the ordinary shares during the period. Calculations of this nature are beyond the scope of the Paper 2.5 syllabus.

4.5 Dilutive potential ordinary shares

According to IAS 33, potential ordinary shares should be treated as dilutive when, and only when, their conversion to ordinary shares would **decrease net profit per share** from continuing operations. This point was illustrated in the question above.

4.6 Restatement

If the number of ordinary or potential ordinary shares outstanding **increases** as a result of a capitalisation, bonus issue or share split, or decreases as a result of a reverse share split, the calculation of basic and diluted EPS for all periods presented should be **adjusted retrospectively**.

If these changes occur **after the balance sheet date** but before the financial statements are authorised for issue, the calculations per share for the financial statements and those of any prior period should be based on the **new number of shares** (and this should be disclosed).

In addition, basic and diluted EPS of all periods presented should be adjusted for the effects of **material errors**, and adjustments resulting from **changes** in **accounting policies**, dealt with in accordance with IAS 8.

An entity **does not restate diluted EPS** of any prior period for changes in the assumptions used or for the conversion of potential ordinary shares into ordinary shares outstanding.

Entities are encouraged to disclose a description of ordinary share transactions or potential ordinary share transactions, other than capitalisation issues and share splits, which occur **after the balance sheet date** when they are of such importance that non-disclosure would affect the ability of the users of the financial statements to make proper evaluations and decisions (see IAS 10). Examples of such transactions include the following.

(a) Issue of shares for cash

(b) Issue of shares when the proceeds are used to repay debt or preferred shares outstanding at the balance sheet date

(c)   Redemption of ordinary shares outstanding

(d)   Conversion or exercise of potential ordinary shares, outstanding at the balance sheet date, into ordinary shares

(e)   Issue of warrants, options or convertible securities

(f)   Achievement of conditions that would result in the issue of contingently issuable shares

EPS amounts are not adjusted for such transactions occurring after the balance sheet date because such transactions **do not affect the amount of capital used** to produce the net profit or loss for the period.

5 Presentation, disclosure and other matters

FAST FORWARD

IAS 33 contains the following requirements on presentation and disclosure.

5.1 Presentation

Basic and diluted EPS should be presented by an entity on the **face of the income statement** for each class of ordinary share that has a different right to share in the net profit for the period. The basic and diluted EPS should be presented with **equal prominence** for all periods presented.

Disclosure must still be made where the EPS figures (basic and/or diluted) are **negative** (ie a loss per share).

5.2 Disclosure

An entity should disclose the following.

(a)   The amounts used as the **numerators** in calculating basic and diluted EPS, and a **reconciliation** of those amounts to the net profit or loss for the period

(b)   The weighted average number of ordinary shares used as the **denominator** in calculating basic and diluted EPS, and a **reconciliation** of these denominators to each other.

5.3 Alternative EPS figures

An entity may present **alternative EPS figures if it wishes**. However, IAS 33 lays out certain rules where this takes place.

(a)   The weighted average number of shares as calculated under IAS 33 **must** be used.

(b)   A **reconciliation** must be given between the component of profit used in the alternative EPS (if it is not a line item in the income statement) and the line item for profit reported in the income statement.

(c)   Basic and diluted EPS must be shown with **equal prominence**.

5.4 Significance of earnings per share

Earnings per share (EPS) is one of the most frequently quoted statistics in financial analysis. Because of the widespread use of the price earnings **(P/E) ratio** as a yardstick for investment decisions, it became increasingly important.

It seems that reported and forecast EPS can, through the P/E ratio, have a **significant effect on a company's share price**. Thus, a share price might fall if it looks as if EPS is going to be low. This is not very rational, as EPS can depend on many, often subjective, assumptions used in preparing a historical statement, namely the income statement. It does not necessarily bear any relation to the value of a company, and of its shares. Nevertheless, the market is sensitive to EPS.

EPS has also served as a means of assessing the **stewardship and management** role performed by company directors and managers. Remuneration packages might be linked to EPS growth, thereby increasing the pressure on management to improve EPS. The danger of this, however, is that management effort may go into distorting results to produce a favourable EPS.

Chapter roundup

- **Earnings per share** is a measure of the amount of profits earned by a company for each ordinary share. Earnings are profits after tax and preferred dividends.

- **Basic EPS** is calculated by dividing the net profit or loss for the period attributable to ordinary shareholders by the weighted average number of ordinary shares outstanding during the period.

- You should know how to calculate **basic EPS** and how to deal with related complications (issue of shares for cash, bonus issue, share splits/reverse share splits, rights issues).

- **Diluted EPS** is calculated by adjusting the net profit attributable to ordinary shareholders and the weighted average number of shares outstanding for the effects of all dilutive potential ordinary shares.

- **Diluted EPS** is complicated, but you should be able to deal with a fairly straightforward situation, eg with convertible loan stock.

Quick quiz

1   How is basic EPS calculated?

2   Give the formula for the 'bonus element' of a rights issue.

3   Define 'dilutive potential ordinary share'.

4   Which numerator is used to decide whether potential ordinary shares are dilutive?

5   Why is the numerator adjusted for convertible bonds when calculating diluted EPS?

Answers to quick quiz

1    $$\dfrac{\text{Net profit/(loss) attributable to ordinary shareholders}}{\text{Weighted average number of ordinary shares outstanding during the period}}$$

2    $$\dfrac{\text{Actual cum} - \text{rights price}}{\text{Theoretical ex} - \text{rights price}}$$

3   See Para 4.1

4   Net profit from continuing operations only.

5   Because the issue of shares will affect earnings (the interest will no longer have to be paid).

Now try the question below from the Exam Question Bank			
Number	**Level**	**Marks**	**Time**
Q14	Examination	25	45 mins

Part C
Consolidated financial statements

Introduction to groups

Topic list	Syllabus reference
1 Group accounts	4(a)
2 IAS 27 *Consolidated and separate financial statements*	4(b)
3 Content of group accounts and group structure	4(c)

Introduction

Consolidation is an extremely important area of your Paper 2.5 syllabus as you are almost certain to face a large compulsory consolidation question in the examination.

The key to consolidation questions in the examination is to adopt a logical approach and to practise as many questions as possible.

In this chapter we will look at the major definitions in consolidation and the relevant accounting standards. These matters are fundamental to your comprehension of group accounts, so make sure you can understand them and then **learn them**.

Study guide

Sections 18 and 19 – Business combinations – introduction

- Describe the concept of a group and the objective and usefulness of consolidated financial statements

- Explain the different methods which could be used to prepare consolidated financial statements

- Explain and apply the definition of subsidiary companies

- Describe the circumstances and reasoning for subsidiaries to be excluded from consolidated financial statements in accordance with relevant accounting standards

- Explain the need for using coterminous year ends and uniform accounting policies when preparing consolidated financial statements

- Describe how the above is achieved in practice

Exam guide

You should have done consolidation at a basic level for Paper 1.1, in which case, treat this chapter as revision.

1 Group accounts

FAST FORWARD

You will probably know that many large businesses actually consist of several companies controlled by one central or administrative company. Together these companies are called a **group**. The controlling company, called the parent or **holding company**, will own some or all of the shares in the other companies, called subsidiary companies.

1.1 Introduction

There are many reasons for businesses to operate as groups; for the goodwill associated with the names of the subsidiaries, for tax or legal purposes and so forth. In many countries, company law requires that the results of a group should be presented as a whole. Unfortunately, it is not possible simply to add all the results together and this chapter and those following will teach you how to **consolidate** all the results of companies within a group.

In traditional accounting terminology, a **group of companies** consists of a **parent company** and one or more **subsidiary companies** which are controlled by the parent company.

1.2 Accounting standards

We will be looking at four accounting standards in this and the next three chapters.

- IAS 27 *Consolidated and separate financial statements*
- IFRS 3 *Business combinations* (goodwill aspects were covered in Chapter 6)
- IAS 28 *Investments in associates*
- IAS 31 *Interests in joint ventures*

These standards are all concerned with different aspects of group accounts, but there is some overlap between them, particularly between IFRS 3 and IAS 27.

In this and the next chapter we will concentrate on IAS 27, which covers the basic group definitions and consolidation procedures of a parent-subsidiary relationship. First of all, however, we will look at all the important definitions involved in group accounts, which **determine how to treat each particular type of investment** in group accounts.

1.3 Definitions

We will look at some of these definitions in more detail later, but they are useful here in that they give you an overview of all aspects of group accounts.

Exam focus point

> All the definitions relating to group accounts are extremely important. You must **learn them** and **understand** their meaning and application.

Key terms

- **Control**. The power to govern the financial and operating policies of an entity so as to obtain benefits from its activities. *(IFRS 3, IASs 27, 28, 31)*

- **Subsidiary**. An entity that is controlled by another entity (known as the parent). *(IFRS 3, IASs 27, 28)*

- **Parent**. An entity that has one or more subsidiaries. *(IFRS 3, IAS 27)*

- **Group**. A parent and all its subsidiaries. *(IAS 27)*

- **Associate**. An entity, including an unincorporated entity such as a partnership, in which an investor has significant influence and which is neither a subsidiary nor a joint venture of the investor. *(IAS 28)*

- **Significant influence** is the power to participate in the financial and operating policy decisions of an investee or an economic activity but is not control or joint control over those policies. *(IASs 28, 31)*

- **Joint venture**. A contractual arrangement whereby two or more parties undertake an economic activity which is subject to joint control. *(IAS 31)*

We can summarise the different types of investment *and* the required accounting for them as follows.

Investment	Criteria	Required treatment in group accounts
Subsidiary	Control	Full consolidation
Associate	Significant influence	Equity accounting (see Chapter 18)
Joint venture (jointly controlled entity)	Contractual joint control	Either: proportional consolidation Or: equity accounting (see Chapter 18)
Investment which is none of the above	Asset held for accretion of wealth	As for single company accounts per IAS 39 (see Chapter 10)

1.4 Investments in subsidiaries

The important point here is **control**. In most cases, this will involve the holding company or parent owning a majority of the ordinary shares in the subsidiary (to which normal voting rights are attached). There are circumstances, however, when the parent may own only a minority of the voting power in the subsidiary, *but* the parent still has control.

Both IFRS 3 and IAS 27 state that control can usually be assumed to exist when the parent **owns more than half (ie over 50%) of the voting power** of an entity *unless* it can be clearly shown that **such ownership does not constitute control** (these situations will be very rare).

What about situations where this ownership criterion does not exist? IFRS 3 and IAS 27 list the following situations where control exists, even when the parent owns only 50% or less of the voting power of an entity.

    (a)   The parent has power over more than 50% of the voting rights by virtue of **agreement with other investors**

    (b)   The parent has power to **govern the financial and operating policies** of the entity by statute or under an agreement

    (c)   The parent has the power to **appoint or remove a majority of members of the board of directors** (or equivalent governing body)

    (d)   The parent has power to cast a **majority of votes at meetings of the board of directors**

IAS 27 also states that a parent loses control when it loses the power to govern the financial and operating policies of an investee. Loss of control can occur without a change in ownership levels. This may happen if a subsidiary becomes subject to the control of a government, court administrator or regulator (for example, in bankruptcy).

Exam focus point

> You should learn the contents of the above paragraph as you may be asked to apply them in the exam.

1.4.1 Accounting treatment in group accounts

IAS 27 requires a parent to present consolidated financial statements, in which the accounts of the parent and subsidiary (or subsidiaries) are combined and presented **as a single entity**.

1.5 Investments in associates

This type of investment is something less than a subsidiary, but more than a simple investment (nor is it a joint venture). The key criterion here is **significant influence**. This is defined as the 'power to participate', but *not* to 'control' (which would make the investment a subsidiary).

Significant influence can be determined by the holding of voting rights (usually attached to shares) in the entity. IAS 28 states that if an investor holds **20% or more** of the voting power of the investee, it can be presumed that the investor has significant influence over the investee, *unless* it can be clearly shown that this is not the case.

Significant influence can be presumed *not* to exist if the investor holds **less than 20%** of the voting power of the investee, unless it can be demonstrated otherwise.

The **existence of significant influence** is evidenced in one or more of the following ways.

    (a)   Representation on the **board of directors** (or equivalent) of the investee
    (b)   Participation in the **policy making process**
    (c)   **Material transactions** between investor and investee
    (d)   Interchange of **management personnel**
    (e)   Provision of **essential technical information**

1.5.1 Accounting treatment in group accounts

IAS 28 requires the use of the **equity method** of accounting for investments in associates. This method will be explained in detail in Chapter 17.

1.6 Accounting for investments in joint ventures

There are situations where venturers control jointly either operations or assets of the joint venture. The case of a **jointly controlled entity** will be considered in detail in Chapter 17.

1.6.1 Accounting treatment in group accounts

IAS 31 allows two treatments for investments in joint entities.

(a)   **Either**: proportionate consolidation
(b)   **Or**: equity method

1.7 Other investments

Investments which do not meet the definitions of any of the above should be accounted for according to IAS 39 *Financial instruments: recognition and measurement.*

Question	Treatments

The section summary after this question will give an augmented version of the table given in Paragraph 1.3 above. Before you look at it, see if you can write out the table yourself.

1.8 Section summary

Investment	Criteria	Required treatment in group accounts
Subsidiary	Control (> 50% rule)	Full consolidation (IAS 27)
Associate	Significant influence (20%+ rule)	Equity accounting (IAS 28)
Joint venture (jointly controlled entity)	Contractual joint control	Either: proportionate consolidation Or: equity accounting (IAS 31)
Investment which is none of the above	Asset held for accretion of wealth	As for single company accounts (IAS 39)

2 IAS 27 *Consolidated and separate financial statements*

FAST FORWARD

> IAS 27 requires a parent to present consolidated financial statements.

2.1 Introduction

Key term

> **Consolidated financial statements**. The financial statements of a group presented as those of a single economic entity.   *(IAS 27)*

When a parent issues consolidated financial statements, it should consolidate **all subsidiaries**, both foreign and domestic.

2.2 Exemption from preparing group accounts

A parent **need not present** consolidated financial statements if and only if all of the following hold:

(a)   The parent is itself a **wholly-owned subsidiary** or it is a **partially owned subsidiary** of another entity and its other owners, including those not otherwise entitled to vote, have been informed about, and do not object to, the parent not presenting consolidated financial statements

(b)   Its securities are **not publicly traded**

(c)   It is **not in the process of issuing securities** in public securities markets; and

(d)   The **ultimate or intermediate parent** publishes consolidated financial statements that comply with International Financial Reporting Standards

A parent that does not present consolidated financial statements must comply with the IAS 27 rules on separate financial statements (discussed later in this section).

2.3 Potential voting rights

An entity may own share warrants, share call options, or other similar instruments that are **convertible into ordinary shares** in another entity. If these are exercised or converted they may give the entity voting power or reduce another party's voting power over the financial and operating policies of the other entity (potential voting rights). The **existence and effect** of potential voting rights, including potential voting rights held by another entity, should be considered when assessing whether an entity has control over another entity (and therefore has a subsidiary).

In assessing whether potential voting rights give rise to control, the entity examines all facts and circumstances that affect the rights (for example, terms and conditions), except the intention of management and the financial ability to exercise the rights or convert them into equity shares.

2.4 Exclusion of a subsidiary from consolidation

The rules on exclusion of subsidiaries from consolidation are necessarily strict, because this is a common method used by entities to manipulate their results. If a subsidiary which carries a large amount of debt can be excluded, then the gearing of the group as a whole will be improved. In other words, this is a way of taking debt **off the balance sheet**.

The previous version of IAS 27 required a subsidiary to be excluded from consolidation where **control is intended to be temporary**: the subsidiary was acquired and is held *exclusively* with a view to its subsequent disposal within twelve months from acquisition *and* management is actively seeking a buyer. This exclusion has now been **removed**; subsidiaries held for sale must be included in the consolidated financial statements.

Subsidiaries held for sale are accounted for in accordance with IFRS 5 *Non-current assets held for sale and discontinued operations*.

It has been argued in the past that subsidiaries should be excluded from consolidation on the grounds of **dissimilar activities**, ie the activities of the subsidiary are so different to the activities of the other companies within the group that to include its results in the consolidation would be misleading. IAS 27 rejects this argument: exclusion on these grounds is not justified because better (relevant) information can be provided about such subsidiaries by consolidating their results and then giving additional information about the different business activities of the subsidiary, eg under IAS 14 *Segment reporting*.

The previous version of IAS 27 permitted exclusion where the subsidiary operates under **severe long-term restrictions** and these significantly impair its ability to transfer funds to the parent. This exclusion has now been **removed**. Control must actually be lost for exclusion to occur.

2.5 Different reporting dates

In most cases, all group companies will prepare accounts to the same reporting date. One or more subsidiaries may, however, prepare accounts to a different reporting date from the parent and the bulk of other subsidiaries in the group.

In such cases the subsidiary may prepare additional statements to the reporting date of the rest of the group, for consolidation purposes. If this is not possible, the subsidiary's accounts may still be used for the consolidation, *provided that* the gap between the reporting dates is **three months or less**.

Where a subsidiary's accounts are drawn up to a different accounting date, **adjustments should be made** for the effects of significant transactions or other events that occur between that date and the parent's reporting date.

2.6 Uniform accounting policies

Consolidated financial statements should be prepared using **the same accounting policies** for like transactions and other events in similar circumstances.

Adjustments must be made where members of a group use different accounting policies, so that their financial statements are suitable for consolidation.

2.7 Date of inclusion/exclusion

The results of subsidiary undertakings are included in the consolidated financial statements from:

(a)   the date of 'acquisition', ie the **date control passes to the parent**, to
(b)   the date of 'disposal', ie the **date control passes from the parent**.

Once an investment is no longer a subsidiary, it should be treated as an associate under IAS 28 (if applicable) or as an investment under IAS 39.

2.8 Accounting for subsidiaries, jointly controlled entities and associates in the parent's separate financial statements

A parent company will usually produce its own, single company financial statements. In these statements, investments in subsidiaries, jointly controlled entities and associates included in the consolidated financial statements should be *either*:

(a)   Accounted for at **cost**, *or*
(b)   In accordance with **IAS 39**.

Where subsidiaries are **classified as held for sale** in accordance with IFRS 5 they should be accounted for in accordance with IFRS 5 (see Chapter 12).

2.9 Disclosure

The disclosure requirements for **consolidated financial statements** are as follows.

(a)   **Summarised financial information** of **subsidiaries** that are **not consolidated**, either individually or in groups, including the amounts of total assets, total liabilities, revenues and profit or loss

(b)   The nature of the **relationship** between the parent and a **subsidiary** of which the **parent** does **not own**, directly or indirectly through subsidiaries, **more than half of the voting power**

(c)   For an investee of which more than half of the voting or potential voting power is owned, directly or indirectly through subsidiaries, but which, because of the absence of control, is not a subsidiary, the reasons **why** the **ownership** does **not constitute control**

(d)   The reporting date of the financial statements of a subsidiary when such financial statements are used to prepare consolidated financial statements and are as of a reporting date or for a period that is different from that of the parent, and the **reason** for using a **different reporting date or different period**

(e)   The nature and extent of any **restrictions** on the ability of subsidiaries to **transfer funds** to the parent in the form of cash dividends, repayment of loans or advances (ie borrowing arrangements, regulatory restraints etc)

Where a parent chooses to take advantage of the exemptions from preparing consolidated financial statements (see above) the **separate financial statements** must disclose:

(a)   the fact that the financial statements are separate financial statements; that the exemption from consolidation has been used; the name and country of incorporation of the entity whose consolidated financial statements that comply with IFRSs have been published; and the address where those consolidated financial statements are obtainable

(b)   a list of significant investments in subsidiaries, jointly controlled entities and associates, including the name, country of incorporation, proportion of ownership interest and, if different, proportion of voting power held

(c)   a description of the method used to account for the investments listed under (b)

When a parent prepares separate financial statements in addition to consolidated financial statements, the separate financial statements must disclose:

(a)   the fact that the statements are separate financial statements and the reasons why they have been prepared if not required by law

(b)   information about investments and the method used to account for them, as above.

2.10 Section summary

IAS 27 covers the basic rules and definitions of the parent-subsidiary relationship. You should learn:

- **Definitions**
- Rules for **exemption** from preparing consolidated financial statements
- **Disclosure**

3 Content of group accounts and group structure

FAST FORWARD   You are expected to be able to deal with a number of possible group structures.

3.1 Introduction

The information contained in the individual statements of a parent company and each of its subsidiaries does not give a picture of the group's total activities. A **separate set of group statements** can be prepared from the individual ones. Remember that a group has no separate (legal) existence, except for accounting purposes.

Consolidated accounts are one form of group accounts which combines the information contained in the separate accounts of a holding company and its subsidiaries as if they were the accounts of a single entity. 'Group accounts' and 'consolidated accounts' are terms often used synonymously.

In simple terms a set of consolidated accounts is prepared by **adding together** the assets and liabilities of the parent company and each subsidiary. The **whole** of the assets and liabilities of each company are included, even though some subsidiaries may be only partly owned. The 'equity and liabilities' side of the balance sheet will indicate how much of the net assets are attributable to the group and how much to outside investors in partly owned subsidiaries. These **outside investors** are known as **minority interests**.

Key term

> **Minority interest.** That part of the profit or loss and of net assets of a subsidiary attributable to equity interests which are not owned directly, or indirectly through subsidiaries, by the parent.
>
> *(IFRS 3, IAS 27)*

Minority interests should be presented in the consolidated balance sheet **within equity, separately from the parent shareholders' equity**.

Most parent companies present their own individual accounts and their group accounts in a single **package**. The package typically comprises the following.

- **Parent company financial statements**, which will include 'investments in subsidiary undertakings' as an asset in the balance sheet, and income from subsidiaries (in dividends) in the income statement

- **Consolidated balance sheet**

- **Consolidated income statement**

- **Consolidated cash flow statement**

It may not be necessary to publish all of the parent company's financial statements, depending on local or national regulations.

3.2 Group structure

With the difficulties of definition and disclosure dealt with, let us now look at group structures. The simplest are those in which a parent company has only a **direct interest** in the shares of its subsidiary companies. For example:

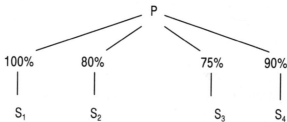

S_1 Co is a wholly owned subsidiary of P Co. S_2 Co, S_3 Co and S_4 Co are partly owned subsidiaries; a proportion of the shares in these companies is held by outside investors.

Often a parent will have **indirect holdings** in its subsidiary companies. This can lead to more complex group structures.

(a)

P Co owns 51% of the equity shares in S Co, which is therefore its subsidiary. S Co in its turn owns 51% of the equity shares in SS Co. SS Co is therefore a subsidiary of S Co and consequently a subsidiary of P Co. SS Co would describe S Co as its parent (or holding) company and P Co as its ultimate parent company.

Note that although P Co can control the assets and business of SS Co by virtue of the chain of control, its interest in the assets of SS Co is only 26%. This can be seen by considering a dividend of $100 paid by SS Co: as a 51% shareholder, S Co would receive $51; P Co would have an interest in 51% of this $51 = $26.01.

(b)

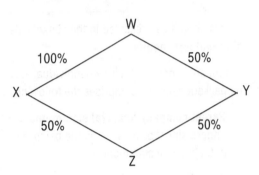

W Co owns 100% of the equity of X Co and 50% of the equity of Y Co. X Co and Y Co each own 50% of the equity of Z Co. Assume that:

(i) W Co does not control the composition of Y Co's board, nor can it cast a majority of votes on the board

(ii) W Co does not hold or control more than 50% of the **voting rights** in Y Co, either directly or by agreement with other investors

(iii) W Co does not have the power to govern the financial or operating policies of Y Co by virtue of statute or an agreement

(iv) None of the above apply to either X Co's or Y Co's holdings in Z Co

In other words, because W Co is not in co-operation with the holder(s) of the other 50% of the shares in Y Co, neither Y nor Z can be considered subsidiaries.

In that case:

(i) X Co is a subsidiary of W Co

(ii) Y Co is not a subsidiary of W Co

(iii) Z Co is not a subsidiary of either X Co or Y Co. Consequently, it is not a subsidiary of W Co

If Z Co pays a dividend of $100, X Co and Y Co will each receive $50. The interest of W Co in this dividend is as follows.

	$
Through X Co (100% × $50)	50
Through Y Co (50% × $50)	25
	75

Although W Co has an interest in 75% of Z Co's assets, Z Co is not a subsidiary of W Co.

(c)

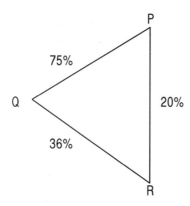

Q Co is a subsidiary of P Co. P Co therefore has indirect control over 36% of R Co's equity. P Co also has direct control over 20% of R Co's equity. R Co is therefore a subsidiary of P Co, although P Co's interest in R Co's assets is only 20% + (75% × 36%) = 47%.

Examples (b) and (c) illustrate an important point: in deciding whether a company A holds more than 50% of the equity (or equivalent) of an entity B it is necessary to aggregate:

- Shares (or equivalent) in B held directly by A
- Shares (or equivalent) in B held by entities which are subsidiaries of A

| Question | Consolidated accounts |

During the time until your examination you should obtain as many sets of the published accounts of large companies in your country as possible. Examine the accounting policies in relation to subsidiary and associated companies and consider how these policies are shown in the accounting and consolidation treatment. Consider the effect of any disposals during the year. Also, look at all the disclosures made relating to fair values, goodwill etc and match them to the disclosure requirements outlined in this chapter and in subsequent chapters on IFRS 3 and IAS 28.

Alternatively (or additionally) you should attempt to obtain such information from the financial press.

Chapter roundup

- This chapter has explained the concept of a **group** and introduced several important **definitions**.

- The principal **regulations** governing the preparation of group accounts have been explained.

- A number of possible **group structures** have been illustrated to show that a company may hold an interest in the net assets of another company which exceeds 50%, without conferring control of the other company. The converse is also true.

Quick quiz

1   Define a 'subsidiary'.

2   When can control be assumed?

3   What accounting treatment does IAS 27 require of a parent company?

4   What accounting treatments are permitted by IAS 31 for investments in jointly controlled entities in the consolidated accounts?

5   When is a parent exempted from preparing consolidated financial statements?

6   Under what circumstances should subsidiary undertakings be excluded from consolidation?

7   How should an investment in a subsidiary be accounted for in the separate financial statements of the parent?

8   What is a minority interest?

Answers to quick quiz

1   An entity that is controlled by another entity.

2   When the parent owns more than half (ie over 50%) of the voting power of an entity, **unless** it can be clearly shown that such ownership does not constitute control.

3   The accounts of parent and subsidiary are combined and presented as a single entity.

4   Proportionate consolidation and the equity method.

5   When the parent is itself a wholly owned subsidiary, or a partially owned subsidiary and the minority interests do not object.

6   Very rarely, if at all. See section 2.4.

7   (a)   At cost, or
    (b)   In accordance with IAS 39.

8   The part of the net profit or loss and the net assets attributable to interests not owned by the parent.

Number	Level	Marks	Time
Q15	Introductory	n/a	n/a

Now try the question below from the Exam Question Bank

BPP
PROFESSIONAL EDUCATION

15

Consolidated balance sheet

Topic list	Syllabus reference
1 IAS 27: Summary of consolidation procedures	4(c)
2 Cancellation and part cancellation	4(c)
3 Minority interests	4(c)
4 Dividends payable by a subsidiary	4(c)
5 Goodwill arising on consolidation	4(c)
6 A technique of consolidation	4(c)
7 Intra-group trading	4(c)
8 Intra-group sales of non-current assets	4(c)
9 Summary: consolidated balance sheet	4(c)

Introduction

This chapter introduces the **basic procedures** required in consolidation and gives a formal step plan for carrying out a balance sheet consolidation. This step procedure should be useful to you as a starting guide for answering any question, but remember that you cannot rely on it to answer the question for you.

Each question must be approached and **answered on its own merits**. Examiners often put small extra or different problems in because, as they are always reminding students, it is not possible to 'rote-learn' consolidation.

The **method of consolidation** shown here uses schedules for workings (reserves, minority interests etc) rather than the ledger accounts used in some other texts. This is because we believe that ledger accounts lead students to 'learn' the consolidation journals without thinking about what they are doing - always a dangerous practice in consolidation questions.

There are plenty of questions in this chapter - work through *all* of them carefully.

Study guide

Section 18 and 19 – Business combinations – introductions

- Prepare a consolidated balance sheet for a simple group dealing with pre– and post-acquisition profits, minority interests and consolidated goodwill

Section 20 Business combinations – intra-group adjustments

- All aspects

1 IAS 27: summary of consolidation procedures

FAST FORWARD

How are consolidated financial statements prepared? IAS 27 lays out the basic procedures and we will consider these in the rest of this chapter.

1.1 Basic procedure

The financial statements of a parent and its subsidiaries are **combined on a line-by-line basis** by adding together like items of assets, liabilities, equity, income and expenses.

The following steps are then taken, in order that the consolidated financial statements should **show financial information about the group as if it was a single entity**.

(a) The carrying amount of the parent's **investment in each subsidiary** and the parent's **portion of equity** of each subsidiary are **eliminated or cancelled** (see Sections 2, 7 and 8)

(b) **Minority interests in the net income of consolidated subsidiaries** are adjusted against group income, to arrive at the net income attributable to the owners of the parent

(c) **Minority interests** in the net assets of consolidated subsidiaries should be presented separately in the consolidated balance sheet (see Section 3)

Other matters to be dealt with include the following.

(a) **Goodwill on consolidation** should be dealt with according to IFRS 3 (see Section 5)
(b) **Dividends payable** by a subsidiary must be accounted for (see Section 4)

IAS 27 states that all intragroup balances and transactions, and the resulting **unrealised profits**, should be **eliminated in full. Unrealised losses** resulting from intragroup transactions should also be eliminated *unless* cost can be recovered. This will be explained later in this chapter.

2 Cancellation and part cancellation

2.1 Procedure

The preparation of a consolidated balance sheet, in a very simple form, consists of two procedures.

(a) Take the individual accounts of the parent company and each subsidiary and **cancel out items** which appear as an asset in one company and a liability in another.

(b) **Add together all the uncancelled assets and liabilities** throughout the group.

Items requiring cancellation may include the following.

(a) The asset **'shares in subsidiary companies'** which appears in the parent company's accounts will be matched with the liability 'share capital' in the subsidiaries' accounts.

(b)   There may be **intra-group trading** within the group. For example, S Co may sell goods on credit to P Co. P Co would then be a receivable in the accounts of S Co, while S Co would be a payable in the accounts of P Co.

2.2 Example: cancellation

P Co regularly sells goods to its one subsidiary company, S Co, which it has owned since S Co's incorporation. The balance sheets of the two companies on 31 December 20X6 are given below.

P CO
BALANCE SHEET AS AT 31 DECEMBER 20X6

	$	$	$
Assets			
Non-current assets			
Tangible assets			35,000
Investment in 40,000 $1 shares in S Co at cost			40,000
			75,000
Current assets			
Inventories		16,000	
Receivables: S Co	2,000		
Other	6,000		
		8,000	
Cash at bank		1,000	
			25,000
Total assets			100,000
Equity and liabilities			
Equity			
70,000 $1 ordinary shares		70,000	
Reserves		16,000	
			86,000
Current liabilities			
Payables			14,000
Total equity and liabilities			100,000

S CO
BALANCE SHEET AS AT 31 DECEMBER 20X6

	$	$	$
Assets			
Non-current assets			
Tangible assets			45,000
Current assets			
Inventories		12,000	
Receivables		9,000	
			21,000
Total assets			66,000
Equity and liabilities			
Equity			
40,000 $1 ordinary shares		40,000	
Reserves		19,000	
			59,000
Current liabilities			
Bank overdraft		3,000	
Payables: P Co		2,000	
Payables: other		2,000	
			7,000
Total equity and liabilities			66,000

Required

Prepare the consolidated balance sheet of P Co at 31 December 20X6.

Solution

The cancelling items are:

(a)   P Co's asset 'investment in shares of S Co' ($40,000) cancels with S Co's liability 'share capital' ($40,000);

(b)   P Co's asset 'receivables: S Co' ($2,000) cancels with S Co's liability 'payables: P Co' ($2,000).

The remaining assets and liabilities are added together to produce the following consolidated balance sheet.

P CO
CONSOLIDATED BALANCE SHEET AS AT 31 DECEMBER 20X6

Assets	$	$
Non-current assets		
Tangible assets (35,000 + 45,000)		80,000
Current assets		
Inventories (16,000 + 12,000)	28,000	
Receivables (6000 + 9,000)	15,000	
Cash at bank P's Co (1,000)	1,000	
		44,000
		124,000
Total assets		
Equity and liabilities		
Equity		
70,000 $1 ordinary shares P's Co	70,000	
Reserves (16,000 + 19,000)	35,000	
	105,000	105,000
Current liabilities		
Bank overdraft S's Co (3,000)	3,000	
Payables (14,000 + 2,000)	16,000	
		19,000
Total equity and liabilities		124,000

Note the following.

X (a)   P Co's bank balance is **not netted off** with S Co's bank overdraft. To offset one against the other would be less informative and would conflict with the principle that assets and liabilities should not be netted off.

(b)   The share capital in the consolidated balance sheet is the **share capital of the parent company alone**. This must *always* be the case, no matter how complex the consolidation, because the share capital of subsidiary companies must *always* be a wholly cancelling item.

2.3 Part cancellation

An item may appear in the balance sheets of a parent company and its subsidiary, but not at the same amounts.

(a)   The parent company may have acquired **shares in the subsidiary** at a price **greater or less than their par value**. The asset will appear in the parent company's accounts at cost, while the liability will appear in the subsidiary's accounts at par value. This raises the issue of **goodwill**, which is dealt with later in this chapter.

(b) Even if the parent company acquired shares at par value, it **may not** have **acquired all the shares of the subsidiary** (so the subsidiary may be only partly owned). This raises the issue of **minority interests**, which are also dealt with later in this chapter.

(c) The inter-company trading balances may be out of step because of **goods or cash in transit**.

(d) One company may have **issued loan stock** of which a **proportion only** is taken up by the other company.

The following question illustrates the techniques needed to deal with items (c) and (d) above. The procedure is to **cancel as far as possible**. The remaining uncancelled amounts will appear in the consolidated balance sheet.

(a) **Uncancelled loan stock** will appear as a **liability of the group**.

(b) **Uncancelled balances on intra-group accounts** represent **goods or cash in transit**, which will appear in the consolidated balance sheet.

Question   Cancellation

The balance sheets of P Co and of its subsidiary S Co have been made up to 30 June. P Co has owned all the ordinary shares and 40% of the loan stock of S Co since its incorporation.

P CO
BALANCE SHEET AS AT 30 JUNE

	$	$
Assets		
Non-current assets:		
Tangible assets	120,000	
Investment in S Co, at cost		
80,000 ordinary shares of $1 each	80,000 ✓	
$20,000 of 12% loan stock in S Co	20,000 ✓	
		220,000
Current assets:		
Inventories	50,000	
Receivables	40,000	
Current account with S Co	18,000 ✓	
Cash	4,000	
		112,000
Total assets		332,000
Equity and liabilities		
Equity:		
Ordinary shares of $1 each, fully paid	100,000	
Reserves	95,000	
		195,000
Non-current liabilities:		
10% loan stock		75,000
Current liabilities:		
Payables	47,000	
Taxation	15,000	
		62,000
Total equity and liabilities		332,000

S CO
BALANCE SHEET AS AT 30 JUNE

	$	$
Assets		
Tangible non-current assets		100,000
Current assets		
Inventories	60,000	
Receivables	30,000	
Cash	6,000	
		96,000
Total assets		196,000
Equity and liabilities		
Equity		
✱ 80,000 ordinary shares of $1 each, fully paid	80,000 ✓	
Reserves	28,000	
		108,000
Non-current liabilities		
✳ 12% loan stock		50,000 ✓
Current liabilities		
Payables	16,000	
Taxation	10,000	
✳ Current account with P Co	12,000 ✓	
		38,000
Total equity and liabilities		196,000

The difference on current account arises because of goods in transit. (18,000 – 12000) 6,000

Required

Prepare the consolidated balance sheet of P Co.

Answer

P CO
CONSOLIDATED BALANCE SHEET AS AT 30 JUNE

	$	$
Assets		
Tangible non-current assets (120 +100)		220,000
Current assets :		
Inventories (50 +60)	110,000	
Goods in transit (18– 12)	6,000	
Receivables (40,000 +30,000)	70,000	
Cash (4,000 + 6,000)	10,000	
		196,000
Total assets		416,000

	$	$
Equity and liabilities		
Equity :		
Ordinary shares of $1 each, fully paid	100,000	
Reserves *(95 + 28)*	123,000	
		223,000
Non-current liabilities :		
10% loan stock	75,000	
✱ 12% loan stock *(50 ~20)*	30,000 ✓	
		105,000
Current liabilities :		
Payables *(47+16)*	63,000	
Taxation *(15+10)*	25,000	
		88,000
Total equity and liabilities		416,000

Note especially how:

(a) The uncancelled loan stock in S Co becomes a liability of the group
(b) The goods in transit is the difference between the current accounts ($18,000 – $12,000)

3 Minority interests

In the consolidated balance sheet it is necessary to distinguish minority interests from those net assets attributable to the group and financed by shareholders' equity.

3.1 Introduction

It was mentioned earlier that the total assets and liabilities of subsidiary companies are included in the consolidated balance sheet, even in the case of subsidiaries which are only partly owned. A proportion of the net assets of such subsidiaries in fact belongs to investors from outside the group (**minority interests**).

The net assets of a company are financed by share capital and reserves. The consolidation procedure for dealing with partly owned subsidiaries is to **calculate the proportion of ordinary shares, preferred shares and reserves attributable to minority interests**.

3.2 Example: minority interests

P Co has owned 75% of the share capital of S Co since the date of S Co's incorporation. Their latest balance sheets are given below.

P CO
BALANCE SHEET

	$	$
Assets		
Non-current assets :		
Tangible assets	50,000	
✱ 30,000 $1 ordinary shares in S Co at cost	30,000 ✓	
		80,000
Current assets		45,000
Total assets		125,000

	$	$
Equity and liabilities		
Equity :		
80,000 $1 ordinary shares	80,000	
Reserves	25,000	
		105,000
Current liabilities		20,000
Total equity and liabilities		125,000

S CO
BALANCE SHEET

	$	$
Assets		
Tangible non-current assets		35,000
Current assets		35,000
Total assets		70,000
Equity and liabilities		
Equity :		
40,000 $1 ordinary shares	40,000	
Reserves	10,000	
		50,000
Current liabilities,		20,000
Total equity and liabilities		70,000

Required

Prepare the consolidated balance sheet.

Solution

All of S Co's net assets are consolidated despite the fact that the company is only 75% owned. The amount of net assets attributable to minority interests is calculated as follows.

	$
Minority share of share capital (25% × $40,000)	10,000
Minority share of reserves (25% × $10,000)	2,500 ·
* Minority interest.	12,500 x

Of S Co's share capital of $40,000, $10,000 is included in the figure for minority interest, while $30,000 is cancelled with P Co's asset 'investment in S Co'.

The consolidated balance sheet can now be prepared.

P GROUP
CONSOLIDATED BALANCE SHEET

	$	$
Assets		
Tangible non-current assets (50,000 + 35,000)		85,000 ·
Current assets (45,000 + 35,000)		80,000 ·
Total assets		165,000
Equity and liabilities		
Equity .		
Share capital	80,000 ·	
Reserves $(25,000 + (75% × $10,000))	32,500	
		112,500
* Minority interest		12,500 x
		125,000
Current liabilities (20,000 + 20,000)		40,000
Total equity and liabilities		165,000

This method of disclosure of minority interests is required by IAS 1 *Presentation of financial statements*.

3.3 Procedure

In more complicated examples the following technique is recommended for dealing with minority interests.

Step 1   **Cancel common items** in the draft balance sheets. If there is a minority interest, the subsidiary company's share capital will be a partly cancelled item. Ascertain the proportion of ordinary shares and the proportion (possibly different) of preferred shares held by the minority.

Step 2   Produce a working for the **minority interest**. Add in the amounts of preferred and ordinary share capital calculated in step 1: this completes the cancellation of the subsidiary's share capital.

Add also the minority's share of each reserve in the subsidiary company. Reserves belong to equity shareholders; the proportion attributable to minority interests therefore depends on their percentage holding of *ordinary* shares.

Step 3   Produce a **separate working for each reserve** (capital, revenue etc) found in the subsidiary company's balance sheet. The initial balances on these accounts will be taken straight from the draft balance sheets of the parent and subsidiary company.

Step 4   The closing balances in these workings can be entered directly onto the **consolidated balance sheet**.

Question

Part cancellation

Set out below are the draft balance sheets of P Co and its subsidiary S Co. You are required to prepare the consolidated balance sheet.

P CO

	$	$
Assets		
Non-current assets		
Tangible assets		31,000
Investment in S Co		
12,000 $1 ordinary shares at cost	12,000	
4,000 $1 preferred shares at cost	4,000	
$4,000 10% debentures at cost	4,000	
		20,000
		51,000
Current assets		21,000
Total assets		72,000
Equity and liabilities		
Equity		
Ordinary shares of $1 each	40,000	
Revenue reserve	22,000	
		62,000
Current liabilities		10,000
Total equity and liabilities		72,000

S CO

	$	$
Assets		
Tangible non-current assets		34,000
Current assets		32,000
Total assets		66,000
Equity and liabilities		
Equity		
✓ Ordinary shares of $1 each	20,000 ✓	
✓ Preferred shares of $1 each	16,000 ✓	
Capital reserve	6,000	
Revenue reserve	4,000	
		46,000
Non-current liabilities		
✓ 10% debentures		10,000 ✓
Current liabilities		10,000
Total equity and liabilities		66,000

Answer

Partly cancelling items are the components of P Co's investment in S Co, ie ordinary shares, preferred shares and debentures. Minorities have an interest in 75% (12,000/16,000) of S Co's preferred shares and 40% (8,000/20,000) of S Co's ordinary shares, including reserves.

You should now produce workings for minority interests, capital reserve and revenue reserve as follows.

Workings

1   Minority interests

	$
Ordinary share capital (40% of 20,000)	8,000
Reserves: capital (40% × 6,000)	2,400
revenue (40% × 4,000)	1,600
	12,000
Preferred share capital (75% × 16,000)	12,000
	24,000

2   Capital reserve

	$
P Co	–
Share of S Co's capital reserve (60% × 6,000)	3,600
	3,600

3   Revenue reserve

	$
P Co	22,000
Share of S Co's revenue reserve (60% × 4,000)	2,400
	24,400

The results of the workings are now used to construct the consolidated balance sheet (CBS).

P GROUP
CONSOLIDATED BALANCE SHEET

	$	$
Assets		
Tangible non-current assets (31,000 + 34,000)		65,000
Current assets (21,000 + 32,000)		53,000
Total assets		118,000
Equity and liabilities		
Equity		
Ordinary shares of $1 each	40,000	
Capital reserve (W2) (60% of 6000)	3,600	
Revenue reserve (W3) [(60% of 4000) + 22,000]	24,400	
		68,000
Minority interests (W1)		24,000
		92,000
Non-current liabilities :		
10% debentures (10,000 - 4000)		6,000
Current liabilities (10,000 + 10,000)		20,000
Total equity and liabilities		118,000

Notes

(a) S Co is a subsidiary of P Co because P Co owns 60% of its ordinary capital. It is unimportant how little of the preferred share capital is owned by P Co.

(b) As always, the share capital in the consolidated balance sheet is that of the parent company alone. The share capital in S Co's balance sheet was partly cancelled against the investment shown in P Co's balance sheet, while the uncancelled portion was credited to minority interest.

(c) The figure for minority interest comprises the interest of outside investors in the share capital and reserves of the subsidiary. The uncancelled portion of S Co's debentures is not shown as part of minority interest but is disclosed separately as a liability of the group.

4 Dividends payable by a subsidiary

4.1 Introduction

When a subsidiary company pays a **dividend** during the year the accounting treatment is not difficult. Suppose S Co, a 60% subsidiary of P Co, pays a dividend of $1,000 on the last day of its accounting period. Its total reserves before paying the dividend stood at $5,000.

(a) $400 of the dividend is paid to minority shareholders. The cash leaves the group and will not appear anywhere in the consolidated balance sheet.

(b) The parent company receives $600 of the dividend, debiting cash and crediting the income statement.

(c) The remaining balance of reserves in S Co's balance sheet ($4,000) will be consolidated in the normal way. The group's share (60% × $4,000 = $2,400) will be included in group reserves in the balance sheet; the minority share (40% × $4,000 = $1,600) is credited to the minority interest account in the balance sheet.

5 Goodwill arising on consolidation

FAST FORWARD

In the examples we have looked at so far the cost of shares acquired by the parent company has always been equal to the par value of those shares. This is seldom the case in practice and we must now consider some more complicated examples.

5.1 Accounting

To begin with, **we will examine the entries made by the parent company in its own balance sheet when it acquires shares.**

When a company P Co wishes to **purchase shares** in a company S Co it must pay the previous owners of those shares. The most obvious form of payment would be in **cash**. Suppose P Co purchases all 40,000 $1 shares in S Co and pays $60,000 cash to the previous shareholders in consideration. The entries in P Co's books would be:

DEBIT	Investment in S Co at cost	$60,000	
CREDIT	Bank		$60,000

However, the previous shareholders might be prepared to accept some other form of consideration. For example, they might accept an agreed number of **shares** in P Co. P Co would then issue new shares in the agreed number and allot them to the former shareholders of S Co. This kind of deal might be attractive to P Co since it avoids the need for a heavy cash outlay. The former shareholders of S Co would retain an indirect interest in that company's profitability via their new holding in its parent company.

Continuing the example, suppose the shareholders of S Co agreed to accept one $1 ordinary share in P Co for every two $1 ordinary shares in S Co. P Co would then need to issue and allot 20,000 new $1 shares. How would this transaction be recorded in the books of P Co?

The simplest method would be as follows.

DEBIT	Investment in S Co	$20,000	
CREDIT	Share capital		$20,000

However, if the 40,000 $1 shares acquired in S Co are thought to have a value of $60,000 this would be misleading. The former shareholders of S Co have presumably agreed to accept 20,000 shares in P Co because they consider each of those shares to have a value of $3. This view of the matter suggests the following method of recording the transaction in P Co's books.

DEBIT	Investment in S Co	$60,000	
CREDIT	Share capital		$20,000
	Share premium account		$40,000

The second method is the one which should normally be used in preparing consolidated accounts.

The amount which P Co records in its books as the cost of its investment in S Co may be more or less than the book value of the assets it acquires. Suppose that S Co in the previous example has nil reserves and nil liabilities, so that its share capital of $40,000 is balanced by tangible assets with a book value of $40,000. For simplicity, assume that the book value of S Co's assets is the same as their market or fair value.

Now when the directors of P Co agree to pay $60,000 for a 100% investment in S Co they must believe that, in addition to its tangible assets of $40,000, S Co must also have intangible assets worth $20,000. This amount of $20,000 paid over and above the value of the tangible assets acquired is called **goodwill arising on consolidation** (sometimes **premium on acquisition**).

Following the normal cancellation procedure the $40,000 share capital in S Co's balance sheet could be cancelled against $40,000 of the 'investment in S Co' in the balance sheet of P Co. This would leave a $20,000 debit uncancelled in the parent company's accounts and this $20,000 would appear in the consolidated balance sheet under the caption 'Intangible non-current assets: goodwill arising on consolidation'.

5.2 Goodwill and pre-acquisition profits

Up to now we have assumed that S Co had nil reserves when its shares were purchased by P Co. Assuming instead that S Co had earned profits of $8,000 in the period before acquisition, its balance sheet just before the purchase would look as follows.

	$
Total tangible assets	48,000
Share capital	40,000
Reserves	8,000
	48,000

If P Co now purchases all the shares in S Co it will acquire total tangible assets worth $48,000 at a cost of $60,000. Clearly in this case S Co's intangible assets (goodwill) are being valued at $12,000. It should be apparent that any **reserves** earned by the subsidiary **prior to its acquisition** by the parent company must be **incorporated in the cancellation** process so as to arrive at a figure for goodwill arising on consolidation. In other words, not only S Co's share capital, but also its **pre-acquisition reserves**, must be cancelled against the asset 'investment in S Co' in the accounts of the parent company. The uncancelled balance of $12,000 appears in the consolidated balance sheet.

The consequence of this is that **any pre-acquisition reserves of a subsidiary company are not aggregated with the parent company's reserves** in the consolidated balance sheet. The figure of consolidated reserves comprises the reserves of the parent company plus the **post-acquisition reserves only of subsidiary companies**. The post-acquisition reserves are simply reserves now *less* reserves at acquisition.

5.3 Example: goodwill and pre-acquisition profits

Sing Co acquired the ordinary shares of Wing Co on 31 March when the draft balance sheets of each company were as follows.

SING CO
BALANCE SHEET AS AT 31 MARCH

	$
Assets	
Non-current assets	
Investment in 50,000 shares of Wing Co at cost	80,000
Current assets	40,000
Total assets	120,000
Equity and liabilities	
Equity	
Ordinary shares	75,000
Revenue reserves	45,000
Total equity and liabilities	120,000

WING CO
BALANCE SHEET AS AT 31 MARCH

	$
Current assets	<u>60,000</u>
Equity	
50,000 ordinary shares of $1 each	50,000
Revenue reserves	10,000
	<u>60,000</u>

Prepare the consolidated balance sheet as at 31 March.

Solution

The technique to adopt here is to produce a new working: 'Goodwill'. A proforma working is set out below.

Goodwill

	$	$
Cost of investment		X
Share of net assets acquired as represented by:		
Ordinary share capital	X	
Share premium	X	
Reserves on acquisition	<u>X</u>	
Group share a%		<u>(X)</u>
		X
b% preferred shares		<u>(X)</u>
Goodwill		<u><u>X</u></u>

Applying this to our example the working will look like this.

	$	$
Cost of investment		80,000
Share of net assets acquired as represented by:		
Ordinary share capital	50,000	
Revenue reserves on acquisition	<u>10,000</u>	
	<u>60,000</u>	
Group share 100%		60,000
Goodwill		<u>20,000</u>

SING CO
CONSOLIDATED BALANCE SHEET AS AT 31 MARCH

	$
Assets	
Non-current assets	
Goodwill arising on consolidation	20,000
Current assets	<u>100,000</u>
	<u>120,000</u>
Equity	
Ordinary shares	75,000
Revenue reserves	<u>45,000</u>
	<u>120,000</u>

5.4 IFRS 3 *Business combinations*

Goodwill arising on consolidation is one form of **purchased goodwill**, and is governed by IFRS 3. As explained in an earlier chapter IFRS 3 requires that goodwill arising on consolidation should **be capitalised in the consolidated balance sheet** and **reviewed for impairment every year**.

Goodwill arising on consolidation is the difference between the cost of an acquisition and the value of the subsidiary's net assets acquired. This difference can be **negative**: the aggregate of the fair values of the separable net assets acquired may exceed what the parent company paid for them. The treatment of this 'negative goodwill' was discussed in Chapter 6. To recap:

(a) An entity should first **re-assess** the amounts at which it has measured both the cost of the combination and the acquiree's identifiable net assets. This exercise should **identify any errors.**

(b) Any **negative goodwill remaining** should be **recognised immediately in profit or loss**, that is in the **income statement.**

6 A technique of consolidation

FAST FORWARD

We have now looked at the topics of cancellation, minority interests and goodwill arising on consolidation. It is time to set out an approach to be used in tackling **consolidated balance sheets**.

The approach we recommend consists of seven stages.

Stage 1 Update the draft balance sheets of subsidiaries and parent company to take account of any proposed dividends not yet accrued for.

Stage 2 Agree intra-group current accounts by adjusting for items in transit.

Stage 3 Cancel items common to both balance sheets.

Stage 4 Produce working for minority interests as shown in Paragraph 3.2.

Stage 5 Produce a goodwill working as shown in example 5.3 above.

Stage 6 Produce a working for capital reserves and revenue reserves.

Stage 7 Produce the consolidated balance sheet as required by the question. Cross reference all workings and notes.

You should now attempt to apply this technique to the following question.

Question

Consolidated balance sheet

The draft balance sheets of Ping Co and Pong Co on 30 June 20X4 were as follows.

Parent

PING CO
BALANCE SHEET AS AT 30 JUNE 20X4

	$	$
Assets		
Non-current assets		
Tangible assets	50,000	
20,000 ordinary shares in Pong Co at cost *80%*	30,000	
		80,000
Current assets		
Inventory *5000 = 2000 + 3,000*	3,000	
Receivables (including $4,000 dividend proposed by Pong Co)	20,000	
Cash	2,000	
		25,000
Total assets		105,000
Equity and liabilities		
Equity		
Ordinary shares of $1 each	45,000	
Capital reserves	12,000	
Revenue reserves	30,000	
		87,000
Current liabilities		
Owed to Pong Co *√ - payables 10,000 = 2000 -*	8,000	
Trade payables	10,000	
		18,000
Total equity and liabilities		105,000

Subsidiary

PONG CO
BALANCE SHEET AS AT 30 JUNE 20X4

	$	$
Assets		
Tangible non-current assets		40,000
Current assets		
Inventory	8,000	
Owed by Ping Co *√*	10,000	
Receivables	7,000	
		25,000
Total assets		65,000
Equity and liabilities		
Equity		
Ordinary shares of $1 each	25,000	
Capital reserves	5,000	
Revenue reserves —— *6000* ——	23,000	
		53,000
Current liabilities		
Trade payables	7,000	
Proposed dividends	5,000	
		12,000
Total equity and liabilities		65,000

Parent

Ping Co acquired its investment in Pong Co on 1 July 20X1 when the revenue reserves of Pong Co stood at $6,000. There have been no changes in the share capital or capital reserves of Pong Co since that date.

At 30 June 20X4 Pong Co had invoiced Ping Co for goods to the value of $2,000 which had not been received by Ping Co.

Goodwill arising on consolidation is to be capitalised. There is no impairment of goodwill.

Prepare the consolidated balance sheet of Ping Co as at 30 June 20X4.

Answer

Stage 1   Ensure parent company and subsidiary balance sheets have correctly taken account of the proposed dividends.

     Ping Co has $4,000 included in receivables for its share (80%) of Pong Co's proposed dividend, so there is no adjustment to make. Similarly, Pong Co has correctly accounted for its dividend payable.

Stage 2   Agree current accounts.

     Ping Co has goods in transit of $2,000 making its total inventory $3,000 + $2,000 = $5,000 *Receivable* and its liability to Pong Co $8,000 + $2,000 = $10,000. — *Payable*

Stage 3   Cancel common items: these are the current accounts between the two companies of $10,000 each and the dividends payable by Pong to Ping. This leaves a payable for the dividend owed to the minority in Pong.

Stage 4   Calculate the minority interest.

Minority interest

	$
Ordinary share capital (20% × 25,000)	5,000
Capital reserves (20% × 5,000)	1,000
Revenue reserves (20% × 23,000)	4,600
	10,600

Note. In this particular case, where there are no preferred shares or adjustments to Pong Co's revenue reserves, the minority interest figure may simply be calculated as 20% of Pong Co's net assets of $(65,000 – 12,000), ie 20% × $53,000. Because, however, such adjustments and complications often arise, it is a good idea to get into the habit of producing the working as shown.

Stage 5   Calculate goodwill.

Goodwill

	$	$
Cost of investment		30,000
Share of assets acquired as represented by:		
Ordinary share capital	25,000	
Capital reserves on acquisition	5,000	
Revenue reserves on acquisition	6,000	
	36,000	
Group share 80%		28,800
Goodwill		1,200

This goodwill must be capitalised in the consolidated balance sheet.

Stage 6 Calculate consolidated reserves.

Consolidated capital reserve

	$
Ping Co	12,000
Share of Pong Co's post acquisition capital reserve	–
	12,000

Consolidated revenue reserve

	$
Ping Co	30,000
Share of Pong Co's post acquisition revenue reserves: 80% × (23,000 – 6,000)*	13,600
	43,600

*Note. Post acquisition reserves of Pong Co are simply reserves now less reserves at acquisition. The working could also be presented as follows.

	Ping	Pong
	$	$
Revenue reserves per question	30,000	23,000
Less pre-acquisition		6,000
		17,000
Share of Pong: 80% × $17,000	13,600	
	43,600	

Stage 7 Prepare the consolidated balance sheet.

PING CO
CONSOLIDATED BALANCE SHEET AS AT 30 JUNE 20X4

	$	$
Assets		
Non-current assets		
Tangible assets ($50,000 + $40,000)		90,000
Intangible asset: goodwill		1,200
Current assets		
Inventories ($5,000 + $8,000)	13,000	
Receivables ($16,000 + $7,000)	23,000	
Cash	2,000	
		38,000
Total assets		129,200
Equity and liabilities		
Equity		
Ordinary shares of $1 each	45,000	
Capital reserves	12,000	
Revenue reserves	43,600	
		100,600
Minority interests		10,600
		111,200
Current liabilities		
Trade payables ($10,000 + $7,000)	17,000	
Minority dividends	1,000	
		18,000
Total equity and liabilities		129,200

<table>
<tr><td>Exam focus point</td><td>A consolidated balance sheet will come up as regularly as clockwork. There will nearly always be an adjustment for intra-group trading, which we look at next.</td></tr>
</table>

7 Intra-group trading

FAST FORWARD

We have already come across cases where one company in a group engages in trading with another group company.

7.1 Unrealised profit

Any receivable/payable balances outstanding between the companies are cancelled on consolidation. No further problem arises if all such intra-group transactions are **undertaken at cost**, without any mark-up for profit.

However, each company in a group is a separate trading entity and may wish to treat other group companies in the same way as any other customer. In this case, a company (say A Co) may buy goods at one price and sell them at a higher price to another group company (B Co). The accounts of A Co will quite properly include the profit earned on sales to B Co; and similarly B Co's balance sheet will include inventories at their cost to B Co, ie at the amount at which they were purchased from A Co.

This gives rise to two problems.

(a) Although A Co makes a profit as soon as it sells goods to B Co, the group does not make a sale or achieve a profit until an outside customer buys the goods from B Co.

(b) Any purchases from A Co which remain unsold by B Co at the year end will be included in B Co's inventory. Their balance sheet value will be their cost to B Co, which is not the same as their cost to the group.

The objective of consolidated accounts is to present the financial position of several connected companies as that of a single entity, the group. This means that **in a consolidated balance sheet the only profits recognised should be those earned by the group** in providing goods or services to outsiders; and similarly, inventory in the consolidated balance sheet should be valued at cost to the group.

Suppose that a holding company P Co buys goods for $1,600 and sells them to a wholly owned subsidiary S Co for $2,000. The goods are in S Co's inventory at the year end and appear in S Co's balance sheet at $2,000. In this case, P Co will record a profit of $400 in its individual accounts, but from the group's point of view the figures are:

Cost	$1,600
External sales	nil
Closing inventory at cost	$1,600
Profit/loss	nil

If we add together the figures for retained reserves and inventory in the individual balance sheets of P Co and S Co the resulting figures for consolidated reserves and consolidated inventory will each be overstated by $400. A **consolidation adjustment** is therefore necessary as follows.

DEBIT   Group reserves   400 Dr

CREDIT   Group inventory (balance sheet)   400 Cr

with the amount of **profit unrealised** by the group.

Question	Unrealised profit

P Co acquired all the shares in S Co one year ago when the reserves of S Co stood at $10,000. Draft balance sheets for each company are as follows.

	P Co		S Co	
	$	$	$	$
Assets				
Non-current assets				
Tangible assets	80,000			40,000
Investment in S Co at cost	46,000			
		126,000		
✳ Current assets		40,000		30,000
Total assets		166,000		70,000
Equity and liabilities				
Equity				
Ordinary shares of $1 each	100,000		30,000	
✳ Reserves	45,000		22,000	
		145,000		52,000
✳ Current liabilities		21,000		18,000
Total equity and liabilities		166,000		70,000

During the year S Co sold goods to P Co for $50,000, the profit to S Co being 20% of selling price. At the balance sheet date, $15,000 of these goods remained unsold in the inventories of P Co. At the same date, P Co owed S Co $12,000 for goods bought and this debt is included in the trade payables of P Co and the receivables of S Co. The goodwill arising on consolidation has been impaired. The amount of the impairment is $1,500.

Required

Prepare a draft consolidated balance sheet for P Co.

Answer	

1   *Goodwill*

	$	$
Cost of investment		46,000
Share of net assets acquired as represented by		
Share capital	30,000	
Reserves	10,000	
	40,000	
Group share (100%)		40,000
Goodwill		6,000

2   *Reserves*

		P Co	S Co
		$	$
Reserves per question		45,000	22,000
Unrealised profit: 20% × $15,000		(3,000)	
		42,000	
Pre-acquisition			(10,000)
			12,000
Share of S Co		12,000	
Goodwill impairment loss		(1,500)	
		52,500	

BPP
PROFESSIONAL EDUCATION

P CO
CONSOLIDATED BALANCE SHEET

	$	$
Assets		
Non-current assets		
Tangible assets	120,000	
Goodwill (6,000 – 1,500)	4,500	
		124,500
Current assets (W1)		55,000
Total assets		179,500
Equity and liabilities		
Equity		
Ordinary shares of $1 each	100,000	
Reserves	52,500	
		152,500
Current liabilities (W2)		27,000
Total equity and liabilities		179,500

Workings

1   *Current assets*

	$	$
In P Co's balance sheet		40,000
In S Co's balance sheet	30,000	
Less S Co's current account with P Co cancelled	(12,000)	
		18,000
		58,000
Less unrealised profit excluded from inventory valuation		(3,000)
		55,000

2   *Current liabilities*

	$
In P Co's balance sheet	21,000
Less P Co's current account with S Co cancelled	(12,000)
	9,000
In S Co's balance sheet	18,000
	27,000

7.2 Minority interests in unrealised intra-group profits

A further problem occurs where a subsidiary company which is **not wholly owned is involved in intra-group trading** within the group. If a subsidiary S Co is 75% owned and sells goods to the parent company for $16,000 cost plus $4,000 profit, ie for $20,000 and if these items are unsold by P Co at the balance sheet date, the 'unrealised' profit of $4,000 earned by S Co and charged to P Co will be partly owned by the minority interest of S Co. As far as the minority interest of S Co is concerned, their share (25% of $4,000) amounting to $1,000 of profit on the sale of goods would appear to have been fully realised. It is only the group that has not yet made a profit on the sale.

There are three different possibilities as regards the treatment of these intra-group profits.

(a)   Remove only the group's share of the profit loading

✓ ☆ (b)   **Remove the whole profit loading, charging the minority with their proportion**

(c)   Remove the whole of the profit without charging the minority (to reduce group reserves by the whole profit loading)

The method given under (b) is usually considered best practice and the double entry is therefore as follows.

Entries to learn

DEBIT	Group reserves
DEBIT	Minority interest
CREDIT	Group inventory (balance sheet)

7.3 Example: minority interests and intra-group profits

P Co has owned 75% of the shares of S Co since the incorporation of that company. During the year to 31 December 20X2, S Co sold goods costing $16,000 to P Co at a price of $20,000 and these goods were still unsold by P Co at the end of the year. Draft balance sheets of each company at 31 December 20X2 were as follows.

	P Co		S Co	
Assets	$	$	$	$
Non-current assets				
Tangible assets	125,000		120,000	
Investment: 75,000 shares in S Co at cost	75,000		–	
		200,000		120,000
Current assets				
Inventories	50,000		48,000	
Trade receivables	20,000		16,000	
		70,000		64,000
Total assets		270,000		184,000
Equity and liabilities				
Equity				
Ordinary shares of $1 each fully paid	80,000		100,000	
Reserves	150,000		60,000	
		230,000		160,000
Current liabilities		40,000		24,000
Total equity and liabilities		270,000		184,000

Required

Prepare the consolidated balance sheet of P Co at 31 December 20X2.

Solution

The profit earned by S Co but unrealised by the group is $4,000 of which $3,000 (75%) is attributable to the group and $1,000 (25%) to the minority. Remove the whole of the profit loading, charging the minority with their proportion.

Reserves	P Co	S Co
	$	$
Per question	150,000	60,000
Less unrealised profit		(4,000)
		56,000
Share of S Co: $56,000 × 75%	42,000	
	192,000	

	$
Minority interest	
Share capital (25% × $100,000)	25,000
Reserves $(60,000 – 4,000) × 25%	14,000
	39,000

P CO
CONSOLIDATED BALANCE SHEET AS AT 31 DECEMBER 20X2

	$	$
Assets		
Tangible non-current assets		245,000
Current assets		
Inventories $(50,000 + 48,000 – 4,000)	94,000	
Trade receivables	36,000	
		130,000
Total assets		375,000
Equity and liabilities		
Equity		
Ordinary shares of $1 each	80,000	
Reserves	192,000	
		272,000
Minority interest		39,000
		311,000
Current liabilities		64,000
Total equity and liabilities		375,000

8 Intra-group sales of non-current assets

As well as engaging in trading activities with each other, group companies may on occasion wish to **transfer non-current assets**.

8.1 Accounting treatment

In their individual accounts the companies concerned will treat the transfer just like a sale between unconnected parties: the selling company will record a profit or loss on sale, while the purchasing company will record the asset at the amount paid to acquire it, and will use that amount as the basis for calculating depreciation.

On consolidation, the usual **'group entity' principle applies**. The consolidated balance sheet must show assets at their cost to the group, and any depreciation charged must be based on that cost. Two consolidation adjustments will usually be needed to achieve this.

(a) An adjustment to alter reserves and non-current assets cost so as to remove any element of unrealised profit or loss. This is similar to the adjustment required in respect of unrealised profit in inventory.

(b) An adjustment to alter reserves and accumulated depreciation is made so that consolidated depreciation is based on the asset's cost to the group.

The double entry is as follows.

(a) *Sale by holding company*

DEBIT   Group reserves
CREDIT   Non-current assets

with the profit on disposal.

DEBIT   Non-current assets
CREDIT   Group reserves (P's share)
CREDIT   Minority interest (MI's share)

with the additional depreciation.

(b)   *Sale by subsidiary*

DEBIT   Group reserves (P's share)
DEBIT   Minority interest (MI's share)
CREDIT   Non-current assets

with the profit on disposal.

DEBIT   Non-current assets
CREDIT   Group reserves

with the additional depreciation.

8.2 Example: intra-group sale of non-current assets

P Co owns 60% of S Co and on 1 January 20X1 S Co sells plant costing $10,000 to P Co for $12,500. The companies make up accounts to 31 December 20X1 and the balances on their revenue reserves at that date are:

P Co after charging depreciation of 10% on plant	$27,000
S Co including profit on sale of plant	$18,000

Required

Show the working for consolidated revenue reserves.

Solution

Revenue reserves

	P Co $	S Co $
Per question	27,000	18,000
Disposal of plant		
Profit		(2,500)
Depreciation: 10% × $2,500	250	15,500
	27,250	
Share of S Ltd: $15,500 × 60%	9,300	
	36,550	

Notes

1   The minority interest in the revenue reserves of S Co is 40% × $(18,000 – 2,500) = $6,200.

2   The asset is written down to cost and depreciation on the 'profit' element is removed. The group profit for the year is thus reduced by a net (($2,500 × 60%) – $250) = $1,250.

9 Summary: consolidated balance sheet

Purpose	To show the net assets which P controls and the ownership of those assets.
Net assets	Always 100% P plus 100% S providing P holds a majority of voting rights.
Share capital	P only.
Reason	Simply reporting to the parent company's shareholders in another form.
Reserves	100% P plus group share of post-acquisition retained reserves of S less consolidation adjustments.
Reason	To show the extent to which the group actually owns total assets less liabilities.
Minority interest	MI share of S's consolidated net assets.
Reason	To show the extent to which other parties own net assets that are under the control of the parent company.

Chapter roundup

- This chapter has covered the mechanics of preparing simple **consolidated balance sheets**. In particular, procedures have been described for dealing with:

    - Cancellation
    - Calculation of minority interests
    - Calculation of goodwill arising on consolidation

- A **seven-stage drill** has been described and exemplified in a comprehensive example.

- The stages are as follows.

    - Update the draft balance sheets to take account of proposed dividends not accrued for
    - Agree intra-group current accounts by adjusting for items in transit
    - Cancel items common to both balance sheets
    - Minority interests
    - Goodwill
    - Reserves
    - Consolidated balance sheet

- We have examined the consolidation adjustments necessary when group companies **trade with or sell non-current assets to each other**.

    - The guiding principle is that the consolidated balance sheet must show assets at their cost to the group.

    - Any profit arising on intra-group transactions must be eliminated from the group accounts unless and until it is realised by a sale outside the group.

- It is important that you have a clear understanding of the material in this chapter before you move on to more complicated aspects of consolidation.

Quick quiz

1   Chicken Co owns 80% of Egg Co. Egg Co sells goods to Chicken Co at cost plus 50%. The total invoiced sales to Chicken Co by Egg Co in the year ended 31 December 20X9 were $900,000 and, of these sales, goods which had been invoiced at $60,000 were held in inventory by Chicken Co at 31 December 20X9. What is the reduction in aggregate group gross profit?

2   Major Co, which makes up its accounts to 31 December, has an 80% owned subsidiary Minor Co. Minor Co sells goods to Major Co at a mark-up on cost of 33.33%. At 31 December 20X8, Major had $12,000 of such goods in its inventory and at 31 December 20X9 had $15,000 of such goods in its inventory.

   What is a permissible amount by which the consolidated profit attributable to Major Co's shareholders should be adjusted in respect of the above?

   Ignore taxation

   A $1,000 Debit
   B $800 Credit
   C $750 Credit
   D $600 Debit

3   What are the components making up the figure of minority interest in a consolidated balance sheet?

4   Fill in the blanks to show the adjustment required before consolidation in cases where a holding company has not accounted for dividends receivable from a subsidiary.

   DEBIT
   CREDIT

   With

5   Goodwill is always positive. True or false?

Answers to quick quiz

1    $60,000 × $\dfrac{50}{150}$ = $20,000

2   D $(15,000 - 12,000) × \dfrac{33.3}{133.3} × 80\%$

3   The minority's share of ordinary shares, preference shares and reserves.

4   DEBIT   Receivables (dividend receivable)
   CREDIT   Revenue reserves

   With the parent company's share of the dividend receivable in the parent's books.

5   False. Goodwill can be negative if the purchaser has 'got a bargain'.

Now try the question below from the Exam Question Bank

Number	Level	Marks	Time
Q16	Examination	25	45 mins

16

Fair value adjustments

Topic list	Syllabus reference
1 Acquisition of a subsidiary during its accounting period	4(c)
2 Dividends and pre-acquisition profits	4(c)
3 IFRS 3: Fair values in acquisition accounting	4(c)

Introduction

This chapter deals with the problems associated with the consolidation of a subsidiary acquired during the accounting period (a fairly common occurrence).

You will not understand the rest of the chapters on consolidation unless you grasp the principles laid out in this chapter. You should pay particular attention to the **determination of pre- and post-acquisition profits** and the **effect of dividends** in Section 2.

Study guide

Section 21 – Business combinations – fair value adjustments

- Explain why it is necessary for both the consideration paid for a subsidiary and the subsidiary's identifiable assets and liabilities to be accounted for at their fair values when preparing consolidated financial statements

- Prepare consolidated financial statements dealing with fair value adjustments (including their effect on consolidated goodwill) in respect of:

   –   Depreciating and non-depreciating non-current assets

   –   Inventory

   –   Monetary liabilities (basic discounting techniques may be required)

   –   Assets and liabilities (including contingencies) not included in the subsidiary's own balance sheet

1 Acquisition of a subsidiary during its accounting period

FAST FORWARD

> When a parent company acquires a subsidiary during its accounting period the only accounting entries will be those recording the **cost of acquisition in the parent company's books**.

1.1 Accounting problem

As we have already seen, at the end of the accounting year it will be necessary to prepare consolidated accounts.

The subsidiary company's accounts to be consolidated will show the subsidiary's profit or loss for the whole year. For consolidation purposes, however, it will be necessary to distinguish between:

   (a)   **Profits earned before acquisition**
   (b)   **Profits earned after acquisition**

In practice, a subsidiary company's profit may not accrue evenly over the year; for example, the subsidiary might be engaged in a trade, such as toy sales, with marked seasonal fluctuations. Nevertheless, the assumption can be made that **profits accrue evenly** whenever it is impracticable to arrive at an accurate split of pre– and post-acquisition profits.

Once the amount of pre-acquisition profit has been established the appropriate consolidation workings (goodwill, reserves) can be produced, as shown in Chapter 16.

Bear in mind that in calculating **minority interests** the distinction between pre– and post-acquisition profits is irrelevant. The minority shareholders are simply credited with their share of the subsidiary's total reserves at the balance sheet date.

It is worthwhile to summarise what happens on consolidation to the reserves figures extracted from a subsidiary's balance sheet. Suppose the accounts of S Co, a 60% subsidiary of P Co, show reserves of $20,000 at the balance sheet date, of which $14,000 were earned prior to acquisition. The figure of $20,000 will appear in the consolidated balance sheet as follows.

	$
Minority interests working: their share of total reserves at balance sheet date (40% × $20,000)	8,000
✗ Goodwill working: group share of pre-acquisition profits (60% × $14,000)	8,400
Consolidated reserves working: group share of post-acquisition profits (60% × $6,000)	3,600
	20,000

Question

Acquisition

Hinge Co acquired 80% of the ordinary shares of Singe Co on 1 April 20X5. On 31 December 20X4 Singe Co's accounts showed a share premium account of $4,000 and revenue reserves of $15,000. The balance sheets of the two companies at 31 December 20X5 are set out below. Neither company has paid or proposed any dividends during the year.

You are required to prepare the consolidated balance sheet of Hinge Co at 31 December 20X5. (There was no impairment of goodwill.)

HINGE CO
BALANCE SHEET AS AT 31 DECEMBER 20X5

	$	$
Assets		
Non-current assets		
Tangible assets	32,000	
✳ 16,000 ordinary shares of 50c each in Singe Co	50,000	
		82,000
Current assets		85,000
Total assets		167,000
Equity and liabilities		
Equity		
Ordinary shares of $1 each	100,000	
Share premium account	7,000	
Accumulated profits	40,000	
		147,000
Current liabilities		20,000
Total equity and liabilities		167,000

SINGE CO
BALANCE SHEET AS AT 31 DECEMBER 20X5

	$	$
Assets		
Tangible non-current assets		30,000
Current assets		43,000
Total assets		73,000
Equity and liabilities		
Equity		
✳ 20,000 ordinary shares of 50c each	10,000	
✳ Share premium account	4,000	
✳ Accumulated profits	39,000	
		53,000
Current liabilities		20,000
Total equity and liabilities		73,000

Answer

Singe Co has made a profit of $24,000 ($39,000 – $15,000) for the year. In the absence of any direction to the contrary, this should be assumed to have arisen evenly over the year; $6,000 in the three months to 31 March and $18,000 in the nine months after acquisition. The company's pre-acquisition accumulated profits are therefore as follows.

	$
Balance at 31 December 20X4	15,000
Profit for three months to 31 March 20X5	6,000
Pre-acquisition accumulated profits	21,000

The balance of $4,000 on share premium account is all pre-acquisition.

The consolidation workings can now be drawn up.

1   Minority interest

	$
Ordinary share capital (20% × $10,000)	2,000
Accumulated profits (20% × $39,000)	7,800
Share premium (20% × $4,000)	800
	10,600

2   Goodwill

	$	$
Cost of investment		50,000
Share of net assets acquired represented by		
Ordinary share capital	10,000	
Accumulated profits (pre-acquisition)	21,000	
Share premium	4,000	
	35,000	
Group share (80%)		28,000
Goodwill		22,000

3   Accumulated profits

	Hinge Co $	Singe Co $
Per question	40,000	39,000
Pre-acquisition (see above)		21,000
		18,000
Share of Singe: $18,000 × 80%	14,400	
	54,400	

4   Share premium account

	$
Hinge Co	7,000
Share of Singe Co's post-acquisition share premium	–
	7,000

HINGE CO
CONSOLIDATED BALANCE SHEET AS AT 31 DECEMBER 20X5

	$
Assets	
Tangible non-current assets	62,000
Goodwill (W2)	22,000
Current assets	128,000
Total assets	212,000

	$
Equity and liabilities	
Equity	
Ordinary shares of $1 each	100,000
Reserves	
Share premium account (W4)	7,000
Revenue reserves (W3)	54,400
	161,400
Minority interest (W1)	10,600
	172,000
Current liabilities	40,000
Total equity and liabilities	212,000

1.2 Example: pre-acquisition losses of a subsidiary

As an illustration of the entries arising when a subsidiary has pre-acquisition *losses*, suppose P Co acquired all 50,000 $1 ordinary shares in S Co for $20,000 on 1 January 20X1 when there was a debit balance of $35,000 on S Co's revenue reserves. In the years 20X1 to 20X4 S Co makes profits of $40,000 in total, leaving a credit balance of $5,000 on revenue reserves at 31 December 20X4. P Co's reserves at the same date are $70,000.

Solution

The consolidation workings would appear as follows.

1 *Goodwill*

	$	$
Cost of investment		20,000
Share of net assets acquired		
as represented by		
Ordinary share capital	50,000	
Revenue reserves	(35,000)	
	15,000	
Group share (100%)		15,000
Goodwill		5,000

2 *Accumulated profits*

	$
P Co	70,000
Share of S Co's post-acquisition	
retained reserves	40,000
Group reserves	110,000

2 Dividends and pre-acquisition profits

FAST FORWARD

A further problem in consolidation occurs when a subsidiary pays out **a dividend soon after acquisition**.

2.1 Pre-acquisition profits

The parent company, as a member of the subsidiary, is entitled to its share of the dividends paid but it is necessary to decide whether or not these dividends come out of the pre-acquisition profits of the subsidiary.

If the dividends come from **post-acquisition** profits there is no problem. The holding company simply **credits** the relevant amount to its **own income statement**, as with any other dividend income. The double entry is quite different, however, if the dividend is paid from **pre-acquisition profits**, being as follows.

DEBIT	Cash
CREDIT	Investment in subsidiary

The parent company's balance sheet would then disclose the investment as 'Investment in subsidiary at cost less amounts written down'.

It is very important that you are clear about the reason for this. Consider the following summarised balance sheets of S_1 Co and S_2 Co as at 31 March 20X4.

	S_1 Co $\$$	S_2 Co $\$$
Goodwill	5,000	5,000
Current assets	30,000	30,000
Current liabilities	10,000	10,000
Ordinary shareholders' equity	25,000	25,000

The companies are identical in every respect, except that the current liabilities of S_1 Co are trade payables while the current liabilities of S_2 Co are a proposed ordinary dividend.

P_1 Co, a prospective purchaser of S_1 Co, is willing to pay $25,000 for 100% of S_1, including goodwill. P_2 Co, a prospective purchaser of S_2 Co, will clearly be willing to pay $35,000 for the acquisition of that company in the knowledge that $10,000 of the cost will immediately be 'refunded' by way of dividend.

Assume that the two purchases are completed on 31 March 20X4 and on 1 April 20X4 S_1 Co and S_2 Co pay off their current liabilities as appropriate. P_1 Co and P_2 Co will then own identical investments, each consisting of $20,000 of current assets plus $5,000 of goodwill, and it is clearly appropriate that the investment figures in their own balance sheets should be identical. This will be the case if P_2 Co sets off the $10,000 dividend receivable against the $35,000 cost of the acquisition, disclosing the investment in S_2 Co at a net cost of $25,000.

The point to grasp is that P_2 Co cannot credit the dividend to profit because no profit has been made. The correct way of looking at it is to say that P_2 Co was willing to pay 'over the odds' for its investment in the presumption that a part of its cost would immediately be repaid. When the dividend is paid, this presumption must be pursued to its conclusion by treating the dividend as a reduction of the cost of the investment.

This accounting treatment is considered **best practice**.

2.2 Example: dividends and pre-acquisition profits

Pip Co acquired 8,000 of the 10,000 $1 ordinary shares of Sip Co on 1 January 20X5 for $25,000. Sip Co's balance sheet at 31 December 20X4 showed a proposed ordinary dividend of $4,000 and retained reserves of $12,000. The balance sheets of the two companies at 31 December 20X5 are given below.

PIP CO
BALANCE SHEET AS AT 31 DECEMBER 20X5

	$\$$	$\$$
Assets		
Non-current assets		
Tangible assets	35,000	
Investment in Sip Co at cost less amounts written down	21,800	
		56,800
Current assets		27,000
Total assets		83,800

	$	$
Equity and liabilities		
Equity		
Ordinary shares of $1 each		50,000
Retained reserves		33,800
Total equity and liabilities		83,800

SIP CO

BALANCE SHEET AS AT 31 DECEMBER 20X5	$
Assets	
Tangible non-current assets	14,500
Current assets	12,500
Total assets	27,000
Equity and liabilities	
Equity	
Ordinary shares of $1 each	10,000
Retained reserves	17,000
Total equity and liabilities	27,000

Required

Prepare the consolidated balance sheet of Pip Co at 31 December 20X5. Goodwill has been impaired – the amount of the impairment is $1,050.

Solution

During the year Sip Co has paid the $4,000 proposed dividend in its 20X4 balance sheet. Pip Co's share (80% × $4,000 = $3,200) has been correctly credited by that company to its 'investment in Sip Co' account. That account appears in the books of Pip Co as follows.

INVESTMENT IN SIP CO

	$		$
Bank: purchase of 8,000 $1 ordinary shares	25,000	Bank: dividend received from pre-acquisition profits	3,200
		Balance c/f	21,800
	25,000		25,000

If Pip Co had incorrectly credited the pre-acquisition dividend to its own income statement, it would have been necessary to make the following adjustments in Pip Co's accounts before proceeding to the consolidation.

DEBIT	Retained reserves	$3,200	
CREDIT	Investment in Sip Co		$3,200

Exam focus point

> This procedure is sometimes necessary in examination questions.

The consolidation workings can be drawn up as follows.

1 *Minority interest*

	$
Share capital (20% × $10,000)	2,000
Reserves (20% × $17,000)	3,400
	5,400

2   *Goodwill*

	$	$
Cost of investment		25,000
Less share of pre-acquisition dividend (80% × $4,000)		3,200
		21,800
Share of net assets acquired as represented by		
Ordinary share capital	10,000	
Reserves	12,000	
	22,000	
Group share (80%)		17,600
Goodwill		4,200

3   *Reserves*

	Pip	*Sip*
	$	$
Per question	33,800	17,000
Pre-acquisition		(12,000)
		5,000
Share of Sip: $5,000 × 80%	4,000	
Impairment of goodwill	(1,050)	
	36,750	

PIP CO
CONSOLIDATED BALANCE SHEET AS AT 31 DECEMBER 20X5

	$	$
Assets		
Non-current assets		
Tangible assets	49,500	
Goodwill (4,200 – 1,050) (W2)	3,150	
		52,650
Current assets		39,500
Total assets		92,150
Equity and liabilities		
Capital and reserves		
Ordinary shares of $1 each	50,000	
Retained reserves (W3)	36,750	
		86,750
Minority interest (W1)		5,400
Total equity and liabilities		92,150

The example above included an ordinary dividend paid from pre-acquisition profits. The treatment would be exactly the same if a **preferred dividend** had been paid from pre-acquisition profits. Any share of such a preferred dividend received by the parent company would be credited, not to income statement, but to the investment in subsidiary account.

2.3 Is the dividend paid from pre-acquisition profits?

We need next to consider how it is decided whether a dividend is paid from pre-acquisition profits. In the example above there was no difficulty: Pip Co acquired shares in Sip Co on the first day of an accounting period and the dividend was in respect of the previous accounting period. Clearly, the dividend was paid from profits earned in the period before acquisition.

The position is less straightforward if shares are acquired **during the subsidiary's accounting period**. An example will illustrate the point.

2.4 Example: acquisition during subsidiary's accounting period

P Co and S Co each make up their accounts to 31 December. P Co buys 80,000 of the 100,000 $1 ordinary shares of S Co for $175,000 on 1 October 20X1. S Co's revenue reserves (after deducting proposed dividends) stood at $50,000 on 31 December 20X0. S Co's profits after tax for the year to 31 December 20X1 were $20,000. In December 20X1 S Co declared a first and final dividend for 20X1 of $10,000. At 31 December 20X1, P Co's reserves stood at $110,000; this does not include any adjustment for dividends receivable from S Co.

Required

Prepare consolidation workings for revenue reserves, minority interest and goodwill as at 31 December 20X1.

Solution

The problem is to decide how much of the dividend paid by S Co comes from pre-acquisition profits. There are several possible ways of doing this but the method we recommend is based on **time-apportionment**. The 20X1 dividend eventually declared by S Co is deemed to have accrued evenly over the year.

Note. Of the $8,000 dividend receivable by P Co, $6,000 is deemed to have come from pre-acquisition profits and is credited to 'Investment in S Co'. $2,000 comes from post-acquisition profits and is added to reserves.

1   *Minority interest*

	$
Share capital (20% × $100,000)	20,000
Revenue reserves (20% × $60,000)	12,000
	32,000

The minority also has an interest ($2,000) in the proposed dividend payable by S Co. This will appear as a current liability in the consolidated balance sheet.

2   *Goodwill*

	$	$
Cost of investment		175,000
Less pre-acquisition dividend		
$10,000 × 9/12 × 80%		6,000
		169,000
Share of net assets acquired as represented by		
Ordinary share capital	100,000	
Revenue reserves		
$(50,000 + 15,000 − 7,500)	57,500	
	157,500	
Group share (80%)		126,000
Goodwill		43,000

3   *Revenue reserves*

	P Co	S Co
	$	$
Per question	110,000	60,000
Dividend receivable	2,000	
Pre-acquisition (W2)		57,500
		2,500
Share of S Co: $2,500 × 80%	2,000	
	114,000	

It has been argued by some that the question as to whether a dividend from a subsidiary to the parent company is available for onward distribution by the parent company depends on whether receipt of the dividend can be regarded as giving rise to a **realised profit** in the financial statements of the parent company and not simply whether it derives from the pre– or post-acquisition profits of the subsidiary.

In other words if the subsidiary **recovers in value** after the distribution, the **loss in value is temporary** and need not be deducted from the cost of the investment (only permanent diminutions should be provided).

Where the investment is carried at fair value, however, it is likely that a dividend which represents a return of pre-acquisition profits would give rise to a **diminution in the value** of the investment and thus should be applied in reducing the cost (carrying value) of that investment.

3 IFRS 3: Fair values in acquisition accounting

FAST FORWARD   Fair values are very important in calculating goodwill.

3.1 Goodwill

To understand the importance of fair values in the acquisition of a subsidiary consider again the definition of goodwill.

Key term

> **Goodwill**. Any excess of the cost of the acquisition over the acquirer's interest in the fair value of the identifiable assets and liabilities acquired as at the date of the exchange transaction.

The **balance sheet of a subsidiary company** at the date it is acquired may not be a guide to the fair value of its net assets. For example, the market value of a freehold building may have risen greatly since it was acquired, but it may appear in the balance sheet at historical cost less accumulated depreciation.

3.2 What is fair value?

Fair value is defined as follows by IFRS 3 and various other standards – it is an important definition.

Key term

> **Fair value**. The amount for which an asset could be exchanged, or a liability settled, between knowledgeable, willing parties in an arm's length transaction.

We will look at the requirements of IFRS 3 regarding fair value in more detail below. First let us look at some practical matters.

3.3 Fair value adjustment calculations

Until now we have calculated goodwill as the difference between the cost of the investment and the **book value** of net assets acquired by the group. If this calculation is to comply with the definition above we must ensure that the book value of the subsidiary's net assets is the same as their **fair value**.

There are two possible ways of achieving this.

(a) The **subsidiary company** might **incorporate any necessary revaluations** in its own books of account. In this case, we can proceed directly to the consolidation, taking asset values and reserves figures straight from the subsidiary company's balance sheet.

(b) The **revaluations** may be made as a **consolidation adjustment without being incorporated** in the subsidiary company's books. In this case, we must make the necessary adjustments to the subsidiary's balance sheet as a working. Only then can we proceed to the consolidation.

Note. Remember that when depreciating assets are revalued there may be a corresponding alteration in the amount of depreciation charged and accumulated.

3.4 Example: fair value adjustments

P Co acquired 75% of the ordinary shares of S Co on 1 September 20X5. At that date the fair value of S Co's non-current assets was $23,000 greater than their net book value, and the balance of retained profits was $21,000. The balance sheets of both companies at 31 August 20X6 are given below. S Co has not incorporated any revaluation in its books of account.

P CO
BALANCE SHEET AS AT 31 AUGUST 20X6

	$	$
Assets		
Non-current assets		
Tangible assets	63,000	
Investment in S Co at cost	51,000	
		114,000
Current assets		82,000
Total assets		196,000
Equity and liabilities		
Equity		
Ordinary shares of $1 each	80,000	
Retained profits	96,000	
		176,000
Current liabilities		20,000
Total equity and liabilities		196,000

S CO
BALANCE SHEET AS AT 31 AUGUST 20X6

	$	$
Assets		
Tangible non-current assets		28,000
Current assets		43,000
Total assets		71,000
Equity and liabilities		
Equity		
Ordinary shares of $1 each	20,000	
Retained profits	41,000	
		61,000
Current liabilities		10,000
Total equity and liabilities		71,000

If S Co had revalued its non-current assets at 1 September 20X5, an addition of $3,000 would have been made to the depreciation charged in the income statement for 20X5/X6.

Required

Prepare P Co's consolidated balance sheet as at 31 August 20X6.

Solution

S Co has not incorporated the revaluation in its draft balance sheet. Before beginning the consolidation workings we must therefore adjust the company's balance of profits at the date of acquisition and at the balance sheet date.

S Co adjusted balance of accumulated profits

	$	$
Balance per accounts at 1 September 20X5 — *Pre acquisition profit*		21,000
Consolidation adjustment: revaluation surplus		23,000
∴ Pre-acquisition profits for consolidation purposes		44,000
Profit for year ended 31 August 20X6 *(41,000 – 21,000)*		
Per draft accounts $(41,000 – 21,000)	20,000	
Consolidation adjustment: increase in depreciation charge	(3,000)	
		17,000
Adjusted balance of accumulated profits at 31 August 20X6		61,000

In the consolidated balance sheet, S Co's non-current assets will appear at their revalued amount: $(28,000 + 23,000 – 3,000) = $48,000. The consolidation workings can now be drawn up.

1 Minority interest

	$
Share capital (25% × $20,000)	5,000
Revenue reserves (25% × $61,000)	15,250
	20,250

2 Goodwill

	$	$
Cost of investment		51,000
Share of net assets acquired as represented by		
Ordinary share capital	20,000	
Revenue reserves		
$(21,000 + 23,000)	44,000	
	64,000	
Group share (75%)		48,000
Goodwill		3,000

3 Accumulated profits

	P Co $	S Co $
Per question	96,000	41,000
Pre acquisition profits		(21,000)
Depreciation adjustment		(3,000)
Post acquisition S Co		17,000
Group share in S Co		
($17,000 × 75%)	12,750	
Group accumulated profits	108,750	

P CO CONSOLIDATED BALANCE SHEET AS AT 31 AUGUST 20X6

	$	$
Assets		
Tangible non-current assets $(63,000 + 48,000)	111,000	
Goodwill (W2)	3,000	
		114,000
Current assets		125,000
		239,000

	$	$
Equity and liabilities		
Equity		
Ordinary shares of $1 each	80,000	
Accumulated profits (W3)	108,750	
		188,750
Minority interest (W1)		20,250
		209,000
Current liabilities		30,000
		239,000

Question   Fair value

An asset is recorded in S Co's books at its historical cost of $4,000. On 1 January 20X5 P Co bought 80% of S Co's equity. Its directors attributed a fair value of $3,000 to the asset as at that date. It had been depreciated for two years out of an expected life of four years on the straight line basis. There was no expected residual value. On 30 June 20X5 the asset was sold for $2,600. What is the profit or loss on disposal of this asset to be recorded in S Co's accounts and in P Co's consolidated accounts for the year ended 31 December 20X5?

Answer

S Co: NBV at disposal (at historical cost) = $4,000 × 1½/4 = $1,500
∴ Profit on disposal = $1,100 (depreciation charge for the year = $500)

P Co: NBV at disposal (at fair value) = $3,000 × 1½/2 = $2,250
∴ Profit on disposal for consolidation = $350 (depreciation for the year = $750).

The minority would be credited with 20% of both the profit on disposal and the depreciation charge as part of the one line entry in the consolidated income statement.

3.5 IFRS 3: Fair values

IFRS 3 sets out **general principles** for arriving at the fair values of a subsidiary's assets and liabilities. The acquirer should recognise the acquiree's identifiable assets, liabilities and contingent liabilities at the acquisition date only if they satisfy the following criteria.

(a)   In the case of an **asset** other than an intangible asset, it is **probable** that any associated **future economic benefits** will flow to the acquirer, and its fair value can be **measured reliably.**

(b)   In the case of a **liability** other than a contingent liability, it is probable that an **outflow** of resources embodying economic benefits will be required to settle the obligation, and its fair value can be **measured reliably**.

(c)   In the case of an **intangible asset** or a **contingent liability**, its fair value can be **measured reliably**.

The acquiree's identifiable assets and liabilities might include assets and liabilities **not previously recognised** in the acquiree's financial statements. For example, a tax benefit arising from the acquiree's tax losses that was not recognised by the acquiree may be recognised by the group if the acquirer has future taxable profits against which the unrecognised tax benefit can be applied.

3.5.1 Restructuring and future losses

An acquirer **should not recognise liabilities for future losses** or other costs expected to be incurred as a result of the business combination.

IFRS 3 explains that a plan to restructure a subsidiary following an acquisition is not a present obligation of the acquiree at the acquisition date. Neither does it meet the definition of a contingent liability. Therefore an acquirer **should not recognise a liability for** such **a restructuring plan** as part of allocating the cost of the combination unless the subsidiary was already committed to the plan before the acquisition.

This **prevents creative accounting**. An acquirer cannot set up a provision for restructuring or future losses of a subsidiary and then release this to the income statement in subsequent periods in order to reduce losses or smooth profits.

3.5.2 Intangible assets

The acquiree may have **intangible assets**, such as development expenditure. These can be recognised separately from goodwill only if they are **identifiable**. An intangible asset is identifiable only if it:

(a) Is **separable**, ie capable of being separated or divided from the entity and sold, transferred, or exchanged, either individually or together with a related contract, asset or liability, or

(b) Arises from **contractual or other legal rights**

3.5.3 Contingent liabilities

Contingent liabilities of the acquirer are **recognised** if their **fair value can be measured reliably**. This is a departure from the normal rules in IAS 37; contingent liabilities are not normally recognised, but only disclosed.

After their initial recognition, the acquirer should measure contingent liabilities that are recognised separately at the higher of:

(a) The amount that would be recognised in accordance with IAS 37
(b) The amount initially recognised

IFRS 3 goes on to list some **general guidelines** for arriving at the fair values of assets and liabilities.

Asset	Fair valuation
Marketable securities	Current market value
Non-marketable securities	Estimated values that take into consideration features such as: (a) price earnings ratios (b) dividend yield (c) expected growth rates of comparable securities of entity with similar characteristics
Receivables, beneficial contracts and other identifiable assets	Present values of the amounts to be received, determined at appropriate current interest rates, less allowances for uncollectability and collection costs if necessary. Discounting is not required for short term receivables when the difference when the difference between the nominal and the discounted amount is not material.
Inventories: finished goods and merchandise	Selling price less the sum of: (a) the costs of disposal, and (b) a reasonable profit allowance for the selling effort of the acquirer based on profit for similar finished goods and merchandise.

Asset	Fair valuation
Inventories: work in progress	Selling price of finished goods less the sum of: (a) costs to complete, (b) costs of disposal, and (c) a reasonable profit allowance for the completing and selling effort based on profit for similar finished goods.
Inventories: raw materials	Current replacement costs
Land and buildings	Market value
Plant and equipment (to be **used** in the business)	Market value normally determined by appraisal. When there is no evidence of market value because of the specialised nature of the plant and equipment or because the items are rarely sold, except as part of a continuing business, they should be valued at their depreciated replacement cost.
Intangible assets, as defined in IAS 38 *Intangible assets*	At a value determined: by reference to an active market as defined in IAS 38, and if no active market exists on a basis that reflects the amount that the acquirer would have paid for the asset in an arm's length transaction between knowledgeable, willing parties based on the best information available.
Net employee benefit assets or liabilities for defined benefit plans	Present value of the defined benefit obligations less the fair value of any plan assets. However, an asset is only recognised to the extent that it is probable that it will be available to the acquirer, in the form of refunds from the plan or a reduction in future contributions.
Tax assets and liabilities	Amount of the tax benefit arising from tax losses or the taxes payable in respect of the net profit or loss, assessed from the perspective of the combined entity. The tax asset or liability is determined after allowing for the tax effect of restating identifiable assets and liabilities to their fair values.
Accounts and notes payable, long-term debt, liabilities, accruals and other claims payable	Present values of amounts to be disbursed in meeting the liability determined at appropriate current interest rates. However, discounting is not required for short-term liabilities when the difference between the nominal amount of the liability and the discounted amount is not material.
Onerous contracts, and other identifiable liabilities of the acquirer.	Present values of amounts to be disbursed in settling the obligations determined at the appropriate current interest rates.
Contingent liabilities	The amounts that a third party would charge to assume those contingent liabilities. Such an amount would reflect all expectations about possible cash flows and not the single most likely or the expected maximum or minimum cash flow.

Some of the above guidelines assume that fair values will be determined by the use of **discounting**. When the guidelines do *not* refer to the use of discounting, discounting may or may not be used in determining the fair values of identifiable assets and liabilities.

3.5.4 Cost of a business combination

The general principle is that the acquirer should measure the cost of a business combination as the total of:

(a)   The **fair values**, at the date of exchange, **of assets given**, liabilities incurred or assumed, and equity instruments issued by the acquirer, in exchange for control of the acquiree, plus

(b)   Any **costs** directly attributable to the business combination

Sometimes all or part of the cost of an acquisition is deferred (ie, does not become payable immediately). The fair value of any deferred consideration is determined by **discounting** the amounts payable to their **present value** at the date of exchange.

Where equity instruments (eg, ordinary shares) of a quoted entity form part of the cost of a combination, the **published price** at the date of exchange normally provides the best evidence of the instrument's fair value and except in rare circumstances this should be used.

Future losses or other costs expected to be incurred as a result of a combination should not be included in the cost of the combination.

Costs **directly attributable** to the combination, for example professional fees, should be included. Costs that cannot be directly attributed to the combination, such as general administrative costs, should not be included: they are recognised as an expense when incurred. **Costs of issuing debt instruments and equity shares** are not directly attributable to the combination. IAS 32 *Financial instruments: disclosure and presentation*, states that such costs should **reduce the proceeds from the debt issue or the equity issue**.

Question	Goodwill on consolidation

Tyzo Co prepares accounts to 31 December. On 1 September 20X7 Tyzo Co acquired 6 million $1 shares in Kono Co at $2.00 per share. The purchase was financed by an additional issue of loan stock at an interest rate of 10%. At that date Kono Co produced the following interim financial statements.

	$m		$m
Property, plant and equipment (note 1)	16.0	Trade payables	3.2
		Taxation	0.6
Inventories (note 2)	4.0	Bank overdraft	3.9
Receivables	2.9	Long-term loans (note 3)	4.0
Cash in hand	1.2	Share capital ($1 shares)	8.0
		Reserves	4.4
	24.1		24.1

Notes

1   The following information relates to the tangible non-current assets of Kono Co at 1 September 20X7.

	$m
Gross replacement cost	28.4
Net replacement cost	16.6
Economic value	18.0
Net realisable value	8.0

The property, plant and equipment of Kono Co at 1 September 20X7 had a total purchase cost to Kono Co of $27.0 million. They were all being depreciated at 25% per annum pro rata on that cost. This policy is also appropriate for the consolidated financial statements of Tyzo Co. No non-current assets of Kono Co which were included in the interim financial statements drawn up as at 1 September 20X7 were disposed of by Kono Co prior to 31 December 20X7. No non-current asset was fully depreciated by 31 December 20X7.

2 The inventories of Kono Co which were shown in the interim financial statements are raw materials at cost to Kono Co of $4 million. They would have cost $4.2 million to replace at 1 September 20X7. Of the inventory of Kono Co in hand at 1 September 20X7, goods costing Kono Co $3.0 million were sold for $3.6 million between 1 September 20X7 and 31 December 20X7.

3 The long-term loan of Kono Co carries a rate of interest of 10% per annum, payable on 31 August annually in arrears. The loan is redeemable at par on 31 August 20Y1. The interest cost is representative of current market rates. The accrued interest payable by Kono Co at 31 December 20X7 is included in the trade payables of Kono Co at that date.

4 On 1 September 20X7 Tyzo Co took a decision to rationalise the group so as to integrate Kono Co. The costs of the rationalisation were estimated to total $3.0 million and the process was due to start on 1 March 20X8. No provision for these costs has been made in the financial statements given above.

Required

Compute the goodwill on consolidation of Kono Co that will be included in the consolidated financial statements of the Tyzo Co group for the year ended 31 December 20X7, explaining your treatment of the items mentioned above. You should refer to the provisions of relevant accounting standards.

Answer

Goodwill on consolidation of Kono Co

	$m	$m
Consideration ($2.00 × 6m)		12.0
Group share of fair value of net assets acquired		
Share capital	8.0	
Pre-acquisition reserves	4.4	
Fair value adjustments		
Tangible non-current assets (16.6 – 16.0)	0.6	
Inventories (4.2 – 4.0)	0.2	
	13.2	
Group share 75%		9.9
Goodwill		2.1

Notes on treatment

(a) It is assumed that the market value (ie fair value) of the loan stock issued to fund the purchase of the shares in Kono Co is equal to the price of $12.0m. IFRS 3 *Business combinations* requires goodwill to be calculated by comparing the cost of acquisition with the fair value of the acquirer's interest in the identifiable net assets of the acquired business or company.

(b) Share capital and pre-acquisition profits represent the book value of the net assets of Kono Co at the date of acquisition. Adjustments are then required to this book value in order to give the fair value of the net assets at the date of acquisition. For short-term monetary items, fair value is their carrying value on acquisition.

(c) IFRS 3 states that the fair value of property, plant and equipment should be determined by market value or, if information on a market price is not available (as is the case here), then by reference to depreciated replacement cost, reflecting normal business practice. The net replacement cost (ie $16.6m) represents the gross replacement cost less depreciation based on that amount, and so further adjustment for extra depreciation is unnecessary.

(d) IFRS 3 also states that raw materials should be valued at replacement cost. In this case that amount is $4.2m.

(e)   The fair value of the loan is the present value of the total amount payable, ie on maturity and in interest. If the quoted interest rate was used as a discount factor, this would give the current par value.

(f)   The rationalisation costs cannot be reported in pre-acquisition results under IFRS 3 as they are not a liability of Kono Co at the acquisition date.

3.6 Goodwill arising on acquisition

Goodwill should be carried in the balance sheet at **cost less any accumulated impairment losses**.

3.7 Adjustments to purchase consideration

An acquisition agreement may provide for adjustments to be made to the purchase consideration **contingent on (ie in the light of) one or more future events**. For example, adjustments may be contingent on a specified future level of earnings being achieved, or perhaps on the maintenance of the market price of the securities issued as part of the purchase consideration.

In these cases, the amount of the adjustment should be **included in the cost of the acquisition** as at the date of acquisition *if.*

(a)   The adjustment is **probable**, *and*

(b)   The amount can be **measured reliably**

If these future events fail to occur or the estimate must be revised, then the cost of the acquisition should be adjusted. **Goodwill** will thus require adjustment (whether positive or negative).

Subsequent changes in the cost of acquisition should be made on the same basis when the contingency becomes resolved *after* the date of the acquisition.

3.8 Adjustments after the initial accounting is complete

Sometimes the fair values of the acquiree's identifiable assets, liabilities or contingent liabilities or the cost of the combination can only be determined **provisionally** by the **end of the period in which the combination takes place**. In this situation, the acquirer **should account for the combination using those provisional values**. The acquirer should **recognise any adjustments** to those provisional values as a result of completing the initial accounting:

(a)   **Within twelve months** of the acquisition date, and

(b)   **From** the acquisition date (ie, retrospectively)

This means that:

(a)   The **carrying amount** of an item that is recognised or adjusted as a result of completing the initial accounting shall be calculated **as if its fair value** at the acquisition date **had been recognised from that date.**

(b)   **Goodwill should be adjusted** from the acquisition date by an amount equal to the adjustment to the fair value of the item being recognised or adjusted.

Any further adjustments after the initial accounting is complete should be **recognised only to correct an error** in accordance with IAS 8 *Accounting policies, changes in accounting estimates and errors*. Any subsequent changes in estimates are dealt with in accordance with IAS 8 (ie, the effect is recognised in the current and future periods). IAS 8 requires an entity to account for an error correction retrospectively, and to present financial statements as if the error had never occurred by restating the comparative information for the prior period(s) in which the error occurred.

Chapter roundup

- In this chapter we have looked at certain problems involved in distinguishing between **pre-acquisition** and **post-acquisition profits** of subsidiary companies.

- When a subsidiary is acquired **during its accounting period**, its **pre-acquisition profits** will include a **proportion of its total profits** for the accounting period.

- In the absence of information to the contrary, the profits earned during the period may be assumed to have **accrued evenly** and should be allocated accordingly.

- **Dividends** paid by a subsidiary to its parent company may only be **credited to the parent's income statement** to the extent that they are paid from **post-acquisition profits**.

- **Dividends** received by the parent company **from pre-acquisition profits** should be credited to 'investment in subsidiary' account and treated as **reducing the cost of the shares** acquired.

- **Goodwill arising on consolidation** is the difference between the purchase consideration and the fair value of the identifiable assets and liabilities acquired.

- **Goodwill** should be calculated **after revaluing** the subsidiary company's assets to fair value.

- If the subsidiary does not incorporate the revaluation in its own accounts, it should be done as a **consolidation adjustment**.

- The accounting requirements and disclosures of the **fair value exercise** are covered by **IFRS 3**.

Quick quiz

1 A parent company can assume that, for a subsidiary acquired during its accounting period, profits accrue evenly during the year. True or false?

2 What entries are made in the consolidated workings accounts to record the pre-acquisition profits of a subsidiary?

3 What entries are made in the holding company's accounts to record a dividend received from a subsidiary's pre-acquisition profits?

4 Describe the requirement of IFRS 3 in relation to the revaluation of a subsidiary company's assets to fair value at the acquisition date.

5 What guidelines are given by IFRS 3 in relation to valuing land and buildings fairly?

Answers to quick quiz

1 True

2 See Para 1.1

3 DEBIT   Cash
  CREDIT   Investment in subsidiary

4 Fair value is not affected by the acquirer's intentions. Therefore any intentions after acquisition are reflected in the income statement after acquisition.

5 Market value

Now try the question below from the Exam Question Bank

Number	Level	Marks	Time
Q17	Examination	25	45 mins

17

Consolidated income statements, associates and joint ventures

Topic list	Syllabus reference
1 The consolidated income statement	4(c)
2 Accounting for associates	4(d)
3 Joint ventures and jointly controlled entities	4(d)

Introduction

Generally speaking, the preparation of the **consolidated income statement** is more **straightforward** than the preparation of the consolidated balance sheet. Complications do arise, however, usually in the form of **inter-company transactions** and accounting for **pre-acquisition profits**.

The consolidated income statement will appear again in Section 2 where we consider the treatment of **associates** and Section 3 where we consider the treatment of **joint ventures**.

Study guide

Sections 18 and 19 – Business combinations – introduction

- Prepare a consolidated income statement for a simple group, including an example where an acquisition occurs during the year and there is a minority interest

Sections 22 and 23 – Business combinations – associates and joint ventures (IAS 28 and 31)

- Define associates and joint ventures (ie jointly controlled operations, assets and entities)

- Distinguish between equity accounting and proportional consolidation

- Describe the two formats of proportional consolidation

- Prepare consolidated financial statements to include a single subsidiary and an associated company or a joint venture

1 The consolidated income statement

> **FAST FORWARD**
>
> As always, the source of the consolidated statement is the individual accounts of the separate companies in the group.

1.1 Consolidation procedure

It is customary in practice to prepare a working paper (known as a **consolidation schedule**) on which the individual income statements are set out side by side and totalled to form the basis of the consolidated income statement.

Exam focus point

> In an examination it is very much quicker not to do this. Use workings to show the calculation of complex figures such as the minority interest and show the derivation of others on the face of the income statement, as shown in our examples.

1.2 Simple example: consolidated income statement

P Co acquired 75% of the ordinary shares of S Co on that company's incorporation in 20X3. The summarised income statements of the two companies for the year ending 31 December 20X6 are set out below.

	P Co $	S Co $
Sales revenue	75,000	38,000
Cost of sales	30,000	20,000
Gross profit	45,000	18,000
Administrative expenses	14,000	8,000
Profit before taxation	31,000	10,000
Taxation	10,000	2,000
Profit for the year	21,000	8,000
Reserves brought forward	87,000	17,000
Reserves carried forward	108,000	25,000

Required

Prepare the consolidated income statement and movement on reserves.

Solution

P CO
CONSOLIDATED INCOME STATEMENT
FOR THE YEAR ENDED 31 DECEMBER 20X6

	$
Sales revenue (75 + 38)	113,000
Cost of sales (30 + 20)	50,000
Gross profit	63,000
Administrative expenses (14 + 8)	22,000
Profit before taxation	41,000
Taxation (10 + 2)	12,000
Profit after taxation	29,000
Minority interest (25% × $8,000)	2,000
Group profit for the year	27,000
Reserves brought forward (group share only: 87 + (17 × 75%))	99,750
Reserves carried forward	126,750

Notice how the minority interest is dealt with.

(a) Down to the line **'profit after taxation'** the **whole** of S Co's results is included without reference to group share or minority share. A **one-line adjustment** is then inserted to deduct the minority's share of S Co's profit after taxation.

(b) The minority's share ($4,250) of S Co's retained profits brought forward is **excluded**. This means that the carried forward figure of $126,750 is the figure which would appear in the balance sheet for group retained reserves.

This last point may be clearer if we revert to our **balance sheet technique** and construct the working for group reserves.

Group reserves

	$
P Co	108,000
Share of S Co's post-acquisition retained reserves (75% × $25,000)	18,750
	126,750

The minority share of S Co's reserves comprises the minority interest in the $17,000 profits brought forward plus the minority interest ($2,000) in $8,000 retained profits for the year.

Notice that a consolidated income statement **links up** with a consolidated balance sheet exactly as in the case of an individual company's accounts: the figure of retained profits carried forward at the bottom of the income statement appears as the figure for retained profits in the balance sheet. (*Note.* Under IAS 1 this would be shown as a movement on reserves; for convenience the reserve movements are shown here with the income statement.)

We will now look at the complications introduced by **inter-company trading, inter-company dividends** and **pre-acquisition profits** in the subsidiary.

1.3 Intra-group trading

Like the consolidated balance sheet, the consolidated income statement should deal with the results of the group as those of a single entity. When one company in a group sells goods to another an identical amount is added to the sales revenue of the first company and to the cost of sales of the second. Yet as far as the entity's dealings with outsiders are concerned no sale has taken place.

The consolidated figures for sales revenue and cost of sales should represent **sales to**, and **purchases from, outsiders**. An adjustment is therefore necessary to reduce the sales revenue and cost of sales figures by the value of intra-group sales during the year.

We have also seen in an earlier chapter that any unrealised profits on intra-group trading should be excluded from the figure for group profits. This will occur whenever goods sold at a profit within the group remain in the inventory of the purchasing company at the year end. The best way to deal with this is to **calculate the unrealised profit on unsold inventories at the year end and reduce consolidated gross profit by this amount**. Cost of sales will be the balancing figure.

1.4 Example: intra-group trading

Suppose in our earlier example that S Co had recorded sales of $5,000 to P Co during 20X6. S Co had purchased these goods from outside suppliers at a cost of $3,000. One half of the goods remained in P Co's inventory at 31 December 20X6. Prepare the revised consolidated income statement.

Solution

The consolidated income statement for the year ended 31 December 20X6 would now be as follows.

	$
Sales revenue (75 + 38 – 5)	108,000
Cost of sales (balancing figure)	(46,000)
Gross profit (45 + 18 – 1*)	62,000
Administrative expenses	(22,000)
Profit before taxation	40,000
Taxation	(12,000)
Profit after taxation	28,000
Minority interest (25% × ($8,000 – $1,000*))	(1,750)
Group profit for the year	26,250
Reserves brought forward	99,750
Reserves carried forward	126,000

*Unrealised profit: ½ × ($5,000 – $3,000)

An adjustment will be made for the unrealised profit against the inventory figure in the consolidated balance sheet, as explained in Chapter 16.

1.5 Intra-group dividends

In our example so far we have assumed that S Co retains all of its after-tax profit. It may be, however, that S Co distributes some of its profits as dividends. As before, the **minority interest** in the subsidiary's profit should be calculated immediately after the figure of after-tax profit. For this purpose, no account need be taken of how much of the minority interest is to be distributed by S Co as dividend.

A complication may arise if the subsidiary has **preferred shares** and wishes to pay a **preferred dividend** as well as an ordinary dividend. In such a case great care is needed in calculating the minority interest in S Co's after-tax profit.

1.6 Example: intra-group dividends

Sam Co's capital consists of 10,000 6% $1 preferred shares and 10,000 $1 ordinary shares. On 1 January 20X3, the date of Sam Co's incorporation, Pam Co acquired 3,000 of the preferred shares and 7,500 of the ordinary shares. The income statements of the two companies for the year ended 31 December 20X6 are set out below.

	Pam Co	Sam Co
	$	$
Sales revenue	200,000	98,000
Cost of sales	90,000	40,000
Gross profit	110,000	58,000
Administrative expenses	35,000	19,000
Profit before tax	75,000	39,000
Taxation	23,000	18,000
Profit after tax	52,000	21,000
Note. Dividends proposed: preferred	–	600
ordinary	14,000	2,000
Reserves brought forward	79,000	23,000

Pam Co has not yet accounted for its share of the dividends receivable from Sam Co.

Prepare Pam Co's consolidated income statement and movements on reserves.

Solution

To calculate the minority interest in Sam Co's after-tax profit it is necessary to remember that the first $600 of such profits goes to pay the preferred dividend. The balance of after-tax profits belongs to the equity shareholders. The calculation is as follows.

	Total		Minority share
	$		$
Profits earned for preferred shareholders	600	(70%)	420
Balance earned for equity shareholders	20,400	(25%)	5,100
Total profits after tax	21,000		5,520

It is irrelevant how much of this is distributed to the minority as dividends: the whole $5,520 must be deducted in arriving at the figure for group profit. The dividends receivable by Pam Co, calculated below, would cancel with the dividends payable by Sam Co to its parent company.

	$
Preferred dividend (30% × $600)	180
Ordinary dividend (75% × $2,000)	1,500
	1,680

PAM CO
CONSOLIDATED INCOME STATEMENT
FOR THE YEAR ENDED 31 DECEMBER 20X6

	$
Sales revenue (200 + 98)	298,000
Cost of sales (90 + 40)	130,000
Gross profit	168,000
Administrative expenses (35 + 19)	54,000
Profit before tax	114,000
Taxation (23 + 18)	41,000
Profit after tax	73,000
Minority interest (as above)	5,520
Group profit for the year	67,480
Dividend proposed (parent company only)	14,000
Profit for the year	53,480
Reserves brought forward (group share only: 79 + (23 × 75%))	96,250
Reserves carried forward	149,730

1.7 Pre-acquisition profits

As explained above, the figure for retained profits at the bottom of the consolidated income statement must be the same as the figure for retained profits in the consolidated balance sheet. We have seen in previous chapters that retained profits in the consolidated balance sheet comprise:

(a)   The **whole of the parent company's** retained profits

(b)   A **proportion of the subsidiary company's** retained profits. The proportion is the **group's share of post-acquisition retained profits** in the subsidiary. From the total retained profits of the subsidiary we must therefore **exclude** both the **minority's share** of total retained profits and the **group's share of pre-acquisition** retained profits.

A **similar procedure is necessary in the consolidated income statement** if it is to link up with the consolidated balance sheet. Previous examples have shown how the minority share of profits is excluded in the income statement. Their share of profits for the year is deducted from profit after tax, while the figure for profits brought forward in the consolidation schedule includes only the group's proportion of the subsidiary's profits.

In the same way, when considering examples which include pre-acquisition profits in a subsidiary, the figure for profits brought forward should include only the group's share of the post-acquisition retained profits. If the subsidiary is **acquired during the accounting year**, it is therefore necessary to apportion its profit for the year between pre-acquisition and post-acquisition elements. The part year method is used.

With the part-year method, the entire income statement of the subsidiary is split between pre-acquisition and post-acquisition proportions. Only the post-acquisition figures are included in the consolidated income statement.

Question		Acquisition

P Co acquired 60% of the equity of S Co on 1 April 20X5. The income statements of the two companies for the year ended 31 December 20X5 are set out below.

	P Co $	S Co $	S Co ($^9/_{12}$) $
Sales revenue	170,000	80,000	60,000
Cost of sales	65,000	36,000	27,000
Gross profit	105,000	44,000	33,000
Administrative expenses	43,000	12,000	9,000
Profit before tax	62,000	32,000	24,000
Taxation	23,000	8,000	6,000
Profit after tax	39,000	24,000	18,000
Dividends (paid 31 December)	12,000	6,000	
Profit for the year	27,000	18,000	
Reserves brought forward	81,000	40,000	
Reserves carried forward	108,000	58,000	

P Co has not yet accounted for the dividends received from S Co.

Prepare the consolidated income statement and movements on reserves.

Answer

The shares in S Co were acquired three months into the year. Only the post-acquisition proportion (9/12ths) of S Co's income statement is included in the consolidated income statement. This is shown above for convenience.

P CO CONSOLIDATED INCOME STATEMENT
FOR THE YEAR ENDED 31 DECEMBER 20X5

	$
Sales revenue (170 + 60)	230,000
Cost of sales (65 + 27)	92,000
Gross profit	138,000
Administrative expenses (43 + 9)	52,000
Profit before tax	86,000
Taxation (23 + 6)	29,000
Profit after tax	57,000
Minority interest (40% × $18,000)	7,200
Group profit for the year	49,800
Dividends (P Co only)	12,000
Profit for the year	37,800
Reserves brought forward*	81,000
Reserves carried forward	118,800

* All of S Co's profits brought forward are pre-acquisition.

Question

Minority interest

The following information relates to the Brodick group of companies for the year to 30 April 20X7.

	Brodick Co $'000	Lamlash Co $'000	Corrie Co $'000
Sales revenue	1,100	500	130
Cost of sales	630	300	70
Gross profit	470	200	60
Administrative expenses	105	150	20
Dividend from Lamlash Co	24	–	–
Dividend from Corrie Co	6	–	–
Profit before tax	395	50	40
Taxation	65	10	20
Profit after tax	330	40	20
Interim dividend	50	10	–
Proposed dividend	150	20	10
Profit for the year	130	10	10
Reserves brought forward	460	106	30
Reserves carried forward	590	116	40

Additional information

(a) The issued share capital of the group was as follows.

    Brodick Co   : 5,000,000 ordinary shares of $1 each.
    Lamlash Co : 1,000,000 ordinary shares of $1 each.
    Corrie Co   : 400,000 ordinary shares of $1 each.

(b) Brodick Co purchased 80% of the issued share capital of Lamlash Co in 20X0. At that time, the revenue reserves of Lamlash amounted to $56,000.

(c) Brodick Co purchased 60% of the issued share capital of Corrie Co in 20X4. At that time, the revenue reserves of Corrie amounted to $20,000.

(d) Brodick Co recognises dividends proposed by other group companies in its income statement.

Required

Insofar as the information permits, prepare the Brodick group of companies' consolidated income statement for the year to 30 April 20X7 in accordance with IASs, and the movement on reserves.

Note. You should append a statement showing the make up of the 'reserves carried forward', and your workings should be submitted.

Answer

BRODICK GROUP
CONSOLIDATED INCOME STATEMENT
FOR THE YEAR TO 30 APRIL 20X7

	$'000
Sales revenue (1,100 + 500 + 130)	1,730
Cost of sales (630 + 300 + 70)	1,000
Gross profit	730
Administrative expenses (105 + 150 + 20)	275
Profit before taxation	455
Tax on profit (65 + 10 + 20)	95
Profit after taxation	360
Minority interests (W1)	16
Profit for the financial year	344
Dividends paid and proposed (parent only)	200
Profit retained for the year	144
Reserves brought forward 1 May 20X6 (W2)	506
Reserves carried forward 30 April 20X7	650

Workings

1   *Minority interests*

	$
In Lamlash (20% × profit after tax)	8,000
In Corrie (40% × profit after tax)	8,000
	16,000

2   *Retained profits brought forward*

	Brodick Co $'000	Lamlash Co $'000	Corrie Co $'000
Per question	460	106	30
Less pre-aqn		56	20
		50	10
Share of Lamlash: 80% × 50	40		
Share of Corrie: 60% × 10	6		
	506		

1.8 Section summary

The table below summarises the main points about the consolidated income statement.

Purpose	To show the results of the group for an accounting period as if it were a single entity.
Sales revenue to profit after tax	100% P + 100% S (excluding dividend receivable from subsidiary and adjustments for inter-company transactions).
Reason	To show the results of the group which were controlled by the parent company.
Inter-company sales	Strip out inter-company activity from both sales revenue and cost of sales.
Unrealised profit on inter-company sales	(a) Goods sold by P. Increase cost of sales by unrealised profit. (b) Goods sold by S. Increase cost of sales by full amount of unrealised profit and decrease minority interest by their share of unrealised profit.
Depreciation	If the value of S's non-current assets have been subjected to a fair value uplift then any additional depreciation must be charged in the consolidated income statement. The minority interest will need to be adjusted for their share.
Transfer of non-current assets	Expenses must be increased by any profit on the transfer and reduced by any additional depreciation arising from the increased carrying value of the asset.

Minority interests	S's profit after tax (PAT) X
	 Less: * unrealised profit (X)
	        * profit on disposal of non-current assets (X)
	        additional depreciation following FV uplift (X)
	 Add: ** additional depreciation following disposal of non-current assets X
	                                 X
	 MI% X
	
	 * Only applicable if sales of goods and non-current assets made by subsidiary.
	
	 ** Only applicable if sale of non-current assets made by parent company.

Reason	To show the extent to which profits generated through P's control are in fact owned by other parties.
Dividends	P's only.
Reason	S's dividend is due (a) to P; and (b) to MI. P has taken in its share by including the results of S in the consolidated income statement. The MI have taken their share by being given a proportion of S's PAT. Remember: PAT = dividends + profit for the year.
Reserves carried forward	As per the balance sheet calculations.

2 Accounting for associates

FAST FORWARD

We looked at investments in associates briefly in Chapter 14. IAS 28 *Investments in associates* covers this type of investment.

2.1 Definitions

We looked at some of the important definitions in Chapter 14; these are repeated here with some additional important terms.

- **Associate**. An entity, including an unincorporated entity such as a partnership, over which an investor has significant influence and which is neither a subsidiary nor a joint venture of the investor.

- **Significant influence** is the power to participate in the financial and operating policy decisions of an economic activity but is not control or joint control over those policies.

- **Joint control** is the contractually agreed sharing of control over an economic activity.

- **Equity method**. A method of accounting whereby the investment is initially recorded at cost and adjusted thereafter for the post acquisition change in the investor's share of net assets of the investee. The profit or loss of the investor includes the investor's share of the profit or loss of the investee.

We have already looked at how the **status** of an investment in an associate should be determined. Go back to Section 1 of Chapter 14 to revise it. (Note that, as for an investment in a subsidiary, any **potential voting rights** should be taken into account in assessing whether the investor has **significant influence** over the investee.)

IAS 28 requires all investments in associates to be accounted for in the consolidated accounts using the equity method, *unless* the investment is classified as 'held for sale' in accordance with IFRS 5 in which case it should be accounted for under IFRS 5 (see Chapter 12), or the exemption in the paragraph below applies.

An investor is exempt from applying the equity method if:

(a) It is a parent exempt from preparing consolidated financial statements under IAS 27, or

(b) All of the following apply:

   (i) The investor is a **wholly-owned subsidiary** or it is a **partially owned subsidiary** of another entity and its other owners, including those not otherwise entitled to vote, have been informed about, and do not object to, the investor not applying the equity method;

   (ii) The investor's securities are **not publicly traded**

   (iii) It is **not in the process of issuing securities** in public securities markets; and

   (iv) The **ultimate or intermediate parent** publishes consolidated financial statements that comply with International Financial Reporting Standards.

The revised version of IAS 28 **no longer allows** an investment in an associate to be excluded from equity accounting when an investee operates under severe long-term restrictions that significantly impair its ability to transfer funds to the investor. Significant influence must be lost before the equity method ceases to be applicable.

The use of the equity method should be **discontinued** from the date that the investor **ceases to have significant influence.**

From that date, the investor shall account for the investment in accordance with IAS 39 *Financial instruments: recognition and measurement.* The carrying amount of the investment at the date that it ceases to be an associate shall be regarded as its cost on initial measurement as a financial asset under IAS 39.

2.2 Separate financial statements of the investor

If an investor **issues consolidated financial statements** (because it has subsidiaries), an investment in an associate should be *either:*

(a)   Accounted for at **cost**, *or*

(b)   In accordance with **IAS 39**

in its separate financial statements.

If an investor that does *not* **issue consolidated financial statements** (ie it has no subsidiaries) has an investment in an associate this should similarly be included in the financial statements of the investor either at cost, or in accordance with IAS 39.

2.3 Application of the equity method: consolidated accounts

Many of the procedures required to apply the equity method are the same as are required for full consolidation. In particular, **intra-group unrealised profits** must be excluded.

Goodwill is calculated as the difference (positive or negative) between the cost of acquisition and the investor's share of the fair values of the net identifiable assets of the associate. This should be treated as required by IFRS 3 (see Chapter 6). Appropriate adjustments should be made to the investor's share of the profits or losses after acquisition, to account for depreciation.

2.3.1 Consolidated income statement

The basic principle is that the investing company (X Co) should take account of its **share of the earnings** of the associate, Y Co, whether or not Y Co distributes the earnings as dividends. X Co achieves this by adding to consolidated profit the group's share of Y Co's profit after tax.

Notice the difference between this treatment and the **consolidation** of a subsidiary company's results. If Y Co were a subsidiary X Co would take credit for the whole of its sales revenue, cost of sales etc and would then make a one-line adjustment to remove any minority share.

Under equity accounting, the associated company's sales revenue, cost of sales and so on are *not* **amalgamated** with those of the group. Instead the group share only of the associate's profit before tax and tax charge for the year is added to the corresponding lines of the parent company and its subsidiaries. In effect, this is the corresponding treatment to the associate's parent company's treatment: the investing company is the minority interest here.

2.3.2 Consolidated balance sheet

A figure for **investment in associates** is shown which at the time of the acquisition must be stated at cost. This amount will increase (decrease) each year by the amount of the group's share of the associated company's profit (loss) for the year.

2.4 Example: associate

P Co, a company with subsidiaries, acquires 25,000 of the 100,000 $1 ordinary shares in A Co for $60,000 on 1 January 20X8. In the year to 31 December 20X8, A Co earns profits after tax of $24,000, from which it pays a dividend of $6,000.

How will A Co's results be accounted for in the individual and consolidated accounts of P Co for the year ended 31 December 20X8?

Solution

In the **individual accounts** of P Co, the investment will be recorded on 1 January 20X8 at cost. Unless there is an impairment in the value of the investment (see below), this amount will remain in the individual balance sheet of P Co permanently. The only entry in P Co's individual income statement will be to record dividends received. For the year ended 31 December 20X8, P Co will:

DEBIT	Cash	$1,500
CREDIT	Income from shares in associated companies	$1,500

In the **consolidated accounts** of P Co equity accounting principles will be used to account for the investment in A Co. Consolidated profit after tax will include the group's share of A Co's profit after tax (25% × $24,000 = $6,000). To the extent that this has been distributed as dividend, it is already included in P Co's individual accounts and will automatically be brought into the consolidated results. That part of the group's profit share which has not been distributed as dividend ($4,500) will be brought into consolidation by the following adjustment.

DEBIT	Investment in associates	$4,500
CREDIT	Income from shares in associates	$4,500

The asset 'Investment in associates' is then stated at $64,500, being cost plus the group share of post-acquisition retained profits.

2.5 Consolidated income statement

A **consolidation schedule** may be used to prepare the consolidated income statement of a group with associates. The treatment of associates' profits in the following example should be studied carefully.

2.6 Illustration

The following consolidation schedule relates to the P Co group, consisting of the parent company, an 80% owned subsidiary (S Co) and an associated company (A Co) in which the group has a 30% interest.

CONSOLIDATION SCHEDULE

	Group $'000	P Co $'000	S Co $'000		A Co $'000
Sales revenue	1,400	600	800		300
Cost of sales	770	370	400		120
Gross profit	630	230	400		180
Distribution costs and administrative expenses (including depreciation, directors' emoluments etc)	290	110	180		80
	340	120	220		100
Interest receivable	30	30	–		–
	370	150	220		100
Interest payable	(20)	–	(20)		
Profit on activities	350	150	200		100
Group share of associated company profit	30	–	–	30%	30
	380	150	200		30
Taxation					
Group	(145)	(55)	(90)		
Associated company	(13)	–	–		(13)
Profit after taxation	222	95	110		17
Minority interest	(22)		(22)		
	200	95	88		17
Inter-company dividends	–	20	(18)		(2)
Group profit	200	115	70		15

Note the following.

(a) **Group sales revenue, group gross profit and costs** such as depreciation etc **exclude** the sales revenue, gross profit and costs etc of **associated companies**.

(b) The **group share** of the associated company **pre-tax profits is credited** to the group income statement (here, 30% of $100,000 = $30,000). If the associated company has been acquired during the year, it would be necessary to deduct the pre-acquisition profits (remembering to allow for tax on current year profits).

(c) **Taxation** consists of the following.

    (i)   Taxation on the **parent company** and subsidiaries in total.

    (ii)   Only the **group's share of the tax charge of the associated company.** A Co's tax would be $43,000, so that the group share is $43,000 × 30% = $13,000.

(d) The minority interest will only ever apply to subsidiary companies.

(e) Inter-company dividends from subsidiaries and associated companies should all be recorded.

2.7 Pro-forma consolidated income statement

The following is a **suggested layout** (using the figures given in the illustration above) for the consolidated income statement for a company having subsidiaries as well as associated companies.

	$'000	$'000
Sales revenue		1,400
Cost of sales		770
Gross profit		630
Distribution costs and administrative expenses		290
		340
Interest and similar income receivable		30
		370
Interest payable and similar charges		(20)
		350
Share of profits (less losses) of associated companies		30
Profit before taxation		380
Taxation		
Parent company and subsidiaries (total amount)	145	
Associated companies (group's share)	13	
		158
Profit for the year		222
Attributable to:		
Equity holders of the parent		200
Minority interest		22
		222

2.8 Consolidated balance sheet

As explained earlier, the consolidated balance sheet will contain an **asset 'Investment in associated companies'.** The amount at which this asset is stated will be its original cost plus the group's share of any **profits earned since acquisition** which have not been distributed as dividends.

2.9 Example: consolidated balance sheet

On 1 January 20X6 the net tangible assets of A Co amount to $220,000, financed by 100,000 $1 ordinary shares and revenue reserves of $120,000. P Co, a company with subsidiaries, acquires 30,000 of the shares in A Co for $75,000. During the year ended 31 December 20X6 A Co's profit after tax is $30,000, from which dividends of $12,000 are paid.

Show how P Co's investment in A Co would appear in the consolidated balance sheet at 31 December 20X6.

Solution

CONSOLIDATED BALANCE SHEET
AS AT 31 DECEMBER 20X6 (extract)

	$
Non-current assets	
Investment in associated company	
Cost	75,000
Group share of post-acquisition retained profits	
(30% × $18,000)	5,400
	80,400

An important point to note is that this figure of $80,400 can be arrived at in a completely different way. It is the sum of:

(a)   the group's share of A Co's net assets at 31 December 20X6, and

(b)   the premium paid over fair value for the shares acquired.

This can be shown as follows.

		$	$
(a)	A Co's net assets at 31 December 20X6		
	Net assets at 1 January 20X6	220,000	
	Retained profit for year	18,000	
	Net assets at 31 December 20X6	238,000	
	Group share (30%)		71,400
(b)	Premium on acquisition		
	Net assets acquired by group on 1 Jan 20X6		
	(30% × $220,000)	66,000	
	Price paid for shares	75,000	
	Premium on acquisition		9,000
	Investment in associated company per balance sheet		80,400

Question   Associate I

Set out below are the draft accounts of Parent Co and its subsidiaries and of Associate Co. Parent Co acquired 40% of the equity capital of Associate Co three years ago when the latter's reserves stood at $40,000.

SUMMARISED BALANCE SHEETS

	Parent Co & subsidiaries $'000	Associate Co $'000
Tangible non-current assets	220	170
Investment in Associate at cost	60	–
Loan to Associate Co	20	–
Current assets	100	50
Loan from Parent Co	–	(20)
	400	200
Share capital ($1 shares)	250	100
Reserves	150	100
	400	200

SUMMARISED INCOME STATEMENTS

	Parent Co & subsidiaries $'000	Associate Co $'000
Net profit	95	80
Taxation	35	30
	60	50

You are required to prepare the summarised consolidated accounts of Parent Co.

Notes

(1)   Assume that the associate's assets/liabilities are stated at fair value.
(2)   Assume that there are no minority interests in the subsidiary companies.

Answer

PARENT CO
CONSOLIDATED INCOME STATEMENT

	$'000
Net profit	95
Share of profits of associated company (80 × 40%)	32
Profit before tax	127
Taxation (35 + (30 × 40%) note (a))	47
Profit attributable to the members of Parent Co	80

Notes

(a)   The note to the tax charge would disclose that $12,000 is the share of Associate's tax.

(b)   The accounts should disclose the amount of the profit attributable to the members of Parent Co which has been dealt with in that company's own accounts. In this example there is insufficient information to do this.

PARENT CO
CONSOLIDATED BALANCE SHEET

	$'000
Assets	
Tangible non-current assets	220
Interest in associated company (see note)	104
Current assets	100
Total assets	424
Equity and liabilities	
Share capital	250
Reserves (W1)	174
Total equity and liabilities	424

Note

	$'000
Interest in associate	
Group's share of net assets (40% × 200)	80
Premium on acquisition (W2)	4
	84
Loan to associate	20
	104

Workings

		Parent & subsidiaries $'000	Associate $'000
1	*Reserves*		
	Per question	150	100
	Pre-acquisition		40
	Post-acquisition		60
	Group share in associate		
	($60 x 40%)	24	
	Group reserves	174	

2   *Premium on acquisition*

	$'000
Share capital	100
Reserves at date of acquisition	40
	140
Net assets acquired (40% × 140)	56
Cost	60
Premium on acquisition	4

Question	Associate II

Alfred Co bought 25,000 ordinary shares on 31 December 20X8 in Grimbald Co at a cost of $38,000 when the balance sheet of Grimbald was as follows.

GRIMBALD CO
DRAFT BALANCE SHEET AT DATE OF SHARE PURCHASE

	$
Assets	
Non-current assets	
Goodwill	30,000
Tangible assets	120,000
	150,000
Current assets	40,000
Total assets	190,000
Equity and liabilities	
Equity	
Called up share capital in ordinary shares of $1	100,000
Reserves	40,000
Non-current liabilities	
12% debentures	50,000
Total equity and liabilities	190,000

During the year to 31 December 20X9 Grimbald Co made a profit before tax of $82,000 and the taxation charge on the year's profits was $32,000. A dividend of $20,000 was paid on 31 December out of these profits.

The balance sheet of Grimbald Co on 31 December 20X9 was as follows.

	$
Assets	
Non-current assets	
Goodwill	30,000
Tangible assets	140,000
	170,000
Current assets	50,000
Total assets	220,000
Equity and liabilities	
Equity	
Called up share capital in ordinary shares of $1	100,000
Reserves	70,000
Non-current liabilities	
12% debentures	50,000
Total equity and liabilities	220,000

Calculate the entries for the associated company which would appear in the consolidated accounts of the Alfred group, in accordance with the requirements of IAS 28. (Assume no impairment of goodwill.)

Answer

Net tangible assets of Grimbald Co at date of acquisition.

	$
Total assets	190,000
Less goodwill	(30,000)
Less non-current liabilities	(50,000)
Net tangible assets	110,000

	$
At the date of the share acquisition	
Alfred Co share of Grimbald's net tangible assets owned	
by equity (25% of $110,000)	27,500
Cost of the shares	38,000
Premium arising on acquisition	10,500

At 31 December 20X8, the investment by Alfred Co in shares of Grimbald would have appeared in the consolidated balance sheet as follows.

	$
Group share of net assets other than goodwill	27,500
Goodwill arising on acquisition	10,500
Total investment in associated company	38,000

	Total	Group share
Grimbald Co	$	$
Profits before taxation for the year to 31.12.X9	82,000	20,500
Taxation	32,000	8,000
Profits after taxation	50,000	12,500
Dividend	20,000	5,000
Retained profit	30,000	7,500

CONSOLIDATED INCOME STATEMENT

	$
Group share of associated company profit	20,500
Associated company taxation	(8,000)

	12,500

CONSOLIDATED BALANCE SHEET

	$
Interest in associated company	45,500

The asset 'interest in associated company' comprises:

Group share of net assets other than goodwill	
($27,500 + retained profits of $7,500)	35,000
Goodwill arising on acquisition	10,500
	45,500

The following points are also relevant and are similar to a parent-subsidiary consolidation situation.

(a)   Use financial statements drawn up to the **same reporting date.**

(b)   If this is impracticable, adjust the financial statements for **significant transactions/ events** in the intervening period. The difference between the reporting date of the associate and that of the investor must be no more than three months.

(c)   Use **uniform accounting policies** for like transactions and events in similar circumstances, adjusting the associate's statements to reflect group policies if necessary.

(d)   If an associate has **cumulative preferred shares** held by outside interests, calculate the share of the investor's profits/losses after adjusting for the preferred dividends (whether or not declared).

2.10 'Upstream' and 'downstream' transactions

'Upstream' transactions are, for example, sales of assets from an associate to the investor. 'Downstream' transactions are, for example, sales of assets from the investor to an associate.

Profits and losses resulting from 'upstream' and 'downstream' transactions between an investor (including its consolidated subsidiaries) and an associate are eliminated to the extent of the investor's interest in the associate. This is very similar to the procedure for eliminating intra-group transactions between a parent and a subsidiary. The important thing to remember is that **only the group's share is eliminated.**

2.11 Example: downstream transaction

A Co, a parent with subsidiaries, holds 25% of the equity shares in B Co. During the year, A Co makes sales of $1,000,000 to B Co at cost plus a 25% mark-up. At the year-end, B Co has all these goods still in inventories.

Solution

A Co has made an unrealised profit of $200,000 (1,000,000 × 25/125) on its sales to the associate. The group's share (25%) of this must be eliminated:

DEBIT	Cost of sales (consolidated income statement)	$50,000	
CREDIT	Investment in associate (consolidated balance sheet)		$50,000

Because the sale was made to the associate, the group's share of the unsold inventory forms part of the investment in the associate at the year-end. If the associate had made the sale to the parent, the adjustment would have been:

DEBIT	Cost of sales (consolidated income statement)	$50,000	
CREDIT	Inventories (consolidated balance sheet)		$50,000

The group's share of the revenue must also be eliminated from the consolidated income statement.

DEBIT	Revenue (25% × 1,000,000)	$250,000
CREDIT	Cost of sales	$250,000

2.12 Associate's losses

When the equity method is being used and the investor's share of losses of the associate equals or exceeds its interest in the associate, the investor should **discontinue** including its share of further losses. The investment is reported at nil value. The interest in the associate is normally the carrying amount of the investment in the associate, but it also includes any other long-term interests, for example, preference shares or long term receivables or loans.

After the investor's interest is reduced to nil, **additional losses** should only be recognised where the investor has incurred obligations or made payments on behalf of the associate (for example, if it has guaranteed amounts owed to third parties by the associate).

2.13 Impairment losses

IAS 39 sets out a list of indications that a financial asset (including an associate) may have become impaired. Any impairment loss is recognised in accordance with IAS 36 *Impairment of assets* for each associate individually.

2.14 Disclosures

The following should be disclosed:

(a) the **fair value** of investments in associates for which there are **published price quotations**

(b) **summarised financial information** of associates, including the aggregated amounts of assets, liabilities, revenues and profit or loss

(c) the **reasons** why the **presumption** that an **investor does not have significant influence** is **overcome** if the investor holds, directly or indirectly through subsidiaries, **less than 20 per cent** of the voting or potential voting power of the investee but **concludes** that it has **significant influence**

(d) the **reasons** why the presumption that an investor has significant influence is overcome if the investor holds, directly or indirectly through subsidiaries, **20 per cent or more** of the voting or potential voting power of the investee but concludes that it **does not have significant influence**

(e) the reporting date of the financial statements of an associate, when such financial statements are used in applying the equity method and are as of a reporting date or for a period that is different from that of the investor, and the **reason** for using a **different reporting date** or different period

(f) the nature and extent of any **restrictions** on the ability of associates to **transfer funds** to the investor in the form of cash dividends, repayment of loans or advances (ie borrowing arrangements, regulatory restraint etc)

(g) the **unrecognised share** of **net losses** of an associate, both for the period and cumulatively, if an investor has discontinued recognition of its share of losses of an associate

(h) the fact that an associate is **not** accounted for using the equity method

(i) **summarised financial information** of associates, either individually or in groups, that are **not** accounted for using the equity method

Investments in associates accounted for using the **equity method** shall be classified **as non-current assets** and disclosed as a **separate item** in the **balance sheet**. The investor's **share of the profit or loss** of such associates shall be disclosed as a **separate item** in the **income statement**. The investor's share of any **discontinued operations** of such associates shall be separately disclosed.

The investor's share of changes in the associate's **equity** is recognised directly in equity by the investor and is **disclosed in the statement of changes in equity** required by IAS 1 *Presentation of financial statements*.

In accordance with IAS 37 *Provisions, contingent liabilities and contingent assets* the investor must disclose:

(a)   Its share of the contingent liabilities of an associate incurred jointly with other investors

(b)   Those contingent liabilities that arise because the investor is severally liable for all liabilities of the associate

Exam focus point

It is not unusual in the exam to have both an associate and a subsidiary to account for in a consolidation.

2.15 Section summary

Income statement	Profit before tax ⎤ Include group share of associate, Tax ⎦ disclosed separately. Disclose net profit for the year retained by associate.
Balance sheet	Interests in associated companies should be stated at: $ (a) Group share of net assets other than goodwill of associate at fair value (at the time of acquisition) X (b) Premium on acquisition so far as it has not already been written off X X Also disclose group's share of post-acquisition reserves of associated companies and movements therein.

3 Joint ventures and jointly controlled entities

FAST FORWARD

Two or more persons may decide to enter into a business venture together without wishing to form a formal long-term partnership.

3.1 Introduction

Usually the venturers agree to place limitations on their activities, for example, a joint venture to manufacture and sell 'total eclipse of the sun' souvenirs could be limited by time, while a joint venture to buy and sell a bankrupt's inventory (a fairly common occurrence in practice) comes to an end when all the inventory has been sold.

Joint ventures are often found when each party can **contribute in different ways** to the venture. For example, one venturer may provide finance, another purchases or manufactures goods, while a third offers his marketing skills.

Joint ventures generally have the following characteristics.

- They are **limited by time and/or activity**
- The venturers usually **carry on their principal businesses** at the same time
- **Separate books** for the venture are **not** normally maintained
- The venturers usually agree to a **profit/ loss sharing ratio** for the purpose of the venture

IAS 31 *Interests in joint ventures* covers all types of joint ventures. It is not concerned with the accounts of the joint venture itself (if separate accounts are maintained), but rather **how the interest in a joint venture is accounted for by each joint venturer** (ie each 'partner' in the joint venture).

The assets and liabilities, income and expenses of the joint venture must be reported in the financial statements of the venturers and investors, whatever the form of the joint venture.

IAS 31 looks at the various forms of joint venture which may be undertaken and then looks at how joint ventures are dealt with in the **individual financial statements** of the venturer *and* the **group financial statements**.

3.2 Definitions

The IAS begins by listing some important definitions.

Key terms

- **Joint venture.** A contractual arrangement whereby two or more parties undertake an economic activity which is subject to joint control.

- **Control.** The power to govern the financial and operating policies of an economic activity so as to obtain benefits from its activities.

- **Joint control.** The contractually agreed sharing of control over an economic activity.

- **Significant influence.** The power to participate in the financial and operating policy decisions of an economic activity but is not control or joint control over those policies.

- **Venturer.** A party to a joint venture that has joint control over that joint venture.

- **Proportionate consolidation**. A method of accounting whereby a venturer's share of each of the assets, liabilities, income and expenses of a jointly controlled entity is combined line-by-line with similar items in the venturer's financial statements or reported as separate line items in the venturer's financial statements.

- **Equity method**. A method of accounting whereby an interest in a jointly controlled entity is initially recorded at cost and adjusted thereafter for the post acquisition change in the venturer's share of net assets of the jointly controlled entity. The income statement reflects the venturer's share of the profit or loss of the jointly controlled entity. *(IAS 31)*

3.3 Forms of joint venture

The **form and structure** of joint ventures can vary enormously. There are, however, three main types identified by the standard.

- **Jointly controlled operations**
- **Jointly controlled assets**
- **Jointly controlled entities**

We will look at each of these below. They are all usually described as joint ventures and fulfil the definition of a joint venture given above.

Whatever the form and structure, every joint venture will have **two characteristics.**

- Two (or more) venturers are bound by a **contractual arrangement**.
- The contractual relationship establishes **joint control**.

3.3.1 Contractual arrangement

The existence of a contractual agreement distinguishes a joint venture from an investment in an associate. **If there is no contractual arrangement, then a joint venture does not exist**.

Evidence of a contractual arrangement could be in one of several forms.

- **Contract** between the venturers
- **Minutes** of discussion between the venturers
- Incorporation in the **articles or by-laws** of the joint venture

The contractual arrangement is usually **in writing**, whatever its form, and it will deal with the following issues surrounding the joint venture.

- Its activity, duration and reporting obligations

- The appointment of its board of directors (or equivalent) and the voting rights of the venturers

- Capital contributions to it by the venturers

- How its output, income, expenses or results are shared between the venturers

It is the contractual arrangement which establishes **joint control** over the joint venture, so that no single venturer can control the activity of the joint venture on its own.

One venturer, identified by the contractual agreement, may be the **operator of the joint venture**. This does *not* mean that the operator controls the joint venture, the operator must act within the policies (financial and operational) agreed by all the venturers as laid out in the contractual arrangement. If this is not the case, if the operator effectively controls the joint venture rather than only acting within the arrangements delegated to it, then the activity is *not* a joint venture.

3.4 Summary: joint ventures

- There are three **common types of joint venture**: jointly controlled operations, assets or entities

- A **contractual arrangement** must exist which establishes joint control

- **Joint control** is important: an **operator** must not be able to govern the financial and operating policies of the joint venture

3.5 Forms of joint venture

3.5.1 Jointly controlled operations

In this type of joint venture, there is no separate entity set up to deal with the joint venture, whether in the form of a corporation, partnership or other entity. Instead, the venturers **use their own assets and resources** for the joint venture, ie their own property, plant and equipment is used and they carry their own inventories.

The venturers also incur their own expenses and liabilities, and raise their own finance which then represent their own obligations. In these situations, the activities of the joint venture will often be performed by the venturers' staff alongside the venturers' **other similar activities**. The way that income and expenses are shared between the venturers is usually laid out in the joint venture agreement.

Question

Joint venture I

Can you think of an example of a situation where such a joint venture might occur?

Answer

IAS 31 uses the example of building an aircraft. Say that Boeing is to build the body of the aircraft and the engines are to be built by Rolls Royce as specified by the airline customer for the aircraft. You can see that different parts of the manufacturing process are carried out by each of the venturers. In the Rolls Royce factory, workers will work on the engines for the Boeing plane alongside others working on engines for different aircraft.

Each venturer, Boeing and Rolls Royce, bears its own costs and takes a share of revenue from the aircraft sale. That share is decided in the contractual arrangement between the venturers.

Can you think of other examples?

3.5.2 Accounting treatment

When a joint venture in the nature of jointly controlled operations exists, IAS 31 requires a venturer to recognise the following in its financial statements.

(a)   The **assets** it controls and the **liabilities** it incurs

(b)   The **expenses** it incurs and the **income** it earns from the sale of goods or services by the joint venture

Separate accounts for the joint venture are not required, although the venturers may prepare management accounts for the joint venture, in order to assess its performance.

3.5.3 Jointly controlled assets

In this type of joint venture, the venturers have **joint control**, and often **joint ownership** of some or all of the assets in the joint venture. These assets may have been contributed to the joint venture or purchased for the purpose of the joint venture, but in any case they are **dedicated to the activities of the joint venture**. These assets are used to produce benefits for the venturers; each venturer takes a share of the output and bears a share of the incurred expenses.

As with jointly controlled operations, this type of joint venture does *not* involve setting up a corporation, partnership or any other kind of entity. The venturers **control their share of future economic benefits** through their share in the jointly controlled asset.

Question

Joint venture II

Can you think of examples of situations where this type of joint venture might take place?

Answer

IAS 31 gives examples in the oil, gas and mineral extraction industries. In such industries companies may, say, jointly control and operate an oil or gas pipeline. Each company transports its own products down the pipeline and pays an agreed proportion of the expenses of operating the pipeline (perhaps based on volume).

A further example is a property which is jointly controlled, each venturer taking a share of the rental income and bearing a portion of the expense.

3.5.4 Accounting treatment

IAS 31 requires each venturer to recognise (ie include in their financial statements) the following in respect of its interest in jointly controlled assets.

(a) Its **share of the jointly controlled assets**, classified by their nature, eg a share of a jointly controlled oil pipeline should be classified as property, plant and equipment

(b) Any **liabilities** it has incurred, eg in financing its share of the assets

(c) Its share of any **liabilities incurred jointly** with the other venturers which relate to the joint venture

(d) Any **income** from the sale or use of its share of the joint venture's output, together with its share of any **expenses** incurred by the joint venture

(e) Any **expenses** which it has incurred in respect of its interest in the joint venture, eg those relating to financing the venturer's interest in the assets and selling its share of the output

This treatment of jointly controlled assets reflects the **substance and economic reality,** and (usually) the legal form of the joint venture. Separate accounting records need not be kept for the joint venture and financial statements for the joint venture need not be prepared. Management accounts may be produced, however, in order to monitor the performance of the joint venture.

3.5.5 Jointly controlled entities

This type of joint venture involves the setting up of a corporation, partnership or other entity. This **operates in the same way as any other entity**, except that the venturers have a contractual arrangement establishing their joint control over the economic activity of the entity.

A jointly controlled entity effectively operates as a **separate entity**: it controls the joint venture's assets, incurs liabilities and expenses and earns income. It can, as a separate entity, enter into contracts in its own name and raise finance to fund the activities of the joint venture. The venturers share the results of the jointly controlled entity, and in some cases they may also share the output of the joint venture.

| Question | Jointly controlled entities |

Can you think of some examples of situations where jointly controlled entities might be set up?

| Answer |

A common situation is where two or more entities transfer the relevant assets and liabilities to a jointly controlled entity in order to combine their activities in a particular line of business.

In other situations, an entity wishing to start operations in a foreign country will set up a jointly controlled entity with the government of the foreign country (or an agency of it).

The **substance** of jointly controlled entities are often similar in substance to the joint ventures discussed above (jointly controlled assets/operations). In the case of the oil/gas pipeline mentioned earlier, the asset might be transferred to a jointly controlled entity for tax or similar reasons. In other circumstances, a jointly controlled entity may be set up to deal with only certain aspects of the jointly controlled operations, eg marketing or after-sales service, design or distribution.

As a separate entity, the jointly controlled entity must maintain its **own accounting records** and will **prepare financial statements** according to national requirements and IASs. The accounting treatment for jointly controlled entities is discussed in the next section.

3.5.6 Transactions between a venturer and a joint venture

A venturer may **sell or contribute assets** to a joint venture. The value attributed to such assets may create a gain or loss. However, any such gain or loss should only be recognised to the extent that it reflects the substance of the transaction.

What this means is that only the **gain** attributable to the interest of the other venturers should be recognised. However, the full amount of any **loss** should be recognised when the transaction shows evidence that the net realisable value of current assets is less than cost, or that there is an impairment loss (determined by applying IAS 36).

Question	Transactions

Kirstan Co contributes inventories to a 50:50 joint venture it has undertaken with Pirstan Co. The recorded historical cost of the inventories in Kirstan Co's accounting records is $2m.

What gain or loss should Kirstan Co recognise in its financial statements when the fair value (net realisable value) of the inventories is estimated at the date of transfer and recorded by the joint venture as:

(a) $2.2m?
(b) $1.8m?

Answer

(a)   Kirstan Co has made a profit of $0.2m, but only 50% of this can be considered as realised, ie that part attributable to the other venturer. Kirstan Co should therefore recognise a gain of $0.1m.

(b)   A loss of $0.2m has been made on the inventories, the entire amount of which should be recognised by Kirstan Co. It is known that the loss will be made, even though the inventories have not yet been sold, and so prudence requires that the full loss should be recognised.

A venturer may **purchase assets** from a joint venture. When it does so, the venturer should not recognise its share of the profit made by the joint venture on the transaction in question until it resells the assets to an independent third party, ie until the profit is realised. Losses should be treated in the same way, *except* losses should be recognised immediately if they represent a reduction in the net realisable value of current assets, or an impairment in the value of non-current assets.

3.5.7 Investors in joint ventures

There may be investors in joint ventures who **do *not* have joint control**. Such interests should be reported in accordance with IAS 39 (see Chapter 10) or IAS 28 *Investments in associates* (see Section 2), depending on the circumstances.

3.5.8 Operators of joint ventures

Operators of joint ventures will often **receive fees** for their work in directly managing the joint venture. Such fees should be accounted for in accordance with IAS 18 *Revenue*. Such management fees will be treated by the joint venture as an expense.

3.6 Disclosure

Disclosure is required in accordance with other relevant standards.

IAS 37 *Provisions, contingent liabilities and contingent assets* requires the disclosure by each venturer of the agreed amount of the following **contingencies** (unless the probability of loss is remote) separately from other contingencies.

- Contingencies incurred by the venturer in relation to its interests in joint ventures and its share of each of the contingencies which has been incurred jointly with the other venturers

- The venturer's share of the contingencies of the joint ventures themselves for which it is contingently liable

- Contingencies that arise because the venturer is contingently liable for the liabilities of the other venturers with a share of the joint venture

IAS 1 *Presentation of financial statements* requires disclosure by each venturer of the aggregate amounts of the following **commitments** in respect of its interests in the joint venture, separately from other commitments.

- The venturer's capital commitments in relation to its interests in joint ventures and its share of the capital commitments incurred jointly with the other venturers

- The venturer's share of the capital commitments of the joint ventures themselves

In addition, a listing and description of interests in **significant joint ventures** and the **proportion of ownership** interest held in jointly controlled entities is required.

3.7 Accounting treatment of jointly controlled entities

3.7.1 Separate financial statements of a venturer

IAS 31 states that where a venturer prepares separate financial statements (as a single company), investments in jointly controlled entities should be *either*:

(a)   accounted for at **cost**, *or*

(b)   in accordance with **IAS 39**.

The same accounting treatment must be applied consistently to all jointly controlled entities.

3.7.2 Consolidated financial statements of a venturer

IAS 31 requires all interests in jointly controlled entities to be accounted for using *either* proportionate consolidation *or* the equity method. There is an exception that where an interest is classified as held for sale it should be accounted for in accordance with IFRS 5 (see Chapter 12).

3.7.3 The proportionate consolidation method

A venturer can report its interest in a jointly controlled entity in its consolidated financial statements using one of the two reporting formats for **proportionate consolidation**.

IAS 31 maintains that this treatment reflects the **substance and economic reality** of the arrangement, ie the control the venturer has over its share of future economic benefits through its share of the assets and liabilities of the venture.

The proportionate consolidation method differs from normal consolidation in that only the group share of assets and liabilities, income and expenses are brought into account. There is therefore **no minority interest**.

There are **two different formats** with which the proportionate consolidation method can be used.

(a)   **Combine on a line-by-line basis** the venturer's share of each of the assets, liabilities, income and expenses of the jointly controlled entity with the similar items in the venturer's consolidated financial statements.

(b)   Include in the venturer's consolidated financial statements **separate line items** for the venturer's share of the assets and liabilities, income and expenses of the jointly controlled entity.

3.8 Example: proportionate consolidation

Both of the above methods produce exactly the same net results and they are demonstrated in this example.

Set out below are the draft accounts of Parent Co and its subsidiaries and of Joint Venture Co. Parent Co acquired 50% of the equity capital of Joint Venture Co three years ago when the latter's reserves stood at $40,000.

SUMMARISED BALANCE SHEETS

	Parent Co & subsidiaries $'000	Joint Venture Co $'000
Tangible non-current assets	220	170
Investment in joint venture	75	–
Current assets	100	50
Loan to Joint Venture	20	–
	415	220
Share capital ($1 shares)	250	100
Reserves	165	100
Loan from Parent Co	–	20
	415	220

SUMMARISED INCOME STATEMENTS

	Parent Co & subsidiaries $'000	Joint Venture Co $'000
Net profit	95	80
Taxation	35	30
	60	50
Dividends proposed	50	10
Retained profit	10	40

Parent Co has taken credit for the dividend receivable from Joint Venture Co.

You are required to prepare the summarised consolidated balance sheet of Parent Co, under each of the formats of proportionate consolidation described by IAS 31.

Solution: line-by-line format

PARENT CO
CONSOLIDATED BALANCE SHEET

	$'000
Goodwill (W1)	5
Tangible non-current assets (220 + (50% × 170))	305
Current assets (100 + (50% × 50))	125
Loan to joint venturer (note)	10
	445

	$'000
Share capital	250
Reserves (W2)	195
	445

Note. The loan is the proportion of the $20,000 lent to the other venturer.

Workings

1   *Goodwill*

	$'000
Cost of investment	75
Share of net assets acquired (50% × 140)	70
Premium on acquisition	5

2   *Reserves*

	Parent Co & subsidiaries $'000	Joint Venture Co $'000
Per question	165	100
Pre-acquisition		(40)
Post-acquisition		60
Group share in joint venture ($60 x 50%)	30	
Group reserves	195	

Solution: separate line method

PARENT CO
CONSOLIDATED BALANCE SHEET

	$'000	$'000
Goodwill (as above)		5
Tangible non-current assets		
Group	220	
Joint venture (170 × 50%)	85	
		305
Current assets		
Group	100	
Joint venture (50% × 50)	25	
		125
Loan to joint venturer		10
		445
Share capital		250
Reserves (as above)		195
		445

In both these cases the **consolidated income statements** would be shown in the same way.

The use of the proportionate consolidation method should be **discontinued** from the date the venturer ceases to have joint control over the entity.

3.9 Allowed alternative: equity method

A venturer can report its interest in a jointly controlled entity in its consolidated financial statements under the **equity method**, as discussed in Section 2. The argument for this method is that it is misleading to combine controlled items with jointly controlled items. It is also felt by some that venturers have significant influence over the entity, not merely joint control.

The use of the equity method should be **discontinued** from the date on which the venturer ceases to have joint control over, or have significant influence in, a jointly controlled entity.

3.10 Summary: jointly controlled entities

In **consolidated accounts**, two treatments are allowed for the consolidation of an investment in a jointly controlled entity.

- **Allowed treatment**: proportionate consolidation, using either of two formats
    - **Line-by-line combined results**
    - **Separate line item method**

- **Allowed alternative**: equity method as under IAS 28

Chapter roundup

- This chapter has explained how to prepare a **consolidated income statement** by combining the income statements of each group company.

- **Adjustments** must be made to:

    - Reduce sales revenue by the amount of any **intra-group trading**, and to deduct from consolidated gross profit any unrealised profit on inventories thus acquired which are held at the year end. Cost of sales will be the balancing figure;

    - Reduce inventory values by the amount of any **unrealised profit** on intra-group trading;

    - Calculate the **minority interest** in subsidiary companies' results for the year;

    - Account for **intra-group dividends**;

    - **Eliminate pre-acquisition** profits.

- IAS 28 requires that, in consolidated accounts, **associates** should be accounted for using **equity accounting principles**.

- In the **consolidated income statement** the investing group takes credit for its **share of the after-tax profits** of associates, whether or not they are distributed as dividends.

- In the **consolidated balance sheet**, the investment in associates should be shown as:

    - **Group share of the associated companies' assets other than goodwill**; plus
    - Any **premium paid on acquisition** of the associated companies' shares.

- There are three usual **forms of joint venture.**

    - Jointly controlled operations – Jointly controlled assets – Jointly controlled entities

- Joint ventures are characterised by **joint control** evidenced by a **contractual arrangement.**

- **Jointly controlled entities** may be accounted for in different ways:

    - **Proportionate consolidation**: combine items on a line by line basis, or on separate lines
    - **Equity method**: as per IAS 28

Quick quiz

1   Barley Co has owned 100% of the issued share capital of Oats Co for many years. Barley Co sells goods to Oats Co at cost plus 20%. The following information is available for the year:

   Revenue   – Barley Co $460,000
   　　　　　 – Oats Co   　$120,000

   During the year Barley Co sold goods to Oats Co for $60,000 of which $18,000 were still held in inventory by Oats at the year end.

   At what amount should revenue appear in the consolidated income statement?

2   Horace Co acquired 75% of the ordinary share capital and 25% of the preference share capital of Sylvia Co several years ago. The income statement of Sylvia Co for the year ended 28 February 20X0 showed the following:

	$	$
Profit on ordinary activities after tax		4,000
Preference dividend	1,000	
Ordinary dividend	2,000	
		(3,000)
		1,000

   What is the minority interest in the consolidated income statement of Horace Co for the year ended 28 February 20X0?

3   Saroti Co owns 70% of the ordinary shares and 40% of the preference shares of Macari Co. An extract from Macari Co's income statement is as follows:

	$
Profit after tax	10,000
Preference dividend paid	(2,000)
Ordinary dividend paid	(5,000)
Retained profit	3,000

   What amount for minority interest should be shown in the consolidated income statement of Saroti Co?

4   Define an associate.

5   How should associates be accounted for in the separate financial statements of the investor?

6   What is the effect of the equity method on the consolidated income statement and balance sheet?

7   How should a venturer account for its share of jointly controlled operations?

8   How should a venturer account for its share of jointly controlled assets?

9   Which standard should an operator of a joint venture follow when dealing with management fees received?

10 What is the procedure for presenting figures under proportionate consolidation?

Answers to quick quiz

1   Revenue: 460 + 120 − 60 = $520,000

2

		$
Preference	75% × 1,000	750
Ordinary	25% × (4,000 − 1,000)	750
		1,500

3

		$
Preference	60% × 2,000	1,200
Ordinary	30% × (10,000 − 2,000)	2,400
Minority interest		3,600

4   An entity in which an investor has a significant influence, but which is not a subsidiary or a joint venture of the investor.

5   Either at cost or in accordance with IAS 39.

6   (a)   *Income statement.* Investing company includes its share of the earnings of the associate, by adding its share of profit after tax.

       (b)   *Balance sheet.* Investment in associates is initially included in assets at cost. This will increase or decrease each year according to whether the associated company makes a profit or loss.

7   (a)   The assets it controls and the liabilities it incurs
       (b)   The expenses it incurs and the income it earns

8   Classified by nature

9   IAS 18 *Revenue*

10   (a)   Line-by-line basis with venturer's own assets, liabilities, income and expenses, or
       (b)   Show as separate line items within the venturer's accounts.

Note: Remember only the venturer's share is included, so there is **no** minority interest.

Now try the questions below from the Exam Question Bank

Number	Level	Marks	Time
Q18	Examination	25	45 mins
Q19	Examination	25	45 mins
Q26*	Examination	25	45 mins

*   This question is at the end of the Exam Question Bank. Detailed guidance is given on approaching this question.

Part D

The theoretical framework of accounting

18

Theoretical aspects of accounting

Topic list	Syllabus reference
1 Comprehensive income	1(c)
2 Fair value	1(c)
3 Current purchasing power (CPP)	1(c)
4 Current cost accounting (CCA)	1(c)
5 Agency theory and the efficient market hypothesis	1(b)

Introduction

The topics covered in this chapter fall neatly into three groups.

- Sections 1 and 2 are the first group examining the meaning of profit and capital.

- Sections 3 and 4 are the second group examining methods of adjusting for changing price levels.

- Section 5 is the third group covering certain theoretical topics.

Ideally, you should study all five topics. However, if you are in a hurry, you would be advised to pick two out of the three groups. We recommend Sections 3–5.

Study guide

Section 2 – Accounting concepts, accounting theory

- Outline the concept of 'comprehensive income'

- Explain the principle of fair value

- Discuss and apply accounting policies

- Describe the deficiencies of historic cost accounts (HCA) during periods of rising prices and explain in principle alternatives to HCA

1 Comprehensive income

Exam focus point

> This topic can only form part of a discussion question in the exam, but it is useful material for any question on convergence issues and it is a new addition to your syllabus, so the examiner expects you to know about it.

FAST FORWARD

> **Comprehensive income** means **all** transactions for the period, other than those between an entity and its owners. It is not currently reported under either UK or International standards, but it is a likely future development.

The concept of **comprehensive income** has been under discussion in since 2002 and illustrates the fact that, while the convergence process of which we are most aware is that between UK and International standards, a similar process is going on between the IASB and the FASB.

1.1 Comprehensive income and the FASB

In the US, public companies have been required since 1997 to report comprehensive income. 'Comprehensive income' is defined as **all** gains and losses for the period, ie. all changes in equity, other than those arising from transactions with equity holders. So it does not include transactions such as share issues and dividend payments.

The requirement to report comprehensive income in the US was prompted by the fact that certain items were bypassing the Statement of Income and going straight to the statement of changes in stockholders' equity, specifically foreign currency translation gains and losses, adjustments to the minimum pension liability and unrealised gains or losses on available-for-sale investments. In this way, users were not being given important information.

1.2 Comprehensive income and the IASB/ASB

Since 2002 the IASB and the ASB have been running a joint project on **reporting financial performance**. Other than the desire to move into line with the FASB, the project has been motivated by the following considerations:

(a)   The conceptual basis of the distinction between the income statement (profit and loss account) and the statement of changes in equity (STRGL) is felt to be unclear.

(b)   The structure of the income statement/profit and loss account could be more clearly defined, with more helpful categorisation of different items.

(c)   The income statement/profit and loss account and the cash flow statement are closely related but not designed to be read together, so their mutual information content could be improved

The work of this project **may** lead to the formulation of a new accounting standard on the presentation of gains and losses, which would replace FRS 3 in the UK. The focus is on the development of a single statement of **comprehensive income,** which would report all gains and losses for the period, replacing in the UK the profit and loss account and the STRGL.

2 Fair value

The concept of **fair value** has become very important since the issue of IAS 39 and now FRS 26 in the UK. Entities are now permitted to remeasure financial instruments to fair value.

Exam focus point

This topic has been newly-added to the syllabus, so ignore it at your peril! Any question involving IAS 39 will require you to know about fair value and a short discussion of it could be added onto the end of an accounts preparation question which includes a financial instrument.

2.1 Background

The fair value concept is relevant to two major areas of accounting.

Following a joint FASB/IASB project on business combinations it was agreed that fair value should be applied to assets and liabilities acquired in a business combination. In many cases this leads to a 'fair value adjustment'.

The EU **Fair Value Directive** required UK and other member states to permit or require companies to account for some of their financial instruments at **fair value**.

The Directive had the declared objective of enabling companies to use more 'transparent' accounting practices and of bringing those practices into line with IAS 39. The UK response to this was the issue of FRS 26.

2.2 Fair value and IAS 39

Fair value is commonly defined by reference to the **current market value** of a financial instrument. IAS 39 defines **fair value** as "the amount for which an asset could be exchanged or a liability settled, between knowledgeable, willing parties in an arm's length transaction."

IAS 39 permits an entity to designate any financial asset or liability on initial recognition as one to be measured at fair value, with changes to fair value recognised in profit or loss.

Measurement at fair value is, of course, no problem in the case of financial instruments for which market prices are readily available. Where this is not the case, fair value will have to be estimated using either the transaction price or valuation techniques using observable market data. There is some degree of judgement implied here, which could lead to different valuations of similar assets/liabilities from one company to the next.

The recognition of changes to fair value in profit or loss means that what are essentially unrealised gains and losses are reported in the income statement. It will be interesting to see how this one plays out.

3 Current purchasing power (CPP)

3.1 Capital maintenance in times of inflation

Profit can be measured as the **difference between how wealthy a company is at the beginning and at the end of an accounting period.**

(a)   This wealth can be expressed in terms of the capital of a company as shown in its opening and closing balance sheets.

(b)   A business which maintains its capital unchanged during an accounting period can be said to have broken even.

(c)   Once **capital has been maintained, anything** achieved **in excess represents profit.**

For this analysis to be of any use, we must be able to draw up a company's balance sheet at the beginning and at the end of a period, so as to place a value on the opening and closing capital. There are particular difficulties in doing this during a **period of rising prices**.

In conventional historical cost accounts, assets are stated in the balance sheet at the amount it cost to acquire them (less any amounts written off in respect of depreciation or impairment in value). Capital is simply the **difference between assets and liabilities**.

<table>
<tr><td>**Exam focus
point**</td><td>If prices are rising, it is possible for a company to show a profit in its historical cost accounts despite having identical physical assets and owing identical liabilities at the beginning and end of its accounting period.</td></tr>
</table>

For example, consider the following opening and closing balance sheets of a company.

	Opening $	Closing $
Inventory (100 items at cost)	500	600
Other net assets	1,000	1,000
Capital	1,500	1,600

Assuming that no new capital has been introduced during the year, and no capital has been distributed as dividends, the profit shown in historical cost accounts would be $100, being the excess of closing capital over opening capital. And yet in physical terms the company is no better off: it still has 100 units of inventory (which cost $5 each at the beginning of the period, but $6 each at the end) and its other net assets are identical. The 'profit' earned has merely enabled the company to keep pace with inflation.

An alternative to the concept of capital maintenance based on historical costs is to express capital in **physical** terms. On this basis, no profit would be recognised in the example above because the physical substance of the company is unchanged over the accounting period. Capital is maintained if at the end of the period the company is in a position to achieve the same physical output as it was at the beginning of the period. You should bear in mind that financial definitions of capital maintenance are not the only ones possible; in theory at least, there is no reason why profit should not be measured as the increase in a company's *physical* capital over an accounting period.

3.2 The unit of measurement

Another way to tackle the problems of capital maintenance in times of rising prices is to look at the **unit of measurement** in which accounting values are expressed.

It is an axiom of conventional accounting, as it has developed over the years, that value should be measured in terms of money. It is also **implicitly assumed** that **money values are stable**, so that $1 at the start of the financial year has the same value as $1 at the end of that year. But when **prices are rising**, this assumption is invalid: **$1 at the end of the year has less value (less purchasing power) than it had one year previously**.

This leads to problems when aggregating amounts which have arisen at different times. For example, a company's non-current assets may include items bought at different times over a period of many years. They will each have been recorded in $s, but the value of $1 will have varied over the period. In effect the

non-current asset figure in a historical cost balance sheet is an aggregate of a number of items expressed in different units. It could be argued that such a figure is **meaningless**.

Faced with this argument, one possibility would be to re-state all accounts items in terms of a stable monetary unit. There would be difficulties in practice, but in theory there is no reason why a stable unit ($ CPP = $s of current purchasing power) should not be devised. In this section we will look at a system of accounting (current purchasing power accounting, or CPP) based on precisely this idea.

3.3 Specific and general price changes

We can identify two different types of price inflation.

When prices are rising, it is likely that the **current value of assets will also rise**, but not necessarily by the general rate of inflation. For example, if the replacement cost of a machine on 1 January 20X2 was $5,000, and the general rate of inflation in 20X2 was 8%, we would not necessarily expect the replacement cost of the machine at 31 December 20X2 to be $5,000 plus 8% = $5,400. The rate of price increase on the machinery might have been less than 8% or more than 8%. (Conceivably, in spite of general inflation, the replacement cost of the machinery might have gone down.)

(a) There is **specific price inflation**, which measures price changes over time for a specific asset or group of assets.

(b) There is **general price inflation**, which is the average rate of inflation, which reduces the general purchasing power of money.

To counter the problems of specific price inflation some system of current value accounting may be used (such as current cost accounting). The capital maintenance concepts underlying current value systems do not attempt to allow for the maintenance of real value in money terms.

Current purchasing power (CPP) accounting is based on a different concept of capital maintenance.

> **CPP** measures profits as the increase in the current purchasing power of equity. Profits are therefore stated after allowing for the declining purchasing power of money due to price inflation.

When applied to historical cost accounting, CPP is a system of accounting which makes adjustments to income and capital values to allow for the general rate of price inflation.

3.4 The principles and procedures of CPP accounting

In CPP accounting, profit is measured after allowing for general price changes. It is a fundamental idea of CPP that capital should be maintained in terms of the same monetary purchasing power, so that:

$$P_{CPP} = D_{CPP} + (E_{t(CPP)} - E_{(t-1)CPP})$$

where P_{CPP} is the CPP accounting profit

D_{CPP} is distributions to shareholders, re-stated in current purchasing power terms

$E_{t(CPP)}$ is the total value of assets attributable to the owners of the business entity at the end of the accounting period, restated in current purchasing power terms

$E_{(t-1)CPP}$ is the total value of the owners' equity at the beginning of the year re-stated in terms of current purchasing power at the end of the year.

A current purchasing power $ relates to the value of money on the last day of the accounting period.

Profit in CPP accounting is therefore measured after allowing for **maintenance of equity capital**. To the extent that a company is financed by loans, there is no requirement to allow for the maintenance of the purchasing power of the non-current liabilities. Indeed, as we shall see, the equity of a business can profit from the loss in the purchasing power value of loans.

3.5 Monetary and non-monetary items

Key term

> A **monetary item** is an asset or liability whose amount is fixed by contract or statute in terms of $s, regardless of changes in general price levels and the purchasing power of the currency.

The main examples of monetary items are cash, receivables, payables and non-current liabilities.

Key term

> A **non-monetary item** is an asset or liability whose value is not fixed by contract or statute.

These include land and buildings, plant and machinery and inventory.

In CPP accounting, the monetary items held must be looked at carefully.

(a)   If a company **borrows money in a period of inflation**, the amount of the debt will remain fixed (by law) so that when the debt is eventually paid, it will be paid in $s of a lower purchasing power.

For example, if a company borrows $2,000 on 1 January 20X5 and repays the loan on 1 January 20X9, the purchasing power of the $2,000 repaid in 20X9 will be much less than the value of $2,000 in 20X5, because of inflation. Since the company by law must repay only $2,000 of principal, it has gained by having the use of the money from the loan for 4 years. (The lender of the $2,000 will try to protect the value of his loan in a period of inflation by charging a higher rate of interest; however, this does not alter the fact that the loan remains fixed at $2,000 in money value.)

(b)   If a company **holds cash in a period of inflation**, its value in terms of current purchasing power will decline. The company will 'lose' by holding the cash instead of converting it into a non-monetary asset. Similarly, if goods are sold on credit, the amount of the debt is fixed by contract; and in a period of inflation, the current purchasing power of the money from the sale, when it is eventually received, will be less than the purchasing power of the debt, when it was first incurred.

In CPP accounting, it is therefore argued that there are **gains from having monetary liabilities and losses from having monetary assets.**

(a)   In the case of **monetary assets**, there is a need to make a charge against profit for the loss in purchasing power, because there will be a need for extra finance when the monetary asset is eventually used for operational activities. For example, if a company has a cash balance of $200, which is just sufficient to buy 100 new items of raw material inventory on 1 January 20X5, and if the rate of inflation during 20X5 is 10%, the company would need $220 to buy the same 100 items on 1 January 20X6 (assuming the items increase in value by the general rate of inflation). By holding the $200 as a monetary asset throughout 20X5, the company would need $20 more to buy the same goods and services on 1 January 20X6 that it could have obtained on 1 January 20X5. $20 would be a CPP loss on holding the monetary asset (cash) for a whole year.

(b)   In the case of **monetary liabilities**, the argument in favour of including a 'profit' in CPP accounting is not as strong. By incurring a debt, say, on 1 January 20X5, there will not be any eventual cash input to the business. The 'profit' from the monetary liabilities is a 'paper' profit, and T A Lee has argued against including it in the CPP income statement.

3.6 Example: CPP accounting

Seep Co had the following assets and liabilities at 31 December 20X4.

(a) All non-current assets were purchased on 1 January 20X1 at a cost of $60,000, and they had an estimated life of six years. Straight line depreciation is used.

(b) Closing inventories have a historical cost value of $7,900. They were bought in the period November-December 20X4.

(c) Receivables amounted to $8,000, cash to $2,000 and short-term payables to $6,000.

(d) There are non-current liabilities of $15,000.

(e) The general price index includes the following information:

Year	Date	Price index
20X1	1 January	100
20X4	30 November	158
20X4	31 December	160
20X5	31 December	180

The historical cost balance sheet of Seep Co at 31 December 20X4 was as follows.

	$	$
Assets		
Non-current assets at cost		60,000
Less depreciation		40,000
		20,000
Current assets		
Inventories	7,900	
Receivables	8,000	
Cash	2,000	
		17,900
Total assets		37,900
Equity and liabilities		
Capital		
Equity		16,900
Loan capital		15,000
		31,900
Current liabilities: payables		6,000
Total equity and liabilities		37,900

Required

(a) Prepare a CPP balance sheet as at 31 December 20X4.

(b) What was the depreciation charge against CPP profits in 20X4?

(c) What must be the value of equity at 31 December 20X5 if Seep Co is to 'break even' and make neither a profit nor a loss in 20X5?

Solution

(a)   CPP BALANCE SHEET AS AT 31 DECEMBER 20X4

	$c	$c
Assets		
Non-current assets, at cost 60,000 × 160/100	96,000	
Less depreciation 40,000 × 160/100	64,000	
		32,000
Inventory* 7,900 × 160/158	8,000	
Receivables**	8,000	
Cash**	2,000	
		18,000
		50,000
Equity and liabilities		
Capital		
Loan capital**		15,000
Equity ***		29,000
		44,000
Current liabilities: payables**		6,000
		50,000

Notes

*Inventories purchased between 1 November and 31 December are assumed to have an average index value relating to the mid-point of their purchase period, at 30 November.

**Monetary assets and liabilities are not re-valued, because their CPP value is the face value of the debt or cash amount.

***Equity is a mixture of monetary and non-monetary asset values, and is the balancing figure in this example.

(b)   Depreciation in 20X4 would be one sixth of the CPP value of the assets at the end of the year, $1/6$ of $96,000 = $16,000. Alternatively, it is:

($1/6$ × $60,000) × 160/100 = $16,000

(c)   To maintain the capital value of equity in CPP terms during 20X5, the CPP value of equity on 31 December 20X5 will need to be:

$29,000 × 180/160 = $32,625

Question	**CPP profits**

Rice and Price set up in business on 1 January 20X5 with no non-current assets, and cash of $5,000. On 1 January they acquired inventories for the full $5,000, which they sold on 30 June 20X5 for $6,000. On 30 November they obtained a further $2,100 of inventory on credit. The index of the general price level gives the following index figures.

Date	Index
1 January 20X5	300
30 June 20X5	330
30 November 20X5	350
31 December 20X5	360

Calculate the CPP profits (or losses) of Rice and Price for the year to 31 December 20X5.

Answer

The approach is to prepare a CPP income statement.

	$c	$c
Sales (6,000 × 360/330)		6,545
Less cost of goods sold (5,000 × 360/300)		6,000
		545
Loss on holding cash for 6 months*	(545)	
Gain by owing payables for 1 month**	60	
		485
CPP profit		60

* ($6,000 × 360/330) – $6,000 = $c 545
**($2,100 × 360/350) – $2,100 = $c 60

3.7 The advantages and disadvantages of CPP accounting

3.7.1 Advantages

(a) The restatement of asset values in terms of a **stable money value** provides **a more meaningful basis of comparison** with other companies. Similarly, provided that previous years' profits are re-valued into CPP terms, it is also possible to compare the current year's results with past performance.

(b) **Profit** is measured in **'real' terms** and excludes 'inflationary value increments'. This enables better forecasts of future prospects to be made.

(c) CPP **avoids the subjective valuations** of current value accounting, because a single price index is applied to all non-monetary assets.

(d) CPP **provides a stable monetary** unit with which to value profit and capital; ie $c.

(e) Since it is based on historical cost accounting, **raw data is easily verified**, and measurements of value can be readily audited.

3.7.2 Disadvantages

(a) It is not **clear what $c means**. 'Generalised purchasing power' as measured by a retail price index, or indeed any other general price index, has no obvious practical significance.

'Generalised purchasing power has no relevance to any person or entity because no such thing exists in reality, except as a statistician's computation.'   (T A Lee)

(b) The use of indices inevitably involves **approximations** in the measurements of value.

(c) The value **of assets in a CPP balance sheet has less meaning than a current value balance sheet**. It cannot be supposed that the CPP value of net assets reflects:

(i) The general goods and services that could be bought if the assets were released

(ii) The consumption of general goods and services that would have to be forgone to replace those assets

In this respect, a CPP balance sheet has similar drawbacks to an historical cost balance sheet.

4 Current cost accounting (CCA)

4.1 Value to the business (deprival value)

Current cost accounting (CCA) reflects an approach to capital maintenance based on maintaining the **operating capability** of a business. The conceptual basis of CCA is that the value of assets consumed or sold, and the value of assets in the balance sheet, should be stated at their **value to the business** (also known as 'deprival value').

Deprival value is an important concept, which you may find rather difficult to understand at first, and you should read the following explanation carefully.

Key term

> The **deprival value** of an asset is the loss which a business entity would suffer if it were deprived of the use of the asset.

(a) A basic assumption in CCA is that 'capital maintenance' should mean maintenance of the 'business substance' or 'operating capability' of the business entity. As we have seen already, it is generally accepted that profit is earned only after a sufficient amount has been charged against sales to ensure that the capital of the business is maintained. In CCA, a **physical** rather than financial definition of capital is used: capital maintenance is measured by the ability of the business entity to keep up the same level of operating capability.

(b) 'Value to the business' is the required method of valuation in current cost accounting, because it reflects the extra funds which would be required to maintain the operating capability of the business entity if it suddenly lost the use of an asset.

Value to the business, or deprival value, can be any of the following values.

(a) **Replacement cost**: in the case of non-current assets, it is assumed that the replacement cost of an asset would be its net replacement cost (NRC), its gross replacement cost minus an appropriate provision for depreciation to reflect the amount of its life already 'used up'.

(b) **Net realisable value** (NRV): what the asset could be sold for, net of any disposal costs.

(c) **Economic value** (EV), or value in use: what the existing asset will be worth to the company over the rest of its useful life.

The choice of deprival value from one of the three values listed will depend on circumstances. In simple terms you should remember that in **CCA deprival value is nearly always replacement cost.**

If the asset is worth replacing, its deprival value will always be net replacement cost. If the asset is not worth replacing, it might have been disposed of straight away, or else it might have been kept in operation until the end of its useful life.

You may therefore come across a statement that deprival value is the **lower of**:

- **Net replacement cost**
- The **higher of net realisable value and economic value**

We have already seen that if an asset is not worth replacing, the deprival value will be NRV or EV. However, there are many assets which will not be replaced either:

(a) Because the asset is **technologically obsolete**, and has been (or will be) superseded by more modern equipment

(b) Because the business is **changing the nature of its operations** and will not want to continue in the same line of business once the asset has been used up

Such assets, even though there are reasons not to replace them, would still be valued (usually) at net replacement cost, because this 'deprival value' still provides an estimate of the **operating capability** of the company.

4.2 CCA profits and deprival value

The deprival value of assets is reflected in the CCA income statement by the following means.

(a) **Depreciation** is charged on non-current assets on the basis of **gross replacement cost** of the asset (where NRC is the deprival value).

(b) Where **NRV or EV** is the deprival value, the charge against CCA profits will be the **loss in value of the asset** during the accounting period; ie from its previous balance sheet value to its current NRV or EV.

(c) **Goods sold** are charged at their **replacement cost**. Thus if an item of inventory cost $15 to produce, and sells for $20, by which time its replacement cost has risen to $17, the CCA profit would be $3.

	$
Sales	20
Less replacement cost of goods sold	17
Current cost profit	3

4.3 Example: CCA v accounting for inflation

Suppose that Arthur Smith Co buys an asset on 1 January for $10,000. The estimated life of the asset is 5 years, and straight line depreciation is charged. At 31 December the gross replacement cost of the asset is $10,500 (5% higher than on 1 January) but general inflation during the year, as measured by the retail price index, has risen 20%.

(a) To maintain the value of the business against inflation, the asset should be revalued as follows.

	$
Gross ($10,000 × 120%)	12,000
Depreciation charge for the year (@ 20%)	2,400
Net value in the balance sheet	9,600

(b) In CCA, the business maintains its operating capability if we revalue the asset as follows.

	$
Gross replacement cost	10,500
Depreciation charge for the year (note)	2,100
NRC; balance sheet value	8,400

Note	$
Historical cost depreciation	2,000
CCA depreciation adjustment (5%)	100
Total CCA depreciation cost	2,100

CCA preserves the operating capability of the company but does not necessarily preserve it against the declining value in the purchasing power of money (against inflation). As mentioned previously, CCA is a system which takes account of specific price inflation (changes in the prices of specific assets or groups of assets) but **not of general price inflation.**

A strict view of current cost accounting might suggest that a set of CCA accounts should be prepared from the outset on the basis of deprival values. In practice, current cost accounts are usually prepared by **starting from historical cost accounts and making appropriate adjustments.**

4.4 Current cost adjustments to historical cost profit

In current cost accounting, profit is calculated as follows

	$
Historical cost profit	X
Less: current cost operating adjustments	(X)
Current cost profit	X

The holding gains, both realised and unrealised, are excluded from current cost profit. The double entry for the debits in the current cost income statement is to credit each operating adjustment to a non-distributable current cost reserve.

4.5 The current cost income statement

The format of the current cost income statement would show the following information, although not necessarily in the order given.

	$	$
Historical cost profit (before interest & taxation)		X
Current cost operating adjustments		
Cost of sales adjustment (COSA)	(X)	
Monetary working capital adjustment (loss or gain) (MWCA)	(X) or X	
Depreciation adjustment	(X)	
		(X)
Current cost operating profit (before interest and taxation)		X
Less interest payable and receivable		(X)
Add gearing adjustment		X
Current cost profit attributable to shareholders		X
Less taxation		(X)
Current cost profit for the year		X

4.6 Cost of sales adjustment (COSA)

The COSA is necessary to **eliminate realised holding gains** on inventory. It represents the difference between the replacement cost and the historical cost of goods sold. The exclusion of holding gains from CC profit is a necessary consequence of the need to maintain operating capability. The COSA represents that portion of the HC profit which must be consumed in replacing the inventory item sold so that trading can continue. Where practical difficulties arise in estimating replacement cost, a simple indexing system can be used.

4.7 Depreciation adjustment

The depreciation adjustment is the **difference between the depreciation charge on the gross replacement cost of the assets and the historical cost depreciation**. This is (as with the COSA) a realised holding gain which is excluded from the CC profit. Where comparison is made with a different asset for the purposes of calculating replacement cost (because of the obsolescence of the old asset), then allowance must be made for different useful lives and different production capabilities.

4.8 Monetary working capital adjustment (MWCA)

Where a company gives or takes credit for the sale or purchase of goods, the goods are paid for at the **end** of the credit period at the replacement cost as at the **beginning** of the credit period. If a company measures profit as the excess of revenue over cost:

(a)   **Outstanding payables protect** the company to some extent from **price changes** because the company lags behind current prices in its payment

(b)   **Outstanding receivables**, in contrast, would be a **burden on profits** in a period of rising prices because sales receipts will always relate to previous months' sales at a lower price/cost/profit level

The MWCA can therefore be **either a gain or a loss**.

4.9 The current cost balance sheet

In the current cost balance sheet:

- **Assets** will be valued at their '**value to the business**'.
- **Liabilities** will be valued at their **monetary amount**.
- There will be a current cost reserve to reflect the revaluation surpluses.

4.10 Example: current cost accounts

At the beginning of a period, Arthur Smith Co has the following balance sheet.

	$
Assets	
Non-current asset (newly acquired)	10,000
Inventories (newly acquired)	2,000
	12,000
Capital	
Equity	8,000
Loan stock (10% interest)	4,000
	12,000

The company gearing is 33%, in terms of both HC and CCA. During the period, sales of goods amounted to $15,000, the replacement cost of sales was $13,200 and the historical cost of sales was $12,000. Closing inventories, at replacement cost, were $4,600 and at HC were $4,400. Depreciation is provided for at 10% straight line, and at the end of the period the non-current assets had a gross replacement cost of $11,000. The HC accounts were as follows.

INCOME STATEMENT

	$
Sales	15,000
Less cost of sales	12,000
	3,000
Depreciation	1,000
Profit before interest	2,000
Interest	400
Profit	1,600

CLOSING BALANCE SHEET

	$
Non-current asset at cost less depreciation	9,000
Inventories	4,400
Cash	200
	13,600
Equity	9,600
Loan stock	4,000
	13,600

Taxation is ignored.

Required

Prepare workings for the CCA accounts. (Depreciation for the period will be based on the end of year value of the non-current asset. All sales and purchases were for cash.)

Solution

The COSA is ($13,200 − $12,000) = $1,200
The depreciation adjustment is $100
The MWCA is nil (there are no purchases or sales on credit).

Note. The small cash balance in the closing balance sheet might be regarded as necessary for business purposes and therefore taken up in the MWCA as monetary working capital. In this example, we will treat the $200 as a cash surplus.

	$	$
Historical cost profit (before interest)		2,000
Current cost adjustments		
COSA	1,200	
MWCA	0	
Depreciation	100	
		1,300
Current cost operating profit		700

The gearing adjustment is calculated by multiplying the three current cost adjustments (here $1,300) by the gearing proportion (by the proportion of the gains which is financed by borrowing and which therefore provides additional profits for equity, since the real value of the borrowing is declining in a period of rising prices).

The gearing proportion is the ratio:

$$\frac{\text{Net borrowing}}{\text{Average net operating assets in the year}}$$

Net operating assets consist of non-current assets, inventories and monetary working capital. They are financed partly by net borrowings and partly by equity. The gearing proportion can therefore equally well be expressed as:

$$\frac{\text{Average net borrowing in the period}}{\text{Average equity interests plus average net borrowing in the period}}$$

Equity interests include the current cost reserve, and also any proposed dividends. Average figures are taken as being more representative than end of year figures.

	$
Opening figures	
Net borrowing	4,000
Equity interests	8,000
Equity plus net borrowing	12,000

Closing figures: since cash is here regarded as a surplus amount, the company is losing value during a period of inflation by holding cash - just as it is gaining by having fixed loans. If cash is not included in MWC, it is:

(a) Deducted from net borrowings
(b) Excluded from net operating assets

(Net operating assets consist of non-current assets, long term trade investments, inventories and monetary working capital.)

The closing figures are therefore as follows.

	$	$
Non-current assets (at net replacement cost $11,000 – $1,100)		9,900
Inventories (at replacement cost)		4,600
Monetary working capital		0
Net operating assets (equals equity interest plus net borrowings)		14,500
Less: net borrowing	4,000	
cash in hand	(200)	
		3,800
Therefore equity interest =		10,700

Average figures	Opening	Closing	Average
Net borrowing	$4,000	$3,800	$3,900
Net operating assets	$12,000	$14,500	$13,250

Divide by 2

The gearing proportion is $\dfrac{3,900}{13,250} \times 100\% = 29.43\%$

Question

CCA accounts

Prepare the CCA accounts based on the above example.

Answer

CCA INCOME STATEMENT

	$	$
Historical cost profit before interest		2,000
Current cost adjustments		
COSA	1,200	
MWCA	0	
Depreciation	100	
		(1,300)
Current cost operating profit		700
Interest	(400)	
Gearing adjustment ($1,300 × 29.43%)	383	
		(17)
Current cost profit		683

CCA BALANCE SHEET (end of year)

	$	$
Non-current assets (net replacement cost)		9,900
Inventories (replacement cost)		4,600
Cash		200
		14,700
Financed by		
Equity at start of year		8,000
Addition to reserves during year		683
Current cost reserve		

500D
683

Excess of net replacement cost over net book value	
(9,900 – 9,000)	900
Depreciation adjustment	100
COSA	1,200
MWCA	0
	2,200
Less gearing adjustment	(383)
	1,817
Add revaluation of year-end inventories	200
	2,017
	10,700
Loan stock	4,000
	14,700

4.11 The advantages and disadvantages of current cost accounting

4.11.1 Advantages

(a) By excluding holding gains from profit, CCA can be used to indicate whether the dividends paid to shareholders will **reduce the operating capability** of the business.

(b) Assets are valued after management has considered the **opportunity cost** of holding them, and the expected benefits from their future use. CCA is therefore a useful guide for management in deciding whether to hold or sell assets.

(c) It is **relevant** to the needs of information users in:

　(i) Assessing the stability of the business entity

　(ii) Assessing the vulnerability of the business (eg to a takeover), or the liquidity of the business

　(iii) Evaluating the performance of management in maintaining and increasing the business substance

　(iv) Judging future prospects

(d) It can be **implemented fairly easily** in practice, by making simple adjustments to the historical cost accounting profits. A current cost balance sheet can also be prepared with reasonable simplicity.

4.11.2 Disadvantages

(a) It is impossible to make valuations of EV or NRV without **subjective judgements**. The measurements used are therefore not objective.

(b) There are several problems to be overcome in deciding how to provide an **estimate of replacement** costs for non-current assets.

　(i) It must be understood from the outset that whereas depreciation based on the historical cost of an asset can be viewed as a means of spreading the cost of the asset over its estimated life, depreciation based on replacement costs does not conform to this traditional accounting view.

　(ii) Depreciation based on replacement costs would appear to be a means of providing that sufficient funds are set aside in the business to ensure that the asset can be replaced at the end of its life. But if it is not certain what technological advances might be in the next few years and how the type of assets required might change between the current time and the estimated time of replacement, it is difficult to argue that depreciation based on today's costs is a valid way of providing for the eventual physical replacement of the asset.

(iii) It is more correct, however, that depreciation in CCA does not set aside funds for the physical replacement of non-current assets.

'CCA aims to maintain no more and no less than the facilities that are available at the accounting date ... despite the fact that the non-current assets which provide those facilities might never be replaced in their existing or currently available form ... In simple language, this means charging depreciation on the basis of the current replacement cost of the assets at the time the facilities are used.' (Mallinson)

(iv) It may be argued that depreciation based on historical cost is more accurate than replacement cost depreciation, because the historical cost is known, whereas replacement cost is simply an estimate. However, replacement costs are re-assessed each year, so that inaccuracies in the estimates in one year can be rectified in the next year.

(c) The mixed value approach to valuation means that some assets will be valued at replacement cost, but others will be valued at net realisable value or economic value. It is arguable that the **total assets** will, therefore, have an **aggregate value** which is **not particularly meaningful** because of this mixture of different concepts.

(d) It can be argued that **'deprival value'** is an **unrealistic concept**, because the business entity has not been deprived of the use of the asset. This argument is one which would seem to reject the fundamental approach to 'capital maintenance' on which CCA is based.

5 Agency theory and the efficient market hypothesis

FAST FORWARD

We are now moving on to some more general theories about behaviour within companies and in the stock market.

5.1 Agency theory and the 'agency problem'

The relationship between **management and shareholders** is sometimes referred to as an **agency relationship**, in which managers act as agents for the shareholders, using delegated powers to run the affairs of the company in the shareholders' best interests.

Key term

Agency theory (Fama and Jensen) proposes that, although individual members of the business team act in their own self-interest, the well-being of each individual depends on the well-being of other team members and on the performance of the team in competition with other teams. The firm is seen as constituted by contracts among the different factors of production.

Agency theory was advanced by two American economists, Jensen and Meckling, in 1976 as a theory to explain relationships within corporations. It has been used to explain management control practices as well as **relationships between management and investors**: here we are concerned with the latter.

Jensen and Meckling proposed that corporations be viewed as a set of contracts between management, shareholders and creditors, with **management as agents** and **providers of finance as principals**. Financial reports and external audit are two mechanisms by which the agents demonstrate compliance with their obligations to the principals.

The agency relationship arising from the separation of ownership from management is sometimes characterised as the **'agency problem'**. For example, if managers hold none or very little of the equity shares of the company they work for, what is to stop them from:

(a)   Working inefficiently?

(b)   Not bothering to look for profitable new investment opportunities?

(c)   Giving themselves high salaries and perks?

One power that shareholders possess is the right to **remove the directors from office**. But shareholders have to take the initiative to do this, and in many companies, the shareholders lack the energy and organisation to take such a step. Even so, directors will want the company's report and accounts, and the proposed final dividend, to meet with shareholders' approval at the AGM.

For **management below director level**, it is the **responsibility of the directors to ensure that they perform well**. Getting the best out of subordinates is one of the functions of management, and directors should be expected to do it as well as they can.

Another reason why managers might do their best to improve the financial performance of their company is that managers' **pay** is often **related to the size or profitability** of the **company**. Managers in very big companies, or in very profitable companies, will normally expect to earn higher salaries than managers in smaller or less successful companies.

Agency theory is based on a number of behavioural and structural assumptions.

(a)   The most important **behavioural assumptions** are individual welfare maximisation, individual rationality, and the assumption that individuals are risk-averse.

(b)   **Structural assumptions** include the assumption that investments are not infinitely divisible, and that individuals vary in their access to funds and their entrepreneurial ability. Some criticisms of the theory have attacked these various assumptions. For example, are individuals satisficers rather than maximisers? And are individuals truly 'rational' or perhaps rather gullible?

The assumptions of the theory suggest that **investors and entrepreneurs** have **incentives for sharing risks and rewards of entrepreneurial activity**, for example where the entrepreneur, who may enjoy limited liability, borrows from investors at fixed rates of interest.

The key feature of an efficient agency contract, for example within a company, is that it allows **full delegation of decision-making authority over the use of invested funds to management without excessive risk of abuse** of that authority. In the real world, an 'agency cost' arises, being the difference between the return expected if managers truly maximised shareholder wealth and the actual return, given that managers will actually be seeking to maximise their own wealth.

'Bonding' and 'monitoring' procedures help to act as **safeguards** to minimise the risk of investors incurring agency costs. An example of 'bonding' is a condition attached to a loan (eg security over assets, conditions not to raise further loans). A bank lending money to a business will also expect information to be supplied to enable it to *monitor* compliance with the loan agreement.

Agency theory suggests that audited accounts of limited companies are an important source of **'post-decision'** information minimising investors' agency costs, in contrast to alternative approaches which see financial reports as primarily a source of **'pre-decision'** information for equity investors. The theory is advanced as an explanation for the continued use of absorption costing and historic costs in management accounts in spite of their apparent lack of relevance in decision making.

5.2 The efficient market hypothesis

It has been argued that certain international stock markets are **efficient capital markets**, that is, markets in which:

(a)   The **prices of securities** bought and sold **reflect all the relevant information** which is available to the buyers and sellers. In other words, share prices change quickly to reflect all new information about future prospects

(b)   **No individual dominates** the market

(c)   **Transaction costs** of buying and selling are **not so high** as to discourage trading significantly

If the stock market is efficient, **share prices should vary in a rational way.**

(a)   If a company makes a profitable investment, shareholders will get to know about it, and the market price of its shares will rise in anticipation of future dividend increases.

(b)   If a company makes a bad investment shareholders will find out and so the price of its shares will fall.

(c)   If interest rates rise, shareholders will want a higher return from their investments, so market prices will fall.

5.2.1 The definition of efficiency

The efficiency of a stock market means the ability of a stock market to price securities fairly and quickly.

Key term

An **efficient market** is therefore one in which the market prices of all the securities traded on it reflect all the available information. There is no possibility of 'speculative bubbles' in which share prices are pushed up or down, by speculative pressure, to unrealistically high or low levels.

5.2.2 Varying degrees of efficiency

There are three degrees or 'forms' of efficiency.

(a)   **Weak form**
(b)   **Semi-strong form**
(c)   **Strong form**

Tests can be carried out on the workings of a stock market to establish whether the market operates with a particular form of efficiency.

5.2.3 Weak form tests and weak form efficiency

The weak form hypothesis of market efficiency explains changes in share prices as the result of **new information** which becomes available to investors.

In other words, share prices only change when new information about a company and its profits have become available. Share prices do **not** change **in anticipation** of new information being announced.

Since new information arrives unexpectedly, changes in share prices should occur in a random fashion: a weak form test seeks to prove the validity of the **random walk theory of share prices**. In addition, since the theory states that current share prices reflect all information available from past changes in the price, if it is correct then chartist or technical analysis cannot be based on sound principles.

Research to prove that the stock market displays weak form efficiency has been based on the principle that:

(a)   If share price changes are random
(b)   If there is no connection between past price movements and new share price changes

then it should be possible to prove statistically there is **no correlation** between successive changes in the price of a share, that is, that **trends in prices cannot be detected.**

Proofs of the absence of trends have been claimed in the work of various writers.

5.2.4 Semi-strong form tests and semi-strong form efficiency

Semi-strong form tests attempt to show that the stock market displays semi-strong efficiency, by which we mean that **current share prices reflect both**:

(a)   **All relevant information about past price movements** and their implications

(b)   **All knowledge** which is **available publicly**

Tests to prove semi-strong efficiency have concentrated on the ability of the market to anticipate share price changes before new information is formally announced. For example, if two companies plan a merger, share prices of the two companies will inevitably change once the merger plans are formally announced. The market would show semi-strong efficiency, however, if it were able to **anticipate** such an announcement, so that share prices of the companies concerned would change in advance of the merger plans being confirmed.

Research in both Britain and the USA has suggested that market prices anticipate mergers several months before they are formally announced, and the **conclusion drawn is that the stock markets in these countries** *do* **exhibit semi-strong efficiency.**

It has also been argued that the market displays sufficient efficiency for investors to **see through 'window dressing'** of accounts by companies which use questionable accounting conventions to overstate profits.

Suppose that a company is planning a rights issue of shares in order to invest in a new project. A semi-strong form efficient market hypothesis (unlike the weak form hypothesis) would predict that if there is public knowledge before the issue is formally announced, of the issue itself and of the expected returns from the project, then the market price (with rights) will change to reflect the anticipated profits before the issue is announced.

5.2.5 Strong form tests and strong form efficiency

A strong form test of market efficiency attempts to prove that the stock market displays a strong form of efficiency, by which we mean that **share prices reflect all information available**:

(a)   **From past price changes**

(b)   **From public knowledge or anticipation**

(c)   **From insider knowledge** available to specialists or experts (such as investment managers)

It would then follow that in order to maximise the wealth of shareholders, management should concentrate simply on maximising the net present value of its investments and it need not worry, for example, about the effect on share prices of financial results in the published accounts because investors will make allowances for low profits or dividends in the current year if higher profits or dividends are expected in the future.

In theory an expert, such as an investment manager, should be able to use his privileged access to additional information about companies to earn a higher rate of return than an ordinary investor. Unit trusts should in theory therefore perform better than the average investor. Research to date has suggested, however, that this expert skill does not exist (or at least, that any higher returns earned by experts are offset by management charges).

5.2.6 How efficient are stock markets?

Evidence so far collected suggests that stock markets show efficiency that is at least weak form, but tending more towards a **semi-strong form**. In other words, current share prices reflect all or most publicly available information about companies and their securities. However, it is very difficult to assess the market's efficiency in relation to shares which are not usually actively traded.

Fundamental analysis and **technical analysis**, which are carried out by analysts and investment managers, play an important role in creating an efficient stock market. This is because an efficient market depends on the widespread availability of cheap information about companies, their shares and market conditions, and this is what the firms of stockbrokers and other financial institutions *do* provide for their clients and for the general investing public.

5.2.7 The implications of the efficient market hypothesis

If the **strong form** of the efficient market hypothesis is correct, **a company's real financial position will be reflected in its share price**. Its real financial position includes both its current position and its expected future profitability.

If the management of a company attempt to maximise the net present value of their investments and to make public any relevant information about those investments then current share prices will in turn be maximised.

The implication for an **investor** is that **if the market shows strong form or semi-strong form efficiency, he can rarely spot shares at a bargain price that will soon rise sharply in value**. This is because the market will already have anticipated future developments, and will have reflected these in the share price. All an investor can do, instead of looking for share bargains, is to concentrate on building up a good spread of shares (a portfolio) in order to achieve a satisfactory balance between risk and return.

Chapter roundup

- **Profit** is an important measure in accounting statements.

  – It measures the efficiency of the company's **management** and helps in decision making.
  – It helps **creditors and investors** to decide whether they can safely lend money.
  – The **government** may use profit as a means of imposing direct taxation.

- **Profit** therefore has a variety of uses and users, but its **measurement depends** on the **methods used to value capital** (assets and liabilities) and on the method, if any, of accounting for price level changes.

- Alternative methods of accounting based on **current value concepts** use **exit values, entry values** or **mixed values**. These principles are developed further in current cost accounting.

- **CPP accounting** is a method of accounting for general (not specific) inflation. It does so by expressing asset values in a stable monetary unit, the $c or $ of current purchasing power.

- In the **CPP balance sheet, monetary items** are stated at their **face value. Non-monetary items** are stated at their **current purchasing power** as at the balance sheet date.

- **CCA** is an alternative to the historical cost convention which attempts to overcome the problems of accounting for **specific price inflation**. Unlike CPP accounting, it does not attempt to cope with general inflation.

- CCA is based on a **physical concept of capital maintenance**. Profit is recognised after the operating capability of the business has been maintained.

- To recognise **holding gains** as part of current cost profit would conflict with the principle of maintaining operating capability.

- The current cost income statement is constructed by taking **historical cost** profit before interest and taxation as a starting point.

  – Current cost **operating adjustments** in respect of **cost of sales**, **monetary working capital** and **depreciation** are made so as to arrive at **current cost operating profit**.

  – A **gearing adjustment** is then necessary to arrive at a figure of current cost profit attributable to shareholders.

- **Agency theory** attempts to explain why companies take decisions which **do not necessarily increase shareholders' wealth.**

Quick quiz

1   Can methods of current value accounting be described as systems for accounting for inflation?

2   Distinguish between specific price inflation and general price inflation.

3   What is an asset's deprival value if it is not worth replacing?

Answers to quick quiz

1   No

2   • Specific price inflation measures price changes over time for a specific asset or group of assets
    • General price inflation measures the continual reduction in the general purchasing power of money

3   The higher of net realisable value and economic value

Now try the question below from the Exam Question Bank

Number	Level	Marks	Time
Q20	Examination	25	45 mins

19

IASB's Framework

Introduction

The IASB's document *Framework for the preparation and presentation of financial statements* represents the **conceptual framework** on which all IASs are based.

A conceptual framework for financial reporting can be defined as an attempt to codify existing **generally accepted accounting principles (GAAP)** in order to reappraise current accounting standards and to produce new standards.

Study guide

Section 1 – Review of basic concepts, *Framework for the Preparation and Presentation of Financial Statements*

- Discuss what is meant by a conceptual framework and GAAP
- Describe the objectives of financial statements and the qualitative characteristics of financial information
- Define the elements of financial statements
- Apply the above definitions to practical situations

1 The IASB's *Framework*

FAST FORWARD We are now going to consider the conceptual framework underpinning IASs.

In July 1989 the IASB (then IASC) produced a document, *Framework for the preparation and presentation of financial statements* (*'Framework'*). The *Framework* is, in effect, the **conceptual** framework upon which all IASs are based and hence which determines how financial statements are prepared and the information they contain.

The *Framework* consists of several sections or chapters, following on after a preface and introduction. These chapters are as follows.

- The objective of financial statements
- Underlying assumptions
- Qualitative characteristics of financial statements
- The elements of financial statements
- Recognition of the elements of financial statements
- Measurement of the elements of financial statements
- Concepts of capital and capital maintenance

We will look briefly at the preface and introduction to the *Framework* as these will place the document in context with the rest of what you have studied for this paper and in particular the context of the *Framework* in the IASB's approach to developing IASs.

Exam focus point

As you read through this chapter think about the impact the *Framework* has had on IASs, particularly the definitions.

1.1 Preface

The preface to the *Framework* points out the fundamental reason why financial statements are produced worldwide, ie to **satisfy the requirements of external users**, but that practice varies due to the individual pressures in each country. These pressures may be social, political, economic or legal, but they result in variations in practice from country to country, including the form of statements, the definition of their component parts (assets, liabilities etc), the criteria for recognition of items and both the scope and disclosure of financial statements.

It is these differences which the IASB wishes to narrow by **harmonising** all aspects of financial statements, including the regulations governing their accounting standards and their preparation and presentation.

The preface emphasises the way **financial statements are used to make economic decisions** and thus financial statements should be prepared to this end. The types of economic decisions for which financial statements are likely to be used include the following.

- Decisions to buy, hold or sell equity investments
- Assessment of management stewardship and accountability
- Assessment of the entity's ability to pay employees
- Assessment of the security of amounts lent to the entity
- Determination of taxation policies
- Determination of distributable profits and dividends
- Inclusion in national income statistics
- Regulations of the activities of entities

Any additional requirements imposed by **national governments** for their own purposes should not affect financial statements produced for the benefit of other users.

The *Framework* recognises that financial statements can be prepared using a **variety of models**. Although the most common is based on historical cost and a nominal unit of currency (ie pound sterling, US dollar etc), the *Framework* can be applied to financial statements prepared under a range of models.

1.2 Introduction

The introduction to the *Framework* lays out the purpose, status and scope of the document. It then looks at different users of financial statements and their information needs.

1.2.1 Purpose and status

The introduction gives a list of the purposes of the *Framework*.

(a) Assist the Board of the IASB in the **development of future IASs** and in its review of existing IASs.

(b) Assist the Board of the IASB in **promoting harmonisation** of regulations, accounting standards and procedures relating to the presentation of financial statements by providing a basis for reducing the number of alternative accounting treatments permitted by IASs.

(c) Assist **national standard-setting bodies** in developing national standards.

(d) Assist **preparers of financial statements** in applying IASs and in dealing with topics that have yet to form the subject of an IAS.

(e) Assist **auditors** in forming an opinion as to whether financial statements conform with IASs.

(f) Assist **users of financial statements** in interpreting the information contained in financial statements prepared in conformity with IASs.

(g) Provide those who are interested in the work of IASB with **information** about its approach to the formulation of IASs (now IFRSs).

The *Framework* is not an IAS and so does not overrule any individual IAS. In the (rare) cases of conflict between an IAS and the *Framework*, the **IAS will prevail**. These cases will diminish over time as the *Framework* will be used as a guide in the production of future IASs. The *Framework* itself will be revised occasionally depending on the experience of the IASB in using it.

1.2.2 Scope

The *Framework* deals with:

(a) The **objective** of financial statements

(b) The **qualitative characteristics** that determine the usefulness of information in financial statements

   (c)   The **definition, recognition and measurement** of the elements from which financial statements are constructed

   (d)   Concepts of **capital and capital maintenance**

The *Framework* is concerned with **'general purpose' financial statements** (ie a normal set of annual statements), but it can be applied to other types of accounts. A complete set of financial statements includes:

   (a)   A balance sheet
   (b)   An income statement
   (c)   A statement of changes in financial position (eg a cash flow statement)
   (d)   Notes, other statements and explanatory material

Supplementary information may be included, but some items are not included in the financial statements themselves, namely commentaries and reports by the directors, the chairman, management etc.

All types of financial reporting entities are included (commercial, industrial, business; public or private sector).

Key term

> A **reporting entity** is an entity for which there are users who rely on the financial statements as their major source of financial information about the entity.
>
> *(Framework)*

1.2.3 Users and their information needs

We have already looked at the users of accounting information in Chapter 1. They consist of investors, employees, lenders, suppliers and other trade creditors, customers, government and their agencies and the public. You should be able to remember enough to do the following exercise.

Question   **Users of financial information**

Consider the information needs of the users of financial information listed above.

Answer

(a)   **Investors** are the providers of risk capital

      (i)   Information is required to help make a decision about buying or selling shares, taking up a rights issue and voting.

      (ii)   Investors must have information about the level of dividend, past, present and future and any changes in share price.

      (iii)   Investors will also need to know whether the management has been running the company efficiently.

      (iv)   As well as the position indicated by the income statement, balance sheet and earnings per share (EPS), investors will want to know about the liquidity position of the company, the company's future prospects, and how the company's shares compare with those of its competitors.

(b)   **Employees** need information about the security of employment and future prospects for jobs in the company, and to help with collective pay bargaining.

(c)   **Lenders** need information to help them decide whether to lend to a company. They will also need to check that the value of any security remains adequate, that the interest repayments are secure, that the cash is available for redemption at the appropriate time and that any financial restrictions (such as maximum debt/equity ratios) have not been breached.

(d)   **Suppliers** need to know whether the company will be a good customer and pay its debts.

(e)   **Customers** need to know whether the company will be able to continue producing and supplying goods.

(f)   **Government's** interest in a company may be one of creditor or customer, as well as being specifically concerned with compliance with tax and company law, ability to pay tax and the general contribution of the company to the economy.

(g)   The **public** at large would wish to have information for all the reasons mentioned above, but it could be suggested that it would be impossible to provide general purpose accounting information which was specifically designed for the needs of the public.

Financial statements cannot meet all these users' needs, but financial statements which meet the **needs of investors** (providers of risk capital) will meet most of the needs of other users.

The *Framework* emphasises that the preparation and presentation of financial statements is primarily the **responsibility of an entity's management**. Management also has an interest in the information appearing in financial statements.

1.3 IAS 1 *Presentation of financial statements*

Much of what IAS 1 states in relation to accounting policies and the formats of financial statements repeats the contents of the *Framework* document. IAS 1 was considered in detail in Chapter 4.

2 The objective of financial statements

FAST FORWARD

The *Framework* states that:

'The objective of financial statements is to provide information about the financial position, performance and changes in financial position of an entity that is useful to a wide range of users in making economic decisions.'

Such financial statements will meet the needs of most users. The information is, however, **restricted**.

(a)   It is based on **past events** not expected future events.
(b)   It does not necessarily contain **non-financial information**.

The statements also show the results of **management's stewardship**.

2.1 Financial position, performance and changes in financial position

It is important for users to assess the **ability of an entity to produce cash and cash equivalents** to pay employees, lenders etc.

Financial position (balance sheet) information is affected by the following and information about each one can aid the user.

(a)   **Economic resources controlled**: to predict the ability to generate cash

(b)   **Financial structure**: to predict borrowing needs, the distribution of future profits/cash and likely success in raising new finance

(c) **Liquidity and solvency**: to predict whether financial commitments will be met as they fall due (liquidity relates to short-term commitments, solvency is longer-term)

Key terms

Liquidity. The availability of sufficient funds to meet deposit withdrawals and other short-term financial commitments as they fall due.

Solvency. The availability of cash over the longer term to meet financial commitments as they fall due.

(Framework)

In all these areas, the capacity to adapt to changes in the environment in which the entity operates is very important.

Financial performance (income statement) information, particularly profitability, is used to assess potential changes in the economic resources the entity is likely to control in future. Information about performance variability is therefore important.

Changes in financial position (ie cash flow statement) information is used to assess the entity's investing, financing and operating activities. They show the entity's ability to produce cash and the needs which utilise those cash flows.

All parts of the financial statements are **interrelated**, reflecting different aspects of the same transactions or events. Each statement provides different information; none can provide all the information required by users.

3 Underlying assumptions

FAST FORWARD   We have already met the two assumptions discussed here.

3.1 Accruals basis

Key term

Accruals basis. The effects of transactions and other events are recognised when they occur (and not as cash or its equivalent is received or paid) and they are recorded in the accounting records and reported in the financial statements of the periods to which they relate.   *(Framework)*

Financial statements prepared under the accruals basis show users past transactions involving cash and also obligations to pay cash in the future and resources which represent cash to be received in the future.

3.2 Going concern

Key term

Going concern. The entity is normally viewed as a going concern, that is, as continuing in operation for the foreseeable future. It is assumed that the entity has neither the intention nor the necessity of liquidation or of curtailing materially the scale of its operations.   *(Framework)*

It is assumed that the entity has no intention to liquidate or curtail major operations. If it did, then the financial statements would be prepared on a **different (disclosed) basis.**

4 Qualitative characteristics of financial statements

FAST FORWARD   The *Framework* states that qualitative characteristics are the attributes that make the information provided in financial statements useful to users.

The four principal qualitative characteristics are **understandability, relevance, reliability and comparability**.

4.1 Understandability

Users must be able to understand financial statements. They are assumed to have some business, economic and accounting knowledge and to be able to apply themselves to study the information properly. **Complex matters should not be left out** of financial statements simply due to its difficulty if it is relevant information.

4.2 Relevance

The **predictive and confirmatory roles** of information are interrelated.

> **Relevance**. Information has the quality of relevance when it influences the economic decisions of users by helping them evaluate past, present or future events or confirming, or correcting, their past evaluations.
>
> *(Framework)*

Information on financial position and performance is often used to predict future position and performance and other things of interest to the user, eg likely dividend, wage rises. The **manner of showing information** will enhance the ability to make predictions, eg by highlighting unusual items.

4.2.1 Materiality

The relevance of information is affected by its **nature and materiality**.

> **Materiality**. Information is material if its omission or misstatement could influence the economic decisions of users taken on the basis of the financial statements.
>
> *(Framework)*

Information may be judged relevant simply because of its nature (eg remuneration of management). In other cases, both the nature and materiality of the information are important. Materiality is not a primary qualitative characteristic itself (like reliability or relevance), because it is merely a threshold or cut-off point.

> There is a more detailed definition of materiality in the revised IAS 1 (see Chapter 1).

4.3 Reliability

Information must also be reliable to be useful. The user must be able to depend on it being a **faithful representation**.

> **Reliability**. Information has the quality of reliability when it is free from material error and bias and can be depended upon by users to represent faithfully that which it either purports to represent or could reasonably be expected to represent.
>
> *(Framework)*

Even if information is relevant, if it is very unreliable it may be **misleading to recognise it**, eg a disputed claim for damages in a legal action.

4.3.1 Faithful representation

Information must represent faithfully the transactions it purports to represent in order to be reliable. There is a risk that this may not be the case, not due to bias, but due to **inherent difficulties in identifying the transactions** or finding an **appropriate method of measurement or presentation**. Where measurement of the financial effects of an item is so uncertain, entities should not recognise such an item, eg internally generated goodwill.

PROFESSIONAL EDUCATION

4.3.2 Substance over form

This concept was discussed in Chapter 1. Faithful representation of a transaction is only possible if it is accounted for according to its **substance and economic reality**, not with its legal form.

Key term

> **Substance over form**. The principle that transactions and other events are accounted for and presented in accordance with their substance and economic reality and not merely their legal form.   *(Framework)*

4.3.3 Neutrality

Information must be **free from bias** to be reliable. Neutrality is lost if the financial statements are prepared so as to influence the user to make a judgement or decision in order to achieve a predetermined outcome.

4.3.4 Prudence

Again, we have already discussed this concept in Chapter 1. **Uncertainties** exist in the preparation of financial information, eg the collectability of doubtful receivables. These uncertainties are recognised through disclosure and through the application of prudence. Prudence does not, however, allow the creation of hidden reserves or excessive provisions, understatement of assets or income or overstatement of liabilities or expenses.

4.3.5 Completeness

Financial information must be complete, within the **restrictions of materiality and cost**, to be reliable. Omission may cause information to be misleading.

4.4 Comparability

Users must be able to compare an entity's financial statements:

  (a)   **Through time** to identify trends

  (b)   **With other entities' statements**, to evaluate their relative financial position, performance and changes in financial position

The consistency of treatment is therefore important across like items over time, within the entity and across all entities.

The **disclosure of accounting policies** is particularly important here. Users must be able to distinguish between different accounting policies in order to be able to make a valid comparison of similar items in the accounts of different entities.

Comparability is **not the same as uniformity**. Entities should change accounting policies if they become inappropriate.

Corresponding information for **preceding periods** should be shown to enable comparison over time.

4.5 Constraints on relevant and reliable information

4.5.1 Timeliness

Information may become irrelevant if there is a delay in reporting it. There is a **balance between timeliness and the provision of reliable information**. Information may be reported on a timely basis when not all aspects of the transaction are known, thus compromising reliability.

If every detail of a transaction is known, it may be too late to publish the information because it has become irrelevant. The overriding consideration is how best to satisfy the economic decision-making needs of the users.

4.5.2 Balance between benefits and cost

This is a pervasive constraint, not a qualitative characteristic. When information is provided, its benefits must exceed the costs of obtaining and presenting it. This is a **subjective area** and there are other difficulties: others than the intended users may gain a benefit; also the cost may be paid by someone other than the users. It is therefore difficult to apply a cost-benefit analysis, but preparers and users should be aware of the constraint.

4.5.3 Balance between qualitative characteristics

A **trade off between qualitative characteristics** is often necessary, the aim being to achieve an appropriate balance to meet the objective of financial statements. It is a matter for professional judgement as to the relative importance of these characteristics in each case.

4.6 True and fair view/fair presentation

The *Framework* does not attempt to define these concepts directly. It does state, however, that the application of the **principal 'qualitative' characteristics** and of **appropriate accounting standards** will usually result in financial statements which show a true and fair view, or present fairly.

5 The elements of financial statements

FAST FORWARD Transactions and other events are grouped together in broad **classes** and in this way their financial effects are shown in the financial statements. These broad classes are the elements of financial statements.

The *Framework* lays out these elements as follows.

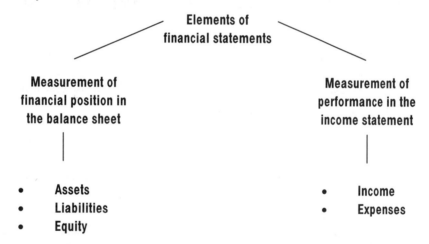

A process of **sub-classification** then takes place for presentation in the financial statements, eg assets are classified by their nature or function in the business to show information in the best way for users to take economic decisions.

5.1 Financial position

We need to define the three terms listed under this heading above.

- **Asset**. A resource controlled by an entity as a result of past events and from which future economic benefits are expected to flow to the entity.
- **Liability**. A present obligation of the entity arising from past events, the settlement of which is expected to result in an outflow from the entity of resources embodying economic benefits.
- **Equity**. The residual interest in the assets of the entity after deducting all its liabilities. *(Framework)*

These definitions are important, but they do not cover the **criteria for recognition** of any of these items, which are discussed in the next section of this chapter. This means that the definitions may include items which would not actually be recognised in the balance sheet because they fail to satisfy recognition criteria particularly, as we will see below, the **probable flow of any economic benefit** to or from the business.

Whether an item satisfies any of the definitions above will depend on the **substance and economic reality** of the transaction, not merely its legal form. For example, consider finance leases (see Chapter 12).

5.2 Assets

We can look in more detail at the components of the definitions given above.

Key term

> **Future economic benefit**. The potential to contribute, directly or indirectly, to the flow of cash and cash equivalents to the entity. The potential may be a productive one that is part of the operating activities of the entity. It may also take the form of convertibility into cash or cash equivalents or a capability to reduce cash outflows, such as when an alternative manufacturing process lowers the cost of production.
>
> *(Framework)*

Assets are usually employed to produce goods or services for customers; customers will then pay for these. **Cash itself** renders a service to the entity due to its command over other resources.

The existence of an asset, particularly in terms of **control**, is not reliant on:

    (a)   **physical form** (hence patents and copyrights); *nor*

    (b)   **legal rights** (hence leases).

Transactions or events **in the past** give rise to assets; those expected to occur in the future do not in themselves give rise to assets. For example, an intention to purchase a non-current asset does not, in itself, meet the definition of an asset.

5.3 Liabilities

Again we can look more closely at some aspects of the definition. An essential characteristic of a liability is that the entity has a **present obligation**.

Key term

> **Obligation**. A duty or responsibility to act or perform in a certain way. Obligations may be legally enforceable as a consequence of a binding contract or statutory requirement. Obligations also arise, however, from normal business practice, custom and a desire to maintain good business relations or act in an equitable manner.
>
> *(Framework)*

It is important to distinguish between a present obligation and a **future commitment**. A management decision to purchase assets in the future does not, in itself, give rise to a present obligation.

Settlement of a present obligation will involve the entity giving up resources embodying economic benefits in order to satisfy the claim of the other party. This may be done in various ways, not just by payment of cash.

Liabilities must arise from **past transactions or events**. In the case of, say, recognition of future rebates to customers based on annual purchases, the sale of goods in the past is the transaction that gives rise to the liability.

5.3.1 Provisions

Is a provision a liability?

Key term

> **Provision**. A present obligation which satisfies the rest of the definition of a liability, even if the amount of the obligation has to be estimated.
>
> *(Framework)*

Assets or liabilities?

Consider the following situations. In each case, do we have an asset or liability within the definitions given by the *Framework?* Give reasons for your answer.

(a)   Pat Co has purchased a patent for $20,000. The patent gives the company sole use of a particular manufacturing process which will save $3,000 a year for the next five years.

(b)   Baldwin Co paid Don Brennan $10,000 to set up a car repair shop, on condition that priority treatment is given to cars from the company's fleet.

(c)   Deals on Wheels Co provides a warranty with every car sold.

Answer

(a)   This is an asset, albeit an intangible one. There is a past event, control and future economic benefit (through cost savings).

(b)   This cannot be classified as an asset. Baldwin Co has no control over the car repair shop and it is difficult to argue that there are 'future economic benefits'.

(c)   This is a liability; the business has taken on an obligation. It would be recognised when the warranty is issued rather than when a claim is made.

5.4 Equity

Equity is defined above as a **residual**, but it may be sub-classified in the balance sheet. This will indicate legal or other restrictions on the ability of the entity to distribute or otherwise apply its equity. Some reserves are required by statute or other law, eg for the future protection of creditors. The amount shown for equity depends on the **measurement of assets and liabilities.** It has nothing to do with the market value of the entity's shares.

5.5 Performance

Profit is used as a **measure of performance**, or as a basis for other measures (eg EPS). It depends directly on the measurement of income and expenses, which in turn depend (in part) on the concepts of capital and capital maintenance adopted.

The elements of income and expense are therefore defined.

ey terms

> - **Income**. Increases in economic benefits during the accounting period in the form of inflows or enhancements of assets or decreases of liabilities that result in increases in equity, other than those relating to contributions from equity participants.
>
> - **Expenses**. Decreases in economic benefits during the accounting period in the form of outflows or depletions of assets or incurrences of liabilities that result in decreases in equity, other than those relating to distributions to equity participants.
>
> *(Framework)*

Income and expenses can be **presented in different ways** in the income statement, to provide information relevant for economic decision-making. For example, distinguish between income and expenses which relate to continuing operations and those which do not.

Items of income and expense can be **distinguished** from each other or **combined** with each other.

5.6 Income

Both **revenue** and **gains** are included in the definition of income. **Revenue** arises in the course of ordinary activities of an entity.

Key term

> **Gains**. Increases in economic benefits. As such they are no different in nature from revenue. *(Framework)*

Gains include those arising on the disposal of non-current assets. The definition of income also includes **unrealised gains**, eg on revaluation of marketable securities.

5.7 Expenses

As with income, the definition of expenses includes losses as well as those expenses that arise in the course of ordinary activities of an entity.

Key term

> **Losses**. Decreases in economic benefits. As such they are no different in nature from other expenses.
>
> *(Framework)*

Losses will include those arising on the disposal of non-current assets. The definition of expenses will also include **unrealised losses**, eg exchange rate effects on borrowings.

5.8 Capital maintenance adjustments

A **revaluation** gives rise to an increase or decrease in equity.

Key term

> **Revaluation**. Restatement of assets and liabilities. *(Framework)*

These increases and decreases meet the definitions of income and expenses. They are **not included** in the income statement under certain concepts of capital maintenance, however, but rather in equity (see Section 8).

5.9 Section summary

Make sure you learn the important definitions.

- **Financial position**:
    - Assets
    - Liabilities
    - Equity
- **Financial performance**:
    - Income
    - Expenses

6 Recognition of the elements of financial statements

As noted in Section 5, items which meet the definition of assets or liabilities may still not be recognised in financial statements because they must also meet certain **recognition criteria**.

Key term

Recognition. The process of incorporating in the balance sheet or income statement an item that meets the definition of an element and satisfies the following criteria for recognition:

(a)   it is probable that any future economic benefit associated with the item will flow to or from the entity; and

(b)   the item has a cost or value that can be measured with reliability.

(Framework)

Regard must be given to **materiality** (see Section 4 above).

6.1 Probability of future economic benefits

Probability here means the **degree of uncertainty** that the future economic benefits associated with an item will flow to or from the entity. This must be judged on the basis of the **characteristics of the entity's environment** and the **evidence available** when the financial statements are prepared.

6.2 Reliability of measurement

The cost or value of an item, in many cases, **must be estimated**. The *Framework* states, however, that the use of reasonable estimates is an essential part of the preparation of financial statements and does not undermine their reliability. Where no reasonable estimate can be made, the item should not be recognised, although its existence should be disclosed in the notes, or other explanatory material.

Items may still qualify for recognition **at a later date** due to changes in circumstances or subsequent events.

6.3 Recognition of items

We can summarise the recognition criteria for assets, liabilities, income and expenses, based on the definition of recognition given above.

Item	Recognised in	When
Asset	The balance sheet	It is probable that the future economic benefits will flow to the entity and the asset has a cost or value that can be measured reliably.
Liability	The balance sheet	It is probable that an outflow of resources embodying economic benefits will result from the settlement of a present obligation and the amount at which the settlement will take place can be measured reliably.
Income	The income statement	An increase in future economic benefits related to an increase in an asset or a decrease of a liability has arisen that can be measured reliably.
Expenses	The income statement	A decrease in future economic benefits related to a decrease in an asset or an increase of a liability has arisen that can be measured reliably.

7 Measurement of the elements of financial statements

Measurement is defined as follows.

Key term

> **Measurement**. The process of determining the monetary amounts at which the elements of the financial statements are to be recognised and carried in the balance sheet and income statement.   *(Framework)*

This involves the selection of a particular **basis of measurement**. A number of these are used to different degrees and in varying combinations in financial statements. They include the following.

Key terms

- **Historical cost**. Assets are recorded at the amount of cash or cash equivalents paid or the fair value of the consideration given to acquire them at the time of their acquisition. Liabilities are recorded at the amount of proceeds received in exchange for the obligation, or in some circumstances (for example, income taxes), at the amounts of cash or cash equivalents expected to be paid to satisfy the liability in the normal course of business.

- **Current cost**. Assets are carried at the amount of cash or cash equivalents that would have to be paid if the same or an equivalent asset was acquired currently.

  Liabilities are carried at the undiscounted amount of cash or cash equivalents that would be required to settle the obligation currently.

- **Realisable (settlement) value**.

  - **Realisable value**. The amount of cash or cash equivalents that could currently be obtained by selling an asset in an orderly disposal.

  - **Settlement value**. The undiscounted amounts of cash or cash equivalents expected to be paid to satisfy the liabilities in the normal course of business.

- **Present value**. A current estimate of the present discounted value of the future net cash flows in the normal course of business.   *(Framework)*

Historical cost is the most commonly adopted measurement basis, but this is usually combined with other bases, eg inventory is carried at the lower of cost and net realisable value.

8 Concepts of capital and capital maintenance

FAST FORWARD

> The concept of capital selected should be appropriate to the needs of the users of an entity's financial statements.

Most entities use a **financial concept of capital** when preparing their financial statements.

8.1 Concepts of capital maintenance and the determination of profit

First of all, we need to define the different concepts of capital. You should be familiar with them from the previous chapter.

Key term

> **Capital**. Under a financial concept of capital, such as invested money or invested purchasing power, capital is the net assets or equity of the entity. The financial concept of capital is adopted by most entities.
>
> Under a physical concept of capital, such as operating capability, capital is the productive capacity of the entity based on, for example, units of output per day.   *(Framework)*

The definition of profit is also important.

Key term

> **Profit**. The residual amount that remains after expenses (including capital maintenance adjustments, where appropriate) have been deducted from income. Any amount over and above that required to maintain the capital at the beginning of the period is profit.
>
> *(Framework)*

The main difference between the two concepts of capital maintenance is the treatment of the **effects of changes in the prices of assets and liabilities** of the entity. In general terms, an entity has maintained its capital if it has as much capital at the end of the period as it had at the beginning of the period. Any amount over and above that required to maintain the capital at the beginning of the period is profit.

   (a)   **Financial capital maintenance**: profit is the increase in nominal money capital over the period.

   (b)   **Physical capital maintenance**: profit is the increase in the physical productive capacity over the period.

Chapter roundup

- The IASB's *Framework* provides a **conceptual framework** for all IASs. It consists of several sections.

- The **objective of financial statements** is to meet the needs of users.

- Important **underlying assumptions** are the **accruals basis** and **going concern**.

- The important **qualitative characteristics** of financial statements are:

    - Understandability
    - Relevance
    - Reliability
    - Comparability

- The elements of financial statements can be broken down into:

    - **Financial position** (balance sheet): assets, liabilities, equity
    - **Financial performance** (income statement): income, expenses

- **Recognition criteria** are very important:

    - Probability of future economic benefits
    - Reliability of measurement

- **Measurement** of elements in financial statements involves selection of one/more of:

    - Historical cost
    - Current cost
    - Realisable (settlement) value
    - Present value

- The **concept of capital and capital maintenance** chosen for financial statements should suit the needs of the user. The choice is between two:

    - Financial capital maintenance
    - Physical capital maintenance

Quick quiz

1   Define a 'conceptual framework'.

2   What are the advantages and disadvantages of developing a conceptual framework?

3   The needs of which category of user are paramount when preparing financial statements?

4   Define 'relevance'.

5   In which two ways should users be able to compare an entity's financial statements?

6   A provision can be a liability. True or false?

7   Define 'recognition'.

8   The cost or value of items in the financial statements is never estimated. True or false?

9   What is the most common basis of measurement used in financial statements?

10 What are the main criticisms of the IASB's approach to a conceptual framework (rather than the document itself)?

Answers to quick quiz

1   This is a statement of generally accepted theoretical principles, which form the frame of reference for financial reporting.

2   *Advantages*

  •   Standardised accounting practice
  •   Less open to criticism
  •   Concentrate on income statement or balance sheet, as appropriate

  Disadvantages

  •   Variety of users, so not all will be satisfied
  •   Variety of standards for different purposes
  •   Preparing and implementing standards not necessarily any easier

3   Needs of investors

4   Information has relevance when it influences the economic decisions of users by helping them evaluate past, present or future events or confirming (or correcting) their past evaluations.

5   •   Through time to identify trends
  •   With other entities' statements

6   True. It satisfies the definition of a liability but the amount may need to be estimated.

7   See Key Term Section 6.

8   False. Monetary values are often estimated.

9   Historical cost.

10 •   Overall approach
  •   Definitions of assets and liabilities

Now try the question below from the Exam Question Bank

Number	Level	Marks	Time
Q21	Examination	25	45 mins

20

Substance of transactions

Topic list	Syllabus reference
1 Off balance sheet finance explained	3(f)
2 Substance over form	3(f)
3 The IASB *Framework*	3(f)
4 Common forms of off balance sheet finance	3(f)

Introduction

This is a very topical area and has been for some time. Companies (and other entities) have in the past used the **legal form** of a transaction to determine its accounting treatment, when in fact the **substance** of the transaction has been very different. We will look at the question of **substance over form** and the kind of transactions undertaken by entities trying to avoid reporting true substance in Sections 1 and 2.

The main weapon in tackling these abuses is the IASB's *Framework for the Preparation and Presentation of Financial Statements* because it applies **general definitions** to the elements that make up financial statements. We will look at how this works in Section 3.

Study guide

Section 17 – Accounting for the substance of transactions

- Explain the importance of recording the substance rather than the legal form of transactions – give examples of previous abuses in this area

- Describe the features which may indicate that the substance of transactions may differ from their legal form

- Explain and apply the principles of recognition and derecognition of assets and liabilities

- Be able to recognise the substance of transactions in general, and specifically account for the following types of transaction:
  - goods sold on sale or return/ consignment goods
  - sale and repurchase/leaseback agreements
  - factoring of accounts receivable

Exam guide

Although there is no IFRS on this subject comparable to the UK's FRS 5 *Reporting the substance of transactions,* the examiner is likely to set a question on this area as he sets both the UK and the international variants. This is borne out by the Pilot Paper.

1 Off balance sheet finance explained

Key term

> **Off balance sheet finance** is the funding or refinancing of a company's operations in such a way that, under legal requirements and traditional accounting conventions, some or all of the finance may not be shown on its balance sheet.

'Off balance sheet transactions' are transactions which meet the above objective. These transactions may involve the **removal of assets** from the balance sheet, as well as liabilities, and they are also likely to have a significant impact on the income statement.

1.1 Why off balance sheet finance exists

Why might company managers wish to enter into such transactions?

(a) In some countries, companies traditionally have a lower level of gearing than companies in other countries. Off balance sheet finance is used to **keep gearing low**, probably because of the views of analysts and brokers.

(b) A company may need to keep its gearing down in order to stay within the terms of **loan covenants** imposed by lenders.

(c) A quoted company with high borrowings is often expected (by analysts and others) to declare a **rights issue** in order to reduce gearing. This has an adverse effect on a company's share price and so off balance sheet financing is used to reduce gearing *and* the expectation of a rights issue.

(d) Analysts' short term views are a problem for companies **developing assets** which are not producing income during the development stage. Such companies will match the borrowings associated with such developing assets, along with the assets themselves, off balance sheet. They are brought back on balance sheet once income is being generated by the assets. This process keeps return on capital employed higher than it would have been during the development stage.

(e) In the past, groups of companies have excluded **subsidiaries** from consolidation in an off balance sheet transaction because they carry out completely different types of business and have different characteristics. The usual example is a leasing company (in say a retail group) which has a high level of gearing.

You can see from this brief list of reasons that the overriding motivation is to avoid **misinterpretation**. In other words, the company does not trust the analysts or other users to understand the reasons for a transaction and so avoids any effect such transactions might have by taking them off balance sheet. Unfortunately, the position of the company is then misstated and the user of the accounts is misled.

You must understand that not all forms of 'off balance sheet finance' are undertaken for cosmetic or accounting reasons. Some transactions are carried out to **limit or isolate risk**, to reduce interest costs and so on. In other words, these transactions are in the best interests of the company, not merely a cosmetic repackaging of figures which would normally appear in the balance sheet.

1.2 The off balance sheet finance problem

The result of the use of increasingly sophisticated off balance sheet finance transactions is a situation where the users of financial statements do not have a proper or clear view of the **state of the company's affairs**. The disclosures required by national company law and accounting standards did not in the past provide sufficient rules for disclosure of off balance sheet finance transactions and so very little of the true nature of the transaction was exposed.

Whatever the purpose of such transactions, **insufficient disclosure** creates a problem. This problem has been debated over the years by the accountancy profession and other interested parties and some progress has been made (see the later sections of this chapter). However, company collapses during recessions have often revealed much higher borrowings than originally thought, because part of the borrowing was off balance sheet.

The main argument used for banning off balance sheet finance is that the true **substance** of the transactions should be shown, not merely the **legal form**, particularly when it is exacerbated by poor disclosure.

2 Substance over form

> **Substance over form.** The principle that transactions and other events are accounted for and presented in accordance with their substance and economic reality and not merely their legal form. *(Framework)*

This is a very important concept. It is used to **determine accounting treatment** in financial statements through accounting standards and so prevent off balance sheet transactions. The following paragraphs give examples of where the principle of substance over form is enforced in various accounting standards.

2.1 IAS 17 *Leases*

In IAS 17, there is an explicit requirement that if the lessor transfers substantially all the **risks and rewards of ownership** to the lessee then, even though the legal title has not necessarily passed, the item being leased should be shown as an asset in the balance sheet of the lessee and the amount due to the lessor should be shown as a liability.

2.2 IAS 24 *Related party disclosures*

IAS 24 requires financial statements to disclose fully any material transactions undertaken with a related party by the reporting entity, **regardless of any price charged**.

2.3 IAS 11 *Construction contracts*

In IAS 11 there is a requirement to account for **attributable profits** on construction contracts under the accruals convention. However, there may be a problem with realisation, since it is arguable whether we should account for profit which, although attributable to the work done, may not have yet been invoiced to the customer. It is argued that the convention of substance over form is applied to justify ignoring the strict legal position.

2.4 IAS 27 *Consolidated and separate financial statements*

This is perhaps the most important area of off balance sheet finance which has been prevented by the application of the substance over form concept. The use of **quasi-subsidiaries** was very common in the 1980s. These may be defined as follows.

Key term

> A **quasi-subsidiary** of a reporting entity is a company, trust, partnership or other vehicle that, though not fulfilling the definition of a subsidiary, is directly or indirectly controlled by the reporting entity and gives rise to benefits for that entity that are in substance no different from those that would arise were the vehicle a subsidiary.

IAS 27 contains a definition of a subsidiary based on **control** rather than just ownership rights, thus substantially reducing the effectiveness of this method of off-balance sheet finance (see Chapter 15). IAS 27 defines control of another entity as:

Key term

> **Control** is the power to govern the financial and operating policies of an entity so as to obtain benefit from its activities.   *(IAS 27)*

The IAS goes on to state that control exists when:

    (a)   The parent has a **majority of the voting rights** in the subsidiary (possibly **by agreement** with other members), *or*

    (b)   The parent can appoint or remove a **majority of the board** of the subsidiary, *or*

    (c)   The parent can **direct the operating and financial policies** through a statute or agreement, *or*

    (d)   The parent can cast the **majority of votes** at a board meeting of directors (or equivalent).

The main effects of this definition on the use of quasi-subsidiaries were as follows.

    (a)   The use of 'voting rights' rather than 'equity shares' prevents the use of **company structures** which give the benefits of ownership to one class of shareholder without the appearance of doing so, eg a company has 100 'A' shares with 10 votes each and 900 'B' shares with one vote each.

    (b)   The right to appoint or remove a majority of the board now means those directors who control a majority of the voting rights at board meetings. This prevents control through **differential voting rights** at board meetings.

IAS 27 therefore **curtailed drastically** the use of quasi-subsidiaries for off balance sheet finance. More complex schemes are likely to be curtailed by the IASB's *Framework* and by various other standards (see below).

PROFESSIONAL EDUCATION

You may also hear the term **creative accounting** used in the context of reporting the substance of transactions. This can be defined simply as the manipulation of figures for a desired result. Remember, however, that it is very rare for a company, its directors or employees to manipulate results for the purpose of fraud. The major consideration is usually the effect the results will have on the company's share price. Some areas open to abuse (although some of these loopholes have been closed) are given below and you should by now understand how these can distort a company results.

(a)   Income recognition and cut-off

(b)   Impairment of purchased goodwill

(c)   Manipulation of reserves

(d)   Revaluations and depreciation

(e)   Window dressing

(f)   Changes in accounting policy

Exam focus point

> Articles on creative accounting appear fairly regularly in *Student Accountant*. Although often based on UK accounting, most of the points can be applied to international accounting.

Question   **Creative accounting**

Creative accounting, off balance sheet finance and related matters (in particular how ratio analysis can be used to discover these practices) often come up in articles in the financial press. Find a library, preferably a good technical library, which can provide you with copies of back issues of such newspapers or journals and look for articles on creative accounting.

3 The IASB *Framework*

As noted above, the IASB *Framework* states that accounting for items according to substance and economic reality and not merely legal form is a key determinant of reliable information.

(a)   For the majority of transactions there is **no difference** between the two and therefore no issue.

(b)   For other transactions **substance and form diverge** and the choice of treatment can give different results due to non-recognition of an asset or liability even though benefits or obligations result.

Full disclosure is not enough: all transactions must be **accounted for** correctly, with full disclosure of related details as necessary to give the user of accounts a full understanding of the transactions.

3.1 Relationship to IASs

The interaction of the *Framework* **with other standards** is also an important issue. Whichever rules are the more specific should be applied, given that IASs should be consistent with the *Framework*. Leasing provides a good example: straightforward leases which fall squarely within the terms of IAS 17 should be accounted for without any need to refer to the *Framework*, but where their terms are more complex, or the lease is only one element in a larger series of transactions, then the *Framework* comes into play. In addition, the *Framework* implicitly requires that its general principle of substance over form should apply in the application of other existing rules.

3.2 Basic principles

How else does the *Framework* enforce the substance over form rule? Its main method is to define the elements of financial statements and therefore to give rules for their recognition. The key considerations are whether a transaction has **given rise to new assets and liabilities**, and whether it has **changed any existing assets and liabilities**.

The characteristics of transactions whose substance is not readily apparent are as follows.

(a) The **legal title** to an item is separated from the ability to enjoy the principal benefits, and the exposure to the main risks associated with it.

(b) The transaction is **linked to one or more others** so that the commercial effect of the transaction cannot be understood without reference to the complete series.

(c) The transaction includes **one or more options**, under such terms that it makes it highly likely that the option(s) will be exercised.

3.3 Definitions

These are perhaps the most important definitions.

Key terms

> - An **asset** is a resource controlled by the entity as a result of past events and from which future economic benefits are expected to flow to the entity.
>
> - A **liability** is a present obligation of the entity arising from past events, the settlement of which is expected to result in an outflow from the entity of resources embodying economic benefits.
>
> *(Framework)*

Identification of **who has the risks** relating to an asset will generally indicate **who has the benefits** and hence **who has the asset**. If an entity is in certain circumstances unable to avoid an **outflow of benefits**, this will provide evidence that it has a liability.

The definitions given in the IASB *Framework* of income and expenses are not as important as those of assets and liabilities. This is because income and expenses are **described in terms of changes in assets and liabilities**, ie they are secondary definitions.

Key terms

> - **Income** is increases in economic benefits during the accounting period in the form of inflows or enhancements of assets or decreases of liabilities that result in increases in equity, other than those relating to contributions from equity participants.
>
> - **Expenses** are decreases in economic benefits during the accounting period in the form of outflows or depletions of assets or incurrences of liabilities that result in decreases in equity, other than those relating to distributions to equity participants.
>
> *(Framework)*

The real importance, then, is the way the *Framework* defines assets and liabilities. This forces entities to acknowledge their assets and liabilities regardless of the legal status.

It is not sufficient, however, that the asset or liability fulfils the above definitions; it must also satisfy **recognition criteria** in order to be shown in an entity's accounts.

3.4 Recognition

Recognition is the process of incorporating in the balance sheet or income statement an item that meets the definition of an element and satisfies the criteria for recognition set out below. It involves the depiction of the item in words and by a monetary amount and the inclusion of that amount in the balance sheet or income statement totals.

The next key question is deciding **when** something which satisfies the definition of an asset or liability has to be recognised in the balance sheet. Where a transaction results in an item that meets the definition of an asset or liability, that item should be recognised in the balance sheet if:

(a)   it is **probable that a future inflow or outflow** of benefit to or from the entity will occur, and

(b)   the item can be **measured at a monetary amount with sufficient reliability.**

This effectively prevents entities abusing the definitions of the elements by recognising items that are vague in terms of likelihood of occurrence and measurability. If this were not in force, entities could **manipulate the financial statements** in various ways, eg recognising assets when the likely future economic benefits cannot yet be determined.

Probability is assessed based on the situation at the balance sheet date. For example, it is usually expected that some customers of an entity will not pay what they owe. The expected level of non-payment is based on past experience and the receivables asset is reduced by a percentage (the general bad debt provision).

Measurement must be reliable, but it does not preclude the use of **reasonable estimates**, which is an essential part of the financial statement preparation.

Even if something does not qualify for recognition now, it may meet the criteria **at a later date**.

3.5 Other standards

The *Framework* provides the general guidance for reporting the substance of transactions and preventing off balance sheet finance. The IASB has developed guidance for specific transactions. These were mentioned in Section 2 and they are covered in various parts of this text. You should consider the particular off balance sheet finance problem they tackle as you study them.

- IAS 17 *Leases* (see Chapter 9)
- IAS 32 *Financial instruments* (see Chapter 8)
- IAS 27 *Consolidated and separate financial statements* (see Chapter 14)
- IAS 24 *Related party disclosures* (see Chapter 23)

3.6 Section summary

Important points to remember from the *Framework* are:

- **Substance over form**
- Definitions of **assets** and **liabilities**
- Definition of **recognition**
- **Criteria** for recognition

4 Common forms of off balance sheet finance

FAST FORWARD How does the theory of the *Framework* **apply in practice**, to real transactions? The rest of this section looks at some complex transactions that occur frequently in practice.

We will consider how the principles of the *Framework* would be applied to these transactions.

- Consignment inventory
- Sale and repurchase agreements
- Factoring of receivables/debts
- Securitised assets
- Loan transfers

Exam focus point

These examples are taken from a UK standard on reporting the substance of transactions, but that standard uses almost the same definitions for assets, liabilities, recognition, etc as the IASB *Framework*, and so these notes are applicable internationally. Note also that, in all the cases discussed, there may be situations somewhere between the two extremes given in each.

4.1 Consignment inventory

Consignment inventory is an arrangement where inventory is held by one party (say a distributor) but is owned by another party (for example a manufacturer or a finance company). Consignment inventory is common in the motor trade and is similar to goods sold on a 'sale or return' basis.

To identify the correct treatment, it is necessary to identify the point at which the distributor or dealer acquired the benefits of the asset (the inventory) rather than the point at which legal title was acquired. If the manufacturer has the right to require the return of the inventory, and if that right is likely to be exercised, then the inventory is *not* an asset of the dealer. If the dealer is rarely required to return the inventory, then this part of the transaction will have little commercial effect in practice and should be ignored for accounting purposes. The potential liability would need to be disclosed in the accounts.

4.1.1 Summary of indications of asset status

The following analysis summarises the range of possibilities in such a transaction.

Indications that the inventory is *not an asset* of the dealer at delivery	Indications that the inventory *is an asset* of the dealer at delivery
Manufacturer can require dealer to **return inventory** (or transfer inventory to another dealer) without compensation.	Manufacturer cannot require dealer to **return or transfer inventory**.
Penalty paid by the dealer to prevent returns/transfers of inventory at the manufacturer's request.	**Financial incentives** given to persuade dealer to transfer inventory at manufacturer's request.
Dealer has unfettered **right to return inventory** to the manufacturer without penalty and actually exercises the right in practice.	Dealer has **no right to return inventory** or is commercially compelled not to exercise its right of return.

Indications that the inventory is *not an asset* of the dealer at delivery	Indications that the inventory *is an asset* of the dealer at delivery
Manufacturer bears **obsolescence risk**, eg:	Dealer bears **obsolescence risk**, eg:
Inventory **transfer price** charged by manufacturer is based on manufacturer's list price at date of transfer of legal title.	Inventory **transfer price** charged by manufacturer is based on manufacturer's list price at date of delivery.
Manufacturer bears **slow movement risk**, eg: transfer price set independently of time for which dealer holds inventory, and there is no deposit.	Dealer bears **slow movement risk**, eg: (a) dealer is effectively charged interest as transfer price or other payments to manufacturer vary with time for which dealer holds inventory, or (b) dealer makes a substantial interest-free deposit that varies with the levels of inventory held.

4.1.2 Required accounting

The following apply where it is concluded that the inventory **is in substance an asset** of the dealer.

(a) The inventory should be recognised as such on the dealer's balance sheet, together with a corresponding liability to the manufacturer.

(b) Any deposit should be deducted from the liability and the excess classified as a trade payable.

Where it is concluded that the inventory is **not in substance an asset** of the dealer, the following apply.

(a) The inventory should not be included on the dealer's balance sheet until the transfer of risks and rewards has crystallised.

(b) Any deposit should be included under 'other receivables'.

Question   Recognition

Daley Motors Co owns a number of car dealerships throughout a geographical area. The terms of the arrangement between the dealerships and the manufacturer are as follows.

(a) Legal title passes when the cars are either used by Daley Co for demonstration purposes or sold to a third party.

(b) The dealer has the right to return vehicles to the manufacturer without penalty. (Daley Co has rarely exercised this right in the past.)

(c) The transfer price is based on the manufacturer's list price at the date of delivery.

(d) Daley Co makes a substantial interest-free deposit based on the number of cars held.

Should the asset and liability be recognised by Daley Co at the date of delivery?

Answer

(a) Legal form is irrelevant
(b) Yes: only because rarely exercised (otherwise 'no')
(c) Yes
(d) Yes: the dealership is effectively forgoing the interest which could be earned on the cash sum

4.2 Sale and repurchase agreements

These are arrangements under which the company sells an asset to another person on terms that allow the company to **repurchase the asset** in certain circumstances. A common example is the sale and repurchase of maturing whisky inventories. The key question is whether the transaction is a **straightforward sale**, or whether it is, in effect, a **secured loan**. It is necessary to look at the arrangement to determine who has the rights to the economic benefits that the asset generates, and the terms on which the asset is to be repurchased.

If the seller has the right to the benefits of the **use of the asset**, and the repurchase terms are such that the **repurchase is likely** to take place, the transaction should be accounted for as a **loan**.

4.2.1 Summary of indications of the sale of the asset

The following summary is helpful.

Indications of *sale* of original asset to buyer (nevertheless, the seller may retain a different asset)	Indications of *no sale* of original asset to buyer (secured loan)
	Sale price does not equal **market value** at date of sale.
No commitment for **seller to repurchase** asset, eg call option where there is a real possibility the option will fail to be exercised.	Commitment for **seller to repurchase** asset, eg: • put and call option with the same exercise price • either a put or a call option with no genuine commercial possibility that the option will fail to be exercised, or • seller requires asset back to use in its business, or asset is in effect the only source of seller's future sales
Risk of **changes in asset value** borne by buyer such that buyer does not receive solely a lender's return, eg both sale and repurchase price equal market value at date of sale/repurchase.	Risk of **changes in asset value** borne by seller such that buyer receives solely a lender's return, eg: • repurchase price equals sale price plus costs plus interest • original purchase price adjusted retrospectively to pass variations in the value of the asset to the seller • seller provides residual value guarantee to buyer or subordinated debt to protect buyer from falls in the value of the asset

Indications of *sale* of original asset to buyer (nevertheless, the seller may retain a different asset)	Indications of *no sale* of original asset to buyer (secured loan)
Nature of the asset is such that it will be used over the life of the agreement, and seller has no rights to **determine its use**. Seller has no rights to determine asset's development or future sale.	Seller retains right to **determine asset's use**, development or sale, or rights to profits therefrom.

4.2.2 Required accounting

Where the substance of the transaction is that of a **secured loan**:

(a)   The seller should continue to recognise the original asset and record the proceeds received from the buyer as a liability.

(b)   Interest, however designated, should be accrued.

(c)   The carrying amount of the asset should be reviewed for impairment and written down if necessary.

Where the transaction is a **sale and leaseback** under a finance lease, then no profit should be recognised on entering in to the arrangement and no adjustment made to the carrying value of the asset. As stated in IAS 17, this represents the substance of the transactions, namely the raising of finance secured on an asset that continues to be held and that is not disposed of.

Where the **seller has a new asset or liability** (eg merely a call option to repurchase the original asset), it should recognise or disclose that new asset or liability on a prudent basis in accordance with the provisions of IAS 37. In particular, the seller should recognise (and not merely disclose) a liability for any kind of unconditional obligation it has entered into. Where doubts exist regarding the amount of any gain or loss arising, full provision should be made for any expected loss; but recognition of any gain, to the extent that it is in doubt, should be deferred until it is realised.

Question	Recognition and sales proceeds

A construction company, Mecanto Co, agrees to sell to Hamlows Bank some of the land within its landbank. The terms of the sale are as follows.

(a)   The sales price is to be at open market value.

(b)   Mecanto Co has the right to develop the land on the basis that it will pay all the outgoings on the land plus an annual fee of 5% of the purchase price.

(c)   Mecanto has the option to buy back the land at any time within the next five years. The repurchase price is based on:

   (i)   original purchase price
   (ii)   expenses relating to the purchase
   (iii)   an interest charge of base rate + 2%
   (iv)   less amounts received from Mecanto by Hamlows

(d)   At the end of five years Hamlows Bank may offer the land for sale generally. Any shortfall on the proceeds relative to the agreed purchase price agreed with Mecanto has to be settled by Mecanto in cash.

Should the asset continue to be recognised by Mecanto Co and the sales proceeds treated as a loan?

Answer

(a) No: the sales price is as for an arm's length transaction.

(b) Yes: Mecanto has control over the asset.
Yes: Mecanto has to pay a fee based on cash received.

(c) Yes: interest is charged on the proceeds paid by Mecanto.
Yes: the repurchase price is based on the lender's return

(d) Yes: options ensure that Mecanto bears all the risk (both favourable and unfavourable) of changes in the market value of the land.

4.3 Factoring of receivables/debts

Where debts or receivables are factored, the original creditor **sells the debts to the factor**. The sales price may be fixed at the outset or may be adjusted later. It is also common for the factor to offer a credit facility that allows the seller to draw upon a proportion of the amounts owed.

In order to determine the correct accounting treatment it is necessary to consider whether the benefit of the debts has been passed on to the factor, or whether the factor is, in effect, providing a loan on the security of the receivable balances. If the seller has to **pay interest** on the difference between the amounts advanced to him and the amounts that the factor has received, and if the seller bears the **risks of non-payment** by the debtor, then the indications would be that the transaction is, in effect, a loan. Depending on the circumstances, either a linked presentation or separate presentation may be appropriate.

4.3.1 Summary of indications of appropriate treatment

The following is a summary of indicators of the appropriate treatment.

Indications the debts are *not an asset* of the seller	Indications that the debts are an *asset* of the seller
Transfer is for a **single non-returnable fixed sum**.	**Finance cost varies** with speed of collection of debts, eg: • by adjustment to consideration for original transfer, or • subsequent transfers priced to recover costs of earlier transfers.
There is **no recourse** to the seller for losses.	There is **full recourse** to the seller for losses.
Factor is paid **all amounts** received from the factored debts (and no more). Seller has no rights to further sums from the factor.	Seller is required to **repay** amounts received from the factor on or before a set date, regardless of timing or amounts of collections from debtors.

4.3.2 Required accounting

Where the seller has retained no significant benefits and risks relating to the debts and has no obligation to repay amounts received from the factors, the receivables should be removed from its balance sheet and no liability shown in respect of the proceeds received from the factor. A profit or loss should be recognised, calculated as the difference between the carrying amount of the debts and the proceeds received.

Where the seller does retain significant benefits and risks, a gross asset (equivalent in amount to the gross amount of the receivables) should be shown on the balance sheet of the seller within assets, and a corresponding liability in respect of the proceeds received from the factor should be shown within liabilities. The interest element of the factor's charges should be recognised as it accrues and included in the income statement with other interest charges. Other factoring costs should be similarly accrued and included in the income statement within the appropriate caption.

Chapter roundup

- The subject of **off balance sheet finance** is a complex one which has plagued the accountancy profession. In practice, off balance sheet finance schemes are often very sophisticated and these are beyond the range of this syllabus.

- Make sure that you have memorised the definitions for **assets and liabilities** (and income and expenses) and the criteria for their **recognition** given in the IASB's *Framework*.

- We have looked at some of the **major types** of off balance sheet finance, including factoring, sale and leaseback and securitisation.

Quick quiz

1   Why do companies want to use off balance sheet finance?

2   How does the *Framework* describe substance over form?

3   What is a quasi subsidiary?

4   What are the common features of transactions whose substance is not readily apparent?

5   When should a transaction be recognised?

Answers to quick quiz

1   The overriding motivation is to avoid misinterpretation. However the result is that users are misled.

2   The principle that transactions and other events are accounted for and presented in accordance with their substance and economic reality rather than merely their legal form.

3   An entity that does not fulfil the definition of a subsidiary but is directly or indirectly controlled by the reporting entity and gives rise to benefits that are in substance no different from those arising if it were a subsidiary.

4   (a)   The legal title is separated from the ability to enjoy benefits.

     (b)   The transaction is linked to others so that the commercial effect cannot be understood without reference to the complete series.

     (c)   The transaction includes one or more options under such terms that it is likely the option(s) will be exercised.

5   When it is probable that a future inflow or outflow of economic benefit to the entity will occur and the item can be measured in monetary terms with sufficient reliability.

Now try the question below from the Exam Question Bank

Number	Level	Marks	Time
Q22	Introductory	n/a	n/a

Part E
Analysing and interpreting financial and related information

Interpretation of financial statements

Topic list	Syllabus reference
1 The broad categories of ratio	5(a), (b)
2 Profitability and return on capital	5(a), (b)
3 Liquidity, gearing/leverage and working capital	5(a), (b)
4 Shareholders' investment ratios	5(a), (b)
5 Accounting policies and the limitations of ratio analysis	5(a), (b)
6 Presentation of financial performance	5(a), (b)

Introduction

You may remember some of the **basic interpretation of accounts** you studied for Paper 1.1. This chapter recaps and develops the calculation of ratios and covers more complex accounting relationships. More importantly, perhaps, this chapter looks at how ratios can be analysed, interpreted and how the results should be presented to management.

Study guide

Section 24 – Analysis and interpretation of financial statements

- Calculate useful financial ratios for single company or group financial statements
- Analyse and interpret ratios to give an assessment of a company's performance in comparison with:

    - a company's previous period's financial statements
    - another similar company for the same period
    - industry average ratios

- Discuss the effect that changes in accounting policies or the use of different accounting policies between companies can have on the ability to interpret performance
- Discuss how the interpretation of value information would differ to that of historical cost information
- Discuss the limitations in the use of ratio analysis for assessing corporate performance, outlining other information that may be of relevance.

1 The broad categories of ratio

FAST FORWARD ▶▶ Your syllabus requires you to **appraise and communicate** the position and prospects of a business based on given and prepared statements and ratios.

If you were to look at a balance sheet or income statement, how would you decide whether the company was doing well or badly? Or whether it was financially strong or financially vulnerable? And what would you be looking at in the figures to help you to make your judgement?

Ratio analysis involves **comparing one figure against another** to produce a ratio, and assessing whether the ratio indicates a weakness or strength in the company's affairs.

1.1 The broad categories of ratios

Broadly speaking, basic ratios can be grouped into five categories.

- Profitability and return
- Long-term solvency and stability
- Short-term solvency and liquidity
- Efficiency (turnover ratios)
- Shareholders' investment ratios

Within each heading we will identify a number of standard measures or ratios that are normally calculated and generally accepted as meaningful indicators. One must stress however that each individual business must be considered separately, and a ratio that is meaningful for a manufacturing company may be completely meaningless for a financial institution. **Try not to be too mechanical** when working out ratios and constantly think about what you are trying to achieve.

The key to obtaining meaningful information from ratio analysis is **comparison**. This may involve comparing ratios over time within the same business to establish whether things are improving or declining, and comparing ratios between similar businesses to see whether the company you are analysing is better or worse than average within its specific business sector.

It must be stressed that ratio analysis on its own is not sufficient for interpreting company accounts, and that there are **other items of information** which should be looked at, for example:

BPP
PROFESSIONAL EDUCATION

(a)   The content of any **accompanying commentary** on the accounts and other statements

(b)   The age and nature of the **company's assets**

(c)   **Current and future developments** in the company's markets, at home and overseas, recent acquisitions or disposals of a subsidiary by the company

(d)   **Unusual** items separately disclosed in the income statement

(e)   Any other **noticeable features** of the report and accounts, such as events after the balance sheet date, contingent liabilities, a qualified auditors' report, the company's taxation position, and so on

1.2 Example: calculating ratios

To illustrate the calculation of ratios, the following **draft** balance sheet and income statement figures will be used.

FURLONG CO INCOME STATEMENT
FOR THE YEAR ENDED 31 DECEMBER 20X8

	Notes	20X8 $	20X7 $
Revenue	1	3,095,576	1,909,051
Operating profit	1	359,501	244,229
Interest	2	17,371	19,127
Profit before taxation		342,130	225,102
Taxation		74,200	31,272
Profit after taxation		267,930	193,830
Dividend		41,000	16,800
Retained profit for the year		226,930	177,030
Earnings per share		12.8c	9.3c

FURLONG CO BALANCE SHEET
AS AT 31 DECEMBER 20X8

	Notes	20X8 $	20X8 $	20X7 $	20X7 $
Assets					
Non-current assets					
Tangible non-current assets			802,180		656,071
Current assets					
Inventory		64,422		86,550	
Receivables	3	1,002,701		853,441	
Cash at bank and in hand		1,327		68,363	
			1,068,450		1,008,354
Total assets			1,870,630		1,664,425
Equity and liabilities					
Equity					
Ordinary shares 10c each	5	210,000		210,000	
Share premium account		48,178		48,178	
Revenue reserve		630,721		393,791	
			888,899		651,969
Non-current liabilities					
10% loan stock 20X4/20Y0			100,000		100,000
Current liabilities	4		881,731		912,456
Total equity and liabilities			1,870,630		1,664,425

NOTES TO THE ACCOUNTS

		20X8 $	20X7 $
1	*Sales revenue and profit*		
	Sales revenue	3,095,576	1,909,051
	Cost of sales	2,402,609	1,441,950
	Gross profit	692,967	467,101
	Administration expenses	333,466	222,872
	Operating profit	359,501	244,229
	Depreciation charged	151,107	120,147
2	*Interest*		
	Payable on bank overdrafts and other loans	8,115	11,909
	Payable on loan stock	10,000	10,000
		18,115	21,909
	Receivable on short-term deposits	744	2,782
	Net payable	17,371	19,127
3	*Receivables*		
	Amounts falling due within one year		
	Trade receivables	884,559	760,252
	Prepayments and accrued income	97,022	45,729
		981,581	805,981
	Amounts falling due after more than one year		
	Trade receivables	21,120	47,460
	Total receivables	1,002,701	853,441
4	*Current liabilities*		
	Trade payables	627,018	545,340
	Accruals and deferred income	81,279	280,464
	Corporate taxes	108,000	37,200
	Other taxes	44,434	32,652
	Dividend	21,000	16,800
		881,731	912,456
5	*Called-up share capital*		
	Authorised ordinary shares of 10c each	1,000,000	1,000,000
	Issued and fully paid ordinary shares of 10c each	210,000	210,000

2 Profitability and return on capital

In our example, the company made a profit in both 20X8 and 20X7, and there was an increase in profit between one year and the next:

(a) Of 52% before taxation
(b) Of 39% after taxation

Profit before taxation is generally thought to be a better figure to use than profit after taxation, because there might be unusual variations in the tax charge from year to year which would not affect the underlying profitability of the company's operations.

Another profit figure that should be calculated is PBIT, **profit before interest and tax**. This is the amount of profit which the company earned before having to pay interest to the providers of loan capital. By providers of loan capital, we usually mean longer-term loan capital, such as debentures and medium-term bank loans, which will be shown in the balance sheet as non-current liabilities.

BPP
PROFESSIONAL EDUCATION

Formula to learn

> **Profit before interest and tax** is therefore:
>
> (a)   the profit on ordinary activities before taxation; **plus**
> (b)   interest charges on long-term loan capital.

Published accounts do not always give sufficient detail on interest payable to determine how much is interest on long-term finance. We will assume in our example that the whole of the interest payable ($18,115, note 2) relates to long-term finance.

PBIT in our example is therefore:

	20X8	20X7
	$	$
Profit on ordinary activities before tax	342,130	225,102
Interest payable	18,115	21,909
PBIT	360,245	247,011

This shows a 46% growth between 20X7 and 20X8.

2.1 Return on capital employed (ROCE)

It is impossible to assess profits or profit growth properly without relating them to the **amount of funds (capital) that were employed in making the profits**. The most important profitability ratio is therefore return on capital employed (ROCE), which states the profit as a percentage of the amount of capital employed.

Formula to learn

> $$\text{ROCE} = \frac{\text{Profit before interest and taxation}}{\text{Capital employed}} \times 100\%$$
>
> Capital employed = Shareholders' equity plus non-current liabilities
> (*or* total assets less current liabilities)

The underlying principle is that we must **compare like with like**, and so if capital means share capital and reserves plus non-current liabilities and debt capital, profit must mean the profit earned by all this capital together. This is PBIT, since interest is the return for loan capital.

In our example, capital employed = 20X8 $1,870,630 − $881,731 = $988,899
20X7 $1,664,425 − $912,456 = $751,969

These total figures are the total assets less current liabilities figures for 20X8 and 20X7 in the balance sheet.

		20X8	20X7
ROCE	=	$360,245	$247,011
		$988,899	$751,969
	=	36.4%	32.8%

What does a company's ROCE tell us? What should we be looking for? There are three comparisons that can be made.

(a)   The **change in ROCE from one year to the next** can be examined. In this example, there has been an increase in ROCE by about 4 percentage points from its 20X7 level.

(b)   The **ROCE being earned by other companies**, if this information is available, can be compared with the ROCE of this company. Here the information is not available.

(c)   A comparison of the ROCE with **current market borrowing rates** may be made.

(i)   What would be the cost of extra borrowing to the company if it needed more loans, and is it earning a ROCE that suggests it could make profits to make such borrowing worthwhile?

(ii)   Is the company making a ROCE which suggests that it is getting value for money from its current borrowing?

(iii)   Companies are in a risk business and commercial borrowing rates are a good independent yardstick against which company performance can be judged.

In this example, if we suppose that current market interest rates, say, for medium-term borrowing from banks, are around 10%, then the company's actual ROCE of 36% in 20X8 would not seem low. On the contrary, it might seem high.

However, it is easier to spot a low ROCE than a high one, because there is always a chance that the company's non-current assets, especially property, are **undervalued** in its balance sheet, and so the capital employed figure might be unrealistically low. If the company had earned a ROCE, not of 36%, but of, say only 6%, then its return would have been below current borrowing rates and so disappointingly low.

2.2 Return on equity (ROE)

Return on equity gives a more restricted view of capital than ROCE, but it is based on the same principles.

Formula to learn

$$ROE = \frac{\text{Profit after tax and preferred dividend}}{\text{Ordinary share capital and other equity}} \times 100\%$$

In our example, ROE is calculated as follows.

	20X8	20X7
ROE =	$\frac{\$267,930}{\$888,899} = 30.1\%$	$\frac{\$193,830}{\$651,969} = 29.7\%$

ROE is **not a widely-used ratio**, however, because there are more useful ratios that give an indication of the return to shareholders, such as earnings per share, dividend per share, dividend yield and earnings yield, which are described later.

2.3 Analysing profitability and return in more detail: the secondary ratios

We often sub-analyse ROCE, to find out more about why the ROCE is high or low, or better or worse than last year. There are two factors that contribute towards a return on capital employed, both related to sales revenue.

(a)   **Profit margin**. A company might make a high or low profit margin on its sales. For example, a company that makes a profit of 25c per $1 of sales is making a bigger return on its revenue than another company making a profit of only 10c per $1 of sales.

(b)   **Asset turnover**. Asset turnover is a measure of how well the assets of a business are being used to generate sales. For example, if two companies each have capital employed of $100,000 and Company A makes sales of $400,000 per annum whereas Company B makes sales of only $200,000 per annum, Company A is making a higher revenue from the same amount of assets (twice as much asset turnover as Company B) and this will help A to make a higher return on capital employed than B. Asset turnover is expressed as 'x times' so that assets generate x times their value in annual sales. Here, Company A's asset turnover is 4 times and B's is 2 times.

Profit margin and asset turnover together explain the ROCE and if the ROCE is the primary profitability ratio, these other two are the secondary ratios. The relationship between the three ratios can be shown mathematically.

Profit margin × Asset turnover = ROCE

$$\therefore \quad \frac{PBIT}{Sales} \times \frac{Sales}{Capital\ employed} = \frac{PBIT}{Capital\ employed}$$

In our example:

		Profit margin		Asset turnover		ROCE
(a)	20X8	$\dfrac{\$360,245}{\$3,095,576}$	×	$\dfrac{\$3,095,576}{\$988,899}$	=	$\dfrac{\$360,245}{\$988,899}$
		11.64%	×	3.13 times	=	36.4%
(b)	20X7	$\dfrac{\$247,011}{\$1,909,051}$	×	$\dfrac{\$1,909,051}{\$751,969}$	=	$\dfrac{\$247,011}{\$751,969}$
		12.94%	×	2.54 times	=	32.8%

In this example, the company's improvement in ROCE between 20X7 and 20X8 is attributable to a higher asset turnover. Indeed the profit margin has fallen a little, but the higher asset turnover has more than compensated for this.

It is also worth commenting on the change in sales revenue from one year to the next. You may already have noticed that Furlong achieved sales growth of over 60% from $1.9 million to $3.1 million between 20X7 and 20X8. This is very strong growth, and this is certainly one of the most significant items in the income statement and balance sheet.

2.3.1 A warning about comments on profit margin and asset turnover

It might be tempting to think that a high profit margin is good, and a low asset turnover means sluggish trading. In broad terms, this is so. But there is a trade-off between profit margin and asset turnover, and you cannot look at one without allowing for the other.

(a) A **high profit margin** means a high profit per $1 of sales, but if this also means that sales prices are high, there is a strong possibility that sales revenue will be depressed, and so asset turnover lower.

(b) A **high asset turnover** means that the company is generating a lot of sales, but to do this it might have to keep its prices down and so accept a low profit margin per $1 of sales.

Consider the following.

Company A		*Company B*	
Sales revenue	$1,000,000	Sales revenue	$4,000,000
Capital employed	$1,000,000	Capital employed	$1,000,000
PBIT	$200,000	PBIT	$200,000

These figures would give the following ratios.

ROCE	=	$\dfrac{\$200,000}{\$1,000,000}$	= 20%	ROCE	=	$\dfrac{\$200,000}{\$1,000,000}$	= 20%
Profit margin	=	$\dfrac{\$200,000}{\$1,000,000}$	= 20%	Profit margin	=	$\dfrac{\$200,000}{\$4,000,000}$	= 5%
Asset turnover	=	$\dfrac{\$1,000,000}{\$1,000,000}$	= 1	Asset turnover	=	$\dfrac{\$4,000,000}{\$1,000,000}$	= 4

The companies have the same ROCE, but it is arrived at in a very different fashion. Company A operates with a low asset turnover and a comparatively high profit margin whereas company B carries out much more business, but on a lower profit margin. Company A could be operating at the luxury end of the market, whilst company B is operating at the popular end of the market.

2.4 Gross profit margin, net profit margin and profit analysis

Depending on the format of the income statement, you may be able to calculate the gross profit margin as well as the net profit margin. **Looking at the two together** can be quite informative.

For example, suppose that a company has the following summarised income statement for two consecutive years.

	Year 1	Year 2
	$	$
Revenue	70,000	100,000
Cost of sales	42,000	55,000
Gross profit	28,000	45,000
Expenses	21,000	35,000
Net profit	7,000	10,000

Although the net profit margin is the same for both years at 10%, the gross profit margin is not.

In year 1 it is: $\dfrac{\$28,000}{\$70,000}$ = 40%

and in year 2 it is: $\dfrac{\$45,000}{\$100,000}$ = 45%

The improved gross profit margin has not led to an improvement in the net profit margin. This is because expenses as a percentage of sales have risen from 30% in year 1 to 35% in year 2.

3 Liquidity, gearing/leverage and working capital

3.1 Long-term solvency: debt and gearing ratios

Debt ratios are concerned with **how much the company owes in relation to its size**, whether it is getting into heavier debt or improving its situation, and whether its debt burden seems heavy or light.

    (a)   When a company is heavily in debt banks and other potential lenders may be unwilling to advance further funds.

    (b)   When a company is earning only a modest profit before interest and tax, and has a heavy debt burden, there will be very little profit left over for shareholders after the interest charges have been paid. And so if interest rates were to go up (on bank overdrafts and so on) or the company were to borrow even more, it might soon be incurring interest charges in excess of PBIT. This might eventually lead to the liquidation of the company.

These are two big reasons why companies should keep their debt burden under control. There are four ratios that are particularly worth looking at, the debt ratio, gearing ratio, interest cover and cash flow ratio.

3.2 Debt ratio

Formula to learn

> The **debt ratio** is the ratio of a company's total debts to its total assets.

    (a)   Assets consist of non-current assets at their balance sheet value, plus current assets.

(b)   Debts consist of all payables, whether they are due within one year or after more than one year.

You can ignore long-term provisions and liabilities, such as deferred taxation.

There is no absolute guide to the maximum safe debt ratio, but as a very general guide, you might regard 50% as a safe limit to debt. In practice, many companies operate successfully with a higher debt ratio than this, but 50% is nonetheless a helpful benchmark. In addition, if the debt ratio is over 50% and getting worse, the company's debt position will be worth looking at more carefully.

In the case of Furlong the debt ratio is as follows.

	20X8	*20X7*
Total debts	$ (881,731 + 100,000)	$ (912,456 + 100,000)
Total assets	$1,870,630	$1,664,425
	= 52%	= 61%

In this case, the debt ratio is quite high, mainly because of the large amount of current liabilities. However, the debt ratio has fallen from 61% to 52% between 20X7 and 20X8, and so the company appears to be improving its debt position.

3.3 Gearing/leverage

Capital gearing or leverage is concerned with a company's **long-term capital structure**. We can think of a company as consisting of non-current assets and net current assets (ie working capital, which is current assets minus current liabilities). These assets must be financed by long-term capital of the company, which is one of two things.

(a)   Issued share capital which can be divided into:

(i)   Ordinary shares plus other equity (eg reserves)
(ii)   Preferred shares

(b)   Long-term debt

Preferred share capital is not debt. It would usually not be included as debt in the debt ratio. However, like loan capital, preferred share capital has a prior claim over profits before interest and tax, ahead of ordinary shareholders. Preferred dividends must be paid out of profits before ordinary shareholders are entitled to an ordinary dividend, and so we refer to preferred share capital and loan capital as **prior charge capital**.

The **capital gearing ratio** is a measure of the proportion of a company's capital that is prior charge capital. It is measured as follows.

ormula to
earn

$$\text{Capital gearing} = \frac{\text{Total prior charge capital}}{\text{Shareholders' equity} + \text{total prior charge capital}} \times 100\%$$

As with the debt ratio, there is **no absolute limit** to what a gearing ratio ought to be. A company with a gearing ratio of more than 50% is said to be high-geared (whereas low gearing means a gearing ratio of less than 50%). Many companies are high geared, but if a high geared company is becoming increasingly high geared, it is likely to have difficulty in the future when it wants to borrow even more, unless it can also boost its shareholders' capital, either with retained profits or by a new share issue.

Leverage is an alternative term for gearing; the words have the same meaning. Note that leverage (or gearing) can be looked at conversely, by calculating the proportion of total assets financed by equity, and which may be called the equity to assets ratio. It is calculated as follows.

Formula to learn

$$\text{Equity to assets ratio} = \frac{\text{Shareholders' equity}}{\text{Shareholders' equity} + \text{total prior charge capital}} \times 100\%$$

or

$$\frac{\text{Shareholders' equity}}{\text{Total assets less current liabilities}}$$

In the example of Furlong, we find that the company, although having a high debt ratio because of its current liabilities, has a low gearing ratio. It has no preferred share capital and its only long-term debt is the 10% loan stock. The equity to assets ratio is therefore high.

		20X8	20X7
Gearing ratio	=	$\dfrac{\$100,000}{\$988,899}$	$\dfrac{\$100,000}{\$751,969}$
		= 10%	= 13%
Equity to assets ratio	=	$\dfrac{\$888,899}{\$988,899}$	$\dfrac{\$651,969}{\$751,969}$
		= 90%	= 87%

As you can see, the equity to assets ratio is the mirror image of gearing.

3.4 The implications of high or low gearing/leverage

We mentioned earlier that **gearing or leverage** is, amongst other things, an attempt to **quantify the degree of risk involved in holding equity shares in a company**, risk both in terms of the company's ability to remain in business and in terms of expected ordinary dividends from the company. The problem with a highly geared company is that by definition there is a lot of debt. Debt generally carries a fixed rate of interest (or fixed rate of dividend if in the form of preferred shares), hence there is a given (and large) amount to be paid out from profits to holders of debt before arriving at a residue available for distribution to the holders of equity. The riskiness will perhaps become clearer with the aid of an example.

	Company A	Company B	Company C
	$'000	$'000	$'000
Ordinary shares	600	400	300
Revenue reserves	200	200	200
Revaluation reserve	100	100	100
	900	700	600
6% preferred shares	-	-	100
10% loan stock	100	300	300
Capital employed	1,000	1,000	1,000
Gearing ratio	10%	30%	40%
Equity to assets ratio	90%	70%	60%

Now suppose that each company makes a profit before interest and tax of $50,000, and the rate of tax on company profits is 30%. Amounts available for distribution to equity shareholders will be as follows.

	Company A	Company B	Company C
	$'000	$'000	$'000
Profit before interest and tax	50	50	50
Interest	10	30	30
Taxable profit	40	20	20
Taxation at 30%	12	6	6
Profit after tax	28	14	14
Preferred dividend	–	–	6
Available for ordinary shareholders	28	14	8

If in the subsequent year profit before interest and tax falls to $40,000, the amounts available to ordinary shareholders will become as follows.

	Company A $'000	Company B $'000	Company C $'000
Profit before interest and tax	40	40	40
Interest	10	30	30
Taxable profit	30	10	10
Taxation at 30%	9	3	3
Profit after tax	21	7	7
Preferred dividend	–	–	6
Available for ordinary shareholders	21	7	1

Note the following.

Gearing ratio	10%	30%	40%
Equity to assets ratio	90%	70%	60%
Change in PBIT	– 20%	– 20%	– 20%
Change in profit available for ordinary shareholders	– 25%	– 50%	– 87.5%

The more highly geared the company, the greater the risk that little (if anything) will be available to distribute by way of dividend to the ordinary shareholders. The example clearly displays this fact in so far as the more highly geared the company, the greater the percentage change in profit available for ordinary shareholders for any given percentage change in profit before interest and tax. The relationship similarly holds when profits increase, and if PBIT had risen by 20% rather than fallen, you would find that once again the largest percentage change in profit available for ordinary shareholders (this means an increase) will be for the highly geared company. This means that there will be greater *volatility* of amounts available for ordinary shareholders, and presumably therefore greater volatility in dividends paid to those shareholders, where a company is highly geared. That is the risk: you may do extremely well or extremely badly without a particularly large movement in the PBIT of the company.

The risk of a company's ability to remain in business was referred to earlier. Gearing or leverage is relevant to this. A highly geared company has a large amount of interest to pay annually (assuming that the debt is external borrowing rather than preferred shares). If those borrowings are 'secured' in any way (and debentures in particular are secured), then the **holders of the debt are perfectly entitled to force the company** to **realise assets to pay their interest** if funds are not available from other sources. Clearly the more highly geared a company the more likely this is to occur when and if profits fall.

3.5 Interest cover

The interest cover ratio shows whether a company is earning enough profits before interest and tax to pay its interest costs comfortably, or whether its interest costs are high in relation to the size of its profits, so that a fall in PBIT would then have a significant effect on profits available for ordinary shareholders.

ɔrmula to
arn

$$\text{Interest cover} = \frac{\text{Profit before interest and tax}}{\text{Interest charges}}$$

An interest cover of 2 times or less would be low, and should really exceed 3 times before the company's interest costs are to be considered within acceptable limits.

Returning first to the example of Companies A, B and C, the interest cover was as follows.

		Company A	Company B	Company C
(a)	When PBIT was $50,000 =	$50,000	$50,000	$50,000
		$10,000	$30,000	$30,000
		5 times	1.67 times	1.67 times
(b)	When PBIT was $40,000 =	$40,000	$40,000	$40,000
		$10,000	$30,000	$30,000
		4 times	1.33 times	1.33 times

Note. Although preferred share capital is included as prior charge capital for the gearing ratio or leverage, it is usual to exclude preferred dividends from 'interest' charges. We also look at all interest payments, even interest charges on short-term debt, and so interest cover and gearing do not quite look at the same thing.

Both B and C have a low interest cover, which is a warning to ordinary shareholders that their profits are highly vulnerable, in percentage terms, to even small changes in PBIT.

Question
Interest cover

Returning to the example of Furlong in Paragraph 1.2, what is the company's interest cover?

Answer

Interest payments should be taken gross, from the note to the accounts, and not net of interest receipts as shown in the income statement.

	20X8	20X7
PBIT	360,245	247,011
Interest payable	18,115	21,909
	= 20 times	= 11 times

Furlong has more than sufficient interest cover. In view of the company's low gearing, this is not too surprising and so we finally obtain a picture of Furlong as a company that does not seem to have a debt problem, in spite of its high (although declining) debt ratio.

3.6 Cash flow ratio

The cash flow ratio is the ratio of a company's **net cash inflow to its total debts**.

(a) **Net cash inflow** is the amount of cash which the company has coming into the business from its operations. A suitable figure for net cash inflow can be obtained from the cash flow statement.

(b) **Total debts** are short-term and long-term payables, including provisions. A distinction can be made between debts payable within one year and other debts and provisions.

Obviously, a company needs to be earning enough cash from operations to be able to meet its foreseeable debts and future commitments, and the cash flow ratio, and changes in the cash flow ratio from one year to the next, provide a **useful indicator of a company's cash position**.

3.7 Short-term solvency and liquidity

Profitability is of course an important aspect of a company's performance and gearing or leverage is another. Neither, however, addresses directly the key issue of *liquidity*.

> **Liquidity** is the amount of cash a company can put its hands on quickly to settle its debts (and possibly to meet other unforeseen demands for cash payments too).

Liquid funds consist of:

(a) Cash

(b) Short-term investments for which there is a ready market

(c) Fixed-term deposits with a bank or other financial institution, for example, a six month high-interest deposit with a bank

(d) Trade receivables (because they will pay what they owe within a reasonably short period of time)

(e) Bills of exchange receivable (because like ordinary trade receivables, these represent amounts of cash due to be received within a relatively short period of time)

In summary, **liquid assets are current asset items that will or could soon be converted into cash, and cash itself.** Two common definitions of liquid assets are:

- All current assets without exception
- All current assets with the exception of inventories

A company can obtain liquid assets from sources other than sales of goods and services, such as the issue of shares for cash, a new loan or the sale of non-current assets. But a company cannot rely on these at all times, and in general, obtaining liquid funds depends on making sales revenue and profits. Even so, profits do not always lead to increases in liquidity. This is mainly because funds generated from trading may be immediately invested in non-current assets or paid out as dividends. You should refer back to the chapter on cash flow statements to examine this issue.

The reason why a company needs liquid assets is so that it can meet its debts when they fall due. Payments are continually made for operating expenses and other costs, and so there is a **cash cycle** from trading activities of cash coming in from sales and cash going out for expenses.

3.8 The cash cycle

To help you to understand liquidity ratios, it is useful to begin with a brief explanation of the cash cycle. The cash cycle describes **the flow of cash out of a business and back into it again as a result of normal trading operations.**

Cash goes out to pay for supplies, wages and salaries and other expenses, although payments can be delayed by taking some credit. A business might hold inventory for a while and then sell it. Cash will come back into the business from the sales, although customers might delay payment by themselves taking some credit.

The main points about the cash cycle are as follows.

(a) The timing of cash flows in and out of a business does not coincide with the time when sales and costs of sales occur. **Cash flows out can be postponed by taking credit. Cash flows in can be delayed by having receivables.**

(b) **The time between making a purchase and making a sale also affects cash flows.** If inventories are held for a long time, the delay between the cash payment for inventory and cash receipts from selling it will also be a long one.

(c) **Holding inventories and having receivables can therefore be seen as two reasons why cash receipts are delayed.** Another way of saying this is that if a company invests in working capital, its cash position will show a corresponding decrease.

(d) Similarly, **taking credit from creditors can be seen as a reason why cash payments are delayed**. The company's liquidity position will worsen when it has to pay the suppliers, unless it can get more cash in from sales and receivables in the meantime.

The liquidity ratios and working capital turnover ratios are used to test a company's liquidity, length of cash cycle, and investment in working capital.

3.9 Liquidity ratios: current ratio and quick ratio

The 'standard' test of liquidity is the **current ratio**. It can be obtained from the balance sheet.

Formula to learn

$$\text{Current ratio} = \frac{\text{Current assets}}{\text{Current liabilities}}$$

The idea behind this is that a company should have enough current assets that give a promise of 'cash to come' to meet its future commitments to pay off its current liabilities. Obviously, a **ratio in excess of 1 should be expected**. Otherwise, there would be the prospect that the company might be unable to pay its debts on time. In practice, a ratio comfortably in excess of 1 should be expected, but what is 'comfortable' varies between different types of businesses.

Companies are not able to convert all their current assets into cash very quickly. In particular, some manufacturing companies might hold large quantities of raw material inventories, which must be used in production to create finished goods inventory. These might be warehoused for a long time, or sold on lengthy credit. In such businesses, where inventory turnover is slow, most inventories are not very 'liquid' assets, because the cash cycle is so long. For these reasons, we calculate an additional liquidity ratio, known as the quick ratio or acid test ratio.

The **quick ratio**, or **acid test ratio**, is calculated as follows.

Formula to learn

$$\text{Quick ratio} = \frac{\text{Current assets less inventory}}{\text{Current liabilities}}$$

This ratio should ideally be **at least 1** for companies with a slow inventory turnover. For companies with a fast inventory turnover, a quick ratio can be comfortably less than 1 without suggesting that the company could be in cash flow trouble.

Both the current ratio and the quick ratio offer an indication of the company's liquidity position, but the absolute figures **should not be interpreted too literally**. It is often theorised that an acceptable current ratio is 1.5 and an acceptable quick ratio is 0.8, but these should only be used as a guide. Different businesses operate in very different ways. A supermarket group for example might have a current ratio of 0.52 and a quick ratio of 0.17. Supermarkets have low receivables (people do not buy groceries on credit), low cash (good cash management), medium inventories (high inventories but quick turnover, particularly in view of perishability) and very high payables.

Compare this with a manufacturing and retail organisation, with a current ratio of 1.44 and a quick ratio of 1.03. Such businesses operate with liquidity ratios closer to the standard.

What is important is the **trend** of these ratios. From this, one can easily ascertain whether liquidity is improving or deteriorating. If a supermarket has traded for the last 10 years (very successfully) with current ratios of 0.52 and quick ratios of 0.17 then it should be supposed that the company can continue in business with those levels of liquidity. If in the following year the current ratio were to fall to 0.38 and the quick ratio to 0.09, then further investigation into the liquidity situation would be appropriate. It is the relative position that is far more important than the absolute figures.

Don't forget the other side of the coin either. A current ratio and a quick ratio can get **bigger than they need to be**. A company that has large volumes of inventories and receivables might be over-investing in working capital, and so tying up more funds in the business than it needs to. This would suggest poor management of receivables (credit) or inventories by the company.

3.10 Efficiency ratios: control of receivables and inventories

A rough measure of the average length of time it takes for a company's customers to pay what they owe is the accounts receivable collection period.

Formula to learn

> The estimated average accounts receivable collection period is calculated as:
>
> $$\frac{\text{Trade receivables}}{\text{Sales}} \times 365 \text{ days}$$

The figure for sales should be taken as the sales revenue figure in the income statement. The trade receivables are not the total figure for receivables in the balance sheet, which includes prepayments and non-trade receivables. The trade receivables figure will be itemised in an analysis of the receivable total, in a note to the accounts.

The estimate of the accounts receivable collection period is **only approximate**.

(a) The balance sheet value of receivables might be abnormally high or low compared with the 'normal' level the company usually has.

(b) Sales revenue in the income statement is exclusive of sales taxes, but receivables in the balance sheet are inclusive of sales tax. We are not strictly comparing like with like.

Sales are usually made on 'normal credit terms' of payment within 30 days. A collection period significantly in excess of this might be representative of poor management of funds of a business. However, some companies must allow generous credit terms to win customers. Exporting companies in particular may have to carry large amounts of receivables, and so their average collection period might be well in excess of 30 days.

The **trend of the collection period over time** is probably the best guide. If the collection period is increasing year on year, this is indicative of a poorly managed credit control function (and potentially therefore a poorly managed company).

3.11 Accounts receivable collection period: examples

Using the same types of company as examples, the collection period for each of the companies was as follows.

Company	Trade receivables sales	Collection period (× 365)	Previous year	Collection period (× 365)
Supermarket	$\frac{\$5,016K}{\$284,986K} =$	6.4 days	$\frac{\$3,977K}{\$290,668K} =$	5.0 days
Manufacturer	$\frac{\$458.3m}{\$2,059.5m} =$	81.2 days	$\frac{\$272.4m}{\$1,274.2m} =$	78.0 days
Sugar refiner and seller	$\frac{\$304.4m}{\$3,817.3m} =$	29.3 days	$\frac{\$287.0m}{\$3,366.3m} =$	31.1 days

The differences in collection period reflect the differences between the types of business. Supermarkets have hardly any trade receivables at all, whereas the manufacturing companies have far more. The collection periods are fairly constant from the previous year for all three companies.

3.12 Inventory turnover period

Another ratio worth calculating is the inventory turnover period. This is another estimated figure, obtainable from published accounts, which indicates the average number of days that items of inventory are held for. As with the average receivable collection period, however, it is only an approximate estimated figure, but one which should be reliable enough for comparing changes year on year.

Formula to learn

> The inventory turnover period is calculated as:
>
> $$\frac{\text{Inventory}}{\text{Cost of sales}} \times 365 \text{ days}$$

This is another measure of how vigorously a business is trading. A lengthening inventory turnover period from one year to the next indicates:

(a)   a slowdown in trading; or

(b)   a build-up in inventory levels, perhaps suggesting that the investment in inventories is becoming excessive.

Generally the **higher the inventory turnover the better**, ie the lower the turnover period the better, but several aspects of inventory holding policy have to be balanced.

(a)   Lead times
(b)   Seasonal fluctuations in orders
(c)   Alternative uses of warehouse space
(d)   Bulk buying discounts
(e)   Likelihood of inventory perishing or becoming obsolete

Presumably if we add together the inventory turnover period and receivables collection period, this should give us an indication of how soon inventory is converted into cash. Both receivables collection period and inventory turnover period therefore give us a further indication of the company's liquidity.

3.13 Inventory turnover period: example

The estimated inventory turnover periods for a supermarket are as follows.

Company	$\dfrac{\text{Inventory}}{\text{Cost of sales}}$	Inventory turnover period (days × 365)	Previous year		
Supermarket	$\dfrac{\$15,554K}{\$254,571K}$	22.3 days	$\dfrac{\$14,094K}{\$261,368K}$	× 365	= 19.7 days

3.14 Accounts payable payment period

Formula to learn

> **Accounts payable payment period** is ideally calculated by the formula:
>
> $$\frac{\text{Trade accounts payable}}{\text{Purchases}} \times 365 \text{ days}$$

It is rare to find purchases disclosed in published accounts and so **cost of sales serves as an approximation**. The payment period often helps to assess a company's liquidity; an increase is often a sign of lack of long-term finance or poor management of current assets, resulting in the use of extended credit from suppliers, increased bank overdraft and so on.

Question

Calculate liquidity and working capital ratios from the accounts of TEB Co, a business which provides service support (cleaning etc) to customers worldwide. Comment on the results of your calculations.

	20X7 $m	20X6 $m
Sales revenue	2,176.2	2,344.8
Cost of sales	1,659.0	1,731.5
Gross profit	517.2	613.3
Current assets		
Inventories	42.7	78.0
Receivables (note 1)	378.9	431.4
Short-term deposits and cash	205.2	145.0
	626.8	654.4
Current liabilities		
Loans and overdrafts	32.4	81.1
Tax on profits	67.8	76.7
Dividend	11.7	17.2
Payables (note 2)	487.2	467.2
	599.1	642.2
Net current assets	27.7	12.2
Notes		
1 Trade receivables	295.2	335.5
2 Trade payables	190.8	188.1

Answer

	20X7	20X6
Current ratio	$\frac{626.8}{599.1} = 1.05$	$\frac{654.4}{642.2} = 1.02$
Quick ratio	$\frac{584.1}{599.1} = 0.97$	$\frac{576.4}{642.2} = 0.90$
Accounts receivable collection period	$\frac{295.2}{2,176.2} \times 365 = 49.5$ days	$\frac{335.5}{2,344.8} \times 365 = 52.2$ days
Inventory turnover period	$\frac{42.7}{1,659.0} \times 365 = 9.4$ days	$\frac{78.0}{1,731.5} \times 365 = 16.4$ days
Accounts payable payment period	$\frac{190.8}{1,659.0} \times 365 = 42.0$ days	$\frac{188.1}{1,731.5} \times 365 = 40.0$ days

The company's current ratio is a little lower than average but its quick ratio is better than average and very little less than the current ratio. This suggests that inventory levels are strictly controlled, which is reinforced by the low inventory turnover period. It would seem that working capital is tightly managed, to avoid the poor liquidity which could be caused by a long receivables collection period and comparatively high payables.

The company in the exercise is a service company and hence it would be expected to have very low inventory and a very short inventory turnover period. The similarity of receivables collection period and payables payment period means that the company is passing on most of the delay in receiving payment to its suppliers.

Question

(a) Calculate the operating cycle for Moribund plc for 20X2 on the basis of the following information.

		$
Inventory:	raw materials	150,000
	work in progress	60,000
	finished goods	200,000
Purchases		500,000
Trade accounts receivable		230,000
Trade accounts payable		120,000
Sales		900,000
Cost of goods sold		750,000

Tutorial note. You will need to calculate inventory turnover periods (total year end inventory over cost of goods sold), receivables as daily sales, and payables in relation to purchases, all converted into 'days'.

(b) List the steps which might be taken in order to improve the operating cycle.

Answer

(a) The operating cycle can be found as follows.

Inventory turnover period: $\dfrac{\text{Total closing inventory} \times 365}{\text{Cost of goods sold}}$

plus

Accounts receivable collection period: $\dfrac{\text{Closing trade receivables} \times 365}{\text{Sales}}$

less

Accounts payable payment period: $\dfrac{\text{Closing trade payables} \times 365}{\text{Purchases}}$

	20X2
Total closing inventory ($)	410,000
Cost of goods sold ($)	750,000
Inventory turnover period	199.5 days
Closing receivables ($)	230,000
Sales ($)	900,000
Receivables collection period	93.3 days
Closing payables ($)	120,000
Purchases ($)	500,000
Payables payment period	(87.6 days)
Length of operating cycle (199.5 + 93.3 – 87.6)	205.2 days

(b) The steps that could be taken to reduce the operating cycle include the following.

(i) Reducing the raw material inventory turnover period.

(ii) Reducing the time taken to produce goods. However, the company must ensure that quality is not sacrificed as a result of speeding up the production process.

(iii) Increasing the period of credit taken from suppliers. The credit period already seems very long – the company is allowed three months credit by its suppliers, and probably could not be increased. If the credit period is extended then the company may lose discounts for prompt payment.

(iv) Reducing the finished goods inventory turnover period.

(v)   Reducing the receivables collection period. The administrative costs of speeding up debt collection and the effect on sales of reducing the credit period allowed must be evaluated. However, the credit period does already seem very long by the standards of most industries. It may be that generous terms have been allowed to secure large contracts and little will be able to be done about this in the short term.

4 Shareholders' investment ratios

These are the ratios which help equity shareholders and other investors to **assess the value and quality of an investment in the ordinary shares of a company.**

They are:

(a)   Earnings per share
(b)   Dividend per share
(c)   Dividend cover
(d)   P/E ratio
(e)   Dividend yield

The value of an investment in ordinary shares in a company **listed on a stock exchange** is its market value, and so investment ratios must have regard not only to information in the company's published accounts, but also to the current price, and the fourth and fifth ratios involve using the share price.

4.1 Earnings per share

It is possible to calculate the return on each ordinary share in the year. This is the earnings per share (EPS). Earnings per share is the amount of net profit for the period that is attributable to each ordinary share which is outstanding during all or part of the period (see Chapter 13).

4.2 Dividend per share and dividend cover

The **dividend per share** in cents is self-explanatory, and clearly an item of some interest to shareholders.

ormula to
earn

Dividend cover is a ratio of: $\dfrac{\text{Earnings per share}}{\text{Dividend per (ordinary) share}}$

It shows the **proportion of profit for the year that is available for distribution to shareholders that has been paid (or proposed) and what proportion will be retained in the business to finance future growth.** A dividend cover of 2 times would indicate that the company had paid 50% of its distributable profits as dividends, and retained 50% in the business to help to finance future operations. Retained profits are an important source of funds for most companies, and so the dividend cover can in some cases be quite high.

A **significant change** in the dividend cover from one year to the next would be worth looking at closely. For example, if a company's dividend cover were to fall sharply between one year and the next, it could be that its profits had fallen, but the directors wished to pay at least the same amount of dividends as in the previous year, so as to keep shareholder expectations satisfied.

4.3 P/E ratio

Formula to learn

> The **Price/Earnings (P/E) ratio** is the ratio of a company's current share price to the earnings per share.

A high P/E ratio indicates strong shareholder **confidence** in the company and its future, eg in profit growth, and a lower P/E ratio indicates lower confidence.

The P/E ratio of one company can be compared with the P/E ratios of:

- Other companies in the same business sector
- Other companies generally

It is often used in **stock exchange reporting** where prices are readily available.

4.4 Dividend yield

Dividend yield is the return a shareholder is currently expecting on the shares of a company.

Formula to learn

$$\text{Dividend yield} = \frac{\text{Dividend on the share for the year}}{\text{Current market value of the share (ex div)}} \times 100\%$$

(a)   The dividend per share is taken as the dividend for the previous year.
(b)   Ex-div means that the share price does *not* include the right to the most recent dividend.

Shareholders look for **both dividend yield and capital growth**. Obviously, dividend yield is therefore an important aspect of a share's performance.

Question	Dividend yield

In the year to 30 September 20X8, an advertising agency declares an interim ordinary dividend of 7.4c per share and a final ordinary dividend of 8.6c per share. Assuming an ex div share price of 315 cents, what is the dividend yield?

Answer

The total dividend per share is (7.4 + 8.6) = 16 cents

$$\frac{16}{315} \times 100 = 5.1\%$$

5 Accounting policies and the limitations of ratio analysis

FAST FORWARD

> We discussed the disclosure of accounting policies in our examination of IAS 1. The choice of accounting policy and the effect of its implementation are almost as important as its disclosure in that the results of a company can be altered significantly by the choice of accounting policy.

5.1 The effect of choice of accounting policies

Where accounting standards allow alternative treatment of items in the accounts, then the accounting policy note should declare which policy has been chosen. It should then be applied consistently.

You should be able to think of examples of how the choice of accounting policy can affect the financial statements eg whether to revalue property in IAS 16, or whether to capitalise the cost of interest in self-constructed assets in IAS 23.

5.2 Changes in accounting policy

The effect of a change of accounting policy is treated as a prior year adjustment according to IAS 8 (see Chapter 12). This just means that the comparative figures are adjusted for the change in accounting policy for comparative purposes and an adjustment is put through reserves.

Under **consistency of presentation** in IAS 1, any change in policy may only be made if it can be justified on the grounds that the new policy is preferable to the one it replaces because it will give a fairer presentation of the result and of the financial position of a reporting entity.

The problem with this situation is that the directors may be able to **manipulate the results** through change(s) of accounting policies. This would be done to avoid the effect of an old accounting policy or gain the effect of a new one. It is likely to be done in a sensitive period, perhaps when the company's profits are low or the company is about to announce a rights issue. The management would have to convince the auditors that the new policy was much better, but it is not difficult to produce reasons in such cases.

The effect of such a change is very **short-term**. Most analysts and sophisticated users will discount its effect immediately, except to the extent that it will affect any dividend (because of the effect on distributable profits). It may help to avoid breaches of banking covenants because of the effect on certain ratios.

Obviously, the accounting policy for any item in the accounts could only be changed once in quite a long period of time. Auditors would not allow another change, even back to the old policy, unless there was a wholly exceptional reason.

The managers of a company can choose accounting policies **initially** to suit the company or the type of results they want to get. Any changes in accounting policy must be justified, but some managers might try to change accounting policies just to manipulate the results.

5.3 Limitations of ratio analysis

The consideration of how accounting policies may be used to manipulate company results leads us to some of the other limitations of ratio analysis. These can be summarised as follows.

(a) Availability of comparable information.
(b) Use of historical/out of date information.
(c) Ratios are not definitive – they are only a guide.
(d) Interpretation needs careful analysis and should not be considered in isolation.
(e) It is a subjective exercise.
(f) It can be subject to manipulation.
(g) Ratios are not defined in standard form.

In the exam, always bear these points in mind; you may even be asked to discuss such limitations, but in any case they should have an impact on your analysis of a set of results.

6 Presentation of financial performance

Exam focus
point

> Examination questions on financial performance may try to simulate a real life situation. A set of accounts could be presented and you may be asked to prepare a report on them, addressed to a specific interested party, such as a bank.

You should begin your report with a heading showing who it is from, the name of the addressee, the subject of the report and a suitable date.

A good approach is often to head up a **'schedule of ratios and statistics'** which will form an appendix to the main report. Calculate the ratios in a logical sequence, dealing in turn with operating and profitability ratios, use of assets (eg turnover period for inventories, collection period for receivables), liquidity and gearing/leverage.

As you calculate the ratios you are likely to be struck by **significant fluctuations and trends**. These will form the basis of your comments in the body of the report. The report should begin with some introductory comments, setting out the scope of your analysis and mentioning that detailed figures have been included in an appendix. You should then go on to present your analysis under any categories called for by the question (eg separate sections for management, shareholders and creditors, or separate sections for profitability and liquidity).

Finally, look out for opportunities to **suggest remedial action** where trends appear to be unfavourable. Questions sometimes require you specifically to set out your advice and recommendations.

6.1 Planning your answers

This is as good a place as any to stress the importance of planning your answers. This is particularly important for 'wordy' questions. While you may feel like breathing a sigh of relief after all that number crunching, you should not be tempted to 'waffle'. The best way to avoid going off the point is to **prepare an answer plan**. This has the advantage of making you think before you write and structure your answer logically.

The following approach may be adopted when preparing an answer plan.

    (a)   Read the question **requirements**.

    (b)   **Skim through the question** to see roughly what it is about.

    (c)   Read through the question carefully, **underlining any key words**.

    (d)   Set out the **headings** for the main parts of your answer. Leave space to insert points within the headings.

    (e)   **Jot down points** to make within the main sections, underlining points on which you wish to expand.

    (f)   Write your **full answer**.

You should allow yourself the full time allocation for written answers, that is 1.8 minutes per mark. If, however, you run out of time, a clear answer plan with points in note form will earn you more marks than an introductory paragraph written out in full.

Question   Ratios

The following information has been extracted from the recently published accounts of DG.

EXTRACTS FROM THE INCOME STATEMENTS TO 30 APRIL

	20X9	20X8
	$'000	$'000
Sales	11,200	9,750
Cost of sales	8,460	6,825
Net profit before tax	465	320
This is after charging:		
Depreciation	360	280
Debenture interest	80	60
Interest on bank overdraft	15	9
Audit fees	12	10

BALANCE SHEETS AS AT 30 APRIL

	20X9		20X8	
	$'000	$'000	$'000	$'000
Assets				
Non-current assets		1,850		1,430
Current assets				
Inventory	640		490	
Receivables	1,230		1,080	
Cash	80		120	
		1,950		1,690
Total assets		3,800		3,120
Equity and liabilities				
Equity				
Ordinary share capital	800		800	
Reserves	1,245		875	
		2,045		1,675
Non-current liabilities				
10% debentures		800		600
Current liabilities				
Bank overdraft	110		80	
Payables	750		690	
Taxation	30		20	
Dividends	65		55	
		955		845
Total equity and liabilities		3,800		3,120

The following ratios are those calculated for DG, based on its published accounts for the previous year, and also the latest industry average ratios:

	DG 30 April 20X8	Industry average
ROCE (capital employed = equity and debentures)	16.70%	18.50%
Profit/sales	3.90%	4.73%
Asset turnover	4.29	3.91
Current ratio	2.00	1.90
Quick ratio	1.42	1.27
Gross profit margin	30.00%	35.23%
Accounts receivable collection period	40 days	52 days
Accounts payable payment period	37 days	49 days
Inventory turnover (times)	13.90	18.30
Gearing	26.37%	32.71%

Required

(a) Calculate comparable ratios (to two decimal places where appropriate) for DG for the year ended 30 April 20X9. All calculations must be clearly shown.

(b) Write a report to your board of directors analysing the performance of DG, comparing the results against the previous year and against the industry average.

Answer

(a)

	20X8	20X9	Industry average
ROCE	$\frac{320+60}{2,275}=16.70\%$	$\frac{465+80}{2,845}=19.16\%$	18.50%
Profit/sales	$\frac{320+60}{9,750}=3.90\%$	$\frac{465+80}{11,200}=4.87\%$	4.73%
Asset turnover	$\frac{9,750}{2,275}=4.29\text{x}$	$\frac{11,200}{2,845}=3.94\text{x}$	3.91x
Current ratio	$\frac{1,690}{845}=2.00$	$\frac{1,950}{955}=2.04$	1.90
Quick ratio	$\frac{1,080+120}{845}=1.42$	$\frac{1,230+80}{955}=1.37$	1.27
Gross profit margin	$\frac{9,750-6,825}{9,750}=30.00\%$	$\frac{11,200-8,460}{11,200}=24.46\%$	35.23%
Accounts receivable collection period	$\frac{1,080}{9,750}\times365=40\text{days}$	$\frac{1,230}{11,200}\times365=40\text{days}$	52 days
Accounts payable payment period	$\frac{690}{6,825}\times365=37\text{days}$	$\frac{750}{8,460}\times365=32\text{days}$	49 days
Inventory Turnover (times)	$\frac{6,825}{490}=13.9\text{x}$	$\frac{8,460}{640}=13.2\text{x}$	18.30x
Gearing	$\frac{600}{2,275}=26.37\%$	$\frac{800}{2,845}=28.12\%$	32.71%

(b) (i) REPORT

To: Board of Directors
From: Accountant
Subject: Analysis of performance of DG

Date: xx/xx/xx

This report should be read in conjunction with the appendix attached which shows the relevant ratios (from part (a)).

Trading and profitability

Return on capital employed has improved considerably between 20X8 and 20X9 and is now higher than the industry average.

Net income as a proportion of sales has also improved noticeably between the years and is also now marginally ahead of the industry average. Gross margin, however, is considerably lower than in the previous year and is only some 70% of the industry average. This suggests either that there has been a change in the cost structure of DG or that there has been a change in the method of cost allocation between the periods. Either way, this is a marked change that requires investigation. The company may be in a period of transition as sales have increased by nearly 15% over the year and it would appear that new non-current assets have been purchased.

Asset turnover has declined between the periods although the 20X9 figure is in line with the industry average. This reduction might indicate that the efficiency with which assets are used has deteriorated or it might indicate that the assets acquired in 20X9 have not yet fully contributed to the business. A longer term trend would clarify the picture.

(ii)   Liquidity and working capital management

The current ratio has improved slightly over the year and is marginally higher than the industry average. It is also in line with what is generally regarded as satisfactory (2:1).

The quick ratio has declined marginally but is still better than the industry average. This suggests that DG has no short term liquidity problems and should have no difficulty in paying its debts as they become due.

Receivables as a proportion of sales is unchanged from 20X8 and are considerably lower than the industry average. Consequently, there is probably little opportunity to reduce this further and there may be pressure in the future from customers to increase the period of credit given. The period of credit taken from suppliers has fallen from 37 days' purchases to 32 days' and is much lower than the industry average; thus, it may be possible to finance any additional receivables by negotiating better credit terms from suppliers.

Inventory turnover has fallen slightly and is much slower than the industry average and this may partly reflect stocking up ahead of a significant increase in sales. Alternatively, there is some danger that the inventory could contain certain obsolete items that may require writing off. The relative increase in the level of inventory has been financed by an increased overdraft which may reduce if the inventory levels can be brought down.

The high levels of inventory, overdraft and receivables compared to that of payables suggests a labour intensive company or one where considerable value is added to bought-in products.

(iii)   Gearing

The level of gearing has increased only slightly over the year and is below the industry average. Since the return on capital employed is nearly twice the rate of interest on the debentures, profitability is likely to be increased by a modest increase in the level of gearing.

Signed: Accountant

Chapter roundup

- This lengthy chapter has gone into quite a lot of detail about basic ratio analysis. The ratios you should be able to calculate and/or comment on are as follows.

    - **Profitability ratios**

        - Return on capital employed
        - Net profit as a percentage of sales
        - Asset turnover ratio
        - Gross profit as a percentage of sales

    - **Debt and gearing/leverage ratios**

        - Debt ratio
        - Gearing ratio/leverage
        - Interest cover
        - Cash flow ratio

    - **Liquidity and working capital ratios**

        - Current ratio
        - Quick ratio (acid test ratio)
        - Accounts receivable collection period
        - Accounts payable payment period
        - Inventory turnover period

    - **Ordinary shareholders' investment ratios**

        - Earnings per share
        - Dividend cover
        - P/E ratio
        - Dividend yield

- With the exception of the last two ratios, where the share's market price is required, all of these ratios **can be calculated from information in a company's published accounts.**

- Ratios provide information through **comparison**.

    - **Trends** in a company's ratios from **one year to the next**, indicating an improving or worsening position.

    - In some cases, **against a 'norm' or 'standard'**.

    - In some cases, **against the ratios of other companies**, although differences between one company and another should often be expected.

- You must realise that, however many ratios you can find to calculate, **numbers alone will not answer a question**. You *must* interpret all the information available to you and support your interpretation with ratio calculations.

Quick quiz

1   List the main categories of ratio.

2   Brainstorm a list of sources of information which would be useful in interpreting a company's accounts.

3   ROCE is $\dfrac{\text{Profit before interest and tax}}{\text{Capital employed}} \times 100\%$

   True ☐

   False ☐

4   Company Q has a profit margin of 7%. Briefly comment on this.

5   The debt ratio is a company's long-term debt divided by its net assets.

   True ☐

   False ☐

6   The cash flow ratio is the ratio of:

   A   Gross cash inflow to total debt
   B   Gross cash inflow to net debt
   C   Net cash inflow to total debt
   D   Net cash inflow to net debt

7   List the formulae for:

   (a)   Current ratio   (c)   Accounts receivable collection period
   (b)   Quick ratio   (d)   Inventory turnover period

8   List six limitations to ratio analysis.

Answers to quick quiz

1   See Section 1.1.

2   There are a number of sources (see Section 1.1). Information on competitors and the economic climate are further items of information.

3   True

4   You should be careful here. You have very little information. This is a low margin but you need to know what industry the company operates in. 7% may be good for a major retailer.

5   False (see Section 3.1)

6   C (see Section 3.6)

7   See Sections 3.9, 3.10 and 3.12.

8   Compare your list to that in paragraph 5.3.

Now try the questions below from the Exam Question Bank

Number	Level	Marks	Time
Q23	Examination	25	45 mins
Q24	Examination	25	45 mins

Cash flow statements

Topic list	Syllabus reference
1 IAS 7 *Cash flow statements*	5(c)
2 Preparing a cash flow statement	5(c)
3 Interpretation of cash flow statements	5(c)

Introduction

You have already covered much of the material on cash flow statements in your earlier studies. Much of this is repeated here for revision. You will tackle group cash flow statements only when you reach Paper 3.6.

The importance of the distinction between cash and profit and the scant attention paid to this by the income statement has resulted in the development of cash flow statements.

This chapter adopts a systematic approach to the preparation of cash flow statements in examinations; you should learn this method and you will then be equipped for any problems in the exam itself.

The third section of the chapter looks at the information which is provided by cash flow statements and how it should be analysed.

Study guide

Sections 25 and 26 – Cash flow statements

- Prepare a cash flow statement, including relevant notes, for an individual company in accordance with relevant accounting standards. (*Note.* Questions may specify the use of the direct or the indirect method)

- Appraise the usefulness of, and interpret the information in, a cash flow statement

Exam guide

Cash flow statements were tested regularly under the old syllabus, and as this syllabus has the same examiner, we may assume that he will also test them regularly.

1 IAS 7 *Cash flow statements*

A cash flow statement is a useful addition to a company's financial statements as a measure of performance.

1.1 Introduction

It has been argued that 'profit' does not always give a useful or meaningful picture of a company's operations. Readers of a company's financial statements might even be **misled by a reported profit figure**.

(a) Shareholders might believe that if a company makes a profit after tax, of say, $100,000 then this is the amount which it could afford to **pay as a dividend**. Unless the company has **sufficient cash** available to stay in business and also to pay a dividend, the shareholders' expectations would be wrong.

(b) Employees might believe that if a company makes profits, it can afford to **pay higher wages** next year. This opinion may not be correct: the ability to pay wages depends on the **availability of cash**.

(c) Survival of a business entity depends not so much on profits as on its **ability to pay its debts when they fall due**. Such payments might include 'revenue' items such as material purchases, wages, interest and taxation etc, but also capital payments for new non-current assets and the repayment of loan capital when this falls due (for example on the redemption of debentures).

From these examples, it may be apparent that a company's performance and prospects depend not so much on the 'profits' earned in a period, but more realistically on liquidity or **cash flows**.

1.2 Funds flow and cash flow

Some countries, either currently or in the past, have required the disclosure of additional statements based on **funds flow** rather than cash flow. However, the definition of 'funds' can be very vague and such statements often simply require a rearrangement of figures already provided in the balance sheet and income statement. By contrast, a statement of cash flows is unambiguous and provides information which is additional to that provided in the rest of the accounts. It also lends itself to organisation by activity and not by balance sheet classification.

Cash flow statements are frequently given as an **additional statement**, supplementing the balance sheet, income statement and related notes. The group aspects of cash flow statements (and certain complex matters) have been excluded as they are beyond the scope of your syllabus.

1.3 Objective of IAS 7

The aim of IAS 7 is to provide information to users of financial statements about the entity's **ability to generate cash and cash equivalents**, as well as indicating the cash needs of the entity. The cash flow statement provides *historical* information about cash and cash equivalents, classifying cash flows between operating, investing and financing activities.

1.4 Scope

A cash flow statement should be presented as an **integral part** of an entity's financial statements. All types of entity can provide useful information about cash flows as the need for cash is universal, whatever the nature of their revenue-producing activities. Therefore **all entities are required by the standard to produce a cash flow statement.**

1.5 Benefits of cash flow information

The use of cash flow statements is very much **in conjunction** with the rest of the financial statements. Users can gain further appreciation of the change in net assets, of the entity's financial position (liquidity and solvency) and the entity's ability to adapt to changing circumstances by affecting the amount and timing of cash flows. Cash flow statements **enhance comparability** as they are not affected by differing accounting policies used for the same type of transactions or events.

Cash flow information of a historical nature can be used as an indicator of the amount, timing and certainty of future cash flows. Past forecast cash flow information can be **checked for accuracy** as actual figures emerge. The relationship between profit and cash flows can be analysed as can changes in prices over time.

1.6 Definitions

The standard gives the following definitions, the most important of which are **cash** and **cash equivalents**.

Key terms

- **Cash** comprises cash on hand and demand deposits.

- **Cash equivalents** are short-term, highly liquid investments that are readily convertible to known amounts of cash and which are subject to an insignificant risk of changes in value.

- **Cash flows** are inflows and outflows of cash and cash equivalents.

- **Operating activities** are the principal revenue-producing activities of the entity and other activities that are not investing or financing activities.

- **Investing activities** are the acquisition and disposal of non-current assets and other investments not included in cash equivalents.

- **Financing activities** are activities that result in changes in the size and composition of the equity capital and borrowings of the entity. *(IAS 7)*

1.7 Cash and cash equivalents

The standard expands on the definition of cash equivalents: they are not held for investment or other long-term purposes, but rather to meet short-term cash commitments. To fulfil the above definition, an investment's **maturity date should normally be within three months from its acquisition date**. It would usually be the case then that equity investments (ie shares in other companies) are *not* cash equivalents. An exception would be where preferred shares were acquired with a very close maturity date.

Loans and other borrowings from banks are classified as investing activities. In some countries, however, **bank overdrafts** are repayable on demand and are treated as part of an entity's total cash management system. In these circumstances an overdrawn balance will be included in cash and cash equivalents. Such banking arrangements are characterised by a balance which fluctuates between overdrawn and credit.

Movements between different types of cash and cash equivalent are not included in cash flows. The investment of surplus cash in cash equivalents is part of cash management, not part of operating, investing or financing activities.

1.8 Presentation of a cash flow statement

IAS 7 requires cash flow statements to report cash flows during the period classified by **operating, investing and financing activities.**

1.9 Example: simple cash flow statement

Flail Co commenced trading on 1 January 20X1 with a medium-term loan of $21,000 and a share issue which raised $35,000. The company purchased non-current assets for $21,000 cash, and during the year to 31 December 20X1 entered into the following transactions.

(a)   Purchases from suppliers were $19,500, of which $2,550 was unpaid at the year end.
(b)   Wages and salaries amounted to $10,500, of which $750 was unpaid at the year end.
(c)   Interest on the loan of $2,100 was fully paid in the year and a repayment of $5,250 was made.
(d)   Sales revenue was $29,400, including $900 receivables at the year end.
(e)   Interest on cash deposits at the bank amounted to $75.
(f)   A dividend of $4,000 was proposed as at 31 December 20X1.

You are required to prepare a historical cash flow statement for the year ended 31 December 20X1.

Solution

FLAIL CO
CASH FLOW STATEMENT FOR
THE YEAR ENDED 31 DECEMBER 20X1

	$	$
Cash flows from operating activities		
Cash received from customers ($29,400 – $900)	28,500	
Cash paid to suppliers ($19,500 – $2,550)	(16,950)	
Cash paid to and on behalf of employees ($10,500 – $750)	(9,750)	
Interest paid	(2,100)	
Net cash used in operating activities		(300)
Cash flows from investing activities		
Purchase of non-current assets	(21,000)	
Interest received	75	
Net cash used in investing activities		
		(20,925)
Cash flows from financing activities		
Issue of shares	35,000	
Proceeds from medium-term loan	21,000	
Repayment of medium-term loan	(5,250)	
Net cash from financing activities		50,750
Net increase in cash and cash equivalents		29,525
Cash and cash equivalents at 1 January 20X1		–
Cash and cash equivalents at 31 December 20X1		29,525

Note that the dividend is only proposed and so there is no related cash flow in 20X1.

Question

The managers of Flail Co have the following information in respect of projected cash flows for the year to 31 December 20X2.

(a)   Non-current asset purchases for cash will be $3,000.

(b)   Further expenses will be:

    (i)   purchases from suppliers – $18,750 ($4,125 owed at the year end);
    (ii)   wages and salaries – $11,250 ($600 owed at the year end);
    (iii)   loan interest – $1,575.

(c)   Sales revenue will be $36,000 ($450 receivables at the year end).

(d)   Interest on bank deposits will be $150.

(e)   A further capital repayment of $5,250 will be made on the loan.

(f)   A dividend of $5,000 will be proposed and last year's final dividend paid.

(g)   Income taxes of $2,300 will be paid in respect of 20X1.

Prepare the cash flow forecast for the year to 31 December 20X2.

Answer

FLAIL CO
STATEMENT OF FORECAST CASH FLOWS FOR
THE YEAR ENDING 31 DECEMBER 20X2

	$	$
Cash flows from operating activities		
Cash received from customers	36,450	
($36,000 + $900 – $450)		
Cash paid to suppliers ($18,750 + $2,550 – $4,125)	(17,175)	
Cash paid to and on behalf of employees		
($11,250 + $750 – $600)	(11,400)	
Interest paid	(1,575)	
Taxation	(2,300)	
Net cash paid from operating activities		4,000
Cash flow from investing activities		
Purchase of non-current assets	(3,000)	
Interest received	150	
Net cash used in investing activities		(2,850)
Cash flows from financing activities		
Repayment of medium-term loan	(5,250)	
Dividend payment	(4,000)	
Net cash used in financing activities		(9,250)
Forecast net decrease in cash and cash equivalents		(8,100)
Cash and cash equivalents as at 31 December 20X1		29,525
Forecast cash and cash equivalents as at 31 December 20X2		21,425

1.10 Activities

The manner of presentation of cash flows between operating, investing and financing activities **depends on the nature of the entity**. By classifying cash flows between different activities in this way users can see the impact on cash and cash equivalents of each one, and their relationships with each other. We can look at each in more detail.

1.10.1 Operating activities

This is perhaps the key part of the cash flow statement because it shows whether, and to what extent, companies can **generate cash from their operations**. It is these operating cash flows which must, in the end pay for all cash outflows relating to other activities, ie paying loan interest, dividends and so on.

Most of the components of cash flows from operating activities will be those items which **determine the net profit or loss of the entity**, ie they relate to the main revenue-producing activities of the entity. The standard gives the following as examples of cash flows from operating activities.

(a)   Cash receipts from the sale of goods and the rendering of services

(b)   Cash receipts from royalties, fees, commissions and other revenue

(c)   Cash payments to suppliers for goods and services

(d)   Cash payments to and on behalf of employees

Certain items may be included in the net profit or loss for the period which do *not* relate to operational cash flows, for example the profit or loss on the sale of a piece of plant will be included in net profit or loss, but the cash flows will be classed as **investing**.

1.10.2 Investing activities

The cash flows classified under this heading show the extent of new investment in **assets which will generate future profit and cash flows**. The standard gives the following examples of cash flows arising from investing activities.

(a)   Cash payments to acquire property, plant and equipment, intangibles and other non-current assets, including those relating to capitalised development costs and self-constructed property, plant and equipment

(b)   Cash receipts from sales of property, plant and equipment, intangibles and other non-current assets

(c)   Cash payments to acquire shares or debentures of other entities

(d)   Cash receipts from sales of shares or debentures of other entities

(e)   Cash advances and loans made to other parties

(f)   Cash receipts from the repayment of advances and loans made to other parties

1.10.3 Financing activities

This section of the cash flow statement shows the share of cash which the entity's capital providers have claimed during the period. This is an indicator of **likely future interest and dividend payments**. The standard gives the following examples of cash flows which might arise under this heading.

(a)   Cash proceeds from issuing shares

(b)   Cash payments to owners to acquire or redeem the entity's shares

(c)   Cash proceeds from issuing debentures, loans, notes, bonds, mortgages and other short or long-term borrowings

(d)   Principal repayments of amounts borrowed under finance leases

Item (d) needs more explanation. Where the reporting entity uses an asset held under a finance lease, the amounts to go in the cash flow statement as financing activities are repayments of the **principal (capital)** rather than the **interest**. The interest paid will be shown under operating activities.

1.11 Example: finance lease rental

The notes to the financial statements of Hayley Co show the following in respect of obligations under finance leases.

Year ended 30 June	20X5	20X4
	$'000	$'000
Amounts payable within one year	12	8
Within two to five years	110	66
	122	74
Less finance charges allocated to future periods	(14)	(8)
	108	66

Interest paid on finance leases in the year to 30 June 20X5 amounted to $6m. Additions to tangible non-current assets acquired under finance leases were shown in the non-current asset note at $56,000.

Required

Calculate the capital repayment to be shown in the cash flow statement of Hayley Co for the year to 30 June 20X5.

Solution

OBLIGATIONS UNDER FINANCE LEASES

	$'000		$'000
Capital repayment (bal fig)	14	Bal 1.7.X4	66
Bal 30.6.X5	108	Additions	56
	122		122

1.12 Reporting cash flows from operating activities

The standard offers a choice of method for this part of the cash flow statement.

(a) **Direct method:** disclose major classes of gross cash receipts and gross cash payments

(b) **Indirect method:** net profit or loss is adjusted for the effects of transactions of a non-cash nature, any deferrals or accruals of past or future operating cash receipts or payments, and items of income or expense associated with investing or financing cash flows

The **direct method is the preferred method** because it discloses information, not available elsewhere in the financial statements, which could be of use in estimating future cash flows. The example below shows both methods.

1.12.1 Using the direct method

There are different ways in which the **information about gross cash receipts and payments** can be obtained. The most obvious way is simply to extract the information from the accounting records. This may be a laborious task, however, and the indirect method below may be easier. The example and question above used the direct method.

1.12.2 Using the indirect method

This method is undoubtedly **easier** from the point of view of the preparer of the cash flow statement. The net profit or loss for the period is adjusted for the following.

(a) Changes during the period in inventories, operating receivables and payables

(b) Non-cash items, eg depreciation, provisions, profits/losses on the sales of assets

(c) Other items, the cash flows from which should be classified under investing or financing activities.

A **proforma** of such a calculation, taken from the IAS, is as follows and this method may be more common in the exam. (The proforma has been amended to reflect changes to IFRS.)

	$
Cash flows from operating activities	
Profit before taxation	X
Adjustments for:	
Depreciation	X
Foreign exchange loss	X
Investment income	(X)
Interest expense	X
Operating profit before working capital changes	X
Increase in trade and other receivables	(X)
Decrease in inventories	X
Decrease in trade payables	(X)
Cash generated from operations	X
Interest paid	(X)
Income taxes paid	(X)
Net cash from operating activities	X

It is important to understand why **certain items are added and others subtracted**. Note the following points.

(a) Depreciation is not a cash expense, but is deducted in arriving at the profit figure in the income statement. It makes sense, therefore, to eliminate it by adding it back.

(b) By the same logic, a loss on a disposal of a non-current asset (arising through underprovision of depreciation) needs to be added back and a profit deducted.

(c) An increase in inventories means less cash – you have spent cash on buying inventory.

(d) An increase in receivables means the company's debtors have not paid as much, and therefore there is less cash.

(e) If we pay off payables, causing the figure to decrease, again we have less cash.

1.12.3 Indirect versus direct

The direct method is encouraged where the necessary information is not too costly to obtain, but IAS 7 does not require it. In practice the indirect method is more commonly used, since it is quicker and easier.

1.13 Interest and dividends

Cash flows from interest and dividends received and paid should each be **disclosed separately**. Each should be classified in a consistent manner from period to period as either operating, investing or financing activities.

Dividends paid by the entity can be classified in **one of two ways**.

(a) As a **financing cash flow**, showing the cost of obtaining financial resources.

(b) As a component of **cash flows from operating activities** so that users can assess the entity's ability to pay dividends out of operating cash flows.

1.14 Taxes on income

Cash flows arising from taxes on income should be **separately disclosed** and should be classified as cash flows from operating activities *unless* they can be specifically identified with financing and investing activities.

Taxation cash flows are often **difficult to match** to the originating underlying transaction, so most of the time all tax cash flows are classified as arising from operating activities.

1.15 Components of cash and cash equivalents

The components of cash and cash equivalents should be disclosed and a **reconciliation** should be presented, showing the amounts in the cash flow statement reconciled with the equivalent items reported in the balance sheet.

It is also necessary to disclose the **accounting policy** used in deciding the items included in cash and cash equivalents, in accordance with IAS 1 *Presentation of Financial Statements*, but also because of the wide range of cash management practices worldwide.

1.16 Other disclosures

All entities should disclose, together with a **commentary by management**, any other information likely to be of importance, for example:

(a)   Restrictions on the use of or access to any part of cash equivalents

(b)   The amount of undrawn borrowing facilities which are available

(c)   Cash flows which increased operating capacity compared to cash flows which merely maintained operating capacity

(d)   Cash flows arising from each reported industry and geographical segment

1.17 Example of a cash flow statement

In the next section we will look at the procedures for preparing a cash flow statement. First, look at this **example**, adapted from the example given in the standard (which is based on a group and therefore beyond the scope of your syllabus).

1.17.1 Direct method

CASH FLOW STATEMENT (DIRECT METHOD)
YEAR ENDED 31 DECEMBER 20X7

	$m	$m
Cash flows from operating activities		
Cash receipts from customers	30,330	
Cash paid to suppliers and employees	(27,600)	
Cash generated from operations	2,730	
Interest paid	(270)	
Income taxes paid	(900)	
Net cash from operating activities		1,560
Cash flows from investing activities		
Purchase of property, plant and equipment	(900)	
Proceeds from sale of equipment	20	
Interest received	200	
Dividends received	200	
Net cash used in investing activities		(480)
Cash flows from financing activities		
Proceeds from issue of share capital	250	
Proceeds from long-term borrowings	250	
Dividends paid*	(1,290)	
Net cash used in financing activities		(790)
Net increase in cash and cash equivalents		290
Cash and cash equivalents at beginning of period (Note)		120
Cash and cash equivalents at end of period (Note)		410

* This could also be shown as an operating cash flow

1.17.2 Indirect method

CASH FLOW STATEMENT (INDIRECT METHOD)
YEAR ENDED 31 DECEMBER 20X7

	$m	$m
Cash flows from operating activities		
Profit before taxation	3,570	
Adjustments for:		
Depreciation	450	
Investment income	(500)	
Interest expense	400	
Operating profit before working capital changes	3,920	
Increase in trade and other receivables	(500)	
Decrease in inventories	1,050	
Decrease in trade payables	(1,740)	
Cash generated from operations	2,730	
Interest paid	(270)	
Income taxes paid	(900)	
Net cash from operating activities		1,560
Cash flows from investing activities		
Purchase of property, plant and equipment	(900)	
Proceeds from sale of equipment	20	
Interest received	200	
Dividends received	200	
Net cash used in investing activities		(480)
Cash flows from financing activities		
Proceeds from issue of share capital	250	
Proceeds from long-term borrowings	250	
Dividends paid*	(1,290)	
Net cash used in financing activities		(790)
Net increase in cash and cash equivalents		290
Cash and cash equivalents at beginning of period (Note)		120
Cash and cash equivalents at end of period (Note)		410

* This could also be shown as an operating cash flow

1.17.3 Notes

The following note is required to both versions of the statement.

Note: Cash and cash equivalents

Cash and cash equivalents consist of cash on hand and balances with banks, and investments in money market instruments. Cash and cash equivalents included in the cash flow statement comprise the following balance sheet amounts.

	20X7	20X6
	$m	$m
Cash on hand and balances with banks	40	25
Short-term investments	370	95
Cash and cash equivalents	410	120

The company has undrawn borrowing facilities of $2,000m of which only $700m may be used for future expansion.

2 Preparing a cash flow statement

You must be able to prepare a cash flow statement by both the indirect and the direct methods.

2.1 Introduction

In essence, preparing a cash flow statement is very straightforward. You should therefore simply learn the format and apply the steps noted in the example below. Note that the following items are treated in a way that might seem confusing, but the treatment is logical if you **think in terms of cash**.

(a)   **Increase in inventory** is treated as **negative** (in brackets). This is because it represents a cash **outflow**; cash is being spent on inventory.

(b)   An **increase in receivables** would be treated as **negative** for the same reasons; more receivables means less cash.

(c)   By contrast an **increase in payables is positive** because cash is being retained and not used to settle accounts payable. There is therefore more of it.

2.2 Example: preparation of a cash flow statement

Kane Co's income statement for the year ended 31 December 20X2 and balance sheets at 31 December 20X1 and 31 December 20X2 were as follows.

KANE CO
INCOME STATEMENT FOR THE YEAR ENDED 31 DECEMBER 20X2

	$'000	$'000
Sales		720
Raw materials consumed	70	
Staff costs	94	
Depreciation	118	
Loss on disposal of non-current asset	18	
		300
Operating profit		420
Interest payable		28
Profit before tax		392
Taxation		124
		268
Dividend		72
Profit retained for year		196
Balance brought forward		490
		686

KANE CO
BALANCE SHEETS AS AT 31 DECEMBER

	20X2		20X1	
	$'000	$'000	$'000	$'000
Assets				
Non-current assets				
Cost	1,596		1,560	
Depreciation	318		224	
		1,278		1,336
Current assets				
Inventory	24		20	
Trade receivables	76		58	
Bank	48		56	
		148		134
Total assets		1,426		1,470
Equity and liabilities				
Equity				
Share capital	360		340	
Share premium	36		24	
Retained earnings	686		490	
		1,082		854
Non-current liabilities				
Long-term loans		200		500
Current liabilities				
Trade payables	12		6	
Taxation	102		86	
Proposed dividend	30		24	
		144		116
		1,426		1,470

During the year, the company paid $90,000 for a new piece of machinery.

Required

Prepare a cash flow statement for Kane Co for the year ended 31 December 20X2 in accordance with the requirements of IAS 7, using the indirect method.

Solution

Step 1   **Set out the proforma cash flow statement** with the headings required by IAS 7. You should leave plenty of space. Ideally, use three or more sheets of paper, one for the main statement, one for the notes and one for your workings. It is obviously essential to know the formats very well.

Step 2   Begin with the **cash flows from operating activities** as far as possible. When preparing the statement from balance sheets, you will usually have to calculate such items as depreciation, loss on sale of non-current assets, profit for the year and tax paid (see Step 4). Note that you may not be given the tax charge in the income statement. You will then have to assume that the tax paid in the year is last year's year-end provision and calculate the charge as the balancing figure.

Step 3   Calculate the cash flow figures for **dividends paid, purchase or sale of non-current assets, issue of shares and repayment of loans** if these are not already given to you (as they may be).

Step 4   If you are not given the profit figure, open up a **working for the income statement**. Using the opening and closing balances of retained earnings, the taxation charge and dividends paid and proposed, you will be able to calculate profit for the year as the balancing figure to put in the cash flows from operating activities section.

Step 5   You will now be able to **complete the statement** by slotting in the figures given or calculated.

KANE CO
CASH FLOW STATEMENT FOR THE YEAR ENDED 31 DECEMBER 20X2

	$'000	$'000
Cash flows from operating activities		
Profit before tax	392	
Depreciation charges	118	
Loss on sale of tangible non-current assets	18	
Interest expense	28	
Increase in inventories	(4)	
Increase in receivables	(18)	
Increase in payables	6	
Cash generated from operations	540	
Interest paid	(28)	
Dividends paid (72 – 30 + 24)	(66)	
Tax paid (86 + 124 – 102)	(108)	
Net cash from operating activities		338
Cash flows from investing activities		
Payments to acquire tangible non-current assets	(90)	
Receipts from sales of tangible non-current assets (W)	12	
Net cash used in investing activities		(78)
Cash flows from financing activities		
Issues of share capital (360 + 36 – 340 – 24)	32	
Long-term loans repaid (500 – 200)	(300)	
Net cash used in financing activities		(268)
Decrease in cash and cash equivalents		(8)
Cash and cash equivalents at 1.1.X2		56
Cash and cash equivalents at 31.12.X2		48

Working: non-current asset disposals

COST

	$'000		$'000
At 1.1.X2	1,560	At 31.12.X2	1,596
Purchases	90	Disposals (balance)	54
	1,650		1,650

ACCUMULATED DEPRECIATION

	$'000		$'000
At 31.12.X2	318	At 1.1.X2	224
Depreciation on disposals		Charge for year	118
(balance)	24		
	342		342

	$'000
NBV of disposals	30
Net loss reported	(18)
Proceeds of disposals	12

Question   Prepare a cash flow statement

Set out below are the financial statements of Emma Co. You are the financial controller, faced with the task of implementing IAS 7 *Cash flow statements*.

EMMA CO
INCOME STATEMENT FOR THE YEAR ENDED 31 DECEMBER 20X2

	$'000
Revenue	2,553
Cost of sales	1,814
Gross profit	739
Distribution costs	125
Administrative expenses	264
Operating profit	350
Interest received	25
Interest paid	75
Profit before tax	300
Taxation	140
Profit after tax	160
Dividends	100
Retained profit for the year	60

EMMA CO
BALANCE SHEETS AS AT 31 DECEMBER

	20X2	20X1
Assets	$'000	$'000
Non-current assets		
Tangible assets	380	305
Intangible assets	250	200
Investments	–	25
Current assets		
Inventories	150	102
Receivables	390	315
Short-term investments	50	–
Cash in hand	2	1
Total assets	1,222	948
Equity and liabilities		
Equity		
Share capital ($1 ordinary shares)	200	150
Share premium account	160	150
Revaluation reserve	100	91
Retained earnings	160	100
Non-current liabilities		
Long-term loan	170	50
Current liabilities		
Trade payables	127	119
Bank overdraft	85	98
Taxation	120	110
Dividends proposed	100	80
Total equity and liabilities	1,222	948

The following information is available.

(a)   The proceeds of the sale of non-current asset investments amounted to $30,000.

(b) Fixtures and fittings, with an original cost of $85,000 and a net book value of $45,000, were sold for $32,000 during the year.

(c) The following information relates to tangible non-current assets.

	31.12.20X2	31.12.20X1
	$'000	$'000
Cost	720	595
Accumulated depreciation	340	290
Net book value	380	305

(d) 50,000 $1 ordinary shares were issued during the year at a premium of 20c per share.

(e) The short-term investments are highly liquid and are close to maturity.

Required

Prepare a cash flow statement for the year to 31 December 20X2 using the format laid out in IAS 7.

Answer

EMMA CO
CASH FLOW STATEMENT FOR THE YEAR ENDED 31 DECEMBER 20X2

	$'000	$'000
Cash flows from operating activities		
Profit before tax	300	
Depreciation charge (W1)	90	
Loss on sale of tangible non-current assets (45 – 32)	13	
Profit on sale of non-current asset investments	(5)	
Interest expense (net)	50	
(Increase)/decrease in inventories	(48)	
(Increase)/decrease in receivables	(75)	
Increase/(decrease) in payables	8	
Cash generated from operations	333	
Interest paid	(75)	
Dividends paid	(80)	
Tax paid (110 + 140 – 120)	(130)	
Net cash from operating activities		48
Cash flows from investing activities		
Payments to acquire tangible non-current assets (W2)	(201)	
Payments to acquire intangible non-current assets	(50)	
Receipts from sales of tangible non-current assets	32	
Receipts from sale of non-current asset investments	30	
Interest received	25	
Net cash flows from investing activities		(164)
Cash flows from financing activities		
Issue of share capital	60	
Long-term loan	120	
Net cash flows from financing		180
Increase in cash and cash equivalents (Note)		64
Cash and cash equivalents at 1.1.X2 (Note)		(97)
Cash and cash equivalents at 31.12.X2 (Note)		(33)

NOTES TO THE CASH FLOW STATEMENT

Note: analysis of the balances of cash and cash equivalents as shown in the balance sheet

	20X2 $'000	20X1 $'000	Change in year $'000
Cash in hand	2	1	1
Short term investments	50	–	50
Bank overdraft	(85)	(98)	13
	(33)	(97)	64

Workings

1   *Depreciation charge*

	$'000	$'000
Depreciation at 31 December 20X2		340
Depreciation 31 December 20X1	290	
Depreciation on assets sold (85 – 45)	40	
		250
Charge for the year		90

2   *Purchase of tangible non-current assets*

TANGIBLE NON-CURRENT ASSETS (COST)

	$'000		$'000
1.1.X2 Balance b/d	595	Disposals	85
Revaluation (100 – 91)	9		
Purchases (bal fig)	201	31.12.X2 Balance c/d	720
	805		805

3 Interpretation of cash flow statements

FAST FORWARD

> IAS 7 *Cash flow statements* was introduced on the basis that it would provide better, more comprehensive and more useful information than what was already shown in the financial statements.

3.1 Introduction

So what kind of information does the cash flow statement, along with its notes, provide?

Some of the main areas where IAS 7 should provide information not found elsewhere in the financial statements are as follows.

(a)   The **relationships between profit and cash** can be seen clearly and analysed accordingly.

(b)   **Cash equivalents** are highlighted, giving a better picture of the liquidity of the company.

(c)   **Financing inflows and outflows must be shown, rather than simply passed through reserves**.

One of the most important things to realise at this point is that it is wrong to try to assess the health or predict the death of a reporting entity solely on the basis of a single indicator. When analysing cash flow data, the **comparison should not just be between cash flows and profit, but also between cash flows over a period of time** (say three to five years).

Cash is not synonymous with profit on an annual basis, but you should also remember that the 'behaviour' of profit and cash flows will be very different. **Profit is smoothed out** through accruals, prepayments, provisions and other accounting conventions. This does not apply to cash, so the **cash flow figures** are likely to be **'lumpy'** in comparison. You must distinguish between this 'lumpiness' and the trends which will appear over time.

The **relationship between profit and cash flows will vary constantly**. Note that healthy companies do not always have reported profits exceeding operating cash flows. Similarly, unhealthy companies can have operating cash flows well in excess of reported profit. The value of comparing them is in determining the extent to which earned profits are being converted into the necessary cash flows.

Profit is not as important as the extent to which a company can **convert its profits into cash on a continuing basis.** This process should be judged over a period longer than one year. The cash flows should be compared with profits over the same periods to decide how successfully the reporting entity has converted earnings into cash.

Cash flow figures should also be considered in terms of their specific relationships with each other over time. A form of **'cash flow gearing'** can be determined by comparing operating cash flows and financing flows, particularly borrowing, to establish the extent of dependence of the reporting entity on external funding.

Other relationships can be examined.

(a)   Operating cash flows and investment flows can be related to match cash recovery from investment to investment.

(b)   Investment can be compared to distribution to indicate the proportion of total cash outflow designated specifically to investor return and reinvestment.

(c)   A comparison of tax outflow to operating cash flow minus investment flow will establish a 'cash basis tax rate'.

The 'ratios' mentioned above can be monitored **inter- and intra-firm** and the analyses can be undertaken in monetary, general price-level adjusted, or percentage terms.

3.2 The advantages of cash flow accounting

The advantages of cash flow accounting are as follows.

(a)   Survival in business depends on the **ability to generate** cash. Cash flow accounting directs attention towards this critical issue.

(b)   Cash flow is **more comprehensive** than 'profit' which is dependent on accounting conventions and concepts.

(c)   **Creditors** (long and short-term) are more interested in an entity's ability to repay them than in its profitability. Whereas 'profits' might indicate that cash is likely to be available, cash flow accounting is more direct with its message.

(d)   Cash flow reporting provides a better means of **comparing the results** of different companies than traditional profit reporting.

(e)   Cash flow reporting **satisfies the needs of all users** better.

(i)   For **management**, it provides the sort of information on which decisions should be taken (in management accounting, 'relevant costs' to a decision are future cash flows); traditional profit accounting does not help with decision-making.

(ii)   For **shareholders and auditors**, cash flow accounting can provide a satisfactory basis for stewardship accounting.

(iii)   As described previously, the information needs of **creditors and employees** will be better served by cash flow accounting.

(f)   Cash flow forecasts are **easier to prepare**, as well as more useful, than profit forecasts.

(g)   They can in some respects be **audited more easily** than accounts based on the accruals concept.

(h)   The accruals concept is confusing, and cash flows are **more easily understood**.

(i)   Cash flow accounting should be both retrospective, and also include a forecast for the future. This is of **great information value** to all users of accounting information.

(j)   **Forecasts** can subsequently be **monitored** by the publication of variance statements which compare actual cash flows against the forecast.

Question

Disadvantages

Can you think of some possible disadvantages of cash flow accounting?

Answer

The main disadvantages of cash accounting are essentially the advantages of accruals accounting (proper matching of related items). There is also the practical problem that few businesses keep historical cash flow information in the form needed to prepare a historical cash flow statement and so extra record keeping is likely to be necessary.

3.3 Criticisms of IAS 7

The inclusion of **cash equivalents** has been criticised because it does not reflect the way in which businesses are managed: in particular, the requirement that to be a cash equivalent an investment has to be within three months of maturity is considered **unrealistic**.

The management of assets similar to cash (ie 'cash equivalents') is not distinguished from other investment decisions.

Chapter roundup

- **Cash flow statements** are a useful addition to the financial statements of companies because it is recognised that accounting profit is not the only indicator of a company's performance.

- **Funds statements** essentially consist of income statement and balance sheet information re-arranged so as to highlight the sources from which funds have been generated and the ways in which they have been utilised.

- Cash flow statements concentrate on the sources and uses of cash and are a useful indicator of a company's **liquidity and solvency**.

- You need to be aware of the **format** of the statement as laid out in **IAS 7**; setting out the format is an essential first stage in preparing the statement, so this format must be learnt.

- Remember the **step-by-step preparation procedure** and use it for all the questions you practise.

- Note that you may be expected to **analyse** or **interpret** a cash flow statement.

Quick quiz

1   What is the aim of a cash flow statement?

2   The standard headings in IAS 7 *Cash flow statements* are:

   - O................... a................

   - I.................... a....................

   - F..................... a......................

   - Net.................... in C........................ and ....

3   Cash equivalents are current asset investments which will mature or can be redeemed within three months of the year end.

   True   ☐

   False   ☐

4   Why are you more likely to encounter the indirect method as opposed to the direct method?

5   List five advantages of cash flow accounting.

Answers to quick quiz

1   To indicate an entity's ability to generate cash and cash equivalents.

2   • Operating activities
     • Investing activities
     • Financing activities
     • Net increase (decrease) in cash and cash equivalents

3   False. See the definition in paragraph 1.6 if you are not sure about this.

4   The indirect method utilises figures which appear in the financial statements. The figures required for the direct method may not be readily available.

5   See paragraph 3.2

Now try the question below from the Exam Question Bank

Number	Level	Marks	Time
Q25	Examination	25	45 mins

Related parties; segment information

Topic list	Syllabus reference
1 IAS 24 *Related party disclosures*	5(e)
2 IAS 14 Segment reporting	5(e)
3 Identifying reportable segments	5(e)
4 Disclosure of segment information	5(d)

Introduction

IAS 24 *Related party disclosures* is an important standard in maintaining the transparency of financial statements.

IAS 14 on segment reporting requires quoted entities to provide additional information on their results, breaking them down by different types of product and service and by geographical areas.

Study guide

Section 27 – Related party disclosures

- Define and apply the definition of related parties in accordance with relevant accounting standards
- Describe the potential to mislead users when related party transactions are included in a company's financial statements
- Adjust financial statements (for comparative purposes) for the effects of non-commercial related party transactions
- Describe the disclosure requirements for related party transactions

Section 28 – Segment reporting

- Discuss the usefulness and problems associated with the provision of segment information
- Define a reportable segment and the information that is to be reported (primary and secondary formats)
- Prepare segment reports in accordance with relevant accounting standards
- Assess the performance of a company based on the information contained in its segment report

1 IAS 24 *Related party disclosures*

FAST FORWARD 〉〉 IAS 24 is basically a disclosure statement.

1.1 Introduction

In the absence of information to the contrary, it is assumed that a reporting entity has **independent discretionary power** over its resources and transactions and pursues its activities independently of the interests of its individual owners, managers and others. Transactions are presumed to have been undertaken on an **arm's length basis**, ie on terms such as could have obtained in a transaction with an external party, in which each side bargained knowledgeably and freely, unaffected by any relationship between them.

These assumptions may not be justified when **related party relationships** exist, because the requisite conditions for competitive, free market dealings may not be present. Whilst the parties may endeavour to achieve arm's length bargaining the very nature of the relationship may preclude this occurring.

1.2 Objective

This is the related parties issue and IAS 24 tackles it by ensuring that financial statements contain the disclosures necessary to draw attention to the possibility that the reported financial position and results may have been affected by the existence of related parties and by material transactions with them. In other words, this is a standard which is primarily concerned with **disclosure**.

1.3 Scope

The standard requires disclosure of related party transactions and outstanding balances in the **separate financial statements** of a parent, venturer or investor presented in accordance with IAS 27.

This is a **change** from the previous version of IAS 24, which did not require disclosure about related party transactions in the parent separate financial statements when they are made available or published with consolidated financial statements for the group.

An entity's financial statements disclose related party transactions and outstanding balances with other entities in a group. **Intragroup** transactions and balances are **eliminated** in the preparation of consolidated financial statements.

1.4 Definitions

The following important definitions are given by the standard. Note that the definitions of **control** and **significant influence** are now the same as those given in IASs 27, 28 and 31.

Key terms

- **Related party**. A party is related to an entity if:

    (a)   directly, or indirectly through one or more intermediaries, it:

        (i)   controls, is controlled by, or is under common control with, the entity (this includes parents, subsidiaries and fellow subsidiaries);

        (ii)   has an interest in the entity that gives it significant influence over the entity; or

        (iii)   has joint control over the entity;

    (b)   it is an associate;

    (c)   it is a joint venture in which the entity is a venturer;

    (d)   it is a member of the key management personnel of the entity or its parent;

    (e)   it is a close member of the family of any individual referred to in (a) or (d);

    (f)   it is an entity that is controlled, jointly controlled or significantly influenced by; or for which significant voting power in such entity resides with, directly or indirectly, any individual referred to in (d) or (e); or

    (g)   it is a post-employment benefit plan for the benefit of employees of the entity, or of any entity that is a related party of the entity.

- **Related party transaction**. A transfer of resources, services or obligations between related parties, regardless of whether a price is charged.

- **Control** is the power to govern the financial and operating policies of an entity so as to obtain benefits from its activities.

- **Significant influence** is the power to participate in the financial and operating policy decisions of an entity, but is not control over those policies. Significant ownership may be gained by share ownership, statute or agreement.

- **Joint control** is the contractually agreed sharing of control over an economic activity.

- **Key management personnel** are those persons having authority and responsibility for planning, directing and controlling the activities of the entity, directly or indirectly, including any director (whether executive or otherwise) of that entity.

- **Close members of the family of an individual** are those family members who may be expected to influence, or be influenced by, that individual in their dealings with the entity. They may include:

    (a)   the individual's domestic partner and children;
    (b)   children of the domestic partner; and
    (c)   dependants of the individual or the domestic partner.   *(IAS 24)*

The most important point to remember here is that, when considering each possible related party relationship, attention must be paid to the **substance of the relationship, not merely the legal form**.

IAS 24 lists the following which are **not necessarily related parties**.

(a)   **Two entities simply because they have a director or other key management in common** (notwithstanding the definition of related party above, although it is necessary to consider how that director would affect both entities)

(b)   **Two venturers, simply because they share joint control over a joint venture.**

(c)   Certain other bodies, simply as a result of their **role in normal business dealings** with the entity

    (i)   Providers of finance
    (ii)   Trade unions
    (iii)   Public utilities
    (iv)   Government departments and agencies

(d)   **Any single customer, supplier, franchisor, distributor, or general agent** with whom the entity transacts a significant amount of business, simply by virtue of the resulting economic dependence.

1.5 Disclosure

As noted above, IAS 24 is almost entirely concerned with disclosure and its provisions are meant to **supplement** those disclosure requirements required by national company legislation and other IASs (particularly IASs 1, 27 and 28 and IFRS 3).

The standard lists some **examples** of transactions that are disclosed if they are with a related party:

- Purchases or sales of goods (finished or unfinished)
- Purchases or sales of property and other assets
- Rendering or receiving of services
- Leases
- Transfers of research and development
- Transfers under licence agreements
- Provision of finance (including loans and equity contributions in cash or in kind)
- Provision of guarantees and collateral security
- Settlement of liabilities on behalf of the entity or by the entity on behalf of another party.

Relationships between **parents and subsidiaries** must be **disclosed irrespective** of **whether** any **transactions** have **taken place between** the related parties. An entity must disclose the **name** of its **parent** and, if different, the **ultimate controlling party**. This will enable a reader of the financial statements to be able to form a view about the effects of a related party relationship on the reporting entity.

If neither the parent nor the ultimate controlling party produces financial statements available for public use, the name of the next most senior parent that does so shall also be disclosed.

An entity should disclose **key management personnel compensation** in **total** and for **each** of the following **categories**.

(a)   **Short-term employee benefits** (eg, wages, salaries, social security contributions, paid annual leave and paid sick-leave, profit sharing and bonuses and non-monetary benefits such as medical care, housing, cars and free or subsidised goods or services)

(b)   **Post-employment benefits** (eg, pensions, other retirement benefits, life insurance and medical care)

(c)   **Other long-term benefits** (eg, long-service leave, sabbatical leave, long-term disability benefits and, if they are not payable within twelve months after the end of the period, profit sharing bonuses and deferred compensation)

    (d)   **Termination benefits**, and

    (e)   **Equity compensation benefits**

Compensation includes amounts paid on behalf of a parent of the entity in respect of the entity.

Where **transactions have taken place** between related parties, the entity should disclose the **nature** of the related party relationships, as well as information about the **transactions and outstanding balances** necessary for an understanding of the potential effect of the relationship on the financial statements. As a minimum, disclosures must include:

    (a)   The **amount of the transactions**

    (b)   The **amount of outstanding balances** and

        (i)   Their terms and conditions, including whether they are secured, and the nature of the consideration to be provided in settlement

        (ii)   Details of any guarantees given or received

    (c)   Provisions for **doubtful debts** related to the amount of outstanding balances

    (d)   The **expense** recognised during the period in respect of **bad or doubtful debts** due from related parties.

The above disclosures shall be made separately for **each** of the following categories:

    (a)   The parent
    (b)   Entities with joint control or significant influence over the entity
    (c)   Subsidiaries
    (d)   Associates
    (e)   Joint ventures in which the entity is a venturer
    (f)   Other related parties

Items of a similar nature may be **disclosed in aggregate** *unless* separate disclosure is necessary for an understanding of the effect on the financial statements.

Disclosures that related party transactions were made on terms equivalent to those that prevail in arm's length transactions can be made only if such disclosures can be substantiated.

1.6 Section summary

IAS 24 is primarily concerned with **disclosure**. You should learn the following.

- **Definitions**: these are very important
- Relationships covered
- Relationships that **may not** necessarily be between related parties
- **Disclosures**: again, very important, representing the whole purpose of the standard

2 IAS 14 *Segment reporting*

FAST FORWARD

IAS 14 adopts a management approach to determining reporting segments.

2.1 Background

Large entities produce a wide range of products and services, often in several different countries. Further information on how the overall results of entities are made up from each of these product or geographical areas will help the users of the financial statements. This is the reason for **segment reporting**.

(a)   The entity's **past performance** will be better understood

(b)   The entity's **risks and returns** may be better assessed

(c)   More **informed judgements** may be made about the entity as a whole

Risks and returns of a **diversified, multi-national company** can only be assessed by looking at the individual risks and rewards attached to groups of products or services or in different geographical areas. These are subject to differing rates of profitability, opportunities for growth, future prospects and risks.

2.2 Scope

Only entities whose **equity or debt securities are publicly traded** (ie on a stock exchange) need disclose segment information. This includes entities in the process of issuing securities. Other entities that produce financial statements which comply with IASs are encouraged to disclose segment information voluntarily (in such cases IAS 14 must be followed entirely, not simply in part).

There are further points to mention regarding group accounts, but these are considered in Part D of this text.

2.3 Definitions

There are so many definitions in the standard that they are broken down by category.

2.3.1 Definitions from other standards

The definitions of **operating activities, accounting policies** and **revenue** as given by IAS 8 (see above) and IAS 18 are reproduced.

2.3.2 Definitions of business segment and geographical segment

These are the most important definitions in the standard, and it is vital that you learn the listed factors for business and geographical segments as these affect the rest of the standard.

Key terms

> - A **business segment** is a distinguishable component of an entity that is engaged in providing an individual product or service or a group of related products or services and that is subject to risks and returns that are different from those of other business segments. Factors that should be considered in determining whether products and services are related include:
>
>   (a)   The nature of the products or services
>
>   (b)   The nature of the production processes
>
>   (c)   The type or class of customer for the products or services
>
>   (d)   The methods used to distribute the products or provide the services
>
>   (e)   If applicable, the nature of the regulatory environment, for example, banking, insurance, or public utilities
>
> - A **geographical segment** is a distinguishable component of an entity that is engaged in providing products or services within a particular economic environment and that is subject to risks and returns that are different from those of components operating in other economic environments. Factors that should be considered in identifying geographical segments include:
>
>   (a)   Similarity of economic and political conditions
>
>   (b)   Relationships between operations in different geographical areas
>
>   (c)   Proximity of operations
>
>   (d)   Special risks associated with operations in a particular area
>
>   (e)   Exchange control regulations
>
>   (f)   The underlying currency risks

- A **reportable segment** is a business segment or a geographical segment identified based on the foregoing definitions for which segment information is required to be disclosed by IAS 14.

  (IAS 14)

All the products or services produced by a segment will be similar with respect to a **majority of the factors** in the definition of a **business segment** (these factors are given in no particular order).

The case is similar for **geographical segments**. These may consist of one country, two or more countries or a region within a country, but they do not include operations in economic environments with significantly differing risks and returns.

IAS 14 argues that entities are organised and managed according to the predominant sources of risk. Their structure and financial reporting systems can therefore be used to identify segments. These should indicate whether the entity's risks and returns are influenced mainly by the geographical **location of its operations** or by the **location of its markets**. Either method can be used to identify geographical segments (ie either by origin or destination of sales).

There is obviously a significant level of judgement required to determine the composition of a segment. The qualitative characteristics of financial statements, as laid out in the IASB's *Framework* (see Chapter 20) should be considered.

2.3.3 Definitions of segment revenue, expense, result, assets and liabilities

These definitions come into play **once segments have been identified**. Some of the group aspects have been excluded here, but we will look at these in Part D.

- **Segment revenue** is revenue reported in the entity's income statement that is directly attributable to a segment and the relevant portion of entity revenue that can be allocated on a reasonable basis to a segment, whether from sales to external customers or from transactions with other segments of the same entity. Segment revenue does *not* include:

  (a)   Interest or dividend income, including interest earned on advances or loans to other segments, unless the segment's operations are primarily of a financial nature

  (b)   Gains on sales of investments or gains on extinguishment of debt unless the segment's operations are primarily of a financial nature

- **Segment expense** is expense resulting from the operating activities of a segment that is directly attributable to the segment and the relevant portion of an expense that can be allocated on a reasonable basis to the segment, including expenses relating to sales to external customers and expenses relating to transactions with other segments of the same entity. Segment expense does not include:

  (a)   Interest, including interest incurred on advances or loans from other segments, unless the segment's operations are primarily of a financial nature

  (b)   Losses on sales of investments or losses on extinguishment of debt unless the segment's operations are primarily of a financial nature

  (c)   Income tax expense

  (d)   General administrative expenses, head office expenses, and other expenses that arise at the entity level and relate to the entity as a whole. However, costs are sometimes incurred at the entity level on behalf of a segment. Such costs are segment expenses if they relate to the segment's operating activities and they can be directly attributed or allocated to the segment on a reasonable basis

Key terms

> - **Segment result** is segment revenue less segment expense. Segment result is determined before any adjustments for minority interest.
>
> - **Segment assets** are those operating assets that are employed by a segment in its operating activities and that either are directly attributable to the segment or can be allocated to the segment on a reasonable basis.
>
>   (a)   If a segment's segment result includes interest or dividend income, its segment assets include the related receivables, loans, investments, or other income-producing assets.
>
>   (b)   Segment assets do not include income tax assets.
>
> - **Segment liabilities** are those operating liabilities that result from the operating activities of a segment and that either are directly attributable to the segment or can be allocated to the segment on a reasonable basis.
>
>   (a)   If a segment's segment result includes interest expense, its segment liabilities include the related interest-bearing liabilities.
>
>   (b)   Segment liabilities do not include income tax liabilities.
>
> - Segment accounting policies are the accounting policies adopted for preparing and presenting the financial statements of the consolidated group or entity as well as those accounting policies that relate specifically to segment reporting.   (*IAS 14*)

You can see from these definitions that only those amounts **directly attributable** to a segment should be included in the segment information.

Normally, internal financial reporting will be along these lines. Occasionally, however, amounts may be allocated to segments for management purposes which seem arbitrary or subjective. Alternatively, an entity may not allocate all items to segments which should be on a reasonable basis. In both these cases, the segment figures would **require adjustment**.

In relation to **segment assets**, if depreciation or amortisation is included as a segment expense, then the **respective asset** must be shown as a segment asset. Such assets may be shared between segments, but assets **held for the head office or for general purposes should be excluded.**

Segment liabilities do *not* include borrowings, liabilities resulting from finance leases, and other liabilities undertaken for **financing rather than operating purposes**. As with depreciation, if interest expense is included in the segment result, the related interest-bearing debt must be included in segment liabilities.

3 Identifying reportable segments

FAST FORWARD

> IAS 14 allows management to choose their primary segment reporting format.

3.1 Introduction

IAS 14 requires management to assess the dominant source and nature of an entity's risks and returns in order to assess whether the **primary segment reporting format** will be by business segment or geographical segment. The other format will then be given as a **secondary segment report**.

Dominant source and nature	Primary segment report	Secondary segment report
Business	Business	Geographical
Geographical	Geographical	Business

How is this decision made? IAS 14 states that it should be based on:

(a) An entity's internal organisational and management structure

(b) The system of internal financial reporting to the board of directors and chief executive officer

There are borderline or difficult cases which must be considered, although these will be very rare: in most cases the choice should be fairly obvious.

Dominant source and nature	Primary segment report	Secondary segment report
Both	Business	Geographical
Neither	Management choice, but show one as primary and one as secondary	

Where risks and rates of return are strongly affected by **both** products/services **and** by geography, this will usually be evidenced by a 'matrix approach' to managing the company and internal reporting. A '**matrix**' **presentation**, where both business and geographical segments are reported as primary segment reporting formats, will often be useful in such situations. This is neither required nor prohibited by IAS 14.

An organisation may be based around neither products/services nor geographical areas, but, say, by legal entity. Management should be able to assess which of the product/ service or geographical influences is dominant, thus allowing **comparability** with other similar entities by the disclosure of segment information.

3.2 Business and geographical segments

Both types of segment, for external reporting purposes, should be those **organisational units** for which information is reported to the board/CEO.

Where directors have had to make a **choice** of which should be the primary reporting format, in the circumstances laid out in Paragraph 8.1 above, then they should use the factors given in the **definitions of business, geographical and reporting segments** in Section 7 above, rather than on the basis of internal financial reporting. There are, however, various rules to be followed.

(a) Internally reported segments that meet the definitions (given in Section 7 above) **should not be further segmented**, even when other segments exist which do not meet the definitions.

(b) For those segments which do not meet the definitions, management should look at the **next lower level of segmentation** that reports information along product/ service or geographical lines according to the definitions in Section 7.

(c) Where lower-level segments identified in (b) meet the relevant definitions, the criteria discussed in Paragraph 8.3 below for identifying reportable segments should be applied to those segments.

If this procedure were not followed, an entity would be creating segments for external reporting purposes only. The approach adopted by the standard, of looking at the organisational and management structure and internal financial reporting system, is often called the '**management approach**'. The components for which information is reported internally are sometimes called '**operating segments**'.

3.3 Reportable segments

There are various rules on what comprises a reportable segment.

3.3.1 Combining segments

Internally reported business segments (two or more) can be **combined** to form a single business or geographical segment if they are **substantially similar**. This will only be the case if:

(a)   They demonstrate similar **long-term financial performance** *and*

(b)   They are similar in **all the factors** given in the definition of segments (see Section 2)

3.3.2 Material segments: 10% threshold rule

There is a **materiality rule**, which we could call the 10% rule. A business or geographical segment is a reportable segment if the majority of its revenue is earned from sales to external customers *and* any of the following applies.

(a)   Segment internal and external **revenue** is 10% or more of total internal and external revenue of all segments.

(b)   Segment **result** (profit *or* loss) is 10% or more of the combined result of all segments in profit *or* the combined result of all segments in loss (whichever is greater in absolute amount).

(c)   Segment **assets** are 10% or more of the total assets of all segments.

3.3.3 Non-material segments

The question then arises as to what should be done with an internally reported segment which is below all the thresholds of significance given above. The choice is as follows.

(a)   The segment is designated as a reportable segment **despite its size**

(b)   If not, **combine with other segments that are also below the thresholds** to form a separately reportable segment. These must be similar, according to the definition of business/geographical segments.

(c)   If neither of the above, include the segment as an **unallocated reconciling item**.

3.3.4 75% rule

There is yet another rule! This, presumably, is to prevent entities from avoiding reporting some segmental information by bundling it up in 'unallocated reconciling items'. This rule states that the total revenue of identified reportable segments must represent **75% or more of the total revenue of the entity**. Where this is not the case, the management must identify further reportable segments, even where they do not meet the 10% threshold (see Paragraph 3.3.2). This will carry on until the 75% of total has been achieved.

3.4 Segment accounting policies

An entity should adopt the **same accounting policies** for preparing segment information as it uses for preparing the financial statements of the entity. Additional segment information prepared on the basis of other policies (eg for internal purposes) may be disclosed, as long as it *is* reported internally *and* the basis of measurement used is reported.

Assets that are jointly used can be allocated to each relevant segment *only if* their related revenues and expenses are also allocated to those segments.

IAS 14 provides a **decision tree** which applies all of these rules, which you may find helpful.

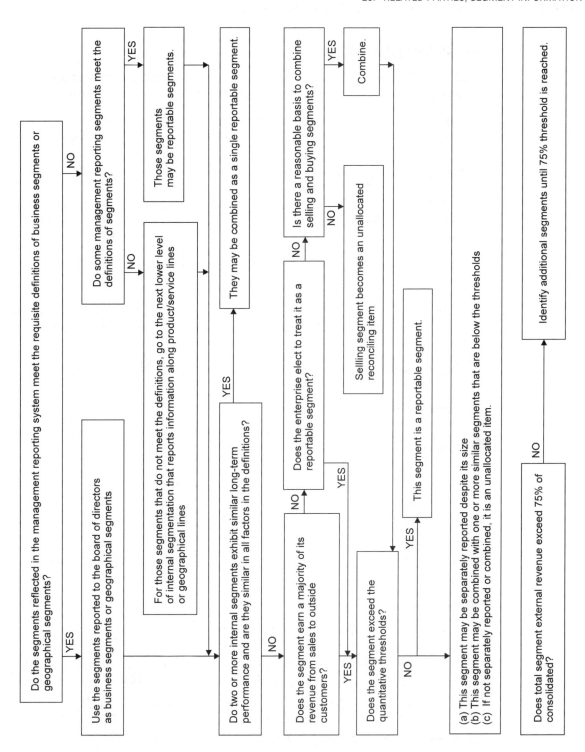

4 Disclosure of segment information

Do not worry too much about the detailed disclosure requirements; try to learn this summary instead.

The disclosure requirements of IAS 14 are long and complicated, but they can be summarised in the following tables.

Primary format is:	Business segment	Geographical segment by location of assets	Geographical segment by location of customers
Item	**Required primary disclosures by:**	**Required primary disclosures by:**	**Required primary disclosures by:**
Revenue from external customers	Business segment	Location of assets	Location of customers
Revenue from transactions with other segments	Business segment	Location of assets	Location of customers
Segment result	Business segment	Location of assets	Location of customers
Carrying amount of segment assets	Business segment	Location of assets	Location of customers
Segment liabilities	Business segment	Location of assets	Location of customers
Cost to acquire property, plant, equipment, and intangibles	Business segment	Location of assets	Location of customers
Depreciation and amortisation expense	Business segment	Location of assets	Location of customers
Non-cash expenses other than depreciation and amortisation	Business segment	Location of assets	Location of customers
Share of net profit or loss of and investment in equity method associates or joint ventures	Business segment (if substantially all within a single business segment)	Location of assets (if substantially all within a single segment)	Location of customers (if substantially all within a single segment)
Reconciliation of revenue, result, assets and liabilities	Business segment	Location of assets	Location of customers

Item	**Required secondary disclosures by:**	**Required secondary disclosures by:**	**Required secondary disclosures by:**
Revenue from external customers	Location of customers	Business segment	Business segment
Carrying amount of segment assets	Location of assets	Business segment	Business segment
Cost to acquire property, plant, equipment, and intangibles	Location of assets	Business segment	Business segment
Revenue from external customers	-	Geographical customers if different from location of assets	-
Carrying amount of segment assets	-	-	Location of assets if different from location of customers

Item	Required secondary disclosures by:	Required secondary disclosures by:	Required secondary disclosures by:
Cost to acquire property, plant, equipment, and intangibles	-	-	Location of assets if different from location of customers

Other required disclosures whatever the primary format
• Revenue for any business or geographical segment whose external revenue is more than 10% of entity revenue but that is not a reportable segment because a majority of its revenue is from internal transfers
• Basis of pricing inter-segment transfers and any change therein
• Changes in segment accounting policies
• Types of products and services in each business segment
• Composition of each geographical segment

The standard also gives the following examples of disclosure, which would be accompanied by a written commentary. The primary disclosures are by business segment (see overleaf) while the secondary disclosures by geographical segments are below.

GEOGRAPHICAL SEGMENTS (note)

	Sales revenue by geographical market	
	20X2	20X1
	$m	$m
United Kingdom	19	22
Other European Union countries	30	31
Canada and the United States	28	21
Mexico and South America	6	2
Southeast Asia (principally Japan and Taiwan)	18	14
	101	90

	Carrying amount of segment assets		Additions to property, plant, equipment, and intangible assets	
	20X2	20X1	20X2	20X1
	$m	$m	$m	$m
United Kingdom	72	78	8	5
Other European Union countries	47	37	5	4
Canada and the United States	34	20	4	3
Indonesia	22	20	7	6
	175	155	24	18

Question

The Multitrade Co has three divisions (all based in the home country, the UK), A, B and C. Details of their revenue, results and net assets are given below.

	Paper products 20X2 $m	Paper products 20X1 $m	Office products 20X2 $m	Office products 20X1 $m	Publishing 20X2 $m	Publishing 20X1 $m	Other operations 20X2 $m	Other operations 20X1 $m	Eliminations 20X2 $m	Eliminations 20X1 $m	Consolidated 20X2 $m	Consolidated 20X1 $m
Revenue												
External sales	55	50	20	17	19	16	7	7				
Inter-segment sales	15	10	10	14	2	4	2	2	(29)	(30)		
Total revenue	70	60	30	31	21	20	9	9	(29)	(30)	101	90
Result												
Segment result	20	17	9	7	2	1	0	0	(1)	(1)	30	24
Unallocated corporate expenses											(7)	(9)
Operating profit											23	15
Interest expense											(4)	(4)
Interest income											2	3
Share of net profits of associates	6	5					2	2			8	7
Income taxes											(7)	(4)
Profit											22	17
Other information												
Segment assets	54	50	34	30	10	10	10	9			108	99
Investment in equity method associates	20	16					12	10			32	26
Unallocated corporate assets											35	30
Consolidated total assets											175	155
Segment liabilities	25	15	8	11	8	8	1	1			42	35
Unallocated corporate liabilities											40	55
Consolidated total liabilities											82	90
Capital expenditure	12	10	3	5	5	5	4	3				
Depreciation	9	7	9	7	5	3	3	4				
Non cash expenses other than depreciation	8	2	7	3	2	2	2	1				

Division A	$'000
Sales to B	304,928
Other UK sales	57,223
Middle East export sales	406,082
Pacific fringe export sales	77,838
	846,071

Division B	
Sales to C	31,034
Export sales to Europe	195,915
	226,949

Division C	
Export sales to North America	127,003

	Division A $'000	Division B $'000	Division C $'000
Operational profit/(loss) before tax	162,367	18,754	(8,303)
Re-allocated costs from			
Head office	48,362	24,181	24,181
Interest costs	3,459	6,042	527

	Head office $'000	Division A	Division B	Division C
Non-current assets	49,071	200,921	41,612	113,076
Current assets	47,800	121,832	39,044	92,338
Current liabilities	28,636	16,959	6,295	120,841

Required

Prepare a segment report in accordance with IAS 14 for publication in Multitrade's accounts, on the basis that the primary report will be based on business segments.

Answer

Ignoring comparative figures, Multitrade Co's segment report would look like this.

BUSINESS SEGMENTS

	Group $'000	Division A $'000	Division B $'000	Division C $'000
Revenue				
Total sales	1,200,023	846,071	226,949	127,003
Inter-segment sales	335,962	304,928	31,034	–
Sales to third parties	864,061	541,143	195,915	127,003
Result				
Segment profit/(loss)	172,818	162,367	18,754	(8,303)
Common costs **	96,724			
Operating profit	76,094			
Net interest	10,028			
Group profit before tax	66,066			
Net assets				
Segment assets	608,823	322,753	80,656	205,414
Unallocated assets	96,871			
Total assets	705,694			
Unallocated liabilities	172,731			
Total liabilities	172,731			

Tutor's hint. As the interest charge is presented as a group item, it is probably best not to present any segmentation of the liabilities on which the interest has presumably been incurred.

GEOGRAPHICAL SEGMENTS

	Group $'000	United Kingdom $'000	Middle East $'000	Pacific fringe $'000	Europe $'000	North America $'000
Revenue by destination ***						
Sales to third parties	864,061	57,223	406,082	77,838	195,915	127,003

*   Revenue, profit, net interest and net assets should be the same as those shown in the accounts.

**   Common costs and unallocated assets are those items in the accounts which cannot reasonably be allocated to any one segment. An example of a common cost is the cost of maintaining the holding company share register, and an example of an unallocated asset might be the head office building.

***   Revenue may be disclosed by origin or destination. Here all sales originate in the UK, so it is sensible to disclose sales by destination.

Chapter roundup

- **IAS 24** is basically a disclosure statement.

- Another important aspect of reporting financial performance is **segment reporting**.

- **IAS 14** adopts a **management approach** to determining reporting segments.

- The most important **definitions** are of:

  - Business segments
  - Geographical segments

- These definitions include **factors** which are used to determine whether products/services are related or whether a geographical segment exists. You must **learn these** as the rest of the standard is based on them.

- Other definitions are also important. You should be particularly careful about what is **included in and excluded from**:

  - Segment revenue
  - Segment expense
  - Segment assets
  - Segment liabilities

- Do not worry too much about the detailed **disclosure requirements**. These are unlikely to be of great importance in the exam.

Quick quiz

1 A managing director of an entity is a related party.

   True ☐

   False ☐

2 What approach should normally be taken when deciding whether business or geographical segments should be the primary reporting format?

Answers to quick quiz

1 True. A member of the key management of an entity is a related party of that entity.

2 See Para 3.1

Exam question bank

Examination standard questions are indicated by the mark and time allocations.

1 Revision of accounting concepts

Explain the following accounting concepts.

(a)   The business entity concept
(b)   The money measurement concept
(c)   The historical cost convention
(d)   The stable monetary unit
(e)   Objectivity
(f)   The realisation concept
(g)   The duality concept

2 Regulators

State three different regulatory influences on the preparation of the published accounts of quoted companies and briefly explain the role of each one. Comment briefly on the effectiveness of this regulatory system.

3 Standard setters

There are those who suggest that any standard setting body is redundant because accounting standards are unnecessary. Other people feel that such standards should be produced, but by the government, so they are legislated.

Required

Discuss the statement that accounting standards are unnecessary for the purpose of regulating financial statements.

4 IAS 1

IAS 1 (revised) states that there are overall considerations that ensure the fair presentation of financial statements and compliance with International Accounting Standards.

Required

(a)   List and explain briefly three of the overall considerations.

   (i)   Materiality and aggregation
   (ii)   Offsetting
   (iii)   Consistency of presentation

   as the terms are used in IAS 1 (Revised).

(b)   Explain and give an example of the effect on a set of published financial statements of a company, if the going concern convention is held not to apply.

(c)   The IASB has produced a document called the 'Framework for the Preparation and Presentation of Financial Statements'.

   Required

   Explain in general terms what the Framework is trying to achieve. Do you think that IAS 1 (Revised) is consistent with this aim? Give reasons for your answer.

5 Jenson (25 marks)

45 mins

The timing of revenue (income) recognition has long been an area of debate and inconsistency in accounting. Industry practice in relation to revenue recognition varies widely, the following are examples of different points in the operating cycle of businesses that revenue and profit can be recognised.

(a)   On the acquisition of goods
(b)   During the manufacture or production of goods
(c)   On delivery/acceptance of goods
(d)   When certain conditions have been satisfied after the goods have been delivered
(e)   Receipt of payment for credit sales
(f)   On the expiry of a guarantee or warranty

In the past the 'critical event' approach has been used to determine the timing of revenue recognition. The International Accounting Standards Board (IASB) in its Framework for the Preparation and Presentation of Financial Statements (Framework) has defined the 'elements' of financial statements, and it uses these to determine when a gain or loss occurs.

Required

(a)   Explain what is meant by the critical event in relation to revenue recognition and discuss the criteria used in the Framework for determining when a gain or loss arises.   (5 marks)

(b)   For each of the stages of the operating cycle identified above, explain why it may be an appropriate point to recognise revenue and, where possible, give a practical example of an industry where it occurs.   (12 marks)

(c)   Jenson has entered into the following transactions/agreements in the year to 31 March 20X0.

  (i)   Goods, which had a cost of $20,000, were sold to Wholesaler for $35,000 on 1 June 20W9. Jenson has an option to repurchase the goods from Wholesaler at any time within the next two years. The repurchase price will be $35,000 plus interest charged at 12% per annum from the date of sale to the date of repurchase. It is expected that Jenson will repurchase the goods.

  (ii)   Jenson owns the rights to a fast food franchise. On 1 April 20W9 it sold the right to open a new outlet to Mr Cody. The franchise is for five years. Jenson received an initial fee of $50,000 for the first year and will receive $5,000 per annum thereafter. Jenson has continuing service obligations on its franchise for advertising and product development that amount to approximately $8,000 per annum for each franchised outlet. A reasonable profit margin on the provision of the continuing services is deemed to be 20% of revenues received.

  (iii)   On 1 September 20W9 Jenson received subscriptions in advance of $240,000. The subscriptions are for 24 monthly publications of a magazine produced by Jenson. At the year end Jenson had produced and despatched six of the 24 publications. The total cost of producing the magazine is estimated at $192,000 with each publication costing a broadly similar amount.

Required

Describe how Jenson should treat each of the above examples in its financial statements in the year to 31 March 20X0.   (8 marks)

6 D'Urberville (25 marks)

45 mins

The financial controller of D'Urberville Inc is preparing forecast balance sheets as at 31 December 20X4, 20X5, 20X6 and 20X7.

The 20X4 forecast has been prepared and shows the following figure in respect of motor vehicles.

	$'000
Cost	540
Accumulated depreciation	130
Net book value	410

Depreciation on motor vehicles is charged at 25% on the reducing balance. A full year's depreciation is charged in the year of purchase and none in the year of sale.

The assistant accountant has collated the following information in order to help the financial controller prepare his forecast.

FORECAST PURCHASES OF MOTOR VEHICLES
FOR THE YEARS ENDED 31 DECEMBER

	20X5 $'000	20X6 $'000	20X7 $'000
List price			
Cash purchase	180	300	450
Leased vehicles	-	400	500
Trade discount (20%)			
Cash purchase	36	60	90
Leased vehicles	-	80	100
Cash discount (5% of net price)	7	12	18
Delivery costs (paid to supplier)	10	12	15
Costs of valeting old vehicles to prepare them for sale	2	3	4
Trade-in allowances on old vehicles to be set off against finance lease first year rental		15	20
Finance lease first year rental		65 (80 – 15)	90 (110 – 20)
Total cash to be paid to the suppliers of the new vehicles in the year of outright purchase	147 (180 – 36 – 7 + 10)	77 (65 + 12)	105 (90 + 15)

FORECAST DISPOSALS OF MOTOR VEHICLES (AT COST)
IN THE YEARS ENDED 31 DECEMBER

	20X5 $'000	20X6 $'000	20X7 $'000
Vehicle			
Originally acquired in years ended 31 December			
20X0	30		
20X1	40		
20X2		45	
20X3		65	
20X4			75

The following methods of purchase will be used to acquire the vehicles.

Year ended 31 December 20X5: cash purchase.

Year ended 31 December 20X6: cash purchase and finance lease agreement. A rental of $80,000 will be payable in arrears for six years. The fair value of the vehicles was $320,000.

Year ended 31 December 20X7: cash purchase and finance lease agreement. A rental of $110,000 will be payable in arrears for six years. The fair value of the vehicles was $400,000.

Required

For the non-current asset (motor vehicles) in the forecast balance sheets of D'Urberville Inc as at 31 December 20X5, 20X6, 20X7, produce a schedule showing cost, accumulated depreciation and net book value. You should show all your workings and make all calculations to the nearest $'000.

7 Winger (25 marks)   45 mins

The following list of account balances relates to Winger at 31 March 20X1.

	$'000	$'000
Sales revenue (note 1)		358,450
Cost of sales	185,050	
Distribution costs	28,700	
Administration expenses	15,000	
Lease rentals (note 2)	20,000	
Debenture interest paid	2,000	
Interim dividends (note 6)	12,000	
Property at cost (note 3)	200,000	
Plant and equipment cost	154,800	
Depreciation 1 April 20X0 – plant and equipment		34,800
Development expenditure (note 4)	30,000	
Profit on disposal of non-current assets		45,000
Trade accounts receivable	55,000	
Inventories: 31 March 20X1	28,240	
Cash and bank	10,660	
Trade accounts payable		29,400
Taxation: over provision in year to 31 March 20X0		2,200
Equity shares of 25c each		150,000
8% debenture (issued in 20W9)		50,000
Accumulated profits 1 April 20X0		71,600
	741,450	741,450

The following notes are relevant.

(a)   Included in sales revenue is $27 million, which relates to sales made to customers under sale or return agreements. The expiry date for the return of these goods is 30 April 20X1. Winger has charged a mark-up of 20% on cost for these sales.

(b)   A lease rental of $20 million was paid on 1 April 20X0. It is the first of five annual payments in advance for the rental of an item of equipment that has a cash purchase price of $80 million. The auditors have advised that this is a finance lease and have calculated the implicit interest rate in the lease as 12% per annum. Leased assets should be depreciated on a straight-line basis over the life of the lease.

(c)   On 1 April 20X0 Winger acquired a new property at a cost of $200 million. For the purpose of calculating depreciation only, the asset has been separated into the following elements.

BPP
PROFESSIONAL EDUCATION

Separate asset	Cost	Life
	$'000	
Land	50,000	freehold
Heating system	20,000	10 years
Lifts	30,000	15 years
Building	100,000	50 years

The depreciation of the elements of the property should be calculated on a straight-line basis. The new property replaced an existing one that was sold on the same date for $95 million. It had cost $50 million and had a carrying value of $80 million at the date of sale. The profit on this property has been calculated on the original cost. It had not been depreciated on the basis that the depreciation charge would not be material.

Plant and machinery is depreciated at 20% on the reducing balance basis.

(d)   The figure for development expenditure in the list of account balances represents the amounts deferred in previous years in respect of the development of a new product. Unfortunately, during the current year, the government has introduced legislation which effectively bans this type of product. As a consequence of this the project has been abandoned. The directors of Winger are of the opinion that writing off the development expenditure, as opposed to its previous deferment, represents a change of accounting policy and therefore wish to treat the write off as a prior period adjustment.

(e)   A provision for income tax for the year to 31 March 20X1 of $15 million is required.

(f)   The company has paid an interim equity dividend and half of the annual debenture interest. The average annual dividend yield (interim plus final) for companies in Winger's market sector is 4%. The current market price of Winger's equity shares is $1.25. In March 20X1 the directors declared, but have not yet accounted for, a final dividend which will give Winger's equity shareholders a return equal to the average gross yield for the sector.

Required

(a)   Prepare the income statement of Winger for the year to 31 March 20X1.   (9 marks)

(b)   A balance sheet as at 31 March 20X1 in accordance with International Accounting Standards as far as the information permits.   (11 marks)

(c)   Discuss the acceptability of the company's previous policy in respect of non-depreciation of property.   (5 marks)

8 C Co

C Co is a civil engineering company. It started work on two construction projects during the year ended 31 December 20X0. The following figures relate to those projects at the balance sheet date.

	Maryhill bypass	Rottenrow Centre
	$'000	$'000
Contract price	9,000	8,000
Costs incurred to date	1,400	2,900
Estimated costs to completion	5,600	5,200
Value of work certified to date	2,800	3,000
Cash received from contractee	2,600	3,400

An old mineshaft has been discovered under the site for the Rottenrow Centre and the costs of dealing with this have been taken into account in the calculation of estimated costs to completion. C Co's lawyers are reasonably confident that the customer will have to bear the additional costs which will be incurred in stabilising the land. If negotiations are successful then the contract price will increase to $10m.

C Co recognises revenues and profits on construction contracts on the basis of work certified to date.

Required

(a)   Calculate the figures which would appear in C Co's financial statements in respect of these two projects.

(b)   It has been suggested that profit on construction contracts should not be recognised until the contract is completed. Briefly explain whether you believe that this suggestion would improve the quality of financial reporting for long-term contracts.

9 Dennis

The following transactions and events have arisen during the preparation of the draft financial statements of Dennis for the year to 31 March 20X0.

(a)   On 1 April 20W9 Dennis issued $80 million 8% convertible loan stock at par. The stock is convertible into equity shares, or redeemable at par, on 31 March 20X4, at the option of the stockholders. The terms of conversion are that each $100 of loan stock will be convertible into 50 equity shares of Dennis. A finance consultant has advised that if the option to convert to equity had not been included in the terms of the issue, then a coupon (interest) rate of 12% would have been required to attract subscribers for the stock.

The value of $1 receivable at the end of each year at a discount rate of 12% can be taken as:

Year	$
1	0.89
2	0.80
3	0.71
4	0.64
5	0.57

Required

Calculate the income statement finance charge for the year to 31 March 20X0 and the balance sheet extracts at 31 March 20X0 in respect of the issue of the convertible loan stock.   (5 marks)

(b)   On 1 January 20X0 Dennis acquired Steamdays, a company that operates a scenic railway along the coast of a popular tourist area. The summarised balance sheet at fair values of Steamdays on 1 January 20X0, reflecting the terms of the acquisition was:

	$'000
Goodwill	200
Operating licence	1,200
Property – train stations and land	300
Rail track and coaches	300
Two steam engines	1,000
Purchase consideration	3,000

The operating licence is for ten years. It was renewed on 1 January 20X0 by the transport authority and is stated at the cost of its renewal. The carrying values of the property and rail track and coaches are based on their value in use. The engines are valued at their net selling prices.

On 1 February 20X0 the boiler of one of the steam engines exploded, completely destroying the whole engine. Fortunately no one was injured, but the engine was beyond repair. Due to its age a replacement could not be obtained. Because of the reduced passenger capacity the estimated value in use of the whole of the business after the accident was assessed at $2 million.

Passenger numbers after the accident were below expectations even allowing for the reduced capacity. A market research report concluded that tourists were not using the railway because of their fear of a similar accident occurring to the remaining engine. In the light of this the value in use of the business was re-assessed on 31 March 20X0 at $1.8 million. On this date Dennis received an offer of $900,000 in respect of the operating licence (it is transferable). The realisable value of the other net assets has not changed significantly.

Required

Calculate the carrying value of the assets of Steamdays (in Dennis's consolidated balance sheet) at 1 February 20X0 and 31 March 20X0 after recognising the impairment losses.

(c)   Dennis is in the intermediate stage of a construction contract for the building of a new privately owned road bridge over a river estuary. The original details of the contract are:

Approximate duration of contract: 3 years
Date of commencement: 1 October 20W8
Total contract price: $40 million
Estimated total cost: $28 million

An independent surveyor certified the value of the work in progress as follows:
– on 31 March 20W9 $12 million
– on 31 March 20X0 $30 million (including the $12 million in 20W9)

Total costs incurred at:
– 31 March 20W9 $9 million
– 31 March 20X0 $28.5 million (including the $9 million in 20W9)

Progress billings at 31 March 20X0 were $25 million.

On 1 April 20W9 Dennis agreed to a contract variation that would involve an additional $5 million contract revenue with associated additional estimated costs of $2 million.

The costs incurred during the year to 31 March 20X0 include $2.5 million relating to the replacement of some bolts which had been made from material that had been incorrectly specified by the firm of civil engineers who were contracted by Dennis to design the bridge. These costs were not included in the original estimates, but Dennis is hopeful that they can be recovered from the firm of civil engineers.

Dennis calculates profit on construction contracts using the percentage of completion method. The percentage of completion of the contract is based on the value of the work certified to date compared to the total contract price.

Required

Prepare the income statement and balance sheet extracts in respect of the contract for the year to 31 March 20X0 only.

10 Bulwell (25 marks)   45 mins

Bulwell Aggregates Co wish to expand their transport fleet and purchased three heavy lorries with a list price of $18,000 each. Robert Bulwell has negotiated lease finance to fund this expansion, and the company has entered into a finance lease agreement with Granby Garages Co on 1 January 20X1. The agreement states that Bulwell Aggregates will pay a deposit of $9,000 on 1 January 20X1, and two annual instalments of $24,000 on 31 December 20X1, 20X2 and a final instalment of $20,391 on 31 December 20X3.

Interest is to be calculated at 25% on the balance outstanding on 1 January each year and paid on 31 December each year.

The depreciation policy of Bulwell Aggregates Co is to write off the vehicles over a four year period using the straight line method and assuming a scrap value of $1,333 for each vehicle at the end of its useful life.

The cost of the vehicles to Granby Garages is $14,400 each.

Required

(a)   Account for the above transactions in the books of Bulwell Aggregates Co showing the entries in the income statement and balance sheet for the years 20X1, 20X2, 20X3. This is the only lease transaction undertaken by this company. (15 marks)

(b)   Account for the above transactions in the books of Granby Garages Co, showing the entries in the lease trading account for the years 20X1, 20X2 and 20X3. This is the only lease transaction undertaken by this company. (10 marks)

Calculations to the nearest $.

11 Corax (25 marks)   45 mins

Corax Inc has an allotted capital of $350,000 in fully paid 50c ordinary shares. At 31 December 20X6 the following balances were included in the company's balance sheet. Corax operates in a country where the imputation tax system applies.

	$
Agreed corporation tax liability on 20X5 profits	16,300
Estimated corporation tax liability on 20X6 profits	5,000
Deferred taxation account	29,400
Retained earnings (credit)	43,000

(No dividends had been paid or proposed in respect of 20X6)

The following information relates to the year ended 31 December 20X7.

(a)   Corporation tax liability for 20X5 profits was settled (January).

(b)   Interim dividend of 3c per share was paid (August).

(c)   Advanced tax on the interim dividend was paid (October).

(d)   Corporation tax liability for 20X6 was agreed at $3,800 (December), paid January 20X8.

(e)   Net profit for 20X7 (before tax) was calculated at $100,000.

(f)   Corporation tax based on the 20X7 profits was estimated at $36,000.

(g)   Directors proposed a final dividend of 4.5c per share (December).

(h)   A transfer to the deferred taxation account of $7,000 for 20X7 is to be made in respect of capital allowances in excess of depreciation charges (the entire balance on the deferred tax account being of a similar nature).

Required

(a)   Make all relevant entries in the ledger accounts (except bank and share capital). (7 marks)

(b)   Complete the Income Statement for 20X7 and show how the final balances would be included the balance sheet at 31 December 20X7. Show the details given in the notes to the accounts. (18 marks)

Assume advanced tax at $1/4$ of the net dividend.

12 Provisions (25 marks)   45 mins

IAS 37 *Provisions, contingent liabilities and contingent assets* was issued in July 1998. Prior to its publication, there was no International Accounting Standard that dealt with the general subject of accounting for provisions.

Extract prepares its financial statements to 31 December each year. During the years ended 31 December 20X0 and 31 December 20X1, the following event occurred.

Extract is involved in extracting minerals in a number of different countries. The process typically involves some contamination of the site from which the minerals are extracted. Extract makes good this contamination only where legally required to do so by legislation passed in the relevant country.

The company has been extracting minerals in Copperland since January 20W8 and expects its site to produce output until 31 December 20X5. On 23 December 20X0, it came to the attention of the directors of Extract that the government of Copperland was virtually certain to pass legislation requiring the making good of mineral extraction sites. The legislation was duly passed on 15 March 20X1. The directors of Extract estimate that the cost of making good the site in Copperland will be $2 million. This estimate is of the actual cash expenditure that will be incurred on 31 December 20X5.

Required

(a)   Explain why there was a need for an accounting standard dealing with provisions, and summarise the criteria that need to be satisfied before a provision is recognised.   (12 marks)

(b)   Compute the effect of the estimated cost of making good the site on the financial statements of Extract for BOTH of the years ended 31 December 20X0 and 20X1. Give full explanations of the figures you compute.

The annual discount rate to be used in any relevant calculations is 10%.   (13 marks)

13 Tree (25 marks)   45 mins

Tree Co is a listed company. The following is a summary of its account balances at 31 March 20X6.

	$'000	$'000
Sales revenues		224,000
Inventories 1 April 20X5	12,580	
Purchases of goods	92,340	
Wages (operating cost)	34,690	
Distribution costs	11,240	
Administration costs	16,780	
Interest expense	200	
Interim ordinary dividend	4,000	
Tangible non-current assets (net of government grants of $4 million, note 1)	112,680	
Depreciation of tangible non-current assets at 1 April 20X5		7,800
Intangible non-current assets, net book value at 1 April 20X5 (note 1)	22,500	
Net surplus on the sale of non-current assets (note 2)		1,800
Research and development costs (note 3)	4,500	
Construction contract balance (note 4)		1,400
Trade receivables/payables	16,800	10,260
Long term investment: 8% Bonds dated 20Y1	14,000	
Bond interest – net receipts (note 5)		840
Tax paid (note 5)	850	
Cash and bank	10,600	
Deferred income tax (note 5)		3,800
Ordinary shares 25 cents each		80,000
Retained earnings 1 April 20X5		23,860
	353,760	353,760

The following information is relevant.

(a) Tangible non-current assets are depreciated at 20% on the cost of assets owned at the year end. The government grant was received during the current year. Tree discloses capital grants as deferred income in its balance sheet. Intangible assets represent software and brands that were all purchased on 1 April 20X3 and are being amortised over five years.

(b) On 1 September 20X5 Tree closed its publishing division. The publishing division's operating results from 1 April 20X5 to the date of closure which are included in the figures in the above list of account balances are:

	$'000
Sales revenues	30,800
Operating costs	(31,766)
Attributable tax relief	200

The operating costs figure above includes estimates of the division's wages and depreciation costs for the period.

The net assets of the division were sold at a gross loss of $1.2 million. This has been deducted from a $3 million surplus on the sale of other land and buildings. Tax relief of $300,000 is attributable to the loss on disposal.

(c) The research and development costs relate to a single project to develop a new electronic keyboard and sampler called the 'Techno'. This was completed during the current year. Full details of its cost are:

	Research	Development
	$'000	$'000
Year to 31 March 20X4	4,500	nil
Year to 31 March 20X5	2,800	2,400
Year to 31 March 20X6	1,200	3,300

Prior to the current year the directors have written off all research and development costs as incurred in compliance with IAS 38 *Intangible assets*. At the beginning of the current year the directors became confident of a profitable outcome to the project. The auditors are satisfied that the expenditure now meets the criteria for asset recognition in IAS 38.

Production of the 'Techno' started immediately after the completion of its research and development and is expected to last for five years. A full year's amortisation is to be calculated for the current year.

(d)   The accountant of Tree was unsure how to record the transactions relating to a construction contract. The figure in the list of account balances represents progress billings received of $5.4 million less the costs incurred to date of $4 million. The following details have been obtained.

	$m
Contract revenue (fixed)	10
Cost incurred to date	4
Estimated cost to complete	2
Progress billings	6

There is a 10% retention from progress billings.

The company believes that the outcome of this contract can be estimated reliably. The company policy for measuring the percentage of completion of a contract is:

$$\frac{\text{Progress billings}}{\text{Total contract revenue}} \times 100\%$$

Note. The billed contract revenue is not included in the sales revenue figure in the list of account balances.

(e)   Tree operates in a country where tax of 25% is deducted at source from bond interest received/paid. Investment income is to be shown gross in the income statement. Tax deducted at source is reclaimed by the suffering company as a reduction of the payment of its income tax liability of the year in which the tax has been deducted. Tax on corporate income is paid 6 months after a company's year end.

The balance on the taxation account of $850,000 in the list of account balances represents the tax provision for the year to 31 March 20X5 of $8,500,000 finally settled on 31 December 20X5 for $9,350,000.

The provision for income tax for the year to 31 March 20X6 is estimated at $10 million. This figure includes the tax effects of the disposal of property and the closure of the publishing division.

Deferred tax is calculated on all temporary differences under the comprehensive (full provision) method. The tax rate is 25%.

Temporary differences at 31 March 20X6 were:

	$'000
Accelerated tax depreciation	23,200
Other temporary differences	(3,400)

(f)   A final dividend of 3 cents per ordinary share has been proposed. Dividends are charged to the income statement of the year to which they relate, not the year in which they are paid.

(g)   Inventories at cost on 31 March 20X6 were $11 million.

Required

Prepare:

(a)   An income statement for Tree for the year to 31 March 20X6.   (11 marks)

(b)   A balance sheet as at 31 March 20X6.   (10 marks)

(c)   A note, suitable for publication, on four important accounting policies relating to the financial
        statements of Tree.   (4 marks)

Show your workings and state any assumptions you make.

14 Cher (25 marks)   45 mins

Note. To answers parts (b) and (c) of this question, you will need to refer to the income statements in the
appendix at the end of the question.

(a)   'Reported earnings per share is a very important indicator of performance for a quoted company.'

        Why do you think that this is, and do you agree?   (8 marks)

(b)   Cher Inc was formed fifteen years ago. As at 1 July 20X3, the issued share capital of the group was
        as follows, all shares being issued at par.

	Shares
Ordinary $1 shares fully paid	800,000
Ordinary $1 shares 60c paid	200,000
	1,000,000

        On 1 October 20X3, Cher Inc received the monies due on the partly paid shares.

        Required

        Calculate the basic earnings per share figure for the year ended 30 June 20X4, as it would appear
        in the financial statements of the group.   (5 marks)

(c)   On 28 February 20X5 Cher Inc made a 1 for 4 rights issue at $1.30 per share. The actual cum
        rights price was $1.90 per share on the last day of quotation cum rights.

        Required

        (i)   Calculate the basic earnings per share for the year ended 30 June 20X5. Show the
                comparative figure for 20X4.   (7 marks)

        (ii)   Explain the reasoning behind your calculation in part (c)(i).   (5 marks)

        APPENDIX: INCOME STATEMENTS

	Cher Inc	
Year ended 30 June	*20X4*	*20X5*
	$'000	$'000
Revenue	2,000	3,400
Cost of sales	900	800
Gross profit	1,100	2,600
Distribution costs	150	240
Administrative expenses	260	410
Profit before tax	690	1,950
Taxation	230	640
Profit after tax	460	1,310
Dividends	100	200
Retained earnings for the year	360	1,110

15 Group accounts

In many countries, companies with subsidiaries have been required to publish group accounts, usually in the form of consolidated accounts. You are required to state why you feel the preparation of group accounts is necessary and to outline their limitations, if any.

16 Arlene and Amanda (25 marks)   45 mins

Arlene Co acquired 135,000 shares in Amanda Co in 20X3. The reserves of Amanda Co at the date of acquisition comprised: retained earnings $20,000; capital reserve $10,000. The draft balance sheets of both companies are given below as at 31 December 20X5.

	Arlene Co $'000	Arlene Co $'000	Amanda Co $'000	Amanda Co $'000
Assets				
Non-current assets				
Tangible assets	350		210	
Investment in Amanda at cost	190		–	
		540		210
Current assets				
Inventories	83		42	
Receivables	102		48	
Current a/c: Amanda	5		–	
Bank and cash	40		12	
		230		102
Total assets		770		312
Equity and liabilities				
Capital and reserves				
Issued shares: $1	400		150	
Accumulated profits	190		99	
Capital reserve	60		15	
		650		264
Current liabilities				
Payables	90		37	
Current a/c: Arlene	–		1	
Proposed dividends	30		10	
		120		48
Total equity and liabilities		770		312

Arlene Co has not yet accounted for its share of the dividend proposed by Amanda Co. Assume the dividend was proposed before the year end.

On 29 December 20X5 Amanda Co sent a cheque for $4,000 to Arlene Co, which was not received until 3 January 20X6.

Required

Prepare the consolidated balance sheet of Arlene Co as at 31 December 20X5. (Goodwill arising on consolidation has been impaired. The amount of the impairment is $21,000).

17 Hand (25 marks)   45 mins

The following are the draft balance sheets as at 31 December 20X1 of Hand Co and its subsidiary Finger Co.

	Hand Co $'000	Hand Co $'000	Finger Co $'000	Finger Co $'000
Assets				
Non-current assets				
Tangible assets	100		76	
Investment in Finger at cost:				
40,000 $1 ordinary shares	50		–	
		150		76
Current assets				
Sundry	195		62	
Current account with Finger	8		–	
		203		62
Total assets		353		138
Equity and liabilities				
Capital and reserves				
Issued capital: $1 shares	100		60	
Accumulated profits	90		36	
		190		96
Current liabilities				
Sundry	163		36	
Current account with Hand	–		6	
		163		42
Total equity and liabilities		353		138

You ascertain the following information.

(a)   Hand Co purchased its shareholding in Finger Co on 30 June 20X1.

(b)   The accumulated profits of Finger Co consist of the following.

	$
Balance at 31 December 20X0	18,000
Profit for the year	18,000
	36,000

(c)   On 30 June 20X1 the fair value of Finger Co's tangible non-current assets exceeded their book value by $3,000. It is group policy to depreciate such assets over five years.

(d)   In July 20X1 Finger Co paid an ordinary dividend for 20X0 of $6,000. The dividend had been provided for in Finger Co's balance sheet at 31 December 20X0. Hand Co has credited its share of the dividend received to income.

(e)   The difference in the current account balances represents cash in transit.

(f)   Any goodwill on consolidation (positive or negative) should be treated in accordance with IFRS 3.

Required

Prepare Hand Co's consolidated balance sheet as at 31 December 20X1.

BPP
PROFESSIONAL EDUCATION

18 Corrie (25 marks)   45 mins

Corrie Co has a 75% subsidiary, Brookie Co, of which it also owns 25% of the preferred shares. Corrie has an associated company, Eastend Co, in which it has a 25% interest. Set out below are the balance sheets of the three companies as at 31 December 20X7. (Investment in subsidiary and associate are shown at cost.)

	Corrie Co		Brookie Co		Eastend Co	
	$m	$m	$m	$m	$m	$m
Assets						
Non-current assets						
Tangible assets	4,920		4,350		–	
Investments					1,500	
Shares in Brookie	3,960		–		–	
Shares in Eastend	900		–		–	
		9,780		4,350		1,500
Current assets						
Inventory	780		600		–	
Receivables	610		360		–	
Cash at bank and in hand	260		30		–	
		1,650		990		–
Total assets		11,430		5,340		1,500
Equity and liabilities						
Capital and reserves						
Ordinary $1 shares	6,000		2,400		1,500	
5% preferred $1 shares	–		1,200		–	
Share premium account	1,490		100		–	
Accumulated profits	1,600		790		–	
		9,090		4,490		1,500
Non-current liabilities		1,730		440		–
Current liabilities		610		410		–
Total equity and liabilities		11,430		5,340		1,500

You are the new assistant financial controller of Corrie Co and have been asked to prepare a consolidated balance sheet for the Corrie Group. The following further information is available.

(a)   Brookie Co was acquired on 1 January 20X7. Corrie Co paid $3,960m for the ordinary and preferred shares. On that date Brookie Co's retained earnings had a credit balance of $898m.

(b)   The preferred shares of Brookie Co are redeemable on 31 December 20Y6 at a premium of 10%. They were originally issued at par on 1 January 20X7. The premium has not yet been accounted for and is to be dealt with using a straight line method.

(c)   The balance on the share premium account of Brookie Co represents the premium on the issue of the ordinary shares.

(d)   When Brookie Co was acquired the fair value of its net assets was equal to their book value except for some non-material differences.

(e)   Goodwill arising on consolidation was found to be impaired. The amount of the impairment is $212,200.

(f)   Eastend Co is an investment company. It has no assets other than a portfolio of investments, the market value of which is $2,200m. In the above balance sheet, the investments are shown at their book value of $1,500m. Corrie Co acquired its interest in Eastend Co on 31 December 20X7.

(g)   Brookie Co paid a dividend for the year of 2c per ordinary $1 share and also paid the 5% preferred dividend. There was no dividend proposed at 31 December 20X7. As assistant financial controller, you have advised the directors of Corrie Co that the dividend payment of Brookie Co should be treated as if it were out of pre-acquisition profits, that is as a deduction from the value of the investment.

(h)   Brookie Co manufactures and sells industrial machinery. On 1 January 20X7 it sold a machine to Corrie Co which Corrie Co correctly classified as a non-current asset. The item was sold at a mark up of 25% of cost and is shown in the books of Corrie Co at $720m. Of this amount, $20m is still owed to Brookie Co. Corrie Co has charged a year's depreciation on the machine of 25%.

Required

(a)   'When a subsidiary pays a dividend out of pre-acquisition profits there are different ways of treating the dividend in the accounts of the holding company.'

Discuss.

(b)   Prepare the consolidated balance sheet for the Corrie Group as at 31 December 20X7.

19 War (25 marks)   45 mins

(a)   When an acquisition takes place, the purchase consideration may be in the form of share capital. Where no suitable market price exists (for example, shares in an unquoted company) how may the fair value of the purchase consideration be estimated?   (4 marks)

(b)   On 1 May 20X7, War Co acquired 70% of the ordinary share capital of Peace Co by issuing 500,000 ordinary $1 shares at a premium of 60c per share. The costs associated with the share issue were $50,000.

As at 30 June 20X7, the following financial statements for War Co and Peace Co were available.

INCOME STATEMENTS
FOR THE YEAR ENDED 30 JUNE 20X7

	War Co	Peace Co
	$'000	$'000
Revenue	3,150	1,770
Cost of sales	(1,610)	(1,065)
Gross profit	1,540	705
Distribution costs	(620)	(105)
Administrative expenses	(325)*	(210)
Profit from operations	595	390
Interest payable	(70)	(30)
Dividends from Peace Co	42	–
Profit before taxation	567	360
Tax on profit	(283)	(135)
Profit after tax	284	225
Dividends paid	(38)	(60)
Retained profit for the year	246	165

*Note. The issue costs of $50,000 on the issue of ordinary share capital are included in this figure.

BALANCE SHEETS AS AT 30 JUNE 20X7

	War Co		Peace Co	
	$'000	$'000	$'000	$'000
Assets				
Non-current assets				
Tangible non-current assets	1,750		350	
Investment in Peace Co	800		–	
		2,550		350
Current assets				
Inventory	150		450	
Receivables	238		213	
Cash	187		112	
		575		775
Total assets		3,125		1,125
Equity and liabilities				
Capital and reserves				
Shares of $1 each	750		100	
Share premium	300		150	
Accumulated profits	625		450	
		1,675		700
Non-current liabilities		1,050		175
Current liabilities		400		250
Total equity and liabilities		3,125		1,125

You have been asked to prepare the consolidated financial statements, taking account of the following further information.

(i)   There was no impairment in the value of goodwill.

(ii)   War Co accounts for pre-acquisition dividends by treating them as a deduction from the cost of the investment. Peace Co paid an ordinary dividend of 10c per share on 1 June 20X7. No dividends were proposed as at 30 June 20X7.

(iii)   The profit of Peace Co may be assumed to accrue evenly over the year.

(iv)   The tangible non-current assets of Peace Co had a net realisable value of $400,000 at the date of acquisition. Their open market value was $500,000. It has been decided that, as Peace Co was acquired so close to the year end, no depreciation adjustment will be made in the group accounts; the year end value will be taken as the carrying value of the tangible non-current assets in the accounts of Peace Co. The remaining assets and liabilities of Peace Co were all stated at their fair value as at 1 May 20X7.

(v)   Peace Co did not issue any shares between the date of acquisition and the year end.

(vi)   There were no intercompany transactions during the year.

Required

Prepare the consolidated balance sheet and the consolidated income statement of the War Group Co for the year ended 30 June 20X7. You should work to the nearest $'000. You do not need to prepare notes to the accounts.   (21 marks)

20 CPP and CCA (25 marks)   45 mins

(a)   'It is important that management and other users of financial accounts should be in a position to appreciate the effects of inflation on the business with which they are concerned.'

Required

Consider the above statement and explain how inflation obscures the meaning of accounts prepared by the traditional historical cost convention, and discuss the contribution which CPP accounting could make to providing a more satisfactory system of accounting for inflation.

(b) Compare the general principles underlying CPP and CCA accounting.

(c) Define the term 'realised holding gain'.

(d) Explain briefly the use in CCA accounting of:

    (i) The cost of sales adjustment
    (ii) The monetary working capital adjustment
    (iii) The depreciation adjustment
    (iv) The gearing adjustment

21 Alpha (25 marks)   45 mins

In producing the Framework for the Preparation and Presentation of Financial Statements (Framework) and some of the current International Accounting Standards, the International Accounting Standards Board (IASB) has had to address the potential problem that the management of some companies may choose to adopt inappropriate accounting policies. These could have the effect of portraying an entity's financial position in a favourable manner. In some countries this is referred to as 'creative accounting'. Included in the Framework, and a common feature of many recent International Accounting Standards, is the application of the principle of 'substance over form'.

Required

(a) Describe in broad terms common ways in which management can manipulate financial statements to indulge in 'creative accounting' and why they would wish to do so.   **(7 marks)**

(b) Explain the principle of substance over form and how it limits the above practice; and for each of the following areas of accounting describe an example of the application of substance over form.

    (i) Group accounting
    (ii) Financing non-current assets
    (iii) Measurement and disclosure of current assets   **(8 marks)**

(c) Alpha, a public listed corporation, is considering how it should raise $10 million of finance which is required for a major and vital non-current asset renewal scheme that will be undertaken during the current year to 31 December 20X6. Alpha is particularly concerned about how analysts are likely to react to its financial statements for the year to 31 December 20X6. Present forecasts suggest that Alpha's earnings per share and its financial gearing ratios may be worse than market expectations. Mr Wong, Alpha's Finance Director, is in favour of raising the finance by issuing a convertible loan. He has suggested that the coupon (interest) rate on the loan should be 5%; this is below the current market rate of 9% for this type of loan. In order to make the stock attractive to investors the terms of conversion into equity would be very favourable to compensate for the low interest rate.

Required

    (i) Explain why the Finance Director believes the above scheme may favourably improve Alpha's earnings per share and gearing.

    (ii) Describe how the requirements of IAS 33 *Earnings per share* and IAS 32 *Financial instruments: disclosure and presentation* are intended to prevent the above effects.

        (10 marks)

22 Reporting substance

Shaky Co enters into an agreement with Farant Factors Co with the following principal terms.

(a) Shaky Co will transfer (by assignment) to Farant Factors Co such trade debts as Shaky Co shall determine, subject only to credit approval by Farant Factors Co and a limit placed on the proportion of the total that may be due from any one debtor. Farant Factors Co levies a charge of 0.15 per cent of revenue, payable monthly, for this facility.

(b) Shaky Co continues to administer the sales ledger and handle all aspects of collection of the debts.

(c) Shaky Co may draw up to 80% of the gross amount of debts assigned at any one time, such drawings being debited in the books of Farant Factors Co to a factoring account operated by Farant Factors Co for Shaky Co.

(d) Weekly, Shaky Co assigns and sends copy invoices to Farant Factors Co as they are raised.

(e) Shaky Co is required to bank the gross amounts of all payments received from debts assigned to Farant Factors Co direct into an account in the name of Farant Factors Co. Credit transfers made by debtors direct into Shaky Co's own bank account must immediately be paid to Farant Factors Co.

(f) Farant Factors Co credits such collections from debtors to the factoring account, and debits the account monthly with interest calculated on the basis of the daily balances on the account using a rate of base rate plus 2.5%. Thus this interest charge varies with the amount of finance drawn by Shaky Co under the finance facility from Farant Factors Co, the speed of payment of the debtors and base rate.

(g) Farant Factors Co provides protection from bad debts. Any debts not recovered after 90 days are credited to the factoring account, and responsibility for their collection is passed to Farant Factors Co. A charge of 1% of the gross value of all debts factored is levied by Farant Factors Co for this service and debited to the factoring account.

(h) Farant Factors Co pays for the debts, less any advances, interest charges and credit protection charges, 90 days after the date of purchase, and debits the payment to the factoring account.

(i) On either party giving 90 days' notice to the other, the arrangement will be terminated. In such an event, Shaky Co will transfer no further debts to Farant Factors Co, and the balance remaining on the factoring account at the end of the notice period will be settled in cash in the normal way.

Required

Consider the nature of the above agreement and resulting transactions and state how these should be reflected in the accounts of Shaky Co.

23 Biggerbuys (25 marks)   45 mins

Biggerbuys has carried on business for a number of years as a retailer of a wide variety of consumer products. The entity operates from a number of stores around the United Kingdom. In recent years the entity has found it necessary to provide credit facilities to its customers in order to maintain growth in revenue. As a result of this decision the liability to its bankers has increased substantially. The statutory financial statements for the year ended 30 June 20X9 have recently been published and extracts are provided below, together with comparative figures for the previous two years.

INCOME STATEMENTS FOR THE YEARS ENDED 30 JUNE

	20X7	20X8	20X9
	$m	$m	$m
Revenue	1,850	2,200	2,500
Cost of sales	(1,250)	(1,500)	(1,750)
Gross profit	600	700	750
Other operating costs	(550)	(640)	(700)
Operating profit	50	60	50
Interest from credit sales	45	60	90
Interest payable	(25)	(60)	(110)
Profit before taxation	70	60	30
Tax payable	(23)	(20)	(10)
Profit after taxation	47	40	20
Dividends	(30)	(30)	(20)
Retained profits	17	10	–

BALANCE SHEETS AT 30 JUNE

	20X7	20X8	20X9
	$m	$m	$m
Tangible non-current assets	278	290	322
Inventories	400	540	620
Trade receivables	492	550	633
Cash	12	12	15
	1,182	1,392	1,590
Share capital	90	90	90
Reserves	252	262	262
	342	352	352
Bank loans	320	520	610
Other interest bearing borrowings	200	200	320
Trade payables	270	270	280
Tax payable	20	20	8
Proposed dividends	30	30	20
	1,182	1,392	1,590

Other information

- Depreciation charged for the three years in question was as follows.

Year ended 30 June	20X7	20X8	20X9
	$m	$m	$m
	55	60	70

- The other interest bearing borrowings are secured by a floating charge over the assets of Biggerbuys. Their repayment is due on 30 June 20Y9.

- The bank loans are unsecured. The maximum lending facility the bank will provide is $630m.

- Over the past three years the level of credit sales has been:

Year ended 30 June	20X7	20X8	20X9
	$m	$m	$m
	300	400	600

The entity offers extended credit terms for certain products to maintain market share in a highly competitive environment.

Given the steady increase in the level of bank loans which has taken place in recent years, the entity has recently written to its bankers to request an increase in the lending facility. The request was received by the bank on 15 October 20X9, two weeks after the financial statements were published. The bank is concerned at the steep escalation in the level of the loans and has asked for a report on the financial performance of Biggerbuys for the last three years.

Required

As a consultant management accountant employed by the bankers of Biggerbuys, prepare a report to the bank which analyses the financial performance of the company for the period covered by the financial statements. Your report may take any form you wish, but you are aware of the particular concern of the bank regarding the rapidly increasing level of lending. Therefore it may be appropriate to include aspects of prior performance that could have contributed to the increase in the level of bank lending.

24 Webster (25 marks)   45 mins

Webster is a publicly listed diversified holding company that is looking to acquire a suitable engineering company. Two private limited engineering companies, Cole and Darwin, are available for sale. The summarised financial statements for the year to 31 March 20X9 of both companies are as follows.

INCOME STATEMENT

	Cole		Darwin	
	$'000	$'000	$'000	$'000
Sales revenue (note (a))		3,000		4,400
Opening inventory	450		720	
Purchases (note (b))	2,030		3,080	
	2,480		3,800	
Closing inventory	(540)		(850)	
		(1,940)		(2,950)
Gross profit		1,060		1,450
Operating expenses		(480)		(964)
Profit from operations		580		486
Loan note interest		(80)		–
Overdraft interest		–		(10)
Net profit for period		500		476

BALANCE SHEETS

	Cole		Darwin	
	$'000	$'000	$'000	$'000
Non-current assets				
Property, plant and equipment (note (c) and (d))		2,340		3,100
Current assets				
Inventory	540		850	
Accounts receivable	522		750	
Bank	20		–	
		1,082		1,600
Total assets		3,422		4,700
Equity and liabilities				
Capital and reserves				
Equity shares of $1 each		1,000		500
Reserves				
Revaluation reserve		–		700
Accumulated profits – 1 April 20X8		684		1,912
Profit – year to 31 March 20X9		500		476
		2,184		3,588
Non-current liabilities				
10% Loan note		800		–
Current liabilities				
Accounts payable	438		562	
Overdraft	–		550	
		438		1,112
Total equity and liabilities		3,422		4,700

Webster bases its preliminary assessment of target companies on certain key ratios. These are listed below together with the relevant figures for Cole and Darwin calculated from the above financial statements:

		Cole		Darwin
Return on capital employed	(500+80)/(2,184+800)		(476/3,588)	
	×100	19·4 %	× 100	13·3 %
Asset turnover	(3,000/2,984)	1·01 times	(4,400/3,588)	1·23 times
Gross profit margin		35·3 %		33·0 %
Net profit margin		16·7 %		10·8 %
Accounts receivable				
collection period		64 days		62 days
Accounts payable				
payment period		79 days		67 days

Note. Capital employed is defined as shareholders' funds plus non-current debt at the year end; asset turnover is sales revenues divided by gross assets less current liabilities.

The following additional information has been obtained.

(a)   Cole is part of the Velox Group. On 1 March 20X9 it was permitted by its holding company to sell goods at a price of $500,000 to Brander, a fellow subsidiary. The sale gave Cole a gross profit margin of 40% instead of its normal gross margin of only 20% on these types of goods. In addition Brander was instructed to pay for the goods immediately. Cole normally allows three months credit.

(b)   On 1 January 20X9 Cole purchased $275,000 (cost price to Cole) of its materials from Advent, another member of the Velox Group. Advent was also instructed by Velox to depart from its normal trading terms, which would have resulted in a charge of $300,000 to Cole for these goods. The

Group's finance director also authorised a four-month credit period on this sale. Cole normally receives two months credit from its suppliers. Cole had sold all of these goods at the year-end.

(c)   Non-current assets:

Details relating to the two companies' non-current assets are:

	Cost/revaluation $'000	Depreciation $'000	Book value $'000
Cole: property	3,000	1,860	1,140
plant	6,000	4,800	1,200
			2,340
Darwin: property	2,000	100	1,900
plant	3,000	1,800	1,200
			3,100

The two companies own very similar properties. Darwin's property was revalued to $2,000,000 at the beginning of the current year (ie 1 April 20X8). On this date Cole's property, which is carried at cost less depreciation, had a book value of $1,200,000. Its current value (on the same basis as Darwin's property) was also $2,000,000. On this date (1 April 20X8) both properties had the same remaining life of 20 years.

(d)   Darwin purchased new plant costing $600,000 in February 20X9. In line with company policy a full year's depreciation at 20% per annum has been charged on all plant owned at year-end. The equipment is still being tested and will not come on-stream until next year. The purchase of the plant was largely financed by an overdraft facility, which resulted in the interest cost shown in the income statement. Both companies depreciate plant over a five-year life and treat all depreciation as an operating expense.

(e)   The bank overdraft that would have been required but for the favourable treatment towards Cole in respect of items in (a) and (b) above, would have attracted interest of $15,000 in the year to 31 March 20X9.

Required

(a)   Restate the financial statements of Cole and Darwin in order that they may be considered comparable for decision making purposes. State any assumptions you make.   (10 marks)

(b)   Recalculate the key ratios used by Webster and, referring to any other relevant points, comment on how the revised ratios may affect the assessment of the two companies.   (10 marks)

(c)   Discuss whether the information in notes (a) to (d) above would be publicly available, and if so, describe its source(s).   (5 marks)

25 Spice (25 marks)

45 mins

The following financial statements relate to Spice Inc.

INCOME STATEMENT FOR THE YEAR TO 31 MARCH 20X6

	$m	$m
Revenue		710
Cost of sales		(314)
Gross profit		396
Distribution costs	(62)	
Administrative costs	(54)	
		(116)
Operating profit		280
Interest payable	(14)	
Interest receivable	6	
		(8)
Profit before tax		272
Taxation		(64)
Profit for the year		208
Dividends		(40)
Retained profit for the year		168

SUMMARISED BALANCE SHEETS

	20X6		20X5	
	$m	$m	$m	$m
Assets				
Non-current assets at cost less depreciation		550		400
Current assets				
Inventory	280		310	
Trade receivables	260		220	
Interest receivable	2		4	
Investments	190		–	
Cash	12		42	
		744		576
Total assets		1,294		976
Equity and liabilities				
Capital and reserves				
Share capital: ordinary shares ($1)	220		180	
10% preference shares ($1)	–		40	
Share premium	88		70	
Capital redemption reserve	40		–	
Revaluation reserve	14		–	
Retained earnings	270		162	
		632		452
Non-current liabilities				
Borrowings	140		164	
Deferred tax	24		16	
		164		180
Current liabilities				
Trade and other payables		498		344
		1,294		976

The following information is relevant.

(a) During the year Spice Inc issued 20 million $1 ordinary shares at a premium of 100%, incurring issue costs of $2 million. Subsequent to this a bonus issue of 1 for 10 shares held was made from accumulated profits. On 1 September 20X5 Spice Inc decided to purchase and cancel all of its preference shares at a premium of 20c per share. The premium has been charged to the income statement as an administrative cost. Company law in the country of incorporation of Spice Inc requires a transfer to the capital redemption reserve equal to the nominal value of the shares redeemed.

(b)   Tangible non-current assets include certain properties which were revalued during the year giving a surplus of $14 million. Assets capitalised under finance lease agreements during the year amounted to $56 million. Disposals of assets having a net book value of $38 million realised $42 million. Depreciation for the year was $76 million.

(c)   All the short term investments of $190 million fall within the definition of cash equivalents under IAS 7.

(d)   *Analysis of liabilities*

	31 March 20X6 $m	31 March 20X5 $m
Repayable within one year:		
Bank overdraft (repayable on demand)	16	40
Obligations under finance leases	10	6
Trade payables	424	254
Corporate tax	32	20
Advanced tax	2	4
Dividends	8	16
Interest payable	6	4
	498	344
Non-current liabilities		
Obligations under finance leases	100	84
6% borrowings 20X6/20Y1	40	80
	140	164

(e)   Some of the borrowings were redeemed at par on 31 March 20X6.

(f)   Advanced tax recoverable at each year end has been offset against deferred tax.

(g)   Interest on finance leases of $6 million is included in the interest charge in the income statement.

Required

(a)   Prepare a cash flow statement for Spice Inc for the year ended 31 March 20X6 in compliance with IAS 7 *Cash flow statements* together with the accompanying notes.   (17 marks)

(b)   Prepare an analysis of the movement on share capital and reserves during the year.   (4 marks)

(c)   The IASB would prefer companies to use the direct method of presenting cash flow information, but almost all companies use the 'indirect' method of presentation. What arguments exist in favour of the direct method?   (4 marks)

26 Hepburn (25 marks)   45 mins

(a)   On 1 October Hepburn acquired 80% of the equity share capital of Salter by way of a share exchange. Hepburn issued five of its own shares for every two shares in Salter. The market value of Hepburn's shares on 1 October 20X0 was $3 each. The share issue has not yet been recorded in Hepburn's books. The summarised financial statements of both companies are:

INCOME STATEMENTS
YEAR TO 31 MARCH 20X1

	Hepburn		Salter	
	$'000	$'000	$'000	$'000
Sales revenues		1,200		1,000
Cost of sales		(650)		(660)
Gross profit		550		340
Operating expenses		(120)		(88)
Debenture interest		Nil		(12)
Operating profit		430		240
Income tax expense		(100)		(40)
Profit after tax		330		200
Dividends: interim	(40)		nil	
final	(40)		nil	
		(80)		(–)
Retained profit for the year		250		200

BALANCE SHEETS
AS AT 31 MARCH 20X1

Non current assets				
Property, plant and equipment		620		660
Investments		20		10
		640		670
Current assets				
Inventory	240		280	
Accounts receivable	170		210	
Bank	20		40	
		430		530
Total assets		1,070		1,200
Equity and liabilities				
Equity shares of $1 each		400		150
Accumulated profits		410		700
		810		850
Non current liabilities				
8% debentures		nil		150
Current liabilities				
Trade accounts payable	170		155	
Taxation	50		45	
Dividends	40		–	
		260		200
		1,070		1,200

The following information is relevant:

(i)   The fair values of Salter's assets were equal to their book values with the exception of its land, which had fair value of $125,000 in excess of its book value at the date of acquisition.

(ii)   In the post acquisition period Hepburn sold goods to Salter at a price of $100,000, this was calculated to give a mark-up on cost of 25% to Hepburn. Salter had half of these goods in inventory at the year end.

(iii)   Consolidated goodwill is impaired. The amount of the impairment is $20,000.

(iv)   The current accounts of the two companies disagreed due to a cash remittance of $20,000 to Hepburn on 26 March 20X1 not being received until after the year end. Before adjusting for this, Salter's debit balance in Hepburn's books was $56,000.

(v)   Hepburn follows the required treatment in IFRS 3 *Business combinations* to record the fair value of assets and minority interests.

Required

Prepare a consolidated income statement and balance sheet for Hepburn for the year to 31 March 20X1.   (20 marks)

(b)   At the same date as Hepburn made the share exchange for Salter's shares, it also acquired 6,000 'A' shares in Woodbridge for a cash payment of $20,000. The share capital of Woodbridge is made up of:

Equity voting A shares	10,000
Equity non-voting B shares	14,000

All of Woodbridge's equity shares are entitled to the same dividend rights; however during the year to 31 March 20X1 Woodbridge made substantial losses and did not pay any dividends.

Hepburn has treated its investment in Woodbridge as an ordinary long-term investment on the basis that:

(i)   It is only entitled to 25% of any dividends that Woodbridge may pay

(ii)   It does not have any directors on the board of Woodbridge

(iii)   It does not exert any influence over the operating policies or management of Woodbridge

Required

Comment on the accounting treatment of Woodbridge by Hepburn's directors and state how you believe the investment should be accounted for.   (5 marks)

Note. You are not required to amend your answer to part (a) in respect of the information in part (b).

Approaching the answer

(a) On 1 October Hepburn acquired 80% of the equity share capital of Salter by way of a share

> Note group structure

exchange. Hepburn issued five of its own shares for every two shares in Salter. The market value of Hepburn's shares on 1 October 20X0 was $3 each. The share issue has not yet been recorded in Hepburn's books. The summarised financial statements of both companies are:

> You can work out the cost of the investment for the goodwill calculation

INCOME STATEMENTS
YEAR TO 31 MARCH 20X1

	Hepburn		Salter	
	$'000	$'000	$'000	$'000
Sales revenues		1,200		1,000
Cost of sales		(650)		(660)
Gross profit		550		340
Operating expenses		(120)		(88)
Debenture interest		Nil		(12)
Operating profit		430		240
Income tax expense		(100)		(40)
Profit after tax		330		200
Dividends: interim	(40)			nil
final	(40)		–	
		(80)		(–)
Retained profit for the year		250		200

BALANCE SHEETS
AS AT 31 MARCH 20X1

Non current assets				
Property, plant and equipment		620		660
Investments		20		10
		640		670
Current assets				
Inventory	240		280	
Accounts receivable	170		210	
Bank	20		40	
		430		530
Total assets		1,070		1,200
Equity and liabilities				
Equity shares of $1 each		400		150
Accumulated profits		410		700
		810		850
Non current liabilities				
8% debentures		nil		150
Current liabilities				
Trade accounts payable	170		155	
Taxation	50		45	
Dividends	40		–	
		260		200
		1,070		1,200

The following information is relevant.

(i)   The fair values of Salter's assets were equal to their book values with the exception of its land, which had fair value of $125,000 in excess of its book value at the date of acquisition.

(ii) In the post acquisition period Hepburn sold goods to Salter at a price of $100,000, this was calculated to give a mark-up on cost of 25% to Hepburn. Salter had half of these goods in inventory at the year end.

(iii) Consolidated goodwill is impaired. The amount of the impairment is $20,000.

(iv) The current accounts of the two companies disagreed due to a cash remittance of $20,000 to Hepburn on 26 March 20X1 not being received until after the year end. Before adjusting for this, Salter's debit balance in Hepburn's books was $56,000.

(v)   Hepburn follows the required treatment in IFRS 3 *Business combinations* to record the fair value of assets and minority interests.

ie minority interests are credited with their share of the fair value adjustment

Required

Prepare a consolidated income statement and balance sheet for Hepburn for the year to 31 March 20X1.   (20 marks)

(b)   At the same date as Hepburn made the share exchange for Salter's shares, it also acquired 6,000 'A' shares in Woodbridge for a cash payment of $20,000. The share capital of Woodbridge is made up of:

Equity voting A shares	10,000
Equity non-voting B shares	14,000

All of Woodbridge's equity shares are entitled to the same dividend rights; however during the year to 31 March 20X1 Woodbridge made substantial losses and did not pay any dividends.

Hepburn has treated its investment in Woodbridge as an ordinary long-term investment on the basis that:

(i)   It is only entitled to 25% of any dividends that Woodbridge may pay

(ii)   It does not have any directors on the board of Woodbridge

(iii) It does not exert any influence over the operating policies or management of Woodbridge

Required

Comment on the accounting treatment of Woodbridge by Hepburn's directors and state how you believe the investment should be accounted for.   (5 marks)

This is a big hint that the treatment may be wrong

Note. You are not required to amend your answer to part (a) in respect of the information in part (b).

BPP
PROFESSIONAL EDUCATION

Exam answer bank

1 Revision of accounting concepts

> **Tutorial note**. This is straightforward revision from your earlier studies. Remember to give examples.

(a) **The business entity concept**

This concept is that accountants regard a business as a separate entity, distinct from its owners or managers. The concept applies whether the business is a limited liability company (and so recognised in law as a separate entity) or a sole proprietorship or partnership (in which case the business is not separately recognised by the law).

(b) **The money measurement concept**

This concept states that accounts will only deal with those items to which a monetary value can be attributed. For example, in the balance sheet of a business monetary values can be attributed to such assets as machinery (eg the original cost of the machinery; or the amount it would cost to replace the machinery) and inventories (eg the original cost of the goods, or, theoretically, the price at which the goods are likely to be sold).

The money measurement concept introduces limitations to the subject-matter of accounts. A business may have intangible assets such as the flair of a good manager or the loyalty of its workforce. These may be important enough to give it a clear superiority over an otherwise identical business, but because they cannot be evaluated in monetary terms they do not appear anywhere in the accounts.

(c) **The historical cost convention**

A basic principle of accounting (some writers include it in the list of fundamental accounting assumptions) is that resources are normally stated in accounts at historical cost, ie at the amount which the business paid to acquire them. An important advantage of this procedure is that the objectivity of accounts is maximised: there is usually objective, documentary evidence to prove the amount paid to purchase an asset or pay an expense.

In general, accountants prefer to deal with costs, rather than with 'values'. This is because valuations tend to be subjective and to vary according to what the valuation is for. For example, suppose that a company acquires a machine to manufacture its products. The machine has an expected useful life of four years. At the end of two years the company is preparing a balance sheet and has to decide what monetary amount to attribute to the asset.

Numerous possibilities might be considered.

(i) The original cost (historical cost) of the machine

(ii) Half of the historical cost, on the ground that half of its useful life has expired

(iii) The amount the machine might fetch on the secondhand market

(iv) The amount it would cost to replace the machine with an identical machine

(v) The amount it would cost to replace the machine with a more modern machine incorporating the technological advances of the previous two years

(vi) The machine's economic value, ie the amount of the profits it is expected to generate for the company during its remaining life

> **Tutorial note**. Here we clarify what historical cost means by reference to other alternative bases of measurement.

515

All of these valuations have something to commend them, but the great advantage of the first two is that they are based on a figure (the machine's historical cost) which is objectively verifiable. (Some authors regard objectivity as an accounting concept in its own right.) The subjective judgement involved in the other valuations, particularly (f), is so great as to lessen the reliability of any accounts in which they are used.

(d) **Stable monetary unit**

The financial statements which an accountant prepares must be expressed in terms of a monetary unit (eg in the UK the £, in the USA the $). It is assumed that the value of this unit remains constant.

In practice, of course, the value of the unit is not usually constant and comparisons between the accounts of the current year and those of previous years may be misleading.

(e) **Objectivity**

An accountant must show objectivity in his work. This means he should try to strip his conclusions of any personal opinion or prejudice and should be as precise and as detailed as the situation warrants. The result of this should be that any number of accountants will give the same answer independently of each other.

In practice, objectivity is difficult. Two accountants faced with the same accounting data may come to different conclusions as to the correct treatment. It was to combat subjectivity that accounting standards were developed.

(f) **The realisation concept**

The realisation concept states that revenue and profits are not anticipated but are recognised by inclusion in the income statement only when *realised* in the form either of cash or of other assets the ultimate cash realisation of which can be assessed with reasonable certainty. Provision is made for all known liabilities (expenses and losses) whether the amount of these is known with certainty or is a best estimate in the light of the information available.

There are some exceptions to the rule, notably for land and buildings. With dramatic rises in property prices in some countries, it has been a common practice to revalue land and buildings periodically to a current value, to avoid having a misleading balance sheet. Even if the sale of the property is not contemplated, such revaluations create an unrealised profit:

DEBIT   Land and buildings account
CREDIT   Reserve account

This profit is sometimes known as a *holding gain*, because it is a profit which arises in the course of holding the asset as a result of its increase in value above cost.

In spite of such exceptions, however, the realisation principle has long been accepted by all practising accountants and it is standard practice that only profits realised at the balance sheet date should be included in the income statement.

> **Tutorial note**. This may change in the future if a single performance statement is adopted reporting both realised and unrealised profits and losses arising in the period.

Unfortunately there is no standard definition of realised profits and losses; it could be said that they are such profits or losses of a company as fall to be treated as realised in accordance with principles generally accepted at the time when the accounts are prepared, with respect to the determination for accounting purposes of realised profits.

BPP
PROFESSIONAL EDUCATION

(g) **The duality concept**

This convention underpins double entry bookkeeping. Every transaction has two effects. For example, if goods are purchased for cash, the accounts must reflect both the purchase and the payment of cash.

2 Regulators

Tutorial note. It is best to use headings to divide up your answer, as we do here.

Stock Exchange

A quoted company is a company whose shares are bought and sold on a stock exchange. This involves the signing of an agreement which requires compliance with the rules of that stock exchange. This would normally contain amongst other things the stock exchange's detailed rules on the information to be disclosed in quoted companies' accounts. This, then, is one regulatory influence on a quoted company's accounts. The stock exchange may enforce compliance by monitoring accounts and reserving the right to withdraw a company's shares from the stock exchange: ie the company's shares would no longer be traded through the stock exchange. In many countries there is, however, no statutory requirement to obey these rules.

Local legislation

In most countries, companies have to comply with the local companies legislation, which lays down detailed requirements on the preparation of accounts. Company law is often quite detailed, partly because of external influences such as EU Directives. Another reason to increase statutory regulation is that quoted companies are under great pressure to show profit growth and an obvious way to achieve this is to manipulate accounting policies. If this involves breaking the law, as opposed to ignoring professional guidance, company directors may think twice before bending the rules – or, at least, this is often a government's hope.

Standard-setters

Professional guidance is given by the national and international standard-setters. Prescriptive guidance is given in accounting standards which must be applied in all accounts intended to show a 'true and fair view' or 'present fairly in all material respects'. International Financial Reporting Standards and national standards are issued after extensive consultation and are revised as required to reflect economic or legal changes. In some countries, legislation requires details of non-compliance to be disclosed in the accounts. 'Defective' accounts can be revised under court order if necessary and directors signing such accounts can be prosecuted and fined (or even imprisoned).

The potential for the IASB's influence in this area is substantial. It must pursue excellence in standards with absolute rigour to fulfil that potential.

3 Standard setters

Tutorial note. This is a rather open-ended, discursive question, in which many relevant points could be valid.

The users of financial information – creditors, management, employees, business contacts, financial specialists, government and the general public – are entitled to information about a business entity to a greater or lesser degree. However, the needs and expectations of these groups will vary.

The preparers of the financial information often find themselves in the position of having to reconcile the interests of different groups in the best way for the business entity. For example whilst shareholders are looking for increased profits to support higher dividends, employees will expect higher wage increases; and yet higher profits without corresponding higher tax allowances (increased capital allowances for example) will result in a larger corporation tax bill.

Without accounting standards to prescribe how certain transactions should be treated, preparers would be tempted to produce financial information which meets the expectations of the favoured user group. For example creative accounting methods, such as off balance sheet finance could be used to enhance a company's balance sheet to make it more attractive to investors/lenders.

The aim of accounting standards is that they should regulate financial information in order that it shows the following characteristics.

(a) Objectivity
(b) Comparability
(c) Completeness
(d) Consistency

4 IAS 1

> **Tutorial note**. Easy marks are to be gained in Part (a). Parts (b) and (c) require more thought.

(a)   (i)   **Materiality and aggregation**. Items which are material need to be shown separately in the financial accounts. Amounts which are not material, can be added together and the sub total can be shown.

      (ii)   **Offsetting**. Assets and liabilities, and income and expenses, should not be set off, unless it is permitted in a standard. This is because it hinders the users of financial statements understanding what the transactions are.

      (iii)   **Consistency**. Transactions should be treated on a similar basis from year to year. Also, transactions of the same kind should be treated in the same way in each accounting period.

(b)

> **Tutorial note**. Start with a simple explanation of what the concept means.

The **going concern assumption** is that an entity will continue in operational existence for the foreseeable future. This means that the financial statements of an entity are prepared on the assumption that the entity will **continue** trading. If this were not the case, various adjustments would have to be made to the accounts: provisions for losses; revaluation of assets to their possible market value; all non-current assets and liabilities would be reclassified as current; and so forth.

Unless it can be assumed that the business is a going concern, other accounting assumptions cannot apply.

> **Tutorial note**. Having made this assertion, you need to clarify it with examples.

For example, it is meaningless to speak of consistency from one accounting period to the next when this is the final accounting period.

The **accruals basis** of accounting states that items are recognised as assets, liabilities, equity, income and expenses when they satisfy the definitions and recognition criteria in the *Framework*.

The effect of this is that revenue and expenses which are related to each other are matched, so as to be dealt with in the same accounting period, without regard to when the cash is actually paid or received. This is particularly relevant to the purchase of non-current assets. The cost of a non-current asset is spread over the accounting periods expected to benefit from it, thus matching costs and revenues. In the absence of the going concern convention, this cannot happen, as an example will illustrate.

Suppose a company has a machine which cost $10,000 two years ago and now has a net book value of $6,000. The machine can be used for another three years, but as it is obsolete, there is no possibility of selling it, and so it has no market value.

If the going concern assumption applies, the machine will be shown at **cost less depreciation** in the accounts (ie $6,000), as it still has a part to play in the continued life of the entity. However, if the assumption cannot be applied, the machine will be given a nil value and other assets and liabilities will be similarly revalued on the basis of winding down the company's operations.

(c)   IAS 1 (revised) is the standard whose overall objectives are to further the user's understanding of financial statements by promoting an improvement in the quality of information disclosed. To achieve this it follows the principles and guidance in the **Framework** document by the IASB.

> **Tutorial note**. You now need to state what problems the *Framework* was brought in to address.

One of the ideas behind such a Framework is to **avoid the fire-fighting approach**, which has characterised the development of accounting standards in the past, and instead develop an underlying philosophy as a basis for consistent accounting principles so that each standard fits into the whole framework. Research began from an analysis of the fundamental objectives of accounting and their relationship to the information needs of accounts users. The Framework has gone behind the requirements of existing accounting standards, which define accounting treatments for particular assets, liabilities, income and expenditure, to define the nature of assets, liabilities, income and expenditure.

IAS 1 (revised) is a consistent and positive step towards the adoption of such a framework as it includes the **basis for presenting the items in the financial statements** in order to give the users of financial statements the maximum disclosure in a clear and **understandable, neutral fashion**.

5 Jenson

> **Tutorial note**. This is an important conceptual subject and it is closely linked with the IASB's *Framework*, which you should have discussed, rather than IAS 18, the accounting standard on revenue recognition. You need to use your imagination to come up with examples in (b).

(a)   In revenue recognition, the 'critical event' is the point in the earnings process or operating cycle at which the transaction is deemed to have been **sufficiently completed** to allow the **profit** arising from the transaction, or a distinct component part of it, to be **recognised** in income in a particular period. This has to be addressed in order to allocate transactions and their effects to different accounting periods and is a direct result of the episodic nature of financial reporting. For most companies the **normal earnings cycle** is the purchase of raw materials which are transformed through a manufacturing process into saleable goods, for which orders are subsequently received, delivery is made and then payment received.

In the past the approach has been to **match costs with revenues** and record both once the critical event has passed; in most systems this critical event has been full or **near full performance of the transaction**, so that no material uncertainties surround either the transaction being completed or the amounts arising from the transaction. This is encompassed in the notion of prudence, so that

7revenue is recognised only in cash or near cash form. However, any point in the cycle could be deemed to be the critical event. This approach leaves the balance sheet as a statement of uncompleted transaction balances, comprising unexpired costs and undischarged liabilities.

In contrast, the IASB's **Framework** defines gains and losses (or income and expenses) in terms of **changes** in assets and liabilities other than those arising from transactions with owners as owners, not in terms of an earnings or matching process. The balance sheet thus assumes primary importance in the recognition of earnings and profits. A gain **can only be recognised** if there is an **increase** in the equity (ie net assets) of an entity not resulting from contributions from owners. Similarly, a loss is recognised if there is a **decrease** in the ownership interest of an entity not resulting from distributions to owners. Thus gains arise from recognition of assets and derecognition of liabilities, and losses arise from derecognition of assets and recognition of liabilities. The IASB explains that it is not possible to reverse this definitional process, ie by defining assets and liabilities in terms of gains and losses, because it has not been possible to formulate robust enough base definitions of gains and losses (partly because the choice of critical event can be subjective). Nevertheless commentators often attempt to link the two approaches by asserting that **sufficient evidence** for recognition or derecognition will be met at the critical event in the operating cycle.

(b)

> **Tutorial note**. You can argue these examples either way – what matters is that you marshal your arguments properly. Remember that this matter is still being clarified, for example by standard setters in the UK.

On the acquisition of goods

This would be **unlikely** to be a critical event for most businesses. However, for some the acquisition of the raw materials is the most important part of the process, eg extraction of gold from a mine, or the harvesting of coffee beans. Only where the goods in question could **be sold immediately in a liquid market** would it be appropriate to recognise revenue, ie they would have to have a **commodity value.**

During the manufacture or production of goods

This is also **unlikely** to be the critical event for most businesses because **too many uncertainties** remain, eg of damaged goods or overproduction leading to obsolete inventory. An **exception** would **be long-term contracts** for the construction of specific assets, which tend to earn the constructing company revenues over the length of the contract, usually in stages, ie there is a **series of critical events** in the operating cycle (according to the Framework). It would **not** be appropriate to recognise all the revenue at the end of the contract, because this would reflect profit earned in past periods as well as the present period. Profit is therefore recognised during manufacture or production, usually through certification by a qualified valuer. Some would argue that this is not really a critical event approach, but rather an 'accretion approach'.

On delivery/acceptance of goods

Goods are frequently sold on **credit**, whereby the vendor hands over the inventory asset and receives in its place **a financial asset of a debt** due for the price of the goods. At that point legal title passes and **full performance** has taken place. In general, the bulk of the risks of the transaction have gone and the only ones remaining relate to the creditworthiness of the purchaser and any outstanding warranty over the goods. Many trade sales take place in this way, with periods of credit allowed for goods delivered, eg 30 days. This therefore tends to be the critical event for many types of business operating cycles.

Where certain conditions have been satisfied after the goods have been delivered

In these situations the customer has a right of return of the goods without reason or penalty, but usually within a time and non-use condition. A good example is clothes retailers who **allow non-faulty goods to be returned.** Another example is where the goods need only be paid for once they are sold on to a third party. Traditionally, recognition of revenue is delayed until, eg **the deadline to allowed return passes.** However, in circumstances where goods are never returned, it might be argued that the substance of the transaction is a sale on delivery.

Receipt of payment for credit sales

Once payment is received, only warranty risk remains. A company may wait until this point to recognise income if receipt is considered uncertain, eg when goods have been sold to a company resident in a country that has exchange controls. It would otherwise be **rare** to delay recognition until payment.

On the expiry of a guarantee or warranty

Many businesses may feel unable to recognise revenue in full because of **outstanding warranties,** eg a construction company which is subject to fee retention until some time after completion of the contract. Other businesses, such as car manufacturers, may make a **general provision** for goods returned under warranty as it will not be possible to judge likely warranty costs under individual contracts.

(c) (i) This agreement is worded as a **sale,** but it is fairly obvious from the terms and assessed substance that it is in fact a **secured loan.** Jenson should therefore continue to recognise the inventory on balance sheet and should treat the receipt from Wholesaler as a loan, not revenue. Finance costs will be charged to the income statement, of $35,000 \times 12\% \times 9/12 = \$3,150$.

(ii) Years 2 to 5 of the franchise contract would be **loss making** for Jenson and hence, under IAS 18, part of the initial fee of $50,000 should be **deferred over the life of the contract.** Since Jenson should be making a profit margin of 20% on this type of arrangement, revenues of $10,000 will be required to match against the costs of $8,000. The company will receive $5,000 pa and so a further $5,000 \times 4 = \$20,000$ of the initial fee should be deferred, leaving $50,000 - \$20,000 = \$30,000$ to be recognised in the first year. However, this may not represent a liability under IAS 37 *Provisions, Contingent Liabilities and Contingent Assets*, where a liability is defined as an obligation to transfer economic benefits as a result of past transactions or events. It will be necessary to consider the terms of the initial fee and whether it is returnable.

(iii) The cost of the first 6 months' publications is $192,000 \div 24 \times 6 = \$48,000$. On an accruals basis, income of $240,000 \div 24 \times 6 = \$60,000$ should be recognised. This would leave deferred income of $240,000 - \$60,000 = \$180,000$ in Jenson's balance sheet (ie as a liability). As in (ii), however, this may not represent a liability. In fact, the liability of the company may only extend to the cost of the future publications, ie $192,000 - \$48,000 = \$144,000$. This would allow Jenson to **recognise all the profit** on the publications **immediately.** In want of an updated accounting standard on revenue recognition, it will be necessary to consider the extent of Jenson's commitments under this arrangement.

6 D'Urberville

> **Tutorial note**. The figures for 20X5 are fairly easy. For 20X6 and 20X7 you have a finance lease to deal with, which requires a bit more thought.

Non-current assets

SCHEDULE OF MOTOR VEHICLES
FOR THE YEARS ENDED 31 DECEMBER 20X5, 20X6, 20X7

		$'000
20X5		
Cost: At 1 January 20X5		540
Additions		147
Disposals		70
At 31 December 20X5		617
Accumulated depreciation:	At 1 January 20X5	130
	Disposals (W1)	50
	Charge for year 25% × (617 − (130 − 50))	134
	At 31 December 20X5	214
Net book value at 31 December 20X5		403

		$'000
20X6		
Cost: At 1 January 20X6		617
Additions*		252
Held under finance leases		320
Disposals		110
At 31 December 20X6		1,079
Accumulated depreciation:	At 1 January 20X6	214
	Disposals (W2)	68
	Charge for year 25% (759 − (214 − 68)) + (25% × 320)	233
	At 31 December 20X6	379
Net book value at 31 December 20X6		700

> ***Tutorial note**. The acquisitions in 20X6 are capitalised at cash price less trade discount (for cash purchases), plus delivery costs $(300 − 60 + 12) = $252,000$. Disclosure of the value of the assets held subject to finance leases is required by IAS 17.

		$'000
20X7		
Cost: At 1 January 20X7		1,079
Additions**		375
Held under finance leases		400
Disposals		75
At 31 December 20X7		1,779
Accumulated depreciation: At 1 January 20X7		379
	Disposals (W3)	(43)
	Charge for year 25% (1,379 − (379 − 43) + (400 × 25%))	361
	At 31 December 20X7	697
Net book value at 31 December 20X7		1,082

> ****Tutorial note**. The acquisitions in 20X7 are capitalised at cash price less trade discount (for cash purchase) plus delivery cost: $(450 − 90 + 15) = $375,000$.

Workings

1   *Accumulated depreciation on 20X5 disposals*

Vehicles acquired in 20X0:

		$
20X0	25% × $30,000	7,500
20X1	25% × $(30,000 − 7,500)	5,625
20X2	25% × $(30,000 − (7,500 + 5,625))	4,219
20X3	25% × $(30,000 − (7,500 + 5,625 + 4,219))	3,164
20X4	25% × $(30,000 − (7,500 + 5,625 + 4,219 + 3,164))	2,373
Total		22,881

Vehicles acquired in 20X1:

		$
20X1	25% × $40,000	10,000
20X2	25% × $(40,000 − 10,000)	7,500
20X3	25% × $(40,000 − (10,000 + 7,500))	5,625
20X4	25% × $(40,000 − (10,000 + 7,500 + 5,625))	4,219
Total		27,344

Total accumulated depreciation on disposals: $(22,881 + 27,344) = $50,225.

2   *Accumulated depreciation on 20X6 disposals*

Vehicles acquired in 20X2:

		$
20X2	25% × $45,000	11,250
20X3	25% × $(45,000 − 11,250)	8,438
20X4	25% × $(45,000 − (11,250 + 8,438))	6,328
20X5	25% × $(45,000 − (11,250 + 8,438 + 6,328))	4,746
Total		30,762

Vehicles acquired in 20X3:

		$
20X3	25% × $65,000	16,250
20X4	25% × $(65,000 − 16,250)	12,188
20X5	25% × $(65,000 − (16,250 + 12,188))	9,141
Total		37,579

Total accumulated depreciation on 20X6 disposals $(30,762 + 37,579) = $68,341

3   *Accumulated depreciation on 20X7 disposals*

Vehicles acquired in 20X4:

		$
20X4	25% × $75,000	18,750
20X5	25% × $(75,000 − 18,750)	14,063
20X6	25% × $(75,000 − (18,750 + 14,063)	10,547
Total		43,360

Tutorial note. Note that the question does not ask for the details of the obligations under the finance leases which would be disclosed under non-current and current liabilities in accordance with the requirements of IAS 17.

7 Winger

Tutorial note. As with consolidated accounts questions, a question on the preparation of a single company's accounts needs a methodical approach. Lay out proformas and fill the numbers in gradually by systematically working through the question. Points are as follows

(a) Exclude 'sale or return' goods from both sales and cost of sales.

(b) Abandonment of research project hits retained profit as well as current year profits.

(c) Exclude from the finance lease interest charge the $20m down payment – interest does not accrue on this.

(d) When calculating the base creditor, you need to accrue one year's interest but no more. You know that $20m is due within one year, so the long term liability is the balance of the total creditor.

(a) WINGER
INCOME STATEMENT FOR THE
YEAR ENDED 31 MARCH 20X1

	$'000
Sales revenues (358,450 – 27,000)	331,450
Cost of sales (W1)	(208,550)
Gross profit	122,900
Distribution expenses	(28,700)
Administration expenses	(15,000)
Operating profit	79,200
Profit on disposal of land and buildings (95,000 – 80,000)	15,000
Loss on abandonment of research project	(30,000)
Profit before interest	64,200
Finance cost (W3)	(11,200)
Profit before tax	53,000
Income tax (15,000 – 2,200)	(12,800)
Profit after tax	40,200
Retained profit for the period (40,200 – 12,000 – 18,000 (W4)	10,200
Accumulated profits b/f (71,600 + 30,000)	101,600
Accumulated profits c/f	111,800

(b) BALANCE SHEET
AS AT 31 MARCH 20X1

	$'000	$'000
Assets		
Tangible non current assets		
Property (200,000 – 6,000 (W2))		194,000
Plant and equipment (W5)		160,000
		354,000
Current assets		
Inventories (28,240 + 22,500 (W1))	50,740	
Accounts receivable (55,000 – 27,000 (W1))	28,000	
Cash	10,660	
		89,400
Total assets		443,400

BPP)))
PROFESSIONAL EDUCATION

	$'000	$'000
Equity and liabilities		
Capital and reserves		
Equity shares 25c each		150,000
Accumulated profits (see (a))		111,800
		261,800
Non-current liabilities		
Leasing obligations (W6)	47,200	
8% loan notes	50,000	
		97,200
Current liabilities		
Trade and other accounts payable (W7)	51,400	
Income tax	15,000	
Proposed dividends	18,000	
		84,400
Total equity and liabilities		443,400

Workings

1	*Cost of sales*	$'000
	Per question	185,050
	Less sale/return goods (27,000 × 100/120)	(22,500)
	Add depreciation (W2)	46,000
		208,550

2	*Depreciation*	$'000
	Building (100,000 ÷ 50)	2,000
	Heating system (20,000 ÷ 10)	2,000
	Lifts (30,000 ÷ 15)	2,000
		6,000
	Leased plant (80,000 × 20%)	16,000
	Owned plant (154,800 − 34,800) × 20%	24,000
		46,000

3	*Finance cost*	$'000
	Debenture interest (50,000 × 8%)	4,000
	Finance lease (80,000 − 20,000) × 12%	7,200
		11,200

4	*Final dividend*	$'000
	Total dividend required $1.25 × 4% × (150,000 × 4)	30,000
	Interim dividend paid	(12,000)
	Final dividend required	18,000

5	*Plant and equipment*	$'000
	Cost: owned plant	154,800
	leased plant	80,000
		234,800
	Depreciation: owned plant (34,800 + 24,000 (W2))	(58,800)
	Leased plant (80,000 × 20%)	(16,000)
		160,000

6	*Leasing obligations*	$'000
	Total payments due	80,000
	Less amount paid	(20,000)
		60,000
	Add accrued interest (60,000 × 12%)	7,200
	Total creditor	67,200
	Due within one year	20,000
	Due after one year	47,200

7	*Trade and other payables*	$'000
	Trial balance	29,400
	Lease creditor (W7)	20,000
	Accrued debenture interest	2,000
		51,400

(c) Companies often used to justify the non-depreciation of buildings on several grounds, including:

(i) That the current value of the buildings was **higher than cost.**

(ii) That the level of **maintenance** meant that no deterioration or consumption had taken place.

(iii) That the depreciation charge would **not be material.**

However, IAS 16 requires the **depreciable amount** of an asset to be charged against profit over its useful life. That depreciable amount is obtained by comparing the cost of the asset with its **estimated residual value** at the end of its useful economic life. By requiring the residual value to be estimated at **current prices**, the standard removes any **potential inflationary effects** which would otherwise increase the residual value and hence reduce, even to zero, the depreciable amount. This overcomes the argument that high residual values remove the need for depreciation, unless the value of a second-hand asset has greater value than the same asset new – an unlikely proposition.

The argument regarding **immateriality** of the depreciation charge because of a long economic life may have some validity. Although it is not addressed directly by IAS 16, accounting standards generally only apply to **material items,** according to the *Framework.* However, under this principle, it will be necessary to consider not only each year's potential depreciation charge, but also the **accumulated depreciation** that would need to be provided against the asset. Over time, this latter amount would inevitably become material and the 'long life' argument would cease to hold.

Thus, Winger's **previous policy** was not appropriate and the change to depreciate assets was necessary to comply with IAS 16.

The directors' treatment of the deferred development expenditure is also incorrect. It needs to be written off because its **value** has become **impaired due to adverse legislation, not a change of accounting policy.** It now has no effective value. There has therefore not been a change of accounting policy, so it cannot be treated as a prior period adjustment. It must be written off to the income statement.

8 C Co

> **Tutorial note.** Calculate profit or loss on the contract and cost of sales comes out as a balancing figure. You can then work out the accrued cost of sales and accrued future losses.

(a)

	Maryhill bypass	Rottenrow centre
	$'000	$'000
Revenue	2,800	3,000
Profit/(loss) (W1)	622	(100)
Cost of sales	2,178	3,100
Current liabilities		
Due to customers for contract work (W2)	578	600

Workings

1. Maryhill: $(9,000 - (1,400 + 5,600)) \times \dfrac{2,800}{9,000} = 622$

    Rottenrow: $8,000 - (2,900 + 5,200) = 100$

2.

	Maryhill	Rottenrow
	$'000	$'000
Costs incurred to date	1,400	2,900
Recognised profits/(losses)	622	(100)
Progress billings	(2,600)	(3,400)
	(578)	(600)

(b) Construction contracts are recognised as such when they cover at **least two accounting periods**. If they were not to be treated as they are under IAS 11 then the costs incurred during the early years of the contract would be recognised but with no corresponding revenue. This would lead to several years of losses then one year of high profits regardless of how profitable the contract really was. The advantage of this approach however would be that there would be no need to use estimates and forecasts.

The current treatment **matches an element of the revenue to the costs incurred**. There is an attempt to maintain **prudence** by ensuring that any **foreseeable** losses are **accounted for immediately**. This gives a fairer representation of the underlying financial substance of the transaction and makes it easier for the user of the accounts to assess the financial position of the company.

9 Dennis

> **Tutorial note.** Compound or hybrid instruments such as convertible loan stock (part (a)) are required by IASs 32 and 39 to be treated according to the substance of the contractual agreement. Here, the equity element and liability (debt) element must be separately identified on the balance sheet. Although in theory this split can be calculated in many ways, with the information available in the question, the only available methodology is the 'residual value of equity' approach. This involves calculating the present value of the cash flows attributable to the 'pure' debt element and treating the difference with the proceeds received as the equity component.

(a)   INCOME STATEMENT (EXTRACTS)

	$'000	$'000
Loan stock interest paid ($80m × 8%)	6,400	
Required accrual of finance cost	1,844	
Total finance cost ($68.704m (W) × 12%)		8,244

BALANCE SHEET (EXTRACTS)

Equity	$'000	$'000
Share options (W)		11,296
Non-current liabilities		
8% loan stock 20X4 (W)	68,704	
Accrual of finance costs	1,844	
		70,548

Working

Year		Cash flow	Factor	PV cash flow
		$'000		$'000
1	Interest	6,400	0.89	5,696
2	Interest	6,400	0.80	5,120
3	Interest	6,400	0.71	4,544
4	Interest	6,400	0.64	4,096
5	Interest + capital	86,400	0.57	49,248
PV of debt cash flows				68,704
Residual equity element (= share options)				11,296
				80,000

(b)

> **Tutorial note**. Impairment is a difficult subject, so make sure you understand where you went wrong – if at all!

The impairment losses are allocated as required by IAS 36 *Impairment of assets*.

	Asset @ 1.1.20X0 $'000	1st loss (W1) $'000	Assets @ 1.2.20X0 $'000	2nd loss (W2) $'000	Revised asset $'000
Goodwill	200	(200)	–	–	–
Operating licence	1,200	(200)	1,000	(100)	900
Property: stations/land	300	(50)	250	(50)	200
Rail track/coaches	300	(50)	250	(50)	200
Steam engines	1,000	(500)	500	–	500
	3,000	(1,000)	2,000	(200)	1,800

Workings

1   *First impairment loss*

$500,000 relates directly to an engine and its recoverable amount can be assessed directly (ie zero) and it is no longer part of the cash generating unit.

IAS 36 then requires goodwill to be written off. Any further impairment must be written off the remaining assets pro rata, except the engine which must not be reduced below its net selling price of $500,000.

2   *Second impairment loss*

The first $100,000 of the impairment loss is applied to the operating licence to write it down to net selling price.

The remainder is applied pro rata to assets carried at other than their net selling prices, ie $50,000 to both the property and the rail track and coaches.

(c) *Income statement*

	$m
Contract revenue (W2)	18.0
Cost of sales (balancing figure)	(14.1)
Profit (W3)	3.9

Balance sheet $m

Current assets

Receivables: amounts recoverable on long-term
                        contracts (W5)   11.0

Workings

1   *Percentage completion*

$$\text{Percentage completion} = \frac{\text{Work certified}}{\text{Contract price}}$$

20W9	*20X0 (including variation)*
$\dfrac{\$12m}{\$40m} = 30\%$	$\dfrac{\$30m}{\$45m} = 66.7\%$ (ie $\frac{2}{3}$)

2   *Contract revenue*

Accumulated revenue to 31 March 20X0 = $45m × $\frac{2}{3}$ = $30m

In 20X0 revenue = $30m – $12m (20W9) = $18m

3   *Profit*

Revised estimated total profit = $45m – $30m = $15m

Accumulated to 31 March 20X0 = $15m × $\frac{2}{3}$ = $10m

Total profit for year ended 31 March 20X0:

	$m
Accumulated to date	10.0
Less 20W9 profit taken (W4)	(3.6)
Less rectification costs	(2.5)
	3.9

4   *Profit for 20W9*

	$m
Revenue	12.0
Cost of sales (bal fig)	(8.4)
Profit = ($40m – $28m) × 30%	3.6

5   *Receivables due from customers*

	$m
Costs incurred to date	28.5
Add recognised profits (3.6 + 3.9)	7.5
Less progress billings	(25.0)
	11.0

10 Bulwell

Tutorial note. The most important part of this question is the working apportioning the lease instalments between interest and the capital. The rest of the accounting follows on from this.

(a)   BOOKS OF BULWELL AGGREGATES CO

LORRIES ACCOUNT

20X1		$			$
1 Jan	Granby Garages	54,000			

ACCUMULATED DEPRECIATION ON LORRIES

20X1		$	20X1			$
			31 Dec	Income statement: ¼ ×		
31 Dec	Balance c/d	12,500		$(54,000 − (3 × 1,333))		12,500
20X2			20X2			
31 Dec	Balance c/d	25,000	1 Jan	Balance b/d		12,500
			31 Dec	Income statement		12,500
		25,000				25,000
20X3			20X3			
31 Dec	Balance c/d	37,500	1 Jan	Balance b/d		25,000
			31 Dec	Income statement		12,500
		37,500				37,500
20X4			20X4			
31 Dec	Balance c/d	50,000	1 Jan	Balance b/d		37,500
			31 Dec	Income statement		12,500
		50,000				50,000
			20X5			
			1 Jan	Balance b/d		50,000

Tutorial note. The above workings are very straightforward and can be done without worrying about the leasing aspects.

LEASE INTEREST PAYABLE

20X1		$	20X1		$
31 Dec	Bank (W)	11,250	31 Dec	Income statement	11,250
20X2			20X2		
31 Dec	Bank (W)	8,063	31 Dec	Income statement	8,063
20X3			20X3		
31 Dec	Bank (W)	4,078	31 Dec	Income statement	4,078

GRANBY GARAGES CO

20X1		$	20X1		$
1 Jan	Bank – deposit	9,000	1 Jan	Lorries a/c	54,000
31 Dec	Bank (W)	12,750			
	Balance c/d	32,250			
		54,000			54,000

20X2			*20X2*		
31 Dec	Bank (W)	15,937	1 Jan	Balance b/d	32,250
	Balance c/d	16,313			
		32,250			32,250
20X3			*20X3*		
31 Dec	Bank (W)	16,313	1 Jan	Balance b/d	16,313

INCOME STATEMENTS (EXTRACTS)

	20X1	*20X2*	*20X3*	*20X4*
	$	$	$	$
Lease interest	11,250	8,063	4,078	
Depreciation on lorries	12,500	12,500	12,500	12,500

BALANCE SHEETS AT 31 DECEMBER (EXTRACTS)

	20X1	*20X2*	*20X3*	*20X4*
	$	$	$	$
Non-current assets				
Lorries: at cost	54,000	54,000	54,000	54,000
Depreciation	12,500	25,000	37,500	50,000
	41,500	29,000	16,500	4,000
Current liabilities				
Finance lease obligations	15,937	16,313	-	-
Non-current liabilities				
Finance lease obligations	16,313	-	-	-

(b)

> **Tutorial note**. As you will see, the lessor's books are a mirror image of the lessee's.

BOOKS OF GRANBY GARAGES CO

BULWELL AGGREGATES CO

		$			$
20X1			*20X1*		
1 Jan	Sales	54,000	1 Jan	Bank	9,000
			31 Dec	Bank	12,750
				Balance c/d	32,250
		54,000			54,000
20X2			*20X2*		
1 Jan	Balance b/d	32,250	31 Dec	Bank	15,937
				Balance c/d	16,313
		32,250			32,250
20X3			*20X3*		
1 Jan	Balance b/d	16,313	31 Dec	Bank	16,313

LEASE INTEREST RECEIVABLE

		$			$
20X1			*20X1*		
31 Dec	Income statement	11,250	31 Dec	Bank	11,250
20X2			*20X2*		
31 Dec	Income statement	8,063	31 Dec	Bank	8,063

20X3

			20X3		
31 Dec	Income statement	4,078	31 Dec	Bank	4,078

INCOME STATEMENTS (EXTRACTS)

		20X1	20X2	20X3
	$	$	$	$
Sales	54,000		–	–
Cost of sales on lease	43,200		–	–
Gross profit on lease sales		10,800	–	–
Lease interest receivable		11,250	8,063	4,078

Working

Apportionment of lease instalments between interest and capital repayment.

	20X1	20X2	20X3
	$	$	$
Opening liability (after deposit)	45,000	32,250	16,313
Add interest at 25%	11,250	8,063	4,078
	56,250	40,313	20,391
Less instalment	24,000	24,000	20,391
Closing liability	32,250	16,313	Nil
Interest element as above	11,250	8,063	4,078
∴ Capital repayment	12,750	15,937	16,313
Total instalment	24,000	24,000	20,391

11 Corax

Tutorial note. Since advance tax has been abolished in the UK, it remains to be seen how it will be examined in the international variant.

(a)

CORPORATE TAX (20X5) ACCOUNT

	$		$
Bank	16,300	Balance b/f	16,300

CORPORATE TAX (20X6) ACCOUNT

	$		$
Income statement over provision	1,200	Balance b/f	5,000
Balance c/d	3,800		
	5,000		5,000

CORPORATE TAX (20X7) ACCOUNT

	$		$
Advanced tax a/c (offset)	5,250	Income statement	36,000
Balance c/d	30,750		
	36,000		36,000

ADVANCED TAX ACCOUNT

	$		$
Bank ($1/4 \times 700{,}000 \times \$0.03$)	5,250	Corporation tax 20X7	5,250
		Deferred taxation – Advanced tax on proposed dividend	
Balance c/d	7,875	($1/4 \times 700{,}000 \times \$0.045$)	7,875
	13,125		13,125

DEFERRED TAXATION ACCOUNT

	$		$
Advanced tax on proposed dividend	7,875	Balance b/f	29,400
		Income statement	
Balance c/d	28,525	(increase in provision)	7,000
	36,400		36,400

(b)   INCOME STATEMENT
FOR THE YEAR ENDED 31 DECEMBER 20X7 (EXTRACT)

	Note	$
Net profit for the year before tax		100,000
Tax on profit for the year	4	(41,800)
Profit for the financial year		58,200
Movement on reserves		
Dividends paid and proposed	2	(52,500)
Retained earnings for the year		58,200
Retained earnings brought forward		43,000
Retained earnings carried forward		48,700

BALANCE SHEET AS AT 31 DECEMBER 20X7 (EXTRACT)

	$	Note
Equity and liabilities		
Issued capital of 700,000 50c ordinary shares fully paid	350,000	
Accumulated profits	48,700	
Current liabilities		
Current tax	42,425	1
Dividends payable	31,500	2
Non current liabilities		
Deferred tax	28,525	3

Notes to the balance sheet and income statement

1   *Current tax comprises*

	$
Corporate tax (3,800 + 30,750)	34,550
Advanced tax on proposed dividend	7,875
	42,425

2   *Dividends payable and paid on ordinary share capital*

	$
Paid 3c per share on 700,000 shares	21,000
Proposed 4.5c per share on 700,000 shares	31,500
	52,500

3   *Deferred tax*

	$
Balance at 1.1.20X7	29,400
Deferred tax expense related to temporary differences	7,000
Advanced tax recoverable on proposed dividend offset	(7,875)
Balance at 31.12.20X7	28,525

4   *Tax on profit for the year*

	$m
Corporate tax (at X% on taxable profits of 20X7)	36,000
Less overprovision on profits of 20X6	(1,200)
Transfer to deferred tax for temporary differences	7,000
	41,800

12 Provisions

> **Tutorial note.** A good knowledge of IAS 37 is needed in this question. Do not disregard the discounting aspects, these calculations are quite straightforward as you are given the formulae in the exam.

(a)   **Why there was a need for an accounting standard dealing with provisions**

IAS 37 *Provisions, contingent liabilities and contingent assets* was issued to prevent entities from using provisions for creative accounting. It was common for entities to recognise material provisions for items such as future losses, restructuring costs or even expected future expenditure on repairs and maintenance of assets. These could be combined in one large provision (sometimes known as the 'big bath'). Although these provisions reduced profits in the period in which they were recognised (and were often separately disclosed on grounds of materiality), they were then released to enhance profits in subsequent periods. To make matters worse, provisions were often recognised where there was no firm commitment to incur expenditure. For example, an entity might set up a provision for restructuring costs and then withdraw from the plan, leaving the provision available for profit smoothing.

The criteria that need to be satisfied before a provision is recognised

IAS 37 states that a provision should not be recognised unless:

(i)   An entity has a present obligation to transfer economic benefits as a result of a past transaction or event, and

(ii)   It is probable that a transfer of economic benefits will be required to settle the obligation, and

(iii)   A reliable estimate can be made of the amount of the obligation.

An obligation can be legal or constructive. An entity has a constructive obligation if:

(i)   It has indicated to other parties that it will accept certain responsibilities (by an established pattern of past practice or published policies), and

(ii)   As a result, it has created a valid expectation on the part of those other parties that it will discharge those responsibilities.

(b)   Extract should recognise a provision for the estimated costs of making good the site because:

(i)   It has a present obligation to incur the expenditure as a result of a past event. In this case the obligating event occurred when it became virtually certain that the legislation would be passed. Therefore the obligation existed at 31 December 20X0, and

(ii)   A transfer of economic benefits is probable, and

(iii)   It is possible to make a reliable estimate of the amount.

Effect on the financial statements

For the year ended 31 December 20X0:

- A provision of $1,242,000 (2,000,000 × 0.621) is reported as a liability under provisions.

- A non-current asset of $1,242,000 is also recognised. The provision results in a corresponding asset because the expenditure gives the company access to future economic benefits; there is no effect on the income statement for the year.

For the year ended 31 December 20X1:

- Depreciation of $248,400 (1,242,000 × 20%) is charged to the income statement. The non-current asset is depreciated over its remaining useful economic life of 5 years from 31 December 20X0 (the site will cease to produce output on 31 December 20X5).

- Therefore at 31 December 20X1 the net book value of the non-current asset will be $993,600 (1,242,000 – 248,400).

- At 31 December 20X1 the provision will be $1,366,000 (2,000,000 × 0.683).

- The increase in the provision of $124,000 (1,366,000 – 1,242,000) is recognised in the income statement as a finance cost. This arises due to the unwinding of the discount.

13 Tree

Tutorial note. This is a wide-ranging 'published accounts' question. Points to watch are as follows.

(a)   Revenue and cost of sales: include the construction contract in both.
(b)   Cost of sales: include the loss on the closure of the publishing division.
(c)   Depreciation: don't forget the development expenditure.
(d)   Change in accounting policy: don't forget to put this through reserves.

(a)   TREE CO
       INCOME STATEMENT
       FOR THE YEAR ENDED 31 MARCH 20X6

	$'000	$'000
Revenue (W1)		230,000
Cost of sales (W2)		(162,306)
Gross profit		67,694
Distribution costs		(11,240)
Administration costs		(16,780)
Operating profit		39,674
Income from investments (W4)		1,120
Interest expense		(200)
Profit before tax		40,594
Income taxes (W5)		(12,000)
Profit after tax		28,594
Dividends: interim	4,000	
final	9,600	
		13,600

NOTES TO THE INCOME STATEMENT

Included in operating profit are the following items.

1   *Discontinued operations*

On 1 September 20X6 Tree closed its publishing division. The loss on disposal of the division was $900,000 ($1,200,000 gross less tax relief of $300,000). The operating loss up to the date of closure was $766,000 made up of sales of $30,800,000 and operating costs were $31,766,000, with attributable tax relief of $200,000.

2   *Profit on disposal of property*

During the year the company disposed of some property, resulting in a surplus of $3,000,000.

(b)   TREE CO
BALANCE SHEET AS AT 31 MARCH 20X6

	$'000	$'000
Assets		
Non-current assets		
Tangible assets (W8)	85,544	
Intangible assets (W7)	20,040	
Investments	14,000	
		119,584
Current assets		
Inventories	11,000	
Gross amount due on construction contracts (W9)	1,000	
Receivables	16,800	
Cash and bank	10,600	
		39,400
Total assets		158,984
Equity and liabilities		
Capital and reserves		
Ordinary shares 25c	80,000	
Accumulated profits (W11)	41,254	
		121,254
Non-current liabilities		
Deferred tax	4,950	
Deferred income: government grant ($4m × 20% × 3)	2,400	
		7,350
Current liabilities		
Trade and other payables (W10)		30,380
		158,984

(c)   *Accounting policies*

Any four of the following.

1   Depreciation has been provided on a straight line basis in order to write off the cost of depreciable non-current assets over their estimated useful lives. The rates used are:

Tangible non-current assets 20% on cost

Intangible non-current assets
    Software   20% on cost
    Development expenditure over the expected period of production

2   Development expenditure relating to specific projects intended for commercial exploitation is carried forward and amortised over the period expected to benefit commencing with the

period in which related sales are first made where it complies with the relevant requirements of IAS 38. Expenditure on research is written off as incurred.

3   Inventories have been valued at the lower of cost and net realisable value.

4   Deferred taxation is provided using the liability method on all temporary differences (the comprehensive basis) as required by IAS 12.

5   The company accrues for profit (by recognising revenue and costs) on construction contracts when their outcome is reasonably foreseeable in accordance with IAS 11.

6   Government grants are treated as deferred income and allocated to the income statement over the expected useful lives of the related assets.

Workings

1   *Revenue*

	$'000
Per list of balances	224,000
Contract*	6,000
Continuing operations	230,000

$$\text{* Invoiced work certified} = 5.4 \times \frac{10}{9} = 6$$

$$\therefore \text{Percentage completion} = \frac{6}{10} = 60\%$$

$$\therefore \text{Revenue} = 60\% \times \$10m = \$6m$$

2   *Cost of sales*

	$'000
Opening inventories	12,580
Purchases	92,340
Contract costs $(10 - 4) \times 60\%$	3,600
Wages	34,690
Research	1,200
Government grant ($4m × 20%)	(800)
Depreciation (W3)	31,496
Profit on sale of property	(3,000)
Loss on closure of publishing division	1,200
	173,306
Closing inventories	11,000
	162,306

3   *Depreciation*

	$'000	$'000
Tangible non-current assets per list of balances	112,680	
Add back government grants	4,000	
	116,680	
Depreciation: 116,680 × 20%		23,336
Intangible non-current assets		
NBV 1.4.X5:	22,500	
$\therefore$ Cost 22,500 × ^{5}/3:	37,500	
Depreciation = 37,500 × 20%		7,500
Development expenditure 20% × 3,300		660
		31,496

4   *Income from non-current asset investments*

	$'000
8% bonds (840 × 100/75)	1,120

5   *Taxation charge*

	$'000
Provision for the year at 25%	10,000
Underprovided in 20X5	850
Transfer to deferred tax (see below)	1,150
	12,000

	$'000
Deferred tax provision required at 31 March 20X6 (23.2m – 3.4m) × 25%	4,950
Provision b/f	(3,800)
∴ Increase in provision required	1,150

6   *Taxation (B/S)*

	$'000
Provision for the year	10,000
Tax suffered at source	(280)
	9,720

7   *Intangible non-current assets*

	Cost	Amortisation	NBV
	$'000	$'000	$'000
Software and brands	37,500	22,500*	15,000
Development costs	5,700	660	5,040
	43,200	23,160	20,040

* 37,500 × $^3/5$ (ie three years' amortisation)

8   *Tangible non-current assets*

	Cost	Depreciation	NBV
	$'000	$'000	$'000
	116,680	31,136*	85,544

* (116,680 × 20%) + 7,800

9   *Construction contracts*

	$'000
Costs incurred + recognised profit to date (4,000 + 2,400)	6,400
Progress billings	(6,000)
	400
Retentions (6,000 – 5,400)	600
Gross amount due from customers	1,000

10   *Trade and other payables*

	$'000
Trade payables	10,260
Incomes taxes (W6)	9,720
Proposed dividend	9,600
Deferred income	
Government grant ($4m × 20%)	800
	30,380

11   *Accumulated profits*

	$'000
Balance 1 April 20X5 as previously reported	23,860
Change in accounting policy	2,400
Restated balance at 1 April 20X5	26,260
Profit for year	14,994
Balance at 31 March 20X6	41,254

14 Cher

> **Tutorial note**. The calculations involved in this question are not particularly complicated. However, a large number of marks are available for explanations and understanding.

(a) Earnings per share (EPS) is one of the most frequently quoted statistics in financial analysis. Because of the widespread use of the price earnings (P/E) ratio as a yardstick for investment decisions, it became increasingly important.

It seems that reported and forecast EPS can, through the P/E ratio, have a significant effect on a company's share price. Thus, a share price might fall if it looks as if EPS is going to be low. This is not very rational, as EPS can depend on many, often subjective, assumptions used in preparing a historical statement, namely the income statement. It does not necessarily bear any relation to the value of a company, and of its shares. Nevertheless, the market is sensitive to EPS.

EPS has also served as a means of assessing the stewardship and management role performed by company directors and managers. Remuneration packages might be linked to EPS growth, thereby increasing the pressure on management to improve EPS. The danger of this, however, is that management effort goes into distorting results to produce a favourable EPS.

The IASB believed that the comparison of different entities' performance should be possible and issued IAS 33 in order to achieve this.

(b) CHER INC
EARNINGS PER SHARE FOR THE YEAR ENDED 30 JUNE 20X4

Earnings		$460,000
Number of shares		
In issue for full year		800,000
In issue 1.7.X3 – 30.9.X3		
$200,000 \times {}^{3}/_{12} \times 60\%$	30,000	
In issue 1.10.X3 – 30.6.X4		
$200,000 \times {}^{9}/_{12} \times 100\%$	150,000	
		180,000
		980,000

$$\text{Earnings per share} = \frac{460,000}{980,000} = 46.9c$$

(c) (i) *Theoretical ex rights price per share*

	$
Value of 4 shares before rights issue (4 × 1.90)	7.60
Value of 1 rights issue share	1.30
Value of 5 shares after rights issue	8.90

$$\text{Theoretical ex rights price} \frac{8.90}{5} = \$1.78$$

Earnings		$1,310,000
Number of shares in issue		
1.7.X4 – 28.2.X5		
$1,000,000 \times \dfrac{8}{12} \times \dfrac{1.90}{1.78}$	711,610	
1.3.X5 – 30.6.X5		
$1,250,000 \times {}^{4}/_{12}$	416,667	
		1,128,277

$$EPS \ \frac{1,310,000}{1,128,277} = 116.1c$$

Revised EPS calculation for 20X4

$$46.9c \times \frac{1.78}{1.90} = 43.9c$$

CHER INC
EARNINGS PER SHARE FOR THE YEAR ENDED 30 JUNE

	20X5	20X4
	116.1c	43.9c

(ii)

> **Tutorial note.** The main point to get across is that a rights issue is like a bonus issue combined with an issue at full market price

A rights issue is a popular method through which public companies are able to access the stock market for further capital. Under the terms of such an issue, existing shareholders are given the opportunity to acquire further shares in the company on a pro-rata basis to their existing shareholdings.

The 'rights' shares will usually be offered at a discount to the market price. In such cases, the issue is equivalent to a bonus issue combined with an issue at full market price. Bonus issues are treated as though they have been in issue for the whole year and are also taken into account in the previous year's EPS calculation to give a comparable result.

The bonus element of the rights issue is given by the following fraction, sometimes referred to as the *bonus fraction*.

$$\frac{\text{Actual cum rights price on last day of quotation cum rights}}{\text{Theoretical ex rights price}}$$

The 'cum rights price' is the *actual* price at which the shares are quoted inclusive of the right to take up the future shares under the rights issue.

The 'ex rights price' is the *theoretical* price at which the shares would be quoted, other stock market factors apart, after the rights issue shares have been issued.

In order to calculate earnings per share with a rights issue, the shares are time apportioned before and after the date of the rights issue. The number of shares is calculated in two stages as follows.

Before rights issue

Number of shares $\times$ Bonus fraction $\times$ Fraction of year
before rights issue $\quad$ before rights issue

After rights issue

Number of shares after rights issue $\times$ Fraction of year after rights issue

The two figures produced by the above calculations are added together to give the denominator for the fraction required in calculating earnings per share.

When calculating the revised earnings per share for the previous year, the latter has to be adjusted to take account of the bonus element by multiplying it by the following

$$\frac{\text{Theoretical ex rights price}}{\text{Actual cum rights price}}$$

This makes the previous year's figure comparable with that of the current year.

15 Group accounts

> **Tutorial note.** This is a general question to get you thinking about the nature of a group. The question strongly hints that there *are* limitations to group accounts.

The object of annual accounts is to help shareholders exercise control over their company by providing information about how its affairs have been conducted. The shareholders of a holding company would not be given sufficient information from the accounts of the holding company on its own, because not enough would be known about the nature of the assets, income and profits of all the subsidiary companies in which the holding company has invested. The primary purpose of group accounts is to provide a true and fair view of the position and earnings of the group as a whole, from the standpoint of the shareholders in the holding company.

A number of arguments have been put forward, however, which argue that group accounts have certain limitations.

(a) Group accounts may be misleading.

    (i) The solvency (liquidity) of one company may hide the insolvency of another.

    (ii) The profit of one company may conceal the losses of another.

    (iii) They imply that group companies will meet each others' debts (this is certainly not true: a parent company may watch creditors of an insolvent subsidiary go unpaid without having to step in).

(b) There may be some difficulties in defining the group or 'entity' of companies, although company law and accounting standards have removed many of the grey areas here.

(c) Where a group consists of widely diverse companies in different lines of business, a set of group accounts may obscure much important detail unless supplementary information about each part of the group's business is provided.

16 Arlene and Amanda

> **Tutorial note**
>
> | | | $ | $ |
> |---|---|---|---|
> | DEBIT | Dividends receivable (90% × $10,000) | 9,000 | |
> | CREDIT | Retained earnings | | 9,000 |

Stage 1 Amanda Co has accounted for a proposed dividend of $10,000, but Arlene Co has not yet accounted for its share of the dividend receivable. Arlene's draft balance sheet is therefore adjusted as follows.

    The adjusted balance on Arlene's retained earnings is $199,000.

Stage 2 The current accounts are agreed once $4,000 cash in transit is recognised.

Stage 3 There are two part-cancelling items: Amanda Co's share capital and the dividend receivable/payable.

Stage 4 *Minority interests*

	$
Issued shares (10% × 150,000)	15,000
Retained earnings (10% × 99,000)	9,900
Capital reserves (10% × 15,000)	1,500
	26,400

Stage 5

Goodwill

	$	$
Cost of investment		190,000
Share of net assets acquired as represented by:		
Ordinary share capital	150,000	
Accumulated profits on acquisition	20,000	
Capital reserves on acquisition	10,000	
	180,000	
Group share 90%		162,000
Goodwill		28,000
Impairment to date		21,000

Consolidated retained earnings

	Arlene Co	Amanda Co
	$	$
Per question	190,000	99,000
Add dividend	9,000	
	199,000	
Pre-acquisition		(20,000)
		79,000
Share of Amanda Co: 79 × 90%	71,100	
Impairment of goodwill	(21,000)	
	249,100	

Consolidated capital reserve

	Arlene Co	Amanda Co
	$	$
Per question	60,000	15,000
Pre-acquisition		(10,000)
		5,000
Share of Amanda Co: 5,000 × 90%	4,500	
	64,500	

ARLENE CO
CONSOLIDATED BALANCE SHEET AS AT 31 DECEMBER 20X5

	$	$
Assets		
Non-current assets		
Tangible assets	560,000	
Goodwill (28 – 21)	7,000	
		567,000
Current assets		
Inventories	125,000	
Receivables	150,000	
Bank and cash	56,000	
		331,000
Total assets		898,000
Equity and liabilities		
Capital and reserves		
Issued shares: $1	400,000	
Accumulated profits	249,100	
Capital reserves	64,500	
Minority interest	26,400	
		740,000
Current liabilities		
Payables	127,000	
Proposed dividend to members of Arlene	30,000	
Proposed dividend to minority (10% × $10,000)	1,000	
		158,000
Total equity and liabilities		898,000

17 Hand

Tutorial note. This is quite a complex question which brings together a number of complications. It is important in dealing with such questions to be methodical in following the recommended five-stage approach.

Stage 1   All dividends have been accounted for by both companies, but Hand Co has treated its share of Finger Co's 20X0 dividend incorrectly. The dividend comes from pre-acquisition profits of Finger Co and should be credited not to income, but to the 'investment in subsidiary' account. The following adjustment is therefore necessary to Hand Co's draft balance sheet.

DEBIT	Retained earnings (40/60 × $6,000)	$4,000	
CREDIT	Investment in Finger Co		$4,000

Hand Co now has a balance of $(90,000 – 4,000) = $86,000 on accumulated profits, while its investment in Finger Co is stated at cost less amounts written down $(50,000 – 4,000) = $46,000.

Stage 2   The current accounts differ by $2,000, being cash in transit from Finger Co to Hand Co. $2,000 cash in transit will appear in the consolidated balance sheet as an asset.

Stage 3   The only cancelling items, apart from the current accounts, are Hand Co's investment in subsidiary and Finger Co's share capital. These will be dealt with in the goodwill calculation.

Stage 4

		$
Minority interests		
Share capital ($^1/_3 \times$ $60,000)		20,000
Retained earnings ($^1/_3 \times$ $38,700) (W)		12,900
		32,900

Stage 5

Goodwill

		$
Cost of investment		50,000
Less dividend from pre-acquisition profits		4,000
		46,000
Share of net assets acquired, as represented by		
Share capital	60,000	
Reserves (W)	30,000	
	90,000	
Group share ($^2/_3$)		60,000
Negative goodwill		14,000

This is credited to the income statement in the year of acquisition.

Accumulated profits

	Hand Co	Finger Co
	$	$
Per question	90,000	38,700
Less dividend	4,000	
	86,000	
Pre-acquisition		30,000
		8,700
Share of Finger: 8,700 × 40/60	5,800	
Negative goodwill	14,000	
	105,800	

Working: accumulated profits of Finger Co

	$	$
Pre-acquisition		
Balance at 31.12.X0	18,000	
Profit for 6 months to 30.6.X1 ($^6/_{12} \times$ $18,000)	9,000	
Consolidation adjustment: revaluation surplus *	3,000	
		30,000
Post-acquisition		
Profit for 6 months to 31.12.X1 ($^6/_{12} \times$ $18,000)	9,000	
Consolidation adjustment: increase in dep'n charge		
($^1/_5 \times$ $3,000 × $^6/_{12}$)*	(300)	
		8,700
		38,700

* These consolidation adjustments are necessary so that the assets of Finger Co are revalued to their fair value on acquisition.

HAND CO
CONSOLIDATED BALANCE SHEET AS AT 31 DECEMBER 20X1

	$	$
Assets		
Non-current assets		
Tangible assets		178,700
Current assets		
Sundry	257,000	
Cash in transit	2,000	
		259,000
Total assets		437,700
Equity and liabilities		
Capital and reserves		
Issued shares: $1	100,000	
Accumulated profits	105,800	
Minority interest	32,900	
		238,700
Current liabilities		199,000
Total equity and liabilities		437,700

18 Corrie

Tutorial note. The tricky aspect here is the treatment of the pre-acquisition dividends, which is tested both as a written question and as a computational question.

(a)   Generally, a dividend paid out of pre-acquisition profits should be applied to reduce the cost of the investments in the balance sheet of the holding company. It should not be treated as realised profit.

The thinking behind this is that the holding company cannot credit the dividend to profit because no profit has been made. The holding company was willing to pay 'over the odds' for its investment in the presumption that part of its cost would be immediately re-paid. When the dividend is paid, this presumption must be pursued to its conclusion by treating the dividend as a reduction of the cost of investment or a return of capital.

However, this accounting treatment is not a requirement, and it is possible to argue that, provided the investment will eventually recover the value that has been removed from it by the distribution, then it is unnecessary to write it down and the dividend to the holding company may be distributed. This implies that, provided the level of profits made by the subsidiary is to be maintained, those profits may be distributed by the holding company.

Best practice would seem to be that a dividend should be applied to reduce the carrying value of the investment in a subsidiary at least to the extent that this is necessary to provide for any diminution in value. Any other amount is probably realised profit in the hands of the parent company.

(b)

Tutorial note. Make sure your treatment of the dividends accords with your answer to part (a), assuming you got that right!

CORRIE GROUP
CONSOLIDATED BALANCE SHEET AS AT 31 DECEMBER 20X7

	$m	$m
Assets		
Non-current assets		
Tangible assets (W4)	9,162.0	
Goodwill: subsidiary (W2)	848.8	
Investment in associate (W6)	900.0	
		10,910.8
Current assets		
Inventories	1,380.0	
Receivables	950.0	
Cash at bank and in hand	290.0	
		2,620.0
Total assets		13,530.8
Equity and liabilities		
Capital and reserves		
Share capital: $1 shares	6,000.0	
Share premium account	1,490.0	
Accumulated profits (W9)	1,177.8	
Minority interests (W5)	1,693.0	
		10,360.8
Non-current liabilities		2,170.0
Current liabilities (W8)		1,000.0
Total equity and liabilities		13,530.8

Workings

1   *Dividends paid by Brookie Co*

	Total		Corrie Co
	$m		$m
Ordinary dividend	48	× 75%	36
Preferred dividend	60	× 25%	15
	108		51

As these dividends are paid out of pre-acquisition profits, they should be charged against the cost of Corrie Co's investment in Brookie Co.

2   *Goodwill*

	$m	$m
Brookie		
Cost of investment in Brookie Co		3,960
Less dividend from pre-acquisition profits (W1)		51
		3,909
Net assets acquired:		
Share capital	2,400	
Share premium	100	
Retained earnings	898	
	3,398	
Group share 75%		2,548
		1,361
5% preference shares	1,200	
Group share 25%		300.0
Goodwill		1,061.0
Impairment		212.2
Consolidated b/s		848.8

3   *Intercompany inventory/non-current asset*

		$m	$m
Intercompany profit = 720 × 25/125			144
DEBIT	Minority interest reserves 25%	36	
DEBIT	Group reserves 75%	108	
CREDIT	Non-current assets		144

		$m	$m
Amortisation adjustment			
Excess depreciation: 25% of 144 = $36m			
DEBIT	Provision for depreciation	36	
CREDIT	Group reserves		36

4   *Tangible non-current assets*

	$m
Corrie	4,920
Less intercompany profit	(144)
Add back excess depreciation	36
	4,812
Brookie	4,350
	9,162

5   *Minority interest*

	$m	$m
Ordinary shares		
Share capital	2,400	
Share premium	100	
Retained earnings (790 – 12)	778	
	3,278	
MI @ 25%		820
Less intercompany profit		36
		784
Preferred shares		
Preferred shares	1,200	
Premium on redemption	12	
	1,212	
MI @ 75%		909
		1,693

6   *Investment in associate*

	$m
Cost of investment	900
Share of fair value of investments acquired 25% × 2,200	550
Goodwill	350

As the holding was purchased at the year end will be no impairment of goodwill.

7   *Receivables*

	$m
Corrie	610
Brookie	360
Less intercompany	(20)
	950

8   *Current liabilities*

	$m
Corrie	610
Brookie	410
Less intercompany	(20)
	1,000

9   *Accumulated profits*

	Corrie $m	Brookie $m
Per question	1,600.0	790
Less pre-acquisition dividends wrongly accounted for (W1)	(51.0)	
Over depreciation of non-current assets (W4)	36.0	
Share of deemed dividend/premium		
((1,200 × 10%)/10) × 25%	3.0	
	1,588.0	
Profit on sale of non-current asset		(144)
Premium on redemption of preferred shares (1,200 × 10%)/10		(12)
		634
Pre-acquisition		(898)
		(264)
Share of Brookie: $264m × 75%	(198.0)	
Impairment of goodwill	(212.2)	
	1,177.8	

19 War

Tutorial note. This question may look intimidating because it involves an acquisition part of the way through the year, some fair value issues and both the consolidated income statement and balance sheet. It is, however, fairly straightforward.

(a)   IFRS 3 *Business combinations* states that shares offered as consideration should be valued at fair value, which for listed shares will be market price on the date of acquisition. However, the standard acknowledges that the market price may be difficult to determine if it is unreliable because of an inactive market. In particular, where the shares are not listed, there may be no suitable market. In such cases the value must be estimated using the best methods available. This may involve the use of:

(i)   The value of similar listed securities
(ii)   The present value of the cash flows of the shares
(iii)   Any cash alternative which was offered
(iv)   The value of any underlying security into which there is an option to convert

It may be necessary to undertake a valuation of the company in question should none of the above methods prove feasible.

(b)   WAR GROUP
      CONSOLIDATED BALANCE SHEET AS AT 30 JUNE 20X7

	$'000	$'000
Assets		
Non-current assets		
Tangible assets (1,750 + 500)	2,250	
Goodwill (W3)	189	
		2,439
Current assets		
Inventories	600	
Receivables	451	
Cash at bank and in hand	299	
		1,350
Total assets		3,789
Equity and liabilities		
Capital and reserves		
Ordinary shares of $1 each	750	
Share premium (W6)	250	
Accumulated profits (W5)	659	
Minority interests (W4)	255	
		1,914
Non-current liabilities		1,225
Current liabilities		650
Total equity and liabilities		3,789

WAR GROUP
CONSOLIDATED INCOME STATEMENT FOR THE YEAR ENDED 30 JUNE 20X7

	$'000
Revenue	3,445
Cost of sales	(1,788)
Gross profit	1,657
Distribution costs	(638)
Administrative expenses (W7)	(310)
Operating profit	709
Interest payable	(75)
Profit before tax	634
Tax on profit	(306)
Profit after tax	328
Minority interests (W8)	(11)
	317
Dividends paid	38
Retained profit for the financial year attributable to the group	279

Workings

1   *Revaluation surplus*

	$'000
Peace Co: tangible non-current assets at market value	500
Carrying value	350
Revaluation surplus	150

IFRS 3 *Business combinations* states that open market values should be used to value
tangible non-current assets, and it is this figure which is compared with the carrying value
here, rather than the net realisable value. The latter is lower because the costs of realisation
are deducted. However, as the group does not intend to dispose of the asset, the market
value is more appropriate.

> **Tutorial note**. Before you can work out the goodwill, you need to work out the pre-acquisition element of the dividend, as this will give you the cost of the investment.

2   *Pre-acquisition dividend*

Dividend paid by Peace to War: $42,000

Pre-acquisition element $^{10}/_{12} \times \$42,000 = \$35,000$

3   *Goodwill*

	$'000	$'000
Cost of investment		800
Less pre-acquisition dividend (W2)		(35)
		765
Share capital	100	
Share premium	150	
Revaluation surplus	150	
Accumulated profits		
Prior year: 450 – 165	285	
Current year: $^{10}/_{12} \times 165$	138	
	823	
Group share: 70%		576
Goodwill		189

4   *Minority interests (balance sheet)*

	$'000
Share capital	100
Share premium	150
Revaluation surplus	150
Retained earnings	450
	850

MI = $850,000 \times 30\% = \$255,000$.

5   *Retained earnings*

	$'000
War Co	625
Less pre-acquisition dividend	(35)
	590
Add back issue costs	50
	640
Peace Co $165 \times {}^2/_{12} \times 70\%$	19
	659

6   *Share premium account*

	$'000
War Co	300
Less issue costs	(50)
	250

7   *Administrative expenses*

	$'000
War Co	325
Peace Co $({}^2/_{12} \times 210)$	35
	360
Less issue costs	(50)
	310

8   *Minority interests (income statement)*

$225 \times {}^2/_{12} \times 30\% = \$11,250$

20 CPP and CCA

> **Tutorial note**. It is unlikely that a detailed computation will be asked for, but you must have an understanding of the principles of CPP and CCA, the differences between them and the ways in which they try to improve on HCA.

(a)   In accounting, the value of income and capital is measured in terms of money. In simple terms, profit is the difference between the closing and opening balance sheet values (after adjustment for new sources of funds and applications such as dividend distribution). If, because of inflation, the value of assets in the closing balance sheet is shown at a higher monetary amount than assets in the opening balance sheet, a profit has been made. In traditional accounting, it is assumed that a monetary unit of $1 is a stable measurement; inflation removes this stability.

CPP accounting attempts to provide a more satisfactory method of valuing profit and capital by establishing a stable unit of monetary measurement, $1 of current purchasing power, as at the end of the accounting period under review.

A distinction is made between monetary items, and non-monetary items. In a period of inflation, keeping a monetary asset (eg trade receivables) results in a loss of purchasing power as the value of money erodes over time. Non-monetary assets, however, are assumed to maintain 'real' value over time, and these are converted into monetary units of current purchasing power as at the year end, by means of a suitable price index. The equity interest in the balance sheet can be determined as a balancing item.

The profit or deficit for the year in CPP terms is found by converting sales, opening and closing inventory, purchases and other expenses into year-end units of $CPP. In addition, a profit on holding net monetary liabilities (or a loss on holding net monetary assets) is computed in arriving at the profit or deficit figure.

CPP arguably provides a more satisfactory system of accounting since transactions are expressed in terms of 'today's money' and similarly, the balance sheet values are adjusted for inflation, so as to give users of financial information a set of figures with which they can:

(i)   Decide whether operating profits are satisfactory (profits due to inflation are eliminated)
(ii)   Obtain a better appreciation of the size and 'value' of the entity's assets

(b)   CPP and CCA accounting are different concepts, in that CPP accounting makes adjustments for general inflationary price changes, whereas CCA makes adjustments to allow for specific price movements (changes in the deprival value of assets). Specific price changes (in CCA) enable a company to determine whether the operating capability of a company has been maintained; it is not a restatement of price levels in terms of a common unit of money measurement. The two conventions use different concepts of capital maintenance (namely operating capability with CCA, and general purchasing power with CPP).

In addition CPP is based on the use of a general price index. In contrast, CCA only makes use of a specific price index where it is not possible to obtain the current value of an asset by other means (eg direct valuation).

(c)   In CCA, holding gains represent the difference between the historical cost of an asset and its current cost. If the asset is unsold, and appears in the balance sheet of a company at current cost, there will be an 'unrealised' holding gain, which must be included in a current cost reserve. When the asset is eventually sold, the profit (equal to the sale price minus the historical cost) may be divided into:

(i)   An operating profit which would have been made if the cost of the asset were its current value

(ii)   A *realised* holding gain which has arisen because of the appreciation in value of the asset between the date of its acquisition and the date of its sale

(d)   (i)   The cost of sales adjustment is the difference between the historical cost of goods sold and their current cost. In a CCA statement, the COSA is therefore used to adjust 'historical cost profit' towards 'current cost profit' by, in effect, changing the cost of sales from an historical cost to a current cost basis.

(ii)   The COSA does not allow for the fact that purchased goods are acquired on credit and finished goods are likewise sold on credit. In a period of inflation, a company benefits from creditors (because payments are made at 'yesterday's prices') but loses with debtors, because a delay in the receipt of cash means that more money is required to purchase replacement assets (at 'tomorrow's prices') in order to maintain the operating capability of the business. The MWCA is therefore a charge, if the company has positive, rather than negative, monetary working capital (MWC defined roughly as receivables minus payables) which takes account of the effect of deferred payments on business substance in arriving at the current cost operating profit.

(iii)   The depreciation adjustment is the difference between the depreciation charge based on the historical cost of non-current assets and the charge based on their current cost. In a CCA statement, the depreciation adjustment is therefore used to adjust 'historical cost profit' towards 'current cost operating profit' in order to reflect the current value of non-current assets 'consumed'.

(iv)   The gearing adjustment is calculated after the current cost operating profit has been determined. A company is financed not only by share capital, but also by debt capital, which falls in 'real' value over time in a period of inflation. There is no need to maintain the operating capability of the business with respect to assets financed by debt capital. The usual gearing adjustment is the amount of holding gains (ie a proportion of the three adjustments described in (i) to (iii) above) which is attributable to assets financed by debt capital rather than equity. These gains, because they will never be paid to the holders of debt capital, are 'free' to the equity shareholders, and the gearing adjustment is therefore added to the current cost operating profit in order to arrive at a value for 'current cost profit attributable to shareholders' of the company.

21 Alpha

> **Tutorial note**. Creative accounting and substance over form are important concepts. You must relate your answer to the situation given in part (c) of the question and not just write a general essay. One or two examples would be enough in (a).

(a)   **Creative accounting**, the manipulation of figures for a desired result, takes many forms. Off-balance sheet finance is a major type of creative accounting and it probably has the most serious implications.

It is very rare for a company, its directors or employees to manipulate results for the purpose of fraud. The major consideration is usually the effect the results will have on the share price of the company. If the share price falls, the company becomes vulnerable to takeover. Analysts, brokers and economists, whose opinions affect the stock markets, are often perceived as having an outlook which is both short-term and superficial. Consequently, companies will attempt to produce the results the market expects or wants. The companies will aim for steady progress in a few key numbers and ratios and they will aim to meet the market's stated expectation.

The number of methods available for creative accounting and the determination and imagination of those who wish to perpetrate such acts are endless. It has been seen in the past that, wherever an accounting standard or law closes a loophole, another one is found. This has produced a change of approach in regulators and standard setters, towards general principles rather than detailed rules.

Here are a few examples of creative accounting.

(i)   **Income recognition and cut-off**

Manipulation of cut-off is relatively straightforward. A company may issue invoices before the year end and inflate sales for the year when in fact they have not received firm orders for the goods. Income recognition can be manipulated in a variety of ways.

(ii)   **Reserves**

Reserves are often used to manipulate figures, avoiding any impact on the income statement. This occurs particularly in situations where an accounting standard allows a choice of treatments, eg foreign exchange losses or gains on foreign subsidiaries can be taken as a movement on reserves.

(iii)   **Revaluations**

The optional nature of the revaluation of non-current assets leaves such practices open to manipulation. The choice of whether to revalue can have a significant impact on a company's balance sheet.

(iv)   **Window dressing**

This is where transactions are passed through the books at the year end to make figures look better, but in fact they have not taken place and are often reversed after the year end. An example is where cheques are written to creditors, entered in the cash book, but not sent out until well after the year end.

(v)   **Change of accounting policies**

This tends to be a last resort because companies which change accounting policies know they will not be able to do so again for some time. The effect in the year of change can be substantial and prime candidates for such treatment are depreciation, inventory valuation, changes from current cost to historical cost (practised frequently by privatised public utilities) and foreign currency losses.

(vi)   **Manipulation of accruals, prepayments and contingencies**

These figures can often be very subjective, particularly contingencies. In the case of impending legal action, for example, a contingent liability is difficult to estimate, the case may be far off and the lawyers cannot give any indication of likely success, or failure. In such cases companies will often only disclose the possibility of such a liability, even though the eventual costs may be substantial.

Tutorial note. This part of the question is useful preparation for Paper 3.6, where you will often be asked to consider the effects of different accounting policies on the financial statements and of key accounting ratios.

(b)   The phrase 'substance over form' has been described as follows.

> 'Transactions and other events should be accounted for and presented in accordance with their substance and financial reality and not merely with their legal form.'

This is a very important concept and it has been used to determine accounting treatment in financial statements through accounting standards and so prevent off balance sheet transactions.

(i)   **Group accounting** is perhaps the most important area of off balance sheet finance which has been prevented by the application of the substance over form concept. A number of IASs have tackled abuses by enforcing the substance over form concept.

The most important point is that the definition of a subsidiary (under IAS 27) is based upon the **principle of control rather than purely ownership.** Where an entity is controlled by another, the controlling entity can ensure that the benefits accrue to itself and not to other parties. Similarly, one of the circumstances where a subsidiary may be excluded from consolidation is where there are severe long-term restrictions that prevent effective control.

(ii)   Finance leases and their accounting treatment under IAS 17 *Leases* are an example of the application of substance over form.

Operating leases do not really pose an accounting problem. The lessee pays amounts periodically to the lessor and these are charged to the income statement. The lessor treats the leased asset as a non-current asset and depreciates it in the normal way. Rentals received from the lessee are credited to the income statement in the lessor's books.

For assets held under **finance leases** this accounting treatment would not disclose the reality of the situation. If a lessor leases out an asset on a finance lease, the asset will probably never be seen on his premises or used in his business again. It would be inappropriate for a lessor to record such an asset as a non-current asset. In reality, what he owns is a stream of cash flows receivable from the lessee. The asset is a receivable rather than a non-current asset.

Similarly, a lessee may use a finance lease to fund the 'acquisition' of a major asset which he will then use in his business perhaps for many years. The substance of the transaction is that he has acquired a non-current asset, and this is reflected in the accounting treatment prescribed by IAS 17, even though in law the lessee may never become the owner of the asset.

(iii)   With regard to **measurement or disclosure of current assets**, a common example where substance over form is relevant are sale and repurchase agreements. There are arrangements under which the company sells an asset to another person on terms that allow the company to repurchase the asset in certain circumstances. A common example of such a transaction is the sale and repurchase of maturing whisky inventories. The key question is whether the transaction is a straightforward sale, or whether it is, in effect, a secured loan. It is necessary to look at the arrangement to determine who has the rights to the economic benefits that the asset generates, and the terms on which the asset is to be repurchased.

If the seller has the right to the benefits of the use of the asset, and the repurchase terms are such that the repurchase is likely to take place, the transaction should be accounted for as a loan.

Another example is the factoring of **trade receivables**. Where debts are factored, the original creditor sells the receivables to the factor. The sales price may be fixed at the outset or may be adjusted later. It is also common for the factor to offer a credit facility that allows the seller to draw upon a proportion of the amounts owed.

In order to determine the correct accounting treatment it is necessary to consider whether the benefit of the receivables has been passed on to the factor, or whether the factor is, in effect, providing a loan on the security of the receivables. If the seller has to pay interest on the difference between the amounts advanced to him and the amounts that the factor has received, and if the seller bears the risks of non-payment by the debtor, then the indications would be that the transaction is, in effect, a loan.

(c) (i) The finance director may be right in believing that renewing the non-current assets of the company will contribute to generating higher earnings and hence improved earnings per share. However, this will not happen immediately as the assets will need to have been in operation for at least a year for results to be apparent. Earnings will be higher because of the loan being at a commercially unrealistic rate, namely 5% instead of 9%.

As regards gearing, the finance director may well wish to classify the convertible loan stock as equity rather than debt; thus gearing will be lower. He may argue that because the loan is very likely to be converted into shares, the finance should be treated as equity rather than as debt.

(ii) IAS 33 *Earnings per share* requires the calculation of **basic earnings per share**. This calculation would permit a scheme like that of the finance director. The issuing of the loan stock would not increase the number of shares and the earnings figure would be calculated on the basis of interest payments at 5%.

However, IAS 33 requires the calculation and disclosure of **diluted EPS**.

The need to disclose diluted earnings per share arose because of the limited value of a basic EPS figure when a company is financed partly by convertible debt. Because the right to convert carries benefits, it is usual that the interest rate on the debt is lower than on straight debt. Calculation of EPS on the assumption that the debt is non-convertible can, therefore, be misleading since:

(1) Current EPS is higher than it would be under straight debt

(2) On conversion, EPS will fall – diluted EPS provides some information about the extent of this future reduction, and warning shareholders of the reduction which will happen in the future

IAS 32 *Financial instruments: disclosure and presentation* affects the proposed scheme in that IAS 32 requires that convertible loans such as this should be split on the balance sheet and presented partly as equity and partly as debt. Thus the company's gearing will probably increase as the convertible loan cannot be 'hidden' in equity.

22 Reporting substance

> **Tutorial note**. Although you are not given the amount of the debt, you have enough information to do an illustrative example as shown below.

The commercial effect of this arrangement is that, although the debts have been legally transferred to Farant Factors Co, Shaky Co continues to bear significant benefits and risks relating to them. Shaky Co continues to bear slow payment risk as the interest charged by Farant Factors Co varies with the speed of collections of the debts. Hence, the gross amount of the debts should continue to be shown on its balance sheet until the earlier of collection and transfer of all risks to Farant Factors Co (ie 90 days).

However, Shaky Co's maximum downside loss is limited since any debts not recovered after 90 days are in effect paid for by Farant Factors Co, which then assumes all slow payment and credit risks beyond this time. Thus, even for debts that prove to be bad, Shaky Co receives some proceeds. (For a debt of 100 that subsequently proves to be bad, the proceeds received would be 100, less the credit protection fee of 1, less an interest charge calculated for 90 days at base rate plus 2.5%.)

Hence, assuming the conditions for linked presentation for non-recourse finance arrangements are met, a linked presentation should be adopted. The amount deducted on the face of the balance sheet should be the lower of the proceeds received and the gross amount of the debts less all charges to the factor in respect of them. In the above example, for a debt of 100 this latter amount would be calculated at 100 less the credit protection fee of 1 and the maximum finance charge (calculated for 90 days at base rate plus 2.5%). Assuming the proceeds received of 80 are lower than this, and accrued interest charges at the year end are 2, the arrangement would be shown as follows.

	$	$
Current assets		
Inventory		X
Debts factored without recourse		
Gross debts (after providing for credit protection fee and accrued interest)	97	
Less non-returnable proceeds	(80)	
		17
Other receivables		X

Tutorial note. It is always a good idea to present the figures 'in context' as above.

In addition, the non-returnable proceeds of 80 would be included within cash and the income statement expenses would include both the credit protection expense of 1 and the accrued interest charges of 2.

23 Biggerbuys

REPORT

To:	The bankers of Biggerbuys
From:	Consultant management accountant
Subject:	Financial performance 20X7 – 20X9
Date:	30 October 20X9

1 Introduction

1.1 In accordance with your instructions, I set out below a review of the entity's financial performance over the last three years.

1.2 The main focus of this report is on the reasons for the increase in the level of bank loans.

1.3 Appropriate accounting ratios are included in the attached appendix.

2 Bank lending

2.1 The main reason for the steep increase in bank lending is due to the entity not generating sufficient cash from its operating activities over the past three years.

2.2 For the year ended 30 June 20X8, the entity had a **net cash deficiency on operating activities** of $18m.

2.3 In addition, for at least the past two years, the cash generated from operating activities has not been sufficient to cover interest payable. Therefore those payments, together with tax and dividends, have had to be covered by borrowings.

2.4 As at 30 June 20X9, bank borrowings were $610m out of a total facility of $630m. Payment of the proposed dividends alone would increase the borrowings to the limit.

3 Operating review

3.1 Although revenue has been rising steadily over the period, operating profit has remained almost static.

3.2 Over this period the profit margin has risen, but not as much as would be expected. The cost of sales have risen in almost the same proportion as sales. This may be due to increased costs of raw materials, as inventories have risen steeply; but the turnover of inventory has been falling or static over the same period.

3.3 There has also been a large increase in trade receivables. Both the increase in inventories and trade receivables have had to be financed out of operating activities leading to the present pressure on borrowings.

3.4 Although the number of days sales in trade receivables has fallen steadily over the period, the trade receivables at the end of June 20X9 still represent nearly a year's credit sales. This is excessive and seems to imply a poor credit control policy, even taking into account the extended credit terms being granted by the company.

4 Recommendations

4.1 The entity needs to undertake an urgent review of its credit terms in order to reduce the levels of trade receivables.

4.2 Inventory levels are also extremely high (representing over four months' sales) and should be reviewed.

4.3 Operating costs also need to be kept under control in order to generate more cash from sales.

Please contact me if you need any further information.

Signed: An Accountant

Appendix: Accounting ratios

		20X7	20X8	20X9
1	Profit margin			
	$\dfrac{\text{Profit before interest}}{\text{Revenue}} \times 100$	$\dfrac{(50+45)}{1,850} \times 100\%$	$\dfrac{(60+60)}{2,200} \times 100\%$	$\dfrac{(50+90)}{2,500} \times 100\%$
		= 5.1%	= 5.5%	= 5.6%
2	Operating costs			
	$\dfrac{\text{Other operating costs}}{\text{Revenue}} \times 100$	$\dfrac{550}{1,850} \times 100\%$	$\dfrac{640}{2,200} \times 100\%$	$\dfrac{700}{2,500} \times 100\%$
		= 29.7%	= 29.1%	= 28.0%
3	Inventory turnover			
	$\dfrac{\text{Cost of sales}}{\text{Inventory}}$	$\dfrac{1,250}{400}$	$\dfrac{1,500}{540}$	$\dfrac{1,750}{620}$
		= 3.1 times	= 2.8 times	= 2.8 times
4	Trade receivables turnover			
	$\dfrac{\text{Trade receivables}}{\text{Credit sales}} \times 365$	$\dfrac{492}{(300+45)} \times 365$	$\dfrac{550}{(400+60)} \times 365$	$\dfrac{633}{(600+90)} \times 365$
		= 523 days	= 436 days	= 334 days

5   *Cash generated from operations*

	20X8 $m	20X9 $m
Profit before interest	120	140
Depreciation	60	70
Increase in inventory	(140)	(80)
Increase in trade receivables	(58)	(83)
Increase in trade payables	–	10
	(18)	57

6   *ROCE*

	20X7	20X8	20X9
$\dfrac{\text{Profit before interest}}{\text{Net assets}+\text{borrowings}}\times100\%$	$\dfrac{95}{(342+520)}\times100\%$	$\dfrac{120}{(352+720)}\times100\%$	$\dfrac{140}{(352+930)}\times100\%$
	= 11.0%	= 11.2%	= 10.9%

7   Interest cover

	20X7	20X8	20X9
$\dfrac{\text{Profit before interest}}{\text{Interest payable}}$	$\dfrac{95}{25}$	$\dfrac{120}{60}$	$\dfrac{140}{110}$
	= 3.8	= 2.0	= 1.3

8   Gearing

	20X7	20X8	20X9
$\dfrac{\text{Borrowings}}{\text{Net assets}+\text{borrowings}}$	$\dfrac{520}{862}$	$\dfrac{720}{1,072}$	$\dfrac{930}{1,282}$
	= 60.3%	= 67.2%	= 72.5%

9   Asset turnover

	20X7	20X8	20X9
$\dfrac{\text{Revenue}}{\text{Net assets}+\text{borrowings}}$	$\dfrac{1,850}{862}$	$\dfrac{2,200}{1,072}$	$\dfrac{2,500}{1,282}$
	= 2.1 times	= 2.1 times	= 2.0 times

24 Webster

> **Tutorial note**. This question is at the upper end of the scale of difficulty which you are likely to encounter, particularly part (a). Study the answer carefully.

(a)   INCOME STATEMENTS (RESTATED)

	Cole $'000	Cole $'000	Darwin $'000	Darwin $'000
Revenue (3,000 – 125) (Note 1)		2,875		4,400
Opening inventory	450		720	
Purchases (Note 2)	2,055		3,080	
Closing inventory	(540)		(850)	
		1,965		2,950
Gross profit		910		1,450
Operating expenses	480		964	
Depreciation (Note 3)	40		(120)	
Loan interest	80		–	
Overdraft interest (W3)	15		–	
		(615)		(844)
Net profit		295		606

BALANCE SHEETS (RESTATED)

	Cole		Darwin	
	$'000	$'000	$'000	$'000
Assets				
Non current assets				
Property, plant, equipment (W1)		3,100		2,620
Current assets				
Inventory	540		850	
Receivables (W2)	897		750	
Bank (W3)	–		60	
		1,437		1,660
		4,537		4,280
Equity and liabilities				
Equity shares ($1)		1,000		500
Revaluation reserve (800 – 40)		760		700
Accumulated profit to 31 March 20X9				
(684 + 295 + 40)/(1,912 + 606)		1,019		2,518
		2,779		3,718
Non current liabilities				
10% loan note		800		–
Current liabilities				
Trade payables (W4)		163		562
Overdraft (W3)		795		–
		4,537		4,280

Workings

1   *Non-current assets*

		Cost/valuation	Depreciation	NBV
		$'000	$'000	$'000
Cole:	property	2,000	100	1,900
	plant	6,000	4,800	1,200
				3,100
Darwin:	property	2,000	100	1,900
	plant (3,000 – 600)	2,400	1,680	720
				2,620

2   *Receivables*
    Cole: 522 + 375 (Note 1) = 897

3   *Bank*

	Cole	Darwin
	$'000	$'000
As stated	20	(550)
Reversal of sale (Note 1)	(500)	
Payment for purchases (Note 2)	(300)	
Payment for plant (Note 3)		600
Payment/saving of interest to balance sheet	15	10
	(795)	60

4   *Payables*
    Cole 438 –275 (Note 2) = 163

559

Tutorial notes

1   Sale to Brander is at gross margin 40%, therefore the cost of sale is $500 × 60% = $300.

Had a normal margin of 20% applied, the cost of this sale would represent 80% of the selling price.

The normal selling price would be $\dfrac{300}{0.8}$ = $375.

Sales and receivables would reduce by $125 and the proceeds of $500 would not have been received.

2   Purchase of goods from Advent on normal terms would have increased purchases by $25. Using the normal credit period would mean these goods would have been paid for by the year end, increasing the overdraft and reducing trade payables.

3   The plant bought in February 20X9 has not yet generated income for Darwin, so it is sensible to ignore it in the acquisition comparison.

The effects are:

- Cost of plant – $600, overdraft affected
- Depreciation reduced $600 × 20% = $120

The depreciation charged changes:

	Cole $'000	Darwin $'000
As stated for property	(60)	
Depreciation on revaluation	100	
Reduction (above)		(120)
	40 increase	(120) (decrease)

(b)

Ratios	Cole		Darwin	
Return on capital employed:	(295+80)/(2,779+800)	= 10.5%	606/3,718	= 16.3%
Asset turnover	2,875/(4,537 – 958)	= 0.8 times	4,400/(4,280 – 562)	=1.2 times
Gross profit %	910/2,875	= 31.7%	(unchanged)	= 33%
Net profit %	295/2,875	= 10.3%	606/4,400	= 13.8%
Receivables collection (days)	897/2,875 ×365	= 114	(unchanged)	= 62
Payables period (days)	163/2,055 ×365	= 29	(unchanged)	= 67

Using the unadjusted figures, Cole would be preferred, as its key ratios given are better than those of Darwin. Cole achieves better profitability due to greater unit margins. Both companies have poor asset turnover implying under-utilisation or inefficient methods.

Both companies manage working capital in a similar fashion. Webster should examine liquidity ratios:

Cole: 1,082/438 = 2.5
Darwin: 1,600/1,112 = 1.4

The acid test ratio of Cole is 1.23 whereas Darwin's is 0.67.

Using the adjusted accounts, the above position is reversed showing Darwin to be more profitable and to manage its assets more efficiently. Cole's true liquidity position is not so healthy – Cole controls receivables poorly and appears to pay suppliers earlier.

Darwin's poor liquidity position is probably due to financing non-current assets from its overdraft. Alternative refinancing would be beneficial.

Cole's parent company has produced an initially favourable set of ratios by creating favourable payment terms and trading conditions, and Darwin's original ratios were distorted by revaluations and the timing of new plant purchases.

Other factors to consider include:

(i)   The asking price
(ii)   The future prospects, profits and cash flow forecasts
(iii)   The state of forward order books
(iv)   The quality of the management and labour force
(v)   Other possible acquisitions

(c)   This answer assumes the accounts would be prepared in compliance with extant IAS's and that they would be publicly available.

Notes (a) and (b). This data would need to be disclosed under IAS 24 *Related party disclosures*. Specifically disclosure would be required of:

(i)   The relationship

(ii)   The nature of the transaction

(iii)   The volume of transactions

(iv)   Outstanding items

(v)   Pricing policy

(vi)   Other data to enable users of accounts to understand the transactions such as margins/terms

Note (c). Under IAS 16 *Property, plant and equipment* where assets are revalued, these values would be included in the balance sheet together with supporting information. IAS 16 also encourages disclosure of fair values if materially different from carrying values.

Note (d). Movements on non current assets would disclose acquisitions, but dates of purchase and financing would not normally be disclosed.

Note (e). This information would not be given and could not be calculated from published accounts.

25 Spice

Tutorial note. One possible approach to this question would be to set out the proforma, slot in all the figures except the change in share capital, then do Part (b), then finish the cash flow statement before you finally go back to Part (c).

(a)   SPICE INC: CASH FLOW STATEMENT FOR THE YEAR ENDED 31 MARCH 20X6

	Note	$m	$m
Net cash from operating activities	1		462
Cash flows from investing activities			
Purchase of non-current assets (W1)		(194)	
Sale of non-current assets		42	
Interest received (6 + 4 – 2)		8	
Net cash used in investing activities			(144)
Cash flows from financing activities			
Issue of share capital (40-2)		38	
Borrowings repaid		(40)	
Repurchase of preference shares		(48)	
Repayment of obligations under finance leases (W3)		(36)	
Dividends paid (W4)		(48)	
Net cash used in financing activities			(134)
Net increase in cash and cash equivalents			184
Cash and cash equivalents at start of year	2		2
Cash and cash equivalents at end of year	2		186

NOTES TO THE CASH FLOW STATEMENT FOR THE YEAR ENDED 31 MARCH 20X6

1   Cash flows from operating activities

	$m
Profit before tax	272
Depreciation	76
Profit on sale of non-current asset (42 – 38)	(4)
Net interest expense	8
Decrease in inventories	30
Increase in trade receivables	(40)
Increase in trade payables (424 – 254)	170
Premium on repurchase of preference shares 40 × 20c	8
Cash generated from operations	520
Interest element of finance lease	(6)
Interest paid (14 + 4 – 6 – 6)	(6)
Corporate tax paid (W2)	(46)
Net cash inflow from operating activities	462

2   Cash and cash equivalents

	20X6	20X5
	$m	$m
Cash in hand	12	42
Short term investments	190	
Bank overdraft	(16)	(40)
	186	2

Workings

1   Non-current assets

	$m		$m
Bal b/d 1.4.20X5	400	Depreciation	76
Non-current assets acquired on		Disposals at NBV	38
finance leases	56		
Revaluation	14		
Balancing figure – paid	194	Bal c/d 31.3.X6	550
	664		664

2   Taxation paid

	$m		$m
Balancing figure – paid 31.3.20X6	46	1.4.20X5	
		Bal b/d corporate tax	20
Bal c/d corporate tax	32	Bal b/d advanced tax	4
Bal c/d advanced tax	2	Bal b/d deferred tax	16
Bal c/d deferred tax	24	Income statement	64
	104		104

3   Finance lease obligations

	$m		$m
Balancing figure – paid	36	Bal b/d 1.4.20X5 6 + 84	90
Bal c/d 31.3.20X6 10 + 100	110	Additions	56
	146		146

4   Dividends

	$m		$m
Balancing figure – paid	48	Bal b/d 1.4.20X5	16
Bal c/d 31.3.20X6	8	Income statement	40
	56		56

5   Issue of share capital

See the answer to part (b) of the question.

(b)   Movement on share capital and reserves

	Ordinary shares $m	Preference shares $m	Share premium $m	Capital redemption $m	Revaluation reserve $m	Accum. profits $m
Balance 1.4.20X5	180	40	70	–	–	162
Issue for cash	20		20			
Issue expenses			(2)			
Bonus issue	20					(20)
Repurchase		(40)				
CRR transfer				40		(40)
Revaluation					14	
Retained earnings						208
Dividend						(40)
	220	–	88	40	14	270

(c)   The arguments which can be advanced in favour of the direct method are as follows.

(i)   The direct method shows

	$m
Cash received from customers	X
Cash paid to suppliers	(X)
Cash paid to employees	(X)
Net cash flow from operations	X

The information disclosed is not shown elsewhere in the accounts and could be useful data.

(ii)   The direct method is arguably easier to explain to non financially orientated managers as changes in working capital items are not included.

(iii)   The information may be more relevant for business decisions.

26 Hepburn

> **Tutorial note**. Technique is everything in these questions. You must **always** check for the date of acquisition in a consolidation question, to check whether it is a mid-year, as is this case – you would lose a lot of marks for missing that. Don't neglect part (b): remember that it is **voting rights** which determine the level of control of an investment not rights to dividends.

(a) HEPBURN
CONSOLIDATED INCOME STATEMENT
FOR THE YEAR ENDED 31 MARCH 20X1

	$'000
Sales revenues (W1)	1,600
Cost of sales (W2)	(890)
Gross profit	710
Operating expenses (W3)	(184)
Debenture interest (12 × 6/12)	(6)
Operating profit	520
Taxation (100 + (40 × 6/12))	(120)
Profit after tax	400
Minority interest (200 × 20% × 6/12)	(20)
Profit after tax and minority interest	380

Movement on reserves	
Dividends: interim	(40)
Final	(40)
Retained profit for the year	380
Retained profit b/f (410 – 250)	160
Retained profit c/f	460

HEPBURN
CONSOLIDATED BALANCE SHEET
AS AT 31 MARCH 20X1

	$'000	$'000
Assets		
Non-current assets		
Tangible non-current assets		
Property (400 + 150 + 125)		675
Plant and equipment (220 + 510)		730
Intangible: goodwill 200 (W4) – 20		180
Investments (20 + 10)		30
		1,615
Current assets		
Inventories (240 + 280 – 10 (W2))	510	
Accounts receivable (170 + 210 – 56)	324	
Bank (20 + 40 + 20)	80	
		914
Total assets		2,529

	$'000	$'000
Equity and liabilities		
Capital and reserves		
Equity shares $1 each (400 + 300 (W4))		700
Share premium account (900 – 300 (W4))		600
Accumulated profits (W5)		460
		1,760
Minority interests (W6)		195
Non-current liabilities		
8% debentures		150
Current liabilities		
Accounts payable (170 + 155 – 36)	289	
Taxation (50 + 45)	95	
Dividends	40	
		424
Total equity and liabilities		2,529

Workings

1	*Sales revenues*		$'000
	Hepburn		1,200
	Salter (1,000 × 6/12)		500
	Less: intragroup sales		(100)
			1,600

2	*Cost of sales*		$'000
	Hepburn		650
	Salter (660 × 6/12)		330
	Less: intragroup sales		(100)
	Unrealised profit in inventory (100 × 50% × 25/125)		10
			890

3	*Operating expenses*		$'000
	Hepburn		120
	Salter (88 × 6/12)		44
	Goodwill impairment		20
			184

4	*Goodwill*	$'000	$'000
	Cost of investment in Salter		
	150 × 80% × 5/2 (= 300) × $3		900
	Fair value of net assets acquired		
	Equity shares	150	
	Accumulated profits		
	At 1 April 20X0 (700 – 200)	500	
	Profit to 1 Oct 20X0 (200 × 6/12)	100	
	Fair value adjustment	125	
		875	
	Group share (80%)		700
	Goodwill		200

5	*Accumulated profits*		$'000
	Hepburn		410
	Unrealised profit in inventories (W2)		(10)
	Salter: share of post-acquisition profits 80% × (200 × 6/12)		80
	Impairment of goodwill		(20)
			460

6	*Minority interest*	$'000
	Equity shares: 20% × 150	30
	Accumulated profits: 20% × 700	140
	Fair value adjustment of land: 20% × 125	25
		195

(b)   In **voting rights**, Hepburn's interest in Woodbridge is **60%;** however it is correct that it is only entitled to 6,000/24,000 = 25% of any dividends paid.

The approach taken by Hepburn to its investment in Woodbridge seems to be based on the view that, with a **25% equity holding**, the investment would normally be treated as an associate and equity accounting applied. However, Hepburn is arguing that it does not exert any significant influence over Woodbridge and hence under IAS 28 *Investments in associates* it can rebut the presumption of associate status.

This overlooks the fact that IAS 27 *Consolidated and separate financial statements* bases the treatment of an investment in another entity on the notion of **control** rather than **ownership**. Hepburn can control Woodbridge by virtue of its holding **the majority of the voting rights** in the company.

Woodbridge is thus a **subsidiary** and should be **consolidated in full** in Hepburn's group accounts, **from the date of acquisition.**

Hepburn's directors may wish to avoid consolidation because of Woodbridge's losses. But these **losses** may indicate that the **value of the investment** in Woodbridge in Hepburn's own individual accounts may be **overstated**. A test for **impairment**, as required by IAS 36 *Impairment of assets*, may reveal that the **recoverable amount** of the investment has fallen below $20,000, thus requiring a write down in Hepburn's own accounts and a write down of Woodbridge's assets in the consolidated accounts.

Index

> Note: **Key Terms** and their page references are given in **bold**.

Review Form & Free Prize Draw – Paper 2.5 Financial Reporting (International stream) (6/06)

All original review forms from the entire BPP range, completed with genuine comments, will be entered into one of two draws on 31 January 2007 and 31 July 2007. The names on the first four forms picked out on each occasion will be sent a cheque for £50.

Name: _____   **Address:** _____

_____

_____

How have you used this Text?
(Tick one box only)

☐ Home study (book only)

☐ On a course: college _____

☐ With 'correspondence' package

☐ Other _____

Why did you decide to purchase this Text? *(Tick one box only)*

☐ Have used BPP Texts in the past

☐ Recommendation by friend/colleague

☐ Recommendation by a lecturer at college

☐ Saw advertising

☐ Saw information on BPP website

☐ Other _____

During the past six months do you recall seeing/receiving any of the following?
(Tick as many boxes as are relevant)

☐ Our advertisement in *ACCA Student Accountant*

☐ Our advertisement in *Pass*

☐ Our advertisement in *PQ*

☐ Our brochure with a letter through the post

☐ Our website www.bpp.com

Which (if any) aspects of our advertising do you find useful?
(Tick as many boxes as are relevant)

☐ Prices and publication dates of new editions

☐ Information on Text content

☐ Facility to order books off-the-page

☐ None of the above

Which BPP products have you used?

Text	☑	*Success CD*	☐	*Learn Online*	☐
Kit	☐	*i-Learn*	☐	*Home Study Package*	☐
Passcard	☐	*i-Pass*	☐	*Home Study PLUS*	☐

Your ratings, comments and suggestions would be appreciated on the following areas.

	Very useful	Useful	Not useful
Introductory section (Key study steps, personal study)	☐	☐	☐
Chapter introductions	☐	☐	☐
Key terms	☐	☐	☐
Quality of explanations	☐	☐	☐
Case studies and other examples	☐	☐	☐
Exam focus points	☐	☐	☐
Questions and answers in each chapter	☐	☐	☐
Fast forwards and chapter roundups	☐	☐	☐
Quick quizzes	☐	☐	☐
Question Bank	☐	☐	☐
Answer Bank	☐	☐	☐
Index	☐	☐	☐

Overall opinion of this Study Text   Excellent ☐   Good ☐   Adequate ☐   Poor ☐

Do you intend to continue using BPP products?   Yes ☐   No ☐

On the reverse of this page are noted particular areas of the text about which we would welcome your feedback. The BPP author of this edition can be e-mailed at: janiceross@bpp.com

Please return this form to: Nick Weller, ACCA Publishing Manager, BPP Professional Education, FREEPOST, London, W12 8BR

Review Form & Free Prize Draw (continued)

TELL US WHAT YOU THINK

Please note any further comments and suggestions/errors below

Free Prize Draw Rules

1 Closing date for 31 January 2007 draw is 31 December 2006. Closing date for 31 July 2007 draw is 30 June 2007.

2 Restricted to entries with UK and Eire addresses only. BPP employees, their families and business associates are excluded.

3 No purchase necessary. Entry forms are available upon request from BPP Professional Education. No more than one entry per title, per person. Draw restricted to persons aged 16 and over.

4 Winners will be notified by post and receive their cheques not later than 6 weeks after the relevant draw date.

5 The decision of the promoter in all matters is final and binding. No correspondence will be entered into.